# CORPORATE TAX LAW

## Structure, policy and practice

Structure is something that many corporate tax systems lack. Focusing on structural defects and how they are addressed in practice, this comprehensive and comparative analysis of corporate tax systems uses a conceptual framework to illustrate and analyse the many difficult issues that corporations pose. This framework is enhanced by the examination of a large body of legal rules and practical considerations that demonstrate how corporate tax systems work in practice. While adopting a broad comparative approach, the analysis also drills down into the detail of influential corporate tax systems to illustrate the major issues they face and the options available to them.

PETER HARRIS is a reader at the Law Faculty of the University of Cambridge. He is also Director of the Centre for Tax Law at the Law Faculty and a director of studies and fellow of Churchill College.

# CAMBRIDGE TAX LAW SERIES

Tax law is a growing area of interest, as it is included as a subdivision in many areas of study and is a key consideration in business needs throughout the world. Books in this series will expose the theoretical underpinning behind the law to shed light on the taxation systems, so that the questions to be asked when addressing an issue become clear. These academic books, written by leading scholars, will be a central port of call for information on tax law. The content will be illustrated by case law and legislation.

The books will be of interest for those studying law, business, economics, accounting and finance courses.

*Series Editor*

Dr Peter Harris, Law Faculty, University of Cambridge, Director of the Centre for Tax Law.

Dr Harris brings a wealth of experience to the Series. He has taught and presented tax courses at a dozen universities in nearly as many countries and has acted as an external tax consultant for the International Monetary Fund for more than a decade.

# CORPORATE TAX LAW

## Structure, policy and practice

PETER HARRIS

CAMBRIDGE
UNIVERSITY PRESS

CAMBRIDGE UNIVERSITY PRESS
Cambridge, New York, Melbourne, Madrid, Cape Town,
Singapore, São Paulo, Delhi, Mexico City

Cambridge University Press
The Edinburgh Building, Cambridge CB2 8RU, UK

Published in the United States of America by Cambridge University Press, New York

www.cambridge.org
Information on this title: www.cambridge.org/9781107033535

© Peter Harris 2013

First published 2013

Printed and bound in the United Kingdom by the MPG Books Group

*A catalogue record for this publication is available from the British Library*

*Library of Congress Cataloguing in Publication data*
Harris, Peter, 1938–
Corporate tax law : structure, policy and practice / Peter Harris.
p.  cm. – (Cambridge tax law series)
Includes bibliographical references and index.
ISBN 978-1-107-03353-5 (hardback)
1. Corporations – Taxation – Law and legislation.   I. Title.
K4544.H375 2013
343.06'7 – dc23      2012037580

ISBN 978-1-107-03353-5 Hardback

# CONTENTS

# PREFACE

This book is inspired by a postgraduate course (Comparative Corporate Tax) that I have taught since 1998. That course has been taught annually at the University of Sydney since that time, but has also been taught at Georgetown, Auckland, London and Melbourne and shortly will be taught at Cambridge. Parts of Comparative Corporate Tax have been taught at Leiden, Gainesville, Florida, Pretoria, Utrecht, Oslo and Vienna. Teaching postgraduates is particularly rewarding, because it provides an opportunity to test understanding of the particulars of different corporate tax systems and different theoretical approaches to issues. With no disrespect to the people who have formally taught me, I have learned more from my students than I was ever taught in classes or presentations I have attended.

Nevertheless, the risk of inaccuracy in a book like this is high. Many comparative books deal with this sort of risk by engaging multiple authors who are experts in particular systems. Although that approach, no doubt, is the way to ensure accuracy of the law, it is not the best manner in which to write an internally consistent book that seeks to explain the structural issues faced by a corporate tax system. So this book intentionally runs the risk of inaccuracy in favour of a holistic manner of looking at and analysing corporate tax systems. Corporate tax systems are notoriously complex, and this book seeks to cut through that complexity and get to the core of the central issues for a corporate tax system. Structural analysis is the core feature and purpose of the book, and it is hoped that that analysis is the book's strength and unique contribution.

The book is designed for postgraduate students and junior practitioners. It is more than an introduction to the subject. It challenges the reader to think about tax issues conceptually and holistically, while illustrating the structure with practical examples. More senior tax practitioners and academics may also find it useful as a means of refreshing their understanding of the basics; its conceptual framework may challenge them to think more deeply about tax issues than they currently do. The law in this book is stated as at 30 July 2012, but some projected changes are noted immediately after the Preface.

Emily has reminded me that I have never dedicated a book to her (something about being the third child). As she is first in my heart and the centre of my world, I dedicate this book to her (and not Smash, Nick, Wife or Mum). Although that is a bit corny, why not? She is the most awesome thirteen-year-old daughter a father could ask for and by far the best looking in the family.

Peter Harris
Cambridge

## Postscript

As this book goes to press at the end of November 2012 it is likely that Germany and especially the US will amend certain features of their corporate tax systems for the start of 2013. Germany is likely to make minor adjustments to its *Organschaft* regime of taxing corporate groups. More seriously, after losing an important case before the Court of Justice of the EU, Germany is again considering fully taxing portfolio corporate shareholders (less than 10% holding) on the receipt of dividends and gains on the disposal of shares.

In the US, the Bush tax cuts mentioned at various points in the text are again due to expire. This would result in increased taxation of individuals (both income and capital gains) and especially the return of the full classical system for individual shareholders. It is not yet clear whether these cuts will be extended and if so to what extent and in what form. By the time this book is published in early 2013, I will have posted an update as to what has happened on my university webpage at www.law.cam.ac.uk/people/academic/pa-harris/39.

# TABLE OF CASES

| Case Name | Chapter number followed by footnote number (t = text around footnote) |
|---|---|
| **United States** | |
| *Helvering* v. *Southwest Consolidated Corp* (1942) 315 US 194 (SC) | *7:* 6 |
| *John Kelley Co* v. *Commissioner* (1946) 326 US 521 (SC) | *2:* 26 |
| *Lucas* v. *Earl* (1930) 281 US 111 (SC) | *1:* 505 |
| *Morrissey* v. *Commissioner* (1935) 296 US 344 (SC) | *1:* 31 |
| *Tooley* v. *Donaldson, Lufkin & Jenrette, Inc* (2004) 845 A 2d 1031 (SC Delaware) | *4:* 2 |
| *Waterman Steamship Corp* v. *United States* (1970) 430 F.2d 1185 (5th Cir) | *8:* 29 |

# TABLE OF STATUTES

| Statute Name | Chapter number followed by footnote number (t = text around footnote) |
| --- | --- |
| *Income Tax (Dividends, Interest and Royalties Withholding Tax) Act 1974* | |
| s. 7 | *3:* 40 |
| *Income Tax Assessment Act 1997* | |
| s. 6–1 | *2:* 156 |
| s. 8–1 | *2:* 170, 313 |
| s. 25–85 | *2:* 225 |
| s. 36–55 | *2:* 312 |
| s. 40–300 | *5:* 137 |
| s. 63–10 | *2:* 311 |
| s. 67–25 | *2:* 311 |
| s. 70–90 | *5:* 137 |
| s. 84–5 | *1:* 514 |
| s. 86–15 | *1:* 513, 515 |
| s. 86–30 | *1:* 521 |
| Div. 87 | *1:* 517 |
| s. 102–3 | *5:* 38 |
| s. 102–10 | *5:* 40 |
| s. 104–135 | *6:* 13 |
| s. 104–145 | *6:* 78 |
| s. 110–25 | *7:* 88 |
| s. 112–20 | *5:* 138 |
| s. 115–100 | *5:* 38 |
| s. 116–30 | *5:* 138 |
| s. 124–780 | *7:* 67, 77, 91 |
| s. 124–782 | *7:* 89 |
| s. 124–783 | *7:* 90 |
| s. 124–785 | *7:* 78 |
| s. 124–786 | *7:* 79 |
| s. 125–65 | *7:* 110 |
| s. 125–70 | *7:* 111, 113, 114 |
| s. 125–80 | *7:* 135 |
| s. 125–90 | *7:* 135 |
| s. 125–155 | *7:* 143 |
| Subdiv. 126-B | *7:* 67 |
| s. 165–10 | *5:* 100 |
| s. 165–12 | *5:* 57, 65, 82 |
| s. 165–13 | *5:* 90 |
| s. 165–15 | *5:* 59 |

| Statute Name | Chapter number followed by footnote number (t = text around footnote) |
|---|---|
| Subdiv. 165-B | **5:** 111 |
| s. 165–96 | **5:** 93, 100 |
| Subdiv. 165-CB | **5:** 111 |
| Subdiv. 165-CC | **5:** 121 |
| Subdiv. 165-C | **5:** 122 |
| s. 165–155 | **5:** 75 |
| s. 165–180 | **5:** 58 |
| s. 165–210 | **5:** 91, 94 |
| Div. 166 | **5:** 60 |
| s. 166–225 | **5:** 73 |
| s. 166–240 | **5:** 77 |
| s. 166–245 | **5:** 77 |
| Subdiv. 170-D | **5:** 139 |
| Subdiv. 175-A | **5:** 59, 116, 141 |
| Div. 190 | **6:** 42 |
| s. 202–5 | **2:** 321 |
| s. 202–40 | **6:** 94 |
| s. 202–45 | **2:** 331; **6:** 94 |
| s. 202–55 | **2:** 309, 322 |
| s. 202–60 | **2:** 323 |
| Div. 203 | **2:** 330 |
| s. 205–10 | **2:** 341 |
| s. 205–15 | **2:** 342; **3:** 24 |
| s. 205–30 | **2:** 343 |
| s. 205–45 | **2:** 324, 326, 344 |
| s. 205–70 | **2:** 325, 345, 346 |
| s. 207–20 | **2:** 310 |
| s. 207–70 | **3:** 41 |
| s. 207–125 | **2:** 328 |
| s. 207–130 | **2:** 328 |
| s. 207–145 | **2:** 329; **8:** 60 |
| s. 216–5 | **8:** 21 |
| s. 216–10 | **8:** 52 |
| Div. 220 | **3:** 182 |
| Div. 328 | **1:** 409 |
| s. 701–1 | **1:** 82 |
| Div. 705 | **5:** 147 |
| Subdiv. 707-C | **5:** 130 |
| s. 707–410 | **5:** 166 |

| Statute Name | Chapter number followed by footnote number (t = text around footnote) |
| --- | --- |
| Subdiv. 709-A | *5:* 157 |
| Div. 711 | *5:* 162 |
| Div. 725 | *8:* 24 |
| s. 725–65 | *8:* 28 |
| Div. 727 | *8:* 34 |
| s. 727–250 | *8:* 35 |
| s. 770–75 | *5:* 156 |
| s. 802–15 | *3:* 61 |
| s. 802–30 | *3:* 60 |
| s. 960–100 | |
| 'entity' | *1:* 11 |
| 'company' | *1:* 16 |
| Div. 974 | *2:* 37 |
| s. 974–15 | *2:* 70 |
| s. 974–20 | *2:* 40 |
| s. 974–35 | *2:* 40 |
| s. 974–70 | *2:* 39, 69 |
| s. 974–75 | *2:* 38 |
| s. 995–1 (definition of 'indirectly') | *5:* 76 |
| *Corporations Act 2001* | |
| s. 411 | *7:* 57 |
| | |
| **Brazil** | |
| *Constitution* | |
| Art. 145 | *1:* 421 |
| | |
| **Canada** | |
| *Income Tax Act* | |
| s. 74.1 | *1:* 505 |
| | |
| **European Union** | |
| *Proposal for a Council Directive on a Common Consolidated Corporate Tax Base (CCCTB), COM(2011) 121/3 ('CCCTB Proposal')* | |
| Art. 1 | *1:* 1, 9, 53 |
| Art. 2 | *1:* 19t |
| Art. 3 | *1:* 54 |

| Statute Name | Chapter number followed by footnote number (t = text around footnote) |
|---|---|
| Art. 86 | *1:* 454; *5:* 131 |
| Annex I | *1:* 19t |
| *Second Company Law Directive,* **Council Directive 77/91/EEC of 13 December 1976** | |
| Art. 8 | *4:* 4 |
| *Mergers Directive,* **Council Directive 90/434/EEC of 23 July 1990 (consolidated as 2009/133/EC)** | *7:* 1 |
| *Parent-Subsidiary Directive,* **Council Directive 90/435/EEC of 23 July 1990** | *2:* 13; *3:* 62, 179 |
| *European Company Statute,* **Council Regulation (EC) No 2157/2001** | *1:* 22 |
| *Application of International Accounting Standards,* **Council Regulation (EC) No. 1606/2002** | *1:* 186, 223 |

**Finland**

| | |
|---|---|
| *Laki konserniavustuksesta verotuksessa* (Group Contributions Law) | *1:* 363 |

**Germany**

*Abgabenordnung ('AO')* **(Tax Code)**

| | |
|---|---|
| s. 39 | *8:* 18 |
| s. 42 | *8:* 25, 62 |

*Aktiengesetz ('AktG')* **(Companies Law)**

| | |
|---|---|
| s. 1 | *Intro:* 22 |
| s. 5 | *1:* 64 |
| s. 8 | *4:* 5 |
| s. 53a | *7:* 47 |
| s. 57 | *2:* 4; *7:* 33 |
| s. 67 | *2:* 8 |
| s. 71 | *6:* 29 |
| s. 93 | *1:* 75 |
| s. 117 | *4:* 2 |
| s. 122 | *1:* 72 |
| s. 124 | *1:* 72 |

| Statute Name | Chapter number followed by footnote number (t = text around footnote) |
| --- | --- |
| s. 20 | *1:* 182; *2:* 15, 21, 94, 102, 127, 159, 189, 292; *3:* 144, 145; *5:* 3, 26, 27; *6:* 6, 17, 24, 26, 89; *7:* 31, 45, 46; *8:* 13, 14, 17, 44 |
| s. 21 | *1:* 182 |
| s. 22 | *1:* 182; *4:* 14 |
| s. 23 | *1:* 182 |
| s. 32a | *1:* 452 |
| s. 32d | *2:* 281, 282, 283; *3:* 163; *5:* 26 |
| s. 34 | *5:* 35 |
| s. 34c | *3:* 156 |
| s. 35 | *1:* 453 |
| s. 43 | *2:* 169, 280; *3:* 30 |
| s. 43a | *3:* 30 |
| s. 44a | *3:* 31 |
| s. 49 | *3:* 64; *5:* 44 |
| s. 50 | *3:* 34 |
| s. 50c (former) | *8:* 61 |
| *Gesetz über steuerrechtliche Maßnahmen bei Erhöhung des Nennkapitals aus Gesellschaftsmitteln* (Law on Fiscal Measures to Increase Nominal Capital from Corporate Funds) | |
| s. 1 | *7:* 32 |
| s. 3 | *7:* 40 |
| *Gewerbesteuergesetz* (Trade Tax Law) | *1:* 451 |
| s. 10a | *5:* 154 |
| *Grundgesetz* (Basic Law) | |
| Art. 3 | *1:* 421 |
| *Handelsgesetzbuch* (Commercial Code) | |
| s. 238 | *1:* 410 |
| s. 241a | *1:* 410 |
| s. 252 | *1:* 220 |
| s. 264 | *1:* 184 |
| s. 290 | *1:* 186, 187 |
| s. 297 | *1:* 188 |

| Statute Name | Chapter number followed by footnote number (t = text around footnote) |
|---|---|
| *Investmentsteuergesetz* (Investment Tax Law) | *3:* 139 |
| *Körperschaftsteuergesetz ('KStG')* (Corporate Income Tax Law) | |
| s. 1 | *1:* 1, 18, 22, 23, 30, 63 |
| s. 2 | *3:* 63 |
| s. 3 | *1:* 33t |
| s. 8 | *1:* 8, 178, 191; *2:* 103, 128, 177, 224; *3:* 65, 144; *4:* 10, 22; *5:* 110; *6:* 80 |
| s. 8a | *2:* 57; *5:* 154 |
| s. 8b | *2:* 178, 253, 266; *3:* 157; *5:* 7; *8:* 38 |
| s. 8c | *5:* 61, 63, 68, 71, 72, 80, 99, 102, 123, 154 |
| s. 11 | *6:* 49, 50 |
| s. 14 | *1:* 89, 103, 105, 115, 150, 347, 364, 393; *2:* 254; *3:* 80 |
| s. 15 | *2:* 58 |
| s. 16 | *1:* 381 |
| s. 17 | *3:* 80 |
| s. 23 | *1:* 450 |
| s. 26 | *3:* 7, 156 |
| s. 27 | *2:* 337, 352 |
| s. 28 | *6:* 16, 17, 23, 25 |
| s. 31 | *1:* 8 |
| s. 32 | *3:* 34, 66 |
| s. 37 | *2:* 241 |
| *Korperschaftsteuerricht-linien (KStR)* (Corporate Income Tax Guidelines) | |
| Para. 36 | *2:* 105 |
| *Umwandlungsgesetz* (Reorganisation Law) | |
| s. 20 | *7:* 56 |
| s. 123 | *7:* 116 |
| s. 128 | *7:* 118 |
| s. 174 | *7:* 116 |

| Statute Name | Chapter number followed by footnote number (t = text around footnote) |
|---|---|
| *Umwandlungssteuergesetz* *('UmwStG')* (Reorganisation Tax Law) | |
| s. 1 | *7:* 116 |
| s. 4 | *7:* 96 |
| s. 11 | *7:* 69, 95, 144 |
| s. 12 | *7:* 85, 96, 147 |
| s. 13 | *7:* 83, 137 |
| s. 15 | *7:* 115, 117, 120, 136, 148 |
| s. 20 | *4:* 27, 28, 29, 52t |
| s. 21 | *7:* 68, 80, 81 |
| s. 22 | *4:* 30; *7:* 82 |
| *Wertpapiererwerbs- und* *Übernahmegesetz* (Securities Acquisition and Takeover Law) | |
| s. 39 | *1:* 92 |
| **Ghana** | |
| *Internal Revenue Act 2000* | |
| s. 2 | *7:* 27 |
| **India** | |
| *Income Tax Act, 1961* | |
| s. 115JB | *1:* 474 |
| s. 115O | *2:* 166 |
| *Finance Act, 2012* | |
| First Schedule | *3:* 99 |
| **Ireland** | |
| *Finance Act 1999* | |
| ss. 27, 28 & 71 | *2:* 200 |
| **Mexico** | |
| *Ley del Impuesto sobre la Renta* (Income Tax Law) | |
| Art. 1 | *3:* 20 |
| Art. 6 | *2:* 20 |
| Art. 11 | *2:* 165, 271 |
| Art. 24 | *5:* 30 |

| Statute Name | Chapter number followed by footnote number (t = text around footnote) |
| --- | --- |
| Art. 88 | *2:* 347; *3:* 20 |
| Art. 109 | *5:* 33 |
| Art. 151 | *5:* 30 |
| Art. 193 | *3:* 107 |
| *Ley del Impuesto Empresarial a Tasa Única* (Business Flat-Rate Tax Law) | *1:* 474 |

**Nepal**
*Income Tax Act 2001*

| | |
| --- | --- |
| s. 53 | *7:* 27 |
| s. 57 | *5:* 117 |

**The Netherlands**
*Wet op de inkomstenbelasting* (Income Tax Law)

| | |
| --- | --- |
| s. 2.13 | *1:* 495 |
| s. 5.2 | *1:* 494 |
| s. 5.5 | *1:* 495 |

*Wet op de vennootschapsbelasting 1969* (Corporate Income Tax Act)

| | |
| --- | --- |
| 15 | *1:* 82 |

**New Zealand**
*Income Tax Act 2007*

| | |
| --- | --- |
| s. LP2 | *2:* 243; *3:* 46 |
| s. OA8 | *5:* 158 |
| s. OB41 | *3:* 158 |
| s. RF8 | *2:* 45 |
| s. YA1 (definition of 'supplementary dividend') | *3:* 47 |

**Norway**
*Lov om skatt av formue og inntekt* (Income and Capital Tax Law)

| | |
| --- | --- |
| s. 10–2 to 10–4 | *1:* 363 |
| s. 10–12 | *1:* 495; *2:* 273 |
| s. 10–31 | *5:* 32 |

| Statute Name | Chapter number followed by footnote number (t = text around footnote) |
| --- | --- |
| s. 8 | *1:* 325, 342; *5:* 40 |
| s. 10 | *5:* 42 |
| s. 10B | *5:* 42 |
| s. 13 | *3:* 129 |
| s. 15 | *4:* 12 |
| s. 16 | *5:* 17 |
| s. 16A | *5:* 19, 136 |
| s. 17 | *1:* 256, 289; *2:* 132; *4:* 16, 35; *6:* 72; *7:* 39, 87 |
| s. 18 | *1:* 256, 289; *4:* 16, 35; *5:* 134; *6:* 72 |
| s. 22 | *6:* 37, 40, 47 |
| s. 24 | *6:* 77 |
| s. 29 | *8:* 23 |
| s. 30 | *8:* 33, 41 |
| s. 31 | *8:* 32, 41 |
| s. 37 | *1:* 216; *6:* 39, 48 |
| s. 38 | *7:* 87 |
| s. 39 | *1:* 216 |
| s. 41 | *4:* 40 |
| s. 42 | *6:* 9, 85 |
| s. 53 | *5:* 39, 167 |
| s. 104 | *5:* 4 |
| s. 105 | *5:* 6 |
| s. 106A | *5:* 6 |
| s. 122 | *6:* 9t, 10, 11, 38, 40, 47, 85t; *7:* 128 |
| s. 123 | *7:* 44 |
| s. 126 | *7:* 11, 37 |
| s. 127 | *7:* 10 |
| s. 128 | *7:* 12, 39 |
| s. 130 | *7:* 38, 130 |
| s. 132 | *7:* 13, 24 |
| s. 135 | *7:* 70, 75 |
| s. 136 | *7:* 76, 131, 132 |
| s. 137 | *7:* 71 |
| s. 138 | *7:* 70 |
| s. 139 | *7:* 72, 86, 142, 146 |
| s. 142 | *7:* 54 |
| s. 144 | *7:* 23 |

| Statute Name | Chapter number followed by footnote number (t = text around footnote) |
| --- | --- |
| s. 6 | *3:* 75 |
| s. 8 | *1:* 1 |
| s. 25 | *1:* 411 |
| s. 34 | *1:* 238; *2:* 180 |
| s. 45 | *1:* 404 |
| s. 173 | *1:* 258, 391 |
| s. 177 | *1:* 258; *4:* 31 |
| s. 178 | *1:* 390; *4:* 32 |
| s. 179 | *1:* 258, 390 |
| s. 264 | *3:* 75 |
| s. 271 | *1:* 1 |
| s. 366 | *2:* 93 |
| s. 367 | *2:* 93 |
| s. 368 | *3:* 75 |
| s. 383 | *2:* 162t; *3:* 149, 150; *6:* 22 |
| s. 384 | *2:* 89, 90 |
| s. 385 | *2:* 77; *8:* 11, 15 |
| s. 397 | *2:* 305, 307, 308, 314t; *3:* 44 |
| s. 397A | *3:* 168 |
| s. 397AA | *3:* 168 |
| s. 398 | *2:* 306 |
| s. 402 | *2:* 92, 162t; *3:* 151; *6:* 22 |
| s. 411 | *7:* 52 |
| s. 414 | *7:* 53 |
| s. 415 | *2:* 151 |
| s. 421 | *2:* 151 |
| s. 577 | *3:* 75 |
| ss. 619 to 648 | *1:* 505 |
| s. 689 | *1:* 1 |
| s. 847 | *1:* 36 |
| s. 863 | *1:* 38t |
| *Companies Act 2006* | |
| s. 6 | *Intro:* 20t |
| s. 9 | *1:* 91 |
| s. 10 | *4:* 5 |
| s. 39 | *Intro:* 20 |
| s. 43 | *Intro:* 21 |
| s. 112 | *2:* 6 |
| s. 113 | *2:* 7 |

| Statute Name | Chapter number followed by footnote number (t = text around footnote) |
| --- | --- |
| s. 809AZB | *8:* 7 |
| s. 811 | *3:* 38 |
| s. 825 | *3:* 38 |
| s. 989 (definition of 'body of persons') | *1:* 15 |
| (definition of 'paid') | *2:* 90 |
| s. 992 (definition of 'company') | *1:* 20t |
| s. 993 | *1:* 97 |
| s. 995 | *1:* 108 |
| s. 997 | *1:* 10 |
| ***Corporation Tax Act 2009 ('CTA 2009')*** | |
| s. 1 | *1:* 199t |
| s. 2 | *1:* 195, 199, 455 |
| s. 3 | *1:* 1; *3:* 73 |
| s. 5 | *3:* 72 |
| s. 6 | *1:* 38 |
| s. 8 | *1:* 197 |
| s. 9 | *1:* 198 |
| s. 14 | *1:* 63t |
| s. 15 | *1:* 63t |
| s. 18 | *1:* 68 |
| s. 18A | *3:* 16 |
| ss. 18G to 18ID | *3:* 132 |
| s. 35 | *1:* 231t |
| s. 46 | *1:* 231t, 233t, 235t |
| s. 47 | *1:* 323 |
| s. 53 | *1:* 231t, 233t |
| s. 54 | *1:* 238; *2:* 134, 180 |
| s. 62 | *1:* 324, 340 |
| s. 93 | *1:* 231t, 233 |
| s. 157 | *1:* 233 |
| s. 162 | *1:* 258, 310, 391 |
| s. 166 | *1:* 258 |
| s. 167 | *1:* 310, 389; *4:* 46 |
| s. 168 | *1:* 258, 310 |
| s. 201 | *1:* 200 |
| s. 205 | *1:* 341 |
| s. 210 | *1:* 234 |

| Statute Name | Chapter number followed by footnote number (t = text around footnote) |
| --- | --- |
| s. 211 | *1:* 201 |
| s. 297 | *1:* 204; *2:* 182 |
| s. 299 | *2:* 183 |
| s. 308 | *1:* 235 |
| s. 309 | *1:* 235 |
| s. 321A | *2:* 143 |
| s. 322 | *7:* 15 |
| s. 415 | *2:* 73; *7:* 25 |
| ss. 444 to 446 | *1:* 257 |
| s. 457 | *2:* 184 |
| s. 463 | *2:* 184 |
| s. 464 | *1:* 203 |
| s. 465 | *1:* 205 |
| s. 466 | *1:* 274 |
| s. 472 | *1:* 274 |
| s. 473 | *1:* 112, 274 |
| s. 521B | *2:* 43 |
| s. 521C | *2:* 44 |
| s. 521E | *2:* 44 · |
| s. 545 | *8:* 46 |
| s. 550 | *8:* 45 |
| s. 551 | *8:* 46 |
| s. 573 | *1:* 206, 339 |
| s. 574 | *1:* 207 |
| s. 585 | *2:* 74 |
| s. 597 | *1:* 236 |
| s. 599 | *1:* 236 |
| s. 693 | *1:* 257 |
| s. 716 | *1:* 236 |
| s. 717 | *1:* 236 |
| s. 747 | *1:* 208 |
| s. 752 | *1:* 209 |
| s. 775 | *1:* 309 |
| s. 776 | *1:* 309 |
| s. 803 | *1:* 212 |
| s. 835 | *1:* 274 |
| s. 836 | *1:* 274 |
| s. 837 | *1:* 112, 274 |

| Statute Name | Chapter number followed by footnote number (t = text around footnote) |
| --- | --- |
| s. 845 | *1:* 257 |
| s. 846 | *1:* 257 |
| s. 881 | *1:* 212 |
| s. 906 | *1:* 212 |
| s. 909 | *1:* 210 |
| s. 913 | *1:* 211 |
| s. 931A | *2:* 78, 90, 162; *3:* 148, 150 |
| ss. 931B to 931Q | *3:* 160 |
| s. 931B | *2:* 247; *3:* 161 |
| s. 931D | *2:* 248; *3:* 161 |
| s. 931E | *2:* 249 |
| s. 931F | *2:* 250 |
| s. 931G | *2:* 251 |
| s. 931H | *2:* 252 |
| s. 931R | *3:* 162 |
| s. 931RA | *6:* 48t |
| s. 931S | *2:* 246 |
| s. 931U | *2:* 250 |
| s. 931W | *1:* 213 |
| s. 938 | *4:* 47 |
| s. 941 | *4:* 48 |
| s. 942 | *4:* 49 |
| s. 944 | *4:* 51 |
| s. 948 | *4:* 50 |
| s. 977 | *1:* 215 |
| s. 979 | *1:* 215 |
| s. 982 | *1:* 214 |
| s. 1219 | *2:* 185 |
| s. 1257 | *1:* 36 |
| s. 1273 | *1:* 38t, 124 |
| s. 1298 | *1:* 404 |
| s. 1305 | *2:* 224 |
| *Corporation Tax Act 2010 ('CTA 2010')* | |
| s. 18 | *1:* 460t, 469; *3:* 90 |
| s. 24 | *1:* 461, 464 |
| s. 25 | *1:* 465 |
| ss. 26 to 30 | *1:* 465 |

| Statute Name | Chapter number followed by footnote number (t = text around footnote) |
| --- | --- |
| s. 27 | *1:* 468t |
| s. 34 | *1:* 173, 470; *6:* 52 |
| s. 37 | *1:* 322, 329, 358; *6:* 53 |
| s. 39 | *1:* 330; *6:* 53 |
| s. 45 | *1:* 335, 358 |
| s. 46 | *1:* 338t, 411 |
| ss. 68 to 90 | *5:* 18 |
| s. 99 | *1:* 349, 360 |
| s. 105 | *1:* 350 |
| s. 106 | *1:* 351 |
| s. 107 | *1:* 352; *3:* 82 |
| s. 109 | *1:* 354 |
| ss. 111 to 128 | *1:* 353 |
| s. 130 | *1:* 355, 394 |
| s. 132 | *1:* 397t |
| s. 133 | *1:* 399, 401 |
| s. 134 | *3:* 83 |
| s. 137 | *1:* 356 |
| s. 139 | *1:* 357 |
| s. 140 | *1:* 357 |
| s. 142 | *1:* 357 |
| s. 143 | *1:* 397, 398 |
| s. 144 | *1:* 397 |
| s. 145 | *1:* 400, 402 |
| s. 151 | *1:* 366, 368, 369, 371 |
| s. 152 | *1:* 140, 365 |
| s. 153 | *1:* 153t, 162, 171, 394t, 396 |
| s. 154 | *1:* 370; *6:* 68 |
| s. 158 | *1:* 372t |
| s. 160 | *1:* 372 |
| s. 162 | *1:* 373 |
| s. 165 | *1:* 374t |
| s. 166 | *1:* 374t |
| ss. 170 to 172 | *1:* 374 |
| ss. 173 to 174 | *1:* 374 |
| s. 183 | *1:* 378 |
| s. 185 | *1:* 395 |
| s. 188 | *1:* 170 |
| ss. 382 to 408 | *5:* 151 |

| Statute Name | Chapter number followed by footnote number (t = text around footnote) |
| --- | --- |
| s. 439 | *1:* 152t, 163t, 167 |
| s. 442 | *1:* 172; *3:* 153 |
| s. 444 | *1:* 165 |
| s. 446 | *1:* 166 |
| s. 448 | *1:* 162t, 163t, 279t, 467t, 519 |
| s. 449 | *1:* 120, 465t |
| s. 450 | *1:* 108t, 109, 110, 112, 113, 119t, 123, 148, 152t, 163t, 274t, 281, 287t, 466t, 467t; *6:* 60 |
| s. 451 | *1:* 108t, 119, 154, 162t, 164t, 274t, 466t; *6:* 60 |
| s. 454 | *1:* 153, 155 |
| s. 455 | *2:* 148t; *3:* 154 |
| s. 456 | *2:* 149 |
| s. 458 | *2:* 148, 152 |
| s. 459 | *2:* 150 |
| s. 617 | *1:* 55 |
| s. 618 | *1:* 56 |
| ss. 672 to 730 | *5:* 101 |
| s. 673 | *5:* 84, 85 |
| s. 674 | *5:* 109, 113 |
| ss. 692 to 703 | *5:* 155 |
| s. 719 | *5:* 52, 70 |
| s. 720 | *5:* 67 |
| s. 721 | *5:* 53; *6:* 56 |
| s. 723 | *5:* 78 |
| s. 724 | *5:* 79 |
| s. 726 | *6:* 58 |
| ss. 731 to 751 | *8:* 57 |
| ss. 752 to 757 | *8:* 6 |
| s. 753 | *8:* 7 |
| ss. 782 to 789 | *8:* 20 |
| ss. 805 to 812 | *8:* 50 |
| s. 944 | *5:* 88t |
| s. 1000 | *2:* 10, 31, 32, 63, 86, 91, 115, 117, 139, 154t; *6:* 8, 36; *7:* 29, 30 |
| s. 1002 | *2:* 115, 117 |
| s. 1015 | *2:* 33, 34, 35, 67 |

| Statute Name | Chapter number followed by footnote number (t = text around footnote) |
|---|---|
| s. 371BB | *3:* 120 |
| s. 371BC | *3:* 131 |
| s. 371BD | *3:* 131 |
| s. 371CA | *3:* 121 |
| s. 371CB | *3:* 122 |
| s. 371CC | *3:* 122 |
| s. 371CE | *3:* 123 |
| s. 371CF | *3:* 124 |
| s. 371CG | *3:* 125 |
| Part 9A, Chapter 4 | *3:* 121 |
| Part 9A, Chapter 5 | *3:* 122 |
| Part 9A, Chapter 6 | *3:* 123 |
| Part 9A, Chapter 7 | *3:* 124 |
| Part 9A, Chapter 8 | *3:* 125 |
| Part 9A, Chapter 9 | *3:* 122 |
| Part 9A, Chapter 11 | *3:* 126 |
| Part 9A, Chapter 12 | *3:* 126 |
| Part 9A, Chapter 13 | *3:* 127 |
| Part 9A, Chapter 14 | *3:* 128 |
| Part 9A, Chapter 15 | *3:* 130 |
| Part 9A, Chapter 16 | *3:* 130 |
| Part 9A, Chapter 17 | *3:* 130 |
| Part 9A, Chapter 18 | *1:* 112; *3:* 119 |
| *Finance Act 2012* | |
| s. 1 | *1:* 457; *2:* 285 |
| s. 5 | *1:* 456 |
| s. 7 | *1:* 460 |

**United States**
*American Bar Association's Model*
  *Business Corporation Act ('MBCA')*

| | |
|---|---|
| s. 1.40 | *2:* 4, 5 |
| s. 2.02 | *4:* 6 |
| s. 3.02 | *Intro:* 26 |
| s. 6.31 | *6:* 29 |
| s. 6.40 | *2:* 4; *6:* 4 |
| s. 8.30 | *1:* 75 |
| s. 11.02 | *7:* 56 |
| s. 11.07 | *7:* 56 |

| Statute Name | Chapter number followed by footnote number (t = text around footnote) |
|---|---|
| *General Corporation Law of Delaware ('DGCL')* | |
| s. 102 | *4:* 6 |
| s. 122 | *Intro:* 27 |
| s. 154 | *2:* 333; *6:* 4 |
| s. 160 | *6:* 29 |
| s. 170 | *6:* 4 |
| s. 219 | *2:* 9 |
| s. 220 | *2:* 9 |
| s. 251 | *7:* 56 |
| *Internal Revenue Code ('IRC')* | |
| s. 1 | *1:* 446, 459; *2:* 287, 291, 295, 303; *3:* 164, 165; *5:* 24 |
| s. 11 | *1:* 446, 458, 464t, 471 |
| s. 26 | *3:* 17 |
| s. 53 | *1:* 479 |
| s. 55 | *1:* 475, 476, 478 |
| ss. 56 to 58 | *1:* 477 |
| s. 61 | *1:* 183; *2:* 156t; *3:* 143 |
| s. 63 | *1:* 183 |
| s. 108 | *7:* 14 |
| s. 118 | *4:* 7 |
| s. 144 | *1:* 100 |
| s. 161 | *1:* 183 |
| s. 162 | *1:* 238; *2:* 133, 173 |
| s. 163 | *2:* 47, 48, 49, 50, 51, 52, 53, 54, 174, 175, 176, 296 |
| s. 165 | *1:* 320t; *6:* 54, 76 |
| s. 172 | *1:* 327, 331 |
| s. 179 | *1:* 382, 383, 408 |
| s. 243 | *2:* 256, 257, 260 |
| s. 245 | *3:* 180 |
| s. 246 | *2:* 268, 276 |
| s. 246A | *2:* 269 |
| s. 267 | *1:* 105t, 114, 121, 142, 301, 302; *2:* 49t; *5:* 74t |
| s. 268 | *1:* 99 |
| s. 269 | *1:* 473; *5:* 115; *8:* 56t |

| Statute Name | Chapter number followed by footnote number (t = text around footnote) |
| --- | --- |
| s. 274 | *1:* 404 |
| s. 301 | *2:* 85, 108t, 113, 334; *6:* 14, 15; *7:* 42 |
| s. 302 | *6:* 31, 32, 34, 35 |
| s. 305 | *7:* 34, 35, 36, 43, 48; *8:* 26t |
| s. 307 | *7:* 41 |
| s. 312 | *2:* 17; *6:* 27 |
| s. 316 | *2:* 16, 25t, 107, 350; *6:* 14; *8:* 8 |
| s. 317 | *2:* 108; *3:* 141t |
| s. 318 | *5:* 74; *6:* 35 |
| s. 331 | *6:* 86 |
| s. 334 | *6:* 75 |
| s. 336 | *6:* 73 |
| s. 337 | *6:* 74 |
| s. 338 | *5:* 117, 142 |
| s. 351 | *4:* 17, 18, 23, 26t, 52t |
| s. 354 | *4:* 26; *7:* 4, 65, 73 |
| s. 355 | *7:* 98, 100, 101, 102, 121, 139 |
| s. 356 | *7:* 8, 122 |
| s. 358 | *4:* 20; *7:* 9, 74, 123 |
| s. 361 | *4:* 23t; *7:* 92, 93, 141 |
| s. 362 | *4:* 21; *7:* 85, 87t, 145 |
| s. 368 | *4:* 19, 23; *7:* 5, 58, 59, 60, 61, 62, 64, 65, 99, 103 |
| s. 381 | *4:* 25; *7:* 94, 149 |
| s. 382 | *5:* 48, 49, 51, 66, 74, 81, 97, 100, 104, 105, 106, 107, 108, 109, 114, 118, 119, 120, 138t, 141t, 144t, 153t; *6:* 55; *7:* 94t |
| s. 383 | *5:* 100, 153 |
| s. 384 | *5:* 146, 150 |
| s. 385 | *2:* 25t, 27, 75t |
| s. 446 | *1:* 405 |
| s. 448 | *1:* 406, 472 |
| s. 469 | *2:* 186, 187 |
| s. 482 | *1:* 240, 242t, 259, 261t, 273, 275t; *2:* 130 |
| s. 531 | *1:* 483t |
| s. 532 | *1:* 483 |
| s. 533 | *1:* 484 |
| s. 535 | *1:* 485 |

| Statute Name | Chapter number followed by footnote number (t = text around footnote) |
| --- | --- |
| s. 541 | *1:* 491 |
| s. 542 | *1:* 152, 168, 174, 175 |
| s. 543 | *1:* 176 |
| s. 544 | *1:* 156, 159, 164 |
| s. 561 | *1:* 486 |
| s. 563 | *1:* 486 |
| s. 861 | *3:* 32, 70, 97 |
| s. 871 | *3:* 37, 71; *5:* 43 |
| s. 872 | *3:* 35 |
| s. 881 | *3:* 32, 68 |
| s. 882 | *3:* 35, 67, 87; *5:* 43 |
| s. 884 | *3:* 102, 103, 105 |
| s. 901 | *3:* 10, 17, 167 |
| s. 902 | *3:* 171 |
| s. 904 | *3:* 11, 12 |
| s. 951 | *3:* 110, 112 |
| s. 952 | *3:* 111, 142 |
| s. 957 | *3:* 112 |
| s. 958 | *3:* 113 |
| s. 964 | *3:* 142 |
| s. 1032 | *4:* 8; *6:* 44; *7:* 19 |
| s. 1059 | *8:* 55 |
| s. 1091 | *5:* 5 |
| s. 1211 | *1:* 189, 320; *5:* 25, 40 |
| s. 1212 | *1:* 328, 332 |
| s. 1221 | *1:* 321 |
| s. 1273 | *7:* 21 |
| s. 1291 | *3:* 135 |
| ss. 1293 to 1295 | *3:* 137 |
| s. 1297 | *3:* 136 |
| s. 1361 | *1:* 151, 157, 158, 160, 161, 168, 169; *3:* 92 |
| s. 1362 | *1:* 498 |
| s. 1363 | *1:* 499, 503t |
| s. 1366 | *1:* 500, 504 |
| s. 1367 | *1:* 502, 503 |
| s. 1377 | *1:* 501 |
| s. 1441 | *3:* 35, 37, 71 |
| s. 1442 | *3:* 32, 69 |

# LIST OF ABBREVIATIONS

## General

| | |
|---|---|
| ACT | Advance corporation tax |
| CCCTB Proposal | 'Proposal for a Council Directive on a Common Consolidated Corporate Tax Base (CCCTB)', COM(2011) 121/3 |
| ECJ | Court of Justice of the European Union |
| EU | European Union |
| EU Law | Law of the European Union |
| FEU Treaty | Treaty on the Functioning of the European Union |
| HMRC | Her Majesty's Revenue Commissioners (UK) |
| IRS | Internal Revenue Service (US) |
| LLC | Limited Liability Company |
| OECD | Organisation for Economic Co-operation and Development |
| OECD Model | Organisation for Economic Co-operation and Development's Model Convention on Income and Capital |
| PE | Permanent establishment |
| UK | United Kingdom |
| US | United States |

## German statutes

| | |
|---|---|
| EStG | *Einkommensteuergesetz* (Income Tax Law) |
| KStG | *Körperschaftsteuergesetz* (Corporate Income Tax Law) |
| UmwStG | *Umwandlungssteuergesetz* (Reorganisation Tax Law) |
| AktG | *Aktiengesetz* (Companies Law) |
| AO | *Abgabenordnung* (Tax Code) |

## UK statutes

| | |
|---|---|
| CAA 2001 | Capital Allowances Act 2001 |
| CTA 2009 | Corporation Tax Act 2009 |
| CTA 2010 | Corporation Tax Act 2010 |

| ITA 2007 | Income Tax Act 2007 |
| ITEPA 2003 | Income Tax (Earnings and Pensions) Act 2003 |
| ITTOIA 2005 | Income Tax (Trading and Other Income) Act 2005 |
| TCGA 1992 | Taxation of Chargeable Gains Act 1992 |
| TIOPA 2010 | Taxation (International and Other Provisions) Act 2010 |

## US statutes

| DGCL | General Corporation Law of Delaware |
| IRC | Internal Revenue Code |
| MBCA | American Bar Association's Model Business Corporation Act |

# INTRODUCTION

## Approach and focus

This book is about income taxation of corporations and dealings with and in them. It seeks to provide a conceptual framework, a structure within which to analyse and illustrate the many difficult issues posed by corporations for income taxation. Structure is something that many corporate tax systems lack. The structure offered by this book is generic and may be used to analyse the corporate tax system of any country. The structure is illustrated with a large body of legal rules and practical considerations, which demonstrate how corporate tax systems *work* in practice. The book adopts two approaches to illustrate the operation of corporate tax systems. A broad comparative approach is used to illustrate the major issues faced by and options available for a corporate tax system. Here illustrations are drawn from a wide variety of jurisdictions.

It is also necessary to *drill down* into the detail of corporate tax systems to accurately illustrate the difficulties they face. Here, a broad comparative approach is less appropriate, and so, when it comes to detail, the book focuses on a few influential and highly developed Western systems. Four particularly important systems or approaches are used for this purpose. The first primary corporate tax system used for purposes of illustration is that of the United Kingdom ('UK'). The modern income tax and the common law approach originate in the UK. The UK's approach to income taxation has influenced the development of more income tax laws throughout the world than any other.[1] This influence is waning, but was holistic among common law jurisdictions. The UK approach also influenced the income tax laws of many civil law jurisdictions, particularly at their inception.[2]

The second approach used to illustrate the detailed operation of corporate tax systems is the Continental European approach. Historically, there

[1] For a detailed analysis of this influence, see Harris (2006) and Harris (forthcoming).
[2] Generally regarding the development of the income tax, see Seligman (1914).

1

has been no single approach to income taxation in Continental Europe, but given the common civil law background of many European countries there is a distinct approach that can be contrasted with the common law approach. Of particular importance is Germany, not only as the largest economy in Europe but also as the primary intellectual source for income taxation in Europe for 150 years. The Continental European approach to income taxation has also influenced the development of a large number of income tax laws throughout the world.

Looking to the future, a 2011 proposal of the European Commission (the 'CCCTB Proposal') has the potential to harmonise the corporate tax bases of European Union ('EU') member states along the lines of the traditional Continental European approach.[3] If adopted, this proposal would form the basis of the corporate tax system of the largest economy in the world. Even if it does not become law, the CCCTB Proposal represents a synthesis of a civil law approach to corporate taxation and is likely to have an impact on the future development of the corporate tax systems of member states of the EU. However, the CCCTB Proposal is not a proposal for a complete corporate tax system. Even if it becomes law, many matters would continue to be governed by the corporate tax systems of member states.[4]

The forth corporate tax system used for detailed illustration purposes is that of the United States ('US'). In many cases the US approach is similar to the others, and in its origins the US income tax was influenced especially by the UK approach.[5] As a consequence, although the US income tax law has influenced the development of income taxation in other countries, it has not had as much influence as the UK approach or the Continental European approach. However, unlike the UK and Germany (and most other countries) the US corporate tax system has to respond to the peculiar difficulty of not being underpinned by a single domestic corporate law. Rather, corporate law in the US is governed by the laws of its fifty states. In an increasingly globalised world, countries are now commonly

---

[3] 'Proposal for a Council Directive on a Common Consolidated Corporate Tax Base (CCCTB)', COM(2011) 121/3 ('CCCTB Proposal'). The CCCTB Proposal is undergoing amendment as it is considered by the EU institutions. The most recent amendments are those proposed by the EU Presidency in document 8387/12 of 4 April 2012.

[4] To provide a broader comparison, where the CCCTB Proposal lacks details with respect to a particular issue, the Australian corporate tax system is often used as a supplement.

[5] Waltman (1980). Regarding the US income tax of 1861, Waltman notes at p. 151 that public finance was 'the agenda creating factor and the British statute the source of the legislative details'.

faced with a multitude of corporate laws, and there is much to be learned from the US approach in this regard.[6]

The focus on these systems and approaches ensures the relevance of the discussion in this book to most any corporate tax system in the world. The book does not purport to be comprehensive in its reference and analysis of relevant tax law or academic literature associated therewith, whether with respect to the German, UK or US corporate tax system or the CCCTB Proposal. Any attempt to do so would obscure the book's structure and, therefore, its purpose. In any case, there are many books specifically dedicated to each of these systems.[7] Sufficient references are provided throughout this book to facilitate more detailed investigation of particular issues.

Corporations invade all aspects of life, and it is not surprising that the taxation of corporations is an integral part of all tax systems. In the past few decades, tax systems have become increasingly complex, reflecting this era of globalisation, the information age and the never ending search for greater efficiency. The taxation of corporations and the taxation of dealings in and with them reflect this greater complexity. Many tax laws, and the UK is a prime example, have become so complex that they have largely lost any structure they once might have had. The extent to which corporations cause difficulty for tax systems depends on the type of tax being imposed.

Tax systems distinguish between direct taxes and indirect taxes. Direct taxes are intended to be borne by the person on whom they are imposed, whereas indirect taxes are intended to be passed on in prices. From a legal perspective, the distinction is much deeper and has its origins in the European feudal system.[8] Income tax is the main example of a direct tax, and value-added tax is the main example of an indirect tax, although at the

---

[6] The CCCTB Proposal would also have to grapple with this issue, although it lacks many details that the US system addresses. Regarding EU measures for harmonisation of member states corporate laws, see http://ec.europa.eu/internal_market/company/official/index_en. htm, accessed 16 July 2012.

[7] For example, see the references under 'Sources of tax law' in Part One of Ault & Arnold (2010). For a detailed consideration of the UK corporate tax system, see Bramwell (2002–), and for the US, see Bittker & Eustice (2003–). For a consider of the German corporate tax system (in English) see Ardizzoni (2005) and Whittmann (1983–). For a consideration of the CCCTB Proposal, see Weber (2012).

[8] For example, in England the Magna Carta recognised the distinction between 'aides' and customs. The King required 'the consent of the great council of the realm' to impose aides, whereas customs were largely levied as of right. Generally, see Harris (2006, p. 30) and the references cited therein. This distinction is still reflected in the UK in the types of taxes that are re-imposed annually in the Finance Act and those (such as value-added tax) that are imposed on a perpetual basis.

fringes the distinction between direct and indirect taxation blurs. Because indirect taxes focus on particular activities, the person conducting the activity is largely secondary. To the extent that identifying the person conducting the activity is relevant, corporations cause problems for indirect taxes, but these pale into insignificance compared to the problems that corporations cause for direct taxes.

For direct taxes to achieve their intent as to incidence (i.e. who bears the burden of the tax), activities, resources and income must be allocated to particular persons or tax subjects. With the many and diverse ways in which this allocation may be achieved (or manipulated), particularly in recent years, direct taxes are especially complex. The introduction of corporations makes this task of allocation verge on the impossible. The difficulties that corporations cause for direct taxes in this allocation process pertain to the very nature of a corporation.

## What is a 'corporation' and why is it important?

The importance of corporations in the daily life of every individual is beyond doubt. This is true on both a global and national scale. Corporations employ individuals and pay the wages that support the majority of households. They make the goods that individuals consume, import those goods and own the shops in which they are sold. Funds that individuals save increasingly find their way into the capital of corporations, which provide the return that sustains individuals, particularly in their retirement. And often that saving is made through the intermediation of corporations.

In 2012 there were 2.9 million registered corporations in the UK; the vast majority of these were small unquoted companies.[9] The corporate sector accounts for 60% of total turnover in the UK, compared to 23% for sole proprietors, 13% for partnerships and 4% for the government and non-profit sectors.[10] Despite this dominance, corporations account for only 28% of the total number of business entities in the UK, although this figure is quite high by international standards. The majority of business entities (62%) are sole proprietorships, with partnerships forming the

---

[9] See Companies House *Register of Statistics*, available at www.companieshouse.gov.uk/about/businessRegisterStat.shtml, accessed 16 July 2012. Fewer than 10,000 of the total were public companies.

[10] See Office for National Statistics, *Releases of UK Business: Activity, Size and Location* Tables B5.2a to B5.2d, available at www.ons.gov.uk/ons/publications/all-releases.html?definition=tcm%3A77-21554, accessed 16 July 2012.

smallest portion (10%). These non-corporate business entities account for substantially less turnover and employment than the corporate sector. Just less than half of the corporations registered in the UK are used for investment or other private activity or are dormant (i.e. do not conduct business).[11]

European and US statistics are more difficult to come by, primarily because corporate law is largely regulated by the member states, and a wide variety of business entities may be used. It seems the European Commission does not compile statistics as to the number of corporations formed in member states.[12] In Germany, all persons conducting a trade must register with the Trade Register (*Handelsregister*) of the local district. These registers record sole traders, partnerships and certain other associations and separately record incorporated companies with share capital.[13] Entries in the trade registers are sent to the Federal Gazette (*Bundesanzeiger*) and are available through the central German Business Register (*Unternehmensregister*). There are 3.4 million companies entered on the German Business Register.[14]

US tax administration statistics for 2008 show approximately 6 million corporations.[15] Again, the vast majority of these are small and unquoted. The corporate sector accounted for 82% of total business receipts in the US, compared to 4% for sole proprietors and 14% for partnerships (including limited liability companies). Corporations accounted for only 18% of the total number of business entities in the US, substantially lower than the proportion in the UK. The majority of business entities (72%) were sole proprietorships, with partnerships forming the smallest portion (10%).[16]

---

[11] Department for Business Innovation and Skills, *Business Population Estimates for the UK and Regions*, available at www.bis.gov.uk/analysis/statistics/business-population-estimates, accessed 16 July 2012.

[12] The European Commission does maintain statistics on the number of businesses and their classification as small, medium-sized or large. In 2008 there were approximately 21 million EU businesses in the non-financial sector. Generally, see http://epp.eurostat.ec.europa.eu/portal/page/portal/european_business/introduction, accessed 16 July 2012. The European Business Register does incorporate links to the company registers of many (but not all) member states, available at www.ebr.org, accessed 16 July 2012.

[13] For a shared portal for trade registers of the German states, see www.handelsregister.de/rp_web/welcome.do, accessed 16 July 2012.

[14] Available at www.unternehmensregister.de/ureg, accessed 16 July 2012.

[15] This number would be closer to 8 million if limited liability companies are included. However, limited liability companies are not technically corporations and so are treated as partnerships in the tax administration statistics.

[16] Internal Revenue Service, *Business Tax* Statistics, available at www.irs.gov/taxstats/bustaxstats/index.html, accessed 16 July 2012.

So corporations are undoubtedly important, but what is a 'corporation'? As with so many complexities, the answer you receive may depend on the perspective of the person who is asked. The word is a derivative of the Latin 'corpus' meaning body. The *Oxford English Dictionary* defines 'corporation' in terms of the action or condition of being 'incorporated'. 'Incorporate' is defined, in turn, as 'to embody'. A related phrase is 'body corporate', which on the face of it seems rather an oxymoron. Its sibling phrase 'body politic' seems more straightforward, meaning the embodiment of a group of persons united in a 'polis', typically used with respect to nations or states. Both 'body corporate' and 'body politic' are defined in terms of a corporation. So, 'corporation' is also defined in terms of a 'number of persons united, or regarded as united, in one body; a body of persons'.[17]

A related term, and one that is often confused with 'corporation', is 'company'. When an individual is in the presence of others, we say the individual is 'in company'. Hence 'company' is defined in terms of 'companionship, fellowship, society' or 'in the society of others, amidst other people, as opposed to *alone*'.[18] So, although the terms 'corporation' and 'company' are related, they are not synonymous. A group of individuals may be in company or a company of persons, but that does not mean they are a corporation or 'body of persons'. It is the embodiment of the group or company that makes them a corporation. Similarly, something may be incorporated (embodied) even though it is not a group of persons.

So the key to 'corporation' is embodiment, but embodiment for what purpose? As mentioned, that may depend on the person being asked. For a lawyer, a corporation is embodiment with a separate legal personality. Where a group of persons is embodied in this way, it is a 'corporation aggregate'. Where the embodiment is a position of a single person (and the person's successors), it is a 'corporation sole'. The British crown is a corporation sole. For a lawyer, the key to a corporation is the bestowal of a legal personality separate and independent of the persons who make up the corporation. For an economist, the embodiment may be to act independently in the economy. A political scientist may view the corporation as a means of regulating collective action or investment.[19]

Because this is book about corporate tax *law*, the focus is a legal one. It is the bestowal of legal personality on a corporation that is the primary

---

[17] *Oxford English Dictionary*. For a detailed consideration of the meaning and history of the term 'body corporate', see Montagu (2001).

[18] Ibid.

[19] Generally, see Harris (1996, pp. 40–8).

source, or at least symptomatic of, the complexity caused by corporations for tax laws. That personality is conferred on corporations by statute, though not exclusively. For example, in the UK, the vast majority of corporations are 'companies' (in the sense of that word discussed earlier) registered under the Companies Act 2006. Once a company is registered, section 6 of the Act provides the following effects:

> (2) The subscribers to the memorandum, together with such other persons as may from time to time become members of the company, are a body corporate by the name stated in the certificate of incorporation.

> (3) That body corporate is capable of exercising all the functions of an incorporated company.

In particular, any limitations on a company's legal capacity imposed by the doctrine of *ultra vires* were lifted in 2006.[20] A contract made by a company is subject to the same 'formalities required by law in the case of a contract made by an individual'.[21] The German corporate law is somewhat briefer and simply provides a corporation with 'its own legal personality'.[22]

As noted, corporate law in the US is regulated by its states. There are two legal sources of particular importance in this regard. First, a majority of US states have adopted in whole or in part the American Bar Association's Model Business Corporation Act ('MBCA') as their general corporate law.[23] Second, the State of Delaware boasts that 'more than 900,000 business entities have their legal home in Delaware including more than 50% of all U.S. publicly-traded companies and 63% of the Fortune 500'.[24] Accordingly, Delaware's General Corporation Law ('DGCL') is particularly important.[25] The MBCA provides that, once incorporated,

> every corporation has perpetual duration and succession in its corporate name and has the same powers as an individual to do all things necessary or convenient to carry out its business and affairs.[26]

Similarly, the DGGL provides broad powers to a corporation created under it, including powers to sue and be sued, hold property and engage in contracts.[27]

---

[20] Companies Act 2006 (UK) s. 39.
[21] Companies Act 2006 (UK) s. 43(2).
[22] Companies Law (*Aktiengesetz*) ('AktG') (Germany) s. 1.
[23] The most recent version of this model is American Bar Association (2010).
[24] Delaware Division of Corporations *2011 Annual Report*, available at http://corp.delaware.gov/, accessed 16 July 2012.
[25] For the purposes of this study, these sources are used as representative of US corporate law.
[26] MBCA (US) s. 3.02.
[27] DGCL (US) s. 122.

Tax law rules primarily attach to legal relations between persons, particularly those based on contract. In the context of corporations, this means attaching tax consequences to the legal relations of something that does not per se exist. Corporations are an artificial legal construct.[28] The artificial nature of the corporation is a theme that runs throughout this book, as it is of most any book that deals with law and corporations. Like other corporate laws, the German Companies Law (*Aktiengesetz*), the UK Companies Act 2006 and the US MBCA and DGCL go on to regulate many other activities of registered corporations, including calculation of corporate profits, corporate surplus and the distribution of dividends. Another continuing theme of this book is a consideration of the extent to which tax law follows corporate law classification and regulation of these activities.

## The 'corporate tax system'

As noted earlier, direct taxes, including income tax, are intended to be borne by the person on whom they are imposed. However, as a result of their artificial nature, corporations cannot bear the burden of taxes, irrespective of the intention of the legislature. Only individuals may bear the burden of taxes (i.e. may be the subject of tax incidence):

> Perhaps the most important point to keep in mind when considering company taxation is that it is not meaningful to think about the effects of taxes on companies separately from the effects of those taxes on the individuals associated with companies.[29]

At some level, there is no such thing as direct taxation of a corporation. Any tax on a corporation involves the indirect taxation of individuals. Attempting to subject a corporation to direct taxation invites individuals to hide or shelter their personal tax responsibility behind the legal cloak of a corporation. In the words of a confessed satirist, a corporation is an 'ingenious device for obtaining individual profit without individual responsibility'.[30]

---

[28] 'A corporation is an abstraction. It has no mind of its own any more than it has a body of its own'. *Lennard's Carrying Co Ltd* v. *Asiatic Petroleum Co Ltd* [1915] AC 705 (HL) at 713 per Viscount Haldane. 'The company as such was only a juristic figment of the imagination, lacking both a body to be kicked and a soul to be damned'. *Northern Counties Securities Ltd* v. *Jackson & Steeple Ltd* [1974] 2 All ER 625 (ChD) at 634, a passage usually attributed to Lord Thurlow (1731–1806).

[29] Mirrlees et al. (2011, p. 408).

[30] Bierce (2010, p. 31).

Nevertheless, direct tax laws must and do deal with corporations and dealings with and in them. Commonly, the provisions that address these matters are among the most complex and controversial. This is certainly true of the income tax, which is the main form of direct taxation. In most countries, it is by far the largest direct tax; in many cases, it is the largest tax of all when taxes on income are aggregated.[31] 'Taxes on income' include direct taxes on creations of wealth (i.e. profits, gains or value added, irrespective of label). Many countries impose more than one tax on income, and commonly these taxes are related. So, in the UK, taxes on income include income tax, corporation tax, capital gains tax and national insurance contributions.[32] Germany and the US also separate corporation tax from personal income tax. By contrast, Australia is an example of a country with a unified income tax on individuals and corporations.

As mentioned, this book is about income taxation of corporations and dealings with and in them. More particularly, its primary purpose is to analyse how the introduction of a corporation affects the fundamental features of an income tax. It is not directly concerned with generic issues of income taxation, such as the calculation of business profits, because that calculation is not peculiar to corporations. Rather, it is concerned with the special rules of an income tax law that exist only because of the peculiar nature of a corporation and, in particular, its artificial nature. In this book, these legal rules are referred to as the 'corporate tax system'.

The policy that should underlie a corporate tax system is a matter of continuous debate.[33] This book offers a conceptual framework within which to identify and analyse the options for a corporate tax system and the policy underlying the various options. Particular options are considered at appropriate points throughout this book, but it is useful to make some general observations regarding corporate tax systems and tax policy.

The artificial nature of the corporation is the overpowering consideration in formulating corporate tax policy. That nature often means that

---

[31] With respect to member countries of the Organisation for Economic Co-operation and Development ('OECD'), see the *OECD Tax Database*, available at www.oecd. org/document/60/0,3746,en_2649_37427_1942460_1_1_1_37427,00.html, accessed 16 July 2012.

[32] National insurance contributions are largely imposed on income from employment. This book makes only fleeting reference to national insurance contributions.

[33] For a recent example, compare the differences in Alworth (2010), Auerbach, Devereux & Simpson (2010), Gordon & Hausman (2010), Griffith, Hines & Sørensen (2010), Huizinga (2010), Mintz (2010) and Mirrlees et al. (2011, chapters 17 & 18), all part of the same study.

there is no clear policy path, only points in a spectrum. The distinction (or lack thereof) between widely held and closely held corporations and between debt and equity capital are examples of the spectrum problem. There are many others. Tax laws draw lines in these spectrums, and every time that they do, corporations are structured to manipulate the line drawing. Where a corporation is involved, it seems that nearly all activities are substitutable.

In recent times, tax policy has largely been driven by economics.[34] However, a brief perusal of any tax law reveals how little economics is involved. Tax laws regulate and feed off of legal and business relations. Providing professional advice regarding these relations is the domain of lawyers and accountants. It is the lawyers and accountants who *use* tax laws. Tax planning involves manipulating legal relations to change tax consequences (i.e. the very nature of tax planning is to engage in substitution). Corporations are a base tool in tax planning, precisely because of their artificial and cloaking nature. Although economists should and do provide input into the design of a corporate tax system, no amount of charts, projections and assumptions will provide adequate guidance or protection for a corporate tax system. Ultimately, the detail of corporate tax policy is predominantly a matter for the people using and abusing the system: lawyers and accountants.

Within its conceptual framework, this book considers structural issues that give rise to tax planning through corporations. It considers how corporations may be used to challenge and shift the very foundations of income taxation. However, this is not a book about tax planning, tax avoidance or tax evasion and the difference between these concepts, if one exists. In particular, although this book may make reference to legal tests referring to a tax avoidance motive, the various forms and features of such a motive are not investigated independently as a topic. So this book does not consider what a tax avoidance motive involves, whether it should be tested subjectively or objectively or whether two people conducting the same activities should be taxed differently depending on their motives.[35]

Much abusive tax planning plays on structural defects in the corporate tax system. For a century, as the use of corporations has become increasingly sophisticated, legislatures have attempted to patch these

---

[34] Again, this is illustrated by Mirrlees et al. (2010) and Mirrlees et al. (2011).

[35] There is a wide literature on tax avoidance. For a book dealing with approaches in a number of countries, see Avery Jones et al. (2008). For a greater focus on the UK from a recognised international expert on tax avoidance and the law, see Tiley (2008, Chapter 5).

defects, apparently oblivious to the structural damage the patching causes to the tax system. Most countries suffer from this problem, but the UK is perhaps the most extreme example. It is fair to suggest that at no point was the UK corporate tax system designed on purpose. Indeed, it seems that this system has no *design* to it. Income tax was introduced in the UK in 1799, long before the advent of the modern registered company with legal personality.[36] When the registered company did appear in 1844, the existing income tax structure was applied to it.[37] There were some immediate issues (e.g. problems of corporate residence). However, most cracks from this lack of consideration appeared as the income tax became more sophisticated, particularly with the introduction of high progressive tax rates just before and during the First World War.

Since that time, legislative plugging of the UK corporate tax system, and of the income tax system generally, has continued unabated. The same is true in other countries. The plugging has accelerated dramatically in recent years. In the mid-1990s, the UK government began a project rewriting its income tax laws.[38] Initially dubbed 'simplification', it soon became a simple 'rewrite' with improved expression. What it should have been called was 'fragmentation'. By the time the rewrite project finished in 2010, the tax laws applicable to income tax had been fragmented into the following main categories:

Capital Allowances Act 2001 ('CAA 2001')
Income Tax (Earnings and Pensions) Act 2003 ('ITEPA 2003')
Income Tax (Trading and Other Income) Act 2005 ('ITTOIA 2005')
Income Tax Act 2007 ('ITA 2007')
Corporation Tax Act 2009 ('CTA 2009')
Corporation Tax Act 2010 ('CTA 2010')
Taxation (International and Other Provisions) Act 2010 ('TIOPA 2010')

Despite the rewrite, provisions remain in the Income and Corporation Taxes Act 1988 ('ICTA 1988'), the law from which the majority of provisions were rewritten. The Taxation of Chargeable Gains Act 1992 ('TCGA 1992') has not been rewritten. This book refers to these acts as the UK's 'income tax laws'.[39] The *only* thing that is *clear* from this mess of laws is that the UK corporate tax system has no discernable structure.

---

[36] Regarding the taxation of corporations before and during the Napoleonic income tax, see Harris (2006).
[37] Generally, see Avery Jones (2011).
[38] For a recent reflection on the rewrite, see Tiley (2010a).
[39] Interpretation Act 1978 Schedule 1 defines 'Tax Acts' as being the 'Income Tax Acts' and the 'Corporation Tax Acts'. These terms are further defined, but in an imprecise fashion

By comparison, the income tax laws of Germany and the US are relatively settled as to structure, although they too have suffered from greater complexity in recent years. German income tax law is governed by the Income Tax Law (*Einkommensteuergesetz*, 'EStG') and the Corporate Income Tax Law (*Körperschaftsteuergesetz*, 'KStG'). There are other relevant tax laws of which the Reorganization Tax Act (*Umwandlungssteuergesetz*, 'UmwStG') is relevant in the context of this book. The US has a single Internal Revenue Code ('IRC'), being Title 26 of the US Code. Subtitle A is dedicated to income taxes, including the tax on individuals and the tax on corporations.

As for the European Commission's CCCTB Proposal, it could only ever be an overlay to the existing corporate tax systems of EU member states. The EU has no power to impose direct taxation, and so the Proposal, if it becomes effective, would at best require member states to amend their corporate tax systems in line with it. This is because the Proposal would take effect as a directive and member states are required to implement directives. However, even if a member state does not implement a directive, the directive still has direct effect in that EU nationals are granted rights under the directive that courts of EU member states are required to enforce in priority to national law.[40]

## Scope and structure of the book

A corporate tax system involves the special rules of an income tax law that exist only because of the peculiar nature of a corporation and, in particular, its artificial personality. These special rules are needed to cater for the impact of a corporation on the fundamental features of an income tax. Therefore, to identify the scope of a corporate tax system, it is necessary to consider the scope of income tax. This book does not engage with the long and detailed debate over the nature of income, but rather adopts a working definition based on observations of what income tax laws tax in practice.[41] In particular, it presumes a realisations base.[42]

---

that does not list the acts covered. In particular, it seems that at least capital gains taxation of individuals would be excluded.

[40] See Harris & Oliver (2010, pp. 26, 27 and 40) and the references cited therein.

[41] Generally regarding the concept of 'income', see Harris (1996, pp. 20–7), Holmes (2001) and Dodge (2012), and the references cited in each.

[42] Regarding the prevalence of the realisations requirement, see Ault & Arnold (2010, pp. 232–7). It is clearly expressed in CCCTB Proposal Art. 9(1), which provides that 'profits and losses shall be recognised only when realised'.

An income tax seeks to tax creations of wealth accruing to a person when and if transformed by a payment by another person. The result is that 'payments' are the building blocks of the income tax base. A payment is a bestowal of value in whatever form by one person on another person. Payments have certain fundamental features. A payment must be considered as made by a particular person and received by another person. A payment must be quantified, particularly if it is not in cash. A payment must be considered as made and received at a particular time, so as to determine the time period in which to recognise the payment. Finally, a payment must be given a character or label because payments with different characters are treated differently by an income tax law. The netting off of payments made and payments received by a particular person, at least those recognised by a tax system, gives rise to the person's net or total income or profits (i.e. income subject to tax).[43] An income tax system then applies a tax rate or tax treatment to this net amount.[44]

The nature of a corporation as a separate legal person means that a corporation can, from a legal perspective, make and receive payments. Therefore, a corporation can have or own income. Chapter 1 of this book considers the taxation of income *derived* by a corporation.[45] For purposes of simplicity and focus, other issues are blotted out in this chapter. The chapter presumes an existing and continuing corporation that does not distribute its income / profits. That is, the chapter considers retained profits of a corporation with a static shareholder base. It is concerned with three primary issues: the manner in which an income tax law identifies entities subject to the corporate tax system, special issues in the tax base calculation that arise by reason of the nature of a corporation and the tax treatment of corporate retained profits (i.e. who should be taxed with respect to those profits and at what rate).

The artificial nature of the corporation becomes particularly clear when corporations distribute their profits (i.e. distribute dividends). Invariably, income tax laws treat dividends as income and, in particular, as a separate source of income from the corporate profits from which they are distributed. This means that corporate income possesses a peculiar nature:

---

[43] By reason of this netting, this book often uses the words 'income' and 'profits' interchangeably. It specifically notes where a gross concept of income (i.e. receipts) is intended.

[44] For more regarding matters discussed in this paragraph, see Harris & Oliver (2010, pp. 8–14).

[45] Tax laws use different phrases to identify income with or allocate income to persons. This book uses the term 'derive', but some tax laws, including those in the UK, use multiple terms such as 'earn', 'entitled to', 'realise' and 'receive'.

it is derived twice. It is income first when derived by the corporation and a second time when distributed as dividends. This peculiar nature means that income tax laws invariably incorporate special rules dealing with the taxation of dividends. Those special rules are discussed in Chapter 2. That chapter first discusses the difficult issues of how to identify, for income tax purposes, shares and distributions with respect to shares. It then proceeds to consider the special tax treatment of dividends. As with Chapter 1, Chapter 2 presumes there is no adjustment in shareholding.

Whereas Chapters 1 and 2 focus on domestic tax issues, Chapter 3 extends those issues into an international setting. It notes that most all income tax laws treat resident and non-resident corporations differently, and so the chapter is structured under two primary headings. The first deals with the three scenarios involving the derivation and distribution of profits of resident corporations that involve international factors. Similarly, the second heading deals with the three scenarios involving the derivation and distribution of profits of non-resident corporations.

Corporate profits cause double vision for a tax system, because they are income both when derived and when distributed. This reflects the artificial nature of the corporation. In fact, everything that happens with respect to the corporation reflects its artificial nature. In particular, the assets held by and value of a corporation are reflected in the shares held in the corporation. Chapter 4 begins a series of chapters that focus on dealings in share interests. There are a limited number of ways in which share interests may be dealt with. Share interests may be created, they may be transferred, they may be terminated and they may be varied. Chapters 4 to 7 deal with these matters.

Chapter 4 considers the creation of share interests (i.e. the tax consequences of the issue of shares by a corporation). Shares may be issued for cash or in return for assets. Shares issued for cash raise few income tax issues, but those issued for assets involve both a disposal of assets by the prospective shareholder and an acquisition of shares and so the situation is more involved. This is particularly so with respect to the incorporation of a business or a subsidiary. The issue of incorporation is the primary focus of Chapter 4.

Chapter 5 moves to the transfer of share interests, which may have consequences at the shareholder level and at the corporate level. At the shareholder level, the issues revolve around the treatment of gains and losses on the disposal of shares. A particular issue involves gains on the disposal of shares that reflect taxed retained profits of the corporation. Issues at the corporate level involve the consequences for a corporation where the transfer of shares results in a change of ownership of the corporation. The ownership of a corporation may also change as a result of creating or terminating shares. However, such a change most commonly happens in the context of a transfer of shares, and so issues of change of ownership are discussed in Chapter 5.

Termination of share interests is considered in Chapter 6. In countries that maintain a par value share approach, a reduction of capital may be viewed as a partial termination of an interest in a share. Reduction of capital is the first matter discussed in Chapter 6. The chapter then moves to consider terminations that result in the cancellation of share interests, but that do not involve a termination of the corporation itself. Here the discussion considers partial liquidations involving the buy-back or redemption of shares. Finally, the chapter discusses the tax consequences of dissolving a corporation, whether solvent or insolvent, both from the perspective of the corporation and the perspective of the shareholder.

Chapter 7 discusses variations of share interests. A variation involves a creation, transfer or termination of share interests or a combination of these. This chapter differs from the earlier chapters in an important respect: Chapter 7 presumes that a person has a similar quantum of interest in the corporation both before and after the variation, or at least the interest before the variation is in some way identifiable with the interest after the variation. There are only so many ways in which a share interest may be varied. It may be exchanged or substituted, it may be split or divided or two interests may be consolidated. Further, the interests held before the variation and after the variation may be in the same corporation, or they may be in different corporations. In colloquial terms, this chapter focuses on corporate reconstructions and amalgamations, including, in the context of multiple corporations, mergers and de-mergers.

This book focuses on three primary artificialities faced by a tax system that derive from the nature of a corporation: the artificiality of the corporation as a separate income-deriving entity (Chapter 1), the artificiality of the corporation as a separate source of income in the form of dividends (Chapter 2) and the artificiality of interests in corporations as a separate form of asset from the assets held by corporations (Chapters 4–7). The interaction of the first two artificialities (economic double taxation of distributed corporate income) is considered in Chapter 2. Chapter 5 considers the interaction of the first and third artificialities (economic double taxation of gains on the disposal of shares). The final chapter of this book focuses on the interaction between the second and third artificialities. Chapter 8 considers turning dividends into capital gains on disposal or shares or vice versa in the context of the manipulative practices known as dividend stripping and capital stripping.

Chapters 1–8 cover all aspects that make up a corporate tax system. The issues covered by these chapters can be made as complex as one prefers. They can be, and are, covered by texts consisting of many volumes. In all the discussion that follows this introduction, the focus is on structure, policy options and the interrelationship between issues. An appreciation of the interrelationship between issues is a matter that is poorly lacking in the corporate tax systems of many countries. So although the discussion in this book does illustrate structure, policy and interrelationship issues with practical examples, what it does not do is discuss technical details where none of these considerations are apparent. In other words, what this book does not do is discuss detail for detail's sake.

# Chapter 1

## Taxation of corporate income when derived

Some of the primary features of a corporate tax system involve a corporation deriving income. The fact that a corporation can derive income stems from its separate legal *personality*. A corporation is a 'person' and can make profits from its contracts and dealings just as an individual can. Therefore, income tax laws that refer to 'person' and make liable to tax the 'person receiving or entitled to the income' or 'profits' automatically make corporations taxable with respect to their income.[1] The concept of 'person' is discussed further at 1.1.1.1.

However, just because corporations have, own or derive income as a legal fact does not mean that a tax law must respect the corporation's separate legal identity for tax purposes. A tax law, for its purposes, may override the corporate law prescription that a corporation is a *person* and ignore the separate legal personality of the corporation. Similarly, just because the law does not imbue an entity with separate legal personality does not mean that a tax law may not treat that entity as having and deriving its own income. In identifying entities that are the subject of a corporate tax system, a tax law may be both broader and narrower than the entities that are imbued with separate personality by law. The identification of entities as the subject of the corporate tax system is discussed under the first heading.[2]

The second heading of this chapter considers the calculation of income or profits derived by a corporation for tax purposes. As mentioned in

---

[1] For example, ITTOIA 2005 (UK) ss. 8, 271 & 689. As discussed at 1.3.1, the vast majority of corporations in the UK are subject to corporation tax instead of income tax by reason of CTA 2009 (UK) s. 3. German income tax law makes a distinction between 'physical persons' and 'corporations, unincorporated organizations, and trusts': Income Tax Law (EStG; Germany) s. 1 and KStG (Germany) s. 1, respectively. Similarly, US tax law distinguishes between 'individuals' and 'corporations': IRC (US) Parts I and II. The CCCTB Proposal applies to 'companies': CCCTB Proposal Art. 1.

[2] For simplicity purposes and unless stated otherwise, this book presumes that entities identified as the subjects of a corporate tax system are corporations.

the introduction, only retained profits are considered at this stage and the shareholding is presumed to be static. General issues that arise with respect to the calculation of the income tax base are not specific to corporations and so are not considered in this book. Rather, its focus is on special issues raised for the tax base by the nature of the corporation or the way in which it is regulated.

Like tax law, corporate law also requires corporations to calculate their profits and regulates the manner in which this is done. The purposes for which corporations calculate profits under corporate law and tax law are not the same or at least are not perfectly aligned. So, a primary issue for a tax law is whether and to what extent it accepts and follows corporate law rules for the calculation of profits. This is the first matter discussed under the second heading. Similarly, corporate law generally prescribes reporting of profits for corporate groups. Few countries, if any, accept this reporting for tax purposes, other than in minor respects. However, corporate groups raise particular issues for a corporate tax system, and these are discussed at appropriate points throughout this book. The second heading of this chapter considers special tax base issues raised by corporate groups.

Another issue arising from the existence of corporations is the interface between the tax base used for corporations and that used for individuals. This is particularly an issue for small or closely held corporations, and the interface becomes obvious and acute when an individual seeks to incorporate a business. Although Chapter 4 considers the immediate consequences of incorporation, the second heading of this chapter considers interface issues that pertain to the tax base (i.e. the extent to which the personal and corporate tax bases should be aligned, at least for closely held corporations).

Once a tax law has identified a corporation and prescribed the calculation of its income or profits, it must proceed to prescribe the tax treatment of those profits. The taxation of retained profits of corporations is a particularly contentious issue, which is discussed under the third heading of this chapter. Corporate tax systems typically tax corporations with respect to their income. In this case, the primary issue is the selection of a corporate tax rate. There is no such thing as a 'correct' corporate tax rate, but there are factors that may inform its selection and there may be consequences arising from that choice. These issues are explored in the first part of the third heading.

However, just because a tax law recognises that a corporation has income does not mean that the tax law will prescribe taxation of the corporation with respect to its income. Rather, it may prescribe that another person is taxable with respect to income retained by a corporation, typically the shareholders, but this is not the only possibility. So finally, the chapter considers the *transparent* taxation of a corporation's retained profits. Transparent taxation is not the same as ignoring the existence of the corporation. It is still the corporation's income; it is just that another person is taxed with respect to it.

## 1.1   Identifying and classifying corporations

An income tax law must identify the types of 'entity', from a range of possibilities, that are the subject of its corporate tax system. The term 'entity' has numerous meanings. In tax laws it tends to be used in the sense of a being or body, something having a quality of individual existence as opposed to the 'qualities or relations' of the thing. In particular, an individual is an entity. In tax laws, other entities tend to have some form of relationship with individuals, but can be perceived as independent of them and their activities. These other entities are necessarily artificial in nature and constitute intermediaries through which individuals conduct activities. Of further relevance is 'body', which may be defined in terms of an 'entity; a thing which exists'. A body is that which 'either doeth or suffereth', and this quality seems of particular relevance in identifying entities for income tax law purposes.[3]

The US income tax law is quite direct in identifying entities subject to it. The Internal Revenue Code (IRC) commonly imposes income tax law obligations on 'taxpayers', a term that is defined by reference to 'persons'.[4] 'Person', in turn, is defined to 'mean and include an individual, a trust, estate, partnership, association, company or corporation'.[5] These are the potential range of tax subjects in the US. The IRC proceeds to define some of these entities, including 'partnership' and 'corporation', though not 'trust', 'estate', 'association' or 'company'.[6] The word 'association' is particularly unclear and is also used in the definition of 'corporation', discussed at 1.1.1.1.

The German income tax laws also refer to 'taxpayer' in many places. However, the Income Tax Law only applies to 'physical persons', and so in principle only individuals are 'taxpayers'.[7] Nevertheless, the Corporate

---

[3]  *Oxford English Dictionary*, definitions of 'entity', 'being', 'thing' and 'body'.
[4]  IRC (US) s. 7701(a)(14).
[5]  IRC (US) s. 7701(a)(1).
[6]  IRC (US) s. 7701(a)(2) & (3).
[7]  In particular, EStG (Germany) s. 1.

Income Tax Law applies many provisions of the Income Tax Law, and so, indirectly, non-individual taxpayers are often covered by the latter.[8] Therefore there is no definition of 'person' or 'entity' under German income tax law. Rather, there are physical persons and entities subject to corporate income tax. Entities are largely determined according to available commercial law entities, a matter further discussed at 1.1.1.1. As noted at that point, German income tax law also grapples with the concept of 'unincorporated organisations'. Similarly, there is no definition of 'person' or 'entity' in the Proposal for a Council Directive on a Common Consolidated Corporate Tax Base (CCCTB), which uses 'taxpayer', defined by reference to 'company'.[9]

The position in the UK is comparatively a mess. UK income tax laws use the word 'entity' in numerous places, but without definition. These uses suggest that an individual is not an 'entity', but that a company or corporation is.[10] It seems likely that a trust is an 'entity', even an entity independent of its trustees. Contrast the Australian income tax law, in which a comprehensive definition of 'entity' expressly includes individuals, corporations, partnerships, associations, bodies of persons and trusts.[11] So like the US approach, Australian law uses a concept to identify the range of subjects to which tax law obligations may affix and then uses that concept consistently; however, Australian law labels the concept 'entity', whereas the US law uses 'person'. By comparison, the UK has little structure to its approach, which is fragmented and confusing.[12]

As in the US, the primary term used in the UK to identify the subject of tax law obligations is 'person'. However, UK income tax law does not define this term, and its ordinary legal meaning suggests that it would be limited to individuals and corporations. This meaning is extended by the Interpretation Act 1978 to include 'a body of persons corporate or unincorporate'.[13] However, the Interpretation Act does not define 'body of persons'. Its ordinary meaning suggests it would cover all the types of entity referred to in US or Australian tax law, with the exclusion of individuals and perhaps trusts (as opposed to trustees).[14]

---

[8]  KStG (Germany) ss. 8(1) and 31.
[9]  CCCTB Proposal Arts. 1 and 4.
[10] See Income Tax Act (ITA) 2007 (UK) s. 997, CTA 2010 (UK) s. 1127, and Taxation (International and Other Provisions) Act (TIOPA) 2010 (UK) s. 340.
[11] Income Tax Assessment Act 1997 (Australia) s. 960–100.
[12] Generally, see Harris (2011).
[13] Interpretation Act 1978 (UK) First Schedule.
[14] See Avery Jones (1991, pp. 458–9).

Confusingly, although the Interpretation Act does not define 'body of persons', UK tax law defines it to mean

> any body politic, corporate or collegiate and any company, fraternity, fellowship and society of persons whether corporate or not corporate . . .[15]

This definition incorporates a list of entities that dates back to the land tax and earlier subsidies beginning in 1450. The result is that where the UK income tax laws use the word 'person', a 'body of persons' according to its general meaning is included. However, where those laws use the phrase 'body of persons', only its tax law definition is used. The situation is far from satisfactory.[16]

Having identified possible entities, a tax law must proceed to determine which of them constitute the subjects of its corporate tax system. The manner in which a tax law does this is discussed at 1.1.1. However, just because a tax law identifies an entity as a 'corporation', and intends that all corporations should be the subjects of its corporate tax system, does not mean that the tax law will treat all of those corporations in precisely the same manner. Invariably, tax laws go further and subcategorise the subjects of the corporate tax system. Section 1.1.2 discusses the ways in which corporations may be subcategorised for the purposes of a corporate tax system.

One manner in which corporations may be subcategorised is by reference to their owners and controllers. However, the manner in which a corporation is owned and controlled may call into question whether the corporation is an appropriate subject of the corporate tax system at all. So categorisation of corporations by reference to their owners and controllers crosses the divide between recognition of tax subject and subcategory. For this reason, this book deals separately with such categorisation. The third subheading explores the relationship between a corporation and the persons that own or control it. The fourth subheading discusses how a corporate tax system may respond to various forms of this relationship, and the final subheading considers how a corporation may be subcategorised by reference to its owners and controllers.

---

[15] ITA 2007 (UK) s. 989 and Taxes Management Act 1970 (UK) s. 118(1).

[16] Generally, see Avery Jones (1991) and Harris (2011). By contrast, the Australian income tax law defines 'person' to include a 'company'. This might seem a rather limiting definition of 'person', but for the fact that 'company' is defined to include an 'unincorporated association or body of persons'; Income Tax Assessment Act 1997 (Australia) s. 960–100. The result seems to be similar to that in the UK, but with no definition of 'body of persons' in the income tax law, thus avoiding the UK confusion.

### 1.1.1   Identifying corporations

As mentioned earlier, in selecting the subjects of a corporate tax system, most countries go beyond a literal meaning of 'corporation' and include some entities that do not have separate legal personality. In addition, some tax laws exclude from their corporate tax system entities that are truly corporations. These tax law adjustments are often achieved through a definition of 'corporation' or 'company'. General definitional issues are the first matter dealt with under this subheading. Some tax laws have a habit of indirectly extending the definition, at least for particular purposes. These laws exclude certain entities from the general definition of 'corporation', but then proceed to treat them as corporations for identified purposes, and sometimes generally. These *tack-on* regimes are the other matter dealt with under this subheading.

One should not underestimate the importance of identifying entities as subjects of a corporate tax system. Through this mechanism governments make policy decisions as to how to tax individuals conducting their activities through different intermediaries. Individuals conducting their activities through one form of entity that is within the definition are usually taxed differently from those conducting their activities directly or through another form of entity that is not within the definition. If these activities are similar and the different forms of entity are freely available, the tax system creates a distortion as to the use of one particular type of entity over another.[17] Tax law distortions favouring or disfavouring incorporation are a continuing theme of this book.

#### 1.1.1.1   Definition

Tax laws must identify the entities that are the subject of the corporate tax system. Tax laws of civil law jurisdictions often incorporate a list of entities subject to corporation tax in the charging provision. This is the approach under the German Corporate Income Tax Law.[18] Part One of that law provides further details as to entities subject to the German corporate tax system. The approach in the CCCTB Proposal is quite similar. Article 2 would apply the Directive to 'companies' of a type listed in Annex I of the Proposal that are established under the laws of a member state. The list includes all types of companies subject to the corporate tax laws

---

[17]  Generally, see Crawford & Freedman (2010).
[18]  KStG (Germany) s. 1.

of member states, but in some cases (including that of the UK) only some of these entities are covered.[19]

By contrast, the tax laws of common law jurisdictions tend to incorporate a general collective definition of entities that are the subject of their corporate tax system. The term used by common law jurisdictions is typically 'company', but in some countries is 'corporation'. The term 'company' seems to be used most often for two reasons. First, the registered company is the most common form of corporation. Second, the legislature intends to cover many more entities than just corporations.

The UK corporate tax system applies to 'companies'. Section 992 of ITA 2007 provides that a

> 'company' means any body corporate or unincorporated association, but does not include a partnership, a local authority or a local authority association.

The same definition is found in section 1121 of Corporation Tax Act (CTA) 2010. This definition was adopted in 1965 with the introduction of the corporation tax. Some argue that the definition was intended to cover all 'persons' that were not individuals or partnerships, and so it covers 'bodies of persons' as that phrase is used in the Interpretation Act 1978. This is the reason for the reference to 'body corporate' and 'unincorporated association', but the definition – in particular, 'unincorporated association' – has taken on its own meaning.[20]

This can be contrasted with the US approach, which provides this definition of 'corporation':

> The term 'corporation' includes associations, joint-stock companies, and insurance companies.[21]

It will be noted that the UK's definition is a 'means' definition, and so 'company' does not have its ordinary meaning. By contrast, the US approach uses an 'includes' definition, and so 'corporation' takes its ordinary meaning and, in addition, is extended by the inclusions.

**Corporations**   Corporate tax systems primarily focus on 'corporations' within the general legal meaning of that term. This focus is clear in the

[19] Only 'companies incorporated' in the UK are covered. It seems this phrase is not co-extensive with a 'body corporate' and so would not cover a limited liability partnership.
[20] Generally, see Harris (2011). Contrast the Australian definition of 'company', given at fn 11, which expressly includes both 'unincorporated associations' and 'bodies of persons'.
[21] IRC (US) s. 7701(a)(3).

UK reference to 'body corporate' (in the definition of 'company') and the US inclusive definition of 'corporation'. It is also clear in the German list approach, which includes the primary forms of 'corporation'[22] and residually 'other private law legal entities'.[23] 'Corporation' or 'body corporate' means an artificial entity that is imbued with personality by law.[24] Corporate status is most commonly achieved by statute, but incorporation may also be (largely historically) granted by charter or letters patent.

Having separate legal personality means that these entities own their assets (both legally and beneficially) and are capable of having their own income at general law (i.e. the law as it applies generally and outside specific contexts such as taxation). The most common type of corporation is the registered company limited by shares. However, there are other types of corporation, including companies limited by guarantee, unlimited companies, partnerships granted corporate personality and corporations set up under their own statute for special purposes. The separate personality gives a corporate tax system a certain comfort with these types of entities. This book presumes that a corporation is a registered company limited by shares.

**Unincorporated entities**    Despite their primary focus on corporations, corporate tax systems also typically cover certain types of unincorporated entities. Which types of unincorporated entity are covered varies from country to country, and it is difficult to generalise, although partnerships are usually excluded in one way or another.

In the UK, the definition of 'company' includes 'unincorporated associations'. This acts as a form of residual entity category. Historically, the 'unincorporated' and 'association / society' elements of 'unincorporated association' were interpreted separately, as in the tax law definition of 'body of persons'. However, in *Conservative and Unionist Central Office v Burrell* the Court of Appeal interpreted the two terms as a joint phrase.[25] The question was whether the investment income of the Central Office

---

[22] KStG (Germany) s. 1(1)1. Expressly included as corporations are Europäische Gesellschaften (European companies established under the *European Company Statute*, Council Regulation (EC) No 2157/2001), Aktiengesellschaften (stock corporations or AGs), Kommanditgesellschaften auf Aktien (limited partnerships with shares or KGaAs) and Gesellschaften mit beschränkter Haftung (limited liability companies or GmbHs).

[23] KStG (Germany) s. 1(1)4.

[24] Although matters are never that simple. See Montagu (2001) regarding the history and meaning of 'body corporate'.

[25] (1981) 55 TC 671 (CA).

(of a political party) was subject to corporation tax or income tax, which were imposed at different rates. It was assumed in this case that, if the Central Office was not assessed as an unincorporated association, the income would be subject to income tax.[26]

In *Conservative and Unionist Central Office*, Lawton LJ defined an 'unincorporated association' in the following terms:

> I infer that by 'unincorporated association' in this context Parliament meant two or more persons bound together for one or more common purposes, not being business purposes, by mutual undertakings, each having mutual duties and obligations, in an organisation which has rules which identify in whom control of it and its funds rests and upon what terms and which can be joined or left at will. The bond of union between the members of an unincorporated association has to be contractual.[27]

The Central Office was not such an association, although clearly each individual constituency office would be.[28] The most common forms of unincorporated associations are clubs and trade associations. 'Unincorporated association' does not cover individuals, partnerships or trusts (the latter two are discussed shortly).

One consequence of an association being unincorporated is that at law it does not own property and cannot contract. So, when including unincorporated entities, it might be expected that a corporate tax system would specify that such entities can own property and have income for tax purposes. Yet such a rule is usually not included, and that is the case in the UK. At least indirectly, this exclusion may have consequences. Although not solely concerned with this issue of the unincorporated nature of certain associations, the issue of mutual trading is at least directly related to it. The question is whether the tax law recognises transactions between members and their association such as to give rise to income of the association. Further consideration of mutual trading is beyond the scope of this book.[29]

In Germany as well, the corporate tax system covers certain unincorporated entities. In particular, the entities subject to corporation tax include

---

[26] In *Conservative and Unionist Central Office* v. *Burrell* (1981) 55 TC 671 (CA), presumably, the Central Office was a body of persons, a grouping of persons (singular including the plural) or a trust. This well demonstrates the confused nature of the UK entity structure and why entity classification matters.

[27] (1981) 55 TC 671 (CA) at 699.

[28] For example, as in *Curtis* v. *Old Monkland Conservative Association* [1906] AC 86 (HL).

[29] Generally, see Bramwell et al. (2009, para. A1.2) and the references cited therein.

'unincorporated associations, institutions, foundations and other special-purpose funds without legal personality under private law'.[30] Unlike the approach in the UK, it seems that these entities can include business entities and so, potentially, partnerships (but see the later discussion on exclusions).

The US approach is also similar, with the definition of 'corporation' including 'associations'. However, unlike the UK and German approach, the US tax law contains no exclusions for particular types of unincorporated association, such as partnerships. Consequently, the US courts adopted a substance approach to 'association' as used in the definition of 'corporation'. In *Morrissey v Commissioner* the US Supreme Court suggested that an organisation will be treated as an association if its characteristics are such that the organisation more nearly resembles a corporation than a partnership or trust.[31] Relevant corporate characteristics include an association (more than one person), objective to carry on business and divide the gains, continuity of life, centralization of management, limited liability, free transferability of interests and holding title to property as an entity. These characteristics were reflected in a list set out in US Treasury Regulations on the definition of 'corporation' (now repealed).

As a result, under US tax law, limited partnerships and some trusts may have been taxed as corporations, depending on their characteristics. The substance approach was problematic in itself, but the US states added to the problems by enacting limited liability company (LLC) statutes. These laws played on the federal list, trying to grant organisations as many corporate attributes as possible without resulting in classification as a corporation for US federal tax purposes. In early 1997, the US tax administration gave up on this approach and adopted an elective regime known as the 'check-the-box' regime. Under this regime many business entities, including limited liability companies, partnerships, trusts and sole traders, may elect whether to be treated as a corporation or be transparent for tax purposes.[32]

**Exclusions**   Sometimes entities are specifically excluded from a corporate tax regime. The German Corporate Income Tax Law provides an

---

[30]   KStG (Germany) s. 1(1)5.

[31]   (1935) 296 US 344 (SC). In this case, a trust created to develop certain real estate was treated as a corporation for tax purposes.

[32]   See Title 26 Code of Federal Regulations (US) § 301.7701–1 and following. The election is not available for businesses incorporated under state laws, insurance companies, banks and state-owned corporations. The election is made by filing Form 8832.

example. It lists the types of entity that are subject to corporation tax. As mentioned earlier, in principle this list might include a partnership. However, section 3(1) of the Corporate Income Tax Law (KStG) goes on to provide that unincorporated associations are not subject to corporation tax if their income is subject to corporation tax or to income tax 'directly through another taxpayer'. The Income Tax Law specifically provides that the income of partners from business includes their 'profit shares' from the partnership.[33] Civil law classification applies for the purposes of determining what is a partnership. As a result, partnerships per se are not subject to corporation tax.

As mentioned, the US definition of 'corporation' is an 'includes' definition and contains no express exclusions. The complex case law on whether a partnership or trust could be considered a 'corporation' was replaced in 1997 with the check-the-box regime. The check-the-box regime means that noncorporate business entities may elect out of the corporate tax system (just as they can elect into it). The position under the CCCTB Proposal would be similar. Although it lists the entities contemplated by the concept of 'company', it only applies to companies that 'opted to apply' the CCCTB system.[34]

By comparison, the UK approach is again messy and an explanation of it would be long-winded. Unlike in Germany or the US, in the UK the exclusion of partnerships (and trusts) from the corporate tax system is not based on their income being taxed to someone else or an election. Rather, in the UK 'partnerships' are expressly excluded from the definition of 'company'.[35] There is no useful definition of 'partnership' or its counterpart 'firm' in the income tax laws.[36] Of more relevance is the definition in section 1 of the Partnership Act 1890:

> Partnership is the relation which subsists between persons carrying on a business in common with a view of profit.

It is clear that an association that is unincorporated and carries on a business is a partnership. Anti-intuitively, however, it seems that according

---

[33] EStG (Germany) s. 15(1)2.
[34] CCCTB Proposal Art. 4(1), definition of 'taxpayer'.
[35] Local authorities and local authority associations are also excluded. Regarding the origins of these exclusions, see Harris (2011).
[36] ITTOIA 2005 (UK) s. 847(1) and CTA 2009 (UK) s. 1257(1) describe 'persons carrying on a trade in partnership' as a 'firm', but that seems irrelevant for the purposes of the definition of 'company'.

to Lawton LJ's definition a partnership is not an 'unincorporated association' (see the earlier discussion) where used in the income tax law definition of 'company', because an 'unincorporated association' requires a non-business purpose. This may be inconsistent with the drafter's intention and the history of the definition.[37]

The Partnership Act definition goes on to exclude corporations from 'partnership'. Of particular importance, this means that, despite their origins as partnerships, companies registered under the Companies Act 2006 are not partnerships. Indeed, it seems that the exclusion in the definition of 'company' in the income tax laws must import the meaning of 'partnership' from the Partnership Act. Otherwise, it may be argued that registered companies are not 'companies' for tax purposes. The problem with importing the Partnership Act definition is that it only excludes corporations formed under UK law. This raises some difficult questions with respect to foreign entities, which are briefly discussed later.

The exclusion of 'partnerships' from the definition of 'company' also raises difficult issues with respect to limited liability partnerships registered under UK law. These entities appear to be and are called 'partnerships', but are given corporate personality by section 1 of the Limited Liability Partnership Act 2000. Therefore, limited liability partnerships seem to fall outside the definition of 'partnership' in the Partnership Act 1890. But would they be 'partnerships' for purposes of the exclusion in the definition of 'company' in the income tax laws? Sections 863(2) of the Income Tax (Trading and Other Income) Act (ITTOIA) 2005 and 1273(2) of CTA 2009 specify that references to 'partnership' in the Taxes Acts include a reference to a 'limited liability partnership', and so a limited liability partnership is a 'partnership' as excluded from the definition of 'company'. Like 'partnership', however, 'limited liability partnership' is not defined, and again this lack of clarity raises issues for foreign entities.

An entity that is not expressly excluded from the definition of 'company' is a trust. A trust is primarily an arrangement under which trustees hold property. A trust would not be an 'unincorporated association' according to Lawton LJ's definition in *Conservative and Unionist Central Office*, nor would the trustees as a group or the beneficiaries as a group be an unincorporated association.[38] This contrasts with the position under US case

---

[37] See Harris (2011). Lawton LJ's interpretation gives little scope for the statutory exclusion of general partnerships in the income tax law definition of 'company'.

[38] In any case, profits derived by a company in a fiduciary capacity are not subject to corporation tax; CTA 2009 (UK) s. 6(1).

law where a trust could (if it has sufficient corporate characteristics) be characterised as an 'association' and so a corporation. It is also unlikely that a trust or its trustees or beneficiaries is a 'body of persons' as defined in the UK income tax laws (see text at footnote 15); the closest phrase used in that definition appears to be 'society of persons'. It seems possible that trustees are a 'body of persons' as used in the definition of 'person' in the Interpretation Act 1978, and perhaps also the beneficiaries, and even the trustees and beneficiaries combined. Bringing the trust itself within that definition is more problematic.

**Foreign entities**    Income tax laws typically deal expressly with the types of entities formed under the law of the country in question. Given the variety of foreign entities, it is not possible for an income tax law to expressly deal with all types. Therefore, an income tax law must have some general classification or characterisation rules to deal with foreign entities. There is more than one reason why an income tax law must have such rules (including for purposes of taxing domestic source income and characterising foreign source income), but for present purposes the issue is whether or not a particular foreign entity falls within the corporate tax system.

The UK has no special legislative rules for determining the character of foreign entities for income tax law purposes. Rather, it relies on the definitions outlined earlier and, in particular, that of 'company'. Considering the elements of that definition, historically there was a fundamental question as to whether a foreign entity could be a 'body corporate' for tax purposes:

> The position of a foreign company of any sort in this country is really anomalous. A foreign company is not recognised as a legal entity; there is no definition of or status given to a foreign company. It is only by the comity of nations that we recognize that there are such things as companies which have an entity analogous to the incorporated company as we know it over here.[39]

So, an initial question to ask is whether the foreign entity is granted a separate legal personality (i.e. is a body corporate) under the law of the country in which it is formed.[40]

---

[39]    Lord Hanworth in *Ryall* v. *Du Bois* (1933) 18 TC 431 (CA) at 440. Also, see Lord Hanworth in *Dreyfus* v. *CIR* (1929) 14 TC 560 (CA) at 575–76.

[40]    For example, in *Memec plc* v. *IRC* [1998] STC 754 (CA) at 762 Peter Gibson LJ noted that a 'partnership is not a company [under UK income tax law] and it is an agreed fact that a silent partnership is not a body corporate under German law'.

What about other entities referred to in the UK definition of 'company'? It seems clear that a foreign entity could be an 'unincorporated association' as defined by Lawton LJ in *Conservative and Unionist Central Office*. Whether it could be a 'partnership' is more difficult to determine. As mentioned, the definition in the Partnership Act 1890 is very broad and would include UK registered companies were it not for their specific exclusion. But that exclusion only extends to entities incorporated under UK law.

'Partnership' as used in the income tax law is not expressly defined, but it seems it should largely draw its meaning from the Partnership Act 1890. That could result in 'body corporate' as applied to foreign entities being overridden where a particular foreign entity could be considered a 'partnership', whether corporate or not incorporate.[41] The preferable view seems to be that 'partnership' as used in the tax law definition of 'company' must be read as excluding foreign entities analogous to those UK entities excluded from the definition of 'partnership' in the Partnership Act 1890.[42] So, foreign corporations, including registered companies, must be considered 'companies' for UK income tax purposes and not 'partnerships'.

A similar problem arises with respect to foreign 'limited liability partnerships'. Again, UK income tax law does not define this phrase. Its meaning for tax purposes is largely, but not exclusively, drawn from the Limited Liability Partnerships Act 2000. In an analogous manner to the treatment of UK limited liability partnerships, it seems the better view is that foreign limited liability partnerships must be considered 'partnerships' for UK tax purposes and so excluded from the definition of 'company'.[43]

This is another messy area where UK income tax law could do with some rationalisation. Cutting through that mess, it seems that foreign entities must be classified according to the UK boxes of 'body corporate', 'unincorporated association', 'partnership' and 'limited liability partnership'. Whether a foreign entity is a 'company' for UK tax purposes will be determined accordingly. How does the UK try to fit foreign entities into these boxes? The approach adopted by the UK courts, which is similar to the approach adopted in many other countries, is a two-stage process:

---

[41]  That is, where the foreign entity could be considered to involve 'persons carrying on a business in common with a view of profit'; Partnership Act 1890 (UK) s. 1(1).

[42]  That is, by Partnership Act 1890 (UK) s. 1(2).

[43]  Contrast HMRC, *Business Income Manual*, at para. BIM72145, available at www.hmrc.gov.uk/manuals/bimmanual, accessed 16 July 2012. HMRC suggest that if the foreign limited liability partnership is a body corporate, it will be subject to corporation tax.

(i) Firstly, ask what characteristics are given to the entity by the corporate or commercial law in the country of formation. The treatment or classification under the foreign *tax* law is generally irrelevant in this process.
(ii) Secondly, given those characteristics, ask to which UK entity is the foreign entity most similar (e.g. is it more like a partnership or a corporation?).[44]

UK tax administration guidance largely focuses on whether a foreign business entity is transparent (like a partnership) or opaque (like a corporation). It lists six factors that are considered relevant. This list is similar, but not the same as, that formerly used by the US in determining whether an 'association' was a 'corporation'. The UK factors need to be weighed and balanced to properly characterise a foreign entity. The UK tax administration considers two factors to be particularly important: whether the business is carried on by the entity or jointly by persons with an interest in the entity, and whether the persons with an interest in the entity are entitled to share in profits as they arise or whether they must wait for a decision to distribute the profits. The Guidance includes a presumptive list characterising common foreign entities.[45]

Historically, the US took the classification of foreign entities further than in the UK. In the US, foreign entities were all classified as unincorporated associations (classification under the foreign law of organisation being irrelevant). This meant that foreign entities might only be a corporation for US tax purposes under the 'association' heading.[46] The introduction of the check-the-box regime in 1997 meant all foreign entities would be corporations or transparent at their choice. The Treasury Regulations regulating the check-the-box regime now contain a list of foreign entities that must be considered as corporations.[47] The list has grown substantially in recent years and typically includes the types of entity that may be listed on a foreign stock exchange, such as the UK public limited company and the German stock corporation (AG).[48]

---

[44] Also see Harris & Oliver (2010, pp. 51–4).
[45] See HMRC, *International Manual*, at para. INTM180000, available at www.hmrc.gov.uk/manuals/intmanual, accessed 16 July 2012.
[46] Internal Revenue Service Ruling 88–8, 1988–1 C.B. 403.
[47] Title 26 Code of Federal Regulations (US) § 301.7701–2(b).
[48] Regarding US classification of foreign entities, both before and after the introduction of the check-the-box regime, see Mullis (2011).

The German experience is similar. Historically, German practice suggested that foreign entities could only fall within the residual category in the list as an 'unincorporated association'.[49] In determining whether a foreign entity is subject to the German corporate tax system, German courts use a comparative typology approach similar to that used in the UK: a foreign entity is compared to German entities and classified according to the German criteria. The treatment under the tax law in the country where the foreign entity is established is irrelevant.[50] This approach is clear in the 2004 Federal Ministry of Finance's special letter ruling on the classification of US LLCs for German tax purposes.[51] The assessment process of whether a US LLC is a corporation or partnership for German tax purposes uses criteria very similar to those formerly used in the US for determining whether a partnership was taxable as a corporation.[52]

The approach in the CCCTB Proposal seems to be similar. That Proposal may apply to foreign companies (i.e. entities formed outside of the EU) if they have a 'similar form' to one of the European entities covered by the Proposal.[53] This abstract reference may be detailed by the European Commission's publication of a list of entities considered to meet that test.[54] As for EU companies, the Proposal would apply to foreign companies only if they opted into the regime.

### 1.1.1.2   Extensions

Common law jurisdictions often extend the meaning of 'corporation' or 'company' by treating some entities that do not fall within the general definition as though they did, at least for limited purposes. The UK provides an example of this approach with respect to authorised unit trusts. Unauthorised unit trusts are taxed as trusts. By contrast, the trustees of an authorised unit trust are treated for income tax purposes as a resident company, at least as regards income arising to the trustees. Similarly, the

---

[49] This has changed as a consequence of case law of the Court of Justice of the EU under which Germany must recognise the legal personality of foreign companies with their 'real seat' in Germany; Case C-208/00 *Überseering BV* v. *Nordic Construction Co Baumanagement GmbH* [2002] ECR I-9919 (ECJ).

[50] For example, decision of the Imperial Finance Court (Reichsfinanzhof) of 12 February 1930, RStBl.1930, 444 (the *Venezuela* decision).

[51] Federal Ministry of Finance (Bundesministerium der Finanzen), letter of March 19, 2004, BStBl.I 2004, 411.

[52] See Eckhardt & Woywode (2004).

[53] CCCTB Proposal Art. 1(2).

[54] CCCTB Proposal Art. 3.

rights of unit holders are treated as shares.[55] Although treated as companies, authorised unit trusts are subject to corporation tax at the basic income tax rate, rather than the usual corporate tax rates.[56]

A common rationale for extending the corporate tax system beyond 'corporation' or 'company' as defined is to cover entities that in substance behave like corporations. This rationale seems clear, for example, in the US treatment of publicly traded partnerships, which are treated as corporations for US tax purposes.[57] Australia seems to adopt the same rationale with respect to corporate limited partnerships, corporate unit trusts and public trading trusts.[58] There may be some element of this in the UK treatment of authorised unit trusts, but the dominant rationale for the UK treatment seems to be to avoid trust tax consequences when a trust retains income.

From a policy perspective, this rationale is a serious matter. If an individual can achieve the same economic outcome by deriving income through a registered company or a limited liability partnership, should not the tax consequences be the same in either case? If accepted and taken to the extreme, this would require a substance rather than a form approach to identifying the subjects of a corporate tax system, much in the same way as the US courts approached the definition of 'corporation' prior to the introduction of the check-the-box regime in 1997 (see text at footnote 31).

As mentioned, the factors that the US courts used to assess whether a non-corporate entity was a 'corporation' for tax purposes were similar to the corporate attributes discussed in any basic corporate law course. These include matters such as separate legal personality, separation of ownership and control, limited liability, continuous existence and free transferability of interests.[59] Whether all or any of these criteria provide a sufficient justification for a different treatment of one entity when compared to another entity is a matter of debate. The US found this system very difficult to administer.

On balance, there seems some justification for basing the selection of entities for a corporate tax system on form, with specific additions for cases of high similarity (such as with unit trusts and limited liability

---

[55]  CTA 2010 (UK) s. 617.
[56]  CTA 2010 (UK) s. 618.
[57]  IRC (US) s. 7704.
[58]  Income Tax Assessment Act 1936 (Australia) Part III, Divisions 5A, 6B and 6C, respectively.
[59]  For example, see Bittker & Eustice (2003–, para. 2.02).

partnerships). This approach involves a pragmatic compromise between ease of administration and reducing tax-induced distortions as to one form of intermediary over another. This issue is returned to at various points in this book.

### 1.1.2  Classifying corporations

Having identified the subjects of a corporate tax system, most all tax laws go on to subcategorise these subjects in some fashion. As mentioned earlier, corporate tax systems do this because they do not treat all types of 'corporations' or 'companies' or dealings with or in them the same. There are only so many ways in which the subjects of a corporate tax system may be subcategorised. The options pertain to the fundamental features of a person. Persons may be subcategorised by reference to the time at which they come into existence or cease to exist. They may also be subcategorised by reference to their physical attributes. Corporations do not have physical attributes, but they do have a location or situs, at least by analogy with individuals. Persons may be subcategorised by reference to their relations with other persons or to the activities they conduct.

This subheading first considers subcategorising corporations by their relations with other persons, then by location or situs and then by activities. It does not consider subcategorising by time of existence. The subheading is solely concerned with identifying subcategories and not with the special rules that apply because corporations fall within a particular subcategory. Those special rules are considered at relevant points throughout this book.

#### 1.1.2.1  Based on relations

Individuals may be related to each other by blood or another recognised bond such as marriage, adoption or civil partnership. Artificial entities are not capable of such relations, but do form other bonds. Artificial entities can be owned and controlled. These attributes are either irrelevant or repugnant in the context of individuals. The nature and degree of ownership and control of a corporation may affect the types of rules applied by a corporate tax system with respect to a corporation. The nature of a corporation's ownership and control may also determine whether the corporation is independently an appropriate subject of the corporate tax system.

In this way, ownership and control of corporations are questions not only of subcategorising the subjects of the corporate tax system but also of identifying such subjects. It is an area where subheadings 1.1.1 and 1.1.2 overlap, and for this reason, subcategorising corporations by reference to their ownership and control is dealt with separately. Subheading 1.1.3 explores the relationship between a corporation and the persons that own or control it. Subheading 1.1.4 considers potential responses to ownership and control of corporations. Subheading 1.1.5 then turns to categorising corporations by reference to their owners and controllers.

### 1.1.2.2   Based on situs: resident / non-resident

Typically, a corporate tax system subcategorises corporations according to their location or situs, which is usually determined by reference to the corporation's residence. Taxation based on corporate residence is an internationally accepted jurisdiction to tax. This is not a book about international taxation, but it does consider the extent to which international factors have an impact on a corporate tax system. Corporate tax systems adopt different rules depending on whether the subject corporation is resident or not. These rules are directly explored in Chapter 3. The definitional issue of corporate residence is briefly considered here.[60]

Corporate residence is just another area in which UK tax rules have been adopted more by accident than by design. The original income tax of the Napoleonic Wars focussed on individuals rather than corporations. As the registered company became common during the second part of the nineteenth century, UK courts applied the general wording of the income tax law to these companies, including the concept of residence. In 1906 in the *De Beers* case, the House of Lords finally rejected the argument that a corporation was resident in the country where it was incorporated or registered. Lord Loreburn stated,

> An individual may be of foreign nationality, and yet reside in the United Kingdom. So may a company. Otherwise it might have its chief seat of management and its centre of trading in England under the protection of English law, and yet escape the appropriate taxation by the simple expedient of being registered abroad and distributing its dividends abroad. ... [A] company resides for purposes of income tax where its real business is carried on. ... I regard that as the true rule, and the real business is carried on where the central management and control actually abides.[61]

---

[60] The following consideration relies heavily on Harris & Oliver (2010, pp. 57–68).

[61] *De Beers Consolidated Mines* v. *Howe* [1906] AC 455 (HL) at 458. It was part of the argument in the *De Beers* case that a foreign corporation (having no legal existence in the UK) could not be resident in the UK and if it was resident anywhere it was the place of its incorporation.

The 'central management and control' test has been consistently applied in cases since *De Beers* and is commonly used for tax purposes in countries with common law based on the UK tradition. This central management and control test has come to focus on the highest level of decision making of the business of a corporation.

Civil law jurisdictions developed management tests based on facts and circumstances similar to the UK's test, and this style of test eventually found its way into double tax treaties as a tiebreaker for dual resident corporations. Some countries, however, including the US, adopted the place of formation or incorporation as their test of residence. The US continues to apply a test purely based on whether the corporation is 'created or organized in the United States or under the law of the United States or any State...'[62] By contrast, the majority of countries began to apply dual tests for residence, one based on management and the other on formation, registration or incorporation.

Until 1988, the UK relied solely on the central management and control test. In that year the case law test was supplemented with an incorporation test. Section 14(1) of CTA 2009 states that '[a] company which is incorporated in the United Kingdom is UK resident...' Clearly, this provision cannot apply to an unincorporated association. Section 15 of CTA 2009 is entitled 'Continuation of residence established under common law'. However, the content of the section does not say this, and in any case, it is problematic to apply the section to unincorporated associations. It must be presumed that the central management and control test continues to apply (and could apply to an unincorporated association). Why the legislation is left in this encrypted form is not clear.

By contrast, the German Corporate Income Tax Law subjects corporations 'to unlimited corporation tax liability if their business management or seat of operations is in the country...'[63] So a corporation is resident if it has its statutory seat or its management in Germany. A corporation's statutory seat is the place so designated in its charter (i.e. the place where it is formally registered). A corporation organized under German law must specify a statutory seat in Germany, and therefore this test operates in a manner similar to a place of incorporation test.[64] The Tax Code provides that 'management' of a business is the centre of commercial management of the business (i.e. the centre from which the corporation's activities are

---

[62]  IRC (US) s. 7701(a)(4) defining 'domestic' corporation.
[63]  KStG (Germany) s. 1(1).
[64]  AktG (Germany) s. 5.

directed).[65] Like 'effective management' in the residence tie-breaker of the OECD Model Convention on Income and Capital (the 'OECD Model'), the focus here is on the day-to-day management rather than the top level of management, as it is in the UK.[66]

Not surprisingly, the CCCTB Proposal would also adopt a dual definition of residence of a corporation. A corporation would be considered resident in the member state in which it has its registered office or place of incorporation. In addition, a corporation would be considered resident in a member state if its place of effective management were situated there. Unlike unilateral laws, this may result in a corporation being simultaneously resident in more than one member state. So, as in the OECD Model, the place of effective management is used as a tiebreaker in such a situation. In addition, if a corporation is resident in a third country under any tax treaty (e.g. as a result of a tiebreaker), the corporation is not considered resident in a member state under the Proposal.[67] The UK has a similar rule in its domestic law, and the OECD suggests a similar result under tax treaties.[68]

### 1.1.2.3 Based on activities: size and character

Corporations may also be subcategorised according to their earning activities. Like individuals, this categorisation may depend on the character of their activities. Relevant activities might include trade or business, investment, banking, insurance, agriculture, shipping, and so on. Some types of activities may be dominated by corporations, and a corporate tax system may incorporate special rules for corporations engaged in specified activities. However, in principle, individuals may engage in any earning activity that a corporation may engage in. Therefore, because subcategorisation of corporations according to earning activity is not directly related to the inherent nature of a corporation, this book does not discuss specialised earning activities as discrete topics.

The same can be said of the size or scale of the activities conducted by corporations. Corporations are often subcategorised by reference to size, and a number of examples are noted throughout this book. Of particular

---

[65] Tax Code (*Abgabenordnung*) ('AO') (Germany) s. 10.

[66] Regarding 'effective management' and the difference between it and 'central management and control' (if any), see Harris & Oliver (2010, pp. 66–7).

[67] CCCTB Proposal Art. 6.

[68] CTA 2009 (UK) s. 18. Regarding this provision and the OECD approach, see Harris & Oliver (2010, p. 383).

relevance in the context of EU corporate tax systems is European Commission Recommendation 2003/361/EC. Although this recommendation categorises 'enterprises', the UK, for example, often applies it specifically to corporations. Under the recommendation, an enterprise is 'micro' if it has fewer than ten employees and either turnover or assets of no more than 2 million Euro. An enterprise is 'small' if it has fewer than fifty employees and either turnover or assets of no more than 10 million Euro. An enterprise is 'medium' if it has fewer than 250 employees and either turnover not exceeding 50 million Euro or assets not exceeding 43 million Euro.

### 1.1.3   Exploring relations with owners and controllers

As mentioned at 1.1.2.1, persons are often defined or subcategorised by reference to their relations with other persons. In the context of corporations, relations with their owners and controllers are particularly relevant. This subheading explores those relations. First, it considers the nature of ownership and control of a corporation. Second, it considers the various degrees of ownership and control that persons may have in and over a corporation. Finally, it considers the situation where two or more corporations are owned and controlled by the same persons (i.e. common ownership and control).

#### 1.1.3.1   Nature of ownership and control

Corporations are artificial entities and cannot be or do without individuals. Like an individual, a corporation may act through its agents. However, the acts of an agent are performed on behalf of the principal and are not acts of the principal per se. A corporation exists (is embodied by) and acts through its organs. These organs are clear in the context of registered companies, the focus of the current discussion.

Registered companies typically have two main organs – the general meeting of shareholders and a board of directors or managers – although there may be subcategories of each depending on the corporation and the jurisdiction. The shareholders own the company and typically have three types of rights; the right to participate in the distribution of profits, the right to capital and any surplus should the company be wound up, and the right to vote in general meetings (see discussion at 2.1). By contrast, the board of directors is responsible for the day-to-day management of the company, and members of the board are typically elected and removed by the general meeting.

A reference to the 'ownership' of a company is most directly a reference to rights to dividends and surplus (i.e. a right to share in the economic performance of the company). Therefore, two companies are commonly owned when the same persons have the same rights with respect to dividends and surplus in each of the companies.

A reference to 'control' of a company is most directly a reference to rights exercised by voting in the general meeting in appointing directors (and making other constitutional changes) or by the directors in conducting the day-to-day affairs of the company.[69] There may be lower levels of control, such as where the board properly delegates functions to a chief executive officer or managing director. Nevertheless, the board remains responsible for supervision of such delegates. A company is controlled by a person when the person has sufficient voting rights at general meetings of the company to pass relevant resolutions. A company is controlled at the board level typically by a majority of board members acting together.

### 1.1.3.2   Degrees of ownership and control

Ownership and control of a corporation are questions of degree not absolutes. Ownership may range from complete ownership of the shares in a corporation to a fraction of a per cent. Similarly, control may range from absolute control at one extreme to independence at the other. Nevertheless, it is common to speak of 'majority' ownership or 'control' in the sense of an ability to pass a resolution at a general meeting or the board level by majority. In a registered company structured along standard lines, a person who owns a majority of the shares has the right to appoint all members of the board of directors.[70] As a result, majority owners often have absolute control at the board level.[71] These types of corporations are referred to as 'controlled corporations'.

Many corporations are not owned or controlled by a single person. Where a corporation has a small number of shareholders, the shareholders are capable of acting collectively, and as a result, the ownership and control of the corporation will tend to coincide. This occurs because, at

---

[69] For example, see the discussion of the Court of Appeal in *Steele* v. *EVC International NV* [1996] STC 785 (CA) in holding that 'control' of a close company was to be tested at the shareholder level. See later discussion at 1.1.5.2.

[70] In many civil law jurisdictions other stakeholders may have a right to be represented on the board.

[71] There are corporate law restrictions on the extent of this absolute control. In particular, there is typically no control over a company's constitution without a special majority (e.g. 75% of votes).

the least, the shareholders can vote in a sufficiently coordinated manner so as to consciously control the directors through the power of appointment and removal. Often the shareholders have entrenched rights to be represented on the board of directors. Small corporations of this nature are often referred to as 'quasi-partnerships'. Quasi-partnerships and one-controller corporations are referred to as 'closely held corporations'.

This form of collective control becomes less practical as shareholding becomes more widely dispersed. Where shareholders are so dispersed that a majority is no longer capable of acting in a coordinated fashion, the ownership and control of the corporation are separated. The corporation is still owned by its shareholders, who have the right to profit distributions and surplus. But the shareholders do not have a practical method of exercising their votes so as to control the directors, who have a much greater degree of autonomy in widely held corporations.

This is not to say that shareholders in widely held corporations have no influence. Even in widely held corporations some shareholders may have a sufficient holding in the corporation to have some say in its management (e.g. by appointment of a particular director). Such shareholders are often referred to as 'substantial shareholders'. Corporate law may grant substantial shareholders special rights, including rights to call general meetings and presentation and receipt of information with respect thereto.[72] As ownership and control coincide to some degree in substantial shareholders, a corporation and its substantial shareholders may be loosely referred to as 'associated'.

### 1.1.3.3   Common ownership and control of corporations

A corporation owned and controlled by a particular individual can behave much as the alter ego of that individual. Ever since the introduction of the registered company, there has been no limit on the number of corporate alter egos a particular individual may have. If an individual registers, owns and controls a number of corporations, these corporations share a common bond. That common bond is their sharing a common ownership and control by the individual. In this sense, the corporations are 'related', and the familial metaphor is extended to refer to such corporations as 'sibling' corporations. The formation and ownership of a corporation by an individual create a form of dual vision for a corporate tax system, which sees

---

[72] For example, see AktG (Germany) ss. 122 and 124 and Companies Act 2006 (UK) ss. 303 and 338.

both the corporation and the individual. The formation and ownership of multiple corporations by an individual create multi-vision.

Also since the introduction of the registered company, it has been possible for one corporation to hold shares in and to own and control other corporations. This was a consequence of granting registered companies an independent identity (i.e. corporate status). The ownership and control of multiple corporations by a single individual create multi-vision for a corporate tax system. The ownership and control of corporations by other corporations create multi-dimensional vision that can push the rationality of a corporate tax system to the extreme. This ownership and control of corporations by other corporations also create legal fictions (subsidiaries) within legal fictions (parent) and limited liability within limited liability.

However, the ownership of shares by one corporation in another corporation does not, of itself, mean that the corporations are related. As noted with respect to sibling corporations, this requires a common bond in the form of ownership and control. Where that ownership and control vest in another corporation, the familial metaphor is taken further, and the other corporation is said to be the 'parent'. The owned or controlled corporations are its 'subsidiaries'. Accordingly, subsidiaries are a form of controlled corporation and a form of or subset of the closely held corporation. Many of the issues that this book discusses in the context of closely held corporations are also discussed in the context of subsidiaries.

A parent corporation and its subsidiaries form a 'corporate group'. This is the typical meaning of 'corporate group', and it may extend to multiple depths, such as where there is a subparent or holding corporation. Single-dimension sibling corporations may also be described as a corporate group (although less commonly), but the owning and controlling individuals are not part of that group (because they are not 'corporate').

It is for good reason that familial terminology is applied to corporate groups. Many, if not most of the difficulties that a tax system faces with respect to corporate groups, it faces with respect to families of individuals. The high level of ownership and control by the parent corporation causes a high level of integration between members of a corporate group. The result is that the members of a corporate group tend to act as a single economic unit. A family of individuals also tends to behave as a single economic unit. Members of either type of family (individuals or corporations) often behave to their detriment if they perceive that another member of the economic unit will receive a greater benefit than the detriment

suffered. The result is a form of arbitrage, which is particularly problematic for tax systems.[73]

Further like families of individuals, at the fringes it can be difficult to
determine which corporations are in the corporate family and which are
not. In the context of individuals, some relatives are sufficiently remote
that they are not viewed as part of the family or the 'immediate' family,
although they might fall within a phrase such as 'extended' family. So an
individual might be a 'relative' and yet not a family 'member'. Similarly,
two corporations might be 'related' and yet not part of the same corporate
group (i.e. not group members). This is likely to be the case where one
corporation is a substantial shareholder in the other – they are associated
corporations – but a corporation's 'relatives' form a broader category.

A corporation is related to another person where sufficient ownership
and control or sufficient common ownership and control exist such as to
give rise to a risk that one will act to its detriment (or not fully exploit an
opportunity) to benefit the other. So, a corporation is 'related' to persons
(individuals or corporations) that have a substantial shareholding in it (i.e.
persons that have some degree of control or influence over the corporation
through an ownership interest in the corporation). A corporation is also
'related' to other corporations that are owned and controlled by one of its
substantial shareholders. 'Related corporations' and, with respect to a particular corporation, 'related individual' and 'related entity' are understood
accordingly.

Labels such as 'controlled corporations', 'group corporations', 'closely
held corporations', 'associated corporations' and the catch-all 'related corporations' are merely descriptions of something that can only be measured
by factors of degree rather than absolutes. Nevertheless, these labels and
distinctions are broadly used in many tax laws.

### 1.1.4   Responses to concentrated ownership and control

Corporations where ownership and control coincide to any degree (i.e.
corporations that are related to their owners) raise challenging issues for
a corporate tax system. How should a corporate tax system respond to
these challenges? There are a number of options, each with its advantages,

---

[73] Of course, the situation is deeper than either the corporate family or the family of individuals. Both of these types of families may integrate, and so a family of individuals and
their closely held corporations may act as a single economic unit. Income tax laws often
overlook this possibility and incorporate multiple rules that deal with the same conceptual
issue.

but none without difficulties. Almost inevitably, a corporate tax system will adopt different options in different contexts, and so this book deals with implementation of those options at various points. However, the fundamental policy issue in all these contexts is how a corporate tax system should view or identify a corporation and its related entities. This is properly an issue for this heading.

Before considering definitional issues, it is appropriate to consider the three fundamental options that a corporate tax system has for identifying a corporation with its owners and controllers. First, a corporate tax system may accept the general law approach that each corporation is a separate person that is to be taxed separately, and thus it incorporates no special rules for corporations and their relatives. This is the non-intervention approach, which accepts certain manipulative behaviour between a corporation and its relatives that naturally erodes the separate identity of the corporation.

Alternately, the corporate tax system may seek to directly intervene with special rules that either erode the separate identity of the corporation or reinforce its separateness from its relatives. Rules that erode the separate identity of a corporation may vary. At one extreme, the rules may collapse that identity completely (i.e. consolidate identity with that of the owners or controllers). At the other extreme, the rules may merely facilitate the transfer of certain tax attributes between the corporation and its relatives. Rules that reinforce the separateness of a corporation seek to prevent or ignore the natural behaviour between a corporation and its relatives that blurs the corporation's separate identity granted by corporate law. Each of these three options is considered in turn.

### 1.1.4.1  Non-intervention: separate entity approach

An income tax system must base itself on the transactions and dealings recognised by law. It would be quite impossible for an income tax law to rewrite each and every transaction entered into by every person, and there would be little point in doing so. However, a tax system will intervene in certain behaviour and effectively rewrite it or prescribe specific consequences for tax purposes. The present question is whether it should do so in the context of corporations and their relatives. As noted earlier, it is of the nature of such corporations that they may behave to their individual detriment if they perceive that a related entity will receive a greater benefit from that behaviour than the detriment suffered.

This behaviour is caused by concentration of ownership and control of the corporation in specific persons and is particularly problematic in controlled corporations, such as group corporations. The income tax system faces similar issues with families of individuals. The fundamental question for an income tax system, including its corporate tax system, is how strictly it wishes to enforce the selection of tax subject it has adopted. An income tax is a direct tax that allocates income to persons and taxes them according to their personal circumstances. If the income tax system has adopted the individual and the individual corporation as its tax subjects, how strictly should it seek a 'proper' allocation of income between individuals or corporations and their relatives?

The core of the issue can be demonstrated by reference to group corporations. Group corporations are subject to a high level of common ownership and control and behave like a single economic unit. If the tax system recognises the legal fiction of each group member rather than the economic reality, group corporations will and do manipulate relations between themselves so as to produce the lowest tax result. As a rule of thumb, in a closed economy, this means averaging out the tax liability between each group member, presuming each is taxable at the same rate. If the members are not taxable at the same rates, then the group corporations can be expected to move tax consequences to the members with the least exposure to tax.[74] The same manipulative behaviour exists between families of individuals and between individuals and their controlled corporations and other artificial entities.

The point is that, despite being imbued with separate legal personality by corporate law, controlled corporations do not behave separately from an economic perspective. Corporate law does little to address this disconnect. It commonly prescribes that the board of directors of each corporation, whether in a group or otherwise, should act loyally, avoid conflicts of interest or even exercise 'independent judgement' when making decisions, but this requirement is often ignored or planned around.[75] Even if this requirement is breached, in the context of a solvent corporation, only minority shareholders (if any) are likely to complain, and they have a notoriously difficult time bringing directors to account.[76]

---

[74] Group corporations tend to act in a similar manipulative fashion with respect to other potential liabilities (e.g. corporate group structures are often manipulated to reduce exposure to involuntary creditors).

[75] For example, see AktG (Germany) s. 93, Companies Act 2006 (UK) ss. 172 to 177, MBCA s. 8.30. The DGCL does not codify directors' duties. Generally, see Cahn & Donald (2010, pp. 338–45).

[76] For example, see Cahn & Donald (2010, chapter 20).

A tax system that incorporates no special rules for corporations and their relatives, by doing nothing, accepts the default manipulation available within the limited confines of the general law. In such a system, the usual tax rules attach to transactions between corporations and their relatives. The system accepts that such dealings may be manipulated so as to reduce the overall tax liability that might otherwise be suffered. The potential for manipulation is particularly high with respect to controlled corporations, including group corporations. As the level of control decreases, so does the scope for manipulation. The tax arbitrage that a non-intervention approach permits is often referred to as 'self-help relief'. Obtaining this relief depends on well-informed tax advisers assisting their clients in structuring transactions so as to achieve the averaging result for tax purposes.

Historically, this non-intervention approach was adopted for income tax purposes. However, as the twentieth century progressed, countries increasingly intervened by overriding for tax purposes the consequences of dealings between relatives, particularly between related and group corporations. In a domestic context, Canada is often viewed as one of the few developed countries still taking a largely non-intervention approach in the corporate income tax field, although it is considering introducing special rules for corporate groups.[77] In an increasingly integrated world, non-intervention is a dangerous approach, at least with respect to international transactions. Multinational groups endeavour to and do shift their profits to the lowest tax jurisdictions.[78]

The focus of this discussion (of the non-intervention approach) has been on the propensity of group corporations in particular to behave in a unified manner despite their separate legal personalities. However, the tax system can be faced with the opposite problem: where a person or corporation seeks to use or add artificial entities to secure some tax benefit multiple times. The most common example is where some particular tax benefit (e.g. a lower rate or credit) is attributed to each person. This creates an incentive to incorporate additional artificial entities so that persons can fragment their activities and secure the benefit multiple times. While artificial entities may easily be used or added, things are not so simple for physical persons, for example, by adding members to a family of individuals.

---

[77] See Canada (2010). Regarding the use of tax losses within Canadian corporate groups and the likelihood of the introduction of new rules, see Suarez (2012).
[78] For example, see the figures given in Sullivan (2011).

### 1.1.4.2  Erosion of identity

Rather than do nothing, a corporate tax system may directly intervene and prescribe rules that intentionally erode the separate identity of a corporation. These rules may be either beneficial, because they permit averaging of tax consequences, or detrimental, because they allocate only one tax benefit between the corporation and its owners and controllers (e.g. a threshold for a lower tax rate or credit). Such rules most commonly apply to controlled corporations, but similar rules may apply to less integrated corporations and their owners and controllers. The following discussion focuses on controlled corporations.

The extent to which a corporate tax system erodes the separate identity of controlled corporations is another example of a spectrum issue. At one extreme, the separate identity of a corporation is collapsed (i.e. consolidation of the corporation with its owners and controllers). At the other extreme of the spectrum the separate identity of a corporation is respected, but isolated tax attributes are singled out for transfer between the corporation and its owners and controllers (and other commonly controlled corporations).[79] Between these extremes, there is an array of hybrid approaches. The following discussion considers each in turn, but does not evaluate the advantages and disadvantages of each approach. These are considered in particular contexts throughout the remainder of this book.

Each of these approaches involves the allocation of tax attributes to the owners and controllers of a corporation; the difference in approach is simply one of degree. An issue for all of these approaches is identifying who may be allocated tax attributes and specifically whether minority owners without any degree of control may be allocated tax attributes of the corporation.

**Collapse of separate identity: consolidation**    A corporate tax system may decide to simply ignore the identity of a corporation and identify its activities, assets and liabilities with its owners or controllers. In the current context, it is presumed that the corporation is of a form eligible to fall within the scope of the corporate tax system, but by reason of its relationship with its owners and controllers or an election of them, the corporation in question falls outside that system. This approach is consolidation,

---

[79] Tax attributes are those features of a tax system that attach to tax subjects and that are carried forward from one tax period to another. The prime example is the tax value of particular assets. Other major examples include the carry-forward of losses, credits and even a particular status (e.g. as a resident or exempt institution).

which collapses the identity of a corporation into that of its owners and controllers. It is most common in the context of corporate groups,[80] but can also be adopted where the owners and controllers are non-corporates. In the latter case, because the corporation is taken out of the corporate tax system and its owners and controllers are not corporations, the corporate tax system is not engaged at all.

In its purest form, consolidation allocates all the activities, assets and liabilities of the corporation to the owners and controllers for tax purposes. If the allocation is to a single owner and controller (e.g. a parent corporation), the corporation (subsidiary) may be treated as a branch of the controller, which has important consequences. Transactions between the corporation and its controller (or between commonly controlled corporations) will be ignored, because the corporation (or corporations) is merely part of the controller and a person (the controller) cannot transact with itself.

This has further repercussions with respect to rights held by the controller against the corporation (or between two controlled corporations): these rights are also ignored. So, for example, in the context of pure corporate group consolidation, a loan between two group members is not a loan for the purposes of the corporate tax system. The shares and other rights held by the parent corporation in a subsidiary or by one group member in another group member *disappear* in pure consolidation.

Consolidation was the earliest form of corporate group treatment adopted by the UK. In 1915, the excess profits duty prescribed,

> Where any company … owns the whole of the ordinary capital of any other company carrying on the same trade or business … the provisions … as to excess profits duty … apply as if that other company were a branch of the first-named company, and the profits of the two companies shall not be separately assessed.[81]

This is a standard approach to pure consolidation; the Netherlands and Australian corporate tax systems currently adopt a similar approach.[82] In the UK, the wholly owned requirement was reduced to 90% in the 1937 National Defence Contribution and settled at 75% in 1938. The

---

[80]  In the context of corporate groups it is often called the 'enterprise doctrine'; see Ting (2012, chapter 2).

[81]  Finance (No 2) Act 1915 (UK) Fourth Schedule para. 6.

[82]  See Corporate Income Tax Act (*Wet op de vennootschapsbelasting*) (Netherlands) s. 15 and Income Tax Assessment Act 1997 (Australia) s. 701–1. For an assessment of the Australian consolidation regime, see Cooper (2011).

consolidation approach was repealed when profits tax was repealed in 1965.[83] In the Netherlands and Australia the holding requirement is 95% and 100%, respectively.

Consolidation is most common in the context of corporate groups. However, it can be adopted with respect to other types of owners and controllers of a corporation (e.g. an individual). A good example is the US check-the-box regime. As mentioned earlier, under this regime many non-corporate business entities, including LLCs, may elect whether to be treated as a corporation or be transparent for tax purposes. This is pure consolidation because the identity of the entity disappears for tax purposes whether the controller or controllers are corporations or individuals. This system can be distinguished from a system of attributing to shareholders income that is accepted to be income of a corporation (discussed later at 1.3.3), which is a form of allocating tax attributes.

**Within a separate entity approach: transfer of tax attributes**    Rather than adopt a single entity approach, a corporate tax system might accept the separate identity of a corporation, but erode the normal consequences of doing so for particular purposes by reason of the way the corporation is owned or controlled. For example, the system may facilitate the averaging of tax consequences by permitting the transfer of losses or other tax attributes between the corporation and its controller (and other controlled corporations of the controller). Similarly, the corporate tax system might apportion the benefits of particular rate thresholds and credits between a controller and controlled corporations to prevent problems of fragmentation. Most commonly, these types of rules only apply in the context of corporate groups.

Without specific rules, tax consequences attach to transactions between a controller and a controlled corporation, including group corporations. Further, rights between a controller and a controlled corporation and between commonly controlled corporations are recognised, such as loans and shares held by one group member in another group member. Specific rules that ameliorate the effects of such transactions are common. This is especially the case as between group corporations, but can also occur in the case of individual controllers, particular in the context of the corporation issuing shares.

Erosion of the separate identity of controlled corporations is the primary approach adopted by the UK corporate tax system, particularly with

---

[83] Generally regarding this history, see Harris (2011).

respect to corporate groups. The specific rules that the UK adopts are discussed at appropriate points throughout this book. This approach was first adopted with respect to the transfer of losses between members of a corporate group for income tax purposes in 1953.[84] It was carried through into the corporation tax in 1965 with substantial modifications in 1967.[85]

**Hybrid approaches**    Some countries appear to adopt what might be described as a hybrid of these two extreme approaches. They collapse the separate identity of controlled corporations for some purposes, but respect their separate identity for others. Again, this is most prevalent in the context of group corporations. For example, the US permits group corporations to file a consolidated tax return,[86] but this is not pure consolidation. Losses and certain other tax attributes are recognised at the group level. However, transactions between group members are recognised, but deferred. Shareholdings of one group member in another group member continue to be recognised, with adjustments.

The CCCTB Proposal would, in effect, produce a result very similar to that of the US. It provides that 'the tax bases of the members of a group shall be consolidated'.[87] This is not pure consolidation, and tax attributes would continue to attach to group members, not least of which would be a liability to pay tax on their share of the consolidated result. However, it would ignore transactions between group members.[88]

The German approach is similarly a hybrid, but is very different in form. Under the *organschaft* regime the tax results of group members may be transferred to the business of a controller. A controller is broader than just parent corporations and may include individuals and partnerships.[89] However, transactions between group members continue to be recognised.

**Problems with minority owners**    As mentioned, each of these approaches involves the allocation of tax attributes to the owners and controllers of a corporation, and the difference in approach is simply one of degree. An issue for all of these approaches is identifying who may be allocated

---

[84] Finance Act 1953 (UK) s. 20.
[85] Generally regarding this history, see Harris (2011).
[86] IRC (US) s. 1501.
[87] CCCTB Proposal Art. 57(1).
[88] CCCTB Proposal Art. 59.
[89] KStG (Germany) s. 14.

tax attributes. This allocation may be to all owners of the corporation, irrespective of whether a particular owner also has any degree of control of the corporation. Alternately, only owners that are also controllers may be subject to attribution. Neither approach is entirely satisfactory in its treatment of corporations with minority owners (i.e. owners that have no degree of control of the corporation).

**Attribution to all owners**    Consider a pure consolidation system that collapses the identity of a corporation and allocates its activities, assets and liabilities to all of its owners (e.g. shareholders). The attribution of activities, assets and liabilities of the corporation is proportionate to all owners and not just to those that have some element of control. A consequence is that there are no membership interests (e.g. shares) recognised for tax purposes. The owners are considered to conduct the corporation's activities directly. Where the corporation has multiple owners, the result is fragmentation of the corporation's tax attributes, and this has consequences when owners transact with the corporation.

For example, presume a corporation sells an asset to a 35% shareholder. If before the sale the asset was considered to be owned proportionately by all shareholders, the sale to the 35% shareholder will be recognised as a sale of a 65% interest in the asset by the other shareholders to the 35% shareholder. The other shareholders will recognise a gain or loss on their proportionate interest accordingly.[90] This can become very complex as ownership of the corporation fragments, which means that this approach is only feasible in the context of closely held corporations. This approach also raises questions of fairness. The sale proceeds will be received by the corporation, but a minority shareholder has virtually no influence over whether the corporation distributes those funds. Nevertheless, the minority shareholder may have to report any gain on the proportionate sale of the asset and pay tax.

These difficulties with minority owners are not confined to an approach that collapses the identity of the corporation. Similar difficulties can arise where that identity is respected, but some tax attribute of the corporation is allocated to a minority owner that has negative tax consequences for the owner. These problems are discussed in more detail later at 1.3.3 in the context of allocating a corporation's reportable taxable income to its owners, irrespective of distribution.

---

[90]  For an example of this approach, see CCCTB Proposal Art. 84.

**Attribution to controllers only**    The alternative is to only allocate tax attributes of a corporation to a particular controller or to a group of persons with a sufficient degree of control. However, this approach also does not produce satisfactory results in the context of a corporation with minority shareholders. This is because the approach results in either what may be viewed as an inappropriate indirect transfer of tax attributes or an inappropriate denial of the transfer of tax attributes. There are also difficulties in determining what constitutes a sufficient degree of control.

As a general rule, tax systems do not permit the transfer of tax attributes (e.g. a person is not permitted to sell losses to another person). The point of eroding the identity of a controlled corporation is to break down this rule. Let us return to the example given earlier of a corporation selling an asset to an owner. If the owner holds all of the shares in the corporation, there is some reason for saying that any gain or loss on the sale of the asset should not be recognised. This is because there has been no change in the underlying or economic ownership of the asset such as to justify the recognition that the gain has been realised for tax purposes. This sort of approach involves *looking through* the corporation (i.e. lifting the corporate veil) to see who its owner is.

It is easy to see why non-recognition might be accepted where the corporation is wholly owned by the purchaser or where the transaction is between two corporations that are wholly owned by the same person (e.g. by a parent corporation). But what if the ownership or common ownership is not complete? If the corporation is owned only as to 75% by the purchaser, should the transaction be recognised? There is no correct answer to this sort of question because it involves the spectrum of corporate ownership. If non-recognition is granted (whether through consolidation or otherwise), the tax system has permitted one-quarter of the owners of the corporation to sell their indirect interest in the asset to a stranger without tax consequences. If non-recognition is not granted, the tax system has recognised a gain where the substantial majority of indirect interests in the asset have not changed (i.e. form is applied over substance).

A middle ground might be to apply a proportionate recognition. This would involve eroding the identity of a corporation only to the extent of its controlling owners. The separate identity of the corporation would continue, proportionately, to represent the interests of the minority shareholders (i.e. those who are not allocated any tax attributes of the corporation). Under this approach, the sale of the asset to the 75% owner would be treated as a sale of a 25% interest in the asset, and the corporation would realise a gain or loss to that extent. This approach is different from the full allocation to all owners discussed earlier. The sale is treated as made by the corporation, not by the shareholders.

Not only is proportionate recognition administratively difficult but it is also not an accurate reflection of what has happened. The result is contrary to the very nature of a corporation as a collective investment vehicle. Recognising only 25% of the gain in the example in the preceding paragraph does not result in tax consequences attaching to just the 25% of owners who might be viewed as having disposed of their interest in the asset. Because the shareholders are collective, it treats all shareholders the same. The 25% who no longer have an indirect interest in the asset and the 75% owner who still does are each treated, indirectly, as though they sold 25% of their interest in the asset. This book discusses a number of examples that produce this sort of problem.

The bottom line is that, in the absence of allocation to all owners proportionately, there is no right answer to the question of the degree of ownership and control required to erode the identity of a corporation for tax purposes, but some observations may be made. In the case of full ownership, the case for erosion of the separate identity of the corporation seems clear, at least in a domestic context. That case progressively weakens as ownership is fragmented to the point that it falls away when control by any particular owner is lost (i.e. typically when there is no 50% owner). Between 100% and 50% ownership, it is impossible to draw any clear line: 100% might seem unduly restrictive, whereas closer to 50% makes the issues discussed earlier with respect to minority owners acute.

As noted at 1.1.3.2, the corporate law of most countries recognises other levels of control between 50% and 100%. One is the level of share ownership required to engage in constitutional reform of a registered company. Germany and the UK generally use 75% for this threshold, and that is a common approach. This is the level of share ownership required to pass a special resolution.[91] Although there is not, perhaps, a conclusive argument for use of this level as the threshold of ownership required for erosion of a corporation's identity, it does have some salient features. Such a level of common ownership increases the controller's ability to integrate the activities of the controlled company into the activities of the controller (i.e. it increases the potential that the corporation and controller will act as a single economic unit). Another important threshold that might be

---

[91] AktG (Germany) s. 179 and Companies Act 2006 (UK) s. 9. There is no requirement under either MBCA (US) or DGCL (US). Regarding required majorities for shareholder meetings in Germany, the UK and the US, see Cahn & Donald (2010, pp. 490–2).

relevant is the level of share ownership required by a majority shareholder to force a minority shareholder to sell in a takeover (in countries where that is possible). In the UK, 90% is used for this threshold in some cases, and in Germany it is 95% (plus a court order).[92]

Should the threshold of ownership required for the transfer of tax attributes of a corporation depend on the particular attribute in question? Again, there is no clear answer to this question, but it *is* clear that countries do adopt different approaches. As is discussed later, the threshold for the direct transfer of tax attributes by a corporation (see 1.2.3) is commonly higher than is required for the indirect transfer of tax attributes (see later at 5.2.2). Should consolidation require full ownership? Minority owners do raise acute issues for consolidation regimes, but there are many examples of consolidation regimes with ownership requirements of less than 100%. The former UK profits tax regime is an example, and the Netherlands regime is another. However, given its holistic nature, it might be expected that a consolidation regime would be at the top end of the threshold adopted by a country for erosion of identity of group corporations.[93]

### 1.1.4.3   Reinforcement of identity: independent entity approach

A corporate tax system may adopt the opposite approach and directly intervene to reinforce the separate identity of corporations in which ownership and control coincide (i.e. corporations that are related to their owners). The system will do this by pretending that corporations and their relatives are not integrated and requiring these related parties to transact or, at least, report for tax purposes as though they had transacted as independent entities. This is known as the arm's length standard or independent entity approach and is classically reflected in the independent pricing of transactions between related entities.

The main problem with the independent entity approach is that it is anti-factual: it asks related entities to behave in a manner that is not of their nature. This can be particularly problematic when the level of relationship is very close, such as in the context of controlled corporations and, in particular, group corporations. Inevitably, the result is a *cat and*

---

[92] Companies Act 2006 (UK) s. 979 and Securities Acquisition and Takeover Law (*Wertpapiererwerbs- und Übernahmegesetz*) (Germany) s. 39(a)(1). There is no requirement under either MBCA (US) or DGCL (US). Regarding the treatment of minorities in a takeover in Germany, the UK and the US, see Cahn & Donald (2010, pp. 764, 768–9 & 774).

[93] Regarding ownership requirements in consolidation regimes, see Ting (2012, heading 5.4).

*mouse game* between the legislature and the related entities whereby legislatures continually prescribe rules to impose the arm's length standard and related entities continually attempt to push the boundaries towards their integrated nature. As a result, tax legislation can get messy.

The independent entity approach is noted at a number of points throughout this book. It is particularly prevalent in the international field where the stakes are high. In the international field, this approach is taken to such an extreme as to treat foreign permanent establishments (PEs) of particular entities as though the PE were itself a separate entity.[94] This can create a dislocation between domestic rules and international rules, but such a dislocation can also occur in a purely domestic scenario. For example, there is some inconsistency in requiring group corporations to account on an arm's length basis for transactions between group members while permitting such corporations to freely transfer losses to each other (see the later discussion at 1.2.2 and 1.2.3). The difference is commonly that the independent entity approach is adopted with respect to related parties, whereas the separate identity of group corporations is independently eroded by different rules.

The series or cell LLCs that have become common in the US provide an interesting analogy to the treatment of PEs under international tax rules. The laws that establish these companies permit assets and liabilities to be grouped into separate series or cells, which may be attributed to specific members or insulated from a liability perspective. Legally, it is like establishing a group of corporations within a single corporation. One question is whether each series or cell is to be treated as a separate entity for tax purposes. At the least, this seems possible in the US[95] and so potentially creates the opposite result to pure consolidation; that is, parts of the same legal entity are treated as separate entities for tax purposes, whereas consolidation treats separate legal entities as part of the same entity for tax purposes.[96]

### 1.1.5   Classifying corporations by their owners and controllers

Subheading 1.1.3 explored the relations between corporations and their owners and controllers. It remains to consider how corporations are

---

[94]  Regarding these rules, see Harris & Oliver (2010, pp. 153–67).

[95]  US Federal Register, Vol. 75, No. 177, Tuesday, September 14, 2010 pp. 55699 & 55707 proposing Title 26 Code of Federal Regulations (US) § 301.7701–1(a)(5).

[96]  Generally, see Bishop (2011) and Fuller (2010).

categorised by reference to their owners and controllers for tax purposes. This discussion follows the varying degrees of ownership and control identified at 1.1.3.2 (i.e. controlled corporations, close corporations and corporations more loosely related to a person with a remoter degree of ownership and control).

The focus is on general rules applicable in income tax law. As mentioned, rules applicable to the categories of corporations identified are considered in the remainder of this book. Further, in some specific circumstances the rules of identification are modified, or altogether different rules are used to identify corporations by reference to their owners and controllers. These specific identification rules are considered later in this book in the context in which the variations are relevant.

### 1.1.5.1   Controlled corporations

Tax laws tend to identify three basic types of controlled corporation. The simplest type is a corporation controlled by a single individual. A second simple type is a corporation controlled by another corporation: a parent corporation. In this case, the two corporations form a corporate group. The third basic type of controlled corporation is a commonly controlled corporation (see 1.1.3.3). Two corporations that are controlled by the same person or persons are said to be 'sibling' corporations and may also be considered to form a corporate group. The following discussion considers how tax laws categorise each type of controlled corporation.

A tax law may have specific rules that categorise each type of controlled corporation. However, many income tax laws incorporate a general concept of affiliated, associated, connected or related persons. This concept includes individuals and their relatives, typically within defined limits of consanguinity. It also includes relationships between individuals and artificial entities, usually based on control, as well as relationships between artificial entities, again based on control or common control. Therefore, controlled corporations are often identified by a tax law, at least in part, by reference to such a general concept.

The UK is an example of a country adopting this sort of approach. Its income tax laws incorporate a general concept of 'connected persons'.[97] Although this concept is not used consistently for the purposes of the corporate tax system, it is the most generally used definition and is one way

---

[97] CTA 2010 (UK) s. 1122. 'Connected persons' is defined in similar terms for income tax purposes (ITA 2007 (UK) s. 993), capital allowance purposes (CAA 2001 (UK) s. 575) and capital gains purposes (TCGA 1992 (UK) s. 286). The latter two definitions are considered in more detail at 1.2.2. They are all clearly of the same origin; the CTA 2010 and ITA 2007 definitions are from ICTA 1988 (UK) s. 839.

to categorise controlled corporations.[98] US income tax law less obviously uses a general concept. However, it does incorporate a concept of 'related taxpayers' or 'related persons',[99] which covers issues analogous to those covered by the UK concept of connected persons. In form, that US concept is used for the purpose of identifying relationships to which a particular rule applies (disallowance of losses). However, other provisions pick up and apply the concept of related persons.[100] The definition of 'controlled group of corporations' is used in a similar fashion.[101]

By comparison, Germany has a general concept of 'relative', but it only applies as between individuals.[102] Separately, Germany has a concept of 'controlled company', including control by an individual, but it is for the specific purpose of transfer of income.[103] Similarly, the CCCTB Proposal contains no general concept of related or connected persons. However, it uses a concept of corporate 'group'.[104]

The following discussion is for general illustrative purposes and so focuses on the most general rules for identifying controlled corporations. Further detail and different definitions in different contexts are provided at relevant points throughout this book.

**Control by an individual**    An income tax law may identify a corporation as controlled by a particular individual. In this case, the law must address two primary issues. The first is the test used for determining whether control exists. The second is which rights are attributed to the individual for the purpose of determining whether the test is met. In particular, an individual may be attributed rights held by certain relatives and related entities for this purpose.

**Test of control**    Both Germany and the US have comparatively simple tests for determining whether an individual controls a corporation for tax purposes. In the US, under section 267(b) of the IRC an individual is 'related' to a corporation if the individual owns 'directly or indirectly'

---

[98] CTA 2010 (UK) s. 1176(1) says this definition applies 'unless otherwise indicated (whether expressly or by implication)'. In the context of an expensive rewrite, it is not clear why this type of ambiguity was accepted.

[99] IRC (US) s. 268.

[100] For example, it is applied by IRC (US) s. 144(a).

[101] IRC (US) s. 1563(a).

[102] AO (Germany) s. 15.

[103] KStG (Germany) s. 14.

[104] CCCTB Proposal Arts. 54 and 55.

more than '50 percent in value of the outstanding stock' of the corporation. The value-of-stock test is interesting because in the context of corporate groups it is supplemented with a voting power test.

By contrast, voting power is the sole test used in the German Corporate Income Tax Law to determine whether a corporation is 'controlled' by another person. The controller can be an individual, provided the individual is conducting a business. The test is holding a 'participation in the controlled company ... such that the majority of the voting rights of the shares in the subsidiary are held' by the controller.[105] Germany has a general rule attributing assets to the legal owner unless that person can be excluded by another from the benefits of the asset for its useful life.[106]

The UK approach is again far from simple. As mentioned, UK income tax law incorporates a general concept of 'connected persons'. In particular, a person (including an individual) is connected with a 'corporation' if the person has 'control' of the corporation.[107] Confusingly, 'control' for the purposes of this definition is taken from sections 450 and 451 of CTA 2010, rather than the proximate section 1124.[108] A person is treated as having 'control' of a corporation if the person has an ability to exercise or acquire 'direct or indirect control' over a corporation's affairs.[109] Of course, this does not really define 'control', which, it seems, will take its ordinary meaning.[110]

In *Steele* v. *EVC International NV*, the Court of Appeal decided that 'control of the affairs of the company in [section 450(2)] means control at the level of general meetings of the company' as opposed to at the board or other administrative level.[111] This narrow focus simplifies the concept of 'control' substantially, but not completely. Having more than 50% of the voting rights in a general meeting clearly amounts to control. Whether

---

[105] KStG (Germany) s. 14(1)1.

[106] AO (Germany) s. 39.

[107] CTA 2010 (UK) s. 1122(3).

[108] CTA 2010 (UK) s. 1123(1). Similarly, there is a definition of 'control' proximate to (but not used in) that of 'connected persons' in ITA 2007 (UK) s. 995 and CAA 2001 (UK) s. 574. TCGA 1992 (UK) s. 288 simply defines 'control' by reference to CTA 2010 (UK) ss. 450 and 451.

[109] CTA 2010 (UK) s. 450(2).

[110] CTA 2010 (UK) s. 1124 provides a more general definition of 'control'. Whether this definition can apply for purposes of s. 450(2) depends on whether, expressly or by implication, s. 450(2) indicates otherwise; s. 1176(2). Although not without doubt, the better view seems to be that 'control' in s. 450(2) is interpreted without regard to s. 1124; see *Steele* v. *EVC International NV* [1996] STC 785 (CA) at 794.

[111] *Steele* v. *EVC International NV* [1996] STC 785 (CA) at 794 per Morritt LJ.

anything less could amount to 'control' (e.g. 45% when the rest of the votes are dispersed broadly) is debateable.[112] Section 450(3) of CTA 2010 goes on to treat a person holding certain rights as having control of a corporation. These extensions include holding more than 50% of the share capital or voting rights in the corporation or having more than 50% of the rights to distributions of income or surplus on winding up.[113]

**Attribution of rights**    In determining whether a particular individual controls a corporation, a tax law may attribute to the individual rights held by certain relatives and related entities of the individual. For example, suppose a tax law seeks to test whether a corporation ('A Co') is controlled by an individual ('B'). B holds 35% of the voting rights in A Co, and a relative of B ('C') holds another 20% of such rights. The question is whether the tax law should consider A Co as controlled by B. If C is an individual related to B, the tax law will take one of two approaches: it will either allocate the rights held by C to B for the purposes of the test, or it will not. This is an all-or-nothing approach.

The situation is different if C is a corporation that is related to B because B controls C (under a previous application of the test). Here, if the tax law seeks to attribute the voting rights in A Co held by C to B, it may take one of two primary approaches. As in the case where C is a related individual, it may attribute all of the rights held by C to B (the 'absolute' approach). Then B would have 35% of the direct rights in A Co, plus a further 20% of the rights attributed from C, and so B would control A Co. Alternately, the tax law may only attribute to B the proportion of the rights held by C based on the percentage of the right that B holds in C. So, for example, if B holds 60% of the voting rights in C, B would only be attributed that percentage of the voting rights that C holds in A Co; that is, 12% (60% of 20%, the 'proportionate' approach). In this case, B's total holding would be 47% (35% direct and 12% indirect), and B would not control A Co.

US income tax law uses a mixed approach in attributing rights to a person for the purpose of determining whether the person is 'related' to a corporation. For the purposes of determining the 50% of the value-of-stock test in section 267 of IRC, an individual is attributed stock held by

---

[112] Other provisions deal with such a scenario; for example, CTA 2009 (UK) ss. 473 (loan relationship) and 837 (intangible assets), TIOPA 2010 (UK) s. 160 (transfer pricing) and TIOPA 2010 (UK) Part 9 A, Chapter 18 (controlled foreign companies). So the better view seems to be that more than 50% is required in the context of the definition in section 450 of CTA 2010.

[113] CTA 2010 (UK) s. 450(3).

family members (i.e. an absolute approach). By contrast, an individual is allocated a proportionate share of stock held 'indirectly' through artificial entities (i.e. other corporations, partnerships, estates or trusts). There are extensions for stock held through partnerships.[114] These are examples of a proportionate approach.

The German rules do not attribute voting rights of relatives to an individual for the purposes of determining whether the individual controls a corporation. It does not do so because the question is essentially whether a particular business controls a corporation. On this basis, it is possible for a partnership of individuals to control a corporation.[115] Further, for the purposes of determining whether a majority of voting rights is met, an individual may be attributed voting rights held by a corporation in which the individual holds a majority of voting rights. The law is not express, but it seems this is a proportionate approach.

When attributing rights for the purposes of the definition of 'connected persons', the UK adopts the absolute approach. A person is connected with a corporation if the person has control of the corporation. This is extended so that a person is also connected with a corporation if that person and persons that are connected with the person control the corporation.[116] An individual is connected with certain relatives.[117] This means that a corporation controlled by both an individual and the individual's relatives is connected with the individual and each of the relatives. It also means that a corporation controlled by both an individual and corporations controlled by the individual (or the individual and the individual's relatives) is connected with the individual and those corporations. There are further extensions for partners in a partnership.[118] All of these extensions involve the absolute approach.

That is pretty complex, but when this approach is overlaid with the concept of 'control' from sections 450 and 451 of CTA 2010 the situation becomes dizzying. In particular, in determining whether a person has 'control' of a corporation, certain rights held by 'associates' may be attributed to the person.[119] 'Associate' is defined in section 448, in not dissimilar terms to those used for 'connected persons' in section 1122 (with exclusions). Again, the approach is the absolute approach. Why the

---

[114] IRC (US) s. 267(c).
[115] KStG (Germany) Art. 14(1)2.
[116] For example, CTA 2010 (UK) s. 1122(3)(b).
[117] For example, CTA 2010 (UK) s. 1122(5).
[118] For example, CTA 2010 (UK) s. 1122(7).
[119] CTA 2010 (UK) s. 451(4).

definition of 'connected persons' indirectly incorporates the definition of 'associate' in this way is unclear. No doubt the legislature intended to throw the net wide, but that is little excuse for the lack of clarity. The situation is made worse because of the uncertainty as to whether 'person', where used in the definition of 'connected persons', includes the plural or a body of persons or whether the context otherwise requires (see the earlier discussion at 1.1.1).

**Control by a corporation**    Just as an income tax law may identify a corporation as controlled by a particular individual, it may identify a corporation as controlled by another corporation. Again, two primary issues arise: the test for control and the attribution of rights held by others.

Some countries use multiple definitions to identify corporations controlled by other corporations. The UK is a good example. Two companies are connected if one company controls the other company under the rules discussed earlier. Similarly, such companies are 'associated'.[120] Of more relevance in this regard are the various definitions of 'subsidiary' in section 1154 of CTA 2010. This section defines '51%', '75%' and '90%' subsidiaries in terms of the ownership of 'ordinary share capital' by one 'body corporate' in another body corporate. The reference to 'body corporate' means that an unincorporated association cannot be a parent or a subsidiary of another company.

The US approach is more consistent. Section 1563(a) of IRC contains a definition of a 'Parent-subsidiary controlled group'. A parent is a corporation that holds at least 80% of the voting power or value of shares in another corporation. This test is used in other contexts (e.g. for determining whether two corporations are 'related' under section 267). However, in the case of section 267 the test is modified to a 50% test.[121]

The CCCTB Proposal also contains a definition of 'qualifying subsidiary'.[122] This term is defined in terms of a parent corporation holding more than 50% of the voting rights in the subsidiary together with ownership rights amounting to more than 75% of the rights to capital and profit. Like the UK and US approach, only a parent corporation can hold a subsidiary. This can be contrasted with the German approach discussed earlier. That approach applies the same rules for identifying whether a corporation is controlled by another corporation or controlled by an individual, and so that approach is not further considered in this discussion.

---

[120]   CTA 2010 (UK) s. 449.
[121]   IRC (US) s. 267(f).
[122]   CCCTB Proposal Art. 54.

The relevant degrees of ownership selected for the various types of subsidiaries may have some relevance in corporate law. Broadly, these were discussed earlier at 1.1.4.2 in the context of the problem of minority owners where the tax identity of a corporation is eroded. The 50% holding test in these corporate tax systems is sufficient to pass an ordinary resolution at a general meeting of the shareholders. As noted earlier at 1.1.3.2, without more, this percentage is typically sufficient to elect at least a majority of the board of directors of a corporation and, perhaps, the whole board. A 75% holding may be sufficient to pass a special resolution to alter the corporation's constitution. Higher holding thresholds, such as the UK 90%, are sometimes sufficient to engage in more extreme action, such as a minority buyout (see the earlier discussion at 1.1.4.2).

**Test of control**    The test of 'control' used by the UK to determine whether two corporations are 'connected' or 'associated' was discussed earlier.[123] It is essentially a question of voting power at a general meeting. By contrast, the various definitions of 'subsidiary' in section 1154 of CTA 2010 (UK) refer to ownership of 'ordinary share capital'.[124] 'Ordinary share capital' is defined in terms of 'issued share capital' (by whatever name it is called) other than capital the holders of which have a right to a dividend at a fixed rate, but have no other right to share in the profits of the company.[125] This definition has certain anti-intuitive consequences. Shares may be ordinary shares even if they have no voting rights. Further, preference shares with a right to share in distributions on a winding up are considered ordinary shares.[126]

There are additional peculiarities when it comes to calculating the amount of ordinary share capital held by a body corporate in another body

---

[123]  CTA 2010 (UK) s. 450.

[124]  This requirement means that, even if a company is a body corporate, it cannot be a subsidiary of another company if it does not have a share capital (e.g. a company limited by guarantee or formed by charter, but apparently such a corporation could be a parent of a subsidiary). As noted at 1.1.1.1, a limited liability partnership is a body corporate but is specifically excluded from any reference to 'company' for corporation tax purposes; CTA 2009 (UK) s. 1273(2). Such partnerships are not, however, specifically excluded from any reference to a 'body corporate'. So the question is whether a limited liability partnership could be a parent of a subsidiary corporation.

[125]  CTA 2010 (UK) s. 1119.

[126]  The ordinary share capital requirement can cause particular uncertainty in the application of the 'subsidiary' definition to entities organised under foreign law (e.g. a US LLC). The categorisation of foreign entities as a 'body corporate' was discussed earlier at 1.1.1.1. It seems likely that the same approach should be adopted in determining whether a foreign entity has a 'share capital' (i.e. focus on the foreign commercial law and analogise with UK corporate law).

corporate. It is nominal share capital that is counted and not, for example, paid-up capital. Further, for it to count, the ownership of share capital must be 'beneficial ownership'.[127] Where shares are subject to a contract, it can be difficult to determine when beneficial ownership is lost. If another person has a right to specifically enforce a transfer of the shares, it is the other person that has beneficial ownership and not the legal owner.[128] Beneficial ownership will not normally pass under a contract subject to a condition precedent. However, it seems that beneficial ownership (as opposed to equitable ownership) will pass if the legal owner is 'bereft' of any substantial rights and left with a 'mere legal shell'.[129] In one case, an option to acquire shares did not pass beneficial ownership even though the option was likely to be exercised.[130]

The US test requires that a parent corporation hold

> 'stock possessing at least 80 percent of the total combined voting power of all classes of stock entitled to vote or at least 80 percent of the total value of shares of all classes of stock ...' in the subsidiary.[131]

For this purpose, 'stock' excludes non-voting preference shares, Treasury shares and certain other holdings.[132] The US commonly treats the holder of an option to acquire shares as the owner of the shares.[133] It otherwise deals with issue of shares subject to a contract through the attribution rules discussed later.

The CCCTB Proposal is more prescriptive than either the UK or US approach in that it uses a combination of voting, capital and profit rights tests. It does not incorporate any special rules dealing with preference shares or options. Further, although the Proposal does incorporate a concept of 'economic owner',[134] that concept is not expressly applied for purposes of determining rights to capital and profits. This approach can be contrasted with the general German rule for determining ownership for tax purposes, discussed earlier in the context of individuals controlling corporations.

---

[127] CTA 2010 (UK) s. 1154(6).
[128] *J. Sainsbury plc* v. *O'Connor* [1991] STC 318 (CA) at 331.
[129] *Wood Preservation Ltd* v. *Prior (Inspector of Taxes)* [1969] 1 WLR 1077 (CA) at 1095 (per Lord Donovan) and 1097 (per Harman LJ), respectively.
[130] *J. Sainsbury plc* v. *O'Connor* [1991] STC 318 (CA).
[131] IRC (US) s. 1563(a)(1)(B).
[132] IRC (US) s. 1563(c).
[133] IRC (US) s. 1563(e)(1).
[134] CCCTB Proposal Art. 4(20).

**Attribution of rights**    An individual may be attributed rights of others for the purposes of determining whether the individual controls a corporation (see the earlier discussion). Similarly, a corporation may be attributed rights for the purpose of determining whether the corporation controls another corporation. Again, a tax law incorporating attribution may adopt an absolute or proportionate approach.

The UK absolute rules discussed earlier in the context of individuals controlling corporations are also used in the context of determining whether a corporation is controlled by another corporation (and so the corporations are 'connected persons'). However, the UK uses a proportionate attribution approach in determining whether a corporation is a 'subsidiary' of another corporation. Using this approach, the ownership of ordinary share capital can be calculated directly or indirectly. An indirect holding is a holding held through another body corporate. So, for example, if A Co holds 80% of the shares in B Co, which holds 60% of the shares in C Co, A Co has a 48% indirect holding in C Co (i.e. 80% of 60%). Any direct holding of shares by A Co in C Co would be added to this amount.[135]

The US approach is very different. It attributes very few rights held by others to a corporation for the purposes of determining whether that corporation is a parent of another corporation. It requires the parent corporation to meet the holding requirement directly, other than in the case of rights subject to an option or held through a partnership or trust.[136] In applying these attribution rules, there is generally only one attribution, so only one corporation is treated as owning particular shares, but that attribution is done in a way that creates a controlled group. Further, the option attribution rule takes precedence.[137]

The CCCTB Proposal adopts a mixed approach in allocating rights for the purposes of determining whether one corporation is a parent of another corporation. In the context of the voting rights test, an absolute approach is used. So, for example, presume that A Co holds 60% of the voting rights in B Co, A Co holds 25% of the voting rights in C Co and B Co holds 30% of the voting rights in C Co. Because A Co has a majority of the voting rights in B Co, it is treated as holding all of B Co's voting rights in C Co. So A Co will have 55% (25% direct plus 30% indirect) of the voting rights in C Co and will meet the more than the 50% threshold.

---

[135]  CTA 2010 (UK) ss. 1155–7.
[136]  IRC (US) s. 1563(d)(1).
[137]  IRC (US) s. 1563(f)(2) & (3).

By contrast, the proportionate approach is used to determine whether the capital and profit tests are met (as described two paragraphs earlier).[138]

**Sibling corporations**    As noted earlier at 1.1.3.3, two or more corporations may be under the common control of the same person. These are often referred to as 'sibling' corporations. Sibling corporations are affiliated, associated, related or, in UK terminology, 'connected persons'. Where the controller is another corporation (parent), they are all 'group corporations', including the parent. Corporations with a common non-corporate controller may also be referred to as 'group corporations', but this is less common and, in any case, the controller will not be considered part of the corporate group. Two or more corporations may also be under the control of the same group of persons. Whether or not the persons making up the group are related or connected, the controlled corporations may be considered as connected (i.e. they may also be sibling corporations). The following discussion first considers categorisation of sibling corporations controlled by a single person and then sibling corporations controlled by the same group of persons.

**Control by a single person**    Under UK income tax law, two corporations are 'connected' if they are both controlled by the same person, or each is controlled by a person and/or persons connected with that person.[139] By contrast, although the UK has generic definitions of various levels of 'subsidiary' (discussed earlier), it does not have a general definition of 'group' corporations. It has definitions of 'group' companies for particular purposes, and these tend to use (and adjust) the definition of a 75% subsidiary. As a result, two 75% subsidiaries with a common parent are often considered part of the same 'group'.[140]

The US is more complicated in this regard; a distinction must be made between a 'parent-subsidiary controlled group' of corporations and a 'brother-sister controlled group' of corporations.[141] Corporations falling within either definition are necessarily 'related' persons.[142] Two corporations are in a 'brother-sister controlled group' if the same individual holds

---

[138] CCCTB Proposal Art. 54(2).

[139] CTA 2010 (UK) s. 1122(2).

[140] For example, see CTA 2010 (UK) s. 152 and TCGA 1992 (UK) s. 170(3). Both of these provisions are considered further at 1.2.3.

[141] IRC (US) s. 1563(a).

[142] IRC (US) s. 267(b)(3). Section 267(f)(1) modifies the tests in s. 1563, and so in some cases two corporations will be related despite not meeting the requirements of s. 1563.

50% of the voting rights and the value of both. In determining whether the 50% test is met, the US adopts a proportionate approach in allocating rights held through other artificial entities, including a corporation. This proportionate approach works in the same manner as the UK rules described at footnote 135. One difference is that there is no attribution if the stock owned in another corporation is less than 5% of the total value of stock in that corporation.[143]

For example, presume individual A holds 60% of B Co, A holds 20% of C Co and B Co holds 80% of C Co. Using the proportionate rule, A indirectly holds 48% of C Co (60% of 80%). So A holds more than 50% of both B Co (60% direct) and C Co (20% direct and 48% indirect). Therefore under the US rules B Co and C Co are a 'brother-sister controlled group'. If A held less than 5% of the shares in B Co, A would be attributed none of B Co's holding in C Co.

By contrast, two subsidiaries are part of the same 'parent-subsidiary controlled group' if other members of the group hold 80% of their voting rights and value.[144] This test inherently involves an absolute approach to the attribution of rights. Once a parent corporation holds 80% of a subsidiary, its complete holding in another corporation will count for purposes of determining whether that other corporation is in the group. For example, presume that A Co holds 80% of the shares in B Co, A Co holds 20% of the shares in C Co and B Co holds 60% of the shares in C Co. The holding of B Co in C Co counts in full for determining whether C Co is within the group. So, in the example, each of A, B and C forms a 'parent-subsidiary controlled group'.

The German income tax law contains no general rules for categorising corporations as sibling corporations. By contrast, the CCCTB Proposal expressly includes all subsidiaries of the same parent corporation in the same group.[145] Two corporations controlled by the same individual cannot constitute a group.

**Control by a group of persons** Rather than being controlled by a single person, two or more corporations (the 'tested' corporations) may be under the control of the same group of persons. As mentioned, such corporations may also be considered sibling corporations. For income tax laws that adopt this approach, the primary difficulty is how to identify the

[143] IRC (US) s. 1563(e)(4).
[144] IRC (US) s. 1563(a)(1)(A).
[145] CCCTB Proposal Art. 55.

relevant 'group'. This discussion does not consider a group of related persons, which has effectively been discussed in the context of attributing to a person rights held by related persons for purposes of determining whether the person has control of a corporation. In this context, the group of persons is presumed to be made up of unrelated persons.

At its extreme, the group could be every person in the world, which would produce the ridiculous result that every corporation in the world is related. Therefore the group needs to be limited in some shape or form. The requirement could be simply that the group is made up of persons (and potentially their relatives) that hold shares in both tested corporations. This is still particularly broad and may be further limited in various ways. One approach would be to limit the common control of the tested corporations to rights held by a limited number of shareholders. Here there is an analogy with closely held corporations, discussed later at 1.1.5.2. Other limitations may be used, such as that the persons in the group act in some coordinated fashion, or have a particular level of shareholding or hold shares in the tested corporations in the same proportion.

The US income tax law faces this issue in its definition of 'brother-sister controlled group' of corporations and in doing so identifies the group of persons by reference to number. Two corporations form such a group if

> 5 or fewer persons who are individuals, estates, or trusts own ... stock possessing more than 50 percent of the total ... voting power ... or more than 50 percent of the total value of shares ... of each corporation, taking into account the stock ownership of each such person only to the extent such stock ownership is identical with respect to each such corporation.[146]

Although not without issue, it seems that the lower of the two percentages that a particular person holds in each corporation is what counts towards the 50% threshold. In this context, each of the five individuals may be allocated rights held by relatives, including rights held indirectly through artificial entities under the rules on constructive ownership discussed earlier.[147]

By contrast, the UK provides a good example of the difficulties that can arise when seeking to identify corporations as commonly controlled by a group of persons if the tax law does not prescribe some relationship for identifying the group. Section 1122(2)(d) of CTA 2010 provides that two companies are connected if

---

[146]  IRC (US) s. 1563(a)(2).
[147]  IRC (US) s. 1563(e).

> a group of two or more persons has control of both companies and the groups either consist of the same persons or could be regarded if (in one or more cases) a member of either group were replaced by a person with whom the member is connected.

This provision is deficient in that it fails to identify any limit as to what may constitute a 'group' of persons. A similar issue arises in the context of section 450(5). If 'two or more persons together' hold certain rights 'they are treated as having control' of the company in question. What the difference might be between 'a group of two or more persons' (section 1122) and 'two or more persons together' (section 450) is difficult to fathom. The drafting is sloppy and inconsistent. These difficulties are further examined in the context of transfer pricing at 1.2.2.

Two further points can be made with respect to section 1122(2)(d) of CTA 2010. First, the reference to a 'group of two or more persons' might suggest that the reference to 'person' in the remainder of the section does not include the plural. If it did include the plural, the reference to 'group of two or more persons' seems superfluous.[148] Similarly, perhaps this context requires that a 'person' does not include a 'body of persons'. Second, this provision only connects the two controlled companies and does not, of itself, connect either company with any person in the group or connect persons in the group. This can be contrasted with the provision that treats a partner in a partnership as connected with other partners and their spouses and relatives.[149]

Outside of these examples, which are largely used for anti-abuse purposes, most countries do not include sibling corporations commonly owned by a group of persons within the concept of a corporate group. Usually, tax laws require a corporate group to be commonly controlled by a single parent corporation. This is the situation in the UK, the US and under the CCCTB Proposal. As mentioned above, the exception is Germany, where a corporate group may be headed by an individual or partnership (or even a PE in Germany of a non-resident), as well as a parent corporation.[150]

### 1.1.5.2  Closely held corporations

As noted earlier at 1.1.3.2, shareholders in a closely held corporation are often capable of acting collectively so as to control the corporation in a way

---

[148] For a similar observation in the context of CTA 2010 (UK) s. 450, see footnote 163.
[149] CTA 2010 (UK) s. 1122(7).
[150] KStG (Germany) s. 14.

that shareholders in widely held corporations cannot. As a result, many countries have special rules applicable to closely held corporations, and so it is necessary to identify this category of corporation. A country that makes a distinction between widely and closely held corporations must grabble with the basic issue of why make such a distinction. At an extreme level, there is no obvious reason why the taxation of Wal-Mart Stores, Inc, Royal Dutch Shell plc, Siemens AG or BP plc should be the same as that of a *Mum and Dad* corporation.

In particular, the shareholders in large listed corporations have little or no direct control over the distribution policy of the corporation. The situation is very different in closely held corporations. The importance of this difference is a particular theme of this book. However, drawing an arbitrary line somewhere in the spectrum between the extremes of Wal-Mart Stores, Inc or Royal Dutch Shell plc and a *Mum and Dad* corporation inevitably causes difficulties. Such lines are open to manipulation by corporations marginally on one side or the other of the boundary.

The following discussion considers tax law identification of closely held corporations. Naturally, categorisation of a corporation as a closely held corporation depends on the number of persons holding share interests in or participating in the corporation. For present purposes, such share interests are referred to as 'participations', and the holder of participations are referred to as 'participators'. However, rarely does a corporate tax system adopt such a simple approach. Most contain additional factors that determine more precisely the type of closely held corporation for the purpose in question. These additional factors may pertain to several matters; in particular, the form of threshold, type of participation, attribution of participations, type of participator, level of participation and type of corporation.

Each of these factors is considered in turn in relation to identifying closely held corporations. Rules applicable to closely held corporations are considered at appropriate points in the remainder of this book. For illustration purposes, the discussion uses the UK's close company, close investment holding company and consortium regimes and the US's S corporation and personal holding company regimes. Neither the German income tax law nor the CCCTB Proposal separately categorises closely held corporations. The discussion does not consider controlled foreign corporations, which are a type of closely held corporation and are briefly considered at 3.2.2.1.

**Form of threshold**    Each regime identifying closely held corporations will directly or indirectly select a number of participators as the basis for the regime. For example, the UK has distinguished closely held corporations for special income tax treatment since 1922, and since then the basic number has been five participators. This is still the primary number used in the UK's close company regime. By contrast, the UK indirectly uses a maximum of twenty participators in its consortium regime. The US also uses 5 participators in its personal holding company regime, but uses 100 participators in its S corporation regime.

A closely held corporation regime must also identify a threshold to which the number of participators pertains. The selected number of participators may pertain to all participators in a corporation or just enough to meet a certain threshold such as some form of control. The US S corporation regime provides an example of a threshold applying to the total number of participators. It defines an S corporation as simply a corporation 'which does not . . . have more than 100 shareholders'.[151]

Where the number of participants refers to that sufficient to constitute some level of control, a corporation could have any number of shareholders; however, if its control is concentrated in the hands of just a few, it might nevertheless be categorised as a closely held corporation. The UK close company regime provides an example of this approach. Section 439 of CTA 2010 defines 'close company' in terms of a company under the control of five or fewer 'participators'. It also applies to a company under the control of any number of participators who are directors, an example of a qualification by reference to the type of participator. The section goes on to drop the control test and alternately define 'close company' to include a company in which five or fewer participators or participators who are directors would have a right to more than 50% of the assets of the company in a winding up.

The concept of control in section 450 of CTA 2010 was discussed earlier at 1.1.5.1 and refers to control at the level of the shareholder meeting. It is expressed in the singular: 'a person' is taken to have control. It is clear from the definition of 'close company' that the rights of participators are to be aggregated in determining whether there is control of the company

---

[151]  IRC (US) s. 1361(b)(1)(A). The US legislation defines a 'small business corporation', which becomes an 'S corporation' by making an election, to be subject to the S corporation regime in Subchapter S. The consequences of making an election are that the corporation is treated similarly to a partnership (see the later discussion at 1.3.3.2).

in question. This is confirmed by section 450(5), which provides that '[i]f two or more persons together satisfy any of the' tests for control, they are treated as having control of the company. This seems quite obvious in the context of the definition of 'close company', but is of particular relevance in other contexts where the section 450 definition of 'control' is used; for example, with respect to the small companies' corporation tax rate (see the later discussion at 1.3.2.2 and the discussion of 'connected persons' at 1.1.5.1).

The US personal holding company regime provides a very similar example. It defines a 'personal holding company' to mean, amongst other qualifications, a corporation if 'more than 50 percent in value of its outstanding stock is owned, directly or indirectly, by or for not more than 5 individuals'.[152] Note that the US regime does not directly reference 'control', but the 50% level of shares owned by the individuals is sufficient to pass a resolution at a shareholders meeting.

The UK consortium company regime provides another example. The definition of a company owned by a consortium appears in section 153 of CTA 2010. The initial requirement is that the company is not a 75% subsidiary of any particular company, and hence a consortium company must be owned by two or more shareholders. The second requirement is that at least 75% of the company's 'ordinary share capital' is owned by other companies, each of which beneficially owns at least 5% of that capital. The latter requirements are discussed shortly. However, the result is that a consortium company must be owned by at least two, but not more than twenty, qualifying shareholders. Further, it is sufficient that the 75% threshold is reached by qualifying shareholders. The remaining 25% could be held by any number of shareholders.

**Type of participation**    Other questions in the identification of closely held corporations pertain to the nature of the participation (shares); that is, which type of interests in a corporation must a person hold to be counted towards the number of participators. The UK treatment of close companies has always been punitive, and so 'participator' is defined broadly in terms of 'a person having a share or interest in the capital or income of the company'.[153] So a participator need not be a shareholder or member in a company; it is sufficient that the person hold certain rights with respect to the company. This is made clear by specific inclusions in the definition.

---

[152]  IRC (US) s. 542(a)(2).
[153]  CTA 2010 (UK) s. 454(1).

'Participator' extends to a person who has share capital, voting or distribution rights or a right to acquire such rights. Future rights are accelerated for this purpose.[154] Certain loan creditors are also included.[155] Of course, being a participator is not sufficient of itself; the participators as identified must also 'control' the company in question, as discussed earlier, and this is essentially a question of control at the shareholder level.

Participations under the UK's close company regime can be contrasted with the requirement for holding 'ordinary share capital' under the consortium company regime. Unlike the close company regime, the consortium company regime is beneficial for taxpayers. 'Ordinary share capital' takes its meaning from section 1119 of CTA 2010 and was discussed earlier at 1.1.5.1. It is substantially narrower than participations under the close company regime. In particular, it only includes issued share capital and excludes certain preference shares.

There is a similar dichotomy between the US's personal holding company regime and its S corporation regime: the former is punitive and the latter beneficial. For the purposes of the personal holding company regime, 'outstanding stock' can be extended to include securities convertible into stock if this would cause a corporation to qualify.[156] By contrast, 'stock' for the purposes of the S corporation regime is narrowed. To qualify as an S corporation, a corporation can only have one 'class of stock'.[157] A class of stock essentially pertains to rights to dividends and a difference in voting rights is ignored.[158]

**Attribution of participations**   As with identifying controlled corporations, in identifying closely held corporations there is the issue of whether rights held by related persons should be aggregated to be treated as held by one person. Alternately, rights held by an artificial entity (say a corporation or partnership) might be disaggregated so as to be treated as held by the participators of the entity (i.e. the shareholder or partners). If rights are aggregated or disaggregated then an additional issue is whether the legal owner still counts as a person holding rights in addition to the person who has been attributed the rights (i.e. whether there can be double counting). These issues have important implications for how the number of participants is calculated in determining if a corporation is closely held.

---

[154]   CTA 2010 (UK) s. 451(2).
[155]   CTA 2010 (UK) s. 454(2).
[156]   IRC (US) s. 544(b).
[157]   IRC (US) s. 1361(b)(1)(D).
[158]   IRC (US) s. 1361(c)(4).

The US personal holding company regime only applies to corporations controlled by five or fewer 'individuals'. This means there is no potential overlap of attribution of stock directly to an artificial entity and simultaneously indirectly to participators in the artificial entity. Where a participation is held by an artificial entity, the only question is whether that participation will be attributed to any individual. Section 544 of IRC contains constructive ownership rules for purposes of the personal holding company regime. Any stock owned by an artificial entity (corporation, partnership or trust) is considered owned proportionately by members of the entity. So in this sense there is disaggregation, but no issue of double counting. Further, an individual may be attributed stock owned by a family member or a partner of the individual. In this sense there is aggregation. The issue of double counting (both the legal owner and the constructive owner) could arise here, but is addressed by aggregating 'only if, the effect is to make the corporation a personal holding company'.[159] Stock subject to an option is considered owned by the option holder.

The US S corporation regime is similar in that it focuses on stock held by individuals. Generally, an S corporation may not have other types of shareholder. This means that the focus is on direct holdings, and those holdings held indirectly through artificial entities are irrelevant. This means the attribution rules are simpler. All members of a family are treated as one shareholder and so there cannot be double counting. The definition of 'family' is substantially broader than that in the personal holding company regime.[160] The one exception to the focus on direct holdings is where a corporation is wholly owned by another corporation that qualifies as an S corporation. In this case, the subsidiary is treated as transparent.[161]

The UK consortium company regime is, like the US's S corporation regime, generally favourable to taxpayers, and so like the S corporation regime it focuses on direct holdings. This regime contains no rules for attributing shares held by one person to a related person. However, a corporation cannot be a consortium company if it is a 75% subsidiary of a particular corporation. Because the 75% test is calculated by direct or indirect holdings (see the earlier discussion at 1.1.5.1), the attribution rules for the 75% test are incorporated indirectly. The UK consortium company regime has one direct example of an attribution rule: a company is treated as held

---

[159] IRC (US) s. 544(a)(4).
[160] IRC (US) s. 1361(c)
[161] IRC (US) s. 1361(b)(3).

by a consortium if its main business consists of conducting a trade and it is a 90% subsidiary of a holding company that is owned by a consortium.[162]

By comparison to these examples, the UK close company regime rules are deficient. As in the US, these rules attribute certain rights to a person for purposes of determining whether a company is controlled by five or fewer participators. These are the rules in section 451 of CTA 2010 that were discussed earlier at 1.1.5.1. In particular, a person is attributed rights held by another on the person's behalf. A person is also attributed rights held by associates and any companies that the person or the person's associates control. The term 'associates' is defined in section 448 in the usual way to include certain family members. It also includes partners and certain trustees. The confused relationship between 'associates' and 'connected persons' was discussed earlier at 1.1.5.1.

The definitions of 'participator', 'control' and 'associate' in Chapter 2 of Part 10 of CTA 2010 provide good examples of the problems that can arise for an income tax law in dealing with artificial entities. Consider, for example, the use of the word 'person' in all these definitions. In principle, the word 'person' takes its meaning from the Interpretation Act 1978, unless the context otherwise requires (see 1.1.1). Does 'person' in the close company rules include a 'body of persons'? If so, it seems possible that a partnership or the trustees of a trust might be a person for the purposes of these rules. Yet, do the references to partners and trustees in section 448 suggest that a 'body of persons' is excluded? Without more, perhaps bodies of persons are included, and this would give rise to issues of double counting.

Less clear is whether the singular 'person' is intended to include the plural 'persons'. Why might this matter? The problem is that the definition of 'close company' in section 439 of CTA 2010 specifies a number of participators who have to have control (unless they are directors). If the singular includes the plural, this limit to five might be effectively lifted. Does the context require the plural of 'person' to be excluded in the definitions of 'participator' and 'control'? Section 450(5) seems to suggest such exclusion in the context of the definition of 'control'.[163] By extension, it seems bizarre that 'person' could include the plural in the definition of 'participator'

---

[162] CTA 2010 (UK) s. 153(3). The trading company does not meet this test if it is a 75% subsidiary of another company (other than the holding company).

[163] Lord Neuberger was of the same opinion in *Kellogg Brown & Root Holdings (UK) Ltd* v. *RCC* [2010] EWCA Civ 118 (CA) at para. 31, but refused to decide the matter.

but not in the definition of 'control'. Perhaps the context requires the plural to be excluded for the whole of Part 10 of CTA 2010 on close companies.

Does the apparent exclusion of the plural with reference to 'person' affect whether the context requires that term to include 'bodies of persons'? A body of persons necessarily includes more than one person. If a body of persons is included, that might have an impact on how the limit to five persons is calculated. Further, if a body of persons is included, does this mean that the persons who make up the body are not counted individually? Illustrated simply, if a company is controlled by a partnership of ten unrelated individuals or controlled by a trust with ten unrelated trustees, is the company a close company or not?

Part of the answer may lie in section 451(6) of CTA 2010, which, like its US equivalent,[164] suggests that such rights are to be attributed to associates 'as will result in a company being treated as under the control of 5 or fewer participators if it can be so treated'. So, in principle, the rights of the partners could be attributed to one of them to cause the company to be a close company. But that is not a complete answer, because if the partnership were the person then it would obviously control the company. In the case of the trust, there is nothing that treats the trustees as associates. The trustees, as a body of persons, might cause the company to be a close company. But if a body of persons is not a person for the purposes of the close company rules, would a single trustee (where there are a number of them) have control of the company?

A fundamental problem with the UK rules is that they have the potential to simultaneously attribute the same participation to more than one person without clarification as to whether this is to be the case and, if so, how it is to work. This potential overlap is reflected in the need for some specific exclusions from the UK close company regime. A company is not a close company if it is controlled by non-close companies.[165] A major impact of this provision is to exclude subsidiaries of listed companies from being close companies. A company is not a close company if at least 35% of the voting rights in the company are allotted to the public and quoted.[166] This exception is subject to anti-abuse rules. These exceptions would not be necessary if the UK rules, like the US personal holding company rules, only counted individuals towards the holding requirement.

---

[164]  IRC (US) s. 544(a)(4).
[165]  CTA 2010 (UK) s. 444.
[166]  CTA 2010 (UK) s. 446.

**Type of participator**    The rules identifying a closely held corporation might require the participations in it to be held by a particular type of person. The lack of a limitation in the UK close company regime is one of the factors leading to the difficulties discussed in the previous subheading. One manner in which this regime does specify the type of participator is with respect to participators who are directors. Where participators who are directors control a company, the company is a close company even if it takes more than five of the directors to control the company (i.e. the number limitation is lifted).[167]

As noted, both the US personal holding company regime and the S corporation regime effectively require participators to be individuals. There are limited extensions in both cases for stock held by certain trusts.[168] The S corporation regime incorporates a further limitation in that all participators must be resident.[169]

In the UK consortium company regime, the participators in the consortium company must be 'companies'. Like the definitions of 'subsidiary' discussed at 1.1.5.1, there is a requirement that the 'company' be a body corporate.[170]

**Level of participation**    It may be that a particular participator must have a certain level of participation in a corporation to count towards the number of participators needed to identify the corporation as a closely held corporation. The UK consortium company regime provides an example of this approach. A particular company must hold at least 5% of the ordinary share capital of a consortium company to qualify as a 'member' of the consortium.[171] None of the other regimes (UK close company regime, US personal holding company regime or US S corporation regime) incorporates a similar requirement.

**Type of corporation**    Finally, a corporation might have to be of a particular type or conduct particular activities to be identified as a closely held corporation. For example, originally a company had to be a UK registered company to be a close company. The current definition applies to all types of 'company' (i.e. including unincorporated associations), but

---

[167]  CTA 2010 (UK) s. 439.
[168]  IRC (US) ss. 542(a)(2) & 1361(c)(2).
[169]  IRC (US) ss. 1361(b)(1)(C).
[170]  CTA 2010 (UK) s. 188.
[171]  CTA 2010 (UK) s. 153(2).

non-resident companies cannot be a close company.[172] Additionally, UK income tax law defines 'close investment-holding company' as a subset of a close company and which is important for purposes of determining the applicable corporate tax rate.[173] A close company is a close investment holding company unless it conducts certain activities; in particular, trading activities or holding land for commercial rent.

The US personal holding company and S corporation regimes also exclude corporations conducting particular activities. In particular, they exclude certain financial institutions and insurance companies.[174] The personal holding company regime has other limitations, excluding foreign corporations in particular. Further, a corporation is not a personal holding company if less than '60 percent of its adjusted ordinary gross income…for the taxable year is personal holding company income'.[175] 'Personal holding company income' is defined broadly to catch any attempt to shelter either passive income or income from personal services in a corporation.[176]

### 1.1.5.3   Associated corporations

As discussed earlier at 1.1.3.2, even in the context of widely held corporations, there are some owners that might be viewed as having some degree of control or influence of the corporation despite not holding a majority ownership interest. As noted, corporate law commonly recognises a concept of 'substantial shareholder,' and it has been suggested that a substantial shareholder might be considered as 'associated' with the corporation. Tax laws might also identify certain persons as associated with a corporation. These are persons with a substantial shareholding that are neither controllers of the corporation nor grouped with other persons that together control the corporation. In this way, a corporation might be associated with either an individual or another artificial entity.

Of the tax laws under consideration, only the CCCTB Proposal has a general concept of 'associated enterprises'. The UK, German and US income tax laws do recognise corporate owners that might be viewed as 'substantial' at a number of points, but they do not incorporate a generally applicable definition. One UK example has already been discussed in

---

[172]   CTA 2010 (UK) s. 442. The extension to all 'companies' except non-resident companies was introduced in 1965. See Harris (2011).
[173]   CTA 2010 (UK) s. 34.
[174]   IRC (US) ss. 542(c) & 1361(b)(2).
[175]   IRC (US) s. 542(a)(1).
[176]   IRC (US) s. 543.

the context of a 5% corporate holder of shares in a consortium company. Another common threshold in this regard is a 10% ownership interest, but other thresholds that might be viewed as substantial are used in rules that are considered throughout this book. These rules include those considered later at 1.3.2.2 (personal services corporations), 2.4.3.1 (exemption of inter-corporate dividends), 3.2.2.3 (underlying foreign tax relief), 5.1.3.1 (participation exemption) and 8.2.2.1 (dividend stripping).

Conceptually, the CCCTB Proposal definition of 'associated enterprises' is inspired by Article 9(1) of the OECD Model.[177] However, unlike Article 9, the CCCTB Proposal definition can only apply so as to associate two 'companies'. Two companies cannot be associated if they are members of the same group of companies. As in the discussion at 1.1.5.1, there are two avenues for the potential association of two companies under the Proposal. The first is where one company participates in the 'management, control or capital' of the other. The second is where the 'same persons' have such a participation in two companies. 'Participation' is defined in terms of holding more than 20% of the voting or capital rights in the company in question. In addition, it includes 'being in a position to exercise a significant influence in the management' of a company. Any one of these three thresholds is sufficient to create an association.

The participation may be held 'directly or indirectly'. This introduces the issue of attribution of rights as discussed in the context of controlled corporations and closely held corporations (at 1.1.5.1 and 1.1.5.2.). For purposes of working out the 20% threshold of voting or capital rights, a simple proportionate approach is used. So if A Co holds 40% of B Co and B Co holds 30% of C Co, A Co is attributed a 12% holding in C Co (i.e. 40% of 30%). However, for the purposes of the voting test, once a right to more than 50% of the votes in an intermediate company is reached, an absolute approach is used. So, if A Co held 60% of the voting rights in B Co it would be attributed all of B Co's holding in C Co (i.e. 30%), and A Co and C Co would be associated despite the fact that A Co is only attributed 18% of the capital rights in C Co (i.e. 60% of 30%).

Because two companies may be associated by having a common participator, the CCCTB Proposal must also deal with individuals. For this purpose, it treats an individual and the individual's spouse and 'lineal ascendants or descendants...as a single person', and there is a similarity here with the rule under the US S corporation regime discussed earlier at 1.1.5.2. So, if 10% of A Co is held by Z and 15% by Z's spouse, and 15% of

---

[177] CCCTB Proposal Art. 78.

B Co is held by Z and 10% by Z's spouse, A Co and B Co are associated enterprises. However, because of the limitation of the CCCTB Proposal to companies, neither Z nor Z's spouse is associated with A Co or B Co.

## 1.2    Corporate tax base issues

Once a tax law has identified corporations and determined that they are capable of making and receiving payments (i.e. that they can be attributed income), the manner in which that income is calculated must be determined. For the vast majority of countries, the manner in which corporate income is calculated is the same as the manner in which the income of an individual is calculated, especially the business income of individuals. Even those countries that have a separate corporation tax law tend to define the corporate tax base by reference to rules used to calculate the personal income tax base. Germany and the US are examples of this approach.[178]

Effectively, this was also the UK approach until the tax law rewrite. However, when the corporation tax was rewritten the peculiar step was taken of rewriting all the rules that apply to individuals into CTA 2009 and CTA 2010. The UK may be the only country in the world that does this. It is not clear why it was thought that the duplication was a good idea. There are a number of reasons why this approach seems less than optimal. The volume of the law duplicated is substantial. It seems inevitable that in the future the divergence between the corporate and personal tax bases will increase. There seems no overriding reason why the corporate tax base should be different from that of the personal income tax base. In particular, there is a real need for the corporate tax base to interface properly with the personal income tax base, especially in the context of closely held corporations.

Despite the strange UK approach, general tax base issues such as the calculation of depreciation and the timing of amounts are not peculiar to corporations. According to the definition adopted by this book (see the introduction), they are not features of a corporate tax system and so are not considered in any detail. However, as noted at the start of this chapter, there are a number of special tax base issues that are peculiar to corporations. Some involve the interface between the corporate tax base and

---

[178]  KStG (Germany) s. 8(1) generally applies the provisions of EStG for the determination of corporate income. IRC (US) Subchapter B (ss. 61 to 291) on the 'Computation of Taxable Income' generally applies to both corporations and individuals.

corporate law. This is the first matter discussed under this heading (i.e. whether and to what extent the corporate tax base follows corporate law rules for the calculation of profits).

The subcategorisation of corporations by reference to their owners and controllers was discussed earlier at 1.1.3 to 1.1.5. As noted at 1.1.4, other than doing nothing, a corporate tax system may either reinforce or erode the separate tax identity of controlled or related corporations. Reinforcing rules are discussed under the second subheading of this heading. These primarily involve the issue of an arm's length approach to transfer pricing. Eroding rules are discussed under the third and fourth subheadings. The third subheading specifically considers eroding rules for group corporations. These rules involve both the non-recognition of gain or loss on transactions between related corporations and the use of a loss incurred by one corporation against the profits of a related corporation. The fourth subheading considers eroding rules for corporations otherwise related with another person (i.e. related in a non-group context).

The final subheading considers special corporate tax base rules for corporations arising from the interface with the personal income tax base. This interface may be caused by events occurring during the life of a corporation that raise issues as to the extent to which the corporate tax base and the personal tax base reflect each other. The interface also arises by reason of special tax base rules designed with individuals in mind and raises the issue whether corporations should be excluded from these special rules and, if so, how those rules should be identified.

### 1.2.1   General rules

#### Schedular vs. global

The introduction explained the income tax in terms of a tax on realised creations of wealth and payments as the building blocks of the income tax base. There are limited activities by which wealth can be created, often referred to as 'income-earning activities'. In the context of individuals, every income tax law has to identify income-producing activities to distinguish them from personal activities and, in particular, consumption. There are three main categories of income-earning activity, which reflect resources available to produce new wealth.

Individuals may use just their own labour to generate new wealth. The primary example of this is 'employment', although this term carries a technical legal meaning in all countries that is both broader and narrower than the simple provision of labour. A person may passively use just assets to generate new resources, commonly referred to as 'investment'. Third, a person may use, in a myriad of proportions, a mixture of labour and assets to produce new wealth. The broadest term that is typically used to describe this combination is 'business' or 'enterprise', although it may, as in the case of the UK, encompass narrower concepts such as trade, independent contractor, profession, calling, vocation, occupation, and so on.

A tax law that calculates income separately for each earning activity conducted by a person is referred to as a *schedular* system. The amount of income from each activity is then typically aggregated to produce a total to which tax rates apply, although in some systems different tax rates are applied to different activities. A schedular system is contrasted with a *global* system under which a person makes only one calculation of aggregate income (i.e. there are no separate calculations for particular earning activities).[179] The majority of countries adopt a schedular system, at least to some extent, and especially with respect to the income of individuals. This is true of the UK.[180] Indeed, the UK's early income tax law dating from 1799 taxed different types of income according to different 'schedules' and was the origin of the reference to a *schedular* tax system.[181] The German personal income tax law is also schedular.[182] By contrast, the US income tax law is usually viewed as global.[183]

Just because an income tax law adopts a schedular approach with respect to individuals does not mean that it will do so with respect to corporations. In many countries, corporations (especially registered

---

[179]   Generally, see Ault & Arnold (2010, pp. 197–8).

[180]   For individuals, the schedular system is listed in ITA 2007 (UK) s. 3 and reflected in ITEPA 2003 (UK) (employment); ITTOIA 2005 (UK) Part 2 (trade, profession and vocation), Part 3 (land), Part 4 (debt claims, shares) and Part 5 (intangible property, other income); and TCGA 1992 (UK) (capital gains). Corporations are discussed later.

[181]   Generally, see Harris (2006), pp. 380–420, 426–34.

[182]   EStG (Germany) s. 1 charges income tax under various heads. Income from a particular activity is calculated as either profit or excess of receipts over costs; s. 2(2). The law proceeds to set out rules regarding each of these calculation methods (ss. 4 to 12) and then rules for calculating each type of income; for example, agriculture and forestry (ss. 13 to 14), business activity (ss. 15 to 17), self-employment (s. 18), employment (s. 19), holding capital assets (s. 20), renting and leasing (s. 21) and other income (ss. 22 to 23). The aggregate of income from these categories is taxable income to which tax rates are applied; s. 2(5).

[183]   IRC (US) s. 61(a) defines 'gross income' to mean 'all income from whatever source' (i.e. it is an aggregate concept). 'Taxable income', to which tax rates apply, is defined as gross income less allowable deductions; s. 63(a). Deductions are granted generally in calculating taxable income rather than in calculating income from any particular activity (e.g. s. 161).

companies) are required to prepare financial accounts under commercial or corporate law. For example, this is reflected in Book 3 of the German Commercial Code (*Handelsgesetzbuch*) and in Chapter 4 of Part 15 of the UK Companies Act 2006. These accounts include a requirement to prepare a profit-and-loss account, which gives rise to questions as to the relationship between corporate financial accounts and the corporate tax base for income tax purposes (discussed later). In particular, the accounts must reflect the financial position of the 'company' and so are inherently *global* in nature.[184]

In many countries, including the UK and the US, there is no similar general requirement for individuals to prepare financial accounts. Indeed, in the US there is no general legal requirement for corporations to prepare accounts under corporate laws such as the Model Business Corporation Act (MBCA) or the General Corporation Law of Delaware (DGCL). However, if a corporation's shares are publicly traded and regulated by the Securities Exchange Commission the corporation is required to file certain 'financial statements' under the Securities Act of 1933 and the Securities Exchange Act of 1934. These statements are detailed in regulations, which generally implement (at least implicitly) generally accepted accounting principles.[185]

This requirement to file global financial accounts is extended in the context of group corporations. A parent corporation is typically required to also prepare group financial accounts for corporate law purposes.[186] Corporate group financial accounts must be prepared for a parent corporation and, broadly, for all the corporations it controls (subsidiaries).[187]

---

[184] For example, see Commercial Code (*Handelsgesetzbuch*) (Germany) s. 264(2), which refers to 'a true and fair view of the assets, liabilities, financial position and results of the company.' See also the Companies Act 2006 (UK) s. 396(2).

[185] Title 17 Code of Federal Regulations (US) Part 210. The relevance of generally accepted accounting principles is recognised by Securities Exchange Act of 1934 (US) s. 13(b)(2)(B)(ii) (US Code Title 15 Chapter 2B s. 78m(b)(2)(B)(ii)).

[186] For example, for EU corporations listed on EU stock exchanges; see *Application of International Accounting Standards*, Council Regulation (EC) No. 1606/2002. For Germany, see Commercial Code (*Handelsgesetzbuch*) (Germany) s. 290, and for the UK, see Companies Act 2006 (UK) s. 399. For the US, see Securities Exchange Act of 1934 (US) s. 13(b) (US Code Title 15 Chapter 2B s. 78m(b)) and Title 17 Code of Federal Regulations (US) § 210.3–01 & 02.

[187] 'Subsidiary' is broadly defined in Companies Act 2006 (UK) s. 1162 according to several tests, including a parent holding a majority of voting rights in the subsidiary, having the right to appoint a majority of the board of directors of the subsidiary or having the power to exercise a dominant influence over the subsidiary. Similarly, see Commercial Code (*Handelsgesetzbuch*) (Germany) s. 290(2). By contrast, Title 17 Code of Federal Regulations (US) § 210.3–02 defines 'subsidiary' simply in terms of 'control', which is

Most commonly, these accounts are prepared on a pure consolidation basis (see the earlier discussion at 1.1.4.2), as though the corporations 'included in the consolidation...were a single company'.[188] As with the financial accounts of single corporations, group financial accounts are prepared on a global basis.

Consistent with the global nature of corporations' financial accounts, the US, German and the CCCTB Proposal corporate tax bases adopt a global approach. The US simply applies the same global approach for corporation tax purposes as it applies to individuals.[189] In a manner reminiscent of the US tax base, the CCCTB Proposal defines the tax base as 'revenues less exempt revenues, deductible expenses and other deductible items'.[190] There is only one calculation for each corporation, and so the approach is global. Although Germany applies a schedular approach to the taxation of individuals, this is modified to a global approach when applied to corporations. All income derived by resident corporations is 'treated as income from business operations'.[191]

As noted at 1.1.4.2, the corporate tax systems of the US, Germany and the CCCTB Proposal adopt hybrid forms of consolidation. These regimes are discussed further at 1.2.3. Although these systems adopt a global approach for calculating the income of individual corporations, this is not the case when calculating the consolidated results for corporate groups. Due to their hybrid nature, each of these regimes incorporates schedular aspects (i.e. some corporate tax base attributes are retained by individual members of a group). So in this regard, these systems do not follow the global approach in group financial accounts.

This can be contrasted with the approach in, for example, Australia and the Netherlands, which adopt pure consolidation for corporate groups in their corporate tax system (see the earlier discussion at 1.1.4.2). Although

---

defined as 'the possession, direct or indirect, of the power to direct or cause the direction of the management and policies of a person, whether through the ownership of voting shares, by contract, or otherwise'. However, consolidation of accounts is only required for 'entities that are majority owned'; § 210.3a-02(a).

[188] Large and Medium-sized Companies and Groups (Accounts and Reports) Regulations 2008 (SI 2008/410) (UK) Schedule 6 para. 1(1). For a similar requirement, see Commercial Code (*Handelsgesetzbuch*) (Germany) s. 297(3). By contrast, Title 17 Code of Federal Regulations (US) § 210.3a-04 requires the elimination of 'intercompany items and transactions between persons included in the ... consolidated financial statements'.

[189] The system is not entirely global. In particular, capital losses are quarantined from the global income calculation; IRC (US) s. 1211(a).

[190] CCCTB Proposal Art. 10.

[191] KStG (Germany) s. 8(2).

group consolidated income under these regimes does not follow that in group financial accounts, both countries do adopt an essentially global approach in calculating group consolidated income for tax purposes. However, the level of holding required for tax consolidation is much higher than the quasi-50% requirement for group financial accounts, being 100% and 95% in Australia and the Netherlands, respectively.

Financial accounts are prepared on a yearly basis, and this does not necessarily coincide with the standard tax year under a tax law. Therefore, it is common to permit taxpayers, especially those in business, to calculate their tax base for a year by reference to the period for which their accounts are made up. For example, in Germany, the tax year is the calendar year, and the profits from a business for a particular year are the profits of the business for any accounting period ending in that year.[192] In the US, the taxable year is also commonly the calendar year, but taxpayers may select another fiscal year (12 months) to be their taxable year.[193] Under the CCCTB Proposal, 'tax year' is defined in particularly flexible terms as 'any twelve-month period'.[194] However, just because a corporate tax base is global or is calculated according to the same period as a corporation's financial accounts does not mean that the corporate tax base follows the financial accounts or that there is even a close connection with a corporation's financial accounts. That is discussed further in this section.

As usual, the UK approach is comparatively a mess. The corporate tax base is schedular and is broadly similar to (but not the same as) that adopted for individuals. Corporation tax is charged on the 'profits' of a company for a financial year.[195] The financial year commences on 1 April and finishes on 31 March.[196] However, profits are determined according to accounting periods and then apportioned to financial years, if they are not the same.[197] Accounting periods are determined by reference to the date that a company makes up its accounts.[198] This and the reference to 'profits' might suggest that the UK corporate tax base is global and that there is a close relationship with financial accounts. That, however, is not the case.

---

[192] EStG (Germany) s. 4a.
[193] IRC (US) s. 7701(a)(23) & (24).
[194] CCCTB Proposal Art. 9(4).
[195] CTA 2009 (UK) s. 2(1).
[196] CTA 2010 (UK) s. 1119 and Interpretation Act 1978 Schedule 1.
[197] CTA 2009 (UK) s. 8(5).
[198] CTA 2009 (UK) s. 9.

The word 'profits' is defined in terms of 'income and chargeable gains'.[199] Chargeable gains are calculated under Taxation of Chargeable Gains Act (TCGA) 1992, and income is calculated under the various heads listed in section 1(2) of CTA 2009. This means corporations must calculate their profits separately according to the following activities:

Trading (CTA 2009 Part 3)
Land (property business) (CTA 2009 Part 4)
Debt Claims (loan relationships) (CTA 2009 Parts 5 and 6)
Derivatives (CTA 2009 Part 7)
Intangibles (CTA 2009 Part 8)
Know-how and Patents (CTA 2009 Part 9)
Dividends (CTA 2009 Part 9A)
Miscellaneous Income (CTA 2009 Part 10)
Disposal of Capital Assets (TCGA 1992)

This schedular system produces a significant divorce between a corporation's financial accounts and its tax base. Unlike the other global systems, it means that the system requires reconciliation rules where a particular receipt or expense might otherwise simultaneously fall under two or more heads of charge. These reconciliation rules are confusing, fragmented, difficult to find and unnecessarily complex. Broadly, they involve the following (at least by comparison to trading):

- Property business has priority over trading.[200] However, except in the context of a trade, the loan relationship rules have priority over property business and the same applies with respect to derivatives.[201] By contrast, property business has priority over the intangible assets regime.[202]
- The loan relationship rules have general priority.[203] However, credits and debits for the purposes of trade are accounted for under the trading head.[204] In addition, distributions generally have priority over loan relationships.[205]
- Credits and debits on derivative contracts for the purposes of trade are accounted for under the trading head.[206] Otherwise, most non-trading

[199]  CTA 2009 (UK) s 2(2).
[200]  CTA 2009 (UK) s. 201.
[201]  CTA 2009 (UK) s. 211.
[202]  CTA 2009 (UK) s. 748.
[203]  CTA 2009 (UK) s. 464.
[204]  CTA 2009 (UK) s. 297.
[205]  CTA 2009 (UK) s. 465.
[206]  CTA 2009 (UK) s. 573.

debits and credits from derivative contracts are dealt with under the loan relationship rules.[207]

- Similarly, credits and debits under the intangible assets regime used for the purposes of trade are accounted for under the trading head.[208] However, unlike derivative contracts, non-trading gains on intangible fixed assets are subject to their own charge.[209]
- Trade has priority over the charge on profits from disposal of know-how.[210] Profits on the disposal of patent rights are calculated only using capital amounts.[211] Under either head, as long as the asset in question (if there is one) is used for commercial purposes and was acquired post-2002, is seems (though not clearly) the intangible assets regime applies.[212]
- Trade and property business has priority over distributions,[213] but distributions generally trump loan relationships (see the earlier discussion).
- Miscellaneous income is subject to trading and property business.[214] Annual payments and other income are expressly residual in nature.[215]
- Normal reconciliation rules apply for capital gains. Amounts included in income are excluded from consideration received on disposal, and amounts deductible from income are excluded from the cost base of an asset.[216]

These reconciliation rules have been set out in detail to demonstrate how a country can let a schedular system get out of control. The UK's system is far from the approach that would be taken in financial accounts. However, just as having a global system does not mean a relationship between financial accounting and the tax base, the UK schedular system does not mean there is no such relationship. To find that relationship, it is necessary to investigate each of these heads of charge. First, it is useful to investigate whether a corporate tax base should follow financial accounts.

---

[207] CTA 2009 (UK) s. 574.
[208] CTA 2009 (UK) s. 747.
[209] CTA 2009 (UK) s. 752.
[210] CTA 2009 (UK) s. 909.
[211] CTA 2009 (UK) s. 913.
[212] CTA 2009 (UK) ss. 803, 881 & 906.
[213] CTA 2009 (UK) s. 931W.
[214] CTA 2009 (UK) s. 982.
[215] CTA 2009 (UK) ss. 977 & 979, respectively.
[216] TCGA 1992 (UK) ss. 37 & 39, respectively.

### Should the corporate tax base follow financial accounts?

There is a substantial amount of academic literature debating whether and to what extent the corporate tax base should follow financial accounts.[217] The following short discussion seeks to summarise that debate rather than contribute to it. An income tax law should take an explicit position on the relevance of financial accounts in determining the tax base, particularly the corporate tax base. Unfortunately, because income tax law developed much earlier than the first release of accounting recommendations in the 1930s (US) and 1940s (UK), the approach is typically fragmented.

The main options for a relationship in law between the corporate tax base and financial accounting are as follows:

1. The corporate tax base mirrors the financial accounts (correlation).
2. The corporate tax base mirrors the financial accounts, but in specific cases the tax law overrides these accounts.
3. As for 2 but any adjustment made by reason of the tax law must be reflected in the financial accounts (reverse correlation).
4. There is no direct relationship, but an indirect ad hoc relationship exists when the tax law fails to prescribe rules.
5. There is no relationship.

Options 1 and 5 are extremes that do not exist to an identifiable extent in practice. Option 3 is also rare and does not exist in countries like the UK and the US where accounting standards are not prescribed by law. This means that, in the vast majority of countries, accounts prepared for corporate tax purposes differ from financial accounts. Divergence in the approach adopted by countries is, therefore, primarily a matter of whether the tax law starts with the financial accounts and makes adjustments or starts with a formulaic tax base and accepts that accounting treatment may be relevant at points. There is also the issue of the extent of divergence or convergence.

As mentioned, historically it was not possible for income tax law to follow financial accounts. Income tax law, at least in the UK, was introduced long before the addition of the registered company and even longer before registered companies were required to prepare and file accounts.[218] In any

---

[217]  Much of this literature is referenced in Schön (2008), especially Part 2.

[218]  The UK first prescribed registration of companies by the Joint Stock Companies Act 1844 (UK). Preparation and publication of financial statements were first prescribed by the Companies Act 1862 (UK) s. 42, which only applied to banking and insurance companies. The statement was to follow Form D of the First Schedule and simply involved a statement of assets and liabilities.

case, prior to the twentieth century and well into it, accounting remained very discretionary, inconsistent and underdeveloped – an inappropriate mix for adoption as a tax base.[219] In the last four decades, accounting has developed dramatically. It is more robust, sophisticated and accurate. Nevertheless, many argue that there are features of accounting standards and the manner in which they are set that make them inappropriate for holistic adoption as a tax base. The following discussion briefly considers the main arguments.

A tax law should be certain and, therefore, precise in calculating a person's income. As a matter of fairness, taxpayers should not have a choice as to how much income they declare (i.e. there should be one, *correct* amount of taxable income). This is also necessary for certainty; that is, a taxpayer should know what the tax consequences of a transaction will be before entering into it. In many cases, accounting rules accept a range of results for particular transactions and positions. The sort of discretion that is left to the accountant is viewed as unacceptable, and so financial accounts are inappropriate for holistic adoption as a tax base.

The purposes for which accounts are prepared are inconsistent with or at least different from the reasons why a person must declare income. Accounts are prepared for investor and public consumption, and as a result, conservatism (prudence) can be important. Historically, this involves not overstating profits and so may involve anticipating losses but not profits.[220] This approach may be viewed as inconsistent with the principle of equity in taxation, which involves a fair sharing of taxation between people based on a consistent and balanced calculation of their income. In tax law, the focus should be on accuracy in comparing positions so as to promote fairness.

The Accounting Standards Board, which issues UK accounting standards; the Financial Accounting Standards Board, which issues US accounting standards; and the International Accounting Standards Board,

---

[219] For an overview of the development of accounting and its relationship with direct taxation in the UK before 1820, see Harris (2006).

[220] This is well demonstrated by Commercial Code (*Handelsgesetzbuch*) (Germany) s. 252(1)4. Conservatism (prudence) is no longer a fundamental of accounting policy in the UK, but is a consideration in determining reliability (e.g. see Financial Reporting Standard 18, available at www.frc.org.uk/Home.aspx, accessed 16 July 2012). For the similar position regarding conservatism in US accounting, see Carmichael, Whittington & Graham (2012, pp. 2–78). However, prudence remains a requirement of preparing accounts for the Companies Act 2006 (UK); see the Large and Medium-sized Companies and Groups (Accounts and Reports) Regulations 2008 (SI 2008/410) (UK) Schedule 1 para. 13.

which issues the International Financial Reporting Standards, are independent authorities.[221] They seek to act in an autonomous and dynamic manner in developing accounting standards. If those standards were the sole basis for determination of taxable income, the government and the tax administration would have a direct interest in the setting of those standards. Interference from the government and the tax administration might reduce the flexibility in setting accounting standards and compromise accuracy. It might also confuse the purposes for which accounting standards are made.

Finally, given the independent nature of the bodies that set accounting standards, there is a question of accountability. If tax law followed financial accounts, these bodies would have an ability to alter the tax base by altering their standards. Responsible government suggests that only the legislature should exercise such a power.

Proponents of using accounting standards do not dispute these points so much as take the view that they do not outweigh the convenience and efficiency of using financial accounts as a tax base. They suggest that there is sufficient (though not complete) consistency of purpose. The government retains the power to override accounting standards should they develop in an obscure manner that makes them inappropriate as a tax base. As a result, there is no reason for the government to become directly involved in setting accounting standards. Nevertheless, the government remains responsible for the choice of adopting accounting standards as the tax base and must monitor that adoption on a continuing basis.

## Relationship with accounting in practice

As mentioned, the vast majority of countries accept a relationship between the corporate tax base and financial accounts, but do not holistically accept financial accounts. The relationship tends to be closest in civil law jurisdictions, which have a greater propensity to use financial accounts as the starting point for calculating the corporate tax base. Common law jurisdictions are less likely to use this starting point, although these jurisdictions do use accounting treatment to fill holes in the absence of legislative rules. One reason for this approach in common law jurisdictions is the exclusion or quarantining of capital gains from the income tax base.

---

[221] Apparently (but not clearly), this is true of the German Accounting Standards Committee, which, in accordance with the Commercial Code (*Handelsgesetzbuch*), is contractually bound with the Federal Ministry of Justice regarding the setting of accounting standards. See http://www.drsc.de/service/ueber_uns/index_en.php, accessed 16 July 2012.

Capital gains are an area in which the corporate tax base is likely to diverge from accounting treatment, at least in common law jurisdictions. There are a number of other areas of common divergence, of which depreciation is the leading example. The tax laws of many countries provide for accelerated rates of depreciation when compared with accounting treatment. In addition, some countries, including the UK, refuse to grant any write-down for some types of depreciating assets. Other areas of divergence include trading stock valuation, provisioning, inflation adjustments, long-term contracts (including leasing), interest, foreign currency transactions, pensions, fines, charitable donations, entertainment expenses and losses.[222]

The matters listed in the preceding paragraph are general tax base issues. The tax laws of many countries incorporate special rules, especially concessions, and sometimes these special rules are targeted at corporations. Special rules may involve the provision of investment tax credits and export or research and development incentives. Some countries have special regimes for headquarter companies, financial services and various other matters or simplified rules for calculating the tax base of small and medium-sized businesses (discussed later at 1.2.5). Many countries also have special regimes for group corporations, which never seem to follow accounting treatment (see the discussion at 1.2.3).

The increased importance of fair value accounting creates another potential dislocation between the corporate tax base and financial accounts, particularly where that base requires realisation. The International Accounting Standards Board was formed in 2000, and since that time the scope for use of fair value accounting has been broadened. This is especially so since the adoption of International Financial Reporting Standards for EU listed corporations in 2005.[223] However, the use of fair value accounting as a point of divergence with the corporate tax base should not be overstated. At present, that method of accounting tends to be used only in the areas of financial instruments and investment property of real estate businesses.[224] Some income tax laws accept or require fair value accounting in these areas or explicitly prescribe rules that are not

---

[222] For an analysis of these issues from the perspective of nine different countries (including Germany, the UK and the US), see Ault & Arnold (2010, Part Two).

[223] *Application of International Accounting Standards*, Council Regulation (EC) No 1606/2002.

[224] Generally regarding fair value accounting, its use in Europe and the US and its role in the 2008 financial crisis, see Laux & Leuz (2009). At p. 827 they note that '[u]nder both US GAAP and IFRS, fair values are most frequently used for financial assets and liabilities'.

dissimilar.[225] Generally, historical cost accounting continues to dominate, particularly in the valuation of plant, equipment and intangible assets.

Germany is a good example of a country where there is a close correspondence between the corporate tax base and financial accounts, although historically it was closer. As mentioned earlier, Germany effectively adopts a global approach to the corporate tax base because all income is considered as business income. Under its Income Tax Law, business income is determined as 'profit' from business activity.[226] 'Profit' is defined as 'the difference in amount between the operating assets at the close of the accounting period and the operating assets at the close of the preceding accounting period'.[227] Section 5(1) is particularly important:

> In the case of traders who ... are required to keep books and prepare financial statements regularly ... the operating assets must be evaluated ... [and] recorded according to the commercial law generally accepted accounting principles, unless a different adjustment is or has been made in accordance with the elections provided under tax law.

Therefore the corporate tax base corresponds to financial accounts (principle of correlation), unless the tax law provides an election to the contrary. Before 2009, there was also a principle of reverse correlation whereby an election under a tax law provision was required to be reported in the financial accounts. The amendments were made when International Financial Reporting Standards became generally available in Germany in 2009.

Although the US approach also has a global corporate tax base, the linkage with financial accounting is substantially weaker. Indeed, as a result of the basic tax base formula (gross income minus allowable deductions) there is no express legislative link at all.[228] US tax law does prescribe that '[t]axable income shall be computed under the method of accounting on the basis of which the taxpayer regularly computes his income in keeping his books'.[229] However, this is not a direct reference to generally accepted accounting principles, and the section goes on to provide for overriding the taxpayer's books.

Surprisingly, the CCCTB Proposal adopts the same approach. Initially, it seemed likely that the CCCTB Proposal tax base would at least start with

---

[225]  A clear example is in CCCTB Proposal Art. 23(2) which would prescribe a mark-to-market approach for recognising gains and losses on financial assets or liabilities. For other examples, see Ault & Arnold (2010, pp. 309–16).

[226]  EStG (Germany) s. 2(2)1.

[227]  EStG (Germany) s. 4(1).

[228]  For example, see Ault & Arnold (2010, pp. 190–1).

[229]  IRC (US) s. 446(a).

profits determined under International Financial Reporting Standards, given the importance of those standards within the EU. However, that did not occur, probably because of issues regarding fair value accounting. The CCCTB Proposal goes out of its way to adopt a realisation requirement for profits and losses.[230]

As noted earlier, the relationship between the UK corporate tax base and financial accounts is complex and fragmented. To understand this relationship, it is necessary to investigate each of the schedular heads of charge to corporation tax. There are some heads where there is no connection or no obvious connection, as with the charge on capital gains. TCGA 1992 is prescriptive about how chargeable gains are calculated, and its rules leave little if any scope for the application of accounting treatment. Likewise, it is difficult to see any substantial role for accounting practice in the context of the charge on know-how, patents, dividends or miscellaneous income. These are, however, minor heads of charge by comparison to the other heads of charge.

The most substantial connection in the UK between the corporate tax base and financial accounts is in the charge on trading income. Section 35 of CTA 2009 charges to corporation tax 'on income' the 'profits of a trade'. This formulation is every bit as quirky as it appears. The reference to 'profits' suggests a connection with accounting, but simultaneously the reference to 'income' suggests a judicially developed concept that distinguishes income from capital. This latter aspect is dealt with explicitly by sections 53 and 93: capital expenditure is not deductible and capital receipts are not included in calculating the profits of a trade, respectively. The treatment of these types of payments is largely reserved for Capital Allowances Act (CAA) 2001 and TCGA 1992. This produces a large dislocation between the profits of a trade and a corporation's financial accounts (especially in the context of depreciable assets), even where the corporation's sole activity is one trade.

However, with respect to revenue (income) amounts, there is a presumption that accounting treatment should be followed, at least residually. Section 46(1) of CTA 2009 provides as follows:

> The profits of a trade must be calculated in accordance with generally accepted accounting practice, subject to any adjustment required or authorised by law in calculating profits for corporation tax purposes.

'Generally accepted accounting practice' (GAAP) is defined by reference to section 1127 of CTA 2010. For companies using International Financial

---

[230] CCCTB Proposal Art. 9(1).

Reporting Standards, GAAP is as prescribed by those standards.[231] Residually, 'generally accepted accounting practice' means accounting practice intended to give a 'true and fair view'. Section 393 of the Companies Act 2006 requires directors to be satisfied that their company's annual accounts give a true and fair view. Section 396 of that Act goes on to specify the nature of a company's individual accounts, but most of the detail is left to regulations.[232] Although the legislation could be clearer, it is accepted that the requirement of a true and fair view is an indirect reference to Financial Reporting Standards issued by the Accounting Standards Board.

Even when the relevant standards are identified in accordance with this convoluted procedure, section 46(1) of CTA 2009 overrides those standards with 'any adjustment required or authorised by law'. It is clear that specific statutory provisions, such as the non-recognition of capital expenditure and receipts in sections 53 and 93, override accounting practice. A major issue has been the extent to which 'law' includes case law. Although conceptually tax cases always involve the interpretation of statute, at a more practical level courts have often filled gaps in tax legislation. It is not clear to what extent changes in accounting practice can supersede earlier judicial pronouncements that filled gaps. This thorny issue has not been resolved directly, but rather the approach in recent years has been to legislate judicial rules thought appropriate.[233]

As for other heads of charge with a connection to accounting practice, income from land (property business) is calculated using the rules for trading profits.[234] In particular, the requirement to follow generally accepted accounting practice in section 46(1) of CTA 2009 is adopted for property business. The connection is more direct in the loan relationship provisions, where amounts are credited and debited in accordance with generally accepted accounting practice.[235] This practice may be overridden by express provisions in the loan relationship rules, but there is no general rule excluding capital expenditure or receipts from recognition. A similar approach is adopted with respect to derivatives and intangibles.[236]

---

[231]  CTA 2010 (UK) s. 1127 referring to *Application of International Accounting Standards*, Council Regulation (EC) No 1606/2002.

[232]  See the Small Companies and Groups (Accounts and Directors' Report) Regulations 2008 (SI 2008/409) (UK) and Large and Medium-sized Companies and Groups (Accounts and Reports) Regulations 2008 (SI 2008/410) (UK).

[233]  For example, the non-inclusion of capital receipts under CTA 2009 (UK) s. 93 and the enactment of *Sharkey* v. *Wernher* [1956] AC 58 (HL) in CTA 2009 (UK) s. 157.

[234]  CTA 2009 (UK) s. 210.

[235]  CTA 2009 (UK) ss. 308 & 309.

[236]  CTA 2009 (UK) ss. 597 & 599 (derivatives) and 716 & 717 (intangibles).

## *1.2.2 Reinforcement of corporate identity: transfer pricing*

As discussed earlier at 1.1.4.3, a corporate tax system may respond to a concentration of ownership and control of a corporation by reinforcing the separate identity of that corporation. The primary mechanism for reinforcing the separate identity of controlled entities is the imposition of the arm's length approach to transfer pricing. This subheading focuses on transfer pricing treatment in a domestic context. It is not concerned with international aspects of transfer pricing or arm's length pricing methodology.[237]

'Transfer pricing' is, not surprisingly, concerned with the price at which resources are transferred, especially between related parties. Here, the arm's length approach is commonly adopted, although it may be expressed in different forms. The application of the arm's length standard means that the actual transaction price is not accepted, and so, because arm's length pricing is an exception to the general approach, the scope of application of the rule needs to be delineated. Doing so involves identifying the relevant relationship required between the parties to trigger the arm's length rule. For this purpose, as discussed earlier at 1.1.5, there may be attribution of rights to particular persons for the purposes of determining if the relevant relationship is met. Further questions involve whether the arm's length price applies to both parties of the transaction and whether any tax consequences attach to payments made to bring the transaction price into line with the arm's length price.

### Arm's length pricing

In many countries, especially common law jurisdictions, transfer pricing rules have been largely confined to cross-border transactions. This was the approach of the UK until 2004. Where transfer pricing rules do not apply, a primary question to be asked regarding pricing of transactions between related parties is whether expenses fall within any general limitations on the deduction of expenses. For example, deductions may be denied where a business purpose is lacking.[238] If an expense is largely an effort to

---

[237] Generally regarding these matters, see Harris & Oliver (2010, pp. 228–45).

[238] In Germany, expenses are generally deductible if 'incurred as a result of the business operations'; EStG (Germany) s. 4(4). In the UK, trading expenses can be deducted only if they are incurred 'wholly and exclusively for the purposes of the trade'; CTA 2009 (UK) s. 54(1) and ITTOIA 2005 (UK) s. 34(1). In the US, expenses are deductible if they are 'ordinary and necessary expenses paid or incurred … in carrying on any trade or business'; IRC (US) s. 162(a).

manipulate who derives income as between related parties, it may not meet this test and, therefore, not be deductible.[239] A deduction may also be denied if a payment constitutes a hidden profit distribution or hidden capital contribution (e.g. see the later discussion regarding Germany).

Many countries, however, apply their transfer pricing rules to both domestic and cross-border transactions. This is the case with the US's general transfer pricing provision:

> In any case of two or more organizations, trades, or businesses (whether or not incorporated, whether or not organized in the United States, and whether or not affiliated) owned or controlled directly or indirectly by the same interests, the Secretary may distribute, apportion, or allocate gross income, deductions, credits, or allowances between or among such organizations, trades, or businesses, if he determines that ... necessary in order to prevent evasion of taxes or clearly to reflect the income of any of such organizations, trades, or businesses.[240]

This relatively short provision is supplemented with extensive regulations. These regulations make it clear that in 'determining the true taxable income of a controlled taxpayer, the standard to be applied in every case is that of a taxpayer dealing at arm's length with an uncontrolled taxpayer'.[241] The regulations go on to specify various methods by which an arm's length price may be established. In broad outline, these are similar to those used by the OECD for purposes of the OECD Model. The regulations define, for the purposes of the regulations, many of the terms and phrases used in section 482.[242]

Similarly, the CCCTB Proposal would adopt a singular approach to transfer pricing. Article 79 of the Proposal in essence replicates the wording of Article 9(1) of the OECD Model. In 'relations' between 'associated enterprises', the enterprises must recognise the income that would have accrued as if they had been dealing as 'independent enterprises'. There is no reference to the OECD *Transfer Pricing Guidelines*, but it seems clear that the intention is that those Guidelines should be followed in determining what price would have been agreed between independent enterprises (i.e. what is an arm's length price).

Germany's approach is somewhat fragmented. In its Foreign Tax Law, it adopts the arm's length standard in terms not dissimilar to the OECD

---

[239] For a discussion of the UK rule in the context of expenses incurred by a family company in favour of a family member, see Harris & Oliver (2008, pp. 254–62).

[240] IRC (US) s. 482.

[241] Title 26 Code of Federal Regulations (US) § 1.482–1(b)(1).

[242] Title 26 Code of Federal Regulations (US) § 1.482–1(i).

Model (or the CCCTB Proposal).[243] However, the German provision goes on to incorporate some specifics as to transfer pricing methodology, rather than directly incorporating the OECD *Transfer Pricing Guidelines* (which remain indirectly relevant). The scope of this provision is limited to a 'foreign business relationship with an associated person.'[244] The German Federal Finance Court has held that the Foreign Tax Law provision cannot apply, even by analogy, to domestic relations between two resident corporations.[245] In domestic situations, transfer pricing adjustments may be made only under the vague concepts of hidden profit distribution and hidden capital contribution. These concepts are largely based on case law (see 2.2.2), and neither is defined in detail in German income tax law.

The UK approach is even more fragmented, and again the capital / revenue distinction is a primary source of this fragmentation. In 2004, the UK extended its primary transfer pricing rules to domestic transactions as a response to a decision of the European Court of Justice.[246] These rules now appear in Part 4 of TIOPA 2010.[247] They are long and detailed, perhaps unnecessarily so. In essence, they also draw heavily from the OECD Model. The UK rules are triggered where a transaction is made between related persons, it is not at arm's length and it confers a benefit in relation to UK tax. Where these conditions are met, the 'profits and losses of the potentially advantaged person are to be calculated for tax purposes as if the arm's length provision had been made or imposed instead of the actual provision.'[248] What constitutes an arm's length provision is to be determined consistently with the OECD *Transfer Pricing Guidelines*.[249]

The TIOPA 2010 transfer pricing rules incorporate an important exception. They do not apply if the potentially advantaged person is a small

---

[243] Foreign Tax Law (*Außensteuergesetz*) (Germany) s. 1.

[244] However, see Foreign Tax Law (*Außensteuergesetz*) (Germany) s. 1(3) regarding attempts to shift certain forms of profit potential offshore.

[245] See Endres & Miles (2004).

[246] Case C-324/00 *Lankhorst-Hohorst GmbH* v. *Finanzamt Steinfurt* [2002] ECR 2002 I-11779 (ECJ). This was, perhaps, an overreaction. Case C-524/04 *Test Claimants in the Thin Cap Group Litigation* [2007] ECR I-2107 (ECJ) suggests that the arm's length test can be applied only to international transactions as a proportionate method of countering tax avoidance. Also, see Case C-311/08 *Société de Gestion Industrielle SA (SGI)* v. *Belgium* [2010] ECR 00 (ECJ).

[247] Despite their domestic application, the UK transfer pricing rules are contained in TIOPA 2010 (ss. 146–230), a law primarily dealing with international matters.

[248] TIOPA 2010 (UK) s. 147.

[249] TIOPA 2010 (UK) s. 164. The OECD is an international organisation of which the UK is a member. In terms of indirect delegation of rule-making power, the adoption of the Transfer Pricing Guidelines raises an interesting analogy with the use of accounting standards for determination of the corporate tax base.

or medium-sized enterprise.[250] Confusingly, the transfer pricing rules are couched in terms of a provision between 'persons', but the exceptions refer to 'enterprises', a term more commonly used in civil law jurisdictions. This is because small and medium-sized enterprises are defined by reference to EU law.[251] The relevant EU law contains thresholds defining these enterprises by reference to number of employees, turnover and net assets. That law contains rules to prevent splitting the thresholds between related enterprises ('partnership' and 'linked' enterprises).[252] Not surprisingly, these anti-splitting rules bear little resemblance to those otherwise used in UK income tax law; for example, to prevent splitting of the small companies rate threshold (discussed later at 1.3.2.2).

Where the transfer pricing rules apply, they adjust the 'profits and losses of the potentially advantaged person'. 'Profits' and 'losses' are defined to include revenue amounts, but there is no mention of capital amounts.[253] TIOPA 2010 goes on to expressly provide that the transfer pricing rules do not affect the calculation of any capital allowance, balancing charge, chargeable gain or chargeable loss.[254] The result is fragmentation of the transfer pricing approach. This means that the treatment of related party transactions involving many capital assets must be sought in CAA 2001 and TCGA 1992. Both Acts have provisions dealing with these transactions, but they are very different from those in Part 4 of TIOPA 2010.

CAA 2001 has no general imposition of market value on sales between related parties. A market value rule does apply if plant or machinery is sold at less than market value and the buyer does not hold the acquired asset as plant or machinery.[255] By contrast, TCGA 1992 has a blanket provision

---

[250] TIOPA 2010 (UK) s. 166. There are exceptions to the exclusion from the transfer pricing rules for small and medium-sized enterprises. Medium-sized enterprises may be subject to the transfer pricing rules if served with a notice by the UK tax administration; TIOPA 2010 (UK) s. 168. Small or medium-sized enterprises may be subject to the transfer pricing rules if they are resident in a non-qualifying territory; TIOPA 2010 (UK) s. 167. Qualifying territories are essentially those with double tax treaties with non-discrimination articles; TIOPA 2010 (UK) s. 173.

[251] TIOPA 2010 (UK) s. 172.

[252] European Commission Recommendation 2003/361/EC Annex Arts. 1 to 6.

[253] TIOPA 2010 (UK) s. 156.

[254] TIOPA 2010 (UK) ss. 213 & 214.

[255] CAA 2001 (UK) s. 61(2) & (4)(a). The pooling system for depreciating plant and machinery means there is no other express treatment of below market value sales (such a transaction cannot usually accelerate an allowance). There are special rules designed to prevent sales between 'connected persons' uplifting the qualifying expenditure beyond the original price paid, typically sales above market value; s. 218. Part of the problem is that the connected person disposing of the asset is not required to bring into account as disposal proceeds any more than the original cost of the asset; s. 62. This means any excess is only

treating transfers of assets between 'connected persons' as being made at market value.[256] As for other countries, there are important exceptions to this treatment, many of which are discussed throughout this book. These include exceptions for transfers between group corporations (see 1.2.3.1) and numerous rollovers, especially on incorporation (see 4.2), corporate reorganisations (see 7.1) and mergers and de-mergers (see 7.2).

There are many differences between these rules in CAA 2001 and TCGA 1992 and the transfer pricing rules in TIOPA 2010. Indeed, it seems the differences among these three sets of rules far outweigh their commonality. The CAA 2001 and TCGA 1992 rules are subject to important exceptions, especially for group corporations (discussed later at 1.2.3.1), but the transfer pricing rules are not. There are no exceptions from the CAA 2001 and TCGA 1992 for small and medium-sized enterprises, and the OECD rules are not expressed to be relevant in determining market value. As is discussed shortly, the concepts of 'control' and 'connected persons' used in these three sets of rules are not the same.[257] Simply, the UK income tax law fails to draw the connection among these rules, providing multiple rules where other countries often provide one unified approach.[258]

### Relevant relationship

The US transfer pricing rules speak of 'two or more organizations [etc.] owned or controlled directly or indirectly by the same interests'.[259] The

---

subject to tax as capital gains. In addition, a person buying plant or machinery from a connected person is denied the annual investment allowance or any first-year allowance with respect to the asset; s. 217.

[256] TGCA 1992 (UK) s. 18 triggering the market value rule in s. 17.

[257] By contrast, although the loan relationship rules have provisions that apply to non-arm's length transactions, the transfer pricing rules in TIOPA 2010 generally have priority; CTA 2009 (UK) ss. 444–6. Similarly, the transfer pricing rules apply to derivatives; s. 693. Although the intangible assets regime contains a market value rule similar to that in TCGA 1992, it too gives priority to the transfer pricing rules in TIOPA 2010; CTA 2009 ss. 845 & 846.

[258] Some special rules apply when a person disposes of trading stock on the cessation of a trade. If the sale is to a 'connected person' and that stock constitutes trading stock of the buyer, the sale must be priced at arm's length. This rule applies both for corporation tax and income tax purposes; CTA 2009 (UK) s. 166 and ITTOIA 2005 (UK) s. 177. There are separate definitions of 'connected persons' for this purpose; CTA 2009 (UK) s. 168 and ITTOIA 2005 (UK) s. 179. Confusingly, the TIOPA 2010 transfer pricing rules have priority; CTA 2009 (UK) s. 162(2) and ITTOIA 2005 (UK) s. 173(2). However, it seems that these special rules for trading stock could apply residually if the transaction in question falls within an exception to the TIOPA 2010 rules (e.g. a small or medium-sized enterprise is involved).

[259] IRC (US) s. 482.

legislation does not elaborate further on the relevant relationship, but the Treasury Regulations do. It is noteworthy that the concept of 'related' persons discussed earlier at 1.1.5.1 is not used for this purpose. The Regulations supporting the transfer pricing rule contain a series of definitions including definitions of 'organization', 'trade or business', 'controlled' and 'controlled taxpayer'.[260] 'Organization' covers those entities that could be within the definition of 'taxpayer' in the IRC (see 1.1.1), but it is not necessary to be a US taxpayer. Surprisingly, 'trade or business' includes employment.

The definition of 'controlled taxpayer' does little more than clarify some of the wording used in section 482 of IRC.[261] It repeats the wording of 'owned or controlled directly or indirectly by the same interests', but contains no elaboration of how to determine indirect control nor does it define 'same interests'. The Regulations do clarify that the person owning or controlling the organisations is also a 'controlled taxpayer', which is not clear on the face of section 482.

'Controlled' includes 'any kind of control'. In particular, the control need not be legally enforceable, and control may exist where two persons are acting in concert. It is the reality of control that is decisive, not its form or the mode of its exercise.[262] The definition of 'controlled' is particularly abstract. The US focus seems to be more on the assessment that a transaction is not at arm's length, and so all transactions must be tested if there is a chance that this is not the case.[263] This approach can be contrasted with a more prescriptive definition of the kind of relationship that must exist before a transaction must be tested against the arm's length standard.

The CCCTB Proposal is prescriptive as to the type of relationship that must exist before a transaction would be tested against the arm's length standard. The transaction must involve 'relations between associated enterprises'.[264] The definition of 'associated enterprises' was discussed earlier at 1.1.5.3 and would involve the holding or common holding of 20% of voting or capital rights or a position of 'significant influence' with respect to management.[265] The German international transfer pricing rules (but not the general concepts of hidden profit distribution and hidden capital contribution) similarly incorporate a requirement of

---

[260]  Title 26 Code of Federal Regulations (US) § 1.482–1(i).
[261]  Title 26 Code of Federal Regulations (US) § 1.482–1(i)(5).
[262]  Title 26 Code of Federal Regulations (US) § 1.482–1(i)(4).
[263]  For example, see Bittker & Eustice (2003–, para. 13.20) and the references cited therein.
[264]  CCCTB Proposal Art. 79.
[265]  CCCTB Proposal Art. 78.

'association'. This is defined broadly to be a 25% 'interest', but is expanded to include the 'exercise of a controlling influence' and even an ability 'to exercise influence' in agreeing to the terms of the business relationship for reasons lying outside that relationship.[266]

For purposes of the UK transfer pricing provisions, persons are related if the 'participation condition' is met. This is defined in terms similar to Article 9(1) of the OECD Model referring to one person 'participating in the management control or capital of the other' or the same person or persons doing so.[267] In form, this terminology is the same as used in the CCCTB Proposal associated enterprises provisions. However, TIOPA 2010 goes on to define 'participating' in very different terms that involve a person 'controlling' a 'body corporate or a firm'.[268] Note the reference to 'body corporate' rather than 'company' (see the earlier discussion at 1.1.1.1). Note also that, although these rules can apply to transactions between an individual and a controlled corporation, they cannot apply to transactions between two related individuals.[269] This apparent limitation of scope reflects that in Article 9(1) of the OECD Model.[270]

'Control' was discussed earlier at 1.1.5.1 and 1.1.5.2 in the context of the definition of 'connected persons' and 'close company', respectively. However, 'control' as used in the transfer pricing rules does not seem to bear the same meaning.[271] Rather, it takes its meaning from section 1124 of CTA 2010.[272] This provision defines 'control' of a body corporate in terms of a person holding shares, voting power or other powers conferred in the corporation's constitutional documents such that the affairs of the corporation are 'conducted in accordance with the wishes' of the person. This definition would not easily apply to control at the level of the board of directors.

The provisions in CAA 2001 and TCGA 1992 mentioned earlier are triggered by transactions between 'connected persons'. Each law has its own definition of 'connected persons'.[273] Rather than using 'connected persons' (or 'associated persons') as an aid in defining 'control' (as in the

---

[266] Foreign Tax Law (*Außensteuergesetz*) (Germany) s. 1(2).

[267] TIOPA 2010 (UK) s. 148.

[268] For example, TIOPA 2010 (UK) s. 157.

[269] One consequence of this limitation is the continuing issue of income splitting between related individuals as seen in *Jones* v. *Garnett* [2007] UKHL 35 (HL). See Harris & Oliver (2008).

[270] See Harris & Oliver (2010, p. 234).

[271] See text at footnote 108.

[272] TIOPA 2010 (UK) s. 217(1).

[273] CAA 2001 (UK) s. 575 and TCGA 1992 (UK) s. 286, respectively.

transfer pricing rules and the close company rules), both these sets of provisions use 'control' as an aid in defining 'connected persons'. The CAA 2001 and TCGA 1992 rules for connected persons are essentially the same as discussed earlier at 1.1.5.1 in the context of connected persons under CTA 2010. So, a person is connected with a 'company' (rather than a 'body corporate') if the person controls the company. Two companies are connected if they are commonly controlled. Both CAA 2001 and TCGA 1992 define 'control' by reference to sections 450 and 451 of CTA 2010 (discussed earlier at 1.1.5.1 and 1.1.5.2), although CAA 2001 has a supplemental rule.[274]

## Attribution of rights

As mentioned earlier, the US Treasury Regulations repeat the words 'owned or controlled directly or indirectly by the same interests' from section 482 of IRC, but do not elaborate how to determine indirect control.[275] Therefore they do not contain any rules on the attribution of rights of related parties. Their focus is, rather, on the fact of a non-arm's length price rather than defining a relationship in which an arm's length price must be tested. The wording of the German international transfer pricing rules is similar. They refer to holding 'a direct or indirect interest' and exercising a controlling influence 'directly or indirectly' without any further detail in the law.[276] This can be contrasted with the position under the CCCTB Proposal, which does contain rules for attributing voting and capital rights held by one person to another person for the purposes of testing which two persons are 'associated'.[277] These rules were discussed earlier at 1.1.5.3.

---

[274]  CAA 2001 (UK) s. 575A and TCGA 1992 (UK) s. 288. The supplemental rule is in CAA 2001 (UK) s. 274. As for the loan relationship rules, they sometimes use the concept of 'connected persons' within the meaning in CTA 2010 (UK) s. 1122 and at other times use a differently defined concept of 'connected companies'; CTA 2009 (UK) s. 466. The latter, like the former, uses the word 'control'. The loan relationship rules sometimes use the concept of 'control' within the meaning in CTA 2010 (UK) s. 1124 and other times use a differently defined concept of 'control'; CTA 2009 s. (UK) 472. By contrast, the intangible assets regime uses a concept of 'related party', again defined in terms of 'control'; CTA 2009 s. (UK) 835. 'Control' is again defined separately; CTA 2009 s. (UK) 836. Like the transfer pricing rules, both the loan relationship rules and the intangible assets regime extend to cover control jointly by two 40% owners. This is done through the concept of 'major interest'; CTA 2009 (UK) ss. 473 & 837, respectively.

[275]  Title 26 Code of Federal Regulations (US) § 1.482–1(i)(5).

[276]  Foreign Tax Law (*Außensteuergesetz*) s. 1(2)1.

[277]  CCCTB Proposal Art. 78.

Again, the UK position is anything but straightforward. TIOPA 2010 expressly deals with control by indirect participation. In a manner reminiscent of the similar rules for connected persons and close companies (discussed earlier at 1.1.5), TIOPA 2010 may attribute certain rights to a person for purposes of determining control, including rights held by 'connected persons'.[278] 'Connected persons' does not take its meaning from section 1122 of CTA 2010 (discussed earlier at 1.1.5.1) nor from the similarly defined term 'associated persons' in section 448 of that Act (discussed earlier at 1.1.5.2). Rather and confusingly, it is defined in extremely similar terms in section 163 of TIOPA 2010. Further, indirect participation may arise where two persons each hold 40% of a corporation.[279]

Despite the bewildering array of prescriptions, there are fundamental problems in applying the various UK concepts of 'connected person' and 'control', particularly where control of two corporations is wielded by more than one person (the 'group' of persons). One question is whether either corporation is connected with any one person in the group. This depends on whether the holdings of one person in the group may be attributed to another person in the group for purposes of determining the latter's control status. It seems that the transfer pricing rules do not do this because these rules refer to 'one of the affected persons' controlling the company.[280] An exception is where the persons in the group 'act together' in a financing arrangement with one of the corporations.[281] The persons in the group would only be connected with either corporation for capital allowance purposes if two or more of them are 'acting together to secure or exercise control of the company'.[282] The approach is similar under TCGA 1992.[283]

The situation as to transactions between the two controlled corporations is different. The transfer pricing rules will apply if the two transacting corporations are controlled by 'the same person or persons'.[284] There is no reference in TIOPA 2010 to the persons 'acting together'. By contrast, for two corporations to be connected for the purposes of the capital allowances provisions, both corporations must be 'controlled' by 'a group

---

[278] TIOPA 2010 (UK) s. 159.
[279] TIOPA 2010 (UK) s. 160. This provision was added to deal with joint ventures companies where neither party may have control.
[280] TIOPA 2010 (UK) s. 148(2)(a) & (3)(a).
[281] TIOPA 2010 s. 161(2). Note that similar phraseology is used in the definition of 'control' in CTA 2010 (UK) s. 450(5) (discussed at 1.1.5.1).
[282] CAA 2001 (UK) s. 575(6).
[283] TCGA 1992 (UK) s. 286(7).
[284] TIOPA 2010 (UK) s. 148(2)(b) & (3)(b).

of two or more persons'.[285] Again, the same test is applied for chargeable gains purposes[286] and is also used in the definition of 'connected persons' in CTA 2010 (as noted earlier at 1.1.5.1). Each of these provisions uses the definition of 'control' from section 450 of CTA 2010. Difficulties with this provision were discussed earlier at 1.1.5.2. In particular, in cases of aggregated control it uses the 'two or more persons together' test. How this test is supposed to interface with the 'group of two or more persons' test is anything but clear.

So there are three different possibilities under UK law for aggregating control in this scenario: 'persons acting together', 'the same person or persons', and 'a group of two or more persons'. In the first of these cases, it might seem clear that there must be some conscious intention to coordinate action. That argument seems strong in the context of its use in the transfer pricing rules, but in the convoluted mess of the relationship between section 450 of CTA 2010 and the various definitions of 'connected persons' the situation is unclear. In the latter two cases, it is not clear whether the 'persons' need some sort of connection between them for their control power to be aggregated (e.g. jointly hold the shares). The Court of Appeal has held that the mere fact the persons are shareholders in both corporations is sufficient.[287] If there is a collection (group) of shareholders that owns the majority of shares of each corporation, then the corporations will be connected.[288]

### Corresponding adjustments and subvention payments

The US, German and CCCTB Proposal transfer pricing rules discussed earlier adjust the price of the transaction for both parties (i.e. they are two-directional). The UK market value rule for disposals between connected persons for capital gains purposes operates similarly.[289] The seller is treated as receiving market value consideration and the buyer treated as paying market value consideration.

---

[285]  CAA 2001 (UK) s. 575(5)(d).
[286]  TCGA 1992 (UK) s. 286(5)(b).
[287]  *Kellogg Brown & Root Holdings (UK) Ltd* v. *RCC* [2010] EWCA Civ 118 (CA).
[288]  The UK tax administration accepts that two corporations are only under the control of the same persons if the group that controls one corporation is identical with the group that controls the other. In addition, the group must be narrowed so as to be no more than a group that 'would not have control of it if any one of the persons were excluded from the group'. HMRC, *Company Tax Manual*, at para. CTM03730, available at www.hmrc. gov.uk/manuals/ctmanual, accessed 16 July 2012.
[289]  TCGA 1992 (UK) ss. 17 & 18.

The other UK transfer pricing rules are one-directional. The transfer pricing rules in TIOPA 2010 adjust the tax liability of only one party to a transaction (i.e. the party that benefits from an 'advantage in relation to UK tax').[290] Without more, this could produce economic double taxation. Therefore, the disadvantaged taxpayer can make a claim to the tax administration to make a transfer pricing adjustment (a corresponding adjustment).[291] This adjustment is only available if the relevant activities of the disadvantaged taxpayer are within the charge to corporation tax or income tax. The rules in CAA 2001 also operate on a one-direction basis – sometimes in the direction of the seller and sometimes the buyer – but there are no rules for corresponding adjustments.

Under the UK transfer pricing rules in TIOPA 2010, it is possible for the parties to an adjusted transaction to make a tax-free payment to each other (often called a 'subvention payment') to bring their cash positions into line with the tax result.[292] There is no express provision for subvention payments in the other UK transfer pricing rules (i.e. those in CAA 2001 or TCGA 1992) or in the US, German or CCCTB Proposal transfer pricing rules. In these cases, perhaps the subvention payment would simply be considered to be part of the transaction in question.

### 1.2.3 Erosion of identity: corporate groups

This subheading is concerned with special tax base rules that erode the identity of group corporations. The mechanisms by which erosion may be achieved were considered earlier at 1.1.4.2. This subheading considers the operation of those mechanisms in two primary contexts. The first is in the form of deferral of tax consequences when a transaction occurs between group corporations. This deferral typically involves exceptions from transfer pricing rules (discussed earlier at 1.2.2) under which assets may be transferred between related corporations on a no gain / no loss basis. Second, the erosion may occur in the form of losses incurred by one group corporation reducing profits derived by another group corporation. These two contexts are the focus of this subheading, but erosions

---

[290] 'Advantage in relation to UK tax' is defined in TIOPA 2010 (UK) s. 155 as smaller profits or greater loss.
[291] TIOPA 2010 (UK) ss. 174 & 188. The corresponding adjustment procedure was lifted from double tax treaty practice with little consideration as to whether it is appropriate for application in a purely domestic context.
[292] TIOPA 2010 (UK) s. 196.

can occur in other contexts.[293] Some of these other areas are considered as a residual matter.

### 1.2.3.1   Transaction deferral

The present discussion is concerned with the deferral of tax consequences resulting from a transaction between two corporations that are members of the same corporate group. This deferral can be achieved in different ways, depending on the type of mechanism that has been selected for erosion of the separate identity of group corporations (see earlier discussion at 1.1.4.2). It may be that the transaction is simply not recognised. Alternately, the transaction may be recognised, but it may be valued in a way that produces no tax consequences. Another option is that the transaction is recognised and valued at arm's length, but the tax consequences are deferred until some future point. These options are the first matter considered in the present discussion. The discussion then proceeds to consider how a group is defined for purposes of securing deferral.

The focus of the discussion is on special rules that defer the tax consequences of a transaction between group corporations. However, brief consideration needs to be given to the consequences of recognising such transactions, especially where they fall outside the scope of the transfer pricing rules considered at 1.2.2. Use of the arm's length approach to transfer pricing reinforces the separate tax identity of group corporations. Using any price other than market value as a transfer price between two related corporations enables those corporations to manipulate the comparative size of their tax bases and achieve tax arbitrage. If the income tax law has no express or implicit arm's length pricing rules, then group corporations may engage in such manipulation to the extent permitted by the general law.

The consequences of transfer pricing manipulation between group corporations are usually of two types. First, prices will be manipulated in such a way that unrealised gains will not be realised, thereby producing similar results as deferral mechanisms. Second, prices will be manipulated in such a way that unrealised losses will be triggered and triggered in the group member most likely to be able to use the loss. This emphasises an important feature of deferral mechanisms: they are designed to prevent artificial loss crystallisation and manipulation just as much as they are to defer the taxation of gains in transactions between group members.

---

[293]  Ting (2012, heading 3.4) identifies 'intra-group loss offset and intra-group asset transfer' as 'the two key functions that a group taxation regime is typically designed to achieve'.

Germany is an example of a country that has no express deferral mechanism for transactions between group corporations. Although Germany does not expressly apply transfer pricing rules to domestic transactions between group corporations, the vague concepts of hidden profit distribution and hidden capital contribution may produce similar consequences (see 1.2.2). But real transactions between members of a corporate group have real tax consequences. Other examples are provided later in the discussion of the manner in which deferral mechanisms operate and the limitations on their scope.

**Deferral mechanism** As mentioned, a deferral mechanism may operate in several ways. One of the features of a pure consolidation regime is that deferral of transactions between group corporations is achieved by ignoring transactions for tax purposes. Group members are considered to be parts of a single corporation for tax purposes (often the parent corporation). As the group is a single person for tax purposes and a person cannot transact with itself, the result is non-recognition. This is the manner in which both the Australian and the Netherlands consolidation regimes operate (see earlier discussion at 1.1.4.2).[294] The US check-the-box regime, also mentioned in that earlier discussion, is another example (e.g. where a parent corporation holds LLCs as subsidiaries).

Outside a pure consolidation regime, transactions between group members are, in principle, recognised for tax purposes. Because group members are related, transfer pricing rules (see 1.2.2) may require that such transactions be valued at an arm's length price. Therefore, to produce deferral, a corporate tax system must either override the arm's length pricing requirement or defer its consequences. The UK and, in substance, the CCCTB Proposal provide examples of the override approach, and the US provides an example of the deferral approach.

Section 1501 of IRC (US) provides:

> An affiliated group of corporations shall, subject to the provisions of this chapter, have the privilege of making a consolidated return with respect to the income tax imposed by chapter 1 for the taxable year in lieu of separate returns.

This rule is the subject of extensive Treasury Regulations,[295] which confirm that an affiliated group may elect to (but is not obliged to) file

---

[294] Also, see Ting (2012, heading 7.2).
[295] Title 26 Code of Federal Regulations (US) § 1.1502–0 & following.

a consolidated return.[296] The US approach is not a pure consolidation approach, because each member of a corporate group must still calculate its own taxable income independently. In principle, it is only the results that are consolidated. So, without more, transactions between members of a corporate group would be recognised (as in Germany), and potentially, the transfer pricing rules discussed earlier at 1.2.2 would apply.

The Treasury Regulations confirm that transactions between group corporations are to be quantified on a separate entity basis. So a group corporation selling an asset to another group corporation must recognise gain or loss on the transaction after taking the transfer pricing rules into consideration.[297] However, the timing of the recognition is determined on a single entity basis.[298] This involves the 'matching rule' whereby the selling corporation does not recognise the gain or loss until the buying corporation accounts for the transaction (e.g. when the buying corporation sells the asset outside the group).[299] The selling corporation also realises gain or loss when it or the buyer ceases to be part of the group.[300]

Because consolidation is elective, the US regime would be exposed to the crystallisation of losses through transactions between group corporations that are not consolidated. This is addressed by a special rule that provides that losses on sales or exchanges between related parties are generally disallowed.[301] The definition of 'related' for this purpose was considered earlier at 1.1.5.1. The disallowance is excluded in the case of group corporations (irrespective of whether they file a consolidated return) and replaced with a deferral of the loss until the property is disposed of outside the group.[302] The Treasury Regulations adapt and apply the consolidated return rules for this purpose.[303]

The US deferral approach can be contrasted with the somewhat confused approach under the CCCTB Proposal, which provides that the 'tax bases of the members of a group shall be consolidated'.[304] This is similar to the US consolidation regime in that it does not collapse the separate

---

[296] Title 26 Code of Federal Regulations (US) § 1.1502–75(a)(1).
[297] Title 26 Code of Federal Regulations (US) § 1.1502–80(a).
[298] Title 26 Code of Federal Regulations (US) § 1.1502–13(a)(2).
[299] Title 26 Code of Federal Regulations (US) § 1.1502–13(c)(2).
[300] Title 26 Code of Federal Regulations (US) § 1.1502–13(d)(1)(i)(A).
[301] IRC (US) s. 267(a)(1).
[302] IRC (US) s. 267(f)(2)(B).
[303] Title 26 Code of Federal Regulations (US) § 1.267(f)-1.
[304] CCCTB Proposal Art. 57(1).

identity of the group members.[305] This feature makes the primary approach under the CCCTB Proposal to transactions between group members somewhat confusing. Consistent with a pure consolidation approach, it provides that 'profits and losses arising from transactions directly carried out between members of a group shall be ignored'.[306]

Without more, this approach sits awkwardly in the context of a regime that continues to recognise the separate identity of each group member. If the identity of group members continues to be recognised, then, for example, the asset transferred must be considered as owned by the transferee and must be allocated a tax value. This requirement is provided by Article 59(4) of the CCCTB Proposal: the 'method for recording intra-group transactions shall enable all intra-group transfers and sales to be identified at the lower of cost and value for tax purposes'. With respect to unrealised gains, this rule seems to act as an exception to the transfer pricing rule discussed earlier at 1.2.2. With respect to unrealised losses (where value is lower than cost), it is consistent with that rule.

Whereas the US consolidation regime is elective, it seems that the CCCTB Proposal consolidation regime would be compulsory for parent corporations and qualifying subsidiaries that have opted for the Proposal to apply.[307] Perhaps for this reason, it does not contain a non-recognition rule for losses incurred in transactions with related parties. However, this does mean that related corporations that are not group corporations could artificially crystallise losses by disposing of assets to a related corporation, whereas group corporations could not. Such manipulation would be subject to the general anti-abuse rule in Article 80 of the CCCTB Proposal.

The approach of the UK must be considered in the context of its fragmented approach to use of the arm's length standard (discussed earlier at 1.2.2). Where the TIOPA 2010 transfer pricing rules apply, there is no exception for transactions between group corporations. This is a consequence of the perceived need in 2004 to apply these rules on a non-discriminatory basis to both international transactions and domestic transactions. In an international setting, arm's length rules are

---

[305] So, for example, under the CCCTB Proposal some tax attributes (such as losses) continue to attach to an individual group member during consolidation (e.g. see CCCTB Proposal Art. 64).

[306] CCCTB Proposal Art. 59(1).

[307] CCCTB Proposal Arts. 54 & 55. Individual corporations would be given a choice as to whether the Proposal would apply to them; Art. 6. However, it seems that once two group corporations opt for the Proposal to apply, the consolidation rules would apply compulsorily.

particularly targeted at group corporations in an effort to prevent movement of the source of income outside a tax jurisdiction.

However, where the small or medium-sized enterprise exception to the TIOPA 2010 transfer pricing rules applies, the position in the UK is similar to what it was prior to the domestic introduction of the arm's length rules. There are no other express rules determining the transfer price of particular transactions between related parties for corporate tax base purposes. So, where the TIOPA 2010 rules do not apply, there is substantial freedom to set prices under general law. Provided the transaction is genuine and the consideration not colourable, the prices set as a matter of law by the transaction should be accepted for corporate tax purposes. The same is largely true of the price paid for, say, plant and machinery for capital allowances purposes. As noted, the TIOPA 2010 transfer pricing rules do not apply for the purposes of CAA 2001. Outside the scope of the anti-abuse rules in CAA 2001 (discussed earlier at 1.2.2), related corporations have a relatively broad scope for negotiating prices on the transfer between them of capital assets for which capital allowances are available.[308]

The position is very different for the purposes of TCGA 1992. As noted, TCGA 1992 has a comprehensive market value rule for transactions between connected persons. However, TCGA 1992 does provide an exception to the market value rule for transactions between group corporations. Section 171 provides that where

> a company ('company A') disposes of an asset to another company ('company B') at a time when both companies are members of the same group ... company A and company B are treated for the purposes of corporation tax on chargeable gains as if the asset were acquired by company B for a consideration of such amount as would secure that neither a gain nor a loss would accrue to company A on the disposal.[309]

Note that this provision is non-discretionary. There is no choice as to its application, just as there is no possibility to realise a part gain or loss. Like

---

[308] An exception to this rule applies where a trade is transferred as a going concern between members of a corporate group. In this case, CTA 2010 (UK) Part 22 may provide relief from a balancing charge under CAA 2001. This approach is most commonly used when 'hiving' down a trade to a newly incorporated company, so it is discussed later at 4.2.

[309] Special rules apply where the asset transferred is a capital asset in the hands of one of the group members but trading stock is in the hands of the other; see TCGA 1992 (UK) s. 173. The intangible assets regime broadly follows the approach in TCGA 1992 (UK) s. 171 rather than the approach in CAA 2001. Intangible fixed assets may be transferred between group members and treated as not involving any realisation or any acquisition; CTA 2009 (UK) ss. 775 & 776. The tax history of the asset is effectively taken over by the transferee.

the US rule discussed earlier, the UK rule is just as much about preventing corporate groups from crystallising unrealised losses by disposing of assets between group members as it is about providing relief from any charge on a gain realised on such a disposal.[310]

**What is a group?**   The concept of group corporations was discussed earlier at 1.1.5.1 in the context of one corporation controlling another corporation or two corporations being controlled by the same person or persons. However, just because an income tax law has a general concept of group corporations does not mean that it will use the concept for all purposes. In some cases a definition of group corporations might be used comprehensively. This is the case under the CCCTB Proposal. In other cases, there might be a special or adjusted definition for purposes of a rule deferring the tax consequences of transactions between group members. This is the situation in the US and the UK.

As mentioned earlier, section 1501 of IRC (US) permits an 'affiliated group of corporations' to file a consolidated tax return. This is done by election, which is in principle irrevocable.[311] 'Affiliated group' is defined in section 1504(a)(1) in terms similar to, but not the same as a 'controlled group of corporations' discussed earlier at 1.1.5.1. An 'affiliated group' is 'one or more chains of includible corporations connected through stock ownership with a common parent corporation which is an includible corporation'. The 'includible corporation' concept is used to prevent certain types of corporations from being within a group that files a consolidated return. So, for example, tax-exempt corporations, foreign corporations and S corporations are not includible corporations, although there are exceptions to the exceptions.[312]

To be included in an affiliated group, there are two tests of 'stock ownership' that count. First, the parent corporation must own directly at least

---

[310] Earlier at 1.2.2, brief mention was made of an arm's length pricing rule for trading stock sold between connected persons if the seller ceases to carry on the trade in question. Where this rule applies, it is possible for corporation tax purposes for the parties to the transaction to elect to, in effect, sell the stock at cost; that is, on a no gain / no loss basis; CTA 2009 (UK) s. 167. This election is available for a sale between two body corporates if they are subject to common 'control'; CTA 2009 (UK) s. 168. So this option is potentially much broader than the 75% group requirements for other exceptions. This relief is further considered at 4.2 in the context of incorporation of a subsidiary. As with the arm's length pricing rule, however, this election is not available if the transfer pricing rules in TIOPA 2010 apply; CTA 2009 (UK) s. 162(2).

[311] Title 26 Code of Federal Regulations (US) § 1.1502–75(a)(2).

[312] IRC (US) s. 1504(b).

80% of the total voting power and total stock value of at least one includible corporation.[313] From this point and under the second test, further corporations must be owned directly as to a similar 80% by other corporations included in the group. So, working down from the parent corporation at the head of a group chain, as each corporation is included because it meets the 80% test, its holdings in another corporation may be counted in determining whether the other corporation also meets the 80% test. However, the requirement of a common parent corporation means that two sibling corporations owned by, for example, an individual cannot file a consolidated return. Only direct holdings are counted, and there are no constructive ownership or other attribution of rights rules.

The UK also refines its concept of group corporations depending on the rule in question. For the purposes of the non-recognition rule for capital gains, 'group companies' is defined in section 170(3) of TCGA 1992 by reference to a 'principal company' and its '75% subsidiaries'. A '75% subsidiary' is defined by reference to section 1154 of CTA 2010, which was discussed earlier at 1.1.5.1. TCGA 1992 is peculiarly prescriptive in identifying the types of companies that can be group companies.[314] It is now possible for a non-resident company to qualify as the principal company or a subsidiary, but section 171 applies only to transactions involving a non-resident company if a UK PE of the non-resident company buys or sells the asset in question.[315]

---

[313] 'Stock' excludes certain non-voting preference shares; IRC (US) s. 1504(a)(4). Voting power focuses on the right to elect directors. See Bittker & Eustice (2003–, para. 13.41) and the references cited therein.

[314] Some entities that fall within the definition of 'company' (see the earlier discussion at 1.1.1.1) cannot be group companies. The types of companies that can be group companies are listed in TCGA 1992 (UK) s. 170(9). Bizarrely, this list does not refer to 'body corporate', although clearly most of the entities referred to are corporations. This is even more bizarre because, as discussed at 1.1.5.1, CTA 2010 defines '75% subsidiary' in terms of a 'body corporate' holding 75% of the ordinary shares in another 'body corporate'. If an entity is not a body corporate, it is difficult to see how this definition could apply. A further difficulty is that some of the entities referred to in the TCGA 1992 list might not have a share capital.

[315] A non-resident company can hold shares so as to cause other companies to qualify. So, for example, TCGA 1992 (UK) s. 171 can apply to two UK resident companies that are 75% subsidiaries of a non-resident company. To facilitate this extension, s. 170(9) provides that 'company' includes a 'company ... formed under' foreign law. It is not clear whether 'company' here takes its meaning from the general definition in s. 288, has its ordinary meaning (which could include, for example, a partnership) or only refers to registered companies. In any case, because of the definition of '75% subsidiary', it seems a foreign company would have to be a body corporate and have a share capital. The requirement that a foreign company must be incorporated is confirmed by s. 170(2)(d). This provision

Recall that under the definition of '75% subsidiary', a parent corporation can satisfy the 75% holding requirement by holding shares directly or indirectly. However, the term 'group companies' for the purposes of TCGA 1992 is given an extended meaning. If A Co holds 75% of B Co, which holds 75% of C Co, C Co is not a 75% subsidiary of A Co. This is because A Co's indirect holding in C Co is only 56.25% (i.e. 75% of 75%). 'Group companies' in TCGA 1992 specifically includes 75% subsidiaries of 75% subsidiaries. However, the UK rule contains an additional limitation: each subsidiary must be at least an effective 51% subsidiary of the principal company. Section 170(7) of TCGA 1992 contains a definition of 'effective 51 per cent subsidiary'. Essentially, the principal corporation of the group must be beneficially entitled to 51% of the distributions of profits from the subsidiary or assets in a winding up. In a standard situation, C Co in the example will meet this test.

Tax laws that provide a definition of group corporations with less than a 100% holding requirement often have rules to stop corporations acting as bridges between two groups. To demonstrate the problem, consider the example in the last paragraph. In addition, presume that C Co holds 75% of D Co. Indirectly, A Co holds only 42% of D Co (approximately), and so D Co is not an effective 51% subsidiary of A Co. However, there could be two corporate groups on these facts; the first made up of corporations A, B and C and the second made up of corporations B, C and D. Using section 171 of TCGA 1992, A Co could transfer an asset on a no gain / no loss basis to B Co or C Co based on the first group. Then the acquiring company could transfer the asset on the same basis to D Co based on the second group. If bridge companies were permitted, the tax deferral could go on ad infinitum. For this purpose, section 170(6) provides that a corporation cannot be a member of two groups and provides a series of reconciliation rules for deciding to which group a corporation belongs.

It seems this issue does not arise under the US consolidation regime. On the facts in the last paragraph, if each of the holdings were increased to 80%, then all of A Co, B Co, C Co and D Co would have to combine as a group if they wished to file a consolidated return. This is because the US simply counts direct holdings of includible corporations and, unlike the UK, does not have an indirect holding requirement of the parent corporation in each subsidiary.

prescribes that 'group' and 'subsidiary' be 'construed with any necessary modifications where applied to a company incorporated under' foreign law. Again, the clarity of UK tax law leaves something to be desired.

By contrast, like the UK rules, under the CCCTB Proposal a 'qualifying subsidiary' is defined by reference to direct or indirect holdings of the parent corporation.[316] There is no reconciliation rule as in the UK, and so it seems that on the facts mentioned earlier B Co and C Co would be members of two groups. It is not at all clear whether there would be a single tax base consolidation or two and, if there were two consolidations, which corporations would be in which group. It is also not clear whether assets could be transferred from one group to another without tax recognition of any gain or loss. Contrast the UK rule, discussed later at 1.2.3.2, that a corporation cannot be a parent corporation if it is a 75% subsidiary of another corporation.

### 1.2.3.2  Loss relief

The separate tax identity of related corporations may be eroded when calculating their tax bases by permitting a loss incurred by one corporation to reduce the profits derived by another corporation in the same corporate group. Transaction deferral, considered under the last paragraph, has the propensity to transfer tax attributes between corporations as a result of a transaction. By contrast, loss offset transfers tax attributes between group corporations irrespective of actual transactions between the corporations.

Tax attributes are features of a tax system that attach to tax subjects and that are carried forward from one tax period to another. Losses are tax attributes because typically they can be used in different manners in the tax period in which they are incurred or carried forward or backward to other tax periods.[317] Therefore, to understand how losses may be used in the context of a corporate group, it is necessary to understand how losses may be used by a single independent corporation. That is the first matter discussed in this subheading. It then considers the various mechanisms by which a loss of one corporation may be set against the profits of another corporation in the same corporate group.

Group loss relief mechanisms share several issues. One is what constitutes a corporate group for the purposes of the loss relief mechanism. This is the final matter considered later. Another issue involves the limited liability that usually protects one group member from another group member's losses. A fundamental question is why one group member (including a parent corporation) should benefit from another group member's losses for tax purposes if the first group member is not commercially liable for

---

[316]  CCCTB Proposal Art. 54.
[317]  See footnote 79.

those losses. Most group loss relief mechanisms do not require a connection between tax and commercial reality. However, some group systems do require a group member to be personally liable for the loss of another group member to benefit from it for tax purposes. This is typically a feature of group contribution regimes and is also a feature of the German *Organschaft* regime discussed later. It is not a feature of group loss relief in the UK or the US or under the CCCTB Proposal.

**Losses of an independent corporation** There are three primary aspects to the manner in which corporations may use losses. The first is the manner in which those losses may be used in the year in which they are incurred. This depends on whether an income tax law adopts a global or schedular approach to calculation of the corporate tax base. Second, there is the question of whether a corporation can carry a loss incurred in one year backwards to set against the profits of a previous year. Because this usually involves the refund of taxes paid in the previous year, this type of relief is quite often restricted or not available at all. Finally, any excess loss that cannot be used in the current year or carried backwards is usually permitted to be carried forward. For how long those losses may be carried forward and what type of income they may be set against will depend on the tax law in question.

**Use in year in which incurred** As mentioned, the manner in which a corporation may use a loss in the year in which it is incurred depends on whether the income tax law in question adopts a global or a schedular approach to calculation of the corporate tax base (see 1.2.1). For example, Germany adopts a global approach with respect to corporations and so needs no express rule that losses from one activity may offset profits from another.[318] The position is the same under the CCCTB Proposal.[319]

Despite also adopting a general global approach, the US treatment of current year losses is slightly more complex. This is because the global approach is partly schedularised through the quarantining of certain losses under section 165 of IRC. In particular, 'losses from sales or exchanges of capital assets shall be allowed only to the extent of gains from such sales or exchanges'.[320] 'Capital asset' is defined in terms of 'property',

---

[318] For example, see EStG (Germany) s. 10d(1) referring to losses 'set off upon determination of the total income'.

[319] CCCTB Proposal Art. 43(1) simply refers to a 'loss incurred ... in a tax year'.

[320] IRC (US) s. 1211(a).

but does not include trading stock, depreciable business assets, certain intellectual property and some other types of assets.[321]

The UK position is again complicated by the schedular nature of its corporate tax base. Just as it is possible to have income or profits with respect to each schedular activity, it is possible to have a loss with respect to many such activities. The UK has special rules specifying when a person with a loss from one activity may set that loss against the profits that the person derives from another activity. This is commonly referred to as 'sideways' relief.

For example, if a company makes a loss in carrying on a trade during an accounting period, the company may claim to set that loss against its total profits of that accounting period.[322] Losses of a trade are computed in the same way as income from the trade.[323] This is important because it means that losses of a trade are only revenue losses. Capital losses are dealt with under TCGA 1992. 'Total profits' are the aggregate profits of a corporation subject to corporation tax and include all types of income as well as capital gains. So trading losses can be set against any income or capital gains of the corporation of the accounting period in which the loss is incurred.

Losses from a UK property business can also be set against a company's total profits.[324] Capital losses can be carried forward indefinitely and set against any type of capital gain.[325] This means that capital losses cannot be deducted in calculating income (i.e. they are quarantined, similar to the position in the US).

**Carry-back**   If a loss incurred by a corporation cannot be absorbed in the year in which it is incurred, a tax law may permit that loss to be carried backwards to reduce the profits of previous years. Many countries do not permit this treatment, which often involves the refund of taxes paid in previous years. For example, the CCCTB Proposal incorporates no provision for the carry-back of losses.

Countries that do permit loss carry-back have often restricted loss carry-back when lowering corporate tax rates. Germany is a good example of this approach. Germany permits corporate losses to be carried back

---

[321] IRC (US) s. 1221.
[322] CTA 2010 (UK) s. 37. Relief against total profits is not available for losses of a wholly overseas trade; s. 37(5).
[323] CTA 2009 (UK) s. 47.
[324] CTA 2010 (UK) s. 62.
[325] TCGA 1992 (UK) s. 8.

for one year and in doing so places a financial limit on the amount of carry-back.[326] The carry-back limit is €511,500, which means the carry-back is less useful for larger corporations. By contrast, the US permits a carry-back of two years without such a limitation.[327] An exception is capital losses, which may be carried back for three years.[328]

In the UK, trading losses incurred by a corporation in a particular accounting period may be set against the total profits of the corporation of the previous accounting period (i.e. one-year carry back).[329] There is a special three-year carry-back for losses incurred in the year in which a trade is terminated.[330] By contrast, a loss from a UK property business cannot be carried backwards. There is also no carry-back of capital losses.

**Carry-forward**   If a loss cannot be used in the year in which it is incurred or carried backwards, most income tax laws permit at least some types of losses to be carried forward. Historically, the period for which losses could be carried forward was limited. However, the current value of a loss decreases as the use of the loss against profits is projected further and further into the future. This means that lifting a limit on the period of carry-forward may not be so costly and can simplify the treatment of losses by cutting down on recording and ordering rules. As a result, permanent loss carry-forward is common, although many countries impose some type of limit on the use of carried-forward losses.

The US has a traditional time limit on the use of carried-forward losses: net operating losses may be carried forward for twenty years.[331] With such a substantial loss carry-forward period, it is not clear why the US does not simply permit unrestricted loss carry-forward. Also confusing is why capital losses may be carried forward for five years only.[332] There seems little rationale for the inconsistency.

Germany has a different limitation on the use of carried-forward losses. In 2004, Germany introduced a measure known as the 'minimum tax' to restrict the rate at which carried-forward losses may be used. When a German corporation seeks to use a loss carried forward from a previous year, it may unrestrictedly reduce its profits by a total of €1 million of that loss.

---

[326] EStG (Germany) s. 10d(1)
[327] IRC (US) s. 172(b)(1)(A).
[328] IRC (US) s. 1212(a)(1)(A).
[329] CTA 2010 (UK) s. 37.
[330] CTA 2010 (UK) s. 39.
[331] IRC (US) s. 172(b)(1)(A).
[332] IRC (US) s. 1212(a)(1)(B).

If it wishes to reduce its profits by any more than this amount, the deduction is limited to '60% of the total amount of income exceeding the €1 million'.[333] Any unused losses may still be carried forward in full (i.e. the measure does not cancel losses). This provision has proved quite controversial; it has often been argued that it discriminates against start-up businesses with losses. It also causes taxpayers with carried-forward losses to monitor their taxable income so that the full €1 million is used each year. In particular, it may be sensible for a corporation with losses to accelerate the recognition of income in some years.

The CCCTB Proposal would also allow corporations to carry forward losses indefinitely.[334] The Presidency review of the Proposal mentioned in this book's introduction would introduce the same limitation on the use of carried-forward losses as in Germany.

The UK typically allows permanent carry-forward of unused loses. So, if a corporation cannot obtain relief for a trading loss in either the current accounting period or the previous accounting period, the loss may be carried forward indefinitely. At this stage, however, the UK schedular system intervenes in a peculiar manner. Carried-forward trading losses may only be set against profits of the same trade that made the loss (i.e. trading losses are quarantined when carried forward).[335] Most countries do not quarantine carried-forward losses in this manner, and the UK approach can produce strange results.

One peculiarity results from the capital / revenue distinction. 'Total profits' include capital gains. This means that a revenue loss from a trade can be set against any capital gains, including capital gains arising in the course of the trade, but only in the year in which the loss is incurred or the previous year. If the loss is carried forward, the loss can only be set against 'income' from the same trade. This means that carried-forward trading losses cannot be set against capital gains, even if the capital gains arise in the course of the very trade that incurred the loss.

Another peculiarity results from the pressure that the carry-forward of losses puts on the concept of a 'trade'. A trade is an activity and so is a question of degree. However, the carry-forward and use of losses are an absolute: the whole of a loss is available or none of it is. Activities may be very closely related, but not constitute part of the same trade, in which case no carry-forward loss relief is available between the activities. If the

---

[333]  EStG (Germany) s. 10d(2).
[334]  CCCTB Proposal Art. 43(1).
[335]  CTA 2010 (UK) s. 45.

activities are slightly more related, perhaps they are the same trade, and so full carry-forward loss relief is available. Taxpayers often argue that their activities are related and fall within the same trade,[336] but this is not always the case. For example, the three-year carry-back of losses against total profits depends on a trade having ceased. This might result in a taxpayer arguing a narrow concept of trade.[337]

Another peculiarity results from the reconciliation rules of the schedular system (discussed earlier at 1.2.1). At least historically, it was possible that some amounts that would be included in trading income were subject to corporation tax under another head of charge. This happened because reconciliation rules required priority to be given to the other head of charge over the trading head. This was particularly a problem in the case of the receipt of interest and of dividends from foreign corporations. It could mean that a carried-forward trading loss could not be set against income that properly belonged to the trade because that income was excluded from the trading head of charge (being taxed under another head).

Section 46 of CTA 2010 was intended to provide some relief in this regard. If current trading profits are insufficient, a carried-forward trading loss may be set against any 'interest or dividends' that 'would be brought into account as trading receipts ... of the trade ... but for the fact that they have been subjected to tax under other provisions'. The test here is whether the investment from which the dividends or interest is derived is in some way integral to the trade.[338] Subsequent developments mean that this relief is practically useless. Any interest that meets this test should now be covered by the loan relationship rules and treated as a receipt of the trade in any case.[339] Most inter-corporate dividends are now exempt and so are not 'subject to tax' (see 2.4.3.1).

Despite these peculiarities, there is a real question whether the policy underlying the quarantining of carried-forward trading losses in the UK

---

[336] For example, in *Netlogic Consulting Ltd* v. *RCC* [2005] STC 524 (SCD), the taxpayer failed in an argument that provision of computing consultancy services was the same trade as a previous loss-making activity of dealing in computers and software.

[337] For example, in *Electronics Ltd* v. *HMIT* [2005] STC 512 (SCD) the taxpayer failed in an argument that the closure of a division of its activities constituted the cessation of a separate trade.

[338] *Nuclear Electric plc* v. *Bradley* [1996] STC 405 (HL). Interest received on long-term loans taken out to fund expenses on the eventual decommissioning of nuclear power stations could not be regarded as trading income against which carried-forward trading losses could be used. By international standards, this is a particularly hard case demonstrating the unfair nature of the quarantining of carry-forward trading losses.

[339] CTA 2009 (UK) s. 573.

makes sense. This policy prescribes that to use trading losses in the future the corporation in question must continue to carry on the very trade that makes the loss. Further, it must continue that trade for as long as it takes to use the loss. It seems strange that a corporation should be encouraged to continue a trade that has proven ineffective for making profits, rather than being encouraged to close it and start something else or at least engage in substantial restructuring. As noted later at 5.2.2.1, the same incentive applies when the corporation in question is sold to new owners (i.e. the new owners are encouraged to carry on the same loss-making trade).

As for other types of losses, carried-forward losses from a UK property business can be set against a corporation's total income and not just its income from that business.[340] The property business must continue for the losses to be used in this manner. This is not such a high threshold because, in contrast to the various trades that a corporation may have, all a corporation's income-generating activities from UK land constitute one single property business.[341] Capital losses can be carried forward indefinitely and set against any type of capital gain.[342] There is no requirement that any particular activity be continued. However, as a general rule, capital losses cannot be deducted in calculating income (i.e. they are quarantined).

**Group loss relief mechanism**     There are various mechanisms by which a loss of one corporation may be set against the profits of another corporation in the same corporate group. The set-off may be achieved by directly attacking the identity of group corporations in whole or in part (i.e. pure or partial consolidation). Alternately, the separate identity of corporate group members may be respected in form, but indirectly attacked through the transfer of tax losses between group members. There are two primary methods by which this loss transfer can be achieved. The transfer may be available irrespective of any transaction between the group corporations. Alternately, the loss transfer may be made indirectly by requiring a group corporation with profits to make a financial contribution to the group corporation with losses (i.e. make a payment to the loss corporation). The manner in which each of these mechanisms operates will also depend on the general rules for use of losses of an independent corporation (discussed earlier).

---

[340] CTA 2010 (UK) s. 62.
[341] CTA 2009 (UK) s. 205.
[342] TCGA 1992 (UK) s. 8.

**Pure consolidation**    In a pure consolidation regime there are no independent tax bases for individual group corporations; there is only the single tax base of the corporate group as a whole. As a result, a corporate tax system adopting pure consolidation simply applies the loss rules for an independent corporation to corporate groups (i.e. there is no need for special group loss relief rules). This is the situation under the Australian and the Netherlands pure consolidation regimes and under the US check-the-box regime (see 1.1.4.2). No doubt, there is an aspect of simplicity to this approach, at least for stable corporate groups. However, that simplicity is dramatically offset by complications caused for pure consolidation regimes when corporations join or leave a corporate group. These issues are considered later at 5.2.

**Partial consolidation**    Instead of pure consolidation, a corporate tax system might collapse the separate identity of corporations only for certain purposes. The US consolidated return regime is an example of this approach. As noted earlier at 1.2.3.1, the Treasury Regulations specifically state that group corporations are 'treated as separate entities for some purposes but as divisions of a single corporation for other purposes'.[343] So group corporations are treated as separate entities for the purposes of calculating income, but are treated as a single corporation for the purposes of timing recognition of intra-group transactions.

Group corporations are also treated as a single corporation when it comes to filing tax returns. For the purposes of a consolidated return, the 'consolidated taxable income' is determined, amongst other things, by 'taking into account … [t]he separate taxable income of each member of the group'.[344] The 'separate taxable income' of a group member is computed in the usual way (subject to modifications) and includes 'a case in which deductions exceed gross income' (i.e. includes a loss).[345] The result is that losses of one group member offset the taxable income of another group member in arriving at consolidated taxable income.

By contrast, a 'consolidated capital gain or loss' is determined by reference to the 'aggregate gains and losses of members from sales or exchanges of capital assets for the year'. So the netting of individual gains and losses occurs at the consolidated level, not at the level of individual group members.[346]

---

[343] Title 26 Code of Federal Regulations (US) § 1.1502–13(a)(2).
[344] Title 26 Code of Federal Regulations (US) § 1.1502–11(a)(1).
[345] Title 26 Code of Federal Regulations (US) § 1.1502–12.
[346] Title 26 Code of Federal Regulations (US) § 1.1502–22(a).

**Loss transfer**  A corporate tax system that adopts a consolidation approach to corporate groups ensures that profits and losses of all group members are offset to produce a final single taxable income for the group as a whole. By contrast, a corporate tax system that recognises for tax purposes the individual identities of each group member runs the risk that losses will be stranded in some group members while other group members might be paying tax on profits. Especially for corporate groups, which act as a single economic unit, the taxation of one part of the unit while the other part of the unit suffers a loss may seem harsh and anti-intuitive. It will also give the group an incentive to rearrange its affairs so as to ensure that losses are not stranded.

Adjusting transfer prices may, if accepted for tax purposes, enable a corporate group to manipulate the profits and losses of individual group members so as to ensure that losses are not stranded. Specific tax law erosions of corporate identity that prescribe a no gain / no loss treatment of transactions between related corporations may achieve the same result, although they may also prevent the early recognition of losses, as in the UK rule for transfers of capital assets between group members discussed earler at 1.2.3.1. Such treatment, in effect, enables the transfer of gains and losses between group members. The transfer of gains and losses between related corporations based on transactions between them is often called 'self-help' group relief.

A corporate tax system that recognises the separate identity of each member of a corporate group may, however, expressly permit the transfer of losses from one member to another. It is also possible to permit the transfer of profits, as doing so may achieve the same result. The important point for present purposes is that the individual profits and losses of each member of a group have been determined (i.e. all transactions between group members have been priced and accounted for (if necessary) in calculating those profits and losses). The transfer of profits or losses is commonly referred to as 'group relief'.

There are various ways in which group relief may be structured. It may involve the simple transfer of losses, as in the UK (discussed later). In such a case, there is an issue as to whether there is any restriction on the direction in which the loss may be transferred (e.g. from subsidiary to parent, from parent to subsidiary or from subsidiary to subsidiary). Usually, there is no such restriction. Another issue is whether payment should be made for such a transfer. Some countries, like the UK, leave this to be determined according to corporate law, but ignore the effects of any payment for tax purposes.

It is also possible for the results of individual group members to be transferred in one direction, typically up to the parent of the group. So, the losses of one subsidiary and the profits of another subsidiary might be offset against each other, but they would do so by reason of each being transferred to the parent. Germany has a form of group relief involving the transfer of independent tax results of group corporations to the parent corporation, referred to as the *Organschaft* regime.

Section 14 of the Corporate Income Tax Law (KStG) provides that if a resident corporation enters into an agreement to transfer profits (*Beherrschungsvertrag*) as referred to in section 291(1) of the Companies Law (AktG), in which it must transfer its entire profits to another domestic commercial enterprise, 'then the income of the subsidiary shall be attributed to the primary enterprise (controlling entity)'. There are certain corporate law requirements with respect to such an agreement, and there are additional tax law requirements. The agreement must be registered with the Trade Register, and it must be concluded for a minimum of five years.[347]

The profit-sharing agreement is a legally binding agreement that requires the approval of 75% of the capital represented at a members' meeting of the subsidiary.[348] Under the agreement the subsidiary must transfer all its profits to the parent. The agreement also requires the parent to pay for losses of the subsidiary. An actual 'money transfer' has to take place (in very broad terms with exceptions). The transfer of profits and losses occurs not only for tax purposes but is also reflected in the commercial accounts. The parent shows the subsidiary's profits and losses in its own financial accounts. Subsidiaries still separately file tax returns, but their income is shown as transferred to the parent. The income of subsidiaries is thus reduced to zero if the parent holds 100% of the shares. Minority shareholders are discussed further later.

The *Organschaft* regime is the only possibility in the German corporate tax system for group loss relief. Its holistic approach can be contrasted with the fragmented UK approach, which typically involves the transfer of losses. Under section 99 of CTA 2010 a corporation may surrender trading losses of an accounting period. This, of course, only deals with one aspect of the schedular system, but the provision extends to cover other aspects including excess capital allowances, deficits on loan relationships, losses of a UK property business, management expenses of an investment

---

[347] KStG (Germany) s. 14(1)3.
[348] AktG (Germany) s. 293.

company and non-trading losses on intangible fixed assets. In the case of trading losses and deficits on loan relationships, a corporation can surrender the loss or deficit even if it has other income that it could use the loss against (e.g. foreign income for which a foreign tax credit is available).[349] Otherwise, amounts can be surrendered only if the surrendering corporation cannot use them.[350] The following discussion focuses on trading losses.

There are various restrictions on the type of corporation that may surrender a trading loss. The broadest category that can do so is resident corporations.[351] However, it is also possible for a non-resident corporation to surrender a trading loss. This may happen where the corporation conducts a trade through a PE situated in the UK, and so is subject to corporation tax with respect thereto.[352] Exceptionally, it is possible for a non-resident corporation subject to tax in another member state of the European Economic Area to surrender a loss, but only under very limited conditions.[353] There are also special restrictions for dual resident corporations.[354]

The UK legislation is more prescriptive when it comes to who can claim a loss that is surrendered. Broadly, a corporation (the 'claimant corporation') may make a claim for group relief for an accounting period in relation to a surrendered loss where the following conditions are met:

- The surrendering corporation must consent to the claim.
- The accounting period of the claimant corporation with respect to which the claim is made must overlap with the accounting period of the surrendering corporation in which the loss was incurred.
- The loss is incurred at a time during the overlapping period when the group condition is met.[355]

Where these conditions are met, 'group relief is given by the making of a deduction from the claimant company's total profits of the claim

---

[349]  CTA 2010 (UK) s. 99(3).
[350]  CTA 2010 (UK) s. 105.
[351]  CTA 2010 (UK) s. 106. A loss cannot be surrendered if it was incurred by a foreign PE of a resident company, and that loss can be used by another person under a foreign tax law (e.g. under a group relief system of the country in which the PE is situated).
[352]  CTA 2010 (UK) s. 107. Again, there is a requirement that the UK loss not be relievable in a foreign country.
[353]  CTA 2010 (UK) ss. 111 to 128. This relief follows the decision of the European Court of Justice in Case C-446/03 *Marks & Spencer* v. *Halsey* [2005] ECR I-10837 (ECJ) and see Harris & Oliver (2010, pp. 334–42).
[354]  CTA 2010 (UK) s. 109.
[355]  CTA 2010 (UK) s. 130.

period'.[356] If the accounting periods of the claimant corporation and the surrendering corporation do not coincide, then relief is granted to the extent of the overlap. This is usually done on a time apportionment basis.[357]

The important point is that group relief is only available on a current year basis. A corporation can only surrender a loss of the current year, and a claimant corporation can only claim the loss to the extent of its corresponding current year. In this way, group relief operates as an extension to the ability of a corporation to use current year trading losses against other types of income under section 37 of CTA 2010. A corporate group can also use current year losses of a group member against the total profits (i.e. any income or capital gain) of any other group member. So, indirectly group relief breaks down the separate identities of group members and focuses on the corporate group. However, this break down does not apply for purposes of the one-year loss carry-back or the loss carry-forward.[358] In particular, even in the context of a corporate group, carried-forward losses can only be used by the corporation that incurred the loss and only to reduce profits from the very trade that incurred the loss.[359]

The UK group relief system does not apply to capital losses, and historically it was not possible to transfer capital losses between members of a corporate group. However, it is possible to achieve a similar treatment to transfer of a loss by transferring a capital asset with a latent gain to the group member with a capital loss using section 171 of TCGA 1992 (discussed earlier at 1.2.3.1). That group member then sells the capital asset outside the group, realises the gain and sets the capital loss against it. This route requires an actual transaction, and that can involve substantial transaction costs, in particular the possibility of a stamp duty charge. Relief from the need to transfer the asset with the latent gain was provided in 2000 and liberalised further in 2009.

The relief is provided by section 171A of TCGA 1992. It applies where a member of a corporate group makes a capital gain or loss with respect to an asset. If at that time the company could transfer the asset to another member of the group using section 171, the capital gain or loss may be transferred to the other group member. Both members must elect for the

---

[356] CTA 2010 (UK) s. 137(1).
[357] CTA 2010 (UK) ss. 139, 140 & 142.
[358] CTA 2010 (UK) ss. 37(3)(b) & 45, respectively.
[359] An exception is where the trade is transferred within a group, in which case the carried-forward losses are transferred with the trade. See the later discussion at 4.2.

transfer. It is possible to transfer only part of a gain or loss, and multiple elections may be made with respect to the same gain or loss (not exceeding in total the gain or loss). So, for example, a capital loss may be split between a number of group members.

Although conceptually there is now common ground between section 171A and the transfer of losses under group relief, the methods by which the transfer is achieved are very different, and there is no possibility to transfer profits under group relief. The lack of consistency is underlined by the intangible assets regime. As noted earlier at 1.2.3.1, it has a provision broadly consistent with section 171 of TCGA 1992. However, it has no equivalent to section 171A. Rather, it seems that, if there is a loss on a fixed intangible asset used in a trade, that loss will flow into the calculation of income profits of the trade.[360] If it produces a loss for the trade, group relief will be available. So section 171A is really a function of the quarantining of capital losses.

**Group contribution**    By contrast, under a group contribution regime, the losses / profits are transferred by the very mechanism of a payment. Under this sort of relief, a group member makes a payment to the loss-making company. That payment constitutes income of the loss-making company (thus reducing its loss) and is deductible to the paying company, which thereby gets use of the loss. Because this sort of system requires an actual payment, it can be difficult to determine whether such a payment has, in substance, been made. Again, usually the payments can be made in any direction within a corporate group. This is the sort of system used in Finland, Norway and Sweden. The UK used such a system from 1953 to 1967 for income and corporation tax purposes.[361]

To use the Swedish regime as an example, section 1 of Chapter 35 of the Income Tax Law (*Inkomstskattelagen*) provides: 'Group contributions will be deducted by the giver and be entered by the recipient if the conditions for deductions in this Chapter have been fulfilled'. The chapter goes on to define 'parent corporation' in terms of a 90% holding. Contributions may be made between a parent corporation and its subsidiaries and between subsidiaries.[362] The similar systems in Finland and Norway were in issue

---

[360]    It is also possible to obtain group relief for a non-trading loss on intangible fixed assets; CTA 2010 (UK) s. 99(1)(g).

[361]    See Harris (2011, pp. 203 & 205).

[362]    Income Tax Law (*Inkomstskattelagen*) (Sweden) Chapter 35 ss. 3 & 4.

in two important cases before the ECJ and the Court of the European Free Trade Association, respectively.[363]

**What is a group?** General issues pertaining to the identification of group corporations were discussed earlier at 1.1.5.1. The current discussion is concerned with any special definition or adaptations of a general definition that are used for purposes of group loss relief. As an initial point, there is no obvious reason why the identification of group corporations for this purpose should be the same as that used for identifying the relationship to which arm's length transfer pricing rules apply (discussed earlier at 1.2.2). The rules under present discussion are concerned with the erosion of the separate identity of corporations, whereas the transfer pricing rules are concerned with reinforcing that identity. And that is the general practice of countries (i.e. that the rules for identifying the subjects of the respective rules are not the same).

A second issue is whether the rules for identification of group corporations are the same for group transaction deferral as they are for group loss relief. In the case of the US and the CCCTB Proposal they are the same, because transaction deferral and loss relief are parts of a single group system. So in these cases, groups for loss relief purposes are identified in the same manner as for transaction deferral (see 1.2.3.1). The situation is different in Germany and the UK.

Germany has no rules for group transaction deferral, but it has rules for group loss relief. The tax rules for identifying who may benefit from profit and loss transfers under the German regime were discussed earlier at 1.1.5.1. Recall that for tax purposes, it is sufficient that a person holds a 'participation in the controlled company…such that the majority of the voting rights of the shares in the subsidiary are held' by the controller.[364] Two features of this test are striking when compared to the other systems. First, it is solely based on voting power, and, second, it is sufficient to hold just in excess of 50% of such power. This compares with the 80% test in the US and the 75% tests in the UK and under the CCCTB Proposal. However, this German level is slightly misleading because, as noted earlier, the members of the controlled corporation must pass a 75% resolution under

---

[363] Case C-231/05 *Oy AA* [2007] ECR I-6373 (ECJ) (Finland) and Case E-7/07 *Seabrokers AS* v. *Staten v/Skattedirektoratet* (2008) 10 ITLR 805 (EFTAC) (Norway). Finland has a separate Group Contributions Law (*Laki konserniavustuksesta verotuksessa*) (Finland). The Norwegian group contribution regime is in Income and Capital Tax Law (*Lov om skatt av formue og inntekt*) (Norway) Arts. 10–2 to 10–4.

[364] KStG (Germany) s. 14(1)1.

corporate law to conclude the profit-sharing agreement that triggers the group loss relief regime.

Another peculiar feature of the German system when compared to the other systems is that the controller (person to whom the profit or loss is transferred) is effectively identified as a business. This means that the 'parent' of a corporate group can be an individual conducting a business, a partnership or even a German PE of a non-resident. In the UK, the US and under the CCCTB Proposal, the parent must be a corporation. As discussed earlier at 1.1.5.1, for the purposes of determining whether a majority of voting rights is met, a person may be attributed voting rights held by a corporation in which that person holds a majority of voting rights. The law is not express, but it seems this is a proportionate approach.

Again, the UK approach is fragmented and requires some explanation. The rules for group identification for purposes of deferring the tax treatment of disposal of capital assets (see 1.2.3.1) are the same as those for transferring capital gains and losses between group members. By contrast, the rules for group identification for purposes of transferring revenue losses of a trade are different. Revenue losses of a trade may only be surrendered to and claimed by corporations that are members of the same 'group of companies'. Two corporations are members of the same group of companies if one is a '75% subsidiary' of the other or both are '75% subsidiaries' of a third company.[365]

The definition of '75% subsidiary' in section 1154 of CTA 2010, discussed earlier at 1.1.5.1, is used for the purposes of group relief.[366] As noted at that point, the definition is limiting because the definition of '75% subsidiary' requires that both the parent and the subsidiary be 'body corporates' and that they have an ordinary share capital. Although the group relief provisions refer to 'company', the general definition of 'company' (discussed earlier at 1.1.1.1) does not apply and 'company' is restricted to 'body corporates'.[367] The requirement of ordinary share capital is relaxed for certain industrial or provident societies so as to treat their capital as though it were ordinary share capital.[368]

Another requirement discussed earlier at 1.1.5.1 is that the ordinary share capital in the subsidiary be owned beneficially by the parent corporation. As mentioned at that point, the courts have interpreted the

---

[365]    CTA 2010 (UK) s. 152.
[366]    CTA 2010 (UK) s. 151(1).
[367]    CTA 2010 (UK) s. 188(1).
[368]    CTA 2010 (UK) s. 151(2).

concept of 'beneficial ownership' quite formally and left substantial scope for manipulation of which corporations are within a corporate group. This is particularly the case considering that there is no requirement that the parent hold the shares in the subsidiary for any specified period of time. As a result of these limitations, the concept of 75% subsidiary is narrowed for the purposes of the group relief rules in several respects.

First, shares held as trading stock do not count towards the 75% threshold.[369] Second, two corporations are not treated as members of the same group if there are certain arrangements in place: to transfer one of the corporations out of the group or under which a third party could obtain control of only one of the corporations or under which the trade of one of them could be carried on by a third party.[370]

More substantially, a 75% subsidiary does not qualify unless the parent corporation is 'beneficially entitled' to 75% of profits of the subsidiary available for distribution to 'equity holders' and would be so entitled to 75% of the assets available for distribution on a winding up.[371] 'Equity holder' is defined in section 158 of CTA 2010 in terms of the holder of ordinary shares or the holder of a loan that is not a 'normal commercial loan'. Both phrases, 'ordinary shares' and 'normal commercial loan', are further defined. The former is defined to exclude certain fixed-rate preference shares, but the types of preferences shares excluded are substantially more prescriptive than the definition of 'ordinary share capital' used for the purposes of the definition of '75% subsidiary' (discussed earlier at 1.1.5.1).[372] A loan creditor will constitute an equity holder where the return on the loan is dependent on the results of the corporation's business or its assets.[373]

Section 165 of CTA 2010 defines beneficial entitlement to profits, and similarly section 166 deals with entitlements on winding up. Considering the flexibility of corporate financing, defining such entitlements as a percentage at any point in time is difficult. Depending how they are structured, rights to corporate profits may change in entitlements depending on future events. Accordingly, CTA 2010 continues to prescribe rules for

---

[369] CTA 2010 (UK) s. 151(3).
[370] CTA 2010 (UK) s. 154.
[371] CTA 2010 (UK) s. 151(4).
[372] CTA 2010 (UK) s. 160. To qualify for group relief a parent company's holding must qualify as both 'ordinary share capital' and 'ordinary shares'.
[373] CTA 2010 (UK) s. 162.

determining the entitlement of shares with limited or temporary rights and shares affected by options.[374]

In the result, the definition of group for the purposes of group relief is substantially different from that for transferring capital assets on a no gain / no loss basis discussed earlier at 1.2.3.1 (i.e. under section 171 of TCGA 1992). Under TCGA 1992, a group includes a parent corporation as well as 75% subsidiaries of the parent's 75% subsidiaries and 75% subsidiaries of 75% subsidiaries. There is a requirement that any subsidiary is an effective 51% subsidiary of the parent corporation, but this is dramatically different from the equivalent 75% rule for group relief. Like the corresponding rule in group relief, the 51% subsidiary is defined by reference to distributions of profits or assets in a winding up, and the TCGA 1992 definition borrows the concepts of 'beneficial entitlement' and 'equity holder' for this purpose from the group relief provisions.[375]

There are other differences between groups under group relief and under TCGA 1992. In the latter, there is no exclusion for counting shares held as trading stock or for corporations subject to arrangements for transfer out of the group, and so on. This may be tempered in the TCGA 1992 context by the rules that reconcile to which group a corporation belongs. There is no provision in the group relief rules stating that a corporation cannot simultaneously be a member of two or more groups. Perhaps group relief does not need such a rule, but the contrast between these similar provisions is confusing. Another difference is that group relief is limited to body corporates, whereas the TCGA 1992 rules are more prescriptive.

Why the UK rules on group transaction deferral and group loss relief use different concepts of 'group' is not clear, although no doubt it has to do with the differing historical origins of the provisions. The bizarre result is that a corporation may in effect transfer capital gains and losses to another corporation in circumstances where it could not transfer trading losses, at least not without transferring the trade. This is despite the fact that capital gains and profits of the trade both fall within total profits that are subject to corporation tax. This is just another area in which the UK corporate tax system is a mess.

**Minority shareholders**    As noted earlier at 1.1.4.2, minority owners cause particular problems for corporate tax systems that erode the separate

---

[374]  CTA 2010 (UK) ss. 170–2 and 173–4, respectively.
[375]  TCGA 1992 (UK) s. 170(8).

identity of corporations. These problems arise in various contexts, including group transaction deferral, but it is useful to consider some practical examples in the context of group loss relief, where the issues are illuminated. Each of the group loss relief regimes of Germany, the UK, the US and the CCCTB Proposal may apply in the context of minority shareholders. In other countries, the potential for minority shareholders is often reduced (or eliminated) through high holding requirements (e.g. under the Australian consolidation regime, which in principle requires subsidiaries to be wholly owned).

Each of the German, UK, US and CCCTB Proposal group loss relief regimes adopts the attribution only to controllers approach. That is, these regimes have the potential to allow, for example, a parent corporation to claim 100% of a subsidiary's loss even if the parent holds less than 100% of the shares. Issues with respect to this approach were discussed earlier at 1.1.4.2. Some group loss relief regimes engage, either directly or indirectly, with these issues, whereas others are silent and leave them to corporate law. For example, the US consolidated return regime and that of the CCCTB Proposal are silent on the matter.[376]

UK tax law is similarly silent as to the treatment of minority shareholders, although the issues are indirectly acknowledged in the treatment of subvention payments. Losses may be transferred irrespective of subvention payments. Nevertheless, it is common for group members receiving the benefits of a loss transfer to pay for this benefit.[377] Indeed, there is a question as to whether the directors of the surrendering company are required by corporate law to demand such a payment. In any case, any such payment is expressly not income of the recipient and not deductible to the payer.[378] There is a similar provision in the context of group transaction deferral.[379] The payment that is not recognised can be anything from nothing up to the amount of the loss, although it is typically no more than the tax value of the loss (loss multiplied by the corporate tax rate). Subvention payments (or lack thereof) provide broad scope for shifting value between group members, a matter discussed later at 8.2.2.

---

[376] See Bittker & Eustice (2003–, para. 13.41), which notes that '[p]rivate law problems can be created by an election to file a consolidated return. For example, filing may be beneficial to the group as a whole at the expense of the minority shareholders of one of the included subsidiaries'.

[377] Regarding subvention payments in the US, see Sparagna (2004), p. 717.

[378] CTA 2010 (UK) s. 183.

[379] TCGA 1992 (UK) s. 171(6).

In contrast to group loss relief regimes that have no requirement for payment of losses, the Scandinavian group contribution regimes require full payment. At some level, this requirement over-compensates minority shareholders. What the minority shareholders lose through group loss relief is the tax value of the loss of their corporation (loss multiplied by the corporate tax rate). This is the maximum value of the availability of the loss for the corporation in the future. Instead, minority shareholders indirectly benefit from the face value of the loss, something they could never do in the absence of group loss relief. This may well be an appropriate policy to support minority shareholders, but it is not neutral from a tax perspective.

These positions can be contrasted with the tax law and corporate law requirements of the German *Organschaft* regime. Where a profit-sharing agreement is in place and there are minority shareholders, the minority shareholders of the subsidiary must receive a 'reasonable compensation'.[380] The compensation can be a fixed periodic payment, or it can be dependent on the profit of the parent (but it must be independent of the profit of the subsidiary). The payment may be from the parent or the subsidiary. The tax law then provides that these compensation payments (grossed-up by the corporate tax rate) constitute the taxable income of the subsidiary.[381] The subsidiary is liable to pay corporation tax on this amount of income, irrespective of whether the compensation payment is made by the subsidiary or the parent.

### 1.2.3.3    Other areas

There are other areas where the separate identity of group corporations may be eroded in calculating their respective taxable income. Two examples will suffice. This erosion can occur where there is some threshold for obtaining a relief. So, for example, in the US a 'controlled group' must split the limitation on first-year expensing allowance between members as if it were 'one taxpayer'.[382] 'Controlled group' is defined by reference to section 1563(a) of IRC (discussed earlier at 1.1.5.1), except that the 80% test is replaced with a 50% test.[383]

---

[380]  AktG (Germany) s. 304. Section 305 goes on to require the parent to offer all outstanding shareholders redemption of their shares, either for cash compensation or for shares in the parent.
[381]  KStG (Germany) s. 16.
[382]  IRC (US) s. 179(d)(6).
[383]  IRC (US) s. 179(d)(7).

Similarly in the UK, group corporations are entitled to only one annual investment allowance for capital allowance purposes. For this purpose, a group is identified by reference to the Companies Act rather than any other definition in the Corporation Taxes Acts.[384] There are other rules for related companies and related groups controlled by non-corporates. In particular, there is only one allowance for two companies controlled by the same individual.[385] However, it seems that an individual and a company controlled by the individual each get an annual investment allowance. In the usual way, the definition of control is fragmented.[386]

These allowance restrictions are examples of an unfavourable erosion of the corporate identity, but there are examples of favourable ones. This happens when a corporation is permitted to use some allowance granted to another related corporation. The UK's section 175 of TCGA 1992 provides an example of this approach. Section 152 permits a person that realises a gain on the disposal of an asset used in a trade to 'roll-over' (defer) taxation of that gain. In effect, this is achieved by reducing the cost base of an asset acquired as a replacement for the disposed asset by the amount of the gain. Section 175 extends the roll-over to the situation in which one member of a corporate group disposes of an asset and the replacement asset is acquired by another member of the group.

### 1.2.4   Erosion of identity: other related corporations

Subheading 1.2.3 focussed on the erosion of separate corporate identity in the context of corporate groups. Such erosion can also occur in other related corporation scenarios identified earlier at 1.1.5. For example, it may occur where an individual controls a corporation (1.1.5.1) or where a corporation is closely held by a group of persons (1.1.5.2). Tax laws sometimes deal with these matters, but less commonly than they address group relief. A few examples pertaining to the calculation of the tax base will suffice, but others are discussed in the remainder of this book.

### Control by an individual

To this point, this book has considered a number of situations in which the separate identity of a corporation is eroded because it is controlled by individuals. The US check-the-box regime may be viewed as such an

---

[384] CAA 2001 (UK) s. 51C.
[385] CAA 2001 (UK) ss. 51D & 51E.
[386] CAA 2001 (UK) s. 51F.

example (see 1.1.4.2), although it is not based on control as such, but rather on the type of entity in question. Under this regime, the income of an LLC may be consolidated with that of a controlling individual. Similarly, under the German *Organschaft* regime (see 1.2.3.2), an individual with a business may enter into a profit-sharing agreement with a controlled corporation. The result is that profits and losses of the corporation will be transferred to the controlling individual.

The UK has no similar broad-based regime that may apply to individuals and controlled corporations. However, there are some isolated examples of the erosion of the separate identity of a corporation controlled by an individual. Subheading 1.2.3.1 mentioned a rule providing relief from a balancing charge for excess capital allowances when a trade is transferred between members of a corporate group. A similar rule applies when a trade is transferred from an individual to a body corporate controlled by the individual or vice versa.[387] It is most commonly used when incorporating a trade, and so it is discussed later at 4.2.1.

As for the market value rule in TCGA 1992 (disposals between connected persons), there is no similar exception for corporations and related individuals as there is for disposal between group corporations (i.e. there is no equivalent to section 171). However, it is possible for an individual to dispose of business assets to a corporation in a non-arm's length transaction on a no gain / no loss basis.[388] However, the provision does not operate in the opposite direction (i.e. a disposal from a corporation to a related individual). This provision is also considered in the context of incorporation at 4.2.

At 1.2.2, brief mention was made of an arm's length pricing rule for trading stock sold between connected persons if the seller ceases to carry on the trade in question. As noted at 1.2.3.1, where this rule applies, it is possible for corporation tax purposes for the parties to the transaction to elect to, in effect, sell the stock at cost (i.e. on a no gain / no loss basis).[389] This election is also available for income tax purposes if an individual controls the body corporate in question.[390] The scope of this rule is, therefore, similar to the scope of the rule for capital allowance purposes discussed earlier. Again, although it is not limited to an incorporation scenario, this relief is further considered at 4.2. As with the arm's length pricing rule,

---

[387] CAA 2001 (UK) ss. 266 & 267.
[388] TCGA 1992 (UK) s. 165.
[389] CTA 2009 (UK) s. 167.
[390] ITTOIA 2005 (UK) ss. 178 & 179.

however, this election is not available if the transfer pricing rules in TIOPA 2010 apply.[391]

All of these UK erosions of separate corporate identity involve transactions between a corporation and a related individual. These are similar, though far from the same, as erosions in the context of related corporations discussed earlier at 1.2.3.1. By contrast, there is no similar erosion irrespective of transactions. That is, there is nothing akin to the loss reliefs available for group corporations discussed earlier at 1.2.3.2. Generally, corporations cannot transfer losses or other tax attributes to related individuals or vice versa.

## Closely held corporations

This book also considers a number of situations in which the separate identity of a corporation may be eroded because it is controlled by a limited number of persons (i.e. it is closely held). Again, the US check-the-box regime and the German *Organschaft* regime can operate in this manner. The check-the-box regime can operate, in principle, irrespective of the number of participators. The *Organschaft* regime can operate where a partnership enters into a profit-sharing agreement with a corporation it controls. The loss transferred from the subsidiary to the partnership will then be apportioned between the partners in the usual manner for partnership income and losses.[392] However, the partnership must conduct a separate business, and the shares must be held as part of that business.[393] This is interpreted to require the partnership to provide services to its controlled corporations that go beyond mere management.

The UK consortium relief regime can produce similar results for corporate joint ventures using a corporation as the vehicle, without the requirement that the adventurers constitute a partnership or carry on a business. This relief is particularly flexible and permits trading losses and other amounts for which group relief is available to be transferred between a corporation and substantial corporate shareholders in that corporation. It can operate to treat the corporation, at least with respect to losses, in a similar manner to what might happen if the corporation were a partnership, and so consortium relief erodes the separate identity of the controlled corporation.

---

[391] CTA 2009 (UK) s. 162(2) and ITTOIA 2005 (UK) s. 173(2).
[392] For example, EStG (Germany) s. 15(1)2.
[393] KStG (Germany) s. 14(1)2.

Consortium relief involves a corporation surrendering a trading loss or other amounts under the rules for group relief (see 1.2.3.2). Consortium relief differs from group relief in several respects, including as to who can claim the surrendered amount. Another corporation can claim a surrendered amount if one of three consortium conditions is met.[394] These conditions are premised on there being a corporation 'owned by a consortium' and another corporation being a 'member of a consortium'. These concepts are defined in section 153 of CTA 2010. It is important to appreciate that a 'consortium' is purely a tax concept, without commercial legal implications, used to describe a corporation (the 'consortium company') held by substantial shareholders that are also corporations. The substantial shareholders are 'members' of the consortium.

To qualify as a member of a consortium, a corporation must hold at least 5% of the consortium company's 'ordinary share capital', and the holding of all consortium members must be an aggregate of at least 75% of that capital. This means that the maximum number of consortium members is twenty (i.e. twenty corporations each holding 5% of the shares in the consortium company). The minimum number is two members. A corporation is not owned by a consortium if it is a 75% subsidiary of another corporation, and so consortium relief only applies where group relief is not available. Because there is no reference to indirect holdings, to qualify as a member a corporation must hold 5% of the consortium company directly.

To qualify for consortium relief under any of the consortium conditions, the consortium company must be either a 'trading company' or a 'holding company'. The first is defined as a corporation whose business consists mainly in carrying on trade. A holding company is a corporation whose business consists mainly in holding securities and shares in 90% subsidiaries that are trading companies.[395] The rules described earlier for determining whether a subsidiary is a 75% subsidiary for group relief purposes also apply in determining whether a trading company is a 90% subsidiary. Importantly, a trading company that is a 90% subsidiary of a holding company that is held by a consortium is itself treated as held by the consortium.[396] This means that both the holding company and its 90% trading subsidiaries may be the subject of consortium relief.

---

[394] CTA 2010 (UK) s. 130(2).
[395] CTA 2010 (UK) s. 185.
[396] CTA 2010 (UK) s. 153(3).

The first consortium condition for claiming relief is prescribed by section 132 of CTA 2010. This allows a member of a consortium to claim a portion of a trading loss of the consortium company, for example. As mentioned, this can work like loss relief for partners in a partnership. However, consortium relief is more flexible because it is also possible for the consortium member to surrender a portion of, say, a trading loss to the consortium company, so the relief works in both directions. In either case, the quantum of relief is limited to the ownership proportion of the total amount surrenderable.[397] This is typically the percentage of ordinary share capital held by the consortium member in the consortium company.[398]

The second consortium condition allows a member of the same group of companies as a member of the consortium to claim a portion of a trading loss of the consortium company, for example.[399] So, if A Co is a 75% subsidiary of B Co and B Co holds 20% of the ordinary shares in a consortium company, a loss of the consortium company may be transferred to A Co. The amount that may be claimed by A Co is again limited to 20% of the consortium company's loss (and not 75% of 20%).[400] The third consortium condition involves the reverse scenario. This condition permits a loss incurred by a member of a corporate group to be passed to a consortium company where another group member holds the relevant holding of shares in the consortium company.[401] In the example, this would allow part of a loss of A Co to be claimed by the consortium company. Again, the quantum of relief would be limited to 20% of A Co's loss.[402]

Consortium relief is an interesting and flexible form of relief that can be particularly useful in the context of joint ventures. In this area, it alleviates much of the tax planning that occurs in other countries in seeking loss relief for joint venture partners with respect to the activities of the joint venture. It also mitigates the *knife edge* nature of group relief. In many cases, if a corporate shareholder falls just short of group relief it will be entitled to consortium relief, making the importance of being within a

---

[397] CTA 2010 (UK) ss. 143 & 144.
[398] If lower, consortium relief may be limited to the proportion of profits available for distribution to equity holders of the consortium company, the proportion of assets that would be available to equity holders on a winding up of the consortium company or the proportion of voting power held directly in the consortium company. For example, see CTA 2010 (UK) s. 143(3).
[399] CTA 2010 (UK) s. 133(1).
[400] CTA 2010 (UK) s. 145(2).
[401] CTA 2010 (UK) s. 133(2).
[402] CTA 2010 (UK) s. 145(3).

group of companies less dramatic. However, like group relief, consortium relief is largely restricted to revenue losses. There is no equivalent to consortium relief with respect to capital losses, reinforcing the fragmented nature of the UK corporate tax system.

### 1.2.5    Interface with personal income tax

This heading is concerned with special rules for calculating the corporate tax base that exist fundamentally because of the nature and existence of a corporation. It considers some general rules and, in particular, the relationship between the corporate tax base and financial accounts, which most corporations must prepare. It also considers special corporate tax base rules that exist to reinforce the separate identity of a corporation and special rules that erode the separate identity of corporations related to other persons. Finally, it considers special corporate tax base rules that might exist because of the relationship between a corporation and individuals and, in particular, the interface between the corporate tax base and the personal income tax base.

As noted at the start of heading 1.2, this interface may be caused by events occurring during the existence of a corporation. This happens most clearly when a corporation distributes profits to an individual and so pre-empts Chapter 2, but it can also arise in other contexts. A different type of interface occurs in the face of special tax base rules designed with individuals in mind. Many of these rules obviously do not apply to corporations, and so the focus is on whether corporations are eligible for any simplified tax base rules that may be available to individuals.

### Interface through events

There are a number of events that may occur during the existence of a corporation where the corporate tax base interfaces with the personal income tax base. This interface may have implications for the design of a corporate tax system. The most important of these interfacing events are considered later in this book and include the distribution of corporate profits (Chapter 2), the incorporation of a business (Chapter 4) and the sale of shares in a corporation (Chapter 5). The matters discussed in this subheading are discussed in more detail in those chapters, but it is useful to preface that subsequent discussion with an overview of the interface issue.

One peculiar feature of a corporation is that its income is derived twice. It is derived once by the corporation as profits and a second time by its members on distribution. This is the dual nature of corporate income and reflects the artificial nature of corporations. This means that corporate income is first measured by the corporate tax base and then, on distribution, by the personal tax base. A problem, or at least an issue, for a corporate tax system is the extent to which these two tax bases coincide. Inevitably, in practice they do not and this has consequences. It means that some amounts might constitute taxable income just at the corporate level, some just at the shareholder level but most at both.

There are only two main ways to remedy this dislocation. One is to make the corporate tax base reflect the personal tax base for dividends. Presuming that all dividends are taxable to individuals as such, this largely means making the corporate tax base reflect profits that are available for distribution under corporate law. For many countries, this would require the corporate tax base to reflect profits declared in financial accounts, as discussed earlier at 1.2.1. The second main way to remedy the dislocation between the corporate tax base and the personal tax base is to have the personal tax base reflect the corporate tax base (i.e. only tax dividends to the extent of profits included in the corporate tax base). This option does not, of itself, suggest a scope for the corporate tax base (e.g. alignment with financial accounts). In either case, hidden profits distributions would still cause difficulties, as discussed further at 2.2.2.

Neither of these approaches involving the interface between the corporate tax base and dividends suggests that the tax base for corporate activities should be the same as it is for individuals conducting similar activities. However, such an alignment might be suggested by the potential to incorporate a business of an individual. If the tax system wishes to pursue neutrality, it might be suggested that the tax base faced by an individual when conducting, for example, a trade should be the same as that faced by a corporation. Otherwise, dislocations between these two tax bases might act as an incentive or disincentive to incorporate the business. An individual might accept that the tax rate is different on incorporation. However, the individual might be more surprised to find that different amounts are included in calculating income from the business or different amounts are deducted in that calculation depending on whether the business is conducted by the individual or a corporation.

A different type of interface occurs between the personal tax base and the corporate tax base when an individual sells shares in a corporation. The value of shares typically depends on assets held and prospects of future profits at the corporate level. Assets supported by retained profits may represent amounts that have been included in the corporate tax base and taxed as such. So, to the extent that gains on the disposal of shares included in the personal tax base reflect profits included in the corporate tax base, there is an interface between the personal and corporate tax bases.

This interface is more complex than those occurring on distribution or incorporation and its implications are not clear. It might suggest that gains on the disposal of shares should be taxed only to the extent they reflect retained profits of the corporation. However, it could also suggest the reverse (i.e. that gains on the disposal of shares should only be taxed to the extent that they do not reflect retained profits). Another alternative is to suggest that the corporate tax base should include amounts to the extent realised on a disposal of shares in the corporation in question. For example, this might mean that when a corporation is sold (share sale), it must include all unrealised gains and losses in its corporate tax base (e.g. treat all assets as realised at market values). What is clear is that there is some reason for further investigating the difference between gains on the disposal of shares that reflect retained profits included in the corporate tax base and such gains that do not reflect retained profits.

### Special rules for individuals: focus on simplified tax base

This book focuses on special tax rules that are required because of the particular nature of a corporation as an artificial person. It presumes that such rules can be distinguished from other rules that cannot be identified as special corporate rules. Just as rules might be identified as special corporate rules, income tax laws include numerous rules that are required because of the peculiar nature of individuals. These rules can relate to an individual's dependency and ability to marry, consume, have leisure time and so on.

There is a fundamental question as to where to draw the line between special corporate rules and general rules. This heading has been concerned with special corporate rules for calculating the corporate tax base. Similarly, there is a fundamental question as to where to draw the line between special rules for individuals and general rules. As with the special corporate rules, in some cases the divide will be obvious. Tax rules concerning dividends are clearly special corporate rules. Rules on employment income are clearly rules for individuals (although there may be an interface in the context of corporate intermediaries), as are rules on disposals between married couples. However, at the margins the differences between special corporate rules and special rules for individuals, at each end, and general income tax rules, in the middle, are not so clear. For example, are rules on a basic exemption and progressive tax rates special rules for individuals, or are they general rules that should be applied to corporations as well? This particular issue is discussed further at 1.3.2.

The structure of an income tax law may draw clear lines between general tax base rules, special corporate tax base rules and special individual tax base rules. The US income tax law is a good example. Part VI of IRC is entitled 'Itemized Deductions for Individuals and Corporations'. Part VII goes on to specifically provide for 'Additional Itemized Deductions for Individuals' and Part VIII for 'Special Deductions for Corporations'. By comparison, Germany has some rules in Chapter One of Part Two of the Corporate Income Tax Law (KStG) that modify the personal income tax base rules as they apply to corporations. The Income Tax Law (EStG) does not specifically identify rules only applicable to individuals, although by their nature this must be true of many provisions.

The confused structure of the UK income tax law was discussed in the introduction, and the entire duplication of the personal and corporate tax bases was noted at the start of this heading. This makes it difficult to assess which rules in Income Tax (Earnings and Pensions) Act (ITEPA) 2003, ITTIOA 2005 and ITA 2007 (personal income tax base) are replicated in CTA 2009 and CTA 2010 (corporate tax base). Even if it is found that a particular rule is replicated, the rule may be modified in one context but not the other, or at least the rules are most commonly not expressed in precisely the same language. Some rules are clearly applicable to one tax base but not the other. For example, the loan relationship rules, the derivate contract rules and the intangible fixed assets regime only apply to corporation tax.[403]

The discussion under this heading has focussed on business income of corporations. The question for our present purposes is whether, in principle, there are special tax rules for calculating an individual's income from a business that should not apply to a corporation calculating income from a business. Clearly, there are many tax rules that apply to the calculation of business income because of a relationship with an individual. An example is the denial of a deduction for business entertainment expenses. However, this rule does not suggest that it should be applied differently depending on whether an individual or a corporation is conducting the business.[404]

---

[403] Another example is the concessionary tax treatment of research and development expenditure in Part 13 of CTA 2009 (UK), including the ability to claim research and development credits.

[404] For example, the limitation of entertainment expenses in IRC (US) s. 274 and EStG (Germany) s. 4(5)2 applies to both individuals and corporations. Because of the split nature of the personal and corporate tax bases in the UK, two rules are required. The rules

However, there is one issue in the context of the calculation of income from a business that requires a bit more consideration. A number of countries have a presumptive tax for small business or at least a simplified method of calculation of business income, especially for individuals below the threshold of registration for value added tax. Should such simplified tax base rules also apply to a corporation?

There are reasons to suggest that a simplified method of calculating business income is a matter peculiar to individuals. Such rules are often implemented because of the difficulty that individuals with small businesses have in calculating their income. Sophisticated calculations that comply with accounting standards are beyond the average small business owner. Unlike registered companies, individuals are often not required by law to prepare accounts that meet these standards. To require them to do so for tax purposes would force many to engage professional assistance, and that would impose additional costs that would disproportionately increase the compliance burden for such businesses.

By comparison, a corporation is typically required by corporate law to prepare financial accounts to a given standard (see 1.2.1), and inevitably this involves engaging a professional. The additional costs in getting the professional to adjust the accounts for tax law purposes may be comparatively minimal. Further, just because a corporation has a relatively small business operation does not mean that its owners and controllers are not sufficiently sophisticated to prepare proper accounts or have other activities that justify such accounts. In the result, whatever the arguments for a simplified tax base for small businesses, the arguments are less strong for extending any such rules to corporations. If a simplified regime is available to individuals but not corporations, there will be a disjuncture between the personal tax base and the corporate tax base.

A main issue for persons conducting a small business is whether they are required to use an accrual base for calculating their income from the business. Other particularly important issues are the manner in which depreciation is calculated and the rules for accounting for trading stock. Tax laws that have a weaker connection between financial accounts and the business tax base have a greater propensity to have flexibility as to whether an accrual system must be used.

---

have the same origins, but are showing signs of divergence; ITTOIA 2005 (UK) s. 45 and CTA 2009 (UK) s. 1298. CCCTB Proposal Art. 14(1)(b) contains a limitation on deduction of entertainment expenses, but the nature of the proposal means it would only apply to corporations.

The US has a weak connection between financial accounts and the business tax base (see the earlier discussion at 1.2.1). In the US, small businesses may account for business income on a cash basis.[405] As a general rule, corporations are not permitted to use the cash method of accounting.[406] This position is similar under the CCCTB Proposal (i.e. corporations that adopt it would not be permitted to use a cash basis).[407] Neither system has a dedicated regime for small businesses. However, the US does grant an immediate expensing allowance for certain tangible assets and computer software. It is presently a maximum of $500,000 and is available to both individuals and corporations.[408]

Australia, which also has a weak connection between financial accounts and the business tax base, provides a good example of a country with special tax rules for small businesses.[409] These rules largely pertain to concessionary methods of calculating capital allowances (depreciation) and accounting for trading stock. A former requirement for cash accounting was repealed in 2006, although that is still an option. These rules apply to 'entities', and so both individuals and corporations may qualify.

By contrast, as discussed earlier at 1.2.1, Germany and the UK have stronger links between financial accounts and the business tax base. As a result, in Germany, most business taxpayers must use the accrual method, but there is a modified system for taxpayers who are not obliged by law to maintain accounting records (largely independent services and farming).[410] Because corporations are required to maintain accounts, this option is not available to corporations.

As mentioned earlier, the UK has a substantial link between financial accounts and the business tax base, at least with respect to revenue matters. Both individuals and corporations are required to calculate their profits from a trade in accordance with generally accepted accounting principles, subject to tax law adjustments.[411] The result is essentially an accrual accounting based approach. Unrealistically, this means that individuals conducting small businesses are required to apply accounting principles

---

[405] IRC (US) s. 446.
[406] IRC (US) s. 448.
[407] CCCTB Proposal Arts. 17, 18 & 19.
[408] IRC (US) s. 179.
[409] Income Tax Assessment Act 1997 (Australia) Division 328.
[410] EStG (Germany) s. 4(3). Under the Commercial Code (*Handelsgesetzbuch*) (Germany) s. 238 'traders' are required to maintain accounts. There is an exception for very small businesses; s. 241a.
[411] ITTOIA 2005 (UK) s. 25 and CTA 2009 s. 46. The latter provision was discussed at 1.2.1.

in filling in their tax returns. Without professional assistance, this requirement is likely to be observed in its non-compliance rather than its compliance. The UK tax administration informally recognises the extent of
non-compliance. In limited cases, the individual tax return form permits
the use of simplified calculations that use a modified cash basis, although
at present no tax law rule expressly authorises this use. There have been
numerous calls in the UK for adoption of a formal simplified tax base
for small businesses.[412] The UK Government is currently consulting on
this.[413]

An annual investment allowance for capital expenditure was introduced in the UK in 2008. One of its publicly stated benefits was
that it would effectively relieve 95% of businesses from making complex writing-down allowance calculations. Despite the fact that corporations must calculate depreciation for financial accounting purposes,
the annual investment allowance is equally available to individuals and
corporations.[414]

### 1.3   Tax treatment

This heading builds on the matters considered under the previous two
headings. It presumes that a corporation has been identified for tax purposes and, importantly, that the corporation is as a legal matter capable
of having income for tax purposes. That is, it is presumed that the entity
identified is capable of making and receiving payments and so can have
income or profits. Accordingly, what is not considered is the taxation of
income of entities that are ignored for tax purposes (transparent). It is also
presumed that the quantum of the corporation's income for a given tax
period has been settled. This means that any special rules for determining
the tax base of corporations, such as those discussed under heading 1.2,
have been accounted for.

This heading is concerned with the deceptively simple question of how
the identified income of the corporation should be taxed. A preliminary
question is whether corporate income should be taxed at the point it is
derived, as opposed to when it is distributed or at some other point in time.
It is often argued that corporations are inappropriate subjects of taxation,
primarily because they do not bear the burden of taxes imposed on them,

---

[412] For example, see Truman (2006) (and the survey referred to therein) and Curtis (2011).
[413] See UK (2011) and HMRC (2012a).
[414] CAA 2001 (UK) s. 51A.

whether direct or indirect taxes.[415] This argument, however, confuses the issue. The preliminary issue is not so much whether corporations should be taxed with respect to their income when it is derived, but whether that income should be taxed to *anyone* when it is derived.

The bottom line is that, if other forms of return on personal savings are taxed, then it will be necessary to tax the retained profits of corporations – both from an equity perspective and an efficiency perspective. If it were otherwise, corporations would provide a simple means of deferring, potentially permanently, the taxation of personal income.[416] This is a consequence of the realisations nature of the income tax. The under-taxation of corporate income when derived (especially its non-taxation) is commonly referred to as the 'corporate tax shelter' problem.

Governments are aware that if they do not tax corporate income effectively the result will be an erosion of the personal income tax base. The erosion can be substantial, and it can have critical fiscal consequences. On average, OECD countries raise about 25% of their revenues from the personal income tax; in the UK it is closer to 30% and in the US 33%. If social security contributions are taken into account, the average is 50%. By comparison, the taxation of corporations with respect to their income raises about 8% on average; in Germany it is less than 5%, the UK about 9% and the US 11%. This can be much higher in resource-rich countries (e.g. in Australia it is more like 20%).[417] These figures have been pretty robust over the past few decades.

The taxation of corporate income when it is derived involves two primary issues. The first is the identification of the tax subject (i.e. who is taxable with respect to corporate income). Just because a corporation has income does not mean that it has to be the tax subject with respect to that income. After all, corporations are legal fictions. The second issue is the rate at which retained corporate profits should be taxed. This issue may be informed by the first (i.e. the selection of the tax subject). This heading discusses these issues under three subheadings. The first considers the options and factors in selecting who is to be taxed with respect to corporate income at the point it is derived. The two main approaches are to tax either the corporation itself or the members of the corporation. Each of these is dealt with under the second and third subheadings, respectively.

---

[415] See references at footnote 29 in the introduction.
[416] Generally, see Harris (1996, pp. 100–12) and the references cited therein.
[417] See OECD (2010–).

## 1.3.1   Selecting the tax subject

### Corporate taxation: in search of a philosophy

How should corporate income be taxed when it is derived? Although this may be a philosophical question, it has practical consequences. How do you tax something that is a legal fiction and fit it into an income tax that predominantly applies to individuals? For some, this may raise the issue of why the legal fiction was created in the first place. For others, it is a question of the behaviour of the legal fiction. Whatever the approach, it is clear that there are several philosophical bases for the taxation of corporate income when derived. These bases are competing, sometimes overlapping, and at other times inconsistent. There is no dominant philosophy, and this is borne out in the divergent approaches of countries to the taxation of corporations. It is, however, useful to consider some of the main possibilities because doing so assists us in assessing various approaches to particular issues discussed later in this book.[418]

A simplistic approach is to suggest that corporations are persons, and therefore, they should be taxed with respect to their income like individuals and at the same (progressive) rates. The trouble is that corporations are really amalgams of individual stakeholders, and even if they exist in some economic sense, they are not the same as individuals. Many of the features of human existence that are reflected in the tax system, such as the need for food and shelter, the existence of family relations and aging, do not apply to corporations.

A dominant philosophy for the taxation of individuals with respect to their income is that taxes should be imposed according to *ability to pay*.[419] This is a very old principle and can have religious connotations.[420] It is also sufficiently vague so as to be adaptable across time and societies. Some countries have incorporated the principle in their constitutions either directly or indirectly through a requirement for equality.[421]

---

[418]   For an economic view on why we tax corporate income, see Nicodème (2009, pp. 2–5).

[419]   Generally, see Harris (1996, pp. 14–27) and the references cited therein. For a more recent view, see Dodge (2012).

[420]   For example, the English poll tax of 1380 required individuals to pay tax according to their 'ability' and there was a similar prescription in local taxation at the time. Similarly, the poor laws beginning in 1563 and the famous ship writs of Charles I of England beginning in 1634 expressly referred to 'ability'. See Harris (2006, pp. 45–6, 53, 74–5, & 80–1).

[421]   For example, the Brazilian Constitution Art. 145 specifically requires taxes to be 'graded according to the economic capacity of the taxpayer'. The German Constitutional Court has interpreted the constitutional requirement of equality (Art. 3) as incorporating the ability to pay principle; see Schön (2010, p. 67). Similarly with respect to Japan, see Nakazato, Ramseyer & Nishikori (2010, pp. 96 to 97), and Italy and Spain, see Vanistendael (1996, pp. 22–3).

Ability to pay is broadly accepted to require each person in a given society to make the same comparative (equal) sacrifice or suffer the same (equal) burden in paying taxes.[422] This leads to the justification for progressive as opposed to proportional taxation. As individuals' income or wealth increases, the utility of their next dollar (etc.) decreases. So individuals derive less utility from their millionth dollar than they do from their thousandth dollar. This justifies taxing the millionth dollar at a higher rate than the thousandth dollar so as to equalise the sacrifice or burden in paying the tax. The result is progressive taxation.

Even if ability to pay is legally applicable to corporations (e.g. by constitution), there is a certain irrationality in attempting to do so. The notion of sacrifice suggests an investigation of the incidence of taxation; it is the 'burden' of taxation that should be equalised, and a tax that is shifted or passed on to another person is no burden at all. Although incidence is a particularly slippery concept, as noted in the introduction, it is generally agreed that corporations do not bear the burden of taxation. The incidence of a tax imposed on a corporation is not the corporation itself but the individuals engaging with or having an interest in the corporation. At this level, it simply makes no sense to attempt to apply the concept of ability to pay to corporations. Therefore, ability to pay is at best a flawed philosophy for the taxation of corporations.

The fact that corporations are artificial, do not exist per se and so do not bear the burden of taxation may suggest that corporations should not be taxed with respect to their income. As mentioned earlier, this suggestion does not mean that corporate income should not be taxed at all when it is derived, but just that it should not be taxed to the corporation. So this would be a sort of negative philosophy – 'don't tax the corporation'. Although the corporation would not be taxed, the usual suggestion is that the shareholders in the corporation should be taxed with respect to corporate income, irrespective of distribution (i.e. a transparent treatment).[423] From a practical perspective, this is only possible in certain circumstances and is discussed further at 1.3.3. So inevitably, countries impose income tax on corporations, although maybe not all corporations.

Another potential philosophy is that corporate taxation must be competitive. Corporate taxation should not be such as to deter foreigners from investing in the local economy. It is presumed that foreign investors are marginal investors and any attempt to tax a standard rate of return (such

---

[422] Interpreting ability to pay to require equality of sacrifice was famously advocated by John Stuart Mill; see Mill (1871, p. 392).

[423] See Harris (1996, pp. 107–8) and the references cited therein.

as a risk-free interest rate) will deter such investment. This is because a standard rate of return is set globally and any attempt to tax it will cause foreigners to invest elsewhere. If, however, an above standard rate of return (economic rent) can be derived locally, that is an appropriate subject of taxation. This is because after taxation (presuming taxation is less than 100%) the foreign investor is still left with a better return than a standard rate of return.[424]

This type of analysis regarding economic rents is overly simplified. There are different types of economic rents, and some, if not all, types of economic rents are also subject to international competition. For reasons discussed in the introduction, corporation tax is an indirect tax, a source-based tax. It is a primary mechanism by which countries tax the return to foreign investors derived from activities within a country. Therefore, the tax on corporate income is also a primary mechanism by which a country taxes economic rents derived from that country. Indeed, if interest expense were freely deductible and subject to limited or no taxation at source, that interest may represent the standard rate of return for the activities in question. Because the taxation of corporate income is a tax on profits after the interest deduction, that taxation can approximate a tax on economic rents.[425]

There are problems with adopting taxation of economic rents as a philosophy for the taxation of corporate income. It may indicate something about the taxation of domestic source income derived by foreigners, but indicates little about purely domestic taxation or the taxation of residents with respect to their foreign source income. It could be that the taxation of economic rents is also adopted as a domestic tax philosophy, which might result in no taxation or at least reduced taxation of capital income.[426] However, this is contrary to generally understood notions of the principle of ability to pay and would, in effect, require that the principle be discarded (or interpreted in a dramatically different manner). This is particularly problematic and speculative for countries where the ability to pay principle is constitutionally entrenched.[427]

---

[424] For a lawyers' guide to the taxation of economic rents, see Passant (2011).

[425] Some and, in particular, the UK Institute for Fiscal Studies have championed formalising this position by providing an exemption for the standard rate of return on corporate equity (allowance for corporate equity or 'ACE'). For a recent proposal in this regard, see Mirrlees, Adam, Besley et al. (2011, chapters 17 & 18). And see the later discussion at 2.4.2.1.

[426] For such a proposal (rate of return allowance or 'RRA'), see Mirrlees, Adam, Besley et al. (2011, chapter 14).

[427] It is possible to limit taxation of economic rents to the taxation of the domestic activities of foreigners. In this context, the ability to pay principle could continue to require the

It is difficult to apply the ability to pay principle to corporations because of their artificial nature. Because of that artificiality, it is inevitable or at least a feature of corporations that income derived by a corporation becomes the income of individuals at some point after it is derived by the corporation. This typically occurs on division or distribution of profits, which is a separate taxing event from the deriving of profits (see 2.3). On this basis, a corporation may be viewed as simply a vehicle through which individuals derive income that, when corporate profits are retained, involves the temporary allocation of corporate income to the corporation for tax purposes. This is consistent with the nature of a corporation as a collective investment vehicle, can be consistent with the realisations basis of the income tax (see introduction) and is not inconsistent with the ability to pay principle.

As a result, it is commonly suggested that the philosophy of the taxation of retained corporate profits should be taxation that acts as a temporary surrogate for personal income taxation.[428] When corporate profits are distributed to individuals, taxation should be adjusted in accordance with the ability to pay principle. It was this type of philosophy that caused the proliferation of imputation systems from the 1960s through the 1990s,[429] although it was clear as a philosophy from the introduction of the modern income tax in the UK in 1799. Indeed, historically, corporation tax as a temporary surrogate for personal income tax may be viewed as the dominant philosophy of the corporation tax.

Globalisation has dramatically challenged the domination of this philosophy, some might say fatally.[430] The world now involves individuals resident in a particular country directly or indirectly investing in corporations located in and conducting activities in countries all around the globe. In this context, it is not clear which country's corporate taxation should be acting as a surrogate for which country's individuals. Added to this is the particular difficulty in taxing capital income, issues regarding the exempt taxation of retirement savings (one of the primary forms of saving by individuals) and suggestions that returns on capital should not be taxed at all. These issues assault not just the philosophy of corporation tax as a temporary surrogate for personal income taxation but also the very principle of ability to pay.

holistic taxation of income in a purely domestic setting. Symmetry might then require that residents only be taxed on their standard rate of return with respect to foreign investments.

[428] Generally, see Harris (1996, pp. 102–4).
[429] See Harris (2010).
[430] Ibid.

It would be naive to suggest that ability to pay as the dominant philosophy of taxation is or will become irrelevant. Economics pays scant regard to this principle except to the extent that it constitutes a limitation on possible approaches to taxation. This is because ability to pay is a moral philosophy and not an economic one. It has been the guiding principle of taxation since the Middle Ages (and earlier) and is still under constant discussion. Perhaps globalisation has caused such a fundamental shift in our economies that the principle of ability to pay must be replaced with economic principles. However, it seems more likely that the principle of ability to pay will be adapted (as it has in the past) to the new circumstances.

This discussion considered only the most widely discussed options for a philosophy of corporate taxation. There are other possible philosophies. For example, it might be suggested that the taxation of corporate income should more generally be governed by a principle of competition. Taxation of economic rents might have something to do with this principle, but competition may more broadly govern the structure of a corporate tax system. It might also be suggested that corporate taxation should be governed by the need to promote innovation or wealth maximisation. More recently, economic sustainability and green growth are having a serious impact on the design of tax systems and in the future might serve as a basic philosophy for corporate taxation. There are other possibilities.

## Options for tax subject

It is presumed that corporate profits should be taxed under an income tax irrespective of whether they are distributed, if for no other reason than to protect the individual income tax base from unacceptable deferral. If retained corporate profits are to be taxed, the next issue is *who* should be taxed.[431] As mentioned, just because a corporate tax system recognises a corporation as a person and allocates income to the corporation does not mean that the corporate tax system will necessarily tax the corporation with respect to its income. Clearly, however, a corporation may be taxed with respect to its income, and this is the dominant approach. Here the primary issue is the rate at which corporations should be taxed, discussed later at 1.3.2.

Alternately, a corporation's shareholders may be taxed with respect to the corporation's retained profits. In this case the rate at which shareholders should be taxed is less of an issue. It is presumed that they would be taxed at their usual marginal rates (if the shareholders are individuals).

---

[431] Generally, see Harris (1996, pp. 49–53).

The more difficult issue is how a single amount, the profits of a corporation, should be allocated among multiple shareholders. This issue has two features: identifying the group that is subject to allocation and determining the basis of allocation. These issues are explored further at 1.3.3 in the context of practical examples.

Corporations and shareholders are not the only possible subjects for the taxation of retained corporate profits. As noted earlier at 1.1.3.1, corporations generally have two main organs: the shareholders in general meeting and the board of directors. Therefore the board of directors or at least the management of a corporation is another possible tax subject. Even if management is not the primary tax subject in this regard, it is often a secondary or residual tax subject.[432] Corporations must act through individuals, and so at a physical level corporations are incapable of paying taxes. It is typically a corporation's management that causes the corporation to pay tax. Therefore, if a corporation fails to pay tax, there is reason for making the management personally liable, at least in the case of solvent corporations.

It is also possible to simultaneously select more than one option to be taxed with respect to retained corporate profits. There have been examples of corporations being taxed with respect to their income and at the same time shareholders of the corporation being taxed with respect to that income. This might be done to increase the corporate tax rate to that of the shareholders in question, particularly where the shareholder is subject to progressive tax rates higher than the corporate tax rate.[433]

Selection of a particular tax subject for the taxation of retained corporate profits may depend on the circumstances of the corporation in question. This is an area where the subcategorisation of corporations (see 1.1.2 and following) is particularly relevant. The ability of shareholders in a closely held corporation to coordinate their activities in order to control

---

[432] *Holland* v. *RCC* (2010) [2010] UKSC 51 (SC) involved an argument that a particular individual was a de facto director of a group of corporations that paid insufficient taxes. The actual director of these corporations was another corporation of which the individual was a director. The corporations were set up to be used as corporate tax shelters for other individuals who were seeking access to the UK's small profits rate of corporation tax (see 1.3.2.2). The UK tax administration proceeded to argue that the individual was personally liable for the taxes by reason of causing the corporations to distribute dividends while insolvent. In a split decision, the UK Supreme Court held the individual was not a de facto director.

[433] Such an allocation was made to active shareholders under the former Norwegian imputation system; see Harris (1996, p. 730). A similar allocation may have been made under the former UK surtax apportionment that operated between 1922 and 1988; see Harris (2011), particularly at p. 199.

the corporation was discussed earlier at 1.1.3.2. Shareholders in closely held corporations usually have the ability to control the distribution policy of such corporations. Indeed, such shareholders may have a separate shareholders agreement addressing this issue. In other words, shareholders in closely held corporations have an ability to call for distributions or divisions of profits at their will. It is a small step to suggest that such shareholders have a personal *ability to pay tax* out of profits retained by the corporation.

The situation is very different with widely held corporations. In those corporations, although the shareholders may have a collective ability to control the directors (and so distribution policy), they have no practical mechanism for acting collectively. If realisation is accepted, there is no ground for suggesting that a small shareholder in a large corporation realises any income where the corporation retains profits. The shareholder has no *ability to pay tax* out of those profits.

By contrast, the control possessed by shareholders in closely held corporations may be considered to give rise to a form of constructive receipt or realisation. Accordingly, there seems substantial justification for taxing shareholders in a closely held corporation with respect to retained profits of the corporation, although this is not without practical difficulty. There is less justification for doing so in the context of widely held corporations. In the absence of fundamentally altering the nature of income taxation, there is little choice but to tax widely held corporations directly with respect to their retained profits. A problem with taxing widely and closely held corporations differently is that it puts pressure on the definition of each. As noted at 1.1.5.2, this is a spectrum issue, and any line drawn between these different types of corporations must be arbitrary.

### 1.3.2   Taxing the corporation

Inevitably, countries that impose an income tax impose that tax on corporations with respect to their income. That is the situation with which this subheading is concerned. The primary issue for consideration is the rate at which tax is imposed on the corporation. There is no such thing as a 'correct' corporate tax rate, only a rate the selection of which may be influenced by particular factors.[434] This subheading first discusses the main factors to be considered in selecting a corporate tax rate. The

---

[434] For a comparative analysis of corporate tax rates in G-20 countries (plus some), see Harris (2010).

discussion then draws on practical examples in considering the options in selecting a corporate tax rate.

### 1.3.2.1 Factors in selecting a corporate tax rate

Two categories of issues are relevant in selecting a corporate tax rate for retained profits. First, there is a question of how the corporate tax rate affects the interface between the tax treatment of retained profits and other aspects of the income tax system – in particular, the personal income tax. This discussion focuses on distortions caused by the selection of a particular corporate tax rate, given the fact that no corporate tax rate is entirely neutral. Second, philosophical issues of the type described earlier at 1.3.1 may be considered in selecting a corporate tax rate. These issues provide some insight into how and the extent to which corporate tax rate distortions may be addressed.

**Interfacing issues**   The taxation of retained profits in the hands of a corporation interfaces with any situation that is substitutable with such retention. There are three interfaces that are particularly sensitive to the selection of a corporate tax rate. At a basic level, there is the interface involving selection of the vehicle through which income is derived. Here the issue is how the taxation of retained profits under the corporation tax compares with the taxation of retained profits derived directly or through other types of artificial intermediaries.

At a more direct level, retained profits represent (at least in prospect) a return on one particular manner in which a corporation may be financed (i.e. equity capital, a return for shareholders). Here the issue is how the taxation of retained profits under the corporation tax compares with the taxation of the return on the other major manner in which a corporation may be financed (i.e. debt capital, a return for debenture holders). At the most specific level, retained profits represent a return that can be but is not presently paid to shareholders. Here the issue is how the taxation of retained profits under the corporation tax compares with the taxation of distributed corporate profits.

Some of these issues have been touched on earlier at 1.2.5 in the context of the interface between the corporate tax base and the personal income tax base. In particular, that discussion considered dislocations that might occur on incorporation of a business if the two tax bases are not the same. Similar dislocations occur if the corporate tax rate is not the same as that faced by a sole proprietor. In simple terms, if the corporate tax rate is lower than the marginal tax rate faced by a sole proprietor, there is an incentive to incorporate the business. If the corporate tax rate is higher, there is a disincentive to incorporate. Similar issues arise where the business is conducted by some other entity (e.g. a partnership or trust). Because partnerships are typically transparent, the issues are largely the same as for sole proprietors. The taxation of trusts is beyond the scope of this book.

The same analysis applies as to the form of financing (i.e. whether debt or equity). The distinction between debt and equity financing (or lack thereof) is discussed later at 2.1.2. In principle, the return on debt is obligatory, whereas the return on equity financing is typically discretionary. This means there are two points at which the taxation of the return on debt and equity can be compared (presuming, as the present discussion does, that there is no adjustment of interests in the corporation): where the profits are retained (the present discussion) and where the profits are distributed (discussed later at 2.3 and 2.4). So, unless retained profits are taxed at the same rate as interest in the hands of the financier, there will be either an incentive or disincentive to finance with debt comparative to equity.

The same analysis applies with respect to the decision to retain or distribute profits. If the profits are retained, this means they will be reinvested in the corporation in question. If the profits are distributed, the investor has several options: consume the distribution, reinvest in the distributing corporation or invest in some other form of saving. If the investor's intention is to reinvest in the same corporation, then the level of tax on retained profits when compared with the level of taxation on distributed profits is highly relevant. If the corporate tax on retained profits is higher, there is an incentive to distribute. If the corporate tax on retained profits is lower, then retaining profits is the favoured reinvestment strategy.

However, the difference between the taxation of retained profits and distributed profits can have an impact even where the investor would prefer to engage in consumption or investment elsewhere. If the taxation of retained profits is sufficiently low by comparison to the taxation of distributions, this may cause the investor to choose not to engage in consumption. Similarly, if the taxation of retained profits is sufficiently low, there will be more to reinvest in the corporation in question than there would be in some other investment (i.e. the difference between the two forms of taxation). This may cause the retention of profits in the corporation to be a better investment than the alternate investment, even if the rate of return on the alternative is greater than what the corporation can earn on the retained profits.

Added to this complex mix of factors regarding the form of financing and whether to retain or distribute profits is the fact that the investor may have little or no influence over these factors. This may particularly be the case in widely held corporations where ownership and control are separated. The management of the corporation may not provide a comparable debt option to the option of equity in the corporation. Or it may decide to retain profits in the corporation irrespective of what a particular investor would prefer. At a collective level, management of a corporation is likely to be influenced by market preferences, but these may not reflect the preferences of a particular investor. Each of these options becomes increasingly substitutable in corporations that are controlled by the investor in question (i.e. in the context of closely held corporations).

**Philosophical issues**  With these interfacing issues in mind, it is useful to turn to some of the philosophical issues considered earlier at 1.3.1 and assess whether any of them are instructive when selecting a corporate tax rate for retained profits.

**Same rates as individuals**  One philosophy was to subject corporations to the same (progressive) tax rates as individuals. The discussion at 1.3.1 raised certain conceptual objections to this approach, which can also be illustrated by reference to the interfacing issues. If individuals are subject to progressive rates and corporations are subject to the same progressive rates then, without more, there is an incentive to incorporate, to finance with equity and to retain profits.

These incentives would arise because individuals, through the use of a corporation, could indirectly benefit from more than one set of progressive tax rate thresholds. This would encourage income splitting in a similar manner as the separate taxation of spouses can encourage income splitting. Further, it could encourage an individual to use multiple corporations. It is possible to apportion one set of progressive tax rate thresholds between an individual and the individual's controlled entities. This can be complex (see the later discussion at 1.3.2.2), especially in the case of close corporation controlled by a number of persons. In any case, progressive taxation of corporations raises serious questions as to what should happen when a corporation distributes profits (i.e. how the shareholders should be taxed). The progressive tax rate of the corporation is unlikely to be the same as that of its shareholders. The taxation of distributions is considered later at 2.3 and 2.4.

This philosophy – taxation of corporations at the same rates as individuals – could be reversed. It might be suggested that other forms of business entity (including individuals), debt financing and distributions should be taxed in the same manner as retained profits of a corporation. This is similar to the dual income approach under which individuals are taxable with respect to capital income at a single flat rate while their income from labour (or at least income from employment) is subject to taxation at progressive rates. This approach has been used in Scandinavian countries since the early 1990s and suggested by Griffith, Hines and Sørensen for the UK, though not adopted by the final Mirrlees Review.[435]

This approach suffers from several problems. First, and for many foremost, it is repugnant to the ability to pay principle. Second, it does not of itself suggest a particular rate of corporation tax, although it is typically understood to be a rate that is substantially below the highest personal marginal tax rate. Third, although it may resolve some of the interface issues discussed earlier, it opens up interface issues on other fronts. In particular, it opens up interface issues regarding the difference between sole proprietors and employment and encourages people to try to convert labour income into income from capital. Further, it does not resolve all of the usual interface issues. In particular, the distinction between debt and equity remains an issue for exempt investors and, in particular, pension funds and non-residents.

**Temporary surrogate**    If corporation tax were to perform as a temporary surrogate for the personal income tax, what would that suggest for the corporate tax rate? What would be the best rate to act as a surrogate? That depends on identifying the shareholders of the corporation in question. For the sake of simplicity, presume a corporation, A Co, with four shareholders, each holding a quarter of the shares in the corporation. Three of these shareholders are individuals, one with a marginal tax rate of 40%, one with a marginal tax rate of 20% and one who is exempt. The other shareholder is another corporation, B Co. Presume that B Co is taxable (for whatever reason) at 30%. At what rate should the subject A Co be taxed so that the taxation acts as an appropriate surrogate for the taxation of these shareholders?

Some might suggest that A Co should be taxed at the same rate as B Co so that it would be an appropriate surrogate for the taxation of B Co. However, many people might suggest this tax rate not because it is the

---

[435]  Griffith, Hines & Sørensen (2010).

best rate to act as a surrogate, but because of a belief that two corporations should be taxed at the same rate. This approach has more to do with issues of competition than the temporary surrogate philosophy. In any case, 30% is not an appropriate surrogate for any of the other shareholders, at least not individually.

Others might suggest that the most appropriate tax rate for A Co is 40%, being the highest rate applicable to any of its shareholders. This position is taken by a number of countries, and other countries go further by taxing corporations above the highest marginal rate.[436] A reason for following this position is that if any rate less than 40% is used, A Co may be used as a corporate tax shelter for the 40% shareholder. Again, this approach focuses on one shareholder, and at some level it is not consistent with the collective nature of the corporation. Problems associated with fragmenting a corporation in this way according to its shareholders were discussed earlier at 1.2.3.2 in the context of minority shareholders.

The temporary surrogate philosophy makes sense only if it is applied to the shareholders as a group, much in the way that corporate law often identifies a corporation with its shareholders as a group. The shareholders have invested on equal terms and will be expecting equal treatment, at least until such time as profits are distributed. In other words, the shareholders on the lower rates would not be expecting their share of retained profits to be taxed at a lower rate than the share of shareholders on higher rates. They would expect the profits to be taxed on a homogeneous basis that reflects the reality of those profits as an undivided pool. This suggests that the appropriate surrogate for personal taxation is the taxation of the shareholders as a whole (i.e. the aggregate taxation of the shareholders).

This aggregated view of the shareholders might lead to the suggestion that the corporate tax rate should be the average weighed tax rate of the corporation's shareholders as a group. This is an interesting suggestion because it creates some sense of (but not complete) neutrality in the main interfaces with the corporate tax rate. This is the rate that the shareholders as a group would face in aggregate if they conducted the corporate activities in partnership (assuming partnerships to be transparent). It is not the rate they would individually face in a partnership. It is only possible to achieve neutrality in that sense if the profits are disaggregated (i.e. the corporation is taxed on a transparent basis as discussed later at 1.3.3). The same comments can be made with respect to the distortion between debt and equity financing.

---

[436] See Harris (2010, p. 580).

Using average weighed shareholder tax rates as a corporate tax rate creates a particular form of neutrality in the interface between retention and distribution. Directors tend to consider shareholders as a group, at least in the absence of controlling shareholders, and directors' duties tend to require them to do so. When viewing shareholders in this way, whether there is a tax incentive to retain or distribute becomes a simple question of whether in aggregate more or less tax will be levied when profits are retained or when they are distributed. If the corporate tax rate is the average weighed shareholder tax rate, then in principle no more and no less tax will be levied on distribution when compared with retention.[437] This should provide some neutrality for directors in deciding whether or not to distribute corporate profits.[438]

At a general level, the temporary surrogate philosophy has some logic about it. However, that logic breaks down once the specifics of particular corporations are considered. The problem is that persons on different tax rates invest in different corporations in different proportions. So the average shareholder tax rate for one corporation may not be the same as for another. Further, the average shareholder tax rate for a corporation at one point in time may not be the same as at another point in time. The shareholders' marginal tax rates may vary from year to year or shares in the corporation may be sold between persons on different tax rates.

At a practical level, it is not possible to have a custom tax rate for every corporation. Nevertheless, in the context of widely held corporations, at least listed corporations, it is possible to identify an average shareholder tax rate; this is a commonly referred to concept. So, in the context of widely held corporations, it might be possible to target a corporate tax rate somewhere near the average shareholder tax rate. As corporations become closely held and control enters the picture, any such logic falls away.

If the corporate tax rate is below the highest marginal rate, it can be expected that persons on the highest rate will band together and seek to shelter their income behind the corporate form. Doing so would result not only in an individual benefit for each shareholder but also an aggregate benefit when compared to the average shareholder tax rate. Indeed, if

---

[437] This presumes that in aggregate distributed profits would be taxed at shareholder marginal rates (i.e. taking into account both corporate-level tax and shareholder-level tax).

[438] But see Kaserer, Rapp & Trinchera (2011, p. 21) and the discussion at 2.3.2.3 for an observation that corporations managed by substantial shareholders might distribute more profits.

corporations are to be taxed with respect to retained profits, then, in the context of closely held corporations, the only way to prevent corporations being used as tax shelters is to tax them at the highest marginal rate.

By comparison, persons on marginal tax rates below the corporate tax rate would be discouraged from adopting the corporate form or at least retaining profits in that form, depending on the tax treatment of distributions. They are likely to seek transparent forms of taxation. There are several ways in which this might be achieved. They may use a transparent form of business, such as a sole proprietorship or partnership. They may seek a return from the corporation in a deductible form, such as through wages, royalties or interest. They may also seek distributions instead of retentions if these are taxed overall (corporate and shareholder level taxes) more lightly.

The bottom line is that in the context of closely held corporations and progressive rates, the only manner in which to achieve any sense of neutrality between different forms of doing business, financing the business and retention or distribution is by treating the corporation as transparent. Some of these issues can be partly addressed with a flat tax on capital income, but as discussed earlier, that causes its own problems. Widely held corporations appear to raise different issues. However, distinguishing between widely held and closely held corporations is inherently problematic (see 1.1.5.2). There seems no way out of the circle.

**Competition**   It would be naive to suggest that any country today consciously seeks to follow the temporary surrogate philosophy to corporate taxation, although this approach may be subconsciously considered when grappling with the corporate tax shelter problem. What countries are increasingly attuned to is tax rate competition, particularly in economic blocks such as the EU. The last three decades, and particularly in the last 15 years, have seen a dramatic drop in corporate tax rates around the globe. The average corporate tax rate has dropped from 31.4% in 1999 to 25% in 2012. The drop has been particularly significant in the EU where the drop was more than 10% in the same period. It has been far less dramatic, for example, in Latin America.[439]

Personal income tax rates have dropped over the same period, although not to the same extent; in fact, they seem to have stabilised in recent

---

[439] See KPMG's *Corporate Tax Surveys* for various years, available at http://www.kpmg.com/ Global/en/Pages/default.aspx, accessed 16 July 2012. The steep drop in the EU was partly caused by the admission of Eastern European and other countries during this time period.

years.[440] Especially in OECD countries, this has left a widening gap between the highest marginal tax rate for individuals and the corporate tax rate. In 2012, the average corporate tax rate in OECD countries was 25%, whereas the average highest marginal tax rate (excluding social security contributions) was 40.5%. This is dramatically different from world averages of 25% for the corporate tax rate and 31.7% for the highest marginal tax rate for the same year. It means that developed countries typically have a massive problem with corporate tax shelters because there is the potential to shelter income from on average up to 15.5% tax if income is derived and retained in a corporation. Other countries hardly have this problem at all.

Interestingly, as corporate tax rates have fallen, the number of exempt entities and non-residents holding shares in widely held corporations has risen dramatically. Using UK quoted shares as an example; forty years ago resident individuals held half of UK quoted shares. That figure is now 11.5%, a drop of nearly four fifths. Initially, this drop was taken up by institutional investors and, in particular, pension funds. By the 1990s, resident institutional investors held more than half of quoted shares, with pension funds holding more than 30%. Since this time, the proportion of quoted shares held by institutional investors has halved and there has been more than a threefold increase in shares held by non-residents. Non-residents now hold well in excess of 40% of UK quoted shares.[441]

Pension funds are typically exempt from income tax, as are non-resident shareholders receiving dividends.[442] The result is that average shareholder tax rates, especially for widely held corporations, have dropped dramatically over the same period during which corporate tax rates have dropped. This may be no coincidence, and although it can be suggested that the corporate tax rate has lowered so as to be a better surrogate for shareholder taxation, that is unlikely to be the primary reason for the coincidence. This is because corporation tax is typically not a temporary surrogate for shareholder taxation of non-residents and tax exempts: it is a final tax.

In addition to general competition for portfolio investors, a major factor at work in the lowering of corporate tax rates may be the distortion

---

[440] See KPMG's *Individual Income Tax Rate Surveys* for various years, available at http://www. kpmg.com/Global/en/Pages/default.aspx, accessed 16 July 2012.

[441] Office for National Statistics (2010, p. 4) and Office for National Statistics (2012). It may be presumed that the volume of foreign shares held by resident institutional investors has increased dramatically in the past two decades.

[442] Regarding the taxation of non-resident shareholders receiving dividends from resident corporations, see the later discussion at 3.1.2.

between the taxation of returns on equity compared to those on debt. A flow of funds in the form of interest going to tax-exempt institutions and non-residents is typically untaxed at either the corporate level or the shareholder level by the country where the corporation is located. By contrast, a flow of funds in the form of dividends going to the same investors is likely to be taxed, but only at the corporate level (i.e. by the corporation tax). The substitutability of debt and equity is likely to cause excessive reliance on debt and put downward pressure on the corporate tax rate.[443]

So tax competition is felt most acutely in the context of widely held corporations. These corporations account for a massively disproportionate share of all corporation tax collected and are also held disproportionately by non-residents.[444] However, as noted in the introduction, the overwhelming *number* of corporations are small, closely held corporations, and these most commonly have no tax exempt or non-resident shareholders. For those corporations, tax competition seems less relevant than for widely held corporations, and the debt versus equity interface is likely to be dramatically less acute. By contrast, the corporate versus non-corporate interface and, particularly, the distribution versus retention interface are likely to be particularly acute. An increasing problem for governments is being able to distinguish between these two different types of corporations. As tax competition drives down corporate tax rates because of international factors, it drives up corporate tax shelter problems with the vast majority of corporations. The situation could be different if widely and closely held corporations were subject to different corporate tax treatment.

### 1.3.2.2 Options in selecting a corporate tax rate

Considering the factors discussed earlier at 1.3.2.1, there are a multitude of ways in which a country can set a corporate tax rate. Many, perhaps a slim majority of countries, simply have one corporate tax rate. However, if size of economy is considered, then large economies tend to have multiple rates.[445] If multiple rates are used, they can be set in a number of ways. They might be set by reference to the amount of income derived (i.e. progression) or the type of income derived (i.e. differentiation), or the variation may be caused by additional levies at the regional level. Some countries apply a different rate to an alternate tax base to ensure that a minimum level of corporation tax is levied. Many countries had rules

---

[443] See Harris (2010).

[444] Nearly one quarter of all corporation tax in the UK is collected from the top 100 listed companies; see Symons & Howlett (2010).

[445] Regarding G-20 countries (and some others), see Harris (2010).

applying a higher corporate tax rate to undistributed profits in order to prevent unacceptable deferral of shareholder tax on dividends. The US still has such rules.

**Main rate**    The main issue with respect to the main corporate tax rate is how it compares to the highest marginal tax rate for individuals. For the past decade, the highest US federal corporate tax rate has equalled the highest individual tax rate.[446] The rates were aligned when the Bush (George W.) government introduced temporary rate cuts for individuals.[447] These cuts were due to expire at various times, but have been continually extended. The most recent expiry was to be the end of 2010, but the cuts were extended just two weeks before that time. The cuts are now due to expire at the end of 2012.[448] As a result, the US does not have as large a problem with corporate tax shelters as some other countries, although they can be problematic as a result of progressive corporate rates (discussed later).[449] In addition to the federal corporate tax, US corporations are typically subject to state corporation taxes. The rates vary from state to state, ranging from nil to a maximum of 12%.

Germany is also a federal country, but its municipal-level trade tax rate is substantially higher than that of corporate taxes in US states. Germany imposes a federal corporate tax rate of 15%, which is increased by a surcharge, making it 15.825%.[450] Municipal trade tax is imposed by federal law largely on the same base as the federal corporate tax.[451] The trade tax is imposed at the rate of 3.5%, but municipalities increase this by selecting a multiplier of between 200% and 490%. The result is a trade tax rate of typically around 14%, which yields a combined corporate tax rate of somewhere in the vicinity of 30%. This is still substantially lower than the highest personal marginal rate of 45%, which is increased to approximately 47.5% by the surcharge.[452] So there is some potential to use corporations as tax shelters in Germany. The trade tax would increase this distortion dramatically for individual traders. However, individual traders are given

---

[446] US corporate tax rates are found in IRC (US) s. 11 and individual tax rates in s. 1.

[447] Previously, the highest individual marginal rate was 39.6%.

[448] Tax Relief, Unemployment Insurance Reauthorization, and Job Creation Act of 2010 (US) ss. 101 and 102.

[449] Foreign corporations can pose a corporate tax shelter problem for all countries. Rules for controlled foreign corporations are briefly discussed at 3.2.2.1.

[450] KStG (Germany) s. 23(1).

[451] Trade Tax Law (*Gewerbesteuergesetz*) (Germany).

[452] EStG (Germany) s. 32a.

a lump sum credit against the income tax to offset the imposition of trade tax.[453]

Regional corporate taxes in both the US and Germany are largely imposed on an apportionment of the federal corporate tax base. In contrast, the CCCTB Proposal would impose no central EU tax. Rather, the corporate tax base would be calculated under rules at the EU level, and that tax base would be apportioned between EU member states where the corporation (or group) is conducting business according to a formulary apportionment.[454] The part of the tax base apportioned to a particular member state would be taxed at the prevailing corporate tax rate in that member state. So in this context, there would be only regional levies, and, in principle, the CCCTB Proposal could not, of itself, create a corporate tax shelter problem. Whether there is a problem would be determined by reference to the corporate and personal income tax rate schedules of particular member states.

By contrast, UK corporation tax involves no regional levy, only the imposition by the central government. As for income tax, the UK reimposes corporation tax every year in the annual Finance Act.[455] For the tax year beginning 1 April 2012, the main corporate tax rate is 24%.[456] This is planned to decrease to 22% by 2014. Considering the current highest tax rate for individuals is 50%,[457] the UK suffers a massive corporate tax shelter problem. It is made worse by the difference in tax treatment of an individual trader compared to an incorporated business by the small profits rate, to be discussed later. That discussion also considers the manner in which the UK has reacted to the problem.

**Progressive rates**    If a country imposes corporation tax at progressive rates, it is very unlikely that it will use the individual progressive rate schedule in doing so. The US is a good example. Federally, it applies progressive corporate tax rates according to the schedule shown in Table 1.1.

The thresholds used are very different from those used for individuals. For example, for individuals the 35% rate band applies to income above

---

[453] EStG (Germany) s. 35.

[454] CCCTB Proposal Art. 86. In form, the apportionment always involves a consolidated group because a PE is treated as a member of a group separate from the corporation of which it is a part; Art. 4(7) defining 'group member'.

[455] CTA 2009 s. 2(1).

[456] Finance Act 2012 (UK) s. 5(1).

[457] Finance Act 2012 (UK) s. 1. The UK government plans to reduce this to 45% in 2013.

Table 1.1. *US schedule of*
*progressive corporate tax rates*

| Income (in US dollars) | Rate of tax |
| --- | --- |
| 0–50,000 | 15% |
| 50,000–75,000 | 25% |
| 75,000–100,000 | 34% |
| 100,000–335,000 | 39% |
| 335,000–10,000,000 | 34% |
| 10,000,000–15,000,000 | 35% |
| 15,000,000–18,333,333 | 38% |
| 18,333,333 and above | 35%[458] |

$379,150.[459] Further, for individuals the rates are consistently progressive with no rate exceeding 35%. By comparison, the 39% and 38% corporate rates require some explanation. These rates are designed to claw back the benefit of previous lower rates. So, by the time the 39% rate band has been exhausted, all of a corporation's income has been taxed at 34%. Similarly, by the time the 38% rate band has been exhausted, all of a corporation's income has been taxed at 35%.

The UK also imposes corporation tax at progressive rates, although the rate structure is not as complicated as that of the US. Section 18 of CTA 2010 provides for the imposition of corporation tax at a 'small profits rate'. This rate is also set by the annual Finance Act. Confusingly, however, the small profits rate is usually set by law in the year in which it is imposed, whereas the main rate is usually set a year in advance. This means that reference must be made to two Finance Acts to determine the corporation tax rates for a particular year. The small profits rate for the tax year beginning 1 April 2012 is 20%.[460]

The small profits rate only applies up to a threshold of £300,000. The benefit of the small profits rate is clawed back by a statutory formula for profits between £300,000 and £1,500,000.[461] This formula is commonly understood to simply apply a higher rate to profits between these limits, much in the way that the 39% and 38% US rates discussed earlier do. At present the UK higher rate can be calculated as 26.5%. This means that profits up to £300,000 are taxed at 20%, between £300,000 and £1,500,000

---

[458]  IRC (US) s. 11(b)(1).
[459]  IRC (US) s. 1.
[460]  Finance Act 2012 (UK) s. 7.
[461]  CTA 2010 (UK) s. 24.

at 25% and above £1,500,000 at 24%. This is dramatically different from the situation for individuals where the 40% rate starts to apply around £40,000 of income and the 50% rate at around £150,000.[462]

The distortions caused by this structure are horrendous. In the US, there is some scope for an individual to split income with a controlled corporation in order to secure two sets of progressive rate thresholds. But any such scope pales into insignificance compared to the UK position. Between £40,000 and £150,000 an individual can more than halve his or her tax bill by deriving income through and retaining profits in a corporation. Between £150,000 and £300,000 the saving is potentially one and a half times the tax bill; above £300,000 it is still a saving of more than a half. The result is that any person who is likely to derive more than £40,000 per year will use a closely held corporation, subject to anti-abuse rules discussed later. The savings can be larger if social security contributions are accounted for and a corporation also provides an opportunity to split income with other family members, especially spouses.[463] In the result, it is largely for tax reasons that the UK has a disproportionately large number of small companies (see the introduction).

It is one thing to permit an individual to split income with a controlled corporation. It is quite another to permit individuals to have multiple income splits by using multiple corporations. Using the US as an example, without income-splitting rules, it would be possible for an individual to form a number of corporations to get the benefit of the 15% initial corporate tax rate many times over. This problem does not arise for countries that use a single flat corporate tax rate. Countries that use progressive rates for corporations usually have special rules that apportion the rate bands between corporations that are subject to common control. The UK and the US have such rules.

Section 1561 of the IRC (US) limits the multiple use of certain benefits for a 'controlled group of corporations'. In particular, the income tax bands in section 11(b) must be apportioned between such corporations. In principle, each threshold is equally divided amongst the corporations in question, which can be quite arbitrary if different group members have different amounts of income. 'Controlled group of corporations' is defined in section 1563(a) to include both a 'parent-subsidiary controlled group' and

---

[462] ITA 2007 (UK) s. 10. There is an effective 60% rate because the personal exemption is withdrawn between £100,000 and about £113,000; s. 35.

[463] Regarding income splitting using a family corporation in the UK, see Harris & Oliver (2008).

a 'brother-sister controlled group' or a combination of the two. These definitions were considered earlier at 1.1.5.1. 'Parent-subsidiary controlled group' is defined in terms of an 80% holding by the parent corporation or by other members in the group. By contrast, two corporations are a 'brother-sister controlled group' if they are held as to 50% voting and value by the same persons (not exceeding 5). There are attribution rules for relatives.

The UK rules for use of the small profits rate are similar, though with subtle but important differences. The £300,000 and £1,500,000 small profits rate thresholds are divided evenly between 'associated companies'.[464] Confusingly, the concept 'associated companies' is defined in section 25(4) of CTA 2010 in very similar, though not identical terms as the definition of 'associated company' in section 449 (considered earlier at 1.1.5.1).[465] Two corporations are associated if one is under the 'control' of the other or both are under the 'control of the same person or persons'. 'Control' takes its meaning from sections 450 and 451, which were considered at 1.1.5.1. Generally, 50% ownership is sufficient. Section 25(3) specifically excludes from associated companies a corporation that has not 'carried on any trade or business at any time in the accounting period';[466] presumably because it will be a 'close investment holding company' and the headline rate will apply (see the later discussion).

The attribution of rights for the purpose of determining control under section 450 of CTA 2010 was also considered earlier at 1.1.5.1. In particular, rights held by 'associates' may be attributed to a person for the purposes of determining whether he or she has 'control' of two corporations. 'Associate' is defined by reference to section 448. In particular, an individual is an associate of a relative or a partner. This could have arbitrary results. It meant that a corporation owned by an individual was automatically associated with a corporation owned by the individual's children or remoter issue or siblings. The same applied to corporations owned by business partners. In all these cases the small profits rate thresholds had to be apportioned, irrespective of how independent the corporations

---

[464]  CTA 2010 (UK) s. 24(3).

[465]  The definition of 'associated companies' in CTA 2010 (UK) s. 25 is qualified by a number of rules in ss. 26–30, which deal with, amongst other things, association through preference shares, loans and trusts.

[466]  In *RCC v. Salaried Persons Postal Loans Ltd* [2006] STC 1315 (Ch) it was held that a corporation that merely rented premises was not carrying on a business for the purposes of this rule.

were.[467] This situation is now relieved by section 27 as amended in 2011. Two corporations are associated only if there is 'substantial commercial interdependence' between them.[468]

**Differentiation**  Corporate tax rates may vary depending on the type of activity in which a corporation engages. Both the UK and the US provide examples of differentiation in an effort to prevent perceived abuses of their progressive corporate tax rates. The UK's small profits rate is not available for a 'close investment-holding company' or a non-resident corporation.[469] 'Close investment-holding company' is a subset of 'close company', which was discussed earlier at 1.1.5.2. A close investment-holding company is a close company that

> exists wholly or mainly for the purpose of carrying on a trade or trades on a commercial basis [or] for the purpose of making investments in land, or estates or interests in land, in cases where the land is, or is intended to be, let commercially.[470]

So, close investment-holding companies are taxed at the headline corporate tax rate on all of their profits. Originally, this was designed to prevent individuals from sheltering passive investment income from higher rates of tax. As the main rate of corporation tax has decreased and the gap between the small profits rate and the main corporate tax rate has narrowed, the close investment-holding company regime has become pretty useless in deterring the use of corporations as tax shelters.

By contrast, the US rules are designed to prevent individuals from using corporations as a tax shelter for personal services income. Progressive corporate tax rates do not apply to a 'qualified personal service corporation'. Rather, this type of corporation is taxed at a flat rate of 35% (i.e. the top corporate tax rate equal to the highest personal marginal tax rate).[471]

---

[467]  This was particularly a problem for large professional partnerships, where the partners did not know how many corporations their fellow partners owned. The result was, in effect, that the small profits rate was not available.

[468]  The Corporation Tax Act 2010 (Factors Determining Substantial Commercial Interdependence) Order 2011 outlines the factors to be considered when determining whether there is substantial commercial interdependence.

[469]  CTA 2010 s. 18. Non-resident corporations were discussed at 1.1.2.2. The UK tax administration accepts that the benefit of the small profits rate must be granted to a non-resident corporation if the corporation is resident in a country that has a tax treaty with the UK incorporating a non-discrimination provision.

[470]  CTA 2010 (UK) s. 34.

[471]  IRC (US) s. 11(b)(2).

'Qualified personal service corporation' is defined as a corporation where substantially all its activities involve the performance of professional services and substantially all of the stock of the corporation is held by employees or former employees.[472] The particular services mentioned are those in the 'fields of health, law, engineering, architecture, accounting, actuarial science, performing arts, or consulting'.

This treatment of personal service corporations seems pretty arbitrary – targeted at professions in which the government believes large amounts might be derived and sheltered in corporations to avoid the highest marginal tax rate.[473] For lower tax rate individuals using a corporation in these fields, this treatment can only be unfair. Such individuals are likely to avoid corporations per se and rather use an LLC and the check-the-box regime. Australia and the UK have moved to address this issue in a different manner, by attributing personal services income to the person providing the services. These regimes are discussed further at 1.3.3.3. The important difference with the Australian and UK regimes is that they tax the personal services provider at their marginal rates, producing a result similar to the US check-the-box regime.

**Anti-erosion: alternative minimum tax**    Some countries are concerned that their standard corporate tax base incorporates too many concessions or at least concessions that might be over-exploited. Beginning in 1970, the US introduced the alternative minimum tax to combat the over-use of concessions. Some other countries, though not a dramatic number but including India and Mexico, have enacted rules for a similar purpose.[474] Minimum tax rules vary substantially from country to country. In the US, the alternative minimum tax is calculated by comparing 'tentative minimum tax' with income tax otherwise payable ('regular tax'). If tentative minimum tax is greater, the difference between tentative minimum tax and regular tax is payable as alternative minimum tax.[475] The effect is that a corporation must pay in total the higher of the tentative minimum tax and regular tax.

---

[472] IRC (US) s. 448(d)(2). The stock can be held 'indirectly through 1 or more partnerships, S corporations, or qualified personal service corporations'.

[473] There are other methods that the US tax administration might use to attack this type of corporation, including lifting the corporate veil, assignment of income doctrine, or reallocation under IRC (US) s. 482 (transfer pricing) or s. 269 (corporation acquired for the principal purpose of avoiding federal income tax).

[474] See Income Tax Act, 1961 (India) s. 115JB and Business Flat-Rate Tax Law (*Ley del Impuesto Empresarial a Tasa Única*) (Mexico).

[475] IRC (US) s. 55(a).

For corporations, tentative minimum tax is calculated as 20% of 'alternative minimum taxable income'. The 20% rate is applied after deducting an exempt amount of $40,000 from alternative minimum taxable income.[476] 'Alternative minimum taxable income' is calculated as the regular income tax base subject to specified adjustments, including the addition of certain tax preferences.[477] Corporations with gross receipts not exceeding $7,500,000 (on a three-year average), are exempt from alternative minimum tax.[478] A corporation that pays alternative minimum tax can carry it forward and set it against its regular corporation tax liability of future years. However, the set-off cannot reduce regular corporation tax below the tentative minimum tax amount.[479] In this way, tentative minimum tax is averaged out, and fluctuations between regular tax and tentative minimum tax over a number of years can settle at the overall tentative minimum tax amount.

The purpose of alternative minimum tax is to remove the benefit of preferences in the income tax system. A similar effect can be achieved by restricting dividend relief by reference to profits that have been fully taxed to or tax paid by a corporation. This is referred to as *wash-out* of corporate preferences and is further discussed at 2.4.1.3.

**Anti-deferral: tax on excessive retention**    Historically, when income tax rates were proportionate, distortions as to incorporation, debt versus equity and, typically, retention versus distribution were not substantial. This changed dramatically with the introduction of progressive income tax for individuals, especially around the time of the First World War. The situation was aggravated when classical systems became popular in the 1930s and 40s.[480] In the face of high progressive tax rates for individuals, the result was a massive incentive for retaining profits in a corporation (i.e. the corporate tax shelter problem). As a result, many countries, including the UK and the US, introduced rules to prevent excessive retention by corporations, which was viewed as a means of avoiding shareholder tax. Originally, these rules allocated undistributed profits of corporations to shareholders for the purposes of imposing progressive taxation (at rates

---

[476] IRC (US) s. 55(b)(1)(B) & (d)(2).
[477] IRC (US) ss. 56–8.
[478] IRC (US) s. 55(e)(1).
[479] IRC (US) s. 53.
[480] The classical system involves the taxation of corporate income when derived and the taxation of distributions without relief for one tax against the other. See the later discussion at 2.3.1.

above the corporate rate).[481] These rules were of a type discussed later at 1.3.3.

Concerned about the constitutionality of the allocation to shareholders, in 1920 the US moved to impose instead an additional tax on corporations that retained profits 'beyond the reasonable needs' of their business.[482] This is the origin of the US accumulated earnings tax. This tax remains despite the repeal of similar provisions in other countries, especially during the income tax rate reductions of the 1980s. The severity of the US accumulated earnings tax has decreased in recent years as a result of the introduction of dividend relief in 2003 (see 2.4.3.2). Indeed, if the accumulated earnings tax were considered part of regular corporation tax, the US system looks much like dividend relief in the form of a split rate system, with a higher corporate tax on retained profits than on distributed profits. However, in form, it is an additional tax on retained profits (not a lower tax on distributed profits), and so it is appropriate to consider it at this point.

Section 531 of IRC imposes, in addition to other corporate taxes, a tax of 15% on the 'accumulated taxable income' of corporations. As is discussed at 2.4.3.2, this is equivalent to the highest rate of tax on dividends paid to resident individuals. Nevertheless, the accumulated earnings tax is a penalty tax; shareholders are still taxable on distributions without credit for any accumulated earnings tax paid with respect to the profits distributed. The tax is still couched in terms of corporations being used for the purpose of avoiding shareholder income tax on distributions.[483] Its imposition has no regard to whether the corporation is widely or closely held. If a corporation retains profits 'beyond the reasonable needs' of its business, the corporation is treated as having an avoidance purpose (unless it proves otherwise). Similarly, the fact that a corporation is a holding or investment corporation is prima facie evidence of the avoidance purpose.[484]

'Accumulated taxable income' is taxable income (subject to certain adjustments) less dividends paid and a standard credit.[485] To be deductible, the dividends must be paid during the tax year in question or before the fifteenth day of the third month of the following tax

[481]    See Harris (1996, p. 105 fn. 282) regarding the original rules in Australia, Canada, the UK and the US.
[482]    Revenue Act of 1921 (US) s. 220.
[483]    IRC (US) s. 532.
[484]    IRC (US) s. 533.
[485]    IRC (US) s. 535(a). Under (b)(1), a deduction is provided for regular corporation tax.

year.[486] The credit is equal to profits retained for the reasonable needs of the corporation's business. There is an aggregate minimum credit of $250,000 ($150,000 for personal service corporations) accumulated from past and present profits.[487] This credit is apportioned equally between members of a 'controlled group of corporations' in the same manner as the progressive tax rate thresholds discussed earlier.[488]

Case law suggests that what is required to determine reasonable business needs is a comparison between a corporation's total liquid assets at the end of the year with its reasonable business needs.[489] The Treasury Regulations outline a number of acceptable grounds for reasonable business needs including business expansion and plant replacement, business acquisition, debt retirement and working capital. Not acceptable are loans to shareholders and related parties and investments in areas not related to business.[490] Most corporations avoid paying accumulated earnings tax by ensuring the distribution of sufficient profits.

The US replaces accumulated earnings tax with an equivalent tax for personal holding companies.[491] A 'personal holding company' is a closely held corporation, and the definition of that phrase was considered earlier at 1.1.5.2. The main difference between accumulated earnings tax and the tax on personal holding companies is that the latter does not incorporate a credit for the reasonable needs of a corporation's business.

### 1.3.3  Taxing owners and controllers

When a corporation derives and retains profits, a country may decide to tax owners and controllers of the corporation with respect to those profits, either in substitution for or as a supplement to taxation of the corporation. In the present context, it is presumed that the corporation has been allocated the income, which has been calculated at the corporate level. Therefore, this subheading is not concerned with situations in which the corporation's identity is collapsed, such as under the US check-the-box regime (see the earlier discussion at 1.1.4.2).[492] However, this subheading

---

[486] IRC (US) ss. 561 & 563.
[487] IRC (US) s. 535(c).
[488] IRC (US) s. 1561.
[489] See Bittker & Eustice (2003–, paras. 7.03 to 7.06).
[490] Title 26 Code of Federal Regulations (US) § 1.537–2.
[491] IRC (US) s. 541.
[492] If the identity of the corporation is collapsed, then the corporation has no income and all activities of the corporation are attributed to its owners and controllers.

does consider some hybrid regimes under which the corporation retains its identity and calculates income for tax purposes, but some of its activities are directly attributed to its owners and controllers.

There are a number of ways in which owners and controllers of a corporation may be attributed income as a result of and taxed with respect to retention by the corporation. There are limitations on the use of each option, and so there are factors to consider in adopting an option. These are the first matters discussed under this subheading. The most common method of allocation is the partnership method, which is the second matter discussed under this subheading. Historically, corporate tax systems were generally concerned about the use of corporations as tax shelters. With increasing support for the idea that capital income should be taxed more lightly than income from labour (see the earlier discussion at 1.3.2.1), some countries have become more focussed on the use of corporations to shelter income from personal services from tax. Attribution of personal services income derived through a corporation is the final matter considered by this subheading.

### 1.3.3.1   Factors and options for allocation

There are three primary options for taxing shareholders with respect to retained profits of their corporation. Each faces different issues, and any of these may be used as a substitute or supplement for taxation of the corporation.

**Partnership method**    In the context of a realisation-based income tax, the partnership method is the primary method for taxing shareholders with respect to the retained profits of corporations. Profits are determined at the corporate level including according to the usual realisation basis of the income tax. The aggregate profits are then allocated amongst persons according to their respective interests in the corporation (e.g. in proportion to shareholdings). This method raises several conceptual issues and is impractical in certain circumstances.[493]

A first problem is the manner in which the profits are attributed. Shareholders are being allocated and taxed with respect to profits of a corporation before they are distributed. A risk is that profits will subsequently be distributed in a manner different from that in which they were attributed

---

[493]   Generally, see Harris (1996, pp. 110–12) and the references cited therein.

when the profits were derived. This could particularly happen in corporations that have a number of different classes of shares with different rights as to distributions. The result could be the unacceptable situation in which one shareholder pays tax on profits ultimately distributed to another shareholder. For this reason, attribution might be limited to corporations with one class of share; for example, as under the US S corporation regime (discussed later).

Another difficulty is that a shareholder cannot file a tax return until such time as the corporation has determined its profits and set an allocation. This may not be a problem where a single corporation is involved, but it can be unworkable where corporations hold shares in other corporations. Consider the scenario in which A Co holds shares in B Co, which holds shares in C Co, and C Co holds shares in A Co. Allocation could be virtually impossible in such a case, and even if the circular problem is resolved, long chains of corporations holding shares in other corporations might prevent timely filing of shareholder tax returns.

Further issues involve characterisation of the allocation. Shareholder income is typically in the form of dividends, and this income has a singular character. But a corporation may derive many types of income; for example, exempt income, capital gains, foreign income, and so on. Should the allocation to shareholders follow the character of the various types of income derived by the corporation, or should the allocation have a homogeneous character like dividends? If different types of income are to be allocated to shareholders, in what manner should they be apportioned; for example, according to a discretionary or strictly proportionate rule?

Other timing issues arise if shares are transferred during a tax year. Should the corporate profits be allocated to the shareholder who holds shares at the end of the year or be proportionate to all shareholders who held shares during the year? The former approach may be open to manipulation, and the latter may be impossible in widely held corporations where shares change constantly. In some cases, it may be impossible to identify all the relevant former shareholders for purposes of apportionment. Other issues are caused by potential adjustments to corporate profits by the tax administration, potentially years after the allocation to shareholders was made. It is not practical to seek to find and make adjustments to the tax returns of all former shareholders, and yet it may be unfair to adjust the tax liabilities of current shareholders.

All of these issues mean that the partnership method is only practical in the context of simply structured closely held corporations, of the type often called 'quasi-partnerships'. This is perhaps unsurprising. Part of the reason for the facilitation of registered companies in the UK in the 1840s was the difficulty in allocating liability between many and varied partners. Tax is just one form of liability.

One major difference between the registered company and the traditional partnership is the limited liability of the average shareholder. This raises the issue of what should happen if a corporation makes a loss instead of a profit. Should shareholders be allocated losses and deduct them in calculating tax due on other income? It seems somewhat strange to permit shareholders to deduct losses for which they cannot be directly liable. There is a direct analogy here with permitting parent corporations to deduct the losses of subsidiaries under consolidation or group relief (see the earlier discussion at 1.2.3.2). A sound approach is to permit shareholders to deduct losses to the extent of their cost base in the shares in question (see discussion of US S corporation regime at 1.3.3.2).

**By reference to value of shares**    The partnership method has its limitations, particularly with respect to widely held corporations. These limitations can be overcome by focusing on the value of the shares held in the corporation that is retaining profits. Valuing shares in widely held corporations can be straightforward, particularly if the shares are listed on a stock exchange. By comparison, valuing shares in closely held corporations can be particularly difficult and involve substantial compliance costs. Here there is a particular synergy between the partnership method and methods that use the value of shares as a reference point (i.e. the former are more suited to closely held corporations and the latter are more suited to widely held corporations). There are two main methods by which the value of shares may be used to, at least indirectly, tax the retained profits of corporations.

The more targeted method is to tax shareholders on the increase in the value of their shares. The presumption is that the retention of profits by the corporation increases the value of shares in the corporation and so taxing that increase over the span of a year indirectly taxes the retained profits of the corporation. The current scenario presumes only retained profits, but under this approach dividends would be taxed to the shareholder in the same manner as any other income.

Taxing increases in the value of shares does not produce the same results as the partnership method. The partnership method is usually constructed in a fashion that only taxes profits realised at the corporate level. This is not possible if increases in the value of shares are taxed. Shares may increase in value for all sorts of reasons that do not involve the realisation of profits.

Share values take account of changes in prospects for making profits and so have the potential to reflect realised and unrealised gains and losses. Therefore, to tax shareholders on increases in the value of shares would fundamentally alter the scope of the income tax in this context, perhaps in a way that many would view as unacceptable. Nevertheless, there are examples of countries using this method in an international context (see the discussion at 3.2.2.1).

A more obscure method of using share values to tax shareholders with respect to retained profits is used by the Netherlands. The Netherlands adopts a schedular approach to income taxation of individuals, categorising the income of individuals according to 'boxes'. Box III includes income from non-substantial shareholdings. Dividends from such shareholdings are not directly taxable. Rather, income from such shares is calculated as a fixed 4% of the average value of the shares in question for the year.[494] The resulting notional income is taxed at a flat rate of 30% with a general Box III exemption of about €20,000.[495] So far as retained profits are concerned, this tax is levied in addition to an ordinary corporation tax that is largely based on realisations.

Taxation under the Netherlands Box III is not really taxation of retained profits of a corporation, although it may produce that effect. Rather, in substance it is simply the replacement of taxation of income from shares with taxation of the capital value of shares. This is most clearly demonstrated in loss years when, despite a fall in value in the shares, shareholders are still taxed in a positive amount; that is, 1.2% (30% of 4%) of the reduced value of the shares.

Despite all the objections that have been made with respect to this Netherlands system, the system still remains in place after more than twelve years. For many shareholders the system is simple, and for the tax administration, tax is comparatively stable and robust. However, even if the Netherlands views this system as a success, it has not been adopted by any other major economy. At some level, it is diametrically opposed to an exemption for a standard rate of return at the shareholder level (e.g. as used in Norway).[496] Instead of taxing economic rents, the Netherlands Box III only taxes (at the shareholder level) a standard rate of return. Both

---

[494] Income Tax Law (*Wet op de inkomstenbelasting*) (Netherlands) s. 5.2.
[495] Income Tax Law (*Wet op de inkomstenbelasting*) (Netherlands) ss. 2.13 & 5.5, respectively.
[496] Norway does this by providing an exemption for a standard rate of return on shares, referred to as the shielding allowance (*skjermingsfradrag*); Income and Capital Tax Law (*Lov om skatt av formue og inntekt*) (Norway) Art. 10–12.

these systems of shareholder taxation were introduced as a modernisation of traditional income taxation to deal with issues faced from a globalising world. The fact that they produce opposite results demonstrates continuing uncertainty and controversy over the best way to address the taxation of corporate income.

**Capital gains with deferral charge**    The taxation of shareholders with respect to an annual increase in the value of their shares as a method of taxing retained profits of a corporation is objectionable on the basis that it involves the taxation of unrealised gains. This objection can be removed by simply taxing gains on the disposal of shares (dividends would also be taxable). Taxing such gains is unobjectionable even if it involves taxing unrealised gains of the corporation because it does involve taxing a realised gain of the shareholder. However, waiting until a shareholder sells shares before taxing retained corporate profits would involve an unacceptable deferral of taxation and increase the corporate tax shelter problem. This deferral can be addressed by incorporating an interest charge for deferred tax on gains on the disposal of shares. The interest charge is best demonstrated with an example.

Presume that a shareholder holds shares in A Co for five years and makes a gain of 100 on the sale of the shares. This gain must be apportioned over the five years of ownership. This may be done on a simple time apportionment basis, but to be more accurate, perhaps this should be done on the basis of the average value of the shares during each year. Presume that the apportionment is simply 20 gain to each of the five years. Tax payable by the shareholder on each part of the gain would then be worked out for each of the five years. The tax for the first year of holding would be subject to a compound interest charge for the deferral of that tax in years two, three, four and five. The tax attributable to the second year of holding would be subject to a compound interest charge for years three, four and five and so on. The interest charge is intended to remove the benefits of deferral and, therefore, the corporate tax shelter benefit.

Initially, it might seem that to impose a large tax on the gain and, in addition, to impose what might be a substantial interest charge would increase the lock-in effect of the realisation basis income tax. That is, it might be thought that shareholders would not sell their shares because they would not want to incur the tax and the interest. It is often countered that a rational shareholder would understand that there is no point in delaying disposal as the interest charge will increase the longer the shares are held. This may well be, but it is not clear that all shareholders would be so rational. Many may go on holding shares in the hope of avoiding the tax (e.g. as a result of reform, by moving overseas or on death). In any case, the capital gains with interest charge approach is not used as a basic approach in any major economy. However, the US does use it with respect to passive foreign investments, discussed later at 3.2.2.1.

### 1.3.3.2  Partnership method

The US S corporation regime provides a good example of the partnership method of allocating corporate profits to shareholders irrespective of distribution. It was introduced in 1958 to provide greater neutrality between the taxation of small corporations and that of unincorporated businesses. There was a particular bias against the use of corporations during the years when the US adopted a full classical system; that is, full economic double taxation of corporate profits in the hands of corporations and dividends in the hands of shareholders (see the later discussion at 2.3.1). The S corporation regime has always been popular, but is not a complete solution to the distortions of the classical system, as demonstrated by the proliferation of LLCs from the 1980s and the introduction of dividend relief in the US in 2003. Despite those reforms, the S corporation regime remains popular.[497]

The definition of 'small business corporation' was considered earlier at 1.1.5.2. As noted at that point, a small business corporation must not have more than 100 shareholders, who in principle must be individuals and residents, and must not have more than one class of stock. Corporations meeting these requirements may elect to be an S corporation. The election and termination of election are freely available, but once terminated a new election cannot be made for five years from the date of termination unless the tax administration approves.[498] As a consequence of the election, an S corporation is not subject to corporation tax. The S corporation still has to calculate its taxable income, but does so in the same manner as an individual. This means that, in principle, any elections that affect the calculation of the tax base are made by the S corporation.[499] This is very different from the check-the-box regime, where the identity of the corporation disappears and all such calculations and elections would be made at the shareholder level.

---

[497]  In 2008, there were four million S corporations, more than two-thirds the total number of corporations; Internal Revenue Service, *Business Tax* Statistics, available at http://www.irs.gov/taxstats/bustaxstats/index.html, accessed 16 July 2012.

[498]  IRC (US) s. 1362.

[499]  IRC (US) s. 1363.

Shareholders must include in their taxable income their 'pro rata share' of the corporation's taxable income. Determining the 'pro rata share' is simplified by the fact that an S corporation can have only one class of share. Generally, it is the pool of corporate income that is allocated in this way. However, if separate parts of the income might affect the tax liability of a particular shareholder, those parts are allocated separately. The character of any amount included in a shareholder's share is the same as it is in the hands of the corporation. So, for example, the allocated share of a capital gain, dividend or foreign income of the corporation retains that character when allocated to the shareholder.[500] Importantly, this attribution occurs irrespective of distribution. If the share ownership changes during the year, income is generally prorated over the entire year and attributed to the shareholders before and after the change on a time basis.[501] This is workable because an S corporation can have no more than 100 shareholders.

Attribution of income of an S corporation to its shareholders results in adjustments to the cost base of shares held in the corporation. The attribution increases the shareholder's cost base as if the income had been distributed and then reinvested in the corporation.[502] This prevents the risk of double taxation of the shareholder with respect to the same economic gain, discussed later at 5.1.2. Section 1363 of IRC passes losses through to shareholders. These losses reduce the cost basis of the shares.[503] However, a shareholder's loss is limited to the total of the cost base in the shares held and any debt the corporation owes to the shareholder. Any disallowed loss may be carried forward until there is further investment in the corporation; for example, by additional capital contribution or by the recognition of corporate-level income.[504]

### 1.3.3.3   Personal services income

General regimes, such as the US's S corporation regime, may resolve the corporate tax shelter problem – the particular problem of an individual splitting income with a corporation (i.e. causing the corporation to derive income that might otherwise have been derived by the individual). However, such a general regime does not necessarily solve a basic income-splitting problem, such as the splitting of income between two spouses.

---

[500]  IRC (US) s. 1366(a) & (b).
[501]  IRC (US) s. 1377(a) defining 'pro rata share'.
[502]  IRC (US) s. 1367(a)(1). Distributions reduce the cost base of the shares.
[503]  IRC (US) s. 1367(a)(2).
[504]  IRC (US) s. 1366(d)(1).

Income splitting between spouses (or other relatives) may be achieved directly, but corporations can facilitate income splitting indirectly. Not only may a controlled corporation employ a spouse but also the spouse may be issued shares in the corporation and so be entitled to a share of corporate profits. An attribution regime such as the S corporation regime does not alter an income shift achieved in this way. Without more, it will allocate income to both spouses (because they both hold shares) irrespective of comparative contributions to the corporation.

Generally, income splitting may be addressed by selecting the family as the tax unit. If the individual is the tax unit, income splitting can also be addressed by case law, such as the assignment of income doctrine in the US, or alternately, a country might have a general anti-income-splitting rule, such as in Canada and the UK.[505] These rules commonly accept that income from an outright transfer of assets from one spouse to another spouse is effective in transferring income for tax purposes. What is not accepted is that contractual arrangements can transfer income from personal services from one person to a related person (i.e. income from personal services is inalienable, unlike income from assets). However, use of a corporation may circumvent this inalienability. In the absence of effective transfer pricing rules between an individual and a controlled corporation (see the earlier discussion at 1.2.2), an individual may work for such a corporation at below market value. This would make the corporation more profitable, and those profits (attributable to the individual's personal services) may be distributed to a spouse or other relative who holds shares in the corporation.[506]

Therefore, personal services corporations pose two types of problems for governments. One is the incentive to derive income and retain it in the corporation to avoid higher levels of individual taxation. The second is the ability to use a corporation to split personal services income between related parties in a way that would not be accepted if a direct income split were attempted. A general attribution regime such as the S corporation regime may address the first problem, but requires more to address the second. Some countries have attempted to address both problems in the

---

[505] Generally, see Ault & Arnold (2010, pp. 326–30). The US case law follows *Lucas* v. *Earl* (1930) 281 US 111 (SC). Income Tax Act (Canada) s. 74.1 is a general rule to prevent income splitting between spouses or between individuals and related minors by way of 'transfer of property'. Similarly, the UK settlement rules may prevent income splitting, but appear to be narrower; ITTOIA 2005 (UK) Part 5 Chapter 5.

[506] For a classic example of such an arrangement, see *Jones* v. *Garnett* [2007] UKHL 35 (HL). Generally, see Harris & Oliver (2008).

context of a regime specifically targeted at the provision of personal services through a corporation or other intermediary. The UK and Australia provide examples.[507]

Attribution under the US's S corporation regime is supplemented with a special rule targeted at reallocating attributions between family members. Section 1366(e) of IRC provides as follows:

> If an individual who is a member of the family...of one or more shareholders of an S corporation renders services for the corporation or furnishes capital to the corporation without receiving reasonable compensation therefore, the Secretary shall make such adjustments in the items taken into account by such individual and such shareholders as may be necessary in order to reflect the value of such services or capital.

This is effectively a transfer pricing rule targeted at preventing income splitting of remuneration for personal services between family members through the use of S corporations.[508]

The UK rules apply where an individual personally performs services for another person (the 'client') through a corporation (or other third party) and 'if the services were provided...directly...the worker would be regarded...as an employee of the client'.[509] This rule is peculiarly narrow in being limited to a hypothetical employment scenario. It therefore incorporates all the difficulties of determining whether or not a person is an employee, and it seeks to apply those tests in the context of a hypothetical.[510] These rules were particularly concerned with the outsourcing phenomenon[511] and the risk that it poses to the yield of the wage withholding tax.[512]

---

[507] Both the UK and Australia have particular problems with corporate tax shelters stemming from the gap between the highest individual marginal rate and the corporate tax rate. In the UK, the gap can be in excess of 30% (if National Insurance Contributions are included). In Australia, the gap is 18%.

[508] Generally, see Bittker & Eustice (2003–, para. 6.06[6]) and the references cited therein.

[509] ITEPA 2003 (UK) s. 49(1).

[510] For examples of UK courts grappling with this issue, see *Usetech Ltd* v. *Young (HMIT)* [2004] STC 1671 (Ch) and *Dragonfly Consultancy Ltd* v. *RCC* [2008] EWHC 2113 (Ch). In the latter case the court held that a right in the services contract to substitute the individual services provider pointed towards self-employment rather than employment, but was not necessarily determinative (and was not on the facts).

[511] Employers seek to avoid strict laws on employees' rights by transferring former employees to independent agencies and requiring the employees to provide their services through a corporation. The former employees then seek to access the potential tax benefits associated with the new structure. For an example of this practice in the UK where the Court of Appeal held the individual was still an employee, see *Muscat* v. *Cable & Wireless plc* [2006] EWCA Civ 220 (CA).

[512] The wage withholding tax is typically the most significant proportion of income taxation. For example, in the UK for 2011/12 it accounted for more than 87% of all income

This can be contrasted with the Australian rules, which rather adopt a broad rule and then specify exceptions. These rules provide that an individual must include in taxable income any 'personal services income' that another entity (a 'personal services entity') gains from the individual's personal services.[513] 'Personal services income' is defined by reference to income that is 'mainly a reward for your personal efforts or skills'.[514] The rules do not apply where the corporation conducts a personal services business or promptly pays wages.[515]

In outline, the 'personal services business' test is met if 75% of the personal services income is for producing a result, tools are not supplied by the services acquirer and the corporation or services provider is liable for rectification of defects.[516] There is also a personal services business where the corporation has two or more clients that are not associated with the corporation as a result of general advertising. Alternately, the corporation must have independent employees who perform at least 20% of the work of the corporation. The test can also be met by the corporation having an independent and exclusive business premises.[517]

Where the UK rules apply, the service provider may be treated as receiving a payment from the corporation as employment income.[518] This is important because it means that wage withholding and national insurance contributions apply to the deemed payment. The service provider or an associate must have a 'material interest' in the corporation, defined as 5% of ordinary share capital.[519] The amount of the deemed payment can be as much as 95% of the payments made by the client to the corporation.[520] The corporation itself is not treated as transparent. It still has profits and those profits are still liable to corporation tax. Rather, items in the calculation of those profits (i.e. payments received from the client) are treated as

---

tax receipts (exclusive of corporation tax) or about 30% of all tax receipts. See HMRC, *National Statistics*, available at http://www.hmrc.gov.uk/thelibrary/national-statistics.htm, accessed 16 July 2012. In Germany, wage withholding accounts for about 25% of tax receipts; see Ault & Arnold (2010, p. 69).

[513] Income Tax Assessment Act 1997 (Australia) s. 86–15(1).

[514] Income Tax Assessment Act 1997 (Australia) s. 84–5(1).

[515] Income Tax Assessment Act 1997 (Australia) s. 86–15(3) & (4).

[516] These factors are similar to those used by many countries in determining whether an individual is an employee.

[517] Income Tax Assessment Act 1997 (Australia) Division 87.

[518] ITEPA 2003 (UK) s. 50(1).

[519] ITEPA 2003 (UK) s. 51. 'Associate' is defined in s. 60 by reference to CTA 2010 (UK) s. 448, as to which, see earlier discussion at 1.1.5.1.

[520] ITEPA 2003 (UK) s. 54.

having been paid to the individual. The Australian regime operates similarly, although more expressly.[521]

Tax planners soon found ways to circumvent these UK rules. In particular, unrelated service providers grouped together in a single corporation controlled and managed by a professional, typically a tax advisor. This 'managed service company' structure is now subject to separate anti-abuse rules, discussed later at 2.2.1.4. With such a substantial gap between the taxation of employment income and the taxation of income derived through a corporation, the UK's difficulties seem certain to continue.[522] By contrast, the UK government seems to have no appetite for dealing with the use of corporations to shelter other types of income from higher progressive tax rates. The result is a form of indirect differentiation by which individuals with employment income are subject to greater taxation than other types of income.

---

[521] Income Tax Assessment Act 1997 (Australia) s. 86–30 effectively reduces the corporation's income by the amount attributed to the service provider.

[522] After the government rejected abolition of these rules and further legislative reform, the tax administration responded with draft guidance, see HMRC (2012b).

# 2

# Taxation of corporate income when distributed

The title of this chapter suggests that what is a distribution is driven by the concept of corporate income. However, at a primary level the opposite may be suggested (i.e. the concept of corporate income may be driven or at least refined by the concept of a distribution of corporate income). As explained in the introduction, payments are the building blocks of the income tax base. Payments received are taken into account, and payments made are deducted in calculating taxable income. If a corporation is viewed as a separate entity, then dividends (distributions of corporate profits) are clearly a payment made by a corporation.[1] Normally, corporations seek expensing (deduction) treatment for payments made, and if a corporation is viewed as independent of its shareholders, dividends are, at some level, an expense.

However, if a corporation is identified more closely with its owners and controllers, dividends are a division of net profits. For this reason, distributions are not deductible when calculating accounting profits and, as a general rule, a corporation's taxable income. This means that many payments made – in particular, interest expense – are deductible in calculating income, but payments made in the form of dividends are not deductible. Accordingly, it is necessary to identify particular payments as dividends before taxable income can be definitively calculated.

That dividends are not deductible reveals two important features of dividends. First, it is important to identify dividends because, as payments made by corporations, dividends are singled out for special tax treatment. That is, they are a prime example of the *character* of a payment being particularly important for the purposes of determining tax consequences. Second, any attempt to identify dividends as a distribution of corporate income results in circularity. Corporate income cannot be calculated without identifying which payments are not deductible (i.e. which payments

---

[1] 'Dividends' and 'distributions of corporate income / profits' are used interchangeably in this book. The term 'dividend' is further discussed at 2.2.1.

are dividends). A tax law must be capable of identifying dividends independently of the calculation of corporate income. So how should a tax law identify dividends, and what test should it use?

The identification of dividends is another area where tax law overlaps with corporate law. As with the calculation of corporate profits, an initial question is whether tax law should simply adopt the corporate law position in identifying dividends. For example, the UK's Companies Act 2006 defines 'distribution' to mean 'every description of distribution of a company's assets to its members, whether in cash or otherwise'.[2] The Act proceeds to prescribe that a 'company may only make a distribution out of profits available for the purpose' and then defines available profits.[3] These corporate law rules reveal the two main difficulties in identifying dividends: determining who is a 'member' and what is a 'distribution' of 'company assets' 'out of profits'.[4]

It is often suggested that the corporate law identification of dividends is too formal to be accepted for tax law purposes. No doubt, corporate law, as revealed in the UK provisions, has broadened in recent years, particularly because of influence from the EU. However, corporate law still struggles in identifying members and in dealing with constructive dividends, which typically involve the interception of corporate income before the corporation derives it. These areas cause more acute problems for a corporate tax system than they do for corporate law purposes. Dividends are highly fungible or substitutable with other types of payments made by corporations, particularly with payments of interest. Because dividends are taxed differently from those other payments, there is a high risk that taxpayers will arbitrage the tax treatment of dividends, and the corporate law prescription provides little protection against their doing so.

As an alternative, it is often suggested that a substance approach be adopted with respect to identifying dividends for tax purposes. The debate

---

[2] Companies Act 2006 (UK) s. 829.
[3] Companies Act 2006 (UK) s. 830.
[4] The position in Germany is similar. AktG (Germany) s. 57(3) provides that, before the dissolution of a corporation, only profits may be distributed to shareholders. As discussed earlier at 1.2.1, in the US under the MBCA or the DGCL there is no prescription to record profits or that dividends are only distributable out of profits. However, MBCA (US) s. 1.40(6) defines 'distribution' as 'a direct or indirect transfer of money or other property (except its own shares) or incurrence of indebtedness by a corporation to or for the benefit of its shareholders in respect of any of its shares'. Further, MBCA (US) s. 6.40(d) is permissive in the sense that '[t]he board of directors may base a determination that a distribution is not prohibited ... on financial statements prepared on the basis of accounting practices and principles'. There are no equivalents in DGCL.

then moves to how such an approach might be formulated. As mentioned, there is little utility in seeking to formulate such an approach by reference to a right to corporate profits, because this creates a circularity issue. Rather, the approach must be to focus on the nature of the rights with respect to which a particular payment is made, assuming that the concept of payment is defined broadly. So a dividend is a payment made to a person holding rights similar to those of a typical shareholder. As this chapter discusses, seeking to identify those rights with any particularity is extremely difficult.

The issues faced when a corporation derives income are in many ways encountered when a corporation distributes that income. As noted in the introduction, corporate income is peculiar in that it is treated as income twice: once when it is derived and again when it is distributed. This peculiarity of dual derivation is caused by the artificial nature of the corporation. There are two elements to this artificiality that produce dual derivation. These can be illustrated by a simple example.

Presume an individual conducts a business through a corporation. If the corporation were ignored, the individual would be viewed as conducting the business. Inserting a corporation between the individual and the business triggers two elements of artificiality. The first involves treating the corporation as conducting the business and deriving the income from it. Here the artificiality exists in allocating the activity and payments made and received in the course of that activity to the corporation instead of the individual. The source of income (the business) is real, but the person treated as deriving it is artificial (the corporation).

The situation is reversed on distribution. Here the person deriving the income (the individual) is real, but the source of the income is artificial (the membership rights with respect to which the distributions are made). Accordingly, just as the first heading of the first chapter was concerned with identifying the first artificiality (identifying corporations), the first heading of this chapter is concerned with identifying the source of distributions. That is, the first heading of this chapter is concerned with classifying rights held against corporations and identifying membership rights as a class of corporate rights. As the discussion in the book presumes (unless stated otherwise) a simple registered corporation with freely transferable shares, these membership rights are referred to as shares or share interests.

Once shares have been identified, it is still necessary to identify which payments received by a person owning shares should be considered as made with respect to those shares. Payments received by a person with respect to shares are referred to as 'dividends' or 'distributions'. The manner in which distributions are identified for tax purposes is discussed under the second heading of this chapter. Once shares have been identified, the identification of distributions with respect to those shares involves two primary elements. The first is a nexus issue of identifying a particular payment with the shares in question such that the shares can be said to be the source of the payment. The second issue is one of identifying the type of payments that may constitute a distribution.

The identification of distributions involves identifying the tax base of the shareholder. This is analogous to identifying the corporate tax base under the second heading of Chapter 1. Once a shareholder has been identified as deriving a distribution, the final issue is the tax treatment of the shareholder with respect to the distribution. This is considered under the third, fourth and fifth headings of this chapter, which are analogous to the tax treatment of income derived by a corporation under the third heading of Chapter 1.

However, the main issue under that heading was whether to tax the corporation with respect to its income and if so at what rate. In contrast, the main issue under the third, fourth and fifth headings of this chapter is how the tax treatment of the shareholder should be adjusted, if at all, on the presumption that the profits that have been distributed were already taxed when derived in the hands of the distributing corporation. The discussion under the third heading considers the dual nature of corporate income (i.e. the fact that it is both income of the corporation when derived and income of the shareholder when distributed). This dual nature leads to the potential for economic double taxation (classical system). The third heading analyses the arguments for and against such double taxation (i.e. it discusses the main forms of distortion that are often attributed to the classical system).

The fourth heading of this chapter considers how economic double taxation may be relieved at the point that corporate income is distributed (i.e. dividend relief). Dividend relief may take various forms, each of which involves varying degrees of distortion and/or complexity. Not all distributions made by corporations to shareholders receive the same tax treatment, irrespective of whether dividend relief is adopted. At a minimum, returns of capital are taxed differently from profit distributions. Corporate tax systems that treat different distributions differently necessarily get involved in reconciling the difference between the taxation of corporate income in the hands of the corporation with the taxation of distributions in the hands of shareholders. The final heading of this chapter considers these reconciliation issues.

## 2.1 Classifying corporate rights

This heading is concerned with identifying membership rights in a corporation as a class of corporate rights. In particular, it is concerned with identifying the source of distributions of corporate income. In the context of a corporation limited by shares, this heading is concerned with who is a shareholder for tax purposes. In the context of other types of corporation, it is appropriate to speak of 'membership rights'. The classification of corporate rights as membership rights or shares is a generic issue for a corporate tax system. It is critical for purposes of characterising payments made by corporations as distributions of corporate profits. However, it is important in other circumstances as well.

Identifying shares is also critical in characterising dealings in corporate rights. The tax treatment of a creation, transfer or termination of shares might be different from the tax treatment of dealings in other corporate rights. These are matters discussed in Chapters 4–7. Identifying shares or rights typically attached to shares is also critical in identifying the special relationship between a corporation and a person holding rights in the corporation. These relationships were discussed earlier at 1.1.3 and 1.1.5. The owners of membership rights or shares are the 'owners' of the artificial construct that is the corporation. Through these rights a person may be able to control a corporation. Therefore, identifying shares is critical in determining, for example, whether two corporations are members of a group of corporations. Typically, identifying shares is critical wherever an income tax law seeks to reinforce or erode the separate identity of a corporation.

An important policy issue is whether 'shares' should be identified differently depending on the tax rule in question. In the context of classifying corporations by reference to ownership and control, examples were provided using ordinary share capital, value of shares, rights to distribution, voting power and, simply, control as the test. The first two of these examples require identification of shares as a holistic unit. The latter three are individual rights that may be attached to shares or, in the case of control, be held independently of shares. So a first issue is whether shares are identified holistically or whether the focus is on the individual rights attaching to shares.

Shares are commonly identified holistically as an item of property,[5] but at another level shares are fundamentally an amalgam of rights. There are

---

[5] For example, '[s]hares means the units into which the proprietary interests in a corporation are divided'; MBCA (US) s. 1.40(22). See also Companies Act 2006 (UK) s. 541.

three types of rights or features typically attached to shares or member-ship of a corporation. The first is an investment in a corporation and the assumption of entrepreneurial risk with respect to that investment. This type of investment is usually in the form of 'share capital', but that phrase has particular meaning in the context of corporations limited by shares. The broader phrase 'equity capital' refers to both share capital and accu-mulated profits. The touchstone of this feature of shares is the subordina-tion of any claim with respect to shares (capital or return on capital) to creditors of the corporation. This means an investment in shares is typi-cally for an indefinite period and that on termination of the corporation creditors are paid before anything is paid on the shares.

The second feature of shares is a return on investment that varies with the profitability or performance of the corporation. This is a right to a share of divided profits of the corporation and any surplus left if the cor-poration is terminated. The third feature of shares is the right to participate in the organs of the corporation (see the earlier discussion at 1.1.3.1). This is, at a minimum, a right to participate and vote in the general meeting of members of the corporation. If a majority of voting rights is held, this right to participate will extend to the right to appoint management, although a right to participate in management may be directly attached to shares.

The other primary form of investment in a corporation is debt capital (i.e. a loan or debenture), and debt capital is commonly distinguished from equity capital. The rights typically attached to debt capital may be con-trasted with those attaching to shares. Debt capital is for a limited period, and there is no subordination to other creditors; that is, debt capital (and the return thereon) usually ranks pari passu with other unsecured cred-itors, although it is often secured. Debt capital is entitled to a fixed peri-odic return (interest) calculated as a rate by the effluxion of time, which is payable regardless of whether the corporation makes a profit. However, debt capital confers no right to participate in the organs of a corporation, either at general meeting or in management.

Corporate tax systems focus on different parts of these features depend-ing on the purposes for which shares need to be identified. For exam-ple, rules that reinforce the separate identity of the corporation, such as transfer pricing rules (see the earlier discussion at 1.2.2), tend to focus on the ability to manipulate pricing in transactions with a corporation (control), irrespective of form of manipulation. By contrast, the rules eroding the separate identity of a corporation are more likely to focus on shares holistically, but then reinforce substance by ensuring that the rele-vant percentage is held of each of the rights attaching to shares. In some cases, the reinforcement may only refer to particular rights perceived as most important in the context of the rule in question. So, in the context of group loss relief (see 1.2.3.2), the primary test of owning share capital (or value of share capital) is backed up with a voting test to ensure that there is both substantial ownership and control.

What should be the focus in the context of identifying dividends? Should the focus be holistically on shares, and if so, should tax law follow the manner in which corporate law identifies shares? Or should tax law focus on particular rights attaching to shares? This is the first matter discussed under this subheading. Most tax laws do not accept corporate law identification of shares. Tax law may specifically override the corporate law classification of an instrument or may characterise the return on a particular instrument as dividends, even though the instrument is not a share. The discussion proceeds to consider three circumstances in which corporate law classification may be overridden.

The rights typically attaching to shares and those attaching to debt are the ends of a spectrum. A corporation may create an instrument that is not clearly shares and not clearly debt but rather falls into the grey area between these two extremes. It does so by attaching to the instrument some rights that are consistent with shares and some rights that are more consistent with a debt instrument. These are 'hybrid' instruments because they are not clearly shares and not clearly debt. Nevertheless, a corporation mixing rights attached to a hybrid instrument will put a label on the instrument (i.e. as either shares or debt). Commonly, such labels are accepted by corporate law, and so, if corporate law classification were accepted, there would be substantial scope for tax arbitrage between shares and debt. Therefore many tax laws override corporate law classification of at least some hybrid instruments. This is considered under the second subheading.

The first and second subheadings look at instruments individually. When looked at in this fashion, a corporation may clearly have issued debt or equity. However, when the overall financing of a corporation is considered, this distinction may not be so clear. There may be an imbalance that causes the tax law to override the corporate law classification of some part of the financing. This imbalance particularly arises in the context of excessive debt financing, discussed under the third subheading. Here, the volume of debt financing when compared to equity financing calls into question the substance of the rights attaching to the excessive part of the debt. If the debt-to-equity ratio is too high, in substance the rights attached to the excessive debt might behave more like equity capital than debt capital.

Corporations issue multiple financial instruments. Often there is more than a casual relationship between instruments, and this relationship may be taken into consideration in classifying the instruments for tax purposes. Two or more instruments may be so related that tax law classifies those instruments as a single instrument for tax purposes. Similarly, features that might typically be incorporated in separate instruments might be amalgamated into one combined instrument, in which case tax law might fragment the combined instrument into two instruments. Amalgamation and fragmentation of corporate instruments are the final matter dealt with under this heading.

### 2.1.1  Identification of membership rights with corporate profits

The issue for discussion is the manner in which membership rights are identified for purposes of determining the source of dividends under a corporate tax system. Sometimes the two issues, the source and the income from the source, are conflated and the tax law simply taxes 'dividends'. Nevertheless, in characterising a payment received as a dividend, courts will look to the source of the rights with respect to which the payment is made (i.e. there will be an implicit reference to membership rights). Often, however, a tax law refers to 'shares' or similar rights. This is clear in the context of corporations limited by shares, but is not so appropriate in the context of corporations that do not have capital divided into shares, especially unincorporated associations that might be treated as corporations for tax purposes (see the earlier discussion at 1.1.1.1).

Another issue regarding the identification of shares involves the interface between the corporate tax base and the personal tax base (discussed earlier at 1.2.5). Corporate law often provides a direct interface between the identification of corporate profits and the identification of shares. So, as noted earlier, under the UK's Companies Act 2006 'distribution' is defined by reference to 'members', and there is a prohibition on making distributions except out of corporate profits. 'Member' of a company is defined in terms of a 'person...whose name is entered in its register of members'.[6] In the context of corporations limited by shares, the

---

[6] Companies Act 2006 (UK) s. 112.

register lists the holders of shares.[7] The position in Germany is similar. '[S]hareholders are only those who are entered as such in the share register'.[8] The same is true in the US under the MBCA; the definition of 'distribution' refers to 'shareholders', which is defined as 'the person in whose name shares are registered in the records of a corporation'.[9]

In a typical corporation limited by shares, it is the shareholders who are entitled to the corporate profits, and what they are entitled to is defined by reference to the manner in which profits are calculated for corporate law purposes. As noted earlier at 1.2.1, a corporation's profits for tax law purposes will not equal its profits for corporate law purposes. For corporate law purposes, corporate profits match the shareholders' entitlement to distributions. A corporate tax system cannot simply achieve a similar match. Because the corporate tax base does not equal profits for accounting purposes, there is no particular type of interest in a corporation (similar to members in corporate law) that is entitled to distributions of profits as calculated under tax law. Tax law breaks the logic between corporate profits and shares. As a consequence, it is not clear on what basis a tax law should identify the source of distributions of corporate profits (i.e. how it should identify shares or membership rights).

Some countries do make reference to shares or other membership rights in subjecting distributions of corporate profits to tax. Others only refer to the profit distribution itself. The UK provides an example of the latter approach. It has a comprehensive definition of 'distribution' of a company.[10] Item A of this definition includes 'any dividend paid by the company'. There is no reference to any interest in the company with respect to which the dividend must be paid. Considering the width of the definition of 'company', which includes unincorporated associations (see the earlier discussion at 1.1.1.1), this lack of reference is understandable. However, the UK doctrine of source suggests that there must be at least an implicit right with respect to which a dividend is paid; otherwise the payment would be a simple gift. The UK reference to 'dividends' presumes a calculation of profits and that the payment is made as a division of those profits. These presumptions can be particularly narrow, as is illustrated at

---

[7] Companies Act 2006 (UK) s. 113(3).
[8] AktG (Germany) s. 67(2).
[9] MBCA (US) s. 1.40(21). The position is more obscure under DGCL, but it does define 'stockholder', at least indirectly, by reference to the person entered in the stock ledger; DGCL (US) s. 220(a)(1) together with s. 219(c).
[10] CTA 2010 (UK) s. 1000.

various points in this book. However, it is also broad in the sense that a person may be in receipt of a dividend despite not having what might be described as a membership interest.[11]

The CCCTB proposal adopts a similar approach. It refers to 'dividends and other profits distributions' without reference to the corporate rights with respect to which such payments are made.[12] There is no definition of these terms, and so the approach is similar to that taken in the Parent-Subsidiary Directive.[13] The Australian approach is also similar in that it has a definition of 'dividend' and so 'dividend' takes its ordinary meaning.[14]

By contrast, the German income tax law refers to 'shares of profits (dividends), income and other benefits from shares' and other specified corporate rights.[15] The rights referred to largely follow interests in the entities that are subject to corporation tax, and so commercial law classification is followed. Like the other approaches, however, it is a right to share in 'profits' that is the primary determinative factor.

The US approach is different again in that it refers to the investor in the corporation rather than the investment that is the source of dividends. 'Dividend' is defined to mean 'any distribution of property made by a corporation to its shareholders . . . out of its earnings and profits'.[16] 'Shareholder' is undefined. If the term 'shareholder' were to take a technical meaning, this would be unduly restrictive, especially considering the width of the definition of 'corporation' (i.e. would only cover entities that issue shares). As a result, case law takes a substance approach to what is a shareholder and what are shares. This is discussed in more detail later.

In each of these cases, it is either explicit or implicit that a dividend must be paid in fulfilment of a right to receive 'profits'. But what does the term 'profits' mean in this regard? It does not mean specifically a right to receive profits as calculated for the purposes of the corporate tax base. In the UK, Germany and under the CCCTB Proposal, it seems inevitable that it means 'profits' as normally understood (i.e. by reference to accounting practices), although this meaning is not stated explicitly.

---

[11]   For example, see *AW Walker and Co* v. *CIR* [1920] 3 KB 648 (KB) and *CIR* v. *The Mashona-land Railway Co, Ltd* (1926) 12 TC 1159 (KB). Contrast, *IRC* v. *Pullman Car Co Ltd* [1954] 2 All ER 491 (ChD).

[12]   CCCTB Proposal Art. 4(8).

[13]   Council Directive 90/435/EEC of 23 July 1990.

[14]   Income Tax Assessment Act 1936 (Australia) s. 6(1).

[15]   EStG (Germany) s. 20(1)1.

[16]   IRC (US) s. 316(a)

In the US, earnings and profits have a particular tax law meaning. The IRC sets out some rules for determining earnings and profits, but there is a lot left unsaid.[17] These gaps are filled by the Treasury Regulations, which provide more general rules for determining earnings and profits.[18] Although accounting is important in determining earnings and profits, it is not determinative. Accordingly, "earnings and profits" form a concept peculiar to the income tax law. This concept is similar, but not the same as accounting profits, and is very different from a corporation's taxable income. However, this peculiarity has little impact on the meaning of 'shareholder'.

### 2.1.2 Hybrid instruments

Fixation on a right to a division of corporate profits is not a substantive test of who is a 'shareholder' or member and, as discussed earlier, involves an element of circularity. On this test corporate profits have to be identified so as to determine who is a shareholder, and yet corporate profits cannot be identified until the rights of shareholders have been determined. Corporate profits are determined after accounting for expenses, and expenses are largely a matter of formality (i.e. the payment by the corporation made out of net profits or not). If tax law accepted this formality, taxpayers would largely be able to choose whether to receive interest or dividends by structuring the form of instruments they hold in a corporation. So long as there are substantial differences between the taxation of the return on debt and that on equity, this gives rise to the potential for unacceptable tax arbitrage. The situation would be worse if corporate law were followed and shareholder was identified solely with a person entered on the register of shareholders.[19]

The only way for tax law to break the formality and circularity between profits and shares in profits and registered and unregistered members is to address the question of who in substance is a shareholder. And the only way of engaging with this question is to consider the various rights that typically attach to shares. These were discussed earlier at 2.1. Clearly, the simultaneous existence of subordination, rights to profits and surplus

---

[17] IRC (US) s. 312.

[18] Title 26 Code of Federal Regulations (US) §§ 1.312–1 to 1.312–15 and particularly 1.312–6.

[19] For a comprehensive comparative analysis of the debt / equity divide, see Schoen et al. (2009). See also International Fiscal Association (2012).

and participation in the organs of a corporation would constitute a particular instrument to be in substance a share. The problem arises with hybrids that demonstrate only some of the features of shares. Determining whether a hybrid instrument is in substance a share or, for example, debt raises the question as to whether some of the typical features of a share are more important than others.

In the context of an income tax, which focuses on returns from assets, it might be suggested that a rate of return varying with performance of a corporation and subordination, and so with capital risk associated with the investment in the corporation, are the most important. But just as there is a spectrum with respect to debt on the one hand and shares on the other, there is a spectrum associated with rates of return and risk. The rate of return with respect to ordinary shares in a 'blue chip' corporation may hardly vary at all, the consistency supporting the share price. In contrast, the rate of return from an investment in a corporation engaged in high-risk activity may vary dramatically with those risks. Indeed, in many cases there will be substantially more risk involved in holding straight debt in one corporation compared with holding shares in another.

Given the broad range of shareholder types, there may be no such thing as a typical or standard shareholder. As a matter of practicality, income tax laws must accept as a starting point commercial law characterisation of assets and transactions. It is not surprising that countries typically accept this starting point in classifying debt and shares for tax purposes. Most tax laws then proceed to re-characterise debt and shares or the returns thereon in isolated cases by reference to the substance of the investment in question. So there are two scenarios that require consideration: situations in which an instrument that is debt in form is treated as equity and those in which an instrument that is equity in form is treated as debt. Each is considered in turn.

### 2.1.2.1  Debt instruments

An instrument may be debt in form and yet incorporate substantial features of equity. Two primary examples of this are profit-sharing debentures and convertible notes (debentures). Profit-sharing debentures most clearly incorporate a return varying with the performance of the issuing corporation. However, in other respects, they may incorporate debt-like features. The return of capital investment may rank equally with other debt, there may be no right to share in surplus on a winding up and there is unlikely to be any right to participate in the organs of the corporation. By contrast, convertible notes may behave like debt, but the underlying value of the investment is determined by reference to the shares into which the notes can be converted. Tax laws adopt widely different approaches as to how they treat hybrid debt instruments.

The German approach is quite formal and restricted. As mentioned earlier, profit shares and dividends are identified with shares and certain other corporate rights as classified under commercial law.[20] However, in addition to these formal equity instruments, dividends may also be identified with 'profit participation rights'. This only happens where the rights grant both a 'right to profits and liquidation proceeds'.[21] Accordingly, profit-sharing debentures with a right to surplus on liquidation are treated as equity, but those without a liquidation right are treated in accordance with their form (i.e. as debt and the return thereon as interest). Typically, the treatment of convertible notes also follows their form. In extreme cases, the German concept of 'hidden profit distribution' might have some application to hybrids, but it is most commonly used in the context of constructive dividends to shareholders, discussed later at 2.2.2.[22]

The CCCTB Proposal is even less prescriptive when it comes to hybrid instruments. There is no attempt to deal with hybrid instruments, which, it seems, would be classified for tax purposes according to their form. This position seems to be accepted by the general anti-abuse rule, which generally prescribes respect for 'genuine commercial activities'.[23] Further, this position seems to be confirmed by the definition of 'interest' for purposes of the thin capitalisation rule, which essentially follows the same definition in the OECD Model. It specifically includes 'income from debt-claims...whether or not carrying a right to participate in the debtor's profits'.[24]

---

[20] Fischer & Lohbeck (2012, p. 308) describe the approach as follows: 'With respect to classification as debt or equity for tax purposes, the commercial treatment according to German generally accepted accounting principles (GAAP) is decisive due to the legal principle that tax accounting should be based on commercial accounting, whereby instruments which assume liability towards the creditors are treated as equity, all other instruments as debt'. The legal principle referred to is that in EStG (Germany) s. 5(1), discussed earlier at 1.2.1.

[21] EStG (Germany) s. 20(1)1. Schoen et al. (2009, pp. 39–40) identify these rights as 'jouissance' rights. They suggest that there is no need to share in losses, but the right must pertain to net value, profit of a single branch or dividends paid to shareholders rather than to turnover or other gross figures. Further, redemption at liquidation, rather than a share in the liquidation itself, is sufficient.

[22] Generally regarding the German approach to classification as debt or equity, see Fischer & Lohbeck (2012, pp. 315–19).

[23] CCCTB Proposal Art. 80.

[24] CCCTB Proposal Art. 81(2). This definition would disappear with the EU Presidency amendments.

As mentioned earlier, the US IRC contains no definition of 'shareholder' for the purposes of section 316. However, US courts apply a substance approach to the classification of an investment as debt or equity. The approach of the courts is to take into account various characteristics of the investment in question to determine whether on balance the instrument is debt or equity. The case law is vast.[25] Some of the main factors that courts consider are set out in section 385(b) of IRC:

(1) whether there is a written unconditional promise to pay on demand or a specified date a sum certain in money in return for an adequate consideration in money or money's worth, and to pay a fixed rate of interest,
(2) whether there is subordination to or preference over any indebtedness of the corporation,
(3) the ratio of debt to equity of the corporation,
(4) whether there is convertibility into the stock of the corporation, and
(5) the relationship between holdings of stock in the corporation and holdings of the interest in question.

In *John Kelley Co* v. *Commissioner* the US Supreme Court stated that there is 'no one characteristic, not even exclusion from management, which can be said to be decisive in the determination of whether the obligations are risk investments in the corporations or debts'.[26]

Section 385 of IRC has an instructive history. It authorises the Secretary to the Treasury to make 'regulations determining whether an interest in a corporation is to be treated ... as stock or indebtedness (or as in part stock and in part indebtedness)'.[27] This provision was added in 1969 in an effort to rationalise the case law on the debt / equity distinction. Regulations were introduced that focused on the economic characteristics of the instrument. These rules were complex, revised, suspended and then revoked and withdrawn in 1983.[28] One important feature of section 385 is that the issuer's characterisation of an instrument is binding on the issuer and holders of the instrument, but not on the tax administration or holders who have notified the tax administration.

---

[25] For an overview, see Bittker & Eustice (2003–, chapter 4). Ring (2012, p. 780) suggests that 'the IRS and the courts struggle to determine the true substance of an instrument by taking into account a range of factors'.

[26] *John Kelley Co* v. *Commissioner* (1946) 326 US 521 (SC) at 530.

[27] IRC (US) s. 385(a).

[28] See Bittker & Eustice (2003–, para. 4.02[8]).

The classification of profit-sharing debentures and convertible notes for US income tax purposes as debt or equity depends on the particular features of the instrument in question. Consideration must be give as to whether the instruments have a long maturity date, whether rights to the return are subordinated to general creditors, the variability of that return with the success of the corporation and voting rights. If the instruments have a certain term that is not overly long and ensures a return of capital invested, profit-sharing debentures and convertible notes are likely to be characterised as debt.[29]

The UK's is again a fragmented approach. As noted earlier at 2.1.1, it is possible that interest paid on profit-sharing debentures is a dividend according to case law principles. Although if the interest is payable out of pre-netted profits, that is not the case. However, the definition of 'distribution' includes certain 'interest' paid with respect to 'securities'. 'Security' is broadly defined and includes loans.[30] In particular, interest paid on a security that exceeds a 'reasonable commercial return for the use of the principal' is treated to the extent of the excess as a distribution.[31] That treatment does not necessarily catch profit-sharing debentures, but does catch interest paid at an excessive interest rate, discussed further at 2.1.3.

Profit-sharing debentures will be caught by head F of the definition of 'distribution', which covers interest paid in respect of 'special securities'.[32] There are a number of conditions under which a security may be a special security. In particular, a security is a special security if interest payable on the security 'depends (to any extent) on the results of...the company's business, or...any part of the company's business'.[33] This provision clearly covers profit-sharing debentures. Similarly, convertible notes may be special securities unless the securities are 'listed on a recognised stock exchange [or] issued on terms which are reasonably comparable with the terms of issue of securities listed on a recognised stock exchange'.[34] Debentures with a term of more than fifty years issued between associated companies might also be treated as special securities.[35]

---

[29] See Bittker & Eustice (2003–, paras 4.03[2][f] and [g] and 4.60[1]) and the references cited therein.
[30] CTA 2010 (UK) s. 1117(1).
[31] CTA 2010 (UK) s. 1000(1)E.
[32] CTA 2010 (UK) s. 1000(1)F.
[33] CTA 2010 (UK) s. 1015(4). Under s. 1017 interest under ratchet loans is not caught (i.e. where the interest rate goes up as the corporation's performance goes down or vice versa).
[34] CTA 2010 (UK) s. 1015(3).
[35] CTA 2010 (UK) ss. 1015(6) & 1016. 'Associated companies' is defined by reference to 75% subsidiary (see earlier discussion at 1.1.5.1); s. 1017.

These re-characterisation provisions are extremely broad and were subject to abuse. Corporations with no use for interest deductions (e.g. those in a loss position) found that they could vary the terms of a loan (e.g. with a bank) slightly so that interest came to be characterised as a distribution. There would be no deduction for the corporation, but the lender's receipt would be characterised as a distribution and (if the lender were a corporation) that would mean the interest was exempt. In effect, this form of arbitrage permitted the transfer of losses from a borrower to an unrelated lender. The UK addressed the arbitrage in a most peculiar manner.

The re-characterisation of interest on special securities does not apply to interest paid to a resident corporation.[36] This leads to the bizarre situation under which the characterisation of interest payable on profit-sharing debentures or convertible notes depends on the identity of the holder of those instruments. If the holder is a resident corporation, the interest retains its character as interest. If the holder is other than a resident corporation, the interest is re-characterised as a distribution. As a result, the deductibility of interest paid by the issuing corporation can change when such instruments are sold by a resident corporation to another type of person, or vice versa.

Australia also had difficulty in distinguishing debt from equity for income tax purposes; in 2001 it sought to address these difficulties by focusing on one particular feature of debt when compared with equity.[37] This feature is the obligation to return capital to a debenture holder. The Australian rules begin by asking whether an interest in a corporation is an 'equity interest'. The definition of this term not only includes a membership interest in a corporation but also profit-sharing debentures and convertible notes.[38] However, an instrument is not re-characterised for tax purposes if it meets the 'debt test'.[39] The debt test is worded in particularly obscure language, but is broadly met if a corporation has an 'effectively non-contingent obligation' to make payments to the lender equalling the capital amount of the loan within ten years of issue.[40]

---

[36]   CTA 2010 (UK) s. 1032(1). To the extent the interest is 'beyond a reasonable commercial return' (i.e. within head E of the definition of 'distribution'), it will nevertheless be treated as a distribution.

[37]   Income Tax Assessment Act 1997 (Australia) Div. 974.

[38]   Income Tax Assessment Act 1997 (Australia) s. 974–75.

[39]   Income Tax Assessment Act 1997 (Australia) s. 974–70(1).

[40]   Income Tax Assessment Act 1997 (Australia) s. 974–20. The debt test may be met for longer term loans if the present value of payments to be made is equal to or more than the amount of the loan; s. 974–35.

It is not clear whether Australia's interesting experiment can be viewed as a success. The rules are long and complicated and often obscure and difficult to apply. They are not holistic in their re-characterisation, being largely applied only in the tax treatment of returns on corporate financing instruments. It is not clear that they offer a more principled approach to the classification of hybrid debt instruments than the other approaches mentioned. The ten-year threshold can be just as arbitrary and is a major distortion in the structuring of hybrid instruments.

### 2.1.2.2 Preference shares

An instrument may be shares in form and yet incorporate substantial features of debt. Such shares are generically referred to as 'preference shares'. Dividends and returns on capital on preference shares usually rank above ordinary shares. Further, the right to dividends on preference shares may be fixed (e.g. like an interest rate on the capital value of the shares). In addition, the dividend right may be cumulative; that is, if the right to dividends is not met in one year (due to lack of profits) it is added to the right for the next year. Preference shares may also be denied voting rights at a general meeting of shareholders and be redeemable after a fixed term. Accordingly, non-voting fixed-rate cumulative redeemable preference shares are functionally equivalent to subordinated debt. Nevertheless, tax laws are less likely to re-characterise shares as debt than they are to treat debt as equity.

In Germany, preference shares are treated as shares for tax purposes. One reason may be that German corporate law regulates the issue of preference shares to a greater extent than in most common law jurisdictions. German corporate law permits the exclusion of voting rights on preferred stock and a preferential right to dividends, subject to certain floors and ceilings or fixed terms. However, if the preferential dividend is not paid, corporate law activates certain inalienable rights including voting rights.[41] Similarly, there is no provision for re-characterisation of preference shares under the CCCTB Proposal.

Under US case law, preference shares might be characterised as debt. This depends on weighing up the characteristics of the investment as referred to earlier at 2.1.2.1. At one extreme, preference shares that participate in profits are likely to give 'an invulnerable equity status'.[42] As more

---

[41] AktG (Germany) ss. 139 & 140.
[42] Bittker & Eustice (2003–, para 4.03[1]).

debt-like features are introduced, there is greater risk of the instrument being classified as debt.

The UK had difficulties with preference shares in the same manner (although somewhat later) as it had with hybrid debt instruments re-characterised as equity. Corporations with little value for deductions were issuing preference shares to *lenders* (e.g. banks) in an effort to exempt the return on the loan as dividends and lower borrowing costs. In effect, this style of planning could also indirectly transfer the benefit of losses from a corporation to a lender.

The planning was shut down in 2004 with the 'shares as liabilities' rules. Under these rules, redeemable preference shares that are designed to yield an interest-like return are, subject to conditions, treated as creditor loan relationships for tax purposes.[43] These rules cover only quasi-loans that are treated as a financial liability rather than equity for accounting purposes, and the generation of a tax advantage must be one of the main purposes of the investment.[44] Once again, these rules are lopsided in that they only apply to corporate holders of certain preference shares. If those shares are transferred between corporations and other persons their character changes.

The Australian debt / equity rules do not directly re-characterise preference shares of any type as debt. However, dividends paid on shares that meet the debt test are provided with a different tax treatment from dividends paid on other types of shares. This is discussed further at 2.4.2.1. It can result in dividends on ten-year or less redeemable preference shares being taxed in a manner that is consistent with the tax treatment of interest on debt.

### 2.1.3   Excessive debt

The characterisation of hybrid instruments focuses on the rights attached to a particular instrument. Particular corporate instruments might be clearly debt or clearly equity, and yet the character of part of the financing might be challenged as being excessive. This is particularly an issue in the context of excessive debt financing. The volume of debt financing when compared to equity financing might be such as to call into question the substance of the rights attaching to the excessive part of the debt. This is the issue of 'thin capitalisation'. Thin capitalisation is particularly a problem in an international context due to the vastly different taxing

[43]  CTA 2009 (UK) s. 521B.
[44]  CTA 2009 (UK) ss. 521C & 521E.

rights that a source country has over interest and profits distributed as dividends.[45]

Nevertheless, despite an international focus, thin capitalisation is a conceptual issue of classification of debt and equity interests in a corporation. In recent years, a number of countries have brought their thin capitalisation rules 'onshore'. This is particularly the case within the EU where there are EU law issues in applying thin capitalisation rules only to cross-border financing. However, many countries still only apply their rules to inbound financing.

There are a number of approaches to thin capitalisation. Each approach results in interest paid on excessive debt being non-deductible for the payer. This is the critical issue from an international perspective. However, the rules of some countries re-characterise either the excess debt as equity or the excess interest as a dividend. This can be particularly important in a domestic scenario because re-characterisation can alleviate the otherwise harsh result that the excessive interest is both non-deductible to the payer and fully taxed as interest to the recipient (i.e. economic double taxation). Re-characterisation often results in the availability of dividend relief, discussed later at 2.4.

A common approach adopted by countries to the thin capitalisation problem, especially in an international setting, is the safe haven approach.[46] Under this approach, debt financing received by, say, a corporation from associated entities is compared to the equity financing of the corporation. If the debt, as compared to the equity, exceeds a certain ratio (the debt-to-equity ratio) then interest on the excessive debt is not deductible. Some countries have a simple ratio (e.g. 2:1) applicable to all industries, but other countries adopt different ratios or formulas for particular situations. Each of these different approaches is similar in that each focuses on the volume of debt as compared to equity, rather than the volume of interest paid on debt. Countries that adopt different ratios often tighten the ratio when broadening their tax base and lowering corporate tax rates. Commonly, this approach is combined with the third approach (discussed later), which accepts debt financing that exceeds the ratio if the taxpayer can show that he or she could borrow a similar amount from an independent third party (e.g. a bank).

---

[45] Generally regarding the international issue of thin capitalisation, see Harris & Oliver (2010, pp. 252–9).

[46] For example, Australia, Canada and Japan adopt the safe haven approach with respect to international financing; see Ault & Arnold (2010, pp. 518–20).

A major issue under the safe haven approach is how equity capital is measured. Typically, it includes both share capital and retained profits (e.g. net assets). Another difficult issue is which debt counts – all debt or just debt financing from related parties. If the latter approach is used, then the law must define the related party. Further, this approach must deal with the problem of *back-to-back* arrangements. To avoid related party debt, a parent corporation may place a deposit with an independent bank and then the bank loans funds to the relevant subsidiary. Similar results can be achieved with parent corporation guarantees. It can be difficult to trace back-to-back arrangements, particularly in an international setting. Another issue is the time at which compliance with the ratio is measured: is it at the start of the year, the end or the highest point during the year? The involvement of corporate groups also raises issues. Is the ratio applied to the group or individual members of the group? Where this is relevant, group corporations must be defined.

Another popular approach to thin capitalisation, and an increasingly used method, is to deal with excessive debt financing through earnings stripping rules. Broadly, this approach involves denying a deduction for interest to the extent that it exceeds a certain percentage of income before financing costs. In 1989, the US adopted an earnings stripping rule with a safe haven based on a debt-to-equity ratio. Although this rule is targeted at excessive inbound debt financing, it is instructive to consider its application and the issues it raises.

Under the US rules a corporation may be denied a deduction for 'disqualified interest'.[47] 'Disqualified interest' is interest paid to a 'related person' who is not subject to US tax with respect to that interest, essentially non-residents and tax exempts.[48] 'Related person' is defined by reference to section 267 of IRC (discussed earlier at 1.1.5.1) and so in terms of 50% control or common control of the corporation paying the interest.[49] Any disqualified interest for which a deduction is denied in a particular year is carried forward and treated as disqualified interest incurred in the next year.[50]

The amount denied as a deduction is limited by two rules.[51] A deduction is denied for disqualified interest only to the extent that the

---

[47]  IRC (US) s. 163(j)(1).
[48]  IRC (US) s. 163(j)(3).
[49]  IRC (US) s. 163(j)(4).
[50]  IRC (US) s. 163(j)(2).
[51]  IRC (US) s. 163(j)(2)(A).

corporation's 'net interest expense' exceeds 50% of the corporation's 'adjusted taxable income'. 'Net interest expense' is the difference between interest incurred during the year and interest derived during the year. 'Adjusted taxable income' is essentially a net cash flow concept, determined without regard to depreciation, interest expense and loss carry-forward.[52]

The second limitation is based on the corporation's debt-to-equity ratio. If the corporation's debt is not more than 1.5 times its equity, there is no denial of interest under the earnings stripping rule. In determining the debt-to-equity ratio, it is total indebtedness that counts and not just that owed to related persons.[53] For the purposes of applying these limitations, members of an affiliated group of corporations are treated as a single corporation.[54] 'Affiliated group' is the test for whether a corporate group can consolidate (see the earlier discussion at 1.2.3.1), but in the context of the earnings stripping rule it is irrelevant whether the group members have in fact consolidated.

These US rules may result in a deduction for interest being denied, but do not re-characterise the excess interest as dividends. That may occur if the excessive debt is re-characterised under the US substance approach to the debt / equity distinction (see earlier at 2.1.2). Because of the limited scope of the earnings stripping rule, the debt / equity classification is particularly important in domestic scenarios.

In 2008, Germany adopted an earnings stripping rule (referred to as the 'interest barrier') as part of a package involving a reduction in corporate tax rate.[55] The operative rule is similar to that in the US, but the scope of operation of the rule is substantially different. In particular, the German rule applies to both domestic and international interest (i.e. it is not limited in geographical operation). Further, the German rule applies to all interest paid and so is not limited to interest paid to related persons.

Under section 4h(1) of the Income Tax Law (EStG), interest incurred is fully deductible to the extent of interest income. Any interest incurred in excess of interest income is deductible only to the extent that it does not exceed 30% of profits before interest, taxes, depreciation and amortization. For the purposes of this rule, all interest counts, whether incurred in

---

[52] IRC (US) s. 163(j)(6)(A).
[53] IRC (US) s. 163(j)(2)(C).
[54] IRC (US) s. 163(j)(6)(C).
[55] Before 2008, Germany applied a safe haven approach to both international and domestic related party debt.

respect of related or unrelated party debt. Any interest for which a deduction is denied may be carried forward and treated as interest incurred in the following five years.

As with the US approach, there are important exceptions to the application of the German interest barrier.[56] First, the interest barrier does not apply if total net interest expense (the sum of all interest expenses less interest income) is below €3 million. Once this threshold is reached, the entire amount of the net interest expense is subject to the interest barrier. This threshold is not expressly apportioned between members of a corporate group, which has given rise to some tax planning. Second, the limitation does not apply unless the operations are part of a group. This exception is effective for individuals, but in the case of a corporation the exception is limited by the Corporate Income Tax Law. The interest barrier applies to non-group corporations unless they show that less than 10% of interest incurred over interest income is paid to 25% shareholders or associates, defined by reference to the international rules on transfer pricing (see earlier at 1.2.2). This rule extends to back-to-back arrangements.[57]

The final exception to the interest barrier applies to groups and involves comparing the German part of a group's equity ratio to the worldwide equity ratio of the worldwide group. The interest barrier does not apply if the German equity ratio is equal to or greater than (within a 2% margin) the equity ratio of the worldwide group, known as the 'escape clause'. For this purpose, 'group' is defined in terms of permission to consolidate results under accounting standards. For the purposes of applying the interest barrier, corporations within an *Organshaft* (see earlier at 1.2.3.2) are 'deemed to constitute a single operation'.[58]

As with the US earnings stripping rules, these German rules do not re-characterise excess interest as a dividend, something the former German debt-to-equity ratio rules did do. This is particularly relevant in a domestic scenario because, unlike the US rules, the German rules are generally applicable. Further, unlike in the US, Germany does not apply a substance approach in distinguishing between shares and debt.

A third approach to excessive debt financing is to apply the arm's length standard to the *volume* of debt financing (i.e. apply transfer pricing rules). Under this approach, interest is deductible only to the extent that it is paid on debt that could be borrowed from an independent party. This approach is less common, though of particular relevance when applying tax treaties.

[56]  EStG (Germany) s. 4h(2).
[57]  KStG (Germany) s. 8a(2).
[58]  KStG (Germany) s. 15(3).

It is the approach used by the UK in its domestic law.[59] Since 2004, the UK's transfer pricing rules (discussed earlier at 1.2.2) have been the primary rules regulating thin capitalisation. From the same date, those rules have applied equally to both domestic and international transactions. Therefore these rules may simultaneously restrict the deductibility of interest based on the rate at which interest is charged as well as the amount borrowed.[60]

As with any approach to thin capitalisation based on related party dealings, the transfer pricing approach suffers problems with back-to-back arrangements. A subsidiary may be able to borrow money from an independent bank because of a guarantee provided by its parent corporation. The UK rules specifically provide that in such a case a subsidiary's borrowing capacity that is due to the guarantee is to be ignored for purposes of determining whether the bank would have loaned the funds on an independent basis.[61]

From 2010, the UK has backed up its transfer pricing approach with a worldwide interest deduction cap. Interest deductions granted to UK members of a multinational corporate group are limited to the total net finance costs paid by the worldwide group (including the UK members) to external lenders.[62]

As with the US and German approaches, the UK transfer pricing rules do not re-classify interest paid as a distribution. The exception, mentioned earlier at 2.1.2.1, is where interest paid represents 'more than a reasonable commercial return' for the use of the funds borrowed.[63] This provision's focus on the funds borrowed means that re-characterisation is not generally applicable in a thin capitalisation case. As a result, the UK transfer pricing rules raise a serious risk of economic double taxation of the excessive interest.[64]

As initially drafted, the CCCTB Proposal had no general rule applicable to excessive debt financing, although it did have a rule targeted at interest paid to low-tax third countries.[65] The Presidency amendments would

---

[59] As a rule of thumb, the UK tax administration is not concerned with cases where the level of debt to equity does not exceed a ratio of 1:1 and the level of interest cover (the number of times that operating profits meet interest payments) exceeds 3:1. However, the tax administration denies that this is a 'safe harbour'. See Almand & Sayers (2009).

[60] Consistent with the transfer pricing approach, the UK tax administration makes available an Advance Thin Capitalisation Agreement procedure; see Statement of Practice 04/07.

[61] TIOPA 2010 (UK) s. 153.

[62] TIOPA 2010 (UK) Part 7 (ss. 260–353).

[63] CTA 2010 (UK) s. 1000(1)E.

[64] Under TIOPA 2010 (UK) ss. 191–4 there is some scope for treating a related party guarantor as paying interest for which the borrower is denied a deduction.

[65] CCCTB Proposal Art. 81.

remove this provision and replace it with a general earnings stripping rule similar to that adopted in Germany.[66]

It is interesting to note in passing that the comprehensive Australian rules for distinguishing debt and equity introduced in 2001 and discussed earlier at 2.1.2 do not deal with excessive debt financing. Straight debt does not constitute an 'equity interest', and even if it did, the debt test would typically apply. This is because financial instruments are generally tested on an isolated basis. There is some scope for amalgamating related instruments, a matter to which the discussion now turns.

### 2.1.4  Amalgamation and fragmentation

The thin capitalisation issue is not particularly concerned with individual instruments, but with the overall combined impact of those instruments. As noted, there is often more than a casual relationship between instruments. Two or more instruments issued by a particular corporation may be so related that tax law classifies those instruments as a single instrument for tax purposes. Similarly, a single instrument might be fragmented into two or more instruments for tax purposes. Amalgamation and fragmentation of instruments issued by a particular corporation are the first matters considered in the following discussion.

The issues considered under this heading focus on instruments issued by a particular corporation. The possibility that tax law might combine the effects of related instruments issued by a particular corporation raises the issue of how the tax law should treat instruments that are related but that are issued by different entities. This situation raises the slippery issue of how to deal with third-party intermediation of instruments. This is the final matter considered under this subheading.

Countries do not adopt holistic approaches to the issues considered in this subheading. Indeed, the issues considered here demonstrate most graphically the impossibility of adopting a substance approach to the debt / equity distinction. So, the approach in this subheading is rather to provide some general background and isolated examples.

### 2.1.4.1  Amalgamation

As noted at the start of this heading, shares are at some level an amalgam of particular rights. This becomes abundantly clear when the rights

---

[66]  CCCTB Proposal Art 14a (Presidency amendment).

typically attached to shares are fragmented. The extent to which a particular corporation can achieve a fragmentation depends on the corporate law by which the corporation is regulated. Where that corporate law is particularly flexible, it might be possible to issue non-voting shares that participate in profits and at the same time issue voting shares with few other rights. Now imagine that the two types of shares are 'stapled' such that it is not possible to deal with one type of share without dealing with the other. In substance, there is little difference between holding a stapled pair of shares or a single ordinary share.

This is a simple example that does not play on the shares / debt distinction. However, it can be altered by stapling a share and a debt instrument so that the debt instrument cannot be dealt with independently of the share. Further, the debt instrument might be a profit-sharing debenture. Alternately, a straight debt instrument might be stapled to a participating share, but the right to dividends under the share might be reduced by interest payable on the debt instrument. This option might be particularly attractive if interest on debt is taxed more favourably than dividends on shares. The options for mixing and matching shares with debt are endless, depending on the flexibility of corporate law. The same can be said of the options for stapling the shares and the debt instrument. To make matters more complex, in the context of corporate groups, the shares might be issued by one group member and the debt instrument by another.

How should a corporate tax system respond to this type of issue? If it accepts the flexibility of corporate law classification then the integrity of any distinction in the tax law treatment of debt and equity and the returns thereon is eroded. Taxpayers, or at least those well advised, would in effect be able to select debt or equity treatment, depending on the treatment they prefer. Attempting to reclassify or amalgamate all instruments that might be in some fashion related would appear to be administratively implausible. As a result, tax laws are more likely either to target specific issues or to rely on general anti-avoidance principles. The only manner in which to address the issue holistically would be to treat debt and equity and the returns thereon in the same manner for tax purposes. That would erode any connection between financial accounts and the corporate tax base and cause other problems such as those discussed later at 2.4.2.1.

The UK adopts the targeted measure approach. As noted earlier at 2.1.2.1, it re-characterises interest paid on 'special securities' as a distribution for tax purposes. The definition of special securities includes securities that are 'connected with shares in the company'.[67] Securities are connected with shares if

(a) it is necessary or advantageous for a person who has, or disposes of or acquires, any of the securities also to have, or to dispose of or acquire, a proportionate holding of the shares, and
(b) that is a consequence of the nature of the rights attaching to the securities or shares and, in particular, any terms or conditions attaching to the right to transfer the securities or shares.[68]

There is no requirement that the connected securities be issued by the corporation that has issued the shares or by any person related to the corporation that has issued the shares.

The Australian debt / equity rules deal with the same issue in a more obscure fashion. Two or more related schemes may be 'taken together to give rise to an 'equity interest' in a company if

(a) the company enters into, participates in or causes another entity to enter into or participate in the constituent schemes; and
(b) a scheme with the combined effect or operation of the constituent schemes ... would give rise to an equity interest in the company ... and
(c) it is reasonable to conclude that the company intended, or knew that a party to the scheme or one of the schemes intended, the combined economic effects of the constituent schemes to be the same as, or similar to, the economic effects of an equity interest.[69]

The Australian rule seems messy by comparison to the UK rule and narrower in scope. It seems unlikely to provide more certainty as to classification for taxpayers. A similar rule applies in determining whether the debt test is met.[70]

In the US it is possible that related instruments may be 'bundled' under the substance approach to the debt / equity distinction, although the treatment is often uncertain and there seems a dearth of case law on the topic.[71] Canada has also had difficulties with stapled securities and moved to deny deductions to corporations for debt stapled to shares.[72]

---

[67] CTA 2010 (UK) s. 1015(5).
[68] CTA 2010 (UK) s. 1017(2).
[69] Income Tax Assessment Act 1997 (Australia) s. 974–70(2).
[70] Income Tax Assessment Act 1997 (Australia) s. 974–15(2).
[71] See Bittker & Eustice (2003–, para. 4.03[4]) and the references cited therein.
[72] See Juneja & Crosbie (2011).

### 2.1.4.2 Fragmentation

A single instrument issued as just debt or just equity may incorporate features that are not consistent with that classification or that may be sensibly split from the instrument. The classic example is an instrument with an imbedded option, such as a convertible note. Most commonly, such instruments are treated for tax purposes consistently with their general law classification (i.e. as a single instrument). However, there are exceptions.

For example, in the UK the tax treatment of issuers and corporate holders of convertible notes follows the accounting treatment of these instruments. This means that for tax purposes convertible notes are bifurcated into a debt component and an equity component. The debt component is taxed as if it were an ordinary loan relationship.[73] The equity component (i.e. the right to convert the note into shares) is taxed like an independent derivative contract.[74] As a result, interest payments on convertible bonds are generally tax deductible. The exception is where the interest payments are classified as distributions, discussed earlier at 2.1.2.1.

In the US, the unbundling issue is most likely to arise where, in a reorganisation, the taxpayers must receive only 'shares'. This may be required for the taxpayers to receive a particular tax treatment, usually deferral of recognition of a gain on disposal of the exchanged shares (discussed in Chapter 7). Bittker and Eustice suggest that the critical issue is 'whether a certain right is an attribute of the stock itself or is a separate security that either is not stock at all or that flavors the stock sufficiently to require the recipient to recognize income'.[75] Section 385 of the IRC (discussed earlier at 2.1.2) says that regulations may provide that an instrument is in part share and part debt, but no such regulations have been issued.

### 2.1.4.3 Third-party intermediation

So far, the discussion has only considered instruments issued by a particular corporation or, at most, a related entity. The impossibility of the substance approach to debt / equity for tax purposes is illustrated most clearly once a third party is involved. A particular corporation may have issued ordinary debt or ordinary shares, and yet the holder of the instrument may

---

[73] CTA 2009 (UK) s. 415.
[74] CTA 2009 (UK) s. 585.
[75] Bittker & Eustice (2003–, para. 4.03[4]) make a rather fine distinction between 'bifurcation' and 'unbundling' based on the intention of the issuer.

enter into arrangements with independent third parties that are inconsistent with the holder's rights to the debt or shares. For example, the holder of ordinary shares may assign the right to receive dividends, the right to vote or the right to surplus on winding up. Similarly, the holder may enter into put and call options in such a manner that any capital risk or benefit associated with the shares is transferred to the third party.

There are multifarious complex financial instruments that may be entered into that adjust the substance of a shareholder's position as such. When faced with such instruments, a tax law must address two primary questions: does the shareholder still hold a share for tax purposes, and does the person to whom the rights are transferred or to whom the risk is transferred hold shares for tax purposes? It is clearly possible to transfer the attributes of shares in such a fashion that it must be accepted that the transferee and not the transferor is in substance the shareholder. A bare trust might be such an example. However, tax laws do not adopt such an extreme version of a substance approach to identifying shares.

What tax laws sometimes do is to target or deny certain tax consequences if a person does not hold certain attributes of a share, after considering arrangements with third parties. An example of this approach is found in the Australian and US rules that deny relief from economic double taxation of dividends if shares are not held at risk, discussed later at 2.4.3. Other examples involve special rules for assignment of dividends and the tax treatment of stock-lending and share repurchase agreements, considered later at 8.1 and 8.3, respectively. Other examples were briefly mentioned earlier in the context of determining whether a corporation is part of a group or not. Shares over which options are outstanding or that do not have basic rights to profits and voting may not count for purposes of determining the shareholder threshold necessary to create a corporate group (see earlier discussion at 1.2.3).

## 2.2   Identifying distributions

Once shares have been identified, it is necessary to identify a payment as a distribution of profits with respect to those shares (i.e. identify dividends). Dividends are payments that are recognised for tax purposes. As such, they are one of the building blocks of the income tax (see the introduction). This means that an income tax law must have a mechanism for determining in respect of dividends each of the fundamental features of a payment: allocation, quantification, timing and characterisation. This heading first considers these fundamental features in the context of a simple cash dividend.

Dividends are a division of profits. In identifying dividends, it is presumed that profits are derived and then divided. However, a corporation is often able to control whether it derives income or not. Instead of deriving income directly and distributing the profits as dividends, a corporation may seek to divert its income-earning opportunities directly to its shareholders. In other words, a corporation may be able to manipulate its affairs such that its shareholders intercept its income-earning operations. This type of interception is often referred to as a 'hidden profit distribution' or 'constructive dividend'. Hidden profit distributions raise difficult issues as to the type of value transfers that constitute a payment, the nexus of such payments with shares and, when there is such a payment and sufficient nexus, the fundamental features of a payment. Hidden profit distributions are the second matter considered under this heading.

### 2.2.1 Fundamental features of dividends

The current discussion presumes that a corporation has derived profits and distributes a cash dividend from the profits in fulfilment of a right attaching to shares in that corporation. It may seem that there is little further to discuss in this simple scenario in terms of identifying the dividend for tax purposes. However, for an income tax law to attach tax consequences to the dividend, the tax law must directly or by implication determine the fundamental features of the payment that is the dividend. Each of these features is considered in turn.

#### 2.2.1.1 Allocation

Tax law must treat a dividend as paid by a particular corporation and as received by a particular person. In the usual case this is straightforward, and tax law follows commercial law. There may, however, be cases in which this is not so straightforward. The payment may clearly be a distribution of profits of the paying corporation and the person receiving the dividend may clearly hold shares, but the shares may not match the corporation distributing the profits. For example, a subsidiary corporation may make a cash distribution directly to its parent corporation's shareholders. In some countries corporate law may limit the ability to do this. However, if it happens, how should tax law treat such a situation?

One approach is to treat the situation as involving two payments instead of one. So tax law would view the subsidiary as distributing a dividend to the parent corporation and then the parent corporation as distributing a dividend to its shareholders. It seems that case law in the US can produce such a result.[76] A similar result might be achieved through a concept of 'hidden profit distribution', such as in Germany (see later discussion at 2.2.2) or a general principle of constructive receipt. In the UK, dividends are taxable to the person 'receiving or entitled to the distribution'.[77] The phrase 'entitled to' could catch an attempt to divert a dividend for income tax purposes, but bizarrely the same wording is not used in the context of the charge to corporation tax on distributions.[78] Constructive receipt would more clearly apply where a shareholder attempts to divert a dividend to a related party.

Another approach is to directly treat the dividend from the subsidiary as a dividend in the hands of the parent's shareholders, despite the mismatch between the payer and the shares held. The UK has an express provision dealing with this scenario:

> '[D]istribution', in relation to a company which is a member of a 90% group, includes anything distributed out of assets of the company (whether in cash or otherwise) in respect of shares in or securities of another company in the group.[79]

There is a similar provision that applies in a less than 90% holding scenario where two corporations come to an arrangement regarding a distribution to each other's shareholders.[80]

Constructive receipt might thwart an attempted diversion of a dividend to the person entitled to receive it. For example, the payment of a dividend to a shareholder's relative is unlikely to be effective for tax purposes. However, constructive receipt will not solve attempts to split income between related parties where that attempt involves a transfer of ownership of the shares in question. The holding of shares by family members can be a particularly effective manner of income splitting. Income splitting between relatives using shares was discussed earlier at 1.3.3.3 in the context of personal services corporations. General rules to prevent income splitting discussed at that point may also apply to prevent splitting dividend income.

[76] Bittker & Eustice (2003–, para. 8.05[10]).
[77] ITTOIA 2005 (UK) s. 385.
[78] CTA 2009 (UK) s. 931A is particularly obscure. Its heading refers to 'charge to tax on distributions received', but the charge uses neither the 'received' concept nor the 'entitled' concept.
[79] CTA 2010 (UK) s. 1072(1). Under s. 1072(4) a '90% group' is defined as a company and its 90% subsidiaries. '90% subsidiaries' was discussed earlier at 1.1.5.1.
[80] CTA 2010 (UK) s. 1112.

### 2.2.1.2 Quantification

A dividend payment must be quantified for income tax purposes. This is simple in the context of a cash dividend such as is currently under discussion. However, where an in-kind dividend is involved, the quantification issues are the same as faced in the context of employee fringe benefits and transfer pricing. These problems are well illustrated in the context of hidden profit distributions, discussed later at 2.2.2.

### 2.2.1.3 Timing

In the context of a realisation-based income tax, the tax law must determine the time at which dividends are recognised so as to determine the tax period in which the dividends have tax consequences. This may be determined according to general principles of the timing of receipt. So, for example, in Germany, business income is determined on a profits basis, but other types of income, including dividends, are determined as 'the excess of receipts over costs'.[81] In the context of a cash dividend, this is the time at which a cheque is received.[82] As discussed earlier at 1.2.1, where the dividends are received in the context of a business, recognition follows accounting treatment. This includes all dividends received by corporate shareholders.

Under the CCCTB Proposal, dividends would be recognised when 'the right to receive them arises'.[83] This seems to mean that the timing of the receipt depends on the corporate law of the country under which the corporation is organised. This should be the time at which an enforceable debt arises in favour of the shareholder, which is often when a final dividend is declared in a general meeting. This treatment is only relevant where corporations subject to the CCCTB Proposal receive dividends. The recognition of dividends received by any other entity will be determined under the tax law of the country of residence of the entity, irrespective of whether the distributing corporation is subject to the CCCTB Proposal.

Under US tax law, the recognition of dividends under state corporate law is not directly relevant. As mentioned earlier at 2.1.1, dividends are only taxable to the extent of 'earnings and profits' and 'earnings and profits' is a US tax law concept. This means that timing the recognition of a distribution is relevant for several purposes, including the date at which

---

[81] EStG (Germany) s. 2(2).
[82] Ault & Arnold (2010, p. 300).
[83] CCCTB Proposal Art. 18.

earnings and profits are to be determined, the date of valuing the distribution and the date at which the shareholder becomes taxable, among others. In the context of a dividend paid by cheque, this is generally the date on which the cheque is posted. Taxability for the shareholder may occur at an earlier time if there is constructive receipt, which is when 'the cash or other property is unqualifiedly made subject to [the shareholder's] demands'.[84] These rules apply to all types of shareholders, irrespective of whether they are accounting on a cash or accrual basis and when an enforceable debt arises under local state law.[85]

The UK rules are confusing. In the context of a simple cash dividend, the definition of 'distribution' refers to a 'dividend paid by the company'.[86] 'Paid' in this context is defined for the purposes of corporation tax as the date on which dividends become 'due and payable'.[87] This is the date specified in the corporate resolution confirming the dividend; if no date is specified, it occurs when the dividend is declared. By contrast, an interim dividend is typically unenforceable until it is paid.[88] A problem is that this definition only applies for the purposes of corporation tax. It does not apply for income tax purposes, where the charge is on 'dividends paid and other distributions'.[89] There is a question whether the definition of 'paid' applies for this purpose.[90]

### 2.2.1.4  Dual character

As discussed in the introduction to this chapter, although dividends are often characterised as a distribution of corporate profits, this definition produces circularity. The only way to break this circularity is to characterise dividends by reference to the holding of certain rights (i.e. shares or a similar membership interest). This is a standard procedure under

---

[84]  Title 26 Code of Federal Regulations (US) § 1.301–1(b).

[85]  Generally, see Bittker & Eustice (2003–, para. 8.04[2]) and the references cited therein. As they note, IRC (US) s. 301, which defines 'distribution made by a corporation', refers to an amount 'received', implying a cash basis. Section 301 is further discussed at 2.2.2.

[86]  CTA 2010 (UK) s. 1000(1)A.

[87]  CTA 2010 (UK) s. 1168.

[88]  *Potel* v. *IRC* [1971] 2 All ER 504 (ChD).

[89]  ITTOIA 2005 (UK) s. 384(1).

[90]  It seems the definition of 'distribution' for income tax purposes indirectly incorporates the definition of 'paid'; ITA 2007 (UK) s. 989. However, literally it seems possible for dividends to be charged under ITTOIA 2005 (UK) s. 384(1) irrespective of whether they have become a 'distribution'. Similarly, the corporation tax charge on dividends refers to 'dividend or other distribution', but does not use the word 'paid'; CTA 2009 (UK) s. 931A(1). Perhaps the definition of 'paid' in CTA 2010 (UK) s. 1168 is relevant for all purposes of chargeability, but the legislation is unnecessarily confusing.

an income tax; a payment is characterised by reference to the rights with respect to which the payment is made, and the form of the payment is irrelevant. So a simple cash dividend paid in clear fulfilment of a shareholding right gives few problems of characterisation for tax purposes. The main type of problem in this regard arises by reason of the potential for dual characterisation.

Just because a payment is characterised as a corporate dividend does not mean that it is not simultaneously characterised as something else. In some cases the other character may involve a mere subcategorisation of the dividend. So, in the UK, dividends may be subcategorised as being either of a revenue nature or a capital nature. Historically, only dividends of a revenue nature were chargeable to income tax and capital dividends were not chargeable. This limitation is overcome by specifically including in the definition of 'distribution' a 'capital dividend'.[91] The exception is the income tax (not corporation tax) charge on dividends of non-resident corporations, where the charge is only on 'dividends' and 'dividends of a capital nature' are specifically excluded.[92]

However, dual characterisation may be competing rather than subcategorisation. The categorisation of a payment as dividends is critical for the paying corporation because dividends are not deductible. Here there is unlikely to be any scope for dual characterisation: a payment by a corporation is either a distribution or not. For the recipient of a dividend there seems more potential for dual characterisation. For example, employees are often given shares in their employer in the course of their employment. Dividends paid on employee shares may raise issues as to their appropriate characterisation. Dividends received in the context of a business or on shares held as trading stock may raise similar questions as to appropriate characterisation.

A tax law may provide general reconciliation rules where a payment may be characterised as a dividend and something else. This is particularly important where a country adopts a schedular system. The messy reconciliation rules under the UK schedular corporation tax were discussed earlier at 1.2.1. There are similar rules for individuals under the schedular system. Broadly, employment is given priority, then property business, then trade, then dividends and then other types of income.[93] If there are

---

[91] CTA 2010 (UK) s. 1000(1)A. A 'capital dividend' is a dividend paid out of capital profits; *IRC v. Reid's Trustees* [1949] AC 361 (HL).

[92] ITTOIA 2005 (UK) s. 402.

[93] ITTOIA 2005 (UK) ss. 2, 4, 366 & 367.

no reconciliation rules, then the likely approach is that a payment cannot have dual characterisation and it is a matter for the courts in difficult cases to determine the most appropriate character of a payment.

As noted at 1.2.1, although the German income tax is global for corporations, it is schedular for individuals. This means Germany requires reconciliation rules where dividends fall under more than one schedule. These rules are similar to the UK rules. If dividends fall 'within income from agriculture and forestry, from business enterprises, from independent employment or from renting and leasing, it shall be added to this income' rather than be taxed as income from capital assets.[94]

The character of a dividend may also be affected by tax planning. The incentive to derive and retain profits in a corporation because of a low corporate tax rate (corporate tax shelter) was discussed earlier at 1.3.3.3 in the context of personal services income. This presumed that profits retained in a corporation are taxed more lightly than profits derived directly. However, it may be that profits distributed in the form of dividends are still more lightly taxed than other types of income, even after considering the issue of economic double taxation (see the later discussion at 2.3 and 2.4). In this case, a tax law or the courts might re-characterise a payment that is in legal form a dividend as some other form of payment.

The US provides an example of the risk of re-characterisation by courts. In limited circumstances, individuals might seek to derive dividends instead of wage income so as to avoid wage withholding and social security taxes. This is particularly acute in the context of S corporations. As discussed earlier at 1.3.3.2, this regime may allocate the profits of an S corporation to its shareholders, and in doing so the profits have the same character in the hands of the shareholders as they have in the hands of the corporation. Because a corporation cannot be an employee, the allocation would not in principle be characterised as employment income. Therefore, wage withholding and social security taxes can be avoided by deriving a low wage from an S corporation and taking the remainder of the remuneration as dividends (which are not subject to tax due to the allocation of corporate profits). As a result, a line of US tax cases have held that dividends might be re-characterised as wage income.[95]

The UK provides a tax law example of the re-characterisation of dividends into employment income. The rules on attribution of personal services corporation income were discussed earlier at 1.3.3.3. These rules

---

[94] EStG (Germany) s. 20(3).
[95] Generally, see Bittker & Eustice (2003–, para. 6.06[5]) and the references cited therein.

require the personal service provider (together with associates) to have a material (10%) interest in the corporation in question. As a variation of this requirement, certain professionals set up corporations that they managed and through which others could, for a fee, provide their personal services in return for a mixture of salary, dividends and benefits (especially travel). Many service providers would use the same manager and the same company, even if their businesses were different. This was an avenue for small service provides to have their business managed and at the same time obtain some tax benefits associated therewith, especially avoidance of National Insurance Contributions on employment income.

These 'managed service companies' as a tax planning device were counteracted with rules in 2007. Broadly, the rules apply where a corporation is in the business of providing the services of individuals, and a person is 'involved' with the corporation 'who carries on a business of promoting or facilitating the use of companies to provide the services of individuals'.[96] Where a person provides services through a managed service company and the person (or an associate) receives 'a payment or benefit which can reasonably be taken to be in respect of the services', then the person is deemed to have received a payment of employment income.[97] The employment income is equal to the payment or benefit, subject to certain adjustments.[98] In particular, 'distributions' from a managed service company may be reduced by such deemed employment income.[99]

### 2.2.2 Intercepting corporate profits: hidden profit distributions

Rather than deriving income directly, a corporation may seek to divert its income or income-earning opportunities directly to its shareholders. It may seek to divert its income to a shareholder by making a payment to a shareholder that is not in the form of a dividend. 'Payment' was described in the introduction as a 'bestowal of value' by one person on another. There are only so many ways in which a person may bestow value on another. A person may transfer an asset to the other. So far, this heading has considered cash transfers, but the transfer may be in the form of some other kind of asset. Reversing this, a person may bestow value on another by reducing his or her liabilities (e.g. forgiving a debt or other liability

---

[96] ITEPA 2003 (UK) s. 61B(1). There is a special exclusion for the provision of ordinary legal and accounting services; s. 61B(3).
[97] ITEPA 2003 (UK) s. 61D(1).
[98] ITEPA 2003 (UK) s. 61E & 61F.
[99] ITEPA 2003 (UK) s. 61H.

owed by the other or by satisfying a liability owed by the other person). A person makes a payment by permitting another to use an asset that the person owns, including money. Finally, a person can make a payment by performing personal services for another person.[100]

A hidden profit distribution may take any of these forms of payment by a corporation to a shareholder. Each involves a transaction or dealing between the corporation and its shareholders (or their associates). As a result, each type of hidden profit distribution may give rise to tax consequences at the corporate level and at the shareholder level. At the corporate level, there is the issue as to whether the corporation realises income. At the shareholder level, hidden profit distributions raise issues as to the capacity in which the shareholder receives the benefit (dual characterisation issue), and so the nexus between the benefit and the shares as the source of the benefit may be in issue. Other issues for shareholders include the timing and valuation of the hidden distribution. Each type of hidden profit distribution is considered in turn.

Hidden profit distributions are more common in corporations where ownership and control coincide. As a result, some countries broaden the concept of dividend for tax purposes where a closely held corporation is involved. It is not clear why distribution rules should be limited in such a fashion, but the distinction is commonly a result of tightening defects in loosely drafted definitions of 'dividend'.

### 2.2.2.1   Transfers of assets

A transaction between a corporation and its shareholders may involve the transfer of an asset. If a corporation transfers an asset to a shareholder for less than market value, there is a bestowal of value by the corporation on the shareholder. If a shareholder transfers an asset to a corporation for more than market value, again there is such a bestowal. Focusing on a transfer by the corporation, if the shareholder pays nothing for an asset, an in-kind dividend seems clear. The shareholder may, however, pay anything from nothing up to the market value of the asset. It may seem obvious that any discount on the market value price of the asset is a hidden profit distribution. However, this logic only follows in the face of comprehensive

---

[100] It is also possible to bestow value by creating an asset in another person. Examples include granting another person a lease on beneficial terms and a company issuing shares. Creation cases typically involve the granting of personal rights against the person bestowing the value. In substance, the creation cases involve the other methods of bestowing value (i.e. transfer, use or services).

transfer pricing rules that are applied domestically. As discussed earlier at 1.2.2, this is not always the case.

In most but not all cases the transfer of an asset from a corporation to a shareholder is obvious. A situation of some difficulty occurs where a shareholder appropriates a corporate opportunity. The corporate law of many countries have rules prohibiting a director from misappropriating opportunities that belong to the corporation the director is meant to be serving.[101] If a shareholder appropriates an opportunity, how should this be characterised? In the context of a mature and secure opportunity, perhaps it should be dealt with in the same manner as a transfer of an asset to the shareholder (i.e. raise questions as to a hidden profit distribution). Dealing with this appropriation is more difficult in the context of a developing opportunity.

**Shareholder level**   The question is whether a transfer of an asset at an undervalue that benefits a shareholder should be treated as a dividend for tax purposes. Presuming the transfer occurs outside of a business of the shareholder, transfer pricing rules alone are unlikely to produce a dividend. There may be consequences for the entity disposing of the asset. Where the corporation is the transferor, there may be a gain (discussed later), but there is a mere acquisition by the shareholder and (absent a deemed dividend) only a question of the asset's cost base in the hands of the shareholder. Where the shareholder is the transferor, there may be an increased profit on the disposal, which could have tax consequences. In such a case, the shareholder might benefit from having part of the sale proceeds characterised as a dividend (e.g. because of the availability of dividend relief).

Countries adopt widely different approaches to hidden profit distributions. Germany adopts a comprehensive approach based on the concept of hidden profit distribution. As mentioned earlier at 2.1.1, German income tax law refers to 'shares of profits (dividends), income and other benefits from shares'.[102] This provision continues to specifically include 'constructive dividends' within other benefits. Another provision declares that

---

[101]   For example, in the UK this has been codified as part of the no conflict rule; see Companies Act 2006 (UK) s. 175(2). By contrast, in Germany the rule against taking corporate opportunities is based on case law and is part of the duty of loyalty (*Treupflicht*). The approach in the US is similarly based on case law. Generally see Cahn & Donald (2010, pp. 338–47).

[102]   EStG (Germany) s. 20(1)1.

constructive dividends do not reduce a corporation's income.[103] Germany has a highly developed case law on constructive dividends. Essentially, any transaction between a shareholder and corporation that is not undertaken at arm's length is a potential constructive dividend.[104]

Decisions of the Federal Tax Court define a constructive dividend as any decrease (or prevented increase) in capital that

- is caused by the shareholder relationship
- affects the amount of the corporation's income
- is not based on a shareholders' resolution to declare a dividend
- a monetary benefit to the shareholder or a person related to the shareholder is not required

This case law is reflected in the Corporate Income Tax Guidelines issued by the German tax administration.[105] Any decrease or prevented increase in a corporation's income is caused by the shareholder relationship if the terms would not be agreed upon with the shareholder by a prudent business manager exercising due diligence. If the shareholder is a controlling shareholder, a link with the shareholder relationship will be presumed if there is no clear agreement in writing in advance of the benefit.[106] The approach is extremely broad and effectively amounts to a form of transfer pricing rule. It may extend to encompass the foregoing of a corporate opportunity for profit in favour of a shareholder. As a result, any value passed to a shareholder upon a transfer of assets by a corporation will be treated as a constructive dividend.

The US approach is also relatively comprehensive. As noted earlier at 2.1.1, 'dividend' is defined in terms of a distribution of property.[107] Further, section 301(a) of IRC requires the distribution to be made 'with respect to its stock'. 'Property' is defined broadly to mean 'money, securities, and any other property'.[108] This is far from a statutory framework prescribing the treatment of constructive dividends. However, US case law has developed a substance approach to what is treated as a distribution for tax purposes (i.e. a benefit can be a distribution even though it is not declared in a formal fashion by the corporation).

---

[103]  KStG (Germany) s. 8(3).
[104]  See Ault & Arnold (2010, p. 358).
[105]  Corporate Income Tax Guidelines (*Korperschaftsteuerricht-linien*; KStR) para. 36.
[106]  Whittmann (1983–, para. 32.05[2](d)[i]).
[107]  IRC (US) s. 316(a).
[108]  IRC (US) s. 317(a).

Bittker and Eustice suggest that

> the hallmark of a constructive distribution [is] value passing from, or a sufficiently specific economic benefit conferred by, the corporation to the shareholder, for which the shareholder does not give equivalent value in exchange.[109]

Although German case law is formulated on the basis of the shareholder relationship causing a reduction in corporate income, US case law focuses on the receipt of a benefit in the capacity as shareholder. Accordingly, if the benefit is received in some other capacity (e.g. as creditor or employee), there is no dividend. However, if the shareholder capacity is clear, it is not necessary that the shareholder receive the benefit directly. The courts may imply constructive receive where, for example, the benefit is provided to an entity that is related to a shareholder.[110]

It is clear that a sale by a corporation to a shareholder at an undervalue produces a dividend to the extent that the price paid is less than the 'fair market value' of the property. This is confirmed by Treasury Regulations.[111] Similarly, a shareholder who seizes a corporate opportunity may be found to have received a constructive dividend.[112] If there is a constructive dividend in the context of an asset transferred by a corporation to its shareholders, the shareholder receives a cost base in the asset equal to its fair market value.[113]

By contrast and as usual, the UK makes constructive dividends look difficult. The UK has no comprehensive concept of constructive dividend and has felt the need to target particular types of benefits given to shareholders in the definition of 'distribution'.[114] The sale of an asset at an undervalue could only constitute a 'dividend' where it involves a division of profits. So long as the sale is above the cost of the corporation, this is unlikely to be the case. In addition to 'dividends', 'distribution' expressly includes the following:

> Any other distribution out of assets of the company in respect of shares in the company, except however much (if any) of the distribution...

---

[109] Bittker & Eustice (2003–, para. 8.05[1]).
[110] Bittker & Eustice (2003–, para. 8.05[2]).
[111] Title 26 Code of Federal Regulations (US) § 1.301–1(j).
[112] Bittker & Eustice (2003–, para. 8.05[9]).
[113] IRC (US) s. 301(d).
[114] The Australian approach is similar; see Income Tax Assessment Act 1936 (Australia) s. 6(1) (definition of 'dividend') & Part III Div. 7A.

represents repayment of capital on the shares, or ... is (when it is made) equal in amount or value to any new consideration received by the company for the distribution.[115]

This provision seeks to overcome any argument that such distributions would not be 'dividends'. However, the provision is limited in two respects. First, the distribution must be 'out of assets', and it is not clear exactly what this means in the case at hand. If the shareholder pays at least the amount of the corporation's book value of the asset, could there ever be a distribution 'out of assets'? Even if there was, what would be the amount of that distribution? Further, the distribution must be 'in respect of shares'.[116] There must be a risk that in some cases the shareholder is characterised as a purchaser and so any benefit is not 'in respect of shares'. The point is that this provision is nothing like a proper transfer pricing rule.

However, another head of 'distribution' does function as a transfer pricing rule:

> [I]f on a transfer of assets or liabilities ... by a company to its members, or ... to a company by its members ... the amount or value of the benefit received by a member exceeds the amount or value of any new consideration given by the member .... The company is treated ... as making a distribution to the member of an amount equal to the excess.[117]

The amount or value of a benefit is determined according to market value.[118] This provision applies to a transfer of an asset by a corporation to a shareholder at an undervalue. However, it is not without limitations. It is a one-sided transfer pricing rule and so, as discussed later, will not increase a corporation's profits. Further, it is limited to a 'transfer of assets or liabilities' and so is not easy to apply to other kinds of constructive dividends. In particular, it seems difficult to apply to the appropriation of a corporate opportunity by a shareholder.

The definition of 'distribution' is even broader in the context of a 'close company'.[119] A close company is treated as making a distribution where it

---

[115] CTA 2010 (UK) s. 1000(1)B. This head is excluded in the case of the distribution of assets between non-associated companies; s. 1002.

[116] 'Shares' includes any 'interest of a member in a company'; CTA 2010 (UK) s. 1117.

[117] CTA 2010 (UK) s. 1020(1), which is incorporated into the definition of 'distribution' by s. 1000(1)G. Many such transfers between resident corporations are excluded from the definition of 'distribution'; ss. 1002 & 1021.

[118] CTA 2010 (UK) s. 1020(3).

[119] The definition of 'close company' was considered earlier at 1.1.5.2.

incurs an expense in, or in connection with, the provision for any participator of ... living or other accommodation ... entertainment ... domestic or other services, or ... other benefits or facilities of any kind.[120]

The amount of the distribution to the participator is 'the expense, less ... any part of the expense that the participator makes good to the company'.[121] Initially, this seems a bizarre rule, being focused on the amount of the corporation's expense rather than the value of the benefit to the shareholder. So, if the shareholder at least paid the corporation's cost in providing the benefit, it seems likely the rule could not apply. However, and equally strange, the corporation's expense is defined by reference to the valuation rules for employee fringe benefits.[122] In many cases, the value under the employee fringe benefit rules is the value of the benefit rather than the expense in providing the benefit.[123]

This extended meaning of 'distribution' is further extended to apply to cross-arrangements where close companies agree to benefit each other's participators.[124] Further, the meaning of 'participator' is extended to include an 'associate' of a participator.[125] What is not clear is why these further extensions do not or should not apply in the context of other types of distribution. Further, it is not clear why the general extension to cover in-kind benefits is limited to close companies. The UK approach smacks of the random targeting of particular areas without much thought as to structure.

The CCCTB Proposal has no rules at the shareholder level, which is not surprising because any distributions received would generally be exempt.[126]

**Corporate level**   Where a corporation transfers an asset to a shareholder, the main question at the corporate level is whether the tax law requires the corporation to account for income in an amount that is more than what the shareholder paid for the asset. If transfer pricing rules apply, then

---

[120] CTA 2010 (UK) s. 1064(1). Again, there is an exclusion for certain inter-corporate benefits; s. 1066.

[121] CTA 2010 (UK) s. 1064(2).

[122] CTA 2010 (UK) s. 1064(3).

[123] Despite its strange wording, the UK tax administration is of the opinion that the distribution can exceed the actual costs of the corporation. HMRC, *Company Tax Manual*, at para. CTM60550, available at www.hmrc.gov.uk/manuals/ctmanual, accessed 16 July 2012.

[124] CTA 2010 (UK) s. 1067.

[125] CTA 2010 (UK) s. 1069.

[126] CCCTB Proposal Art. 11(c).

clearly this would be the consequence. However, as mentioned, countries appear to hesitate in applying transfer pricing rules to domestic transactions, including those between corporations and shareholders. If countries do not apply transfer pricing rules so as to include an amount in the corporation's income, they may nevertheless deny the corporation a deduction for expenses incurred in providing the shareholder with the benefit. This approach dislocates the amount of the distribution from the amount realised by the corporation. As a result, a tax law cannot be sure that the full benefit to the shareholder has already been taxed at the corporate level.

Germany adopts a comparatively pure approach to the treatment of corporations with respect to hidden profit distributions. Unlike most countries, Germany seeks a symmetrical treatment of shareholders and corporations. There is one provision in the Income Tax Law incorporating constructive dividends into the shareholder's income.[127] There is a reflective provision in the Corporate Income Tax Law specifying that constructive dividends do not reduce corporate income.[128] This means that where a hidden profit distribution is found of a type that reduces corporate income, there should be symmetry between including that amount in corporate income and taxing that amount to the shareholder.[129]

Other countries struggle with the inclusion of a notional amount in the income of the corporation. In particular, other countries tend not to have a provision that specifically states that hidden profit distributions do not reduce corporate income. As noted with respect to Germany, there is a strong connection here with transfer pricing rules. So, in other countries the transfer pricing rules might have some scope for application to a corporation making hidden profit distributions. However, as noted earlier at 1.2.2, transfer pricing rules often have limited application. In the US, they are limited by reference to 'organizations, trades, or businesses'.[130] Although the Treasury Regulations give these terms a broad meaning so as to include a sole proprietorship and employment, it is not clear that they could extend to include a passive shareholder.[131] It seems unlikely that the appropriation by a shareholder of a corporate opportunity that did not amount to 'property' would have any tax consequences for the corporation.

---

[127]   EStG (Germany) s. 20(1)1.
[128]   KStG (Germany) s. 8(3).
[129]   See Ault & Arnold (2010, p. 358).
[130]   IRC (US) s. 482.
[131]   Title 26 Code of Federal Regulations (US) § 1.482–1(i).

The UK approach is similar, with a potential twist. As discussed earlier at 1.2.2, the UK transfer pricing rules could apply to a 'transaction' between a corporation and a controlling shareholder, but not to a transaction with a non-controlling shareholder. Further, the exceptions from the transfer pricing rules for small and medium-sized enterprises exclude most UK corporations providing shareholder benefits from the scope of the rules. However, a residual argument is that the provision of a shareholder benefit by a corporation is not on revenue account from the corporation's perspective. The corporation is not in the business of providing shareholder benefits. If this were the case, the market value rule in TCGA 1992 might apply (perhaps after an appropriation from trading stock in a relevant case).[132] There would be no exceptions from the application of this rule for shareholders or small corporations. This rule could not apply to appropriation by a shareholder of a corporate opportunity unless that opportunity could be described as a corporate 'asset'.

A country may have no obvious manner of increasing a corporation's income by the amount of notional income siphoned off to a shareholder as a hidden profit distribution. However, there may be consequences on the deduction side for a corporation. Any expenses associated with the provision of a shareholder benefit may not be deductible under a general business purpose test for expenses. So, in the US, expenses in providing the benefit might not be 'ordinary and necessary expenses paid or incurred...in carrying on any trade or business'.[133] In the UK, such expenses might not be incurred 'wholly and exclusively for the purposes of the trade'.[134] Identifying the expenses or relevant part of the expenses might be difficult. At the least, the result should be that a corporation could not make a loss on a transfer of an asset to a shareholder (presuming the asset to be worth more than its cost).

The CCCTB Proposal is peculiar in that it has a special provision dealing with shareholder benefits at the corporate level. As noted earlier at 1.1.2, the transfer pricing rules in the CCCTB Proposal only apply to 'associated enterprises'. The definition of 'associated enterprises' was discussed earlier at 1.1.5.3, and as noted at that point, it does not cover individuals. So the transfer pricing rules may apply to a transfer of assets between two associated corporations, but not to a transfer of an asset to a controlling individual. Perhaps because of this, Article 15 of the CCCTB Proposal

[132] TGCA 1992 (UK) s. 17.
[133] IRC (US) s. 162(a).
[134] CTA 2009 (UK) s. 54(1).

specifically denies a deduction for 'benefits granted' to certain individual shareholders or their relatives.[135] These individuals are identified by reference to a 20% participation of the corporation as used in the definition of 'associated enterprises' (discussed earlier at 1.1.5.3).[136] Under Article 15, expenses in providing such benefits are not deductible 'to the extent that such benefits would not be granted to an independent third party'.

### 2.2.2.2   Assumption or forgiveness of liability

Rather than transfer an asset to a shareholder, a corporation may reduce a liability of a shareholder. The shareholder might owe the liability to the corporation or to some third party. When the shareholder owes the liability to a third party, the corporation clearly makes a payment on the shareholder's behalf. Any issue is essentially one of constructive receipt (e.g. characterising the payment as first made to the shareholder as a distribution, who then discharges the liability). The situation may be less clear where the payment by the corporation serves some legitimate business purpose, despite conferring a benefit on the shareholder (e.g. valuation of shares or payment of a debt guaranteed by a shareholder).

In Germany, the question is whether the shareholder relationship is causative of any reduction in corporate assets. In the US the question is one of 'whether the corporate expenditure was incurred primarily to benefit the corporation's trade or business or primarily for the personal benefit of the shareholders'.[137] In the UK, where the expense is incurred by a close company, the question is whether it is incurred 'in connection with' the provision of any benefit or facility.[138] This seems particularly broad, perhaps too broad for the purposes of creating any certainty. By contrast, the situation is particularly unclear in the context of other corporations. There may be a 'distribution out of assets...in respect of shares',[139] although the nexus with the shares may create some difficulty. Arguably, there is no transfer of 'assets or liabilities' by the company to the member or vice versa, and so the lopsided transfer pricing rule cannot apply.[140]

When the corporation forgives a debt, there is no cash payment by the corporation, but most countries have no difficulty in characterising this

---

[135]   CCCTB Proposal Art. 15.
[136]   CCCTB Proposal Art. 78.
[137]   Bittker & Eustice (2003–, para. 8.05[8]) and see the examples provided there.
[138]   CTA 2010 (UK) s. 1064(1). Again, there is an exclusion for certain inter-corporate benefits; s. 1066.
[139]   CTA 2010 (UK) s. 1000(1)B.
[140]   CTA 2010 (UK) s. 1029.

as a constructive distribution. This is certainly the case in Germany and the US, where the usual tests apply for constructive dividends. In the UK, again there would clearly be a distribution in the context of a close corporation. The position is less clear in the context of other corporations. There is case law recognising forgiveness of debt as a 'distribution out of assets', but this was in the context of a forgiveness entered as a distribution in the corporation's accounts.[141] Clearly, a debt is forgiven out of assets, but there is a question whether a 'distribution' can be interpreted more narrowly to only cover situations in which there is some identifiable transfer or dealing out. In particular, it seems difficult to describe a forgiveness of debt as a transfer of 'assets or liabilities' under the transfer pricing rule.[142]

In a standard situation, a reduction of a shareholder's liability by a corporation does not involve the interception of corporate profits, so there is no question of a corporation realising notional income. However, there is a question of whether the payment or forgiveness is deductible for the corporation. It usually depends on the general rule for deduction of corporate expenses, which may be supported by a specific rule denying a deduction for dividends (discussed later at 2.4.2.1). The latter rule may be particularly important where the payment or forgiveness serves some corporate business purpose. The UK had particular problems with corporations claiming a deduction for the forgiveness of a shareholder loan under its loan relationship rules. This was addressed with a specific rule.[143] Article 15 of the CCCTB Proposal, which denies a deduction for benefits granted to certain shareholders, may also have some relevance here.

### 2.2.2.3 Loans and use of assets

Value may be bestowed by a corporation on a shareholder by permitting the shareholder to use a corporate asset for less than what an independent party would be willing to pay. The most clear and common example of this is where the corporation loans funds to a shareholder at low interest. However, there are examples of use of other types of corporate assets such as a house, car or boat. By providing the use at undervalue, the corporation is forgoing potential income. As discussed earlier, in a transfer of assets case a corporation may forgo an unrealised gain, but equally an undervalue

---

[141] *John Paterson (Motors) Ltd.* v. *IRC* [1978] STC 59 (Crt of Session) applying an earlier version of CTA 2010 s. 1000(1)B.
[142] CTA 2010 (UK) s. 1029.
[143] CTA 2009 (UK) s. 321A.

transfer may involve a payment out of assets of the corporation. A reduction of liability case is unlikely to involve any forgoing of potential income
by a corporation. By contrast, a benefit provided in a use case is likely to
wholly involve the forgoing of potential income and so raises critical issues
at both the shareholder level and the corporate level.

The German constructive dividend rules catch use-type benefits given
to shareholders. Transfer pricing rules are applied to determine the value
of the benefit received, involving all the usual problems in determining
an appropriate transfer price. In some cases it may be difficult to determine the nature of the benefit. For example, the constructive dividend
from a low-interest loan is usually the forgone interest. However, if there
is no intention to repay the loan, the whole amount of the loan may be
treated as a constructive distribution.[144] Again, the treatment at the corporate level is typically symmetrical. Any forgone interest or rent is included
in the corporation's income, and the corporation is taxable with respect
thereto. This symmetry aids in the taxation of dividends to shareholders because it ensures that funds and benefits used for dividends suffer a
similar corporate-level tax.

Similarly, US constructive dividend rules cover use benefits provided
to shareholders. The amount of the benefit is the 'fair rental value' of
the property, less any amount paid by the shareholder, but in some cases
courts have focused on corporate deductions.[145] There is no express rule
that includes the forgone rent in the income of the corporation. This has
become particularly important since the tax rate applicable to dividends
was reduced in 2003 (see the later discussion at 2.4.3.2). This position is
all the more peculiar because there is an express provision dealing with
low-interest loans.

Section 7872 of IRC treats interest forgone in 'any below-market loan'
as transferred by the corporation to the shareholder and then retrans-
ferred by the shareholder to the corporation. The first part of this provision produces a dividend and the second part interest income for
the corporation (i.e. notional income). There is a de minimis exception
for loans not exceeding $10,000.[146] This treatment presumes that the

---

[144] Fischer & Lohbeck (2012, p. 321) discuss the possibility that a loan by a subsidiary to
a parent corporation is treated as a hidden profit distribution. They suggest that '[f]acts
possibly reclassifying such loan are e.g. the shareholder having no intention and ability
to repay the loan, an unusually long loan term, the loan being non-interest bearing, no
collateral being granted, etc.'

[145] Bittker & Eustice (2003–, para. 8.05[4]).

[146] IRC (US) s. 7872(c)(3).

transaction is properly characterised as a loan in the first place. If there is no intention to create a bona fide creditor-debtor relationship then the whole amount advanced to the shareholder might be treated as a dividend.[147]

The UK position with respect to shareholder use benefits is again confused. It does not cope well with these types of benefits, but in some cases its treatment seems to be excessive. There is no 'dividend', because the benefit does not divide profits. There is no 'distribution out of assets' because the benefit represents potential income and not actual 'assets'. There is no obvious 'transfer' of an 'asset or liability'. In the context of a close company, there is clearly a benefit or facility, but it is not necessary that the company 'incurs expense' in connection with the provision. If the company incurs no expense, it is difficult to see how the close company provision can be triggered. If the company incurs a small expense there is a certain disquiet with treating the whole market value of the rent or interest forgone as a distribution when the provision refers to the company's expense. The drafting is sloppy to say the least.

At another extreme, the UK may treat a loan made by a close company to a shareholder in a distribution-like manner. Section 455 of CTA 2010 applies where a close company makes a loan or advance to a participator or associate of a participator. In this case, the company must pay 25% of the amount advanced as 'if it were an amount of corporation tax'. This payment is due irrespective of whether there is an intention to pay back the loan and of whether any interest forgone is treated as a distribution. The 25% rate once made some sense in the context of the former corporate tax system and a 40% personal marginal tax rate. Both of these features have been adjusted substantially, and the tax is now little more than a deposit in case the loan turns out to be in substance a dividend. So, if the loan is repaid, the amount paid as corporation tax is refunded to the company.[148] As in the US, there is a de minimis exception, but the beneficiary of the loan must be a full-time worker.[149] There are provisions to prevent arrangements between two or more corporations to stall the charge on the loan.[150] The loan is only treated as income of the participator if it is released. However, this is still not a distribution, but is subject to a special charge that is similar to that imposed

[147] Bittker & Eustice (2003–, para. 8.05[6]).
[148] CTA 2010 (UK) s. 458.
[149] CTA 2010 (UK) s. 456.
[150] CTA 2010 (UK) s. 459.

on distributions.[151] As a result, on release the corporation is repaid the deposit.[152]

In 2010, Australia felt the need to specifically deal with constructive dividends in the form of use benefits. In the UK style, this is still a fragmented approach and does not attempt to deal with the constructive dividend issue conceptually or holistically. A dividend may now be triggered in Australia on the 'grant of a lease, or a licence or other right to use an asset'.[153] The amount of the dividend is 'the amount that would have been paid for the transfer, lease, licence or other right by parties dealing at arm's length'.[154] However, as in the UK, this provision only applies to closely held corporations (private companies).

At the corporate level, there is no provision in the UK that would include forgone rent or interest in the income of a corporation. In the context of loans by close companies, this lack of a provision is perhaps understandable, because there is a corporate tax charge on the amount of the loan. In other contexts it is less understandable and particularly so where dividend relief is available in respect of most all distributions. The position is similar under the CCCTB Proposal. There is no rule that would include foregone interest in the income of a corporation. Article 15 in denying a deduction for certain shareholder benefits is unlikely to have any substantial application in the case of foregone interest because there may be little expense to the corporation to deny a deduction for.

### 2.2.2.4   Provision of services

Value may also be bestowed on a shareholder by the corporation providing services for the shareholder. The services may be provided in the course of the corporation's normal business operations, but the corporation may also engage externals to provide services for the shareholder. The difference between this case and the case of reduction of liabilities is that in this case the shareholder does not incur a liability that is met by the corporation: the corporation engages the services directly and on its own account. In many cases, the provision of services may be accompanied with a provision (transfer) of assets.

There are few issues involved in this form of constructive dividend in addition to those described earlier. As in the transfer of assets case, there

---

[151]   ITTOIA 2005 (UK) ss. 415 & 421.
[152]   CTA 2010 (UK) s. 458.
[153]   Income Tax Assessment Act 1936 (Australia) s. 109C(3)(d).
[154]   Income Tax Assessment Act 1936 (Australia) s. 109C(4)(d).

is the question of the difference in value between expenses incurred by the corporation in the provision of the services and the market value of those services (e.g. the price that would be charged to an independent third party). Germany, which essentially adopts a transfer pricing approach to constructive dividends, treats the market value of the services as a constructive dividend. If this is in excess of the expenses incurred by the corporation in the provision, the result is likely to be notional income for the corporation. Again, this approach is largely due to Germany's symmetrical treatment of the corporation and the shareholder in these cases. In the US, there is also a constructive dividend in the amount of the fair market value of the services provided. However, the corporation is unlikely to be imputed notional income (beyond consideration provided by the shareholder), but is denied a deduction for expenses in providing the services.

Again the UK situation is more difficult. In the context of a close company, there seems to be a straightforward distribution under section 1064 of CTA 2010, which is valued according to the employee fringe benefit rules. Outside of this provision the position is not so clear. There is no clear 'transfer of assets or liabilities' under section 1020. There may, however, be a 'distribution out of the assets of the company in respect of shares in the company' under section 1000(1)B. Any distribution is likely to be limited to the amount that is out of assets (i.e. expenses incurred by the corporation in providing the benefit). There is no increase to the market value of the services provided. Similarly, there is unlikely to be any income realised at the corporate level (beyond consideration provided by the shareholder), but the corporation will be denied a deduction for expenses incurred in providing the service. The position is likely to be similar under Article 15 of the CCCTB Proposal.

## 2.3 Dual nature of corporate income

Corporate income is peculiar in that it is treated as income twice: once when it is derived and again when it is distributed. As noted at the start of this chapter, this peculiarity of dual derivation is caused by the artificial nature of the corporation, and there are two elements to this artificiality. The first is the artificiality of a corporation as an entity deriving income, and the second is the artificiality that dividends are a separate source of income from the income of the corporation. Most all countries tax both these events, and so the result is economic double taxation unless specific relief is provided. The charge to tax on dividends and the potential for economic double taxation of corporate income are the first matters dealt with under this heading. Once the potential for economic double taxation has been identified, the discussion turns to consider whether it is appropriate that corporate income be subjected to this form of double taxation.

### 2.3.1 *Economic double taxation: the classical system*

Without exception, corporate tax systems treat dividends as income of the shareholder. This may, perhaps, seem intuitive, but at a deeper level it is somewhat disturbing. An income tax seeks to tax creations of wealth accruing to a person when and if transformed by a payment received from another person (i.e. when realised). But where is the creation of wealth when a corporation distributes a dividend? Presuming that dividends are not deductible, a dividend does not cause an erosion of another person's income such as a payment of interest, wages or other disbursements. So the funds that represent the dividend have typically already been taxed as a creation of wealth as income of the corporation.

The questionable nature of dividends as income is given away by the very word. 'Dividend' is a derivative of the word 'divide'. Why should dividing profits result in income separate from the earning of those profits? Most countries' income tax laws do not consider the division of partnership profits as income separate from the earning of those profits. What makes corporations different? Historically, perhaps they were not different. The original UK income tax dating from 1799 did not charge dividends as a separate item of income (excepting dividends from government funds). Indeed, the UK income tax law did not expressly charge dividends until 1965.

However, the modern approach is to subject dividends to income tax and to do so expressly in the tax law. The rationale for this charge to tax seems to be the separate identity of the corporation. That is, unlike in the context of a partnership, the income of a corporation is not in law the income of the shareholders: they have separate identities. The focus here seems to be on legal form rather than economic substance and is particularly problematic where non-corporate entities are identified as subjects of the corporate tax system (see the earlier discussion at 1.1.1). Even in the context of a standard registered corporation, saying that income is legally the income of the corporation does not necessarily lead to the conclusion that a division of that income between the shareholders constitutes a new source of income.

In any case, it is not useful to dwell on the issue of whether dividends should or should not constitute income because inevitably they are treated as income for tax purposes. Nevertheless, this uneasy nature of dividends as income helps to explain why the full consequences of this characterisation are often not followed through in the tax system. Those consequences suggest that dividends should be subjected to tax in the same manner as any other type of income. This would result in full economic double taxation of corporate income – once in the hands of the corporation when the income is derived and a second time in the hands of the shareholders when the income is distributed. A corporate tax system that subjects corporate income to double taxation in this manner without relief for one tax against the other is most commonly referred to as a 'classical system'. Such a system is not 'classical' in the sense of being the earliest form of corporate tax system. Rather, it is 'classical' in the sense that most countries treat corporate income and dividends as separate sources of income and tax them as such.[155]

The following discussion considers two features of the inclusion of dividends in income: the charge to tax and whether the charge is on the gross amount of the dividends or the net amount.

### 2.3.1.1 The charge

The matter for present discussion is the taxation of corporate distributions. The dual nature of corporate income provides two potential taxing events (i.e. the deriving of corporate income and its distribution). There are a number of options for the taxation of corporate income when it is derived. These options were considered earlier at 1.3, where the focus was largely on the taxation of the corporation with respect to its income, taxation of shareholders (e.g. partnership-style taxation) or taxation of both. The options for the taxation of distributions are largely similar. Just as corporate income when derived is typically taxed in the hands of the corporation (i.e. corporation tax), corporate distributions are typically taxed in the hands of the shareholder (i.e. shareholder tax). However, there are examples of corporations being taxed with respect to their own distributions, and examples of both corporations and shareholders being taxed with respect to distributions. Each of these is considered in turn.

**Shareholder taxation**   Most income tax laws list the types of income that are subject to tax, and most commonly this list includes dividends. Where dividends are included in income, the income is the income of the shareholder, and so it is clear that what is envisaged is a shareholder tax. An

---

[155] Regarding the origins of use of the phrase 'classical system', see Harris (1996, p. 60).

example is the US. Section 61(a) of IRC, which identifies 'gross income' in terms of 'all income from whatever source derived'. This is no doubt sufficient to include dividends in gross income, but the provision never-theless proceeds to list certain non-limiting inclusions, and specifically includes '(7) Dividends'. Hence, dividends are taxable to recipients. The Australian approach is similar. Assessable income includes both 'ordinary income' and 'statutory income'.[156] Although dividends are no doubt 'ordinary income' they are nevertheless specifically included in assessable income by statute and so constitute statutory income.[157]

German income tax law also lists the types of income that are subject to charge;[158] however, further investigation is required to identify dividends as one of those types. One of the heads of charge is 'income from cap-ital assets'. It is defined in a separate provision and specifically includes 'profit shares (dividends)'.[159] Again, dividends are seen as the income of the recipient, and so the German law envisages a shareholder tax. Under the CCCTB Proposal, the tax base would be calculated as 'revenues' less deductions.[160] 'Revenues' is defined to include, amongst other items, 'dividends and other profits distributions'.[161]

As usual, for historic reasons, the UK approach is peculiar. In each of the cases of Germany, the US and the CCCTB Proposal, dividends are included in the income of the recipient irrespective of whether dividends are from a resident or non-resident corporation. As mentioned, histor-ically, the UK did not expressly charge dividends. However, dividends from resident corporations were charged as 'other income' (Schedule D Case VI), and dividends from non-resident corporations were charged as foreign income (Schedule D Case V). In 1965, dividends from resident corporations became specifically chargeable (Schedule F), but not divi-dends from non-resident corporations. The tax law rewrite made the sit-uation more confusing. For individuals, Schedule F was rewritten as sec-tion 383(1) of ITTOIA 2005, but the charge on dividends of non-resident corporations was rewritten separately as section 402 of ITTOIA 2005. For corporations, there is only one charge to tax on dividends, irrespective of whether the distribution is from a resident or non-resident corporation.[162]

---

[156] Income Tax Assessment Act 1997 (Australia) s. 6–1(1).
[157] Income Tax Assessment Act 1936 (Australia) s. 44.
[158] EStG (Germany) s. 2(1).
[159] EStG (Germany) s. 20(1)1.
[160] CCCTB Proposal Art. 10.
[161] CCCTB Proposal Art. 4(8).
[162] CTA 2009 (UK) s. 931A.

As discussed earlier at 1.2.1, a tax law may require a person to calculate his or her income separately for each earning activity (schedular approach), or there may be one global calculation. In a global system, dividends are aggregated with other income and then deductions are taken off. In such a context, dividends are not treated differently from other income, and there is no special calculation for them. In contrast, under a schedular system there may be different rules of calculation or a different tax treatment for dividends. These special rules are considered in the remainder of this chapter. It is possible, however, that dividends simultaneously fall under more than one head of charge in a schedular system.

This issue of simultaneous charges under a schedular system is essentially the same as the issue of dual characterisation of a payment discussed earlier at 2.2.1.4. That discussion considered the possibility that a particular payment was simultaneously characterised as a dividend and as something else. It is that dual characterisation that gives rise to the possibility of a dividend simultaneously falling under two or more charges (schedules) of a schedular system. Reconciliation rules that determine under which head dividends are to be charged were considered at that point (including the cross-reference to the discussion at 1.2.1).

**Corporate distributions tax**  Although it is typical to tax shareholders with respect to dividends (i.e. a shareholder tax), there are examples of corporations being taxed with respect to their own distributions. Corporate distributions taxes were commonly used in European imputation systems before the Court of Justice of the EU effectively struck them down.[163] For example, the equalisation taxes levied by Germany, Finland, France and Italy in the 1990s were taxes levied on corporations and calculated by reference to their distributions. Similarly, the advance corporation taxes levied in the UK and Ireland at the same time were corporate distributions taxes.[164] There are still isolated examples of corporate distributions taxes. Argentina and Mexico still levy a corporate equalisation tax on profits distributed out of untaxed funds.[165] Other countries levy a general corporate distributions tax on dividends distributed by a corporation. Two famous

---

[163]  Generally, see Harris (2010).

[164]  Regarding these taxes, see Harris (1996) pp. 579–94 (Finland), 595–612 (France), 613–32 (Germany), 633–50 (Ireland), 651–68 (Italy) and 769–89 (UK).

[165]  Income Tax Law (*Ley de Impuesto a las Ganancias*) (Argentina) Art. 69bis and Income Tax Law (*Ley del Impuesto sobre la Renta*) (Mexico) Art. 11.

examples are the Indian dividend distribution tax and the South African secondary company tax.[166]

A corporation may also be charged with the responsibility of withholding tax from the dividends it distributes. Here, the tax may be formally laid on the shareholder, but in substance there is little to distinguish between a corporate distributions tax and a dividend withholding tax, although there can be important tax treaty consequences.[167] This substitutability of corporate distributions tax and dividend withholding tax is demonstrated by the South African example. From 1 April 2012, South Africa has replaced its secondary company tax with a standard dividend withholding tax imposed at the same rate.[168]

**Withholding and dual taxation**    Earlier at 1.3.1 it was noted that corporate income when derived may be simultaneously taxed in the hands of the corporation and its shareholders. Similarly, both the distributing corporation and shareholders may be simultaneously taxed with respect to corporate distributions. This may formally be the case, as with the former European equalisation taxes and the UK and Irish advance corporation taxes (mentioned earlier), but this is now a rare occurrence. However, this dual taxation may also be achieved indirectly in the form of a dividend withholding tax. When a corporation is required to withhold tax from its dividends, it must calculate the tax and pay it to the tax administration. In substance, this is a form of indirect tax, intended for the shareholder but collected from the corporation. In addition, the shareholder may be taxed with respect to the dividend, but receive a credit for the tax paid at the corporate level.

Withholding taxes are common and are often referred to as a system of 'deduction at source'. Most countries operate a withholding tax system for wage income. The approach is more hit and miss with other types of income. Some countries operate a general withholding tax system for dividends paid by resident corporations. Germany is an example of such an approach. As a general rule, German corporations are required to withhold tax at the rate of 25% from dividend distributions.[169] The tax is withheld even in situations in which the shareholder is exempt or partially

---

[166] Income Tax Act, 1961 (India) s. 115O and Income Tax Act, 1962 (South Africa) s. 64B.
[167] In particular, it is usually accepted that corporate distributions taxes are not subject to dividend withholding tax limitations under tax treaties; see Harris (2010, p. 581).
[168] Regarding this change, see Mazansky (2012).
[169] EStG (Germany) s. 43(1)1.

exempt. The rate may be reduced in certain circumstances (e.g. in the context of a tax treaty).

General dividend withholding taxes are quite common in Europe. They have also become more common because of an increase in the number of countries that apply a final dividend withholding tax to dividend income (see the later discussion at 2.4.3.2). However, many countries do not have a general dividend withholding tax, but do impose a dividend withholding tax on distributions by resident corporations to non-residents. The US and Australia are examples of such an approach, which is considered further at 3.1.2. Some countries, such as the UK, simply impose no dividend withholding tax at all, even with respect to distributions to non-residents.

### 2.3.1.2  Expenses in deriving dividends

Each tax law must address the issue of whether expenses incurred in deriving dividends are deductible. The deduction of expenses is only possible (or at least realistic) in the context of a shareholder tax. Taxes imposed on corporations with respect to their distributions, whether formally as a corporate distributions tax or informally as a dividend withholding tax, can only be imposed on the gross amount of dividends. Accordingly, the following discussion is limited to a consideration of whether shareholders can deduct expenses incurred in deriving dividends.

Most commonly, expenses incurred in deriving dividends involve interest incurred on funds used to purchase shares or fees in managing share portfolios. Where a country adopts a global approach to the calculation of income (see the earlier discussion at 1.2.1) a general deduction provision may permit the deduction of expenses incurred in deriving dividends. For example, this is the case in Australia.[170] In principle, the CCCTB Proposal is also a global system and interest would be deductible under the general deduction provision.[171] However, as a form of dividend relief, dividends are expressly exempt, and there is a special rule for deduction of costs incurred in deriving exempt income.[172] This is discussed further at 2.4.3.1.

By contrast, although the US has a general deduction rule for trade and business expenses,[173] it has specific provisions for other types of expenses. In particular, the US has a specific rule that permits a deduction for

---

[170] Income Tax Assessment Act 1997 (Australia) s. 8–1 is the general deduction rule.
[171] CCCTB Proposal Art. 12.
[172] CCCTB Proposal Art. 14(1)(g).
[173] IRC (US) s. 162.

interest expense.[174] This provision is extraordinarily wide but is then narrowed by limitations. In particular, interest expense incurred by individuals for investment income is quarantined, so that it cannot exceed the amount of investment income.[175] 'Investment income' is defined in terms of 'gross income from property held for investment'.[176] These US rules are an example of what is essentially a global system indirectly adopting schedular features. With respect to corporations holding shares, there is no similar restriction on interest deductibility, but there are special rules reducing dividend relief for debt-financed shares, discussed later at 2.4.3.1.

The German rules for corporate shareholders are similar to those under the CCCTB Proposal. The global approach to calculating the corporate tax base means the general rule on deductibility of business expenses applies to corporations, including expenses incurred in deriving dividend income.[177] However, dividends are expressly exempt, and there is a special rule for deduction of costs incurred in deriving such income.[178] For individuals, the treatment of expenses incurred in deriving dividends depends on whether those dividends constitute income from business or income from capital assets. However, in either case, expenses are in principle deductible.[179] Again, these general rules are qualified in the context of dividend relief, discussed later. The interest barrier rules on the deduction of interest, discussed earlier at 2.1.3, apply to both corporations and individuals, but they are not particularly directed at interest incurred in deriving dividends.

So it may be suggested that as a general rule expenses incurred in deriving dividend income are deductible in the same manner as expenses incurred in deriving other types of income. Once again, the exception is the UK. Here the schedular charge to tax is on 'dividends', and this means dividends as a gross amount (i.e. not net of expenses). Whereas most countries start with the presumption that expenses incurred in deriving dividends are deductible and then overlay this with restrictions, the UK does the opposite. It begins with a denial of a deduction for expenses incurred in deriving dividends, but then grants deductions for some expenses in isolated and quite peculiar circumstances.

---

[174] IRC (US) s. 163(a).
[175] IRC (US) s. 163(d).
[176] IRC (US) s. 163(d)(4)(B).
[177] KStG (Germany) s. 8(1) applying EStG (Germany) s. 4(4).
[178] KStG (Germany) s. 8b.
[179] EStG (Germany) ss. 4(4) and 9(1).

As noted, dividends received in the context of a trade or property business are treated as trade or property business income, and so the general rules on deductibility of expenses apply.[180] From this generality, a distinction must be made between shares held by individuals and shares held by other corporations. In the case of individuals subject to the charge to tax on dividends, the charge is in principle on the gross dividends. However, special rules provide that an individual may be entitled to deduct from net income (aggregation of income charged under various schedules) interest paid on a loan to acquire ordinary shares in a close company that is trading. The individual must be a full-time worker or hold more than 5% of the ordinary shares in the company.[181] These provisions only apply to interest expense.

Similarly, where the shareholder is a corporation, the UK has special rules that would permit the deduction of interest. These are the loan relationship rules. Where the interest is incurred in the course of a trade, it is deductible in calculating the profits of that trade.[182] Where this is not the case, interest incurred is only set against interest derived and so produces a profit or deficit on the corporation's loan relationships. Any profit is charged to corporation tax.[183] Any non-trading deficit can be deducted against profits of the deficit period, carried back to set against any non-trading profits from loan relationships of a previous accounting period or carried forward to set against non-trading profits of future accounting periods.[184] As for other non-trading expenses in deriving dividend income, these may be deductible under special rules for 'companies with investment business'. In particular, 'expenses of management' of a corporation's investment business are deductible from total profits.[185] These rules are peculiar to the UK and a function of its schedular approach with its mixture of charging net and gross amounts to corporation tax.

It is one matter to determine that expenses in deriving dividends are deductible. It is another to determine what happens if those expenses are greater than the dividend income (i.e. produce a loss from the holding of shares). Most countries do not address this issue directly, but many countries have restrictions on the use of passive losses that may affect the use of losses from the holding of shares. The treatment of passive losses is not

---

[180] For example, ITTOIA 2005 (UK) s. 34 and CTA 2009 (UK) s. 54.
[181] ITA 2007 (UK) ss. 383, 392 & 393.
[182] CTA 2009(UK) s. 297.
[183] CTA 2009(UK) s. 299.
[184] CTA 2009 (UK) ss. 457–63.
[185] CTA 2009 (UK) s. 1219.

a matter with which this book is particularly concerned. However, it is useful to make a few observations.

The argument for quarantining passive losses is essentially intertwined with the realisations basis of the income tax. Investors may finance an investment in such a manner as to produce losses in early years, but in the expectation that a gain will be made when the investment is finally realised. In some sense, expenses incurred in early years relate to the gain to be derived in the future. There is some incongruity in permitting the deduction of expenses immediately (reducing tax payable on other income), while the gain accrues untaxed until realisation. Further, many countries have concessions for the taxation of capital gains and so there is the risk that expenses are deducted from fully taxable other income, but the ultimate gain is not fully taxed. These complex issues have led some countries to introduce quarantining of losses from the holding of passive investments.

The US has rules quarantining losses on 'passive activities'.[186] These rules do not apply to deriving dividends and certain other types of investment income,[187] but this means that losses on passive activities cannot be set against investment income. As Ault and Arnold note, the effect of these rules is to require a taxpayer to categorise each of the taxpayer's activities into

> 'normal' business activity, passive activity, and portfolio investments, making an allocation of income and deductions to each category. . . . The rules in effect turn the otherwise global system of income definition into a schedular system in which each activity is potentially a separate income category.[188]

By contrast, Germany directly quarantines losses from the holding of shares to set off against income from other capital assets. 'Losses from capital assets may not be offset against earnings from other sources. . . . However, the losses reduce the earnings of the taxpayer from capital assets in the following assessment periods'.[189] These rules do not apply where the shares are held as part of a business, and so they do not apply to corporations (because all of their income is treated as business income, see the earlier discussion at 1.2.1).

---

[186]  IRC (US) s. 469.
[187]  IRC (US) s. 469(e)(1)(A).
[188]  Ault & Arnold (2010, p. 293).
[189]  EStG (Germany) s. 20(6).

The UK does not need rules like these for the holding of shares, because expenses in deriving dividends are residually not deductible. Where the dividends are received in the context of a business, the general deduction rules apply and the same applies to any resulting loss. As noted earlier, outside the context of a trade, expenses are not deductible without a particular rule allowing such as deduction. Often those rules allow a deduction at the point of aggregation of income from different activities (total income), in which case there is no quarantining. An exception is for corporations with a non-trading deficit on loan relationships, where the carry-back and carry-forward of such deficits are quarantined as discussed earlier.

### 2.3.2 *Should corporate income be taxed twice?*

The artificiality of the corporation leads to the deriving of corporate income twice. Without more, this dual nature of corporate income leads to economic double taxation. However, the schizophrenic nature of the corporation when viewed from a tax perspective does not mean that a corporate tax system will accept that double taxation. The first chapter has already noted numerous examples where a corporate tax system might erode the separate identity of a corporation at the point that corporate income is derived, particularly in the context of closely held corporations. A corporate tax system is even more likely to erode the separate identity of a corporation at the point that corporate income is distributed.

A corporate tax system might accept the separate identity of a corporation when corporate income is derived and then tax the corporation with respect to that income. However, when corporate income is distributed, the system might accept in whole or in part that there is only one creation of income and so provide relief from the economic double taxation that would otherwise result. This is referred to as dividend relief and involves to some extent collapsing the separate identities of the corporation and its shareholders. Issues raised by dividend relief are directly related to any philosophy that a corporate tax system may adopt (see the earlier discussion at 1.3.1). But whether or not a corporate tax system has a clear philosophy, economic double taxation of corporate income has consequences that are real and must be addressed, or at least considered.

Controversy over whether corporate income should be subject to economic double taxation is as old as the income tax and the use of corporations.[190] In the course of that controversy, many arguments have

---

[190] For a historical perspective, see Harris (1996, pp. 72–99).

been raised for subjecting corporate income to economic double taxation. Equally, many arguments have been raised for removing that double taxation and providing dividend relief. That debate over this issue could last so long and still be ongoing is testimony to the fact that there is no categorical answer to whether corporate income should or should not be subjected to economic double taxation. Perhaps the core of the matter is that, once countries create and start taxing fictitious entities, intractable issues are inevitable.

It is not the purpose of this book to recount all of the arguments for or against economic double taxation that have ever been raised.[191] However, it is important for analysis in the remainder of this book that the main issues raised by economic double taxation are considered. These are all related to substitution issues and are therefore largely economic in nature.[192] That is, if distributed corporate profits are subject to double taxation, taxpayers can be expected to find an economic substitute with similar results that does not involve double taxation. Economic double taxation of distributed corporate income involves three fundamental elements. First, it involves a corporation conducting an economic activity. Second, it involves the funding of that activity with equity financing (i.e. share capital). Third, it involves the distribution of the results of the economic activity to the person from whom the equity financing was received. Further substitution effects resulting from the economic double taxation of corporate income occur in the international environment, in particular as to location of investment. These are beyond the scope of this book.[193]

These three elements are the core of the major distortions alleged to be caused by economic double taxation. Economic double taxation involves a bias against using the corporate form to conduct economic activity (i.e. the unincorporated sector is favoured). Economic double taxation involves a bias against financing a corporation with equity finance (i.e. debt as a form of financing is favoured, presuming the return on debt is not subject to economic double taxation). Finally, economic double taxation involves a bias against distributing corporate profits (i.e. there is an incentive to retain corporate profits). Each of these biases is considered in turn.[194]

---

[191] For an overview, see Harris (1996, pp. 112–29).
[192] For an overview of corporate taxation and economic distortions, see Nicodème (2009).
[193] For an overview of these issues, see Nicodème (2009, pp. 9–15).
[194] The US Treasury Blue Book of 2003 identified these three distortions as reasons for the introduction of dividend relief in the US in 2004; US Treasury (2003, p. 11). A fourth reason was a distortion in favour of share buy-backs instead of dividends, which turns on the particular US taxation of share buy-backs, discussed further at 6.2.2. A final reason

## 2.3.2.1 Corporate vs. unincorporated sectors

Where corporate income is subject to two levels of taxation, many individuals who may have used a corporate form for a particular earning activity may choose another form that is not subject to double taxation. So, it is often argued that economic double taxation of corporate income leads to greater use of partnerships and sole proprietorships. This distorts an efficient allocation of resources between the incorporated and the unincorporated sectors.

This form of distortion is well illustrated by experience in the US. The US corporate tax system for many years produced full economic double taxation of corporate income distributed to individuals. Tax planners worked on methods of avoiding the second layer of tax. In the 1950s this avoidance was facilitated through the enactment of the S corporation regime, which produces look-through treatment of certain small corporations (see the earlier discussion at 1.3.3.2).[195] The S corporation regime is limited as to number and type of shareholders, and by the 1970s and 1980s tax planners were trying a little harder to engage in tax avoidance through the use of widely owned partnerships. The situation became extreme with the 'burgeoning in the 1980s of so-called master limited partnerships (MLPs) with hundreds or thousands of limited partners holding publicly traded interests'.[196] The US government reacted in 1987 with the rule that certain publicly trade partnerships are treated as corporations for federal tax purposes (see the earlier discussion at 1.1.1.2).

The 1980s also saw the widespread enactment of state LLC statutes. These laws played on the federal list of corporate characteristics giving rise to classification as a corporation for federal tax purposes. As noted earlier at 1.1.1.1, these statutes tried to grant organisations as many corporate attributes as possible without resulting in classification as a corporation for US federal tax purposes. A driving force for wanting to avoid classification as a corporation was to avoid the economic double taxation that the classification involved. As recounted at 1.1.1.1, in 1997 the US tax administration 'gave up on the business-entity classification game' with the introduction of the check-the-box regime,[197] which permits taxpayers

---

was 'double taxation increases incentives for corporations to engage in transactions for the sole purpose of minimizing their tax liability'.

[195] For background to the S corporation regime, see Bittker & Eustice (2003-, para. 6.01[1]).
[196] Bittker & Eustice (2003–, para. 2.04[4]).
[197] Bittker & Eustice (2003-, para. 2.02[3][a]).

to elect as to whether or not their LLC is a corporation for US tax purposes. Each of these examples demonstrates the sensitivity of the corporate versus unincorporated divide to the issue of economic double taxation.

There are, however, limits on this sensitivity. It has sometimes been argued that economic double taxation is the price paid for the benefits of the corporate form. Here, particular attention might be paid to the benefit of limited liability. The unincorporated sector is favoured because this generally means full personal liability for the people conducting an activity. Shareholders with limited liability do not accept this responsibility. The imposition of economic double taxation as a price for limited liability is unconvincing on at least two grounds. Limited liability is most beneficial in the context of insolvent corporations, corporations that do not pay income tax. Second, limited liability is available when using certain other types of artificial entities, and increasingly so.

More convincing is an argument that the corporate form involves the benefit of access to financial markets for the purposes of raising finance. Here corporate law facilitates the bundling of rights that are freely transferrable, which creates a liquid market that is easily accessible by investors. In addition, the markets are regulated by government. Perhaps this benefit of access to markets should be paid for, but it is unlikely that there is any direct relationship between the amount of the benefit and economic double taxation. However, access to financial markets may mean that conducting an activity in an unincorporated form is not a ready substitute for a corporation. If a corporation cannot be readily substituted with an unincorporated form, then economic double taxation may not cause a distortion in this regard.

This sort of argument is only relevant where the activity in question is likely to need access to financial markets for financing purposes. For example, the vast majority of small businesses do not have sufficient critical mass to facilitate or justify access to financial markets, irrespective of the form in which they are conducted. Such businesses do not access financial markets and therefore do not benefit from the corporate form in this regard. Here, the unincorporated form remains highly substitutable with the corporate form. By contrast, large businesses may find it essential to conduct business in the corporate form in order to gain access to financial markets, and so here the unincorporated form is not a viable option. The result may be an argument that economic double taxation, at least to some extent, is less likely to distort large-scale activities as to form of intermediary than small-scale activities.

This is reflected in the US experience recounted earlier. In the context of small businesses, there was erosion of the separate identity of a corporation for tax purposes, but when it came to widely traded partnerships there was reinforcement of that identity. This is also evident in the extent of dividend relief provided by some countries. Some countries provide higher levels of dividend relief with respect to small corporations than to large corporations. The UK and the US provide examples of this, discussed later at 2.4.3.

Economic double taxation of corporate income is just one factor that may be considered in selecting a vehicle to conduct a particular activity. It is a factor that suggests a bias against use of the corporate form. However, that bias may be offset or completely overcome by other tax benefits resulting from use of the corporate form.[198] First, it may be possible to substantially avoid the impact of economic double taxation by deriving other returns from a corporation, such as interest, gains on the sale of shares or distributions in a buy-back or liquidation. Second, use of a corporation may facilitate the benefits of income splitting between related parties. As discussed earlier at 1.3.3.3, this benefit is particularly important in the context of members of a family using a closely held corporation where a corporation may even be used to split income from personal services.

Finally, if the corporate tax rate is sufficiently low, the beneficial taxation of retained profits of a corporation may offset the detriment of economic double taxation of distributed profits. Here Ireland is a good case study. Its corporate tax system historically provided relief from economic double taxation.[199] In 1999 it began a phased reduction of its corporate tax rate from 32% to the current 12.5%.[200] As a result, it introduced a full classical corporate tax system (i.e. economic double taxation of corporate income). However, the benefits of the low corporate tax rate (personal tax rates run to 41%), particularly on retained profits, offset the detriment of the classical system.

### 2.3.2.2 Dividends vs. other returns

Presuming that a corporation is chosen as the vehicle for an activity, economic double taxation of distributed corporate income may distort the type of income that participators derive from the corporation. Other forms of income that may be derived from a corporation include interest,

---

[198] See Harris (2010, pp. 579–81).
[199] See Harris (1996, pp. 633–4).
[200] Finance Act 1999 (Ireland) ss. 27, 28 & 71.

wages, consultancy fees, royalties, rents, capital gains, liquidation distributions, share buy-back distributions etc. The list is as long as the different types of income recognised by a tax system. If these other types of income are only subject to one level of tax, then dividends will be disfavoured as a particular form of return. It is important to point out that many of these other types of income are fully taxable in the hands of the recipient. In these cases, the distortion occurs because these other types of payment might be deductible for the corporation whereas dividends are typically not deductible.

This distortion against the receipt of dividends compared to other types of income is often framed in terms of a distortion in favour of debt financing over equity financing. Of course, the distortion is broader than that and extends to all returns from a corporation that are subjected to less taxation than dividends. However, for present purposes it is sufficient to focus on that major distortion (i.e. the distortion between debt and equity financing). Further, again it is true that this distortion may be ameliorated by other considerations. Ireland is a useful example. Financing with equity may be favourable if profits are retained in a corporation subject to a low corporate tax rate (i.e. lower than if interest accrued to the investor).

For a corporation, especially a widely held corporation, dividends are similar to interest in that both constitute the cost of capital. That one form of cost of capital is deductible, and the other is not, naturally leads to a tax-induced distortion to excessively rely on debt capital rather than equity capital. The tax planning involved in the debt / equity divide and the complications caused by it for corporate tax systems were discussed earlier at 2.1. It is often suggested that because the classical system induces corporations to overly rely on debt as a source of finance, it can make corporations more vulnerable to insolvency and collapse. If a corporation hits hard times it can legally reduce dividend distributions, but is legally obliged to pay its interest obligations. Indeed, a corporation in difficulties may be legally prohibited from distributing dividends.

Distortions caused by the debt / equity distinction have been particularly poignant in the context of the 2008 financial crisis. In its 2003 report on the introduction of dividend relief, the US Treasury prophetically foretold that '[e]xcessive debt increases the risks of bankruptcy during economic downturns.'[201] Nevertheless, corporate tax systems and, in particular, their cross-border effects continue to heavily favour debt over equity financing:

---

[201]  US Treasury (2003, p. 11).

The incentive is to over rely on debt, with the negative economic effects that that entails. Studies have begun looking at the extent to which the tax distortion between debt and equity and other tax policies contributed to the ongoing economic crisis. At one level, the massive reliance on securitisation that was (and is) at the heart of the crisis is driven by an insatiable preference for debt, which is at least partially caused by the continuing tax distortion between debt and equity. As the proportion of investments held by exempt institutions grows, so will this issue.[202]

The driving distortion continues to be the non-deductibility of the return on equity finance when the return on debt financing is deductible.

If the distortion against equity financing is so bad, why is any equity issued at all? Again, the reason seems to be that there are factors that ameliorate the bias against equity. The core of the bias is that the return on equity capital is subject to both corporation tax and investor tax, whereas the return on debt capital is only subject to investor tax. So the difference is the imposition of corporation tax. However, this additional imposition is only a bias if the investor actually suffers the burden of that tax. This raises the thorny and potentially irresolvable issue of who suffers the burden of corporation tax. As noted in the introduction, one thing seems clear: corporations do not suffer the burden of corporation tax because they do not exist.

But do equity investors suffer the burden of a classical corporation tax? Someone must bear the burden of such a tax, but the question is who. Economists have spent much time analysing this issue for more than eighty years.[203] There are a range of possible subjects of the incidence of corporation tax. It could be shifted to employees in the form of lower wages.[204] It could be shifted to consumers in the form of higher prices, or suppliers in lower prices, or even further to reduce the value of land. Or it could be shifted to shareholders, which many people just presume to be the case. The best guess (and it still seems little more than a guess) is that it all depends on elasticities. Elasticities of inputs and outputs may vary dramatically from country to country, from industry to industry and possibly from corporation to corporation. So the corporation tax may be shifted differently depending on the circumstances. However, one point is clear: corporation tax may and in many circumstances is likely to be shifted to shareholders, at least in part.

---

[202] Harris (2010, p. 588).

[203] For a classic work on shifting the incidence of taxation, see Seligman (1927). For a more recent assessment, see Auerbach (2006).

[204] Regarding this potential, see Nicodème (2009, p. 8).

Even if corporation tax is shifted to shareholders, that still leaves the issue of which shareholders. There is some reason to suggest that it is not shifted to the current holders of shares. The example is commonly run of an existing share market in which there is no classical corporation tax. If a classical corporation tax is then imposed, what would the consequences be? To the extent that the corporation tax is shifted to equity capital, it may have a negative effect on the price of shares. Indeed, the price of shares may fall so that the post-tax return on shares after accounting for the new classical corporation tax is similar to what it was before the imposition of the classical corporation tax. The classical corporation tax is said to be capitalised in the price of shares. In a scenario such as this, it is the people holding shares at the time a classical corporation tax is introduced who bear the burden of that tax for the future.

But is that the only impact? Is there no ongoing effect of the classical corporation tax? There might be no ongoing effect if the market remained stagnant, but that is unlikely. Just as the classical corporation tax is capitalised in the price of existing shares, it will also be capitalised every time a corporation seeks to issue new shares. In other words, the price a corporation might expect for newly issued capital might be discounted under a classical corporation tax. Here a classical corporation tax still creates a distortion between debt and equity financing. Corporations will still find it cheaper to raise debt financing than equity financing. The result can be an inefficient allocation of resources.

Even here there is some uncertainty about the impact of the classical corporation tax. If it is more expensive to raise equity finance in the face of a classical corporation tax, then perhaps that means that the size of the equity market is smaller than it otherwise would be. Again, this is a matter on which inconclusive analysis has been conducted. In particular, there is no evidence that equity markets substantially increase as a result of the introduction of dividend relief. The bottom line seems to be that the size of the equity market is not so reliant on whether or not a classical corporation tax exists. One need only consider that the US equity market went through its periods of highest growth in the face of a full classical corporation tax.

Perhaps this all means that debt and equity financing are not that comparable in any case, even though they may appear substitutable. It is becoming clearer that management and the agency costs associated therewith have much to do with the form of corporate financing. The remuneration of managers is often rewarded on the basis of earnings per share. The issue of debt keeps the pool of shares that need to be serviced down, but in doing so the deductibility of interest on that debt reduces the pool of profits available for shareholders. Further, corporate managers often issue shares as a mechanism of sending signals to the market as to the strength of the corporation's prospects. An issuance of shares may mean that managers believe the corporation will be able to adequately service the return on those shares in the future. The point is that even in the face of a classical corporation tax there are other important factors at work that determine whether and, if so, in what quantity a corporation issues equity capital.

Perhaps the forms of return on debt and equity are also not fully substitutable, at least in arm's length financing scenarios. It is true that both debt and equity constitute the cost of capital for a corporation, but the return on that capital might be fundamentally different. The return on debt capital might be simply a standard rate of return. The return on equity capital might involve in whole or part a participation in economic rents. As noted earlier at 1.3.1, there is some reason for suggesting that economic rents warrant greater taxation than a standard rate of return. In particular, taxation of a standard rate of return is likely to have an inflationary impact, whereas this may not be the case with taxation of economic rents. However, it is likely that at least part of the return on equity capital is a standard rate of return. Here it might be suggested that this part should not be subject to a classical corporation tax, but the part that is a share of economic rents can be. It is this sort of analysis that has driven the allowance for corporate equity proposals (see the earlier discussion at 1.3.1).

If classical corporation tax is not shifted fully or partially to shareholders (past, present or future), but is shifted onto other corporate stakeholders, would that make it acceptable? Clearly there would still need to be an investigation of the incidence of the classical corporation tax to assess the extent to which its impact is harmful. However, it seems strange to accept that, in the context of what is labelled a direct tax, the government accepts that the tax subject does not bear the burden of the tax, but otherwise the government does not really know (or care) who bears its burden. This is consistent with the point made in the introduction that, irrespective of its form, a corporation tax can only ever be an indirect tax.

This sort of analysis – to whom is the classical corporation tax shifted?; if shareholders, is it capitalised in the price of shares?; to what extent is the return on equity capital a share of economic rents? – pushes rationale thinking to the extreme. The bottom line seems to be that we still know little about the precise impact of the classical corporation tax and its distorting effects and we are not likely to see much progress on this front in the near future. However, just because we cannot analyse the precise impact of the distortion does not mean that it is not real.

There can be little doubt that a corporate tax system that provides dividend relief has a neutralising effect on the debt / equity distortion. How far dividend relief can neutralise debt and equity depends on the type of dividend relief selected. There is some reason for believing that, if dividend relief accurately provides relief for corporation tax, then the incidence of corporation tax is removed and there is no issue of shifting. That does not mean that some taxpayers cannot shift their personal tax liability onto others, but that is a different and generic issue.

### 2.3.2.3   Distribution vs. retention

It is presumed that a tax is levied when corporate income is derived and that tax is imposed on the corporation. Whether that tax is appropriate and the types of distortions that it may cause were discussed earlier at 1.3.2. The distribution of dividends is an entirely different event and requires separate consideration. If any tax is imposed by reason of the distribution of dividends, there must be an instinctive response to not do that (i.e. an incentive to not distribute dividends). This incentive to retain corporate profits is most extreme under a classical corporate tax system, in which there is a full imposition of tax on the distribution of dividends. Retaining profits is another method of corporate financing and often is a cheaper source of financing than distributing dividends to existing shareholders and then seeking reinvestment of those funds from those shareholders, whether as new debt or new equity.

As with other distortions caused by economic double taxation of corporate income, whether a tax incentive to retain profits is appropriate is subject to ongoing debate.[205] It is often argued that an incentive to retain profits is a good thing because it encourages saving: the funds never reach individual investors (or at least that is the hope), and so these individuals do not have the choice of consuming those funds and the funds remain available for stimulating further economic activity. It is also pointed out that retaining profits is the cheapest form of financing a corporation because it involves no transaction costs. Both the issue of new debt and that of new equity involve deadweight transaction costs by comparison to retaining profits.

However, it is not clear that the form of saving encouraged by an incentive to retain profits is efficient. In particular, financing in the form of

---

[205] 'Tax effects on the distribution policy of corporations have been at the center of an intense debate in the theoretical and empirical literature on corporate finance and business taxation for over half a century'; Schanz & Theßeling (2011, p. 1).

retained profits is not subject to market competition and is particularly prone to agency costs (i.e. the risk that management will act in a self-interested manner). Even where management behaves, it may only have expertise in running the core activities of the corporation. If these activities are adequately financed, management may have no particular expertise in investing surplus funds. It is often suggested that shareholders (or, in particular, specialist intermediaries such as fund managers) are more efficient in selecting additional investments. Indeed, because individuals increasingly hold their investments in corporations through intermediaries, the risk of individual consumption instead of reinvestment is decreased (and in any case individuals can finance consumption with borrowing). However, these observations do not apply in the context of closely held corporations.

The over-retention of profits by corporations is also blamed for what has been termed 'survival of the fattest'.[206] Economic double taxation of corporate income may suppress the return on shares in the form of dividends. This can have a negative impact on the price of shares, which might be artificially low when compared to the asset backing of a corporation. A low share price encourages takeovers and liquidations. As a result, corporations compete to subsume each other because the total share value of each corporation is less than its asset value. At times the inefficient diversification of corporate investment funded with retained profits has been viewed as a particular problem, especially during the 1990s. It was one of the major rationales for the introduction of dividend relief in the US from 2004:

> [D]ouble taxation lessens the pressure on corporate managers to undertake only the most productive investments because corporate investments funded by retained earnings may receive less scrutiny than investments funded by outside equity or debt financing.[207]

Excessive retention is viewed as increasing the power of corporate managers and making their decisions less open to scrutiny, particularly in widely held corporations. This practice increases exposure to agency risk and the risk of corporate management engaging in excesses that are targeted towards their personal benefit.

However, just as corporate management may continue to issue shares in the face of a classical corporation tax, it is clear that it continues to

---

[206] See Harris (1996, p. 121) and the references cited therein.
[207] US Treasury (2003, p. 11).

distribute dividends in the face of such a tax. As Schanz and Theßeling observe,

> Most of the studies find a rather minor role of taxes. Signalling-, agency- or behavioral effects seem to be at the center of managers' attention when deciding about payout policy.[208]

Nevertheless, they conclude that 'taxation is an important factor for managers deciding on their firm's payout policy'.[209]

Kaserer, Rapp and Trinchera take this analysis further by finding that taxation is likely to be a less important factor in corporations in which management holds a significant number of shares (i.e. where managers are substantial shareholders). By contrast, they find that substantial shareholders who are not managers do not have a significant impact on corporate distribution policy, and there is greater scope for the influence of taxation. Their study

> casts some doubt on the presumption that dividend decisions are driven by controlling activities exerted by external large shareholders. It rather seems that these decisions are driven by agents, giving way to the view that dividend decisions are the outcome of an agency problem (i.e. a private benefit consideration).[210]

Their conclusion is that 'dividend policy is an instrument to extract private benefits of control rather than it is a corporate governance mechanism'.[211]

The impact of corporate insiders on distribution policy has also been confirmed in the US. As noted earlier at 1.3.2.2, in late 2010 the US went through a peculiar episode in which the Bush tax cuts were about to expire. This would have caused the form of dividend relief introduced with those cuts (discussed later at 2.4.3.2) to also expire and would have resulted in the taxation of some dividends increasing from 15% to 39.6%. In the face of this possible impact, many US corporations distributed extraordinary dividends (larger than usual) or accelerated the time of their normal January dividend. Recent evidence suggests that the dividend increases were concentrated in firms largely held by corporate insiders (i.e. management).[212]

---

[208]  Schanz & Theßeling (2011, p. 1).
[209]  Schanz & Theßeling (2011, p. 24). Similarly, Kaserer, Rapp & Trinchera (2011, p. 21).
[210]  Kaserer, Rapp & Trinchera (2011, p. 4). For a similar observation, see Andres, Betzer & Goergen (2012).
[211]  Kaserer, Rapp & Trinchera (2011, p. 22).
[212]  Hanlon & Hoopes (2012).

## 2.4  Dividend relief

There is a substantial consensus that there should be some relief from the economic double taxation of corporate income (i.e. dividend relief), at least in many circumstances. Presuming that is desirable, the next issue is how can it be provided. That is the focus of this heading, which is concerned with identifying and analysing the various methods of providing dividend relief. It begins with a consideration of the options for dividend relief and some of the factors that might be considered in structuring dividend relief.[213]

These options reveal that dividend relief may come in only six essential forms, three at the corporate level and three at the shareholder level. The discussion proceeds to consider the corporate- and shareholder-level forms of dividend relief separately. This discussion analyses the attributes of each method, its benefits and limitations. The discussion is illustrated with examples of what countries do in practice.

### 2.4.1  Options and factors in selecting dividend relief

The purpose of this subheading is to provide some background material before analysing the various forms of dividend relief. It begins by sketching the options for dividend relief. Over the years all sorts of labels have been attached to different forms of dividend relief. The discussion suggests the structural options are limited to six types. Of particular importance in understanding the nature and operation of different forms of dividend relief is the potential difference between the corporation tax base and the shareholder tax base. Critical to this difference is income with respect to which preference (i.e. some form of tax concession) is granted. Preference income causes particular difficulties for dividend relief.

There is also an issue as to whether dividend relief is full or partial. If partial relief is adopted, there are a number of options for implementing the limitation. Finally, different forms of dividend relief give rise to problems with tax arbitrage in the form of dividend streaming. The discussion in this subheading considers dividend streaming from a structural perspective and seeks to explain why it arises. The propensity for particular types of dividend relief to give rise to dividend streaming problems is discussed in other subheadings.

---

[213] This heading follows the approach in Harris (1996, pp. 56–72).

### 2.4.1.1   Types

The options available for relief from economic double taxation of distributed corporate income (i.e. dividend relief) revolve around the dual nature of corporate income. This dual nature provides two potential taxing events: the deriving of corporate income and its distribution. As noted, the levy of tax at both these points without relief for one tax against the other is referred to as the classical system. There are several options for the taxation of corporate income when it is derived. These options were considered earlier at 1.3, where the focus was largely on the taxation of the corporation with respect to its income, taxation of shareholders (e.g. partnership-style taxation) or taxation of both. There are similar options for the taxation of distributions of corporate income; these were considered earlier at 2.3.1.1.

Economic double taxation and relief from it in the form of dividend relief are concerned with the dual nature of corporate income and not who is taxed with respect to that income. The tax on corporate income where derived is generally taxed in the hands of the corporation (i.e. corporation tax), and the tax on corporate profits where distributed is in the hands of the shareholder. So dividend relief typically involves relief from one or the other of these taxes. But this presumption can cloud the issue of dividend relief. Dividend relief is concerned with reconciling any tax levied when corporation income is derived (whether on the corporation or the shareholder) with any tax levied when corporate income is distributed (whether on the corporation or the shareholder).

Another important point to emphasise is that dividend relief involves relief from economic double taxation triggered by the distribution of dividends. It is not concerned with double taxation triggered by other events. So it is not concerned with reconciling taxation of both the corporation and the shareholder when corporate income is derived, or taxation of both the corporation and the shareholder when corporate income is distributed. Further, it is not concerned with reconciling the taxation of corporate income when derived and the taxation of capital gains on the disposal of shares, which might also involve economic double taxation (see the later discussion at 5.1.2). With these qualifications and reservations, the following discussion presumes a single corporation tax is levied on corporate income when derived and a single shareholder tax is levied on dividends when distributed.

The levy of income tax, on either corporate income or shareholder income, involves a tax equation that may be represented as

Taxable Income × Tax Rate = Tax Result

Table 2.1. *Types of dividend relief*

| **Tax on corporate income when derived** | | |
| --- | --- | --- |
| *Reduce* income | tax rate | tax payable |
| *Type* dividend deduction | split rate | corporation tax credit |
| **Tax on corporate income when distributed** | | |
| *Reduce* income | tax rate | tax payable |
| *Type* dividend exclusion | shareholder differentiation | dividend tax credit |

All corporate tax systems that address economic double taxation of corporate income must affect the tax equation at either the corporate or the shareholder level. Accordingly, economic double taxation may be relieved by adjusting the corporation tax equation or the shareholder tax equation or a combination of both. Further, the adjustment must alter (i.e. reduce) one of the three elements of the tax equation: taxable income, the tax rate or the tax result. In each of these cases, the reduction is triggered by and calculated by reference to dividends distributed.

This means that there are six basic types of dividend relief: three at the corporate level reflecting each of the three elements of the corporation tax equation, and three at the shareholder level reflecting each of the three elements of the shareholder tax equation. Each of these types of dividend relief is referred to in Table 2.1 with the usual labels used to refer to each type, which are also used for the purposes of this book.

These different types of dividend relief are explored individually at 2.4.2 and 2.4.3 and illustrated with examples. From a global perspective, there is still a substantial amount of diversity in the types of dividend relief systems adopted by countries.[214] However, the last three decades has seen a dramatic decrease in the number of corporate-level dividend relief systems. The reasons for this decrease are further explored at 2.4.2 and in Chapter 3.

Further, countries may simultaneously adopt more than one type of dividend relief. The type of dividend relief used may vary depending on the type of shareholder or even the type of corporation distributing the dividend, or in a multitude of other ways. In addition, more than two types of dividend relief may be used simultaneously with respect to the same dividend. So, for example, the UK uses two shareholder-level types of

---

[214] For example, see the tables in Ault & Arnold (2010, pp. 408–9).

dividend relief for dividends received by individuals (shareholder differentiation and dividend tax credit). Similarly, before 2000 Germany simultaneously used corporate-level dividend relief (split rate) and shareholder-level dividend relief (dividend tax credit).

There is a difference in the quantum of dividends that may be distributed where dividend relief is provided at the corporate level or where it is provided at the shareholder level. Where full dividend relief is provided at the corporate level, corporation tax is removed, and, therefore, corporations are able to distribute their profits gross of corporation tax. Where relief is provided at the shareholder level, corporation tax is retained. In this case, corporations only have profits net of corporation tax available for distribution and so have the same quantum of dividends available for distribution as under a classical system.

Although total tax levied may be no different whether relief is provided at the corporate level or at the shareholder level, some differences may arise. For example, the time for payment of shareholder tax may be different from that for corporation tax. Where dividend relief is provided at the corporate level, only the calculation of corporation tax requires adjustment. By contrast, where relief is provided at the shareholder level the tax return of each shareholder may require adjustment. Further, because it reduces corporation tax according to distributions and leaves corporations with more profits for distribution, corporate-level dividend relief may affect the distribution policy of corporations.

### 2.4.1.2 Corporation and shareholder tax bases

To analyse the differences among the various methods of dividend relief it is useful to consider some fundamental differences between the corporation tax base and the shareholder tax base. As discussed at the start of this chapter, it is corporate law (not tax law) that regulates the amount corporations may distribute. The profits that corporations are permitted to distribute for corporate law purposes are not likely to correspond with their taxable profits. In particular, corporate profits for corporate law purposes may exceed corporate profits for tax purposes. Therefore, corporations may be able to distribute more profits than they declare for tax purposes.

A major difference between corporation tax levied where corporate income is derived and shareholder tax levied where corporate profits are distributed is the difference between the bases on which each tax is calculated. Where all corporate profits are distributed, the shareholder tax base is not equivalent to the corporation tax base. Rather, the potential tax base for shareholders is, as a general rule, distributable corporate profits as determined by corporate law. This potential tax base is referred to as the 'shareholder tax base'. Of course, a shareholder's taxable income is typically less than this potential amount because only dividends distributed are taxable. This reflects the realisations base of the income tax.

By contrast, the corporation tax base is typically the taxable income of corporations, which may be subject to various forms of adjustment when compared to accounting profits. Further, to be comparable to the shareholder tax base, the corporation tax base must be reduced by corporation tax paid. Even with these adjustments, the difference between the corporation tax base and the shareholder tax base is not an accurate reflection of the difference between how corporate income is taxed when derived and how it might be taxed when distributed. In particular, corporation tax payable may be reduced by concessions other than reductions in amounts of taxable income. Preferences (discussed shortly) also include rate reductions and tax credits. So, at one level, to provide an accurate comparator between the corporation tax base and the shareholder tax base, the corporation tax base may be taken to equal corporation tax paid divided by the headline corporate tax rate. This would then be reduced by corporation tax paid.

Differences between the corporation tax base and the shareholder tax base (in the senses described earlier) are important for the purposes of dividend relief, particularly where full relief from economic double taxation is desired. Incongruence between the corporation tax base and the shareholder tax base may take two forms: the corporation tax base may be larger than the shareholder tax base or vice versa. As a general rule, the shareholder tax base is the larger one. In this case, it is interesting to consider the effects that the incongruence may have where dividend relief is provided at either the corporate level or the shareholder level. In the former case, where the relief is calculated according to dividends distributed and all corporate law profits are distributed, corporations may find themselves in a surplus relief position. Where relief is provided at the shareholder level, but the relief is measured by reference to the corporation tax base, insufficient relief may be generated to provide dividend relief for all dividends distributed.

By contrast, sometimes the corporation tax base may exceed the shareholder tax base.[215] In this case, where full dividend relief is provided at the

---

[215] This can happen where taxable income for corporation tax purposes is greater than distributable profits. One example is where expenses are not deductible for corporation tax purposes, but are for accounting purposes. Entertainment expenses and fines might be an

corporate level the shareholder tax base will generate insufficient relief to eliminate corporation tax completely. Corporation tax levied with respect to profits not available for distribution will remain unrelieved. Where relief is provided at the shareholder level, as the corporation tax base exceeds the shareholder tax base, there will be excess corporation tax base. Because this excess corporation tax base is not available for distribution it is unlikely that shareholders will be provided relief in this regard.

### 2.4.1.3   Preference income

As mentioned, the corporation tax base is likely to be smaller than the shareholder tax base. This results from erosions from the corporation tax base when compared with the shareholder tax base and, in particular, hidden profit distributions. These erosions are commonly referred to as 'preferences' or giving rise to 'preference income'. Preferences encompass exclusions from taxable income, rate reductions and tax credits not suggested by the taxation of income according to a comprehensive definition of income and at full rates. Preferences are also known as 'tax expenditures',[216] but that term is not used in this book because, depending on the type of dividend relief, the preference granted may not be permanent, and in the context of dividend relief it is more usual to refer to preferences.[217] With particular reference to corporation tax, preference income constitutes profits available for distribution that have not been subject to corporation tax at the full rate.

Assuming the corporation tax base is smaller than the shareholder tax base, corporations may have profits available for distribution that are not subject to corporation tax at the full rate (i.e. preference income). In this case, the government must decide the extent to which it will permit corporations to pass through preferences or it will wash out preferences on distribution of corporate profits for which preference is granted. Preferences are 'passed through' where the tax burden suffered by corporate preference income on distribution is the same as if shareholders derived the income distributed and were granted preference directly. Preferences are 'washed out' where they reduce the tax burden on corporate income when derived, but that reduction is not reflected in a matching reduction of taxation of corporate income when distributed. In other words, corporate

---

example. Another example is where corporate taxable income includes gains that are not available for distribution. Certain unrealised gains or income attributed from a controlled corporation might be an example.

[216] For the classic work on tax expenditures, see Surrey and McDaniel (1985).

[217] See Harris (1996, p. 59) and another classic work, being McLure (1979).

tax systems that fully tax on the distribution of corporate profits that were not fully taxed when derived are said to wash out the preference.[218]

### 2.4.1.4 Extent of relief

As noted earlier at 2.3.2, the arguments for relief from economic double taxation of distributed corporate income are not conclusive. Given the ongoing dispute and the fact that many of those arguments are questions of degree, it is not surprising that most countries only provide partial dividend relief. Full dividend relief involves relief that is sufficient to remove the second level of tax. Typically, this involves the removal of corporation tax or shareholder tax. However, it may involve a reduction in both so as to produce what may be considered a single level of tax. Partial dividend relief is relief between full dividend relief and the implementation of a full classical system. A full classical system involves the imposition of corporation tax on corporate income when derived and full shareholder taxation of corporate income when distributed, without relief for one tax against the other.

There are numerous ways in which partial dividend relief can be implemented. Many of these depend on the type of dividend relief selected, and they are explored with practical examples in the remainder of the discussion under this heading. However, there are some broad options for partial dividend relief, which are useful to outline at this point. The most common option is a simple proportional one. The relief that the tax law adopts is simply insufficient to fully relieve economic double taxation of distributed corporate income. So, for example, a full corporation tax is imposed on corporate income when derived. In addition, some shareholder tax is imposed on distributed corporate income, but not a full tax when compared to, say, wages or other income. Alternately, there may be a full shareholder tax, and the normal corporation tax due with respect to corporate income when derived is reduced by reference to dividends distributed, but not to the point to which it is completely removed.

Countries also vary, sometimes dramatically, their level of dividend relief depending on the type of shareholder receiving distributions. Three common divisions depend on whether the shareholder is an individual, a corporation or a non-resident. Even where countries have adopted a

---

[218] For a detailed discussion of preference income and its interrelationship with all forms of integrating corporation and shareholder taxes, see McLure (1979). In particular, see p. 94 regarding pass-through and wash-out of corporate preferences.

full classical system for individuals, dividend relief for inter-corporate dividends is common. This is provided to prevent the cascading of economic double taxation as dividends are distributed through chains of corporations, producing triple taxation or worse. For this reason, most countries provide virtually full dividend relief for many if not most inter-corporate dividends. So, despite only offering partial dividend relief for individuals, Germany, the UK and the US provide virtually full dividend relief for at least some types of inter-corporate dividends. Non-resident shareholders are also often treated very differently from resident shareholders. Sometimes they are not taxed at all, and sometimes they are, subject to tax treaties, taxed more highly than any resident shareholder. These matters are further explored at 3.1.2.

Dividend relief may also vary dramatically depending on the type of corporation distributing a dividend. Here the major distinction is between distributions from resident and non-resident corporations. However, the treatment can also vary depending on other subcategories of corporations. Dividend relief may vary depending on whether a dividend is distributed from a widely or closely held corporation. The treatment may also depend on whether a dividend is received from a group corporation or not. Less commonly, dividend relief may vary depending on the type of funds distributed by the corporation, and here the distribution of foreign income, for example, may be important. Dividend relief may depend on the form of dividend; for example, in some cases hidden profit distributions may not carry dividend relief. Finally, the time at which corporate income is derived or distributed may have an impact. When countries change the form of their corporate tax system they often adopt transitional rules that can grandfather an existing treatment for a certain period.

### 2.4.1.5   Dividend streaming

It has been noted that countries have a habit of adopting different types of dividend relief for different types of shareholders, as well as different levels of dividend relief depending on the circumstances. This can make for a cocktail of complex definitions and operative provisions in the tax law, but has other, potentially more serious effects. Unless all returns derived from a corporation (dividends, interest, rents, wages, gains on disposal of shares, bonus shares, returns of capital and so on) are treated in the same manner in the hands of each taxpayer, then the taxpayer will prefer one type of return over another. This by itself only creates a bias in favour of one return over another, with the risk that there will be more of this type of return in the market than would occur with a more neutral treatment. In practice, however, this never occurs and the consequences are more serious.

Tax laws do tax different (and substitutable) returns differently (i.e. they adopt a schedular approach, at least to some extent). Tax laws also tax different taxpayers differently. What tax laws do not do is tax different taxpayers with respect to different returns differently to the same extent. This can result in a corporation 'streaming' dividends to particular shareholders, which requires some explanation.[219]

**What is dividend streaming?** 'Dividend streaming' is a phrase that is often used to describe a practice that many countries perceive as eroding their income tax system. It is inherently related to a schedular, as opposed to a global income tax. In the context of a schedular income tax, it is impossible to identify a boundary between streaming practices that are perceived as abusive and other practices that countries repeatedly identify as acceptable. If different types of income are taxed differently, taxpayers can be expected to manipulate their circumstances so as to derive the type of income that is subject to least tax.

As the phrase suggests, 'dividend streaming' may be divided into two aspects. The concept of dividends, the difficulty of identifying what is in substance a dividend and the related difficulty of identifying who are in substance shareholders for tax purposes were discussed earlier at 2.1 and 2.2. Any serious attempt to regulate dividend streaming requires the drawing of a line somewhere in the spectrum of shareholder or dividend attributes. Disbursement on one side of the line would be considered typical of shareholding and that on the other would not. Such distinctions are necessarily arbitrary in nature.

Turning to the second aspect of dividend streaming (i.e. 'streaming'), dividends are by definition distributed to shareholders. Therefore, on one view, all dividends are streamed or (to use some synonyms) directed or guided (i.e. to shareholders). Another view suggests that, because the concept of a dividend involves distribution to shareholders, the distribution of dividends to shareholders in the usual, typical or expected manner does not involve streaming, directing or guiding the dividends; rather it simply follows the expected course. Because the direction of dividends to ordinary shareholders may be expected, such distributions should be excluded from any concept of 'dividend streaming'. Streaming of dividends

---

[219] For a more detailed consideration of dividend streaming, see Harris (1998).

appears to suggest that, but for the directing or guiding of dividends to a particular end, the funds or profits constituting the dividends might be expected to take a different form or direction; that is, an alternative course.[220] The concept of dividend streaming, therefore, seems to involve a distribution of dividends in a manner that is contrary to expectations. That is, dividend streaming essentially involves an atypical distribution of dividends.

It appears that the streaming, directing or guiding of dividends contrary to expectations may take one of two forms: funds in the form of dividends may be directed to particular persons, or funds in the form of dividends may be directed away from particular persons. Dividend streaming essentially involves a substance over form approach to the characterisation of dividends. As such, it often involves deriving a non-dividend return in the form of dividends or a dividend return in a non-dividend form.

**Why engage in dividend streaming?**  The essence of the tax rationale for dividend streaming is comparative. From a tax perspective, dividends are either advantaged or disadvantaged when compared with other types of income or gain. The advantage or disadvantage typically relates directly to the amount of tax payable, for example, through tax base, rate or credit mechanisms. Tax incentives for dividend streaming are indicative of a schedular income tax. Indeed, for streaming purposes it is not useful to distinguish between different types of income, but only between income subject to different tax treatments. So, in the context of dividend streaming, it might be relevant to distinguish not only between different types of income subject to different tax treatment but also between different types of dividends that are treated differently for tax purposes.

Dividend streaming may be induced by a direct minimisation of tax or by tax deferral. With respect to direct minimisation, a corporate tax system may provide a general incentive or disincentive for deriving dividend income. The classical system is an example of a general disincentive towards deriving dividend income. Alternatively, the incentive or disincentive may only be directed to particular persons. The full benefit of some types of dividend relief may only be granted to particular shareholders.

For example, a tax law may tax an individual taxpayer at 40% on interest, but 25% on dividends. The taxation of dividends could

---

[220] The assessment of a particular tax treatment by reference to an alternative expected course is a standard approach in tax law rules of an anti-abuse nature; see Harris (2012).

produce full dividend relief (e.g. because corporation tax is imposed at 20%).[221] Inevitably, there will be another taxpayer who is not treated in the same manner. So, for example, there will be a pension fund, government fund or non-resident, for example, that is exempt both with respect to dividends and interest. Here, the individual taxpayer is taxed differently as between dividends and interest, but the exempt taxpayer is not. This can create an incentive to stream interest to tax exempts or, in other words, to stream dividends away from tax exempts and towards individual taxpayers. Similar incentives can be created where a taxpayer is in a loss position (and so effectively an exempt taxpayer).

The same example could be given where different forms of share return are treated differently for different taxpayers. So, an individual shareholder might be taxed at a lower rate on returns of capital or share buybacks than on dividends. By contrast, an exempt entity may be exempt on all returns. In this case, there may be an incentive to stream dividends away from the individual shareholder and to exempt institutions. Similarly, some types of dividends carry dividend relief, but other types of dividends do not. But for an exempt institution there may be no difference (both may be exempt), in which case there is an incentive to stream dividends with dividend relief to shareholders that are subject to tax.

Dividend streaming may also be encouraged through an incentive to distribute or retain corporate profits. This is largely an issue of the relationship between the corporate tax rate and the shareholder tax rate, discussed earlier at 1.3.2. Shareholders taxable with respect to dividends (after allowance for any dividend relief) may prefer that the corporation retain profits; that is, shelter the profits under the lower corporate tax rate. Other shareholders that receive tax benefits with distributions (e.g. dividend tax credits) may prefer that profits be distributed or be neutral as to distributions. So, for example, an exempt fund might like to receive distributions because it does not suffer tax on them and distributions give it an opportunity to reinvest the funds as it desires. By contrast, shareholders that are taxable with respect to distributions might prefer retention, because here they (indirectly through the corporation's reinvestment) get a return on funds that if the funds were distributed would have to be paid in tax.

As these examples with tax-exempt funds demonstrate, incentives to dividend stream can be complex. On the one hand, the tax system might

---

[221] In this example, 100 profit produces 20 corporation tax, leaving 80 dividend; 25% of 80 is a further 20 in shareholder tax, making a total of 40, which is equal to the amount of tax levied on the interest.

discourage tax exempts from receiving dividends when compared with, say, interest on debt. On the other hand, if tax exempts do hold shares, they are likely to prefer distributions over retention. By contrast, persons taxable with respect to dividends may (if there is full dividend relief) be neutral as to holding shares, but if they do they will prefer retention rather than distribution. To neutralise all dividend streaming incentives, a corporate tax system would have to be very global in nature and perhaps do away with the realisation basis.

**Options for dividend streaming**    Dividend streaming is all about directing dividends between investors in such a manner so as to produce the lowest tax result on a fixed distribution. In other words, dividend streaming is essentially a form of tax arbitrage. In practice, it can be facilitated by manipulating rights held in corporations and so is inherently related to the classification of corporate rights as discussed earlier at 2.1. Shares may be issued with rights that will enable dividends to be directed to particular investors. For example, a corporation may issue two classes of shares. One class may be shares on which dividends are regularly payable. The other class may be capital growth shares (e.g. shares on which only bonus shares are received or shares that are redeemable after a set period of time). Alternately, a corporation may issue debt instruments that behave like shares (e.g. profit-sharing debentures or convertible notes). As can be seen, hybrid instruments are commonly used to stream particular types of returns, including dividends.

In these types of streaming, the issuing corporation is designing a particular corporate instrument with particular investors in mind. However, as noted earlier at 2.1.4, a basic corporate investment in the form of shares or debt may be supplemented with a secondary or collateral instrument. In theory, the related instrument may be concluded with the subject corporation, a related corporation or an independent third party (e.g. a merchant bank). The tax planning for implementing dividend streaming and the tax law rules to counter it can be very complex and the tax at stake substantial. Incentives to dividend stream and rules that impede it are considered at various points in this book. However, dividend streaming as a dedicated issue is not pursued further.

### 2.4.2   Corporate-level dividend relief

Relief from economic double taxation of corporate income may be provided at the corporate level when corporations distribute dividends (i.e.

dividend relief from corporation tax may be provided). In this case, dividend relief takes the form of a reduction in one of the elements of the corporation tax equation. Accordingly, it may be provided by a reduction in taxable income, a reduced corporate tax rate for distributed profits or a corporate tax credit calculated according to dividends distributed. Each of these forms of dividend relief at the corporate level may be structured so as to produce similar results. However, there can be subtle differences among them.

In each of these three systems, dividends remain subject to full shareholder tax. As a consequence, there are no special considerations regarding the deduction of expenses incurred by a shareholder in deriving dividend income. As under a classical system, it is likely that such expenses are deductible according to normal principles. The exception would be a country, like the UK, that generally taxes dividends on a gross basis. Accordingly, this subheading does not explore the deduction of expenses incurred in deriving dividends any further. By contrast, dividend relief systems that operate at the shareholder level raise difficult issues regarding the deduction of expenses incurred in deriving dividends. These issues are explored in the context of each shareholder-level dividend relief system at 2.4.3.

Corporate-level dividend relief systems are rarely used because of their international behaviour. In particular, as discussed later at 3.1.2, as a matter of non-discrimination, tax treaties usually require corporate-level relief to be granted for dividends paid to non-resident shareholders if such a relief is available for dividends paid to resident shareholders. In the context of full dividend relief, this would remove corporation tax from profits derived by a non-resident through a resident corporation. This means that corporation tax would not function as a source-based tax. As corporate tax rates have decreased dramatically in recent years, but the right to impose dividend withholding tax under tax treaties has often remained, the international limitations on using corporate-level dividend relief systems may not be as severe as they once were. This is especially the case if a partial dividend relief system is used.

### 2.4.2.1  Dividend deduction system

Relief from double taxation of corporate income may be implemented by reducing the corporate tax base with respect to dividends distributed. Accordingly, a corporation may be permitted a deduction for dividends distributed.

---

### Box 2.1:  Dividend deduction system

Corporate profits of 100 (gross of dividend deduction), a dividend of 50 and a corporate tax rate of 30%:

Corporation tax is $100-50 = 50 \times 30\% = 15$ tax payable

Shareholder has income of 50 taxed at marginal rates

---

The dividend deduction method is the only method capable of fully equating the tax treatment of the return on debt with that of equity, and this is its primary potential benefit. In the past, this system has been used by a number of countries. It was the first corporate tax system adopted by the UK in 1799.[222] It was adopted by Sweden, Finland and Norway beginning in the late 1960s and lasted through to the reforms of the early 1990s.[223] It has also been used more recently in Greece, Mauritius and even Afghanistan.

Currently, there are no major examples of the use of the dividend deduction system. Indeed, many countries specifically provide that dividends are not deductible. This is the case in Germany, the UK and under the CCCTB Proposal.[224] However, there are some isolated instances in which a dividend may be deductible. For example, under the Australian debt / equity rules (see the earlier discussion at 2.1.2) it is possible for shares to meet the debt test. A specific provision permits a deduction for dividends paid on such shares.[225] So, a deduction may be available for dividends paid on, say, ten-year redeemable preference shares. Australia also effectively permits a deduction for dividends distributed by co-operative societies (which are treated as companies for tax purposes) where the imputation system is otherwise not applicable.[226]

### Preference income

The dividend deduction system (see Box 2.1) has an impact on preferences granted at the corporate level. Assuming the shareholder tax base (distributable profits) is larger than the corporate tax base, the dividend deduction system washes out all corporate preferences where a full

---

[222] See Harris (2006, p. 413).
[223] See Harris (1996, p. 96).
[224] See KStG (Germany) s. 8(3), CTA 2009 (UK) s. 1305 and CCCTB Proposal Art. 14(1)(a).
[225] Income Tax Assessment Act 1997 (Australia) s. 25–85(3). Under (5), the deduction is not available if the internal rate of return on the share exceeds a particular benchmark.
[226] Income Tax Assessment Act 1936 (Australia) s. 120.

distribution policy is pursued. Deduction of dividends completely removes the corporate tax base (and corporation tax liability), leaving the shareholder tax base. As a result, under a full distribution policy a full dividend deduction may produce surplus relief at the corporate level in the form of permanent losses. The extent of such losses (assuming full carry-forward and carry-back) represents preferences granted at the corporate level in the form of exclusions from taxable income (e.g. the extent to which distributable profits exceed taxable income for corporation tax purposes).[227] In particular, excess relief may be caused by hidden profit distributions (assuming they give rise to a dividend deduction), particularly where they do not give rise to notional income of the corporation (the usual situation, see 2.2.2).

Other preferences granted at the corporate level, such as tax credits or reduced tax rates, are also washed out on distribution, but are not reflected in permanent losses. The reason why they are washed out on distribution is because they are granted with respect to corporation tax, not shareholder tax, and the dividend deduction system removes corporation tax, leaving the preference-free shareholder tax.[228]

If losses caused by dividend deductions are allowed to be carried forward, they may produce the peculiar consequence of a reinstatement of corporate preferences.[229] For example, presume in year 1 that a corporation has profits of 150 but the tax law specifically excludes 50 of these profits from taxable income. The corporation distributes in year 1 a dividend of 150. As a result, it has no taxable income for year 1, but has a loss of 50 available for carry forward (100 taxable income less dividend deduction of 150). The whole dividend of 150 is taxable to the shareholder, and so the preference granted at the corporate level (the exclusion of 50) is washed out.

However, presume that the corporation has 75 profits in year 2 and this is reduced to 25 by the 50 loss carried forward from year 1. No dividends are distributed in year 2. If the corporate tax rate is 30%, the corporation will have 67.5 in retained profits; 17.5 of these profits represent 25 profits

---

[227] This result can be avoided if dividend deductions are required to be set against all distributable profits rather than just taxable income.

[228] It is possible that some corporate preferences are not washed out on distribution (e.g. where some residual corporation tax liability remains such as where the corporation tax base is greater than the shareholder tax base). Further, a dividend deduction system may be constructed so as to specifically pass through corporate preferences; see McLure (1979, pp. 125–7).

[229] For a discussion of the reinstatement of corporate preferences in the context of imputation systems, see Harris (1996, 217–19).

taxed at the corporate tax rate of 30% (i.e. 25 less corporate tax of 7.5). The other 50 retained profits have not been subjected to tax because the corporate preference from year 1, which was washed out by the dividend of year 1, has been reinstated by reason of the loss carried forward. To prevent reinstatement, a dividend deduction system must deny a deduction for losses generated by dividend deductions.

**Extent of relief**   The level of dividend relief under a dividend deduction system may be limited in several ways. It may be simply limited by reference to the proportion of dividends distributed that are available for deduction. In such a case, a dividend deduction system must decide whether the limited deduction can be set against all corporate profits of a particular year or only a similar percentage of those profits. If there is a limit by reference to a percentage of corporate profits, those profits would have to be identified (e.g. as taxable income or accounting profits). The result of proportional relief is that a partial corporate tax is levied and a full shareholder tax (at marginal rates) is levied.

A dividend deduction system may also be limited by time. This is essentially a question of whether a loss caused by dividend deductions may be carried back and, if so, how far. Such a limitation can create an incentive to distribution dividends and so is discussed later in the context of dividend streaming.

A dividend deduction may also be limited to a deduction for a 'primary', 'normal' or 'basic' dividend.[230] Under this form, a deduction would only be provided for dividends that constitute a standard return for shareholders on their investment. The arguments in favour of such a limitation relate to the taxation of economic rents and were discussed earlier at 1.3.1 and 2.3.2.2. The result would be that the standard return on shares would be treated similarly to interest paid on debt, both being deductible from taxable income for corporation tax purposes. 'The basic idea of this method . . . is of an economic nature and proceeds from the desirability of leaving untaxed a primary interest on the equity capital'.[231] Any return on shares in excess of the standard rate is regarded as excess profits and justifies subjection to economic double taxation. The Brazilian interest on the net equity system may be viewed as adopting this approach.

A variation of this system allows a deduction for a standard rate of return on equity whether or not dividends are distributed.[232] Such a

---

[230]   Norr (1982, p. 100).

[231]   European Communities (1970, p. 34).

[232]   Norr (1982, p. 103). European Communities (1970, p. 34) refers to this as 'the deduction of primary dividend' system.

system does not involve dividend relief because the deduction is not triggered by the distribution of dividends. Versions of this system were used in some German states and Sweden prior to the First World War.[233] The Institute for Fiscal Studies' 'Allowance for Corporate Equity' (or 'ACE') proposal of 1991 involved this approach.[234] The proposal was repeated by the same Institute as part of the Mirrlees review twenty years later.[235] This system and the one mentioned in the last paragraph require a base on which to calculate the standard rate of return. For example, it may be calculated on capital contributed by shareholders.[236] The Institute for Fiscal Studies' ACE is 'based on the accumulated value of retained profits and equity issues, all measured at their historic values, and a nominal rate of return.[237]

**Dividend streaming**  A dividend deduction system can be quite robust against dividend streaming practices. With respect to small business, distributed corporate profits are taxed at marginal rates, and this is likely to be comparable to the treatment of individuals if those profits were derived directly. However, differences still exist. As noted earlier, the corporate tax base is not likely to be the same as the shareholder tax base, and a dividend deduction system washes out preferences granted at the corporate level. Presuming the personal business tax base is similar to the corporate tax base, an individual could secure preferences permanently by deriving business income directly.

The dividend deduction system is even more robust when it comes to the form of return derived from a corporation. The receipt of dividends is not tax advantaged or disadvantaged per se compared to other types of income derived from corporations such as interest and wages. So there is no specific tax incentive to stream dividends to particular types of shareholders. By contrast, the dividend deduction system can have a serious impact on corporate distribution policy (i.e. retention versus distribution). At a simple level, this impact depends particularly on the relationship between shareholder tax rates and the

---

[233] In particular, it was used by Prussia in 1891, Baden in 1884 and Sweden in 1902; see Harris (1996, pp. 83, 85 and 86).

[234] Institute for Fiscal Studies (1991).

[235] Mirrlees, Adam, Besley et al. (2011, chapter 17).

[236] Norr (1982, p. 102).

[237] Institute for Fiscal Studies (1991, p. 26). Also see Mirrlees, Adam, Besley et al. (2011, pp. 421–5). A difficulty with this system is that the deduction is granted irrespective of whether dividends are distributed, which could result in pure non-taxation. The Institute for Fiscal Studies intends this result and would replicate it generally throughout the tax system, including with respect to the receipt of interest.

corporate tax rate, as discussed earlier at 1.3.2.1. At a deeper level, a dividend deduction system might positively encourage distributions depending on how losses caused by dividend deductions are treated. This requires further explanation.

If it were not for the international reasons mentioned earlier, it seems likely that the dividend deduction system would be more popular. Its potential to neutralise the debt / equity divide would be a great temptation to use it. However, that potential neutrality is not so easy to achieve as it might seem. To neutralise the tax treatment of debt and equity, dividends must be treated in the same manner as interest. The same arguments apply for other deductible returns from corporations such as wages. In most jurisdictions, interest incurred is currently deductible. If the deduction produces a loss in the current year the loss can be carried forward and used in future years, sometimes for a limited number of years. As noted earlier at 1.2.3.2, loss carry-back is almost always strictly restricted or not available at all.

It has already been noted that a dividend deduction system that permits losses caused by dividend deductions to be carried forward might reinstate corporate preferences granted in the past. But consider now what would happen with respect to retained profits if this treatment of interest were adopted by a dividend deduction system. Presume a corporation has profits of 100 for year 1, which it retains. There are no dividends distributed, and so it pays corporation tax of, say, 30 (i.e. it has retained profits of 70). Presume it does the same for the next ten years, and so it has retained profits of 700.

In year 11 the corporation has no profits, but distributes all of the profits of previous years. Under a dividend deduction system it will have a loss of 700 for year 11. What should it be permitted to do with this loss? If the loss can only be carried forward, then all of the corporation tax of the first ten years has become permanent (i.e. a classical system is adopted for these years). This would mean that to avoid classical treatment a corporation must distribute all of its profits every year (i.e. there would be a serious incentive to distribute dividends). This would be a major tax distortion of corporate distribution policy.

If the loss may be carried backwards then the tax system must do one of two things. The loss is a reflection of all deductible amounts, including dividends and, for example interest. Presently, most countries do not permit excess interest or other expenses to be carried back as far as ten years. So to permit such loss relief would be a major change to the tax system that goes way beyond dividend relief. Further, if the reinstatement of corporate preferences is to be prevented, carry-forward of losses would have to be denied. This would stand existing loss relief on its head (i.e. only carry-back would be allowed and not carry-forward).

Further, the carry-back of losses results in the refund of corporation tax paid in previous years. Permitting the substantial or permanent carry-back of losses may impose a potentially unaffordable financial burden on governments in economic downturns when corporations make substantial losses. Further, it would be corporations that had paid tax in the past that would be refunded amounts, and this may be viewed as an unfair advantage for established firms compared to start-up firms that would receive no such refund. In other words, a dividend deduction system may exacerbate the distortions already caused by limits on losses.[238]

The second option for carry-back of losses caused by a dividend deduction is to limit it to losses caused by dividends. And to prevent the reinstatement of corporate preferences, perhaps losses caused by dividends could not be carried forward. By contrast, losses caused by other expenses could only be carried forward (or with a limited carry-back). This would require corporations to maintain certain records, and there would need to be ordering rules. These matters are discussed later at 2.5 and can create substantial complexity in a corporate tax system. In any case, once such a division is made, the primary benefit of the dividend deduction system is lost. The returns on debt and equity (i.e. interest and dividends) are no longer treated in the same manner. Both are deductible in the current year, but excess relief for interest could only be carried forward, whereas excess relief for dividends could only be carried backwards. As a result, it would be important to be able to clearly distinguish between debt and equity for tax purposes.

In summary, if losses caused by the deduction of dividends cannot be carried back permanently, there will be an incentive to distribute profits to ensure that the dividend deduction is secured. Also, this might create an incentive not to use the corporate form. Other distortions will be caused if losses caused by the deduction of dividends are not treated the same as losses caused by other types of expenses of corporations. If losses from dividend deductions can be carried back permanently (so as to avoid an incentive to distribute), but losses from other expenses can only be carried forward, there may be a positive incentive to derive dividends instead of

---

[238] The only way to fully neutralise a loss is for a government to make current payments to corporations equal to the corporate tax rate applied to the loss. The free transfer of losses between unrelated parties can go a long way to achieving a similar result.

other returns. Without permanent carry-back of losses generally in the tax system, it is difficult not to cause some distortion under a dividend deduction system.

### 2.4.2.2 Split-rate system

Under a split-rate system dividend relief is granted by reducing the corporate tax rate for dividends distributed. This means there is one corporate tax rate for retained profits and another for distributed profits.

The example in Box 2.2 does not produce full dividend relief. Full dividend relief is only achieved if the corporate tax rate on distributed profits is nil (unless a split-rate system is supplemented with another form of dividend relief).

The most famous split-rate corporate tax system was that of Germany, which operated from 1953 to 2000.[239] Like other corporate-level dividend relief systems, the split-rate system has become unpopular in recent decades for international reasons. So there are no major current examples of a split-rate system, at least no direct examples. The US accumulated earnings tax (see the earlier discussion at 1.3.2.2) may be viewed as an indirect form of a split-rate system. It involves the imposition of an additional corporate tax on retained profits, at least where retention is considered excessive. The result is that retained profits may be subjected to higher corporate-level taxation than distributed profits.

**Preference income**   Like the dividend deduction system, the split-rate system washes out corporate preferences on distribution. The similarity

---

**Box 2.2: Split-rate system**

Corporate profits of 100, a dividend of 50 and a corporate tax rate of 30% on retained profits and 10% on distributed profits:

Corporation tax is
50 retained profits × 30% = 15 tax payable
50 distributed profits × 10% = 5 tax payable

Shareholder has income of 50 taxed at marginal rates

---

[239] From 1977 to 2000 it was supplemented with a full imputation system. See Harris (1996, pp. 613–31).

is not surprising. Corporate preferences are granted with respect to corporation tax, not shareholder tax. Because corporation tax is removed under the split-rate system, so are corporate preferences. Any corporate tax system that ultimately subjects shareholders to marginal tax rates with respect to the shareholder tax base washes out corporate preferences. However, there are subtle differences in the behaviour of a dividend deduction system and a split-rate system. It may be thought that, where the distributed profits tax rate is reduced to zero, the split-rate system is equivalent to the dividend deduction system.[240] In principle, this is not the case because the two systems operate on different elements of the corporation tax equation. Even where the shareholder tax base is larger than the corporate tax base, a full split-rate system is unlikely to result in surplus relief at the corporate level.

Under a split-rate system providing full dividend relief, the corporate tax base is not reduced by the shareholder tax base (as with a dividend deduction system). The corporation tax is systematically removed with dividends by a reduction in the corporate tax rate to zero. Where distributable profits are not included in corporate taxable income (corporate tax exemption), the profits suffer no corporation tax, and so in theory, no rate reduction is available on distribution. Similarly, where corporate income is subject to a preferential rate of corporation tax or tax credits are available with respect to corporate income, the amount of corporation tax reduction available on distribution is limited to actual corporation tax liability. This means that a split-rate system should not result in surplus relief. Because surplus relief is not produced, a split-rate system cannot reinstate corporate preferences (e.g. where surplus relief is carried forward).

**Extent of relief**   The level of dividend relief under a split-rate system may be limited. As noted earlier, this relief can be achieved by simply having a positive corporate tax rate on distributed profits, which produces a proportional relief. Such proportional relief behaves differently than under a dividend deduction system. In particular, there would be no need to identify and limit the profits available for the reduced rate; all profits of a year could be subject to the lower rate if distributed. However, like under a dividend deduction system, the result of proportional relief under a split-rate system is a partial corporate tax and a full shareholder tax (at marginal rates).

Like a dividend deduction system, a split-rate system may also be limited by time. This is essentially a question of whether corporation tax

---

[240] See Harris (1996, p. 64) and the references cited therein.

levied on profits retained from previous years (and so subject to full corporation tax) may be reduced to the distributed profits rate. If there is a limitation on the age of corporate profits that may qualify (e.g. profits retained for no more than six years), the limitation will create an incentive to distribute dividends. This is discussed later in the context of dividend streaming.

As with a dividend deduction system, a split-rate system could be structured so as to only provide dividend relief with respect to the standard rate of return on shares. In this case, the corporate tax rate would only be reduced for dividends that constitute a standard rate of return on equity capital. As with the allowance for corporate equity option, a reduced corporate tax rate to this extent might also be available irrespective of distribution. However, a system that attacked the corporate tax rate is unlikely to produce surplus relief (e.g. in the form of losses).

**Dividend streaming**  Like other corporate-level dividend relief systems, a split-rate system can be quite robust against dividend streaming practices. Where full dividend relief is provided, distributed corporate profits are taxed at marginal rates, and this is likely to be comparable to the treatment of especially individuals if those profits were derived directly. So there should be a high level of neutrality between the corporate and unincorporated forms. However, like a dividend deduction system, a split-rate system washes out corporate preferences. So an individual could secure permanent preferences by deriving income directly.

The split-rate system is unlikely to be as neutral as a dividend deduction system when it comes to the form of return derived from a corporation. Dividends may be taxed comparably to other types of income derived from corporations, but not taxed exactly the same. In particular, corporate payments such as interest and wages are deductible from the corporate tax base, but dividends are not. Nevertheless, because corporation tax is reduced for dividend distributions there can be a high degree of neutrality between these different types of payments. So there may be no specific tax incentive to stream dividends to particular types of shareholders.

As regards distribution versus retention, the split-rate system raises similar issues as the dividend deduction system. Again the relationship between shareholder tax rates and the corporate tax rate is important. Further, a split-rate system has difficult issues to face when profits retained from previous years are distributed. The question is whether the higher corporate tax rate imposed when the profits were retained is reduced in a later year when they are distributed. A reduction could result in the refunding of corporate tax. A failure to refund tax will result in an incentive to distribute profits. This is the case in the US. Once the accumulated earnings tax is applied it is not refundable. This means that the tax functions as a form of penalty, and US corporations typically make sure they distribute sufficient dividends in the current year so as to make sure the tax is not imposed in the first place.

The situation was very different under the former German split-rate system. The higher retained profits corporate tax rate could be reduced to the distributed profits rate irrespective of the length of time between the retention of the profits and their distribution. This caused substantial difficulties when it was announced that the system would be abolished. Corporations quickly distributed dividends to ensure a refund, causing a substantial drain on the German treasury. The legislature responded in April 2003 by freezing the refund until the end of 2005 and extending the transitional rule by a similar period.[241]

### 2.4.2.3 Corporation tax credit system

Under a corporation tax credit system the corporation receives a tax credit calculated by reference to the dividends distributed. The credit directly reduces tax payable and so is fundamentally different from a dividend deduction system, which only reduces the corporate tax base. The credit may be calculated by reference to a dividend withholding tax or corporate distributions tax, but these other types of taxes are not necessary to implement a corporation tax credit system.

The most famous example of this form of corporate tax system is the advance corporation tax system used by the UK from 1971 to 1999. It levied a tax on corporations with respect to corporate distributions ('advance corporation tax' or 'ACT'). This system is often confusing for those not familiar with it because it imposes three taxes: a corporation tax on profits when derived, a corporate tax on distributions and a share-holder tax on distributions. To remove economic double taxation, this means an ACT system must have two mechanisms for relief. Under an ACT system the corporate distributions tax is available for two purposes:

1. The corporate distributions tax is equal to a tax credit provided to shareholders.
2. The corporate distributions tax is deductible against corporation tax levied on corporate income when derived.

---

[241] KStG (Germany) s. 37 and see Daiber (2003).

The important aspect of the ACT system is its second feature (i.e. it provides a deduction against corporation tax levied when corporate income is derived by reference to the dividends distributed). The first aspect – the dividend tax credit – can almost be ignored because it makes ACT effectively equivalent to a dividend withholding tax from the shareholder perspective. This is most clear when considering tax events rather than taxpayers. Like the shareholder tax, ACT is levied with respect to shareholder income. The dividend relief is provided at the corporate level through the credit to reduce the tax on corporate income when derived.

As with the split-rate system example, this example in Box 2.3 does not provide full dividend relief. There remains 12.5 mainstream corporation tax, for which no dividend relief is provided. To provide full dividend relief, a corporation tax credit system must calculate relief at the corporate tax rate. In other words, corporation tax credits should be equivalent to the corporate tax rate applied to gross dividends distributed. On the facts of the example, this would be achieved by granting a corporation tax credit of 30 for every 70 dividend distributed (i.e. by applying ACT at the rate of 42.85% of dividends distributed).

Like other corporate-level dividend relief systems, corporation tax credit systems, including ACT systems, are now rare.[242] A remnant of this style of system is seen in the New Zealand foreign investor tax credit regime. Dividend relief is not granted to non-resident shareholders in New Zealand corporations through the New Zealand imputation system.

---

**Box 2.3:  Advance corporation tax system**

Corporate profits of 100 and all profits distributed after corporation tax, a corporate tax rate of 30% and ACT levied at the rate of 25% of distributed profits:
Corporation tax is

100 profits × 30% = 30 mainstream corporation tax liability
(pre-ACT credit)
70 distributed profits × 25% = 17.5 ACT payable
30−17.5 (ACT credit) = 12.5 mainstream corporation tax payable
(post-ACT credit)

Shareholder has income of 87.5 (70 dividend + 17.5 ACT credit) taxed at marginal rates with a credit for 17.5 (ACT credit)

---

[242] See Harris (2010) regarding the abolition of the Irish, Sri Lankan and UK ACT systems.

Rather, that relief is extended to non-resident shareholders by granting a corporation tax credit calculated by reference to dividends distributed to non-resident shareholders.[243] The system is complex and involves the payment of a supplementary dividend by the corporation to the non-resident shareholders. It is designed to facilitate direct foreign tax credits for New Zealand dividend withholding tax in foreign jurisdictions. It is further considered at 3.1.2.

**Preference income**   The corporation tax credit system, like the dividend deduction system, exposes differences between the corporation tax base and the shareholder tax base. As with the dividend deduction system, assuming the shareholder tax base is larger than the corporation tax base, full distribution of corporate profits may result in surplus relief. Particularly, this may occur where corporation tax credits are calculated at a fixed rate per dividends distributed and not according to corporation tax attributable to profits distributed. Again, hidden profit distributions may cause particular problems. However, unlike a dividend deduction system, this surplus may reflect all corporate preferences and not just exclusions from taxable income. This is because all corporate preferences are reflected in the corporation tax liability (i.e. including rate reductions and tax credits). Further, this surplus may also reflect changes in the corporate tax rate between deriving corporate income and its distribution. Under ACT systems this surplus relief is conventionally referred to as 'surplus ACT'.

Like the dividend deduction system and the split-rate system, a corporation tax credit system providing full dividend relief washes out all corporate preferences on distribution. These corporate preferences reduce corporation tax liability and not shareholder tax levied on distribution. However, like a dividend deduction system, but unlike a split-rate system, a corporation tax credit system may reinstate washed-out preferences where surplus relief is available for carry forward to set against future corporation tax liability (see the example with respect to a dividend deduction system, described earlier at 2.4.2.1).[244]

**Extent of relief**   As with the other corporate-level dividend relief systems, it is a simple matter to proportionately limit the extent of relief under a corporation tax credit system. It is achieved by ensuring that the corporation

---

[243] Income Tax Act 2007 (New Zealand) s. LP2.

[244] The example of reinstatement of corporate preferences in Harris (1996, pp. 218–19) involves an ACT system.

tax credit is calculated at a rate less than the corporate tax rate applied to grossed-up dividends (as in the example in Box 2.3). Like the dividend deduction system, but unlike the split-rate system, there may be a need to limit not only the amount of relief (credit) but also what that relief can be set against (i.e. the amount of corporation tax). Otherwise, surplus relief may be set against corporation tax liability generally, and compromise the proportionate partial nature of the relief. Again, the result of proportional relief under a corporation tax credit system is a partial corporate tax and a full shareholder tax (at marginal rates).

A corporation tax credit system may also be limited by time. Excess corporate tax credits in a particular year (e.g. as a result of the distribution of profits retained from a previous year) may not be available for carry-back or carry-back may be limited to a number of years. Again, any such limitation will create an incentive to the distribution of dividends, which raises dividend streaming issues.

A corporation tax credit system could be structured so as to only allow the credit for dividends that constitute a standard rate of return on equity capital. As with the allowance for the corporate equity option, a corporation tax credit might be allowed to this extent irrespective of distribution. Like a system that attacks the corporate tax base, such a corporation tax credit system might still produce surplus relief (e.g. in the form of unusable credits).

**Dividend streaming**   A corporation tax credit system can also be quite robust against dividend streaming practices. As noted with respect to the split-rate system, in the context of full dividend relief there should be a high level of neutrality between the corporate and unincorporated forms. Again, the wash-out of corporate preferences would produce some disincentive to use of the corporate form.

Similarly, the neutrality of the corporation tax credit system between dividends and other types of income derived from corporations is likely to be similar to that of the split-rate system. Dividends and other returns are similar, but not taxed exactly the same. However, the high degree of neutrality between these different types of payments means that there may be no specific tax incentive to stream dividends to particular types of shareholders.

As regards distribution versus retention, again the assessment of the corporation tax credit system is similar to other corporate-level dividend relief systems. In addition to the difference between the corporate tax rate and shareholder tax rates, problems may occur when profits retained from previous years are distributed. Unless excess corporation tax credits can be carried back without limit, there will be an incentive to distribute dividends. If there is no limit on carry-back, refunds of corporation tax may be substantial, as would the difference in treatment between dividends and deductible returns from a corporation. Under its former ACT system, the UK permitted surplus ACT to be carried back six years. It also permitted surplus ACT to be carried forward permanently, which caused the reinstatement of corporate preferences as discussed earlier.

### 2.4.3 Shareholder-level dividend relief

Dividend relief may be provided at the shareholder level. Such relief is provided with respect to shareholder tax; that is, tax imposed on shareholder income (corporate distributions) whether levied on distributing corporations or their shareholders. In this case, dividend relief takes the form of a reduction in one of the elements of the shareholder tax equation. Dividend relief may be provided by a reduction in taxable income, a reduced shareholder tax rate applicable to dividends received or dividend tax credits calculated according to dividends received. It is difficult to structure these options at the shareholder level so as to produce the same results as produced by the options available at the corporate level. In particular, this difficulty is evident where shareholder tax is part of a progressive personal tax graduated according to total income. Accordingly, there are fundamental differences in dividend relief provided at the corporate level and that provided at the shareholder level.

Conceptually, dividend relief at the shareholder level is simpler than dividend relief at the corporate level. Dividend relief at the corporate level is granted against tax liability arising on the happening of one event (i.e. the deriving of corporate income) by reference to the happening of a second event (i.e. the distribution of dividends). Further, corporation tax is relieved by reference to a standard not incorporated in that levy (i.e. relief is calculated by reference to the shareholder tax base, not the corporation tax base). Where dividend relief is provided at the shareholder level it is calculated by reference to the same standard as tax levied at the shareholder level (i.e. the shareholder tax base). This simplicity erodes where relief provided at the shareholder level is sought to be measured by elements of the corporation tax equation.

#### 2.4.3.1 Dividend exclusion system

A corporate tax system providing dividend relief at the shareholder level by excluding dividends from taxable income is referred to as a dividend exclusion system (see Box 2.4). The level of dividend relief provided

---

**Box 2.4:  Dividend exclusion system**

Corporate tax rate of 30%, corporate profits of 100 and a dividend of 70:

Corporation tax is $100 \times 30\% = 30$ tax payable

Dividend of 70 does not constitute taxable income of the shareholder

---

depends on the percentage of dividends excluded from taxable income for shareholder tax purposes.

The dividend exclusion system removes the shareholder tax base, not the corporation tax base. Where all dividends are excluded from taxable income, shareholder tax is removed completely. Further, assuming the percentage of dividends excluded is similar for all shareholders, the reduction in shareholder tax is made according to each shareholder's marginal tax rate. Shareholder tax relief is greatest for shareholders subject to high marginal tax rates and is nil for shareholders exempt from income tax. Therefore, to the extent that dividends are excluded from taxable income, the effective tax suffered by corporate income is corporation tax. As a result, the dividend exclusion system is often objected to on equity grounds in that it contains no progression according to the ability to pay of shareholders.

Historically, the simplicity of the dividend exclusion system meant that it was often used when the income tax was first imposed. For example, it was used in the US Civil War income tax and the US income tax of 1894, as well as in the early income taxes of Austria, Italy, many German States, India, the Australian States, New Zealand, South Africa and Norway.[245] Under modern income tax systems, it is most commonly used with respect to inter-corporate dividends. As discussed earlier at 1.3.1, the ability to pay principle is difficult to apply to corporations, and so, in the context of inter-corporate dividends, the lack of progression involved in the dividend exclusion system is of little concern.

Historically, the UK had a simple dividend exclusion for inter-corporate dividends distributed by UK resident corporations. It became complicated in 2009 when the exclusion was extended to foreign dividends. Presently, the exemption is applied differently for small companies and other companies. As discussed earlier at 1.1.2.3, the small company distinction

---

[245]  Generally, see Harris (1996, pp. 79–87).

is largely based on EU law.[246] Irrespective of whether the corporation is small or not, the exemption is not available with respect to distributions consisting of interest beyond a reasonable return or interest on special securities (convertible notes, profit-sharing debentures, and so on). These special securities were discussed earlier at 2.1.2.1. Otherwise, for small companies the dividend exemption is only available if it is not part of a tax advantage scheme.[247] By contrast, for other corporations the dividend exclusion is only available if the dividend falls within an 'exempt class'.[248]

A major exempt class of inter-corporate distributions in the UK is those from controlled companies. To qualify, either the recipient must control the corporation or be one of two persons who 'taken together' control the corporation when each holds at least 40% of the distributing corporation. 'Taken together' is defined by reference to the controlled foreign corporation rules.[249] In addition, distributions in respect of non-redeemable ordinary shares are an exempt class.[250] A further exempt class is for distributions in respect of portfolio holdings.[251] Another broad category is dividends derived from transactions not designed to reduce tax.[252] There are other classes as well. Overall, the UK approach seems excessively prescriptive and unnecessarily complex.

By contrast, Germany and the CCCTB Proposal have simple exclusions for inter-corporate dividends. In Germany, dividends as identified under the relevant provision of the Personal Income Tax Law are 'ignored for the purposes of determining income' under the Corporate Income Tax Law.[253] This rule is subject to re-inclusion of 5% of dividends to reflect expenses incurred in deriving dividends as discussed later. In the context of the German group relief system (*Organshaft*, see 1.2.3.2), the profits of the subsidiary are transferred to the parent and so there is no recognition of dividends.[254] Similarly, under the CCCTB Proposal as drafted, 'received profit distributions' are simply exempt.[255] Again, this would be subject to

---

[246] CTA 2009 (UK) s. 931S.

[247] CTA 2009 (UK) s. 931B.

[248] CTA 2009 (UK) s. 931D.

[249] CTA 2009 (UK) s. 931E.

[250] CTA 2009 (UK) s. 931F. Section 931U defines 'redeemable' based on terms of issue and 'ordinary shares' as 'a share that does not carry any present or future preferential right to dividends or to a company's assets on its winding up'.

[251] CTA 2009(UK) s. 931G. A portfolio holding is 10% or less of share capital, distributions and surplus on winding up of the distributing corporation.

[252] CTA 2009 (UK) s. 931H.

[253] KStG (Germany) s. 8b(1).

[254] KStG (Germany) s. 14.

[255] CCCTB Proposal Art. 11(c).

a 5% re-inclusion for expenses. The EU Presidency amendments, however, would limit the exemption to 10% shareholdings on capital account and deny expenses in deriving exempt dividends. For a number of years, Germany has been considering limiting its inter-corporate dividend exemption in the same way.

The US achieves dividend exclusion for inter-corporate dividends through an indirect route. Rather than excluding such dividends from gross income, it grants corporations a deduction for dividends received.[256] This deduction offsets the inclusion of dividends received in income, at least partially. It is not available in computing the accumulated earnings tax or the tax on personal holding companies (see the earlier discussion at 1.3.2.2). In the context of regular corporation tax, the dividends-received deduction is graduated depending on the level of holding that the recipient corporation has in the distributing corporation.

If both corporations are part of an 'affiliated group', the deduction is 100%. The definition of 'affiliated group' was considered earlier at 1.2.3.1 in the context of the US consolidation regime. Recall that an affiliated group is generally defined in terms of an 80% holding by other group corporations. To qualify for the 100% dividends-received deduction, the dividends must be paid from affiliated earnings and profits, and the distributing and recipient corporations must have been affiliated for the period during which the profits were earned.[257] By contrast, where the affiliated members have opted to file a consolidated tax return, the dividends are excluded from gross income.[258] There are, however, complex cost base adjustments to shares held in distributing group members by other group members.[259]

Outside of an affiliated group, an 80% dividends-received deduction is available if the dividend is received from a 20% owned corporation.[260] The 20% requirement is measured by voting rights and value of shares. If neither the affiliated group nor 20% holding requirement is met, then residually the US offers a 70% dividends-received deduction. This means that, for portfolio corporate shareholders, there is a corporate tax charge on 30% of dividends distributed at each link in a corporate chain. By international standards, this is pretty restrictive. Many countries manage to

---

[256] IRC (US) s. 243(a).
[257] IRC (US) s. 243(b).
[258] Title 26 Code of Federal Regulations (US) § 1.1502–13(f)(2).
[259] Title 26 Code of Federal Regulations (US) § 1.1502–32.
[260] IRC (US) s. 243(c).

avoid the taxation of dividends distributed between corporations by one means or another.

Some countries use the dividend exclusion system more broadly and apply it to all shareholders. For example, the dividend exclusion system is available to individuals in Argentina and Brazil.[261] When the German imputation system was repealed in 2000, it was replaced with the inter-corporate dividend exclusion and partial dividend exclusion for individuals. Originally, this exemption was 50% of dividends received by individuals, but when the corporate tax rate was reduced in 2008, the dividend exemption was reduced to its current level of 40% of dividends received.[262] From the start of 2009, this system has been largely replaced with a final dividend withholding tax system. The 40% dividend exclusion continues to apply to dividends received in the context of a business.

When foreign income is exempt, a number of countries take that exempt foreign income into account when determining the tax rate applicable to other income of the taxpayer. In particular, the receipt of exempt income might push an individual into higher progressive rates with respect to his or her other income. This is referred to as exemption with progression.[263] However, when applying a dividend exclusion system, most countries do not adopt exemption with progression. For example, this is the case in Germany. The part of dividends that is exempt is simply excluded from 'taxable income'. Because taxable income is subject to progressive taxation, the exempt part of dividends does not cause the shareholder to be taxed at higher rates with respect to the remainder of those dividends or other income. By contrast, the CCCTB Proposal would expressly permit exemption with progression.[264]

**Expenses in deriving dividends**    Dividend exclusion systems raise difficult issues for the deduction of expenses incurred in deriving excluded dividends. Most countries generally deny a deduction for expenses incurred in deriving exempt income. However, if such a denial is applied to a dividend exclusion, it may reintroduce some of the economic double taxation that the system is designed to relieve. For example, presume an individual incurs interest expense of 60 in deriving an exempt dividend of 100, but is denied a deduction against other income for that expense. If the

---

[261] See Harris (2010, p. 578).
[262] EStG (Germany) s. 3 No. 40(d).
[263] Regarding exemption with progression, see Harris & Oliver (2010, pp. 268–9).
[264] CCCTB Proposal Art. 72.

interest paid is taxable to the recipient, there is a form of economic double taxation. That is, the amount paid as dividends was already taxed to the distributing corporation, but part of the economic gain is taxed again to the recipient of the interest.

This economic double taxation becomes obvious when such a dividend exclusion system is compared to a full classical system. Under a full classical system, the shareholder is likely to get a full deduction for the 60 and only be taxed on 40. So the difference in relief is only the taxation of 40, and could be nothing if the shareholder expenses were the same amount as the dividend. The problem is that dividend relief breaks down the separate identities of the corporation and its shareholders, but the dividend exclusion system isolates expenses at the shareholder level. That is, these expenses of the amalgamated entity (corporation and its shareholders) are not available for deduction against the charge to tax at the corporate level. This problem does not exist with corporate-level dividend relief systems, which are likely to have a full and effective deduction for shareholder expenses.

These issues regarding the deduction of expenses in deriving excluded dividends can give rise to serious dividend streaming issues and distort investment in shares. So it is not surprising that many countries permit shareholders a deduction for such expenses despite the exclusion of dividends. This is most commonly the case with respect to exempt inter-corporate dividends. For example, Germany has a rule that denies a deduction of expenses incurred in deriving exempt income.[265] However, this rule is specifically overridden in the case of corporations claiming an inter-corporate dividend exemption. Corporations that incur expenses, particularly interest, in deriving exempt dividends cannot deduct those expenses to the extent of 5% of dividends received. Any expenses incurred in excess of this amount can be deducted and so reduce tax payable with respect to other income.[266]

The CCCTB Proposal as drafted would have adopted this German rule. Expenses incurred in deriving exempt income would not be deductible, but such expenses would be 'fixed at a flat rate of 5% of that income unless the taxpayer is able to demonstrate that it has incurred a lower cost'.[267] Again, the bottom line is that expenses up to 5% of dividends received are not deductible, but those in excess are deductible. If the taxpayer can prove less than 5% expenses in deriving exempt dividends, the taxpayer

---

[265] EStG (Germany) s. 3c(1).
[266] KStG (Germany) s. 8b(5).
[267] CCCTB Proposal Art. 14(1)(g).

effectively gets a larger exemption. An EU Presidency amendment would remove this rule and provide that expenses incurred in deriving exempt dividends are non-deductible. The potential about-face reflects the controversy surrounding expenses and the dividend exclusion system.

In contrast to the German and CCCTB Proposal approaches, the nature of the UK and US inter-corporate dividend exemptions means that they do not need a specific rule to allow the deduction of expenses in deriving dividends. However, the reasons why the UK and the US do not need such a specific rule are different. In the UK, interest expense is generally deductible under the loan relationship rules, and management expenses are either deductible as general expenses of a trade or as management expenses from total income (see the earlier discussion of these rules at 2.3.1.2).

In the US, dividends received are technically not exempt income. Rather, they are just offset by the dividends-received deduction. Because dividends are prima facie included in gross income, the general deduction rules for expenses apply. Confusingly, this might result in a corporation receiving two sets of deductions when deriving dividends; a deduction for expenses in deriving those dividends and the dividends-received deduction. These dual deductions can be particularly confusing when they interact with loss relief. There are complex rules that seek to ensure that dividends received reduce a current-year loss, but not a carried-forward loss.[268]

Further, there are specific rules restricting the claiming of double deductions in the context of 'debt-financed portfolio stock'. Here the double deduction results from the simultaneous claiming of the dividends-received deduction and a deduction for interest incurred in acquiring the shares in question. 'Portfolio' stock is identified in terms of less than a 50% voting and stock value interest in the distributing corporation. Under these rules, the dividends-received deduction is reduced by a percentage related to the amount of debt incurred to purchase the shares.[269]

In the case of individual shareholders, it is much more likely that an exclusion of dividends from income also means that expenses incurred in deriving dividends are not deductible. This is the case in Germany. Individuals entitled to the 40% exemption for dividends received may

---

[268] IRC (US) s. 246(b). This is achieved in terms of a limit on the dividends-received deduction. The total dividends-received deduction for a particular year is limited to 70% (80% in the case of 20% owned corporations) of the recipient corporation's taxable income, computed without regard to certain deductions (including loss carry-overs and the dividends-received deduction).

[269] IRC (US) s. 246A.

claim as a deduction only 40% of expenses incurred in deriving the dividends.[270]

**Preference income**   A dividend exclusion system that calculates dividend relief by reference to the shareholder tax base does not wash out corporate preferences on distribution. It is shareholder tax that is removed; corporation tax remains as reduced by corporate preferences. Accordingly, preferences granted at the corporate level permanently reduce the effective tax suffered by corporate income. Of course, corporate preferences are equally not passed through, at least not accurately by reference to what would have happened if the shareholder had derived the income directly. Corporate income remains subject to corporation tax, not shareholder tax. Further, the dividend exclusion system does not result in surplus relief.

Dividend relief under a dividend exclusion system is typically calculated according to the shareholder tax base. However, it is possible to limit the dividend exclusion granted to the corporation tax base. For example, dividend exclusion may be granted only with respect to the distribution of corporate profits considered as suffering corporation tax. In this case, the taxable portion of dividends may be subject to progressive tax rates in the hands of shareholders, whereas any excluded portion of dividends would be effectively taxed at the corporate tax rate. Such a system may produce arbitrary results. It washes out corporate preferences, but the extent of wash-out depends on how the dividend exclusion is restricted.

Alternately, a corporate distributions tax may be imposed where profits that have not suffered corporation tax are distributed. Such a tax is referred to as an 'equalisation tax' because it equalises the corporate tax burden on all distributed profits. The corporate distributions tax is usually calculated as the corporate tax rate applied to the distribution of untaxed profits grossed up by the corporate tax rate. For example, a general equalisation tax is levied under both the Mexican and Argentinean dividend exclusion systems.[271] The UK has a bizarre example of an equalisation tax in a very isolated situation. If a corporation makes a capital distribution to a connected shareholder out of a capital gain on which it has not paid corporation tax, the shareholder is liable to pay that corporation tax.[272]

---

[270]   EstG (Germany) s. 3c(2).
[271]   Income Tax Law (*Ley de Impuesto a las Ganancias*) (Argentina) Art. 69bis and Income Tax Law (*Ley del Impuesto sobre la Renta*) (Mexico) Art. 11.
[272]   TCGA 1992 (UK) s. 189.

Equalisation taxes are designed to wash out corporate preferences on distribution.

Dividend exclusion systems are particularly prone to difficulties with hidden profit distributions. As noted earlier at 2.2.2, hidden profit distributions are an interception of potential corporate income by shareholders. Most countries have mechanisms for taxing hidden profit distributions at the shareholder level, but do not tax them at the corporate level (i.e. do not tax notional income of the corporation). Germany was noted as an exception to this generalisation. If notional income is not taxed to the corporation, then this is the equivalent of a corporate tax preference, even though it is likely to be an unintended tax preference. If a dividend exclusion system is adopted and hidden profit distributions are covered by the exclusion, the benefits of a hidden profit distribution are not taxed at all, either at the shareholder or corporate level. The only manner of dealing with this situation is by imposing a special tax on such distributions, either at the corporate or shareholder level (i.e. washing out the unintended preference).

**Extent of relief**  It is a simple matter to proportionately limit the extent of relief under a dividend exclusion system: the exclusion may be limited by reference to a portion of dividends. In particular, the exclusion for higher income tax rate shareholders may be reduced in order to mitigate, at least to a limited extent, the apparent inequity of the dividend exclusion system. If the corporate tax rate is lower than the highest marginal tax rate applicable to individuals, it may be necessary to limit the dividend exclusion. Otherwise, individuals on the highest marginal tax rate may be able to save tax by deriving their income through a corporation.

It is for this reason that Germany limits the dividend exemption available to individuals to 40% of dividends received, although the amount of exemption applies to individual shareholders on all tax rates. In Germany, the corporate tax rate, even when combined with trade tax, is substantially below the highest personal marginal tax rate. If Germany did not reduce the exemption available to individuals, there would be a positive incentive to derive income through a corporation. As it is, there is an incentive to derive and retain profits in German corporations. When profits are distributed, the system is slightly classical for shareholders on the highest marginal rate, but substantially more so for other shareholders, and it is fully classical for exempt shareholders.

Presume profits of 100 subject to 30 corporation tax including surcharge and an average trade tax. Profits net of tax are 70, which are distributed. Forty percent of the distribution is exempt (i.e. 28). The remaining 42 is subject to shareholder tax at the highest rate of 47.5% (including surcharge); that is, 19.95 in tax. The net result is tax of 49.95: 30 at the corporate level and 19.95 at the shareholder level. If the shareholder derived the income directly, the tax is likely to have been 47.5. If the dividend exemption had remained at its 2000 level of 50%, the shareholder tax would have been 16.62 (47.5% of half the dividend; i.e. 35), meaning the combined corporate and shareholder taxes (46.62) would have been less than if the shareholder had derived the income directly.

A dividend exclusion system can be limited so as to only provide exclusion for dividends representing a standard rate of return on equity capital. This is the system used in Norway, where it is referred to as the 'shielding allowance'.[273] The allowance is calculated separately for each share according to the cost of the share and unused allowances may be carried forward. The system is complex in relation to the limited benefit it provides to shareholders, and some shareholders do not claim the allowance because of the high compliance costs. In 2011, the UK Institute for Fiscal Studies made a similar recommendation for the UK. However, the allowance would be generally available for all returns on capital, and it would be supplemented with an allowance for corporate equity at the corporate level (as discussed earlier).[274]

It is also possible to do the opposite; that is, only exempt dividends beyond a standard rate of return and so subject the standard rate of return to economic double taxation. In principle, this is the system adopted by the Netherlands for portfolio shareholders (less than 5% shareholding; Box III). They are deemed to derive a 4% return from shares, irrespective of the amount of dividends received, and any additional amount is not subject to tax. When combined with a flat tax rate of 30%, the Netherlands taxation of shareholders is really a wealth tax of 1.2% (see the earlier discussion at 1.3.3.1).

**Dividend streaming**   When dividend relief is moved to the shareholder level, the nature of and potential for dividend streaming change fundamentally. In the context of a dividend exclusion system, it is impossible to address the distortions that give rise to incentives to stream dividends. The reason for this is simple: the corporation tax remains unrelieved and it is not the same as shareholder taxation.

[273]  Income and Capital Tax Law (*Lov om skatt av formue og inntekt*) (Norway) Art. 10–12.
[274]  See Mirrlees, Adam, Besley et al. (2011, chapter 14).

So a dividend exclusion system encourages individuals on rates higher than the corporate tax rate to derive income through a corporation. Those on individual tax rates below the corporate tax rate are discouraged from using the corporate form. Where the corporate form is used, stakeholders on tax rates higher than the corporate tax rate are encouraged to derive their income from a corporation in the form of dividends. Those on tax rates below the corporate tax rate are encouraged to derive other types of income from corporations, such as wages and interest.

For tax-exempt investors (particularly pension funds and non-residents), this distortion as to the form of return from a corporation is extreme. Interest paid to exempt investors suffers no tax at all. Dividends, however, suffer a full imposition of corporation tax. With the increasing significance of exempt investors, this distortion is extremely important and may cause a general over-reliance on debt in an economy.[275] It may be argued that the corporation tax is shifted away from these investors, but this is only a partial answer. The comparative tax treatment between major forms of investors is still substantially distorted: exempt investors are exempt on the returns on debt and equity, but high-rate taxpayers are fully taxable on one and exempt on the other. This necessarily distorts the type of investor that prefers which type of return. Added to this distortion is the corporate-level distortion that dividends are not deductible, whereas other returns paid by corporations typically are.

The propensity of the dividend exclusion system to cause substantial distortion as to the type of investor that invests in particular corporate investments is well demonstrated by the US response to manipulation of its dividends-received deduction system. That system provides substantial scope for dividend relief for inter-corporate dividends. Less relief is available for other investors, dramatically so for individuals before the reforms of 2003. In other words, it was commonly more tax effective for US corporations to derive dividends than other types of investors. The incentive is for investors that seek a share-like investment to engage in tax planning. Rather than invest directly in shares, they could have a corporation invest in shares and then enter into collateral agreements with the intermediary corporation that effectively transfer the benefits and risks of the shares to the investor. Effectively, the investor might be in substance a shareholder, but not in form and not for the purposes of the tax system.

In 1958, the US enacted a holding-period rule to restrict such tax arbitrage arrangements. Under section 246(c) of IRC, the dividends-received

---

[275] Generally, see Harris (2010) and the references cited therein.

deduction is not available to a corporate shareholder unless the shares are held at risk for more than forty-five days (ninety days for certain preference shares). Periods during which the shares (or substantially identical shares) are subject to options do not count. Further, holding periods do not count where the shareholder has 'diminished his risk of loss by holding 1 or more other positions with respect to substantially similar or related property'.[276] These rules are particularly important where dividend streaming is sought to be effected by buying, selling or varying the shares in question. They are further considered in Chapter 8.

By contrast, a dividend exclusion system is very neutral when it comes to retention or distribution of corporate profits. Because such a system does not subject distributed profits to any tax, retained and distributed profits are treated exactly the same. That a dividend exclusion system can be very distorting in two main indicia of dividend streaming (i.e. distortion as to use of the corporate form and selection of form of financing), but very neutral as to the third (i.e. retention or distribution) demonstrates the conundrum of the corporation tax. It is simply impossible to fit it into an income tax focused on individuals in a non-distorting fashion.

### 2.4.3.2   Shareholder differentiation system

Under a shareholder differentiation system (see Box 2.5), dividend relief is provided by taxing dividends at a rate lower than that applicable to the shareholder's other income.

There are three main methods of reducing the shareholder tax rate, other than a reduction to zero: it may be reduced by a standard rate, reduced to a standard rate or reduced in some proportion.

With respect to the first option, the rate of reduction that suggests itself is one based on the corporate tax rate applicable in the year of distribution. In this case, only shareholders with marginal income tax rates above the corporate tax rate would be liable for shareholder tax. The effect of such a system is to flatten progression with respect to shareholder tax up to the

---

**Box 2.5:  Shareholder differentiation system**

Corporate tax rate of 30%, corporate profits of 100 and a dividend of 70. Fixed shareholder tax of 10%:

Corporation tax is $100 \times 30\% = 30$ tax payable
Dividend of $70 \times 10\% =$ shareholder tax of 7 and a net return of 63

---

[276] IRC (US) s. 246(c)(4)(C).

corporate tax rate. Exempt shareholders would suffer the same effective tax rate as shareholders in a progressive tax bracket equivalent to the corporate rate.

Historically, there were numerous examples of this style of shareholder differentiation system. Income tax would be imposed at a flat rate including on corporate income. Individuals would be subjected to supplementary tax at progressive rates. These supplementary taxes were often referred to as a 'super tax' or 'surtax'. When a corporation derived and distributed income, the corporation would be subject to the normal flat tax, but individuals would not pay normal tax on their dividends. Rather, such individuals would only pay the supplementary progressive rates on dividends. Therefore, this was a form of shareholder differentiation.[277] Such systems are rare in modern income tax systems, although a similar result was achieved for active shareholders under the Scandinavian dual income taxes when they were first introduced.[278]

By contrast, reduction of the shareholder tax to a particular rate is now extremely common; it is probably the most common form of dividend relief.[279] Most often, this flat dividend tax is achieved through a final dividend withholding tax or a corporate distributions tax. The benefit of such a system is primarily its simplicity. The same tax is applied to all shareholders and is collected at the corporate level. It is unnecessary for shareholders to include dividends in their tax returns; they are simply ignored. If interest is treated in a similar manner (and perhaps also passive rent), then the vast majority of the population may not need to file a tax return. The only type of income that the vast majority of individuals are likely to have other than dividends and interest (and rent) is wage income, which can be collected at progressive rates through a wage withholding tax.

Germany adopted a final withholding tax for small shareholdings in 2009 and at the same time applied the same system to certain forms of interest. The system was intended to be simple, but simple often means arbitrary and that raises equity issues. Accordingly, the Germany system includes a number of exceptions and qualifications targeted at the inequity of a final dividend withholding tax. As noted earlier at 2.3.1.1, Germany imposes a general dividend withholding tax of 25% (which is increased by the surcharge).[280] The tax rate for investment income of individuals is now

---

[277] Generally, see Harris (1996, pp. 78–93).
[278] For example, see Harris (1996, p. 728) regarding the former Norwegian treatment of active shareholders.
[279] See Harris (2010, pp. 578–9).
[280] EStG (Germany) s. 43(1)1.

also a flat 25%.[281] Note that investment income does not include dividends received in the context of a business. As discussed earlier at 2.4.3.1, such dividends are taxed at progressive rates with a 40% dividend exclusion.

The scope of the 25% final withholding tax is limited in several respects. An individual can apply for individual taxation instead of the flat tax system if he or she holds at least 25% of the distributing corporation or holds 1% and is an employee of the corporation.[282] In this case, the individual is taxed under the 40% exemption system discussed earlier at 2.4.3.1. This has implications both for deductions (discussed later) and tax rate. In particular, opting out of the 25% final tax means that progressive rates apply, which extend below 25%. In addition, an individual who does not qualify under this opt-out can choose to be taxed at his or her marginal tax rate instead of 25%. However, in this case the tax is still on the gross amount of the dividends, and the 40% exemption is not available.[283]

Under the third method of selecting the tax reduction, shareholder tax rates applicable to dividend income may be reduced in some sort of proportionate manner. Such an approach may also have arbitrary results. The minimum effective tax suffered by corporate income remains the corporation tax. If the proportionate reduction is equal, higher rate taxpayers receive greater relief in terms of tax not levied than low-rate taxpayers. The rate of progression applicable to other income does not apply to dividend income; rather a flatter scale is adopted. Both the UK and the US use this system: the UK in addition to a dividend tax credit but the US exclusively.

Since 1999, the UK corporate tax system has incorporated a combination of a limited dividend tax credit and shareholder differentiation. As noted earlier at 1.3.2.2, the UK charges individuals to tax at the basic, higher or additional rates,[284] and these rates are presently 20%, 40% and 50%, respectively.[285] However, these rates are reduced for dividends to 10%, 32.5% and 42.5%, respectively.[286] Note that the differences between the dividend rates seem to be at least as great as they are between the standard tax rates. In particular, the difference between the 20% and 40% standard rates is 20%, whereas that between the 10% and 32.5% rates is more at 22.5%. Here the UK has increased the rate of progression applicable to dividend income when compared to standard rates. However, this increase in

---

[281] EStG (Germany) s. 32d(1).
[282] EStG (Germany) s. 32d(2)3.
[283] EStG (Germany) s. 32d(6).
[284] ITA 2007 (UK) s. 6(1).
[285] Finance Act 2012 (UK) s. 1.
[286] ITA 2007 (UK) ss. 6(3) & 8(1).

progression is reversed when net returns after tax are considered because profits distributed to all shareholders are subject to the same amount of corporation tax (thereby reducing the overall progressivity of the dividend rates), see the discussion later at 2.4.3.3).

Since 2003, US shareholders have also been taxed at reduced rates on dividends received. The reduction takes the strange form of including 'qualifying dividends' in a taxpayer's net capital gains.[287] Qualifying dividends include dividends from resident corporations. The result is that dividends are taxed at capital gains tax rates, which are lower than full income tax rates. Any net capital gains that would otherwise be taxed at income tax rates of below 25% (income in the 10% and 15% bands) are exempt from taxation. Any net capital gains that would otherwise be taxed at 25% or above (income in the 25%, 28%, 33% and 35% bands) are taxed at 15%. Again, the flattening of individual progressive rates is clear.

If a country adopts a special tax rate or rates for dividend income, the result is a schedular approach. The country must then determine the relationship between the two schedules and, in particular, the impact of dividend income on progressive rates applicable to other income. This is the equivalent of the exemption with progression issue discussed earlier at 2.4.3.1. As noted at that point, the German exclusion of 40% of dividends received by some individuals does not cause other income of those individuals to be taxed at higher rates. Rather, the dividend income is simply not counted in calculating an individual's 'taxable income' subject to progressive taxation. The same approach is adopted when dividends are subject to the final withholding tax: such dividends are expressly excluded from taxable income.[288] Progressive rates are applied to taxable income net of such dividends.

The UK has two progressive rate schedules (one for dividends and another for other income) and so must determine the relationship between the various thresholds at which the different rates apply. In the UK, any dividends that would otherwise fall within the 20% threshold are taxed at 10%, those that would fall within the 40% threshold are taxed at 32.5% and those that would be taxed at 50% are taxed at 42.5%.[289] This substitution approach ensures that each taxpayer in receipt of dividends is only entitled to progressive rate thresholds once. However, because different rates apply to different types of income, the tax law must determine which income is taxed in which tax bracket. For example, the

---

[287] IRC (US) s. 1(h).
[288] EStG (Germany) s. 2(5b).
[289] ITA 2007 (UK) s. 13.

tax law must determine whether a person with both wage income and dividend income is subject first to tax at lower rates on wages and then higher rates on dividends or vice versa. This is a 'slicing' or ordering rule. In the UK, dividends are treated as the highest slice of a person's income and so are taxed at the rates applicable to the highest income thresholds.[290]

The US also has, in effect, two progressive tax rate schedules (one for net capital gains, including dividends, and another for other income) and so faces the same issue as the UK. The US addresses this issue in the same manner as the UK by treating net capital gains (and so dividends) as the top slice of an individual's income. This result is achieved through a complicated limitation on the total amount of tax imposed on an individual's taxable income.[291]

**Expenses in deriving dividends**   The shareholder differentiation system, like the dividend exclusion system, displays difficulties when it comes to the deduction of expenses incurred in deriving income subject to the lower dividend rates. General deductibility would usually be viewed as inappropriate (e.g. under a global system) for fear of expenses incurred in deriving income subject to a lower rate being used to reduce income subject to full rates. So, if expenses are deductible at all, it might be expected that expenses are quarantined. However, it is more likely that a deduction is denied for expenses in deriving income than that those expenses be quarantined.

It is usual for countries that adopt a final withholding tax on dividends to simply deny a deduction for expenses incurred in deriving dividends. This is essentially the approach adopted under the German final withholding tax. However, Germany does permit a fixed deduction of 801 Euros (1602 Euros for couples filing jointly), which is available irrespective of expenses incurred, and so acts as a small exemption.[292] This fixed deduction can cause complex and arbitrary results when considered with the right of individuals to apply for the 40% exemption method if they hold 25% of the distributing corporation or are an employee and have a 1% holding.

Under the 40% dividends exclusion system, 60% of expenses are deductible. If an individual on the highest marginal tax rate (45%) derives dividends with no expenses, the individual is marginally worse off with

[290]   ITA 2007 (UK) s. 16.
[291]   IRC (US) s. 1(h)(1).
[292]   EStG (Germany) s. 20(9).

the 40% exclusion system.[293] However, even if such a shareholder incurs a small amount of interest (say 10% of dividends received), the shareholder is better off under the 40% exclusion system.[294] Shareholders on other tax rates are better off under the 40% exclusion system than the 25% final withholding tax system; in some cases they are substantially better off. Added to this complex mix are the fixed deduction of 801 Euro and the election to be taxed at marginal rates on the gross amount of a dividend.

The US also severely limits deductions under its reduced rate system for dividends. In particular, the lower rates are not available with respect to 'investment income' taken into account under section 163 of IRC.[295] As noted earlier at 2.3.1.2, section 163 provides for a deduction for interest. However, it quarantines interest incurred in deriving passive income so that it can only be set against passive income (i.e. it schedularises the US global calculation of income).[296] Taxpayers are given a choice as to whether to treat dividend income as investment income. If they treat it as investment income, a deduction for interest is available, but quarantined. However, then the lower rate on dividends is not available.

In other words, the only way for an individual shareholder in the US to obtain the lower rates is to be taxed on gross dividends. Most individuals prefer this, unless they have substantial interest expense. However, as with the German shareholder differentiation system, the US limitation works very differently depending on which marginal tax bracket a taxpayer is otherwise in. For example, a taxpayer on a marginal rate below 25% will only make an election to be taxed on a net basis if interest expense exceeds dividend income. By contrast, a person on a 25% marginal rate may make the election if interest expense covers only 40% of dividend income.[297] Again, the system seems complex and arbitrary.

The UK lower rates for dividends fare little better in the expenses department. There are no special rules for deduction of expenses, but the

---

[293] 100 dividends taxed at 25% is 25 shareholder tax; 100 dividends and 40% excluded is 60 × 45%, resulting in 27 shareholder tax. Consideration must also be given to the 801 Euro fixed deduction under the final withholding tax system and the surcharge.

[294] Continuing the example from the previous footnote, 10 interest and so only 6 is deductible. This gives net taxable dividend income of 54 (60 less 6 interest) × 45%, which is a shareholder tax of 24.3.

[295] IRC (US) s. 1(h)(11)(D)(i).

[296] IRC (US) s. 163(d).

[297] 100 dividends taxed at 15% is 15 shareholder tax payable. 100 dividends less 40 interest is 60 net investment income taxed at 25% giving 15 shareholder tax payable. Any more than 40 interest produces less tax if taxed on a net basis.

result can also be peculiar. As noted earlier at 2.3.1.2, the primary rule in the UK for individuals is that they cannot deduct expenses incurred in deriving dividends (i.e. dividends are charged on the gross amount). This is not the case for shareholders receiving dividends as trading income, but in this case the lower rates are not available (because the dividends are charged as trading income, not dividend income). Overall, this rule is similar to the approach in Germany and in the US.

However, as noted earlier at 2.3.1.2, there is a special rule for individuals incurring interest on a loan to acquire ordinary shares in a close company. The individual must be a full-time worker or hold more than 5% of the ordinary shares in the company.[298] Where this rule applies, the individual can deduct the interest from net income (aggregation of income charged under various schedules). As a result, the interest can reduce income taxed at normal (higher) marginal rates. Indeed, this result is ensured. Net income is a global concept in the UK. Once that net income is calculated (as reduced by the qualifying interest), the total is subject to progressive tax rates. One part of the total is subject to the reduced dividend rate and the other part to normal progressive rates. However, the amount of the net income that is subject to the reduced dividend rates is the amount of dividends subject to charge (i.e. the gross amount of dividends), not the dividends as reduced by related expenses. The result is peculiar and perhaps unintended.

**Preference income**   As with the dividend exclusion system, the shareholder differentiation system does not affect the corporation tax base or the quantum of corporation tax levied. Corporate preferences granted reduce the effective tax rate suffered by corporate income. Therefore, the shareholder differentiation system does not wash out corporate preferences on distribution. However, similar to the dividend exclusion system, corporate preferences are not accurately passed to shareholders. Further, the shareholder differentiation system does not result in surplus relief, because dividend distributions have no tax consequences for corporations.

It has been assumed that dividend relief under a shareholder differentiation system is calculated according to the shareholder tax base. However, similar to the dividend exclusion system, it is possible to limit the shareholder tax rate reduction to the corporation tax base. In this case, a

---

[298]  ITA 2007 (UK) ss. 383, 392 and 393.

shareholder tax rate reduction may only be granted with respect to distributions of the profits considered as suffering corporation tax. Such a system is likely to produce arbitrary results similar to where a dividend exclusion system is restricted in this manner. Further, such a system washes out corporate preferences, but the extent of wash-out depends on how the shareholder tax rate reduction is restricted. A more straightforward manner to incorporate such a limitation is to impose a corporate distributions tax on the distribution of preference income (i.e. an equalisation tax).

Without a wash-out of corporate preferences, the shareholder differentiation system, like the dividend exclusion system, is particularly prone to difficulties with hidden profit distributions. If notional income is not taxed to the corporation, hidden profit distributions will be tax preferred. A normal dividend will suffer both corporation tax and reduced shareholder tax, but a hidden profit distribution will potentially suffer only reduced shareholder tax. The UK shareholder differentiation system has the propensity to treat some types of hidden profit distributions in this concessionary manner (i.e. those not giving rise to a charge at the corporate level). The same applies to the US system. As Bittker and Eustice note, '[t]he pain of 'constructive dividend treatment' will be greatly eased by a 15 percent, rather than 35 percent tax rate'.[299] This is not the case in Germany, where the hidden profit distribution is likely to give rise to income taxable to the corporation.

**Extent of relief**    The extent of relief under a shareholder differentiation system depends on whether the overall taxation is being compared to taxation at the corporate level (i.e. corporation tax) or to taxation at the shareholder level. It is usual to compare overall taxation to taxation at the shareholder level. The extent of relief also depends on which of the three methods of shareholder differentiation discussed earlier is used. In each of these cases, the overall taxation is not consistent with progressive tax rates, and each is less beneficial for low-rate taxpayers. The degree of discrimination for low-rate shareholders varies under each system.

Consider a shareholder differentiation system that reduces shareholder tax by a set amount (e.g. the corporate tax rate). In this case, shareholders on individual tax rates at or below the corporate tax rate suffer tax at the corporate tax rate. The result is similar to that under a dividend exclusion system and so produces a full classical treatment for exempt institutions.

---

[299] Bittker & Eustice (2003–, para. 8.06[2][d]).

By contrast, any shareholder on a marginal rate equal to or higher than the corporate tax rate is taxed at that rate (i.e. full dividend relief).

A flat rate applied to dividends is worse than a classical system for shareholders on marginal rates below the dividend rate. For example, the German final dividend withholding tax of 25% is worse than a classical system for individual shareholders on rates below the 25% rate (i.e. an increase in economic double taxation). The harshness of this approach is offset by the ability to request that the shareholder's marginal rate be applied. This produces a full classical system for shareholders on a tax rate of 25% or below, but it must be recalled that expenses are not deductible (unless the election for the 40% exemption system is available). For shareholders in the highest marginal bracket (45%) the final withholding tax produces overall taxation consistent with that rate, presuming no expenses in deriving dividends.[300]

Both the UK and the US apply a form of proportional reduction in tax rates applicable to shareholders. Neither approach relieves any corporation tax (ignoring the US accumulated earnings tax) and so produces a full classical system for exempt shareholders. For other shareholders the analysis is complicated. Both countries apply progressive tax rates to corporations, and so the level of dividend relief varies depending on the level of profits of the corporation. In addition, the UK shareholder differentiation system is supplemented with a dividend tax credit; the overall effect of this system is considered later at 2.4.3.3.

As for the US shareholder differentiation system, the level of dividend relief depends on the rate of corporation tax applied to the profits, the marginal tax bracket of the individual and whether the individual incurs expenses in deriving the dividends. This is a complex mix, but as in Germany, the level of relief is greatest for shareholders in the highest marginal tax bracket (currently 35%) with no expenses. At best for such a shareholder, the US system still imposes at least 10% extra tax on distributed corporate income than would be charged if the shareholder derived the income directly (applying the highest corporate tax rate and ignoring state taxes).[301] To produce full dividend relief for a shareholder in the

---

[300]  100 profits less 30 corporation tax leaves a dividend of 70 subject to 25% withholding tax of 17.5. Net return is 52.5, making total tax collected of 47.5, which is close to the highest personal marginal rate of 45% increased by the surcharge. Application of the surcharge to the dividend withholding tax makes dividends slightly less beneficial.

[301]  100 profits less 35 corporation tax leaves a dividend of 65 subject to 15% tax of 9.75. Net return is 55.25, making total tax collected of 44.25. Thus, economic double taxation consists of the 9.75 shareholder tax, which is the classical element.

highest marginal tax bracket (35%), the corporate tax rate would have to be reduced to approximately 23.5%.[302]

**Dividend streaming**   As with the dividend exclusion system, dividend streaming is an issue under a shareholder differentiation system. If the combined corporation tax and shareholder tax is less than the highest marginal tax rate, there will be an incentive to derive income through a corporation. More likely, however, this combination will be higher than the marginal tax rates of many shareholders, particularly those on lower rates. The result is a disincentive, particularly for small business, to use the corporate form. As with the dividend exclusion system, because the level of dividend relief is likely to be proportionately higher for higher rate shareholders than lower rate shareholders, there may be an incentive to stream dividends to higher rate shareholders. Those on lower rates may be encouraged to derive other types of income from corporations, such as wages and interest. Again, there may be a particular distortion in favour of debt over equity, particularly for exempt investors.

Just as the US recognises the propensity of its inter-corporate dividends-received deduction to facilitate tax arbitrage, the US recognises this propensity in the context of its shareholder differentiation system. The holding-period rule applied in the context of the dividends-received deduction is also applied to the reduced dividend tax rates for individuals.[303] The reduction is not available for individual shareholders unless the shares are held at risk. For individuals, the holding periods are increased to 60 days for ordinary shares and 120 days for preference shares.

The shareholder differentiation system does not encourage distribution of corporate profits. It is neutral as to distribution for shareholders that are not taxed with respect to distributions. However, the most likely effect of a shareholder differentiation system is that shareholders are taxed at a positive rate on dividends and to this extent such as system encourages retention. As with the dividend exclusion system, it is impossible to fit a shareholder differentiation system into an income tax focused on individuals in a non-distorting fashion (unless combined with another form of dividend relief).

---

[302]   A 23.5% corporate tax rate equates to a corporation with income of about $108,000 taxed at the usual corporate marginal rates. This would be further complicated by state corporation taxes.

[303]   IRC (US) s. 1(h)(11)(B)(iii).

---

**Box 2.6:  Dividend tax credit system**

Corporate tax rate of 30%, corporate profits of 100, a dividend of 70 and dividend tax credits calculated as 20% of dividends distributed:

Corporation tax is $100 \times 30\% = 30$ tax payable
Dividend of $70 \times 20\% = 14$ dividend tax credit

Shareholder has income of 84 (70 dividend + 14 tax credit) taxed at marginal rates with a tax credit of 14

---

### 2.4.3.3   Dividend tax credit system

Under a dividend tax credit system shareholders are granted a tax credit calculated according to dividends distributed (see Box 2.6).

Dividend tax credits are typically calculated at a simple fixed rate per dividends received, although there are a number of other ways in which dividend tax credits might be calculated. The rate of dividend tax credit determines the extent of relief (discussed later in more detail). The example in Box 2.6 does not provide full dividend relief: 16 corporation tax (30 less 14 dividend tax credit) remains unrelieved. To provide full relief, the dividend tax credit must be calculated at the corporate tax rate divided by 1 less the corporate tax rate. In the example this would be 30% divided by 1 minus 30% (i.e. 3/7).

The dividend tax credit system remains relatively popular, being used to provide dividend relief in Australia, Canada, Chile, Japan, Korea (Rep.), New Zealand, Taiwan and the UK. It was more popular during the 1990s, particularly in the form of the imputation system (see the later discussion).[304]

As noted earlier at 2.4.2, all corporate-level dividend relief systems broadly operate in a similar manner. Although there are important differences among them, when it comes to expenses in deriving dividends, treatment of preference income, extent of relief and dividend streaming, each system can be structured to produce similar results. The same is not true of shareholder-level dividend relief systems. The operation of the dividend tax credit system is fundamentally different from that of the dividend exclusion system or shareholder differentiation systems in each of these aspects.

---

[304]  Generally, see Harris (2010) particularly at pp. 276–7.

An important issue that does not arise under the other shareholder-level dividend relief systems is that of gross-up (i.e. whether dividend tax credits are considered part of shareholders' taxable income). It is possible to have a dividend tax credit system without gross-up, but this is rare. It is not necessary if shareholders are taxed at a flat rate, but in the face of progression, gross-up is necessary if dividends are to be taxed consistently with marginal tax rates. In any case, gross-up may be justified on the basis that dividend tax credits constitute income and represent an ability to pay taxes.

Further, unlike the other shareholder-level dividend relief systems, the dividend tax credit system can produce surplus relief in the form of excess dividend tax credits. An excess arises when dividend tax credits granted with respect to dividends exceed the shareholder's income tax liability with respect to the dividends. A major issue for a dividend tax credit system is the manner in which excess dividend tax credits may be used. There are a number of options in this regard. Excess dividend tax credits may not be available for use by shareholders. In this case, a dividend tax credit system can produce results similar to those under a shareholder differentiation system.

Alternately, excess dividend tax credits may be available to set against the general income tax liability of shareholders. Again, this may be done in several ways. Excess dividend tax credits may only be available to set against a shareholder's income tax liability of the year in which the dividends are received. Excess dividend tax credits may be available for carry-forward or carry-back to set against other income tax liability of the shareholder. Finally, excess dividend tax credits may be available for refund to shareholders.

As mentioned earlier, the UK corporate tax system uses a dividend tax credit in addition to reduced tax rates for dividends. This combination was adopted in 1999 to replace the advanced corporation tax system (see the earlier discussion at 2.4.2.3), the impetus being international issues discussed in Chapter 3. The tax credit is calculated as one-ninth of the amount of the distribution.[305] The amount of the distribution is increased by the amount of the tax credit (i.e. gross-up is required).[306] So, for every 90 dividend received, the shareholder has a dividend tax credit of 10 (one-ninth of 90) and income of 100 (90 dividend + 10 tax credit). The credit is available to reduce the shareholder tax payable on the dividend at the reduced dividend rates.

---

[305] ITTOIA 2005 (UK) s. 397(1).
[306] ITTOIA 2005 (UK) s. 398(1).

However, there are strict limits on the use of the tax credit, which derive from former dividend streaming issues, discussed later. The tax credit is only available to set against income tax liability, and so it is not available to corporations subject to corporation tax.[307] Further, a tax credit is only granted to the extent that a distribution is

> brought into charge to tax, and accordingly if the person's total income is reduced by any deductions which fall to be made from the distribution, the tax credit for the distribution is reduced in the same proportion as the distribution.[308]

As noted earlier at 2.4.3.2, dividends are treated as the highest part of a person's income. This means that the UK dividend tax credit cannot produce surplus relief (i.e. the tax credit is reduced to ensure that a surplus cannot arise). As a result, dividend tax credits cannot reduce income tax imposed on other income, nor can they be refunded.

This contrasts dramatically with the Australian dividend tax credit system, which provides full dividend relief. The maximum dividend tax credit that can be attached to a dividend is equal to the current corporate tax rate on the grossed-up amount of the dividend.[309] A shareholder that receives a dividend tax credit must include the tax credit in assessable income (i.e. gross-up is required).[310] This gross-up, credit and tax system apply to both individual and corporate shareholders. There are no special tax rates for dividends and no special exemption for inter-corporate dividends (although dividends paid between members of a consolidated group are not recognised).

Until 2000, excess dividend tax credits could be set against income tax due on the shareholder's other income, but could not be carried forward or refunded. The present treatment of excess dividend tax credits depends on the type of shareholder in question. For individuals and superannuation funds (retirement funds) the excess is refundable, resulting in corporate income being taxed at marginal rates.[311] Corporate shareholders are treated differently. Here excess dividend tax credits are most likely to arise by reason of losses. So, borrowing from the New Zealand approach, a corporate shareholder may convert excess dividend tax credits to an

---

[307] ITTOIA 2005 (UK) s. 397(2).
[308] ITTOIA 2005 (UK) s. 397(3).
[309] Income Tax Assessment Act 1997 (Australia) s. 202–55.
[310] Income Tax Assessment Act 1997 (Australia) s. 207–20(1).
[311] Income Tax Assessment Act 1997 (Australia) ss. 63–10 and 67–25.

equivalent amount of tax loss (divide excess credits by the corporate tax rate), which loss can be carried forward in the usual manner.[312]

**Expenses in deriving dividends**   As the Australian system shows, unlike the dividend exclusion or shareholder differentiation systems, a dividend tax credit system can be implemented within a global approach to income calculation. As a result, a dividend tax credit system does not per se suggest any limitation on the deduction of expenses in deriving dividends to which dividend tax credits are attached. For example, in Australia, a shareholder who incurs expenses in deriving dividends to which dividend tax credits are attached is entitled to deduct expenses in the usual fashion under the general deduction rule.[313]

By contrast, the UK's approach with respect to expenses incurred by individuals in deriving dividends is confused and restricted. This was discussed earlier at 2.4.3.2. Broadly, no such deduction is available. However, there is an important exception: interest on a loan to acquire shares in a close company is deductible from total income if certain conditions are met. The question is whether deduction of those expenses causes a reduction in the dividend tax credit. Section 397(3) of ITTOIA 2005 was reproduced earlier, and if the interest reduces the dividends subject to charge then the tax credit is reduced. But the question is whether that interest must reduce dividend income on the shares that the loan was used to purchase.

The better answer seems to be no. The interest deduction is a particular type of relief that can be set against the component parts of an individual's total income 'in the way which will result in the greatest reduction in the taxpayer's liability to income tax'.[314] The exception is if another provision requires the interest 'to be deducted from particular components of income or in a different order'.[315] Section 397(3) of ITTOIA 2005 does not say this. Presuming a taxpayer choice, an individual would be best to set the interest deduction against income that would be taxable at normal marginal rates. Not only would this leave more dividend income to be taxed at lower rates but it would also preserve the dividend tax credit.

---

[312] Income Tax Assessment Act 1997 (Australia) s. 36–55.
[313] Income Tax Assessment Act 1997 (Australia) s. 8–1. Under this provision, there would need to be an objective expectation of sufficient dividend income to offset expenses; *Spassked Pty Ltd* v. *FCT* [2003] FCAFC 282 (FFC).
[314] ITA 2007 (UK) s. 25(2).
[315] ITA 2007 (UK) s. 25(3).

Whether the UK intends this result or not, the drafting of the provisions in question and the manner in which they interrelate are appalling.

**Preference income**  The dividend tax credit system behaves like other forms of dividend relief at the shareholder level when it comes to preference income. The dividend tax credit system does not wash out corporate preferences on distribution because corporate preferences granted permanently reduce the effective tax rate suffered by corporate income. Further, the dividend tax credit system does not accurately pass corporate preferences to shareholders. In particular, many corporate preferences result in exclusions from the tax base. Such preferences are passed through to shareholders in the form of dividend tax credits, which are potentially refundable, which could not happen if the exclusion preference were granted directly to the shareholder.

As a result, a particular problem with the dividend tax credit system is that shareholders may receive dividend tax credits for corporation tax that was never paid by the corporation.[316] Similar problems do occur with the other dividend relief systems at the shareholder level, but those systems have no mechanism for setting the excess dividend relief against other types of income (or a refund of the excess). This is simply a function of the inequity of those systems when compared with a dividend tax credit system. A dividend tax credit system that grants dividend tax credits at a fixed rate per dividends distributed, irrespective of the extent to which profits distributed suffer corporation tax, is conventionally referred to as a 'notional dividend tax credit system'. The UK's dividend tax credit is notional: it is granted irrespective of whether corporation tax has been paid on the profits distributed.

Like other shareholder-level dividend relief systems, the dividend tax credit system might limit relief granted by reference to the corporation tax base rather than the shareholder tax base. In particular, the granting of dividend tax credits may be limited according to corporation tax attributable to the profits distributed. Such a dividend tax credit system imputes to shareholders, on distribution, corporation tax paid by distributing corporations and is referred to as an 'imputation system' (see Box 2.7). Under

---

[316] This conversion of corporate exemptions into dividend tax credits can produce the bizarre result referred to as 'super-integration'; see Harris (1996, p. 135) and the reference cited therein. Presume a corporation derives 100 income that is exempt from tax (for whatever reason). It distributes that income and the shareholder receives a dividend tax credit of 20. Presuming gross-up, the shareholder has income of 120 (100 + 20), which is more than the income derived by the corporation.

---

**Box 2.7:** Imputation system

A dividend tax credit system under which the credit granted to shareholders is calculated according to dividends distributed but limited by reference to corporation tax paid with respect to the profits distributed.

---

the imputation system, corporation tax is often likened to a withholding tax collected on behalf of shareholders.[317]

As with other shareholder-level dividend relief systems that seek to limit relief to the corporation tax base rather than the shareholder tax base, there are two primary options for implementing an imputation system. The question is how to reconcile the dividend tax credit granted with the corporation tax paid. If the two are not equal, then an imputation system must either adjust corporate tax upwards to equal the dividend tax credit, or adjust the dividend tax credit down to equal corporation tax paid. The first is referred to as an 'equalisation tax' and involves a corporate distributions tax on distributions of preference income. The latter is referred to as a 'variable dividend tax credit system', because the rate of the dividend tax credit received with dividends varies depending on corporation tax suffered by the profits considered to be distributed.[318]

Equalisation tax style imputation systems were common in the 1990s, particularly in Europe. However, they became problematic under EU law because they displayed certain discriminatory effects and so were slowly replaced from the late 1990s into the early 2000s. The Australian imputation system is now the only imputation system in G-20 countries, and it is a variable dividend tax credit system. The New Zealand imputation system also survives and is similar.[319] It is useful to briefly consider the main structural features of the Australian imputation system.

The Australian imputation system regulates the manner and extent to which corporations can attach dividend tax credits to their dividends. This is referred to as the 'franking' process.[320] Through this process, corporations allocate corporation tax paid to particular distributions.[321] Only certain types of distributions ('frankable distributions') may have dividend tax credits attached to them, discussed further later. There is no minimum

---

[317] See Harris (1996, p. 71) and the references cited therein.
[318] Generally, see Harris (1996, pp. 154–63).
[319] See Harris (2010) and the references cited therein.
[320] In tax terms, to 'frank' is to prepay tax or free an amount from charge.
[321] Income Tax Assessment Act 1997 (Australia) s. 202–5.

dividend tax credit that may be attached to a dividend, but there is a maximum. The maximum credit that a shareholder can get with a distribution is equal to the current corporate tax rate on the grossed-up amount.[322] The corporation conveys the amount of the credit to the shareholder by specifying the amount in a dividend statement provided to the shareholder.[323]

To ensure that corporations do not attach dividend tax credits to dividends in excess of corporation tax paid, corporations are required to maintain certain records. These records are discussed later at 2.5.1.2. If a corporation does exceed corporation tax paid, it must pay additional corporation tax in the form of franking deficit tax.[324] This is a corporate distributions tax in the nature of an equalisation tax, and so the Australian system incorporates aspects of both primary forms of imputation system: variable dividend tax credit and an equalisation tax. Corporations are encouraged to use the variable dividend tax credit mechanism through the imposition of a penalty should their dividend tax credits exceed corporation tax attributed to the corporation for a year by more than 10%.[325]

Notional dividend tax credit systems experience difficulties with hidden profit distributions. The risk is that dividend tax credits are attached to such distributions even if those distributions have not given rise to any corporation tax liability at the corporate level. The UK dividend tax credit system behaves in this manner. As discussed earlier at 2.2.2, the UK taxes to shareholders many kinds of hidden profit distributions, particularly in the context of closely held corporations. However, such distributions are unlikely to give rise to notional income for the corporation. Nevertheless, it seems that the shareholder would be entitled to dividend relief in the form of reduced rates and a dividend tax credit. The risk is that hidden profit distributions are more tax efficient than standard distributions of profits on which corporation tax has been paid.

As noted, Germany addresses this issue by taxing the corporation on notional income. In effect, this is an equalisation tax for hidden profit distributions. The Australian imputation system would also recapture the benefit of hidden profit distributions (i.e. wash out the corporate-level preference). Because no corporation tax has been paid on the benefit distributed, there would be no dividend tax credit available (or the equalisation tax would be imposed). This is complicated where an Australian corporation has other taxed retained profits on which corporation tax has

---

[322] Income Tax Assessment Act 1997 (Australia) s. 202–55.
[323] Income Tax Assessment Act 1997 (Australia) s. 202–60.
[324] Income Tax Assessment Act 1997 (Australia) s. 205–45(2).
[325] Income Tax Assessment Act 1997 (Australia) s. 205–70(2).

been paid. The Australian corporation might then attach that corporation tax to the hidden profit distribution.

At first blush, this practice might not seem offensive, but there is a deeper issue. If it were possible, it would enable hidden profit distributions to be, in effect, converted into exempt profits at the corporate level. That is, hidden profit distributions would still be effective because they would enable corporations to pass corporation tax paid on to shareholders in the form of dividend tax credits without parting with the profits on which the corporation tax was paid. In effect, this would facilitate funding retention of profits with exempt income. As a result, there are many types of hidden profit distributions to which Australian corporations cannot attach dividend tax credits (i.e. that are 'unfrankable' distributions).[326] Unfrankable distributions are fully taxable to shareholders without dividend relief (i.e. without any dividend tax credits). The list of unfrankable distributions is less than scientific, but it does, in many cases, address this issue of hidden profit distributions.

**Extent of relief**   The extent of relief under a dividend tax credit system can be adjusted proportionately by adjusting the rate of dividend tax credit. As noted earlier, when the dividend tax credit on dividends grossed up by those credits equals the corporate tax rate, the system provides full dividend relief. The Australian imputation system provides full dividend relief except in particular circumstances largely of an anti-abuse nature, several of which are discussed later in the context of dividend streaming.

Dividend tax credit systems may also result in discriminatory levels of dividend relief, much in the same manner as dividend exclusion and shareholder differentiation systems. This happens in particular when the dividend tax credit may only be set against tax chargeable on dividend income, as in the UK. In such a case, dividend tax credits are wasted for shareholders on tax rates below the rate of dividend tax credit. However, unlike the other shareholder-level dividend relief systems, the dividend tax credit system and, in particular, the imputation system have other options that allow them to make progress towards the consistent treatment of corporate income produced by corporate-level dividend relief systems.

A dividend tax credit system can still show some discrimination against low-rate shareholders where excess dividend tax credits can be set against tax due on other income and even where such excess can be carried forward (or back) for use in other years. However, where excess dividend tax credits are refundable, such as under the Australian imputation system,

---

[326] Income Tax Assessment Act 1997 (Australia) s. 202–45.

a dividend tax credit system approaches the treatment obtained under a corporate-level dividend relief system, though not precisely. In particular, such a system could still provide dividend tax credits for tax that was not paid at the corporate level. The result would be less than a full shareholder tax on distributed corporate income. The parity with corporate-level dividend relief systems becomes almost complete when an imputation system is adopted. As with those corporate-level relief systems, all distributed corporate income is effectively taxed at shareholder marginal rates.

The UK dividend relief system incorporates a dividend tax credit, as well as other features that are important in assessing the level of dividend relief provided by it. Generally, it is not a full dividend relief system, but in some respects it can produce that result. In particular, that system must be considered in conjunction with multiple corporate tax rates and reduced shareholder tax rates: the UK system grants higher levels of dividend relief for distributions by corporations subject to lower rates of corporation tax. As noted earlier at 1.3.2.2, the UK has a small profits corporate tax rate of 20% and main corporate tax rate of 24% (being reduced to 22%).

Presume a corporation derives 100 profits, pays corporation tax at 20% and then distributes a dividend of 80 to a shareholder with a marginal tax rate of 40%. In this case, the UK dividend relief system works like this:

| | |
|---|---:|
| Dividend | 80 |
| Dividend tax credit 79 (80) × 1/9 | 8.89 |
| Shareholder income | 88.89 |
| Shareholder Tax at reduced rates | |
| Say 88.89 × 32.5% | 28.89 |
| Less tax credit | 8.89 |
| Net tax | 20 |
| Dividend | 80 |
| Less net tax | 20 |
| Net dividend | 60 |

If the shareholder had derived the income directly, the return would have been the same (i.e. 100 × 40% gives 40 tax and a net return of 60). For shareholders taxable at 20%, the dividend tax rate is reduced to 10%, which is always equal to the dividend tax credit attached to dividends. This means that shareholders in the 20% tax bracket do not pay any tax on dividends received. Again, the net return (80) is the same as would have been derived if the shareholder had derived the income directly. However, a shareholder taxed at less than 20% (e.g. a pension fund, an individual within the exemption threshold or one with losses) is still taxed at 20%, and so the progressive tax scale is reduced.

Shareholders in the 50% tax bracket get a slightly better return through a corporation than directly:

| | |
|---|---|
| Shareholder income | 88.89 |
| Shareholder tax at reduced rates | |
| Say 88.89 × 42.5% | 37.78 |
| Less tax credit | 8.89 |
| | |
| Net tax | 28.89 |
| Dividend | 80 |
| Less net tax | 28.89 |
| | |
| Net dividend | 51.11 |

If the shareholder had derived the income directly, the net return would have been 1.11 less (i.e. 50). Nevertheless, the overall effect of the UK system for corporations taxed on the lower rate is essentially full dividend relief. In the US and Germany, this full relief could only be achieved by selecting a transparent entity to derive the income (or electing S corporation treatment in the US). Of course, the UK treatment of retained profits is very different from the treatment under these transparency regimes.

If the corporate profits are taxed at the full corporate rate of 24%, then the UK does not provide full dividend relief. Again, presume a corporation derives 100 profits, pays corporation tax at 24% and then distributes a dividend of 76 to a shareholder with a marginal tax rate of 40%.

| | |
|---|---|
| Dividend | 76 |
| Dividend tax credit 76 × 1/9 | 8.44 |
| | |
| Shareholder income | 84.44 |
| Shareholder tax at reduced rates | |
| Say 84.44 × 32.5% | 27.44 |
| Less tax credit | 8.44 |
| | |
| Net tax | 19 |
| Dividend | 76 |
| Less net tax | 19 |
| | |
| Net dividend | 57 |

The net return is 3 less than if the shareholder had derived the income directly (57 is 3 less than 60). This is the classical element of the UK corporation tax (i.e. the corporation tax for which dividend relief is not provided). Shareholders on marginal rates below 40% would not suffer any tax on dividends (because the tax credit equals any tax liability), in which case the return would be 76. For a shareholder on a marginal rate of 20%, this is 4 less than if the shareholder derived the income directly (i.e. 76 is 4 less than 80). So the classical element is higher for a 20% shareholder than for a 40% shareholder. Of course it is much worse for shareholders on rates below 20% where the result is the same as a full classical system.

Again, the shareholder on a 50% marginal tax rate fares best:

| | |
|---|---|
| Shareholder income | 84.44 |
| Shareholder tax at reduced rates | |
| Say 84.44 × 42.5% | 35.88 |
| Less tax credit | 8.44 |
| — | |
| Net tax | 27.44 |
| Dividend | 76 |
| Less net tax | 27.44 |
| — | |
| Net dividend | 48.56 |

The net return is now only 1.44 less than if the shareholder had derived the income directly (i.e. 48.56 is 1.44 less than 50), and this is the classical element.

When the main corporate tax rate is reduced to 22% in 2014, the UK system will move even closer to full dividend relief. For 40% shareholders their net return will become 58.5, and so the classical element will be 1.5. For 20% shareholders it will remain slightly higher with a net return of 78 and so a classical element of 2.

**Dividend streaming**   As with other forms of dividend relief at the shareholder level, the dividend tax credit system is particularly prone to dividend streaming. A dividend tax credit system may discourage the use of the corporate form if it does not provide full dividend relief. For lower rate shareholders, there may be a scenario in which excess dividend tax credits are wasted (e.g. are not refundable). However, a dividend tax credit system that provides full relief positively encourages incorporation by individuals on marginal tax rates above the corporate tax rate. This is because funds can be saved in the corporation subject to a lower rate than if derived directly. The UK and Australian dividend tax credit systems, combined with their corporate tax rates, encourage incorporation. For small business there is no particular incentive to stream other types of income to shareholders (e.g. interest and wages). Indeed, in the UK the problem has been the opposite, because dividends are often subject to lower overall tax than other types of income, especially wages.

However, a dividend tax credit system is particularly prone to dividend streaming when some shareholders benefit from dividend tax credits to a greater extent than other shareholders. This is particularly the case in the UK with respect to exempt shareholders (especially pension funds), which do not benefit from the dividend tax credit at all. As a result, it might be expected that UK pension funds hold more debt than they otherwise might because of this distortion. This is very different from the position under the former advance corporation tax system (see the earlier discussion at 2.4.2.3). Under that system, pension funds could obtain a refund of the shareholder tax credit funded with advance corporation tax. That refund would reduce the effective tax rate on corporate profits from 30% if retained to 12.5% if distributed to a pension fund. Not surprisingly, pension funds exercised substantial influence in causing corporations to distribute all of their profits because they would have 17.5% more per 100 profits to reinvest than the corporation if it retained profits. The refund of dividend tax credits to pension funds was abolished in 1997, and since then there has been a substantial shift in portfolios held by UK pension funds away from shares in UK corporations.[327]

Recently, the Australian imputation system has been at risk of similarly causing corporations to excessively distribute profits. For many years since excess dividend tax credits became refundable, retained corporate profits have been taxed at 30%, whereas superannuation funds (retirement funds) have been taxable at 15%. This substantial gap between the tax rate on retained profits and the effective rate on profits distributed to retirement funds is likely to remain for some time.

Before excess dividend tax credits became refundable, Australian corporations had an incentive to stream dividends to shareholders that could

---

[327] 'The investment strategy of pension funds has changed significantly over the past decade.... The removal of the dividend tax credit in 1999 played a major role in reducing the yield attractions of equities to bonds.... There has been a sustained reduction in pension fund exposure to equities and a deliberate move towards higher weightings in bond (gilts and corporate bonds), together with increased diversification.' Southern (2012, p. 751).

best use the dividend tax credits, typically individuals on higher rates. This led to complex anti-streaming rules that are considered shortly. However, even after the refund became available, some shareholders still benefit more from dividend tax credits than others. In particular, as discussed later at 3.1.2.4, non-resident shareholders in Australian corporations tend to get half the benefit that resident shareholders do, and tax-exempt institutions (which exclude retirement funds) get no benefit at all.[328] This created a market for streaming dividends with dividend tax credits to particular types of shareholders. Streaming was made easier by the ability of corporations to attach dividend tax credits to some dividends under the imputation system but not to others.

Australia has a number of rules that seek to address dividend streaming. In particularly, only 'qualifying persons' are entitled to the benefits of dividend tax credits attached to dividends.[329] This means the shareholder must hold the shares on which the dividends are paid at risk for 45 days. This rule was borrowed from the US anti-arbitrage rule for the intercorporate dividends received deduction, discussed earlier at 2.4.3.1. Further, there are rules that prevent corporations from exercising dramatic variation in the rate at which dividend tax credits are attached to different dividends distributed during a year. Broadly, these are the benchmark rules whereby the first dividend in a tax period sets a benchmark, and then the other dividends distributed in the same period must have dividend tax credits attached at the same rate.[330] Further, dividends cannot have dividend tax credits attached to them if they are part of an arrangement to stream dividends to some shareholders and other benefits to others.[331]

As noted earlier, a dividend tax credit system can positively encourage corporate distributions instead of corporate retention. This is particularly a problem where excess dividend tax credits are refundable and the marginal shareholder has a tax rate less than the corporate tax rate. However, an imputation system can also encourage retention of certain profits. Such a system does not grant dividend relief for profits that have not suffered corporation tax. That is, when preference income is distributed, a full shareholder tax is imposed in much the same manner as a classical system would tax distributions.

---

[328] There is no benefit from dividend tax credits if the dividend constitutes exempt income; Income Tax Assessment Act 1997 (Australia) ss. 207–125 and 207–130.

[329] Income Tax Assessment Act 1997 (Australia) s. 207–145(1)(a).

[330] Income Tax Assessment Act 1997 (Australia) Div. 203.

[331] Income Tax Assessment Act 1997 (Australia) s. 202–45(h) referring to Income Tax Assessment Act 1936 (Australia) ss. 45 and 45C.

If the corporation is given a choice as to the order in which it distributes taxed corporate profits or untaxed corporate profits, it will choose to distribute taxed corporate profits in order to delay the full imposition of shareholder tax on the distribution of untaxed corporate profits. Whether this sort of an incentive to retain corporate profits arises depends on the manner in which corporate profits and their tax treatment are recorded and on the ordering rules incorporated in a dividend relief system. These are matters to which the discussion now turns.

## 2.5 Reconciling the corporation and shareholder taxes

All types of dividend relief raise the basic philosophical issue of what the corporate tax system should be trying to tax (see the earlier discussion at 1.3.1). A simple answer that dividend relief should seek to relieve economic double taxation of corporate income says little about the specific manner in which that double taxation is to be relieved. Indeed, it tells us very little about what constitutes double taxation. Does a corporate tax system that taxes corporations at a rate higher than the highest marginal rate but that exempts distributed profits impose economic double taxation? Does a system like Ireland's that taxes corporations at a low rate but also taxes shareholders on distributions at marginal rates constitute economic double taxation? In form, the answers may be no and yes, but the comparative overall taxation in each case might suggest the opposite.

It is for this reason that the discussion of dividend relief typically revolves around a comparison of the taxation of distributed corporate income with taxation at shareholder marginal rates. Any difference between the two gives rise to the distortions associated with the classical system (discussed earlier at 2.3.2). In other words, although a classical system might display these distortions, it is not the sole cause of these distortions. As the earlier discussion at 2.4.2 and 2.4.3 demonstrates, all forms of dividend relief can display these distortions to varying extents depending on the option selected and how it is structured. Therefore it is not useful to label dividend relief 'good' and classical system 'bad'. Each system must be assessed on its merits and particularly by reference to whether it distorts the type of entity through which income is derived, the type of income derived and whether the income is made available to the investor or reinvested (the 'primary distortions').

So the question remains: what should dividend relief seek to achieve? Perhaps it is best to start with what dividend relief cannot achieve. The primary distortions arise because shareholders are not treated as deriving corporate income directly. Dividend relief presumes that the corporation has been taxed with respect to corporate income when derived. So a fundamental premise of dividend relief is that corporate income is *not* treated as derived directly by shareholders. In particular, retained profits are subject to corporation tax, not shareholder tax. Therefore it is impossible for a dividend relief system to cure all of the primary distortions associated with a classical corporate tax system. The only manner in which to achieve that is by ignoring the separate tax identity of the corporation or allocating corporate profits when derived to shareholders. These options were discussed earlier at 1.1.4.2 and 1.3.3.

It seems inevitable that the goal or philosophy of dividend relief should be to minimise the primary distortions, knowing that by definition dividend relief cannot eliminate them. However, such a philosophy does not tell us what comparative weight should be given to each of the distortions, which are often competing. For example, the only manner to ensure that there is no distortion between retention and distribution is to adopt a dividend exclusion system. However, such a system distorts the selection of entity and type of return to a much greater extent than other types of dividend relief. A dividend deduction system is the only manner in which to treat the return on debt and equity the same, but such a system may distort distribution policy.

Perhaps it is best to remember what is being assessed, and that is distributed corporate profits (i.e. income realised by shareholders). Taxing distributions according to shareholder marginal rates neutralises the form of return derived from a corporation, for example, in comparison to wages or interest (presuming they are taxed similarly). Further, it does not necessarily result in substantial distortions as to form of entity or retention or distribution; whether those distortions are displayed will depend on other features of the tax system. In particular, if distributed profits are taxed at shareholder marginal rates, distortions as to the choice of entity and retention or distribution are largely a function of the corporate tax rate selected for retained profits and the comparative sizes of the corporation tax base and the shareholder tax base. Issues surrounding the selection of a corporate tax rate were discussed earlier at 1.3.2.2. Differences between the corporation tax base and the shareholder tax base require some further consideration.

Corporate preferences were discussed earlier at 2.4.1.3. The discussion at 2.4.2 and 2.4.3 demonstrated that different types of dividend relief treat the distribution of preference income differently. Corporate-level dividend relief tends to wash out corporate preferences on distribution. Shareholder-level dividend relief tends to pass through corporate preferences, but not in the manner in which the preference would have been granted had the shareholder derived the income directly. Further, in practice a number of shareholder-level dividend relief systems seek to intentionally wash out corporate preferences on distribution. This result is consistent with anti-erosion measures such as the US alternative minimum tax that also seek to limit the benefits of various preferences (see the earlier discussion at 1.3.2.2). Of course, the difference is that the US system washes out preferences at the point corporate income is derived, whereas various forms of dividend relief only wash out those preferences on distribution.

At issue is the question of which tax base is superior: the corporation tax base or the shareholder tax base. In the context of a realisation-based income tax, most would suggest that the shareholder tax base is superior (i.e. dividends are what should be subjected to tax at marginal rates). Using a shareholder tax base necessarily involves the wash-out of corporate preferences. However, it is likely to also mean that distributed corporate income is not taxed in the same manner as it would be if the shareholder derived the income directly. This is because if the income were derived directly the preferences would have reduced tax liability, at least in the absence of an alternative minimum tax.

But again it must be remembered that, even if corporate preferences are not washed out on distribution, there can be no perfect equivalence with income derived directly. This is because there is no form of dividend relief that naturally passes corporate preferences through a corporation to shareholders in the same form in which the preferences were granted to the corporation. An unacceptable amount of complexity is needed to achieve such a result.[332] These problems are no more clearly illustrated than in the context of hidden profit distributions discussed earlier at 2.4. Dividend relief systems that do not wash out corporate preferences typically produce arbitrary results in this regard.

In principle, most countries adopting a dividend relief system (and perhaps even a classical system) wish to tax all distributed corporate income uniformly. For corporate-level dividend relief systems, achieving this result means making sure that the distribution of dividends does not give rise to excess relief. For shareholder-level dividend relief systems, it

---

[332] See the discussion in Harris (1996, pp. 200–14).

usually means making sure that all distributed corporate income suffers the same corporate tax burden, and here a corporate equalisation tax on distribution of untaxed profits is important. In the context of a dividend tax credit system, a similar result can be achieved by limiting dividend tax credits granted to corporation tax paid. In all these cases, the issue is reconciling the corporation tax base with the shareholder tax base at the time of distribution.

To engage in that reconciliation, the corporate tax treatment of the profits considered distributed must be compared with shareholder taxation. This process gives rise to three major issues. The first is identifying a particular corporate tax treatment with particular corporate profits. The second issue is identifying particular profits (suffering a particular tax treatment under the first issue) as distributed rather than retained. The third issue is the reconciliation itself, which ensures that all distributed profits are taxed uniformly. The third issue can be dealt with briefly. The other two require more detailed consideration.

There are two primary mechanisms for reconciling the corporation tax base with the shareholder tax base. First, and the one used most commonly, that reconciliation may be achieved through an equalisation tax. Such a tax considers which profits have been distributed and, if they have not been subject to sufficient corporation tax when derived, imposes a top-up tax at the corporate level to ensure that all distributed corporate profits have been taxed uniformly at the corporate level. The second mechanism is to reduce the amount of dividend relief by reference to the corporation tax treatment of the profits distributed. This reconciliation mechanism produces different results depending on which of the six primary methods of dividend relief is used. These mechanisms are further discussed later in the context of recording corporate tax treatment and the allocation of profits as retained or distributed.

### 2.5.1   Recording corporate tax treatment

Many corporate tax systems require corporations to maintain some form of records of funds available for distribution to shareholders that affect the tax treatment of distributions. As is discussed at 6.1.1, at a minimum, most countries do not tax returns of share capital in the same manner as distributions of profits. In principle, this means that corporations must record share capital and identify it with particular distributions to shareholders. All returns of share capital are likely to be treated similarly for tax purposes, so there is unlikely to be any subcategorisation of recorded capital for tax purposes, although this does sometimes happen. By contrast, with corporate profits, some forms of dividend relief require a different tax treatment depending on which profits are distributed. In this case, a corporation must retain records of the relevant different types of profits or at least their corporate tax treatment.

### 2.5.1.1   Recording share capital

In many countries, corporate law requires corporations to maintain records of share capital, and the corporate tax system may simply accept those records for tax law purposes. Generally, this is the approach under the German and UK corporate tax systems. By contrast, if there are multiple corporate laws that can apply, perhaps the corporate law records will not be acceptable for tax purposes.

For example, corporate law in the US is largely regulated by state corporate law. This means that, if corporate law classification of share capital were relied on, there might be fifty different ways in which it would be determined. And the majority of state corporate laws no longer incorporate any such classification in any case.[333] Instead, the IRC requires uniformity by requiring corporations to maintain records of 'earnings and profits'. This concept was discussed earlier at 2.1.1. In particular, 'earnings and profits' is a tax law concept, and corporations must maintain records of earnings and profits as prescribed by IRC and supplemented with Treasury Regulations. Any distribution that is out of earnings and profits is a dividend and taxed as income. Any distribution not out of earnings and profits is effectively treated as a return of capital. In particular, such a distribution is not directly included in income, but reduces the cost base of the shares in question. If that cost base is exceeded, the excess is treated as a gain on disposal of the shares.[334]

By comparison, the CCCTB Proposal contains no particular provisions on recording share capital or the tax treatment of returns of share capital. 'Dividends and other profit distributions' are included in 'revenues' and so in the calculation of the tax base.[335] There is no reference to returns of capital, which are presumed to fall outside the corporate tax base. As noted earlier at 2.1.1, there is no definition of 'dividends and other profit

---

[333] The DGCL demonstrates the possible flexibility of state corporate law in this regard. If a corporation issues no par value shares, the stated or legal capital of the corporation is whatever the directors decide; DGCL (US) s. 154. The MBCA (US) intentionally removed any reference to stated or legal capital.

[334] IRC (US) s. 301(c).

[335] CCCTB Proposal Art. 4(8).

distributions'. The presumption seems to be that this definition will be determined by the corporate laws of the various member states and that such laws will distinguish between returns of capital and profit distributions. This area does benefit from some harmonisation of EU corporate law.[336]

Corporate law records of share capital might also be viewed as in some respects inadequate in ensuring the accuracy of tax law. Such records typically only record formal contributions to share capital, but shareholders might make informal contributions. Informal contributions occur when a shareholder passes some benefit to a corporation for inadequate consideration. They are like the reverse of a hidden profit distribution. Germany is one of the few countries to expressly deal with 'hidden capital contributions' in its Corporate Income Tax Law. Corporations must maintain for tax purposes a contributions account that records shareholder contributions other than formal share capital contributions.[337] In countries where there is no express provision, accountants are likely to adopt the practice of recognising a loan whenever a shareholder passes a benefit to a corporation. In this way, returns to the shareholder will be recognised as a return of loan capital and not taxed.

### 2.5.1.2  Recording profits

All countries will require corporations to record share capital (including negatively as in the US), even if corporate law records are adopted for this purpose. However, some countries also need to record different categories of profits or their corporate tax treatment if the distribution of those profits gives rise to different tax consequences than the distribution of other profits. This is particularly an issue for some types of dividend relief systems. There are a number of methods for maintaining records of profits. The types of records that must be maintained and the options available may depend on which aspect of the tax equation is adjusted by dividend relief, whether at the corporate level or at the shareholder level.

This is not the place for a detailed consideration of the different types of records that may be maintained for the purposes of dividend relief.[338] However, the types of records maintained can have a serious impact on

---

[336]  Generally, regarding EU regulation of corporate law, see Dine & Hughes (2007–).
[337]  KStG (Germany) s. 27.
[338]  This is considered in detail in Harris (1996, pp. 135–87).

the behaviour of dividend relief systems and the types of distortions they incorporate. So a brief consideration is appropriate. Records may be composed of three basic elements: distributable profits, corporation tax and corporate taxable income. Distributable profits must be recorded with either corporation tax or taxable income, typically the former. Corporation tax and taxable income may be recorded in isolation. Each of these options is considered in turn in the light of different forms of dividend relief.

**Corporate profits with tax treatment**   This is the most accurate and complex form of records that dividend relief may require. It involves recording corporate profits in some relationship with their tax treatment. The most complete records itemise all corporate profits available for distribution with their particular tax treatment. In this case, there may be any number of different types of corporate profits that must be recorded. Alternately, corporate profits may be pooled and a fixed corporate tax treatment assigned to the pool. There may be one or more pools; the more pools, the more like the itemised approach this option becomes. Finally, there may simply be two pools: one being profits (distributable or taxable) and the other being corporation tax paid. Under this approach, the tax treatment of particular distributions varies depending on the ratio of profits in the profits pool to corporation tax in the tax pool. The difference between these approaches can be illustrated with an example using a dividend deduction system.

Presume a dividend deduction system under which the deduction for dividends may be carried back to previous years. A corporation derives and retains profits over a five-year period and the profits are subject to various tax treatments. Some profits are excluded from the corporate tax base, some profits receive some sort of credit relief (e.g. a research and development credit) and other profits are taxed at different rates (e.g. as a result of concessions or changes in the corporate tax rate). The carry-back of a dividend deduction involves a refund of corporation tax paid in previous years. To determine how much refund to provide, the tax law must identify which of these profits is distributed and how much corporation tax was paid with respect to those profits.

The itemised approach would require records to be maintained for each of the five years and, within each year, would record each item of income and its particular tax treatment. By contrast, there may simply be one pool of profits considered taxed at a particular rate. Most simply, this type of record would be achieved by dividing corporation tax paid by the particular rate selected.[339] There would be no record of the precise corporation tax treatment of particular profits, but only a record of all corporate profits considered to have suffered tax at a particular rate. A distribution of those profits would give rise to a refund of corporation tax at a set rate. This simple approach gives rise to what has been referred to as 'super-stacking' and is particularly a problem if hidden profit distributions do not give rise to notional corporate income.[340] By contrast, the corporation might maintain a pool of distributable profits and another pool of total corporation tax paid. The refund of corporation tax in this case would be calculated as the ratio of the profit pool to the corporation tax pool and so would vary from time to time depending on the level in each pool.

Any of these methods could be used for purposes of imposing a corporate equalisation tax to ensure that all corporate profits distributed suffer an equal tax treatment, irrespective of the type of dividend relief. The same is not true if the amount of dividend relief is sought to be limited by reference to the tax treatment when corporate profits were derived (i.e. dividend relief is denied for the distribution of preference income). As noted earlier at 2.4.3, denying dividend relief in this way produces a non-uniform taxation of different dividend distributions (and so arbitrary results), except in the context of full dividend relief that taxes distributed corporate income at shareholder marginal rates.

So, for example, a dividend deduction system can produce excess relief where distributable profits are greater than the corporation's taxable income. The only way to prevent this excess is to require the deduction to be set against not only taxable income but also all distributable profits of a corporation. Dividends distributed out of profits in excess of the corporation's taxable income would not give rise to a dividend deduction (or refund). By contrast, a split-rate system should not give rise to excess relief; there can be no reduction in tax rate applicable to the distribution of profits that have not suffered corporation tax. A corporation tax credit system may also give rise to excess relief, but it is more difficult to

---

[339] This system is very similar to a system that simply records corporation tax paid.

[340] Dividend relief will not be restricted until all taxed profits have been exhausted. So, provided some taxed profits are retained, hidden profit distributions will be granted dividend relief and so they will be tax preferred (because they are not properly taxed at the corporate level). See the discussion of different types of relief at the shareholder level at 2.4.3. Generally regarding super-stacking, see Harris (1996, pp. 219–21) and the references cited therein.

prevent that excess relief, even if distributable profits are recorded. Preventing that excess relief can only be achieved by setting all dividends against distributable profits (not taxable income) and limiting the credit to the amount of tax paid on the profits distributed.

Moving to the shareholder level, the dividend exclusion system can produce arbitrary and confusing results. How would the exclusion be limited by reference to corporation tax paid at the corporate level? One approach is to limit the exclusion to the amount of profits considered subject to full corporation tax. This would be difficult if an itemised approach were adopted. It would be more straightforward under a pooling approach. The shareholder differentiation system fares no better. By contrast, any of these profit-recording approaches could be applied appropriately to a dividend tax credit system. The dividend tax credit would be limited to the corporation tax attributable to the profits distributed. Of course, the result would be a variable dividend tax credit imputation system (see the earlier discussion at 2.4.3.3).

**Corporation tax**    Rather than recording profits with a corporation tax treatment, a dividend relief system may just record a total of corporation tax paid. Again, it is a simple matter to use such records with an equalisation tax approach. Whenever a dividend is distributed, the pool of corporation tax would be reduced by an amount equal to the corporate tax rate applied to the grossed-up amount of the distribution (the dividend plus that reduction). When the pool runs out, every distribution would give rise to equalisation tax calculated in the same manner. This system, like the pooling with a fixed tax treatment recording of profits, can result in super-stacking and so does not work effectively in the context of hidden profit distributions that do not give rise to notional corporate income.

If an equalisation tax mechanism is used, recording corporation tax can work with any form of dividend relief. However, if, instead, the amount of dividend relief is to be restricted according to corporation tax treatment, recording corporation tax only works with some forms of dividend relief. Without a conversion of the tax into profits or a recording of profits with corporation tax, it cannot work with dividend relief systems that operate on the tax base. Simply recording corporation tax paid does not identify when a deduction for dividends should be denied because it gives rise to excess relief. Similarly, it does not assist in determining when a distribution is from tax-preferred income so as to deny exclusion under a dividend exclusion system. Similarly, recording corporation tax does not assist in limiting relief under a split-rate system or a shareholder differentiation system. Each system needs to identify which profits have been distributed to determine whether the relief should be denied.

However, simply recording corporation tax can be used in conjunction with dividend relief systems involving credits. This is true with a corporation tax credit system. Here the credit granted to a corporation for distributions would be debited to the pool of corporation tax paid. Once that pool is exhausted, no further credit would be attached to distributions. The same is true at the shareholder level. The dividend tax credit granted to shareholders could be limited to the amount in the pool of corporation tax paid. Once this pool is exhausted, no further tax credits would be granted to shareholders. The Australian variable dividend tax credit imputation system records corporation tax in a single pool in this manner.

Australian corporations previously recorded profits subject to corporation tax at the headline rate. This was changed in 2002 to require a record of corporation tax paid instead of taxed profits. Each corporation must maintain a 'franking account'.[341] The tax law specifies when a credit arises in this account.[342] Most importantly, a credit occurs when a corporation pays corporation tax. There is also a credit when a corporation receives a dividend with dividend tax credits attached, in which case the account is credited with the dividend tax credit. In this way, the benefits of the imputation system pass between corporations. Debits arise when a corporation attaches dividend tax credits to a dividend that it distributes. Other debits arise as a matter of penalty.[343]

The franking account is a running account that carries over from year to year. It is expected that Australian corporations will adjust the dividend tax credits attached to their distributions so that their account does not go into deficit. If, however, a corporation's franking account is in deficit at the end of a tax year, it is liable to pay a special tax (franking deficit tax)

---

[341] Income Tax Assessment Act 1997 (Australia) s. 205–10.
[342] Income Tax Assessment Act 1997 (Australia) s. 205–15.
[343] Debits are listed in Income Tax Assessment Act 1997 (Australia) s. 205–30. Importantly, a debit arises as a result of certain forms of hidden profit distribution made by closely held corporations. This ensures that corporation tax is treated as paid with respect to such distributions. However, despite this allocation of corporation tax to a hidden profit distribution, the shareholder gets no dividend tax credit. The result can be economic double taxation.

equal to the excess.[344] As noted earlier at 2.4.3.3, this is a simple equalisation tax that can be credited against future corporation tax liability.[345] As mentioned, corporations are discouraged from running deficits. If they run deficits in excess of certain limits, their franking account is debited with the result that valuable franking credits are lost.[346] This can result in corporation tax not being credited to the shareholders (i.e. a classical treatment).

**Taxable income**  A dividend relief system may simply require a corporation to record a single pool of taxed profits for the purposes of adjusting relief granted. Again, this system works simply with an equalisation tax. A corporation distributes profits from its taxed profits account. When the credit in that account is exhausted, any further distributions are subject to equalisation tax at the corporate tax rate applied to the grossed-up distribution (distribution plus equalisation tax). For example, if the corporate tax rate is 30%, a distribution of 70 in excess of taxed profits gives rise to equalisation tax of 30. This is the manner in which the Mexican equalisation tax is imposed (see the earlier discussion at 2.4.3.1).[347]

If an equalisation tax adjustment is not used, recording taxed profits in a single pool only works with dividend relief at the shareholder level. For example, exclusion would not be granted for distributions made in excess of the taxed profits account. A similar approach can be used for denying reduced shareholder rates or dividend tax credits. However, as discussed earlier, the results can be arbitrary. For example, under a dividend exclusion system, dividends from the taxed profits account are subject to tax at the corporate rate, whereas dividends in excess of this amount are taxed at shareholder marginal rates. Similar issues arise with a shareholder differentiation system, but not so much with a dividend tax credit system.

Simply recording taxed profits is not sufficient for any of the corporate-level dividend relief systems. As noted earlier, each of these systems results in a refund of corporation tax paid to the distributing corporation. Simply identifying that distributed profits have been taxed when derived does not determine what is the appropriate amount of the refund. That amount depends on the corporation tax paid with respect to the profits considered

---

[344] Income Tax Assessment Act 1997 (Australia) s. 205–45.
[345] Income Tax Assessment Act 1997 (Australia) s. 205–70(1).
[346] Income Tax Assessment Act 1997 (Australia) s. 205–70(2).
[347] Mexican corporations are required to maintain a 'net taxed income account'; Income Tax Law (*Ley del Impuesto sobre la Renta*) (Mexico) Art. 88.

distributed. Accordingly, these systems tend to require corporate profits to be recorded with their tax treatment. The exception is the corporation tax credit system where, as noted earlier, it is possible to simply maintain a record of total corporation tax paid.

### 2.5.2 Allocation of profits as retained or distributed: ordering rule

The requirements discussed earlier at 2.5.1 record different corporate funds that result in different tax treatment when distributed. Assuming there are at least two different types of corporate funds (e.g. capital and profits, or profits and residual), a corporate tax system requires an ordering rule that determines when a particular distribution is from a particular fund. In broad terms, this involves allocating profits as retained or distributed. The ordering rule may be mandatory in that the tax law specifies the order in which the funds are considered distributed. However, some types of records when combined with some types of dividend relief may involve an implicit ordering rule. The discussion first considers the distribution of capital versus profits. It then considers the distribution of various types of profits.

#### 2.5.2.1 Returns of capital

As noted earlier, most countries tax returns of capital differently from distributions of profits. Further, almost always capital is considered returned after corporate profits. In perhaps the majority of cases this happens implicitly because of a corporate law requirement for maintenance or preservation of capital. This is the case with the German and UK corporate tax systems when it comes to returns of share capital. What is a return of share capital is determined by corporate law and in principle involves distributing corporate profits first.

However, there are two circumstances in which accepting the corporate law classification of a return as a distribution of profits or return of capital is inappropriate or impractical. The first circumstance relates to what might be referred to as 'capital streaming', although it tends to be just a form of dividend streaming. Because returns of capital are typically taxed differently from dividends, some types of taxpayer may prefer returns of capital over receipt of dividends. In particular, a return of capital might shelter a shareholder from higher progressive tax rates applicable to dividends. So it is common for higher rate shareholders to prefer returns of capital. If there were no regulation, corporations may stream dividends to low-rate shareholders and returns of capital to high-rate shareholders.

Traditionally, the corporate law of most countries provided adequate regulation against capital streaming, and the German and UK corporate tax systems presume this to still be the case. Each share is allocated a set capital amount (par value), and such capital can only be returned to shareholders in limited circumstances (capital maintenance). The distinction between par value and non-par value shares is further explored at 4.1.1. Many countries, particularly in Europe, continue to adopt the traditional approach of par value shares with maintenance of capital requirements. It is not easy to capital stream in the face of such requirements, although share premiums might give some scope depending on the corporate law in question.

However, many countries have liberalised maintenance of capital requirements (where they existed). Shares may have no par value, and so the share capital of corporations is a homogeneous pool and is not apportioned to particular shares. In addition, there may be few limitations on corporations returning capital to shareholders, at least where the directors make declarations as to the solvency of the corporation. The tax treatment of returns of capital is further considered at 6.1.1. Liberalisation of returns of capital often makes capital streaming for tax purposes a very simple matter – so simple that the tax law may respond by introducing aspects that reverse to some extent the corporate law liberalisation measures.

This was precisely the Australian experience when it liberalised its corporate law in the late 1990s. Subject to solvency declarations, corporations have a wide discretion in returning capital to shareholders and selecting which shareholders to return capital to. For tax purposes, Australia considered a formal profits first rule, such as that adopted in the US and discussed later, but decided instead to adopt a general anti-abuse approach. The core provision applies where a corporation

> streams the provision of capital benefits and the payment of dividends to its shareholders in such a way that:
>
> (a) the capital benefits are...received by shareholders...who would... derive greater benefit from the capital benefits than other shareholders; and
> (b) it is reasonable to assume that the other shareholders...have received...dividends.[348]

The consequence of applying this provision is that the capital benefit is treated as a dividend with no dividend tax credits attached (i.e. fully

---

[348] Income Tax Assessment Act 1936 (Australia) s. 45A(1).

taxable at marginal rates).[349] In practice, this provision operates to force corporations to make proportional distributions of capital to shareholders and often to distribute profits first.

The second situation in which corporate law classification may be inappropriate is where there are multiple corporate laws that might apply, but they differ substantially in classification of distributions as returns of capital. Here the issue is not so much a question of capital streaming as a question of uniform treatment within a particular country. Historically, this was the problem in the US, although with very liberal corporate laws, capital streaming would have become an additional issue. Corporate law is largely regulated by the states, and it might be viewed as inappropriate to have fifty different definitions of a return of capital (if there is one at all) that could have tax consequences for federal purposes.

As noted earlier at 2.5.1.1, the US has formal rules that in substance identify what is a distribution of profits and what is a return of capital for federal tax purposes. Corporations are required to maintain a record of earnings and profits for this purpose. This record is supplemented with an express ordering rule that considers distributions as 'made out of earnings and profits to the extent thereof, and from the most recently accumulated earnings and profits'.[350] The result is that all distributions are taxable until the corporation runs out of earnings and profits. Classification as a return of capital or otherwise under corporate law is irrelevant. Here, there is some risk of capital streaming. So, if earnings and profits of the current year are insufficient to cover all distributions during the year, what earnings and profits exist are prorated over all the distributions during the year. Earnings and profits are then allocated to dividends in chronological order so that the dividends distributed at the end of the year are most likely to be non-taxable.[351]

Germany has another example of where an express tax law ordering rule is required for returns of capital. As noted earlier at 2.5.1.1, Germany requires corporations to record informal (hidden) capital contributions. The return of such contributions to shareholders is not regulated by the maintenance of capital requirements of corporate law. German tax law requires corporations to maintain not only this capital contributions account but also a record of 'equity capital' – effectively funds available

---

[349] Income Tax Assessment Act 1936 (Australia) s. 45C.
[350] IRC (US) s. 316(a).
[351] Title 26 Code of Federal Regulations (US) § 1.316–2(b).

for distribution as a dividend. This record of 'equity capital' is 'the fiscal balance sheet, less the subscribed capital and the balance of the fiscal contribution account'. Distributions by German corporations are only considered as made from the capital contributions account 'if the sum of the payments made during the fiscal year exceeds the profit for appropriation to dividends established at the end of the preceding fiscal year'.[352] Accordingly, when it comes to returns of hidden capital, Germany adopts an express profits first ordering rule in much the same fashion as the US does generally.

### 2.5.2.2   Different types of profits

Putting returns of capital to one side, a corporate tax system will also require an ordering rule if it distinguishes the tax treatment of the distribution of particular types of profits. Whether such a rule is implicit or explicit depends on the manner in which profits and corporation tax are recorded. If a corporate tax system identifies different types of profits with their corporation tax treatment, it is likely to need an express ordering rule as to which profits are considered as distributed first. For example, under the pre-2000 German imputation system there was an express rule that considered the most highly taxed profits as distributed first.[353]

With some systems there may be an implicit ordering rule. For example, under the Mexican corporate tax system, distributions are exempt from equalisation tax to the extent of credit in the distributing corporation's taxed profits account (see the earlier discussion at 2.4.3.1). This implicitly treats taxed profits as distributed first. A similar result may be achieved with a system that records corporation tax and uses an equalisation tax. For example, under the Australian imputation system, equalisation tax (franking deficit tax) is only payable when dividend tax credits exceed the surplus in the distributing corporation's franking account. Again, the result is the distribution of taxed profits before untaxed profits.

It is also possible to have a discretionary ordering rule. So, as noted earlier at 2.4.3.3, Australian corporations have discretion over the amount of dividend tax credits attached to the dividends they distribute. Subject to various benchmark rules, they can attach dividend tax credits at a rate anywhere between nothing and the corporate tax rate applied to the dividend grossed up by the credit. This means a corporation could choose to distribute untaxed profits before taxed profits. Because doing so would

---

[352]   KStG (Germany) s. 27(1).
[353]   See Harris (1996, p. 624).

result in increased shareholder tax, this is not likely to happen unless a corporation is trying to manipulate the imputation system (e.g. by streaming dividend tax credits away from non-resident shareholders). As noted earlier, Australia has strict anti-abuse rules to deal with dividend streaming.

# 3

# Taxation of corporate income

## International aspects

This is a book about corporate taxation, not international taxation. How-ever, in a globalising world it is inappropriate to ignore the international dimension. A corporate tax system must integrate and interface with the tax system as it applies to cross-border activities. So an international tax book is likely to have to deal at some point with the interface between international tax rules and the rules of the corporate tax system.[1] Similarly, a book about corporate tax law should deal with the interface between the corporate tax system and international tax rules. That is what this chapter does. It takes the issues discussed in Chapters 1 and 2 and projects them into an international setting.

This chapter is not concerned with the content of international tax rules and, in particular, tax treaties based on the OECD Model. So it does not consider source and residence taxation per se, but rather presumes such taxation in accordance with generally accepted international norms. What this chapter is concerned with is analysing how the introduction of inter-national factors affects the behaviour of a corporate tax system. In partic-ular, it is concerned with how the corporate income tax system is adjusted when international factors are introduced.

The main international factor that affects the behaviour of a corporate tax system is the residence of the corporation. Indeed, countries typically adopt one form of corporate tax system for resident corporations and a dif-ferent form for non-resident corporations. To understand why this is the case requires a brief excursion into the different jurisdictions to tax that are recognised with respect to resident and non-resident corporations.[2] The two main recognised jurisdictions to tax are on the bases of source and residence. Much has already been made of the artificial nature of

---

[1] For example, see Harris & Oliver (2010) particularly at pp. 48–68, 181–97, 282–312, 333–42, 346–53, 388–415 and 416–51.

[2] Regarding jurisdiction to tax in an international setting, see Harris and Oliver (2010, chap-ter 2).

corporations as persons and dividends as income; see the discussion at the start of Chapter 2. These two elements of artificiality involving corporations are replicated when it comes to international jurisdictions to tax.

The dual nature of corporate income means that the jurisdiction to tax corporate income should be assessed separately at the point corporate income is derived and when corporate income is distributed. At the point income is derived, the standard rules are used to determine the source of a corporation's income.[3] Jurisdiction to tax on the basis of residence is determined on the basis of the corporation's residence. Rules for determining a corporation's residence were briefly considered earlier at 1.1.2.2. As noted at that point, these rules are particularly artificial, reflecting the artificial nature of the corporation.

At the point corporate income is distributed, a country's source rules must be extended to provide a specific rule for sourcing dividends. Most commonly, the rule is that dividends are sourced where a corporation is resident; this is the rule under double tax treaties.[4] It is a particularly artificial rule, which again reflects the artificial nature of the corporation. Perhaps for this reason, some countries' domestic law sources dividends where the profits from which they are distributed are sourced.[5] By contrast, the residence of a shareholder in receipt of dividends is determined according to the usual rules for residence.

Looked at in the round, the taxation of corporate income involves two standard jurisdictions to tax: the country where the corporation's income is sourced and the country of the ultimate shareholder. It also involves two jurisdictions to tax based on the artificial elements of the corporation (i.e. residence based on corporate personality and source based on dividends as income). This artificiality is reinforced by the nature of these rules: the residence jurisdiction for corporate income when derived is precisely the same as the source jurisdiction for corporate income when distributed.

In a globalising world, countries are learning that there is little substance in these artificial jurisdictions to tax based on corporate residence. From a non-tax perspective, a person resident in a particular jurisdiction seeking to derive profits from another jurisdiction through a corporation may care little where that corporation is resident. However, the location

---

[3] Regarding these rules see Harris & Oliver (2010, chapter 3).
[4] OECD Model Art. 10 and see Harris & Oliver (2010, p. 181).
[5] Ibid., p. 78.

Table 3.1. *Eight scenarios*

| | Source of profits | Corporate residence | Shareholder residence |
|---|---|---|---|
| 1. | Domestic | Domestic | Domestic |
| 2. | Foreign | Domestic | Domestic |
| 3. | Domestic | Domestic | Foreign |
| 4. | Foreign | Domestic | Foreign |
| 5. | Domestic | Foreign | Foreign |
| 6. | Foreign | Foreign | Domestic |
| 7. | Domestic | Foreign | Domestic |
| 8. | Foreign | Foreign | Foreign |

of a corporation's residence has a dramatic effect on which countries have taxing rights. Because of this dramatic difference, countries tend to adopt a different form of corporate tax system for resident corporations than they do for non-resident corporations. Whether this makes any sense from a practical perspective is another matter.

Collapsing these artificial jurisdictions to tax based on corporate residence, the deriving and distribution of corporate income involve three fundamental jurisdictions to tax: the source of the corporation's income, the residence of the corporation and the residence of the shareholder. These three jurisdictions give rise to eight possible scenarios involving corporate income that give rise to different jurisdictions to tax for a particular country. These eight scenarios are shown in Table 3.1.

Note that scenarios 1 to 4 involve resident corporations, whereas scenarios 5 to 8 involve non-resident corporations. Scenario 1 requires no further consideration because it was presumed in Chapters 1 and 2. Scenario 8 requires no consideration because it does not involve a recognised jurisdiction to tax. If the artificiality of the corporation is recognised, and corporate residence as a jurisdiction to tax is ignored, the remaining six scenarios are either linked to each other or to scenario 1 or 8. So, scenario 2 is the same as scenario 6 except for the residence of the corporation. Similarly, scenario 3 is the same as scenario 5 except for the residence of the corporation. In the same vein, scenario 4 is the same as scenario 8 and scenario 7 is the same as scenario 1.

There is another connection between scenarios 2 to 7. In an international setting, at least two countries are involved: one country involving a resident corporation and the other country involving a non-resident corporation. This book is concerned with the corporate tax system of a single country, and so in an international setting, it is concerned with analysing the system from the perspective of only one of the countries involved (although that may account for a presumed treatment in the other country). However, the tax laws of a particular country must deal with each scenario involving a resident corporation and each scenario involving a non-resident corporation. So with respect to a particular scenario involving a resident corporation, it is possible to consider how that country would treat the scenario if it were the country where the corporation is not resident, and vice versa. In this way, each of the three scenarios involving a resident corporation has a matching scenario involving a non-resident corporation.

Scenario 2 involves foreign income of a resident corporation distributed to resident shareholders. From the perspective of the country where the income is sourced, this involves a non-resident corporation deriving domestic source income and distributing it to non-resident shareholders. So scenario 2 matches scenario 5. Similarly, scenario 3 involves domestic source income of a resident corporation distributed to a non-resident shareholder. From the perspective of the shareholder's country of residence, this involves a non-resident corporation distributing foreign source income to a resident shareholder. So scenario 3 matches scenario 6. Following this pattern scenario 4 matches scenario 7. The consistency of a particular corporate tax system can be tested by considering whether it treats these matching scenarios in a symmetrical fashion; that is, does it result in more or less taxation then would be imposed in a purely domestic scenario (scenario 1).

With these thoughts in mind, the purpose of this chapter is to consider the behaviour of corporate tax systems in scenarios 2 through 7. It is structured under two primary headings. The first heading considers the scenarios involving resident corporations. The second heading considers the scenarios involving non-resident corporations. The cross-border scenarios in this chapter consider the interrelationship between two countries' corporate tax systems. The short discussion under the third heading considers which country's corporate tax system should be followed if the countries adopt different levels of dividend relief.

## 3.1   Resident corporations

### 3.1.1   *Foreign income / resident shareholders: scenario 2*

For the sake of simplicity, this scenario presumes a resident corporation that derives business income through a foreign PE (fixed place of business). The profits attributable to the PE are subject to corporation tax in the foreign country. Those profits (net of foreign and domestic corporation tax) are distributed as a dividend to a resident shareholder.

A number of issues arise in scenario 2 when the corporate profits are derived. These are the first matter discussed under this subheading. The discussion then proceeds to consider more complex issues that arise when the corporate profits are distributed. This discussion considers treatment under a classical system, dividend relief at the corporate level and dividend relief at the shareholder level separately.

### 3.1.1.1 Foreign tax relief

At the point corporate income is derived, the primary issue is one of foreign tax relief. The foreign profits are subject to foreign corporation tax, and the question is whether the residence country grants the corporation a credit for this foreign corporation tax or rather exempts the foreign income.[6] There are a few issues here that are peculiar to corporations. If an exemption for foreign profits is adopted, the profits will suffer only foreign corporation tax when derived. If the foreign tax credit method is used and foreign corporation tax is lower than domestic corporation tax, there will be residual domestic corporation tax to pay. The total of the foreign and domestic corporation tax will equal the domestic corporation tax liability.

If the foreign corporation tax is equal to or more than the domestic corporation tax, the foreign tax credit system will behave like an exemption system with one qualification. Where the foreign tax is more than the residence country tax, the result may be excess foreign tax credits. The question then becomes whether those excess credits can be used in any other manner. The vast majority of countries adopt the 'ordinary credit' method. This means that foreign tax credits are limited to domestic corporation tax on foreign income (the 'limitation on credit'). By contrast, a 'full credit' would permit excess foreign tax credits to reduce corporation tax due on domestic source income.

Within the ordinary credit system, there are several ways in which the limitation on the credit may be calculated. All foreign income and foreign tax may be lumped together, in which case the limit would be on a worldwide basis. Alternately, the limitation on credit may be calculated for all income sourced within a particular foreign country (i.e. a country-by-country basis). It might also be calculated separately for different types of income (i.e. a type of income or basket approach to the limitation on

---

[6] Generally, regarding the exemption and the credit methods of foreign tax relief, see ibid., pp. 265–82.

credit). Finally, the limitation on credit might be calculated separately for each item or slice of income (i.e. an item-by-item or slice-by-slice approach). Where any other process than an item-by-item approach is adopted for a foreign tax credit, two issues arise with respect to excess foreign tax credits. The first is whether the corporation may carry the excess forward or backward for use in other years. The second is whether the excess may be transferred to or used by another corporation in the same corporate group as the corporation that paid the foreign tax. This will largely depend on the method by which the separate identity of corporate group members is eroded, if any (see the earlier discussion at 1.2.3).

Countries adopt widely varying approaches in granting foreign tax relief with respect to foreign business profits of corporations. Germany adopts a foreign tax credit calculated on a country-by-country basis,[7] although it most commonly uses the exemption method in its tax treaties. Excess credits may not be carried forward or backward. However, the *Organschaft* procedure transfers the profits of a subsidiary to the parent corporation. The result is that the country-by-country limitation is applied to all corporations in an *Organschaft* arrangement.

By contrast, the CCCTB Proposal would calculate the EU-wide profits of the corporation and then use a formula to apportion the tax base among the member states. However, where a PE is situated in a non-EU country (third country), the Proposal adopts an exemption system.[8] The exemption is denied (and no foreign tax relief provided) where the profits are derived from certain low-tax countries.[9] Because there is no foreign tax credit under this Proposal, the question of the use of excess foreign tax credits by other members of a corporate group does not arise.

The US adopts the foreign tax credit method of foreign tax relief.[10] The limitation on credit is calculated on a worldwide basis, but with separate calculations for active and passive income (i.e. a type of income approach).[11] Excess foreign tax credits can be carried back one year and

---

[7] KStG (Germany) s. 26.

[8] CCCTB Proposal Art. 11(e). As originally drafted, the exemption was subject to a 5% re-inclusion for costs (like inter-corporate dividends; see the discussion at 2.4.3.1), Art. 14(1)(g). The EU Presidency amendments would remove this rule and flatly deny a deduction for expenses incurred in deriving the PE income.

[9] CCCTB Proposal Art. 73. The EU Presidency amendments would move the rules on PEs in low-tax countries to the controlled foreign corporation rules in Art. 82.

[10] IRC (US) s. 901.

[11] IRC (US) s. 904(a) & (d). Regarding these baskets and separate baskets for income re-sourced from the US to foreign under a tax treaty, see Kochman & Rosenbloom (2012).

forward for ten.[12] In the context of a consolidated group, the limitation on credit is applied at the group level.[13] This means that excess credits on foreign income derived by one group member may offset corporation tax due on foreign income of the same type derived by another group member.

The UK has traditionally adopted a foreign tax credit approach to foreign tax relief.[14] The credit is limited on a slice-by-slice basis, with the income from a foreign PE constituting a single slice. Generally, this means that excess foreign tax credits cannot be carried forward or backwards. However, there is an exception for excess foreign tax credits arising with respect to a foreign PE. They may be carried back for three years or forward indefinitely, but only to set against corporation tax liability arising with respect to that PE.[15] Because this is still a slice-by-slice approach, there is no provision for transfer of excess credits between members of a corporate group.

In 2011, the UK supplemented this foreign tax credit with an exemption for profits of a foreign PE of a corporation. The exemption only applies when a corporation elects for it to apply.[16] The election is permanent. Where the foreign tax credit method is used, losses of a foreign PE may offset domestic profits of the same trade. Where the election is made for the exemption to apply, no PE losses are recognised. The UK law proceeds for a dozen pages to outline limitations and qualifications to the exemption, including one where the PE is situated in a low tax country.

### 3.1.1.2 Classical system

Where a classical system is adopted, shareholders are taxed on dividends received irrespective of whether the corporate profits distributed were derived from a foreign or domestic source. Such a system incorporates all the distortions usually associated with the classical system (see the earlier discussion at 2.3.2), but does incorporate a form of neutrality – that between deriving domestic source income or foreign source income. In a domestic scenario (scenario 1), a classical system involves the imposition of corporation tax and a separate imposition of shareholder tax. Scenario 2 produces a similar though not identical result.

If an exemption system of foreign tax relief is used, the foreign country imposes corporation tax and the domestic country imposes shareholder

[12] IRC (US) s. 904(c).
[13] Title 26 Code of Federal Regulations (US) § 1.1502–4.
[14] TIOPA 2010 (UK) s. 9.
[15] TIOPA 2010 (UK) s. 73.
[16] CTA 2009 (UK) s. 18A.

tax. The only difference is the quantum of the corporation tax, which may be different between the foreign country and the domestic country. This is a standard feature of the exemption system of foreign tax relief. If a foreign tax credit system is used and the foreign corporation tax is equal to or more than the domestic corporation tax, the same observations apply. The foreign tax serves as the sole corporation tax imposed on the corporate income. If the foreign corporation tax is lower than the domestic corporation tax, then a foreign tax credit system will result in residual domestic corporation tax liability. Here the total corporation tax levied (foreign and domestic) equals the domestic corporation tax, but part of this corporation tax will be levied by the foreign country and part by the domestic country.

### 3.1.1.3   Dividend relief at the corporate level

Scenario 2 demonstrates the issues with corporate-level dividend relief systems discussed earlier at 2.4.2. The fundamental question is whether foreign corporation tax counts as tax for purposes of dividend relief or whether only domestic corporation tax counts. As noted earlier, the classical system can be neutral in scenario 2 as compared with a purely domestic scenario (scenario 1) because the foreign corporation tax largely sits in the place of and replaces the domestic corporation tax. The country of residence of the shareholder then gets a full shareholder tax. But if the corporation and shareholder taxes are collapsed (as dividend relief does), which country should get that tax? Or should these taxes not be collapsed because they are paid to different countries? This latter approach would create a difference between a domestic perspective and an international perspective. In a globalising world, the international perspective increasingly dominates.

Consider a simple example involving a dividend deduction system. The foreign corporate tax rate is 30%, which is also the domestic corporate tax rate. For foreign profits of 100, there is foreign corporation tax of 30, but due to foreign tax relief there is no domestic corporation tax. How can a dividend deduction system in the domestic country work in such a situation? In order to work from an international perspective, the foreign corporation tax needs to be relieved when the foreign profits are distributed. The domestic country will inevitably refuse to refund the foreign corporation tax. The foreign country will inevitably refuse to grant the PE such a deduction, especially if that country has a classical system or a different form of dividend relief.

From a domestic perspective, the domestic country will view the foreign profits as exempt profits because they have not suffered domestic corporation tax. Corporations will need to keep records of these profits, and the dividend deduction system must have an ordering rule saying when those profits are considered to be distributed. When the foreign profits are distributed they will not give rise to a refund of corporation tax because they are considered tax preferred. Most likely, the shareholder will be fully taxed with respect to dividends received, despite the fact that the profits distributed have suffered unrelieved foreign corporation tax. The result is, in effect, a classical treatment. The corporation tax is levied by the foreign country and the shareholder tax by the domestic country.

So the neutralities that the dividend deduction system was designed to produce in a domestic context are not replicated in this international setting. Dividend relief is granted for domestic activities, but not international activities, and this can be contrasted with the classical system. The classical system is non-neutral in a domestic setting, but is neutral as between domestic and international activities. The dividend deduction system is more neutral in a domestic setting, but is likely to be non-neutral as between domestic and international activities.

The only way to address the international non-neutrality of the dividend deduction system is to accept what dividend relief does. Dividend relief erodes the separate identities of a corporation and its shareholders at the point corporate profits are distributed. In particular, corporate-level dividend relief erodes the separate identity of the corporation. If that is accepted, then what a dividend deduction system should do when foreign profits are distributed is treat the foreign corporation tax paid as paid by the shareholders. The shareholders should then be granted foreign tax relief with respect to the dividends distributed from the foreign profits, either by way of exemption or foreign tax credit. That is, the corporate-level preference that results from foreign tax relief should be *passed through* to the shareholders instead of being *washed out*.

As noted earlier at 2.4.1.3, it can be quite complex to pass corporate-level preferences through a dividend relief system. To do so accurately in the context of a dividend deduction system would require an itemised recording of foreign profits with their corporation tax treatment. The foreign corporation tax would be passed through with dividends from the foreign profits and the shareholders granted a foreign tax credit for this tax. Any domestic corporation tax levied on the foreign profits, such as residually under a foreign tax credit system, would be refunded to the corporation when those profits are distributed (i.e. under the dividend deduction system).

Similar issues arise under other forms of dividend relief at the corporate level. Under a split-rate system, the domestic country cannot reduce the imposition of foreign corporation tax when foreign profits are distributed. However, such a system might attempt to pass foreign tax relief through to shareholders. As noted earlier at 2.4.2.2, the US accumulated earnings tax might be viewed as incorporating a split-rate feature. In the context of distributed foreign profits, the accumulated earnings tax has no application, and the US does not attempt to pass foreign tax credits through to shareholders. The US foreign tax credit cannot be set against accumulated earnings tax, only against regular corporation tax.[17]

Under a corporation tax credit system, corporation tax credits may be granted with respect to the distribution of foreign source income. This was the situation under the former UK advanced corporation tax system. This relief then overlaps with foreign tax relief, particularly if that is granted in the form of a foreign tax credit. During the 1970s, the UK required corporations to set their advanced corporation tax credit against their corporate income tax liability before any foreign tax credit. There was then concern that this approach breached the requirement of providing foreign tax relief under UK tax treaties and the ordering was changed. So UK corporation tax liability was first reduced by foreign tax credits and then by credits for advance corporation tax. The result was mountains of surplus advanced corporation tax credits for corporations with higher levels of foreign income. Originally, there was no attempt to pass foreign tax relief through to shareholders. However, beginning in 1994 there was a rudimentary attempt to pass some relief through in the form of the foreign income dividend regime.[18]

### 3.1.1.4  Dividend relief at the shareholder level

By contrast with corporate-level dividend relief systems, in the context of scenario 2 shareholder-level dividend relief systems demonstrate their natural potential to pass through corporate preferences, though not accurately. Under shareholder dividend relief systems the corporation tax remains unaffected, and so foreign tax relief granted at the corporate level permanently reduces the overall tax liability suffered by corporate income.

---

[17]  IRC (US) s. 901(a) referring to the list in s. 26(b).

[18]  Regarding these features of the former UK advanced corporation tax regime (abolished in 1999) see Harris (1996, pp. 769–89). The UK foreign income dividend scheme was in dispute under EU law in Case C-446/04 *Test Claimants in the FII Group Litigation* [2006] ECR I-11753 (ECJ).

Indeed, a shareholder-level dividend relief system that tries to wash out corporate foreign tax relief on distribution is likely to be a more complex system than one that does not.

Consider, for example, the inter-corporate dividend exclusion systems adopted by Germany, the UK, the US and under the CCCTB Proposal. In each of these cases, dividends are excluded from the recipient corporation's taxable income irrespective of whether the profits distributed are foreign and were sheltered from domestic corporation tax by reason of foreign tax relief.[19] Similarly, the German 40% exclusion of dividends received by individuals is available irrespective of whether the profits distributed have been granted foreign tax relief. In these cases, there is a level of neutrality between a taxpayer deriving domestic source income through a resident corporation or deriving foreign source income through a resident corporation. For reasons discussed earlier at 2.4.3.1, there is unlikely to be neutrality between the taxpayer deriving the foreign source income directly or between financing in the form of debt or equity.

The same is true with respect to shareholder differentiation systems. Inevitably, the special tax rates applied to dividend income are applied irrespective of the source of profits from which a resident corporation makes the distribution. This is the case under both the UK and the US shareholder differentiation systems and the German final withholding tax for individuals. Again, there is a level of neutrality between resident corporations deriving domestic or foreign source income. In principle, the same is true under a notional dividend tax credit system. The UK grants dividends tax credits for dividends distributed by resident corporations irrespective of whether those dividends are distributed from foreign profits that have been sheltered from UK corporation tax by reason of foreign tax relief.

However, as discussed earlier at 2.5, a country may wish to limit the notional amount of relief under shareholder-level dividend relief systems and seek to reconcile the corporation and shareholder taxes. Here there is again the issue of whether an international or domestic perspective is taken, and the manner in which a country records corporate tax treatment will have a dramatic effect on the treatment of foreign source corporate profits when distributed. Where a corporate tax system records

---

[19] Of course, the US inter-corporate dividends received deduction works by first including the dividends in taxable income and then granting an offsetting deduction for at least part of those dividends.

profits, whether with corporation tax treatment or just taxable profits, the question is whether profits that have been granted foreign tax relief are considered fully taxed. From an international perspective, that is clearly the case; however, from a domestic perspective such profits may be considered tax preferred.

So, for example, the Mexican corporate tax system requires Mexican corporations to record profits that have been subjected to Mexican tax. The taxed profits account includes foreign profits of Mexican corporations even if those profits have been sheltered from Mexican corporation tax by reason of foreign tax relief.[20] This is not so problematic where shareholders are granted an exemption, reduced rate or non-refundable and quarantined dividend tax credits. Here, although corporate-level foreign tax relief may not be accurately passed through to shareholders,[21] there is no potential for foreign tax to be refunded by the domestic country or offset domestic tax liability on domestic income. That is, these types of dividend relief system (the most distorting types from a domestic perspective) are broadly consistent with the exemption or ordinary foreign tax credit methods of foreign tax relief.

However, as soon as there is a risk of surplus relief at the shareholder level, notional shareholder relief runs a risk for local revenues. In particular, consider a notional dividend tax credit system under which excess dividend tax credits are refundable or at least permitted to be set against tax liability on other domestic source income. Foreign tax relief in the form of an exemption or ordinary foreign tax credit is not available to set against tax liability on domestic source income. If notional dividend tax credits are granted with respect to the distribution of foreign source income by a resident corporation and excess credits may be used against other tax liability, there will be a distortion. A person may be better off deriving foreign source income through a resident corporation than they are deriving the income directly. By doing the former, the person may lift some of the limits on the use of foreign tax relief.

---

[20] The 'net tax income account' is credited with taxable income, and foreign income is taxable income. A foreign tax credit is available; Income Tax Law (*Ley del Impuesto sobre la Renta*) (Mexico) Arts. 1, 6 & 88.

[21] Foreign tax relief in the form of an exemption may be viewed as accurately passed through to a shareholder, although the quantum of exemption may be an issue. Foreign tax credits are not accurately passed through. In particular, because the shareholder is granted no foreign tax credits, there can be no excess credits and so no carry-forward or carry-back or setting of such excess against other foreign source income of the shareholder.

In a worst case scenario, if excess notional dividend tax credits are refundable, the domestic country may refund to low-rate shareholders tax paid by the distributing corporation to a foreign country. For this reason, most countries that have granted refundable dividend tax credits have limited in some shape or form the amount of dividend tax credits to the amount of corporation tax paid domestically. That is, refundable dividend tax credit systems tend to be imputation systems and reconcile the corporation and shareholder taxes. Only corporation tax paid domestically may fund dividend tax credits and not foreign tax for which foreign tax relief is granted. In other words, the distribution by a corporation of foreign source income for which foreign tax relief has been granted will give rise to a corporate-level distribution tax (equalisation tax) or will not have dividend tax credits attached (variable dividend tax credit).

The result is that imputation systems have tended to replicate or mimic treatment under corporate-level dividend relief systems. They are very neutral from a domestic perspective, particularly as regards the primary distortions of the classical system mentioned earlier at 2.3.2, but they are not neutral as between the deriving of domestic or foreign source income. The fundamental problem is that domestic dividend relief is more generous and more neutral than foreign tax relief. Because a country is not willing to extend that neutrality to an international setting, it ends up creating a disincentive to derive foreign source income through resident corporations.

When faced with these issues of domestic neutrality versus international non-neutrality, a country has three basic choices. First, it may bring the distortions of foreign tax relief onshore and so change its form of dividend relief system to one that is non-neutral and cannot produce excess relief. This approach involves a move to a dividend exclusion system, shareholder differentiation system or dividend tax credit system with no excess credits. This is what happened in Germany, the UK and other EU member states as a result of decisions of the ECJ.[22] Second, it may retain its dividend relief system and adopt a classical system for foreign source income. This approach involves imposing an equalisation tax or denying dividend relief when foreign profits are distributed. It makes the disincentive for corporations to derive foreign source income when compared to domestic source income worse than it is for individuals.

The only other option is to retain the domestic dividend relief system for domestic source income, but try to pass corporate foreign tax relief

---

[22] See Harris (2010).

through to shareholders on distribution of foreign source income. On distribution, shareholders would receive the same amount of foreign tax relief as if they had derived the income directly. There is still a distortion as between deriving domestic source income and foreign source income, but it is simply a reflection of a distortion inherent in the international order. International norms on foreign tax relief (exemption or ordinary foreign tax credit) already incorporate a general disincentive for low-rate taxpayers to derive foreign source income when compared to domestic source income. A bigger problem is that passing foreign tax relief through a dividend relief system is complex and holds a high compliance burden that will often be felt to be not worth the effort.[23]

The Australian imputation system still refuses to pass corporate-level foreign tax relief through to resident shareholders. Only corporation tax paid to Australia is credited to a corporation's imputation account from which dividend tax credits to shareholders are funded.[24] If a corporation derives exempt foreign income (such as profits from a foreign PE), nothing is credited to the corporation's imputation account. When those profits are distributed, shareholders will not receive dividend tax credits (or the corporation will pay equalisation tax). The result is a classical treatment. The foreign country imposes corporation tax, and Australia imposes a full shareholder tax on the foreign profits net of corporation tax.

The resulting distortion is mitigated somewhat by super-stacking and Australia's implicit ordering rule. If an Australian corporation pays any Australian corporation tax, it can immediately fund dividend tax credits with that tax up to the corporate tax rate applied to the grossed-up dividend. This means that a corporation can fund retention with profits that have been wholly exempt from Australian corporation tax, including foreign source income. This approach produces what is often referred to as a 'knife-edged' distribution policy. Corporations are willing to distribute profits with full dividend tax credits attached to the extent permitted by their imputation account. Once a corporation exhausts its imputation account, it is then resistant to distribute profits (i.e. there is an incentive to retain the profits in order to avoid shareholder-level taxation).

---

[23] The UK and some other imputation countries formerly tried to pass foreign tax relief through to shareholders in a simple and somewhat arbitrary fashion; see (Harris 1996, pp. 344–7).

[24] Income Tax Assessment Act 1997 (Australia) s. 205–15.

The Australian government is well aware of the distortion that its imputation system creates. It can have a retarding effect on Australian corporations expanding overseas. However, it does have some positive aspects. Corporations are hungry for imputation account credits. So, all things being equal, Australian corporations would rather pay corporation tax to Australia than to a foreign country. In this way, the distortion in the imputation system is viewed as supporting anti-abuse measures such as transfer pricing rules and controlled foreign corporation rules. If Australian tax is avoided when a corporation derives income, it will be picked up on distribution.

### 3.1.2 Domestic income / non-resident shareholders: scenario 3

In scenario 3, the domestic country is both the source of the profits derived by the corporation and the source of dividends distributed by it. So this scenario does not involve foreign tax relief and its interrelationship with dividend relief. The tax treatment of corporate income when derived is simply as considered in Chapter 1. Nevertheless, scenario 3 does involve some controversial issues. Just as scenario 2 demonstrated the limitations of corporate-level dividend relief systems, scenario 3 demonstrates the limitations of shareholder-level dividend relief systems.

#### 3.1.2.1 Classical system

The international order (and the OECD Model) was designed with the dual nature of corporate income in mind (i.e. it presumes a classical system). In the context of scenario 3, the domestic country applies its usual corporate tax treatment to corporate income when derived. The international factor involves the distribution of that corporate income to a non-resident shareholder. A classical system presumes that a non-resident shareholder is taxable with respect to the receipt of dividends. As the source country of the dividends, the domestic country will, therefore, expect some tax from the non-resident shareholder. A difficult issue is how much tax to expect, but this is not a specific dividend tax issue. A classical system treats dividend income in the same fashion as other income, and so the generic issue is the rate at which a domestic country taxes non-residents.

Here there is usually a distinction between taxation of non-residents on a net basis and on a gross basis.[25] The net basis is typically limited to

---

[25] See Ault & Arnold (2010, pp. 495–515).

situations in which the domestic tax jurisdiction can verify expenses incurred by a non-resident. These situations usually involve a non-resident having a physical presence in a jurisdiction, such as through employment, place of business or holding of land. Here there is still an issue of whether non-residents are subject to the usual progressive tax rates or whether they are subject to a flat rate on the basis that the source country cannot observe their whole tax capacity (i.e. ability to pay). However, dividends usually do not fall into this category and so are taxed on a gross basis at a flat rate. As a matter of necessity, this tax is usually collected by requiring corporations to withhold it from distributions made to non-residents.

Tax treaties based on the OECD Model typically limit the source country's right to tax dividends. The usual limitation is that source country taxation must not exceed 5% of the gross amount of dividends distributed to non-resident parent corporations and otherwise not more than 15% of the gross amount of dividends.[26] The residence country of the shareholder will be required to grant a foreign tax credit for this source country tax. Commonly, this produces neutrality in that the shareholder receives a classical treatment. The domestic / source country receives corporation tax and a limited dividend tax, and the foreign / residence country may receive some dividend tax but grants foreign tax relief. The exception is where the source country's dividend tax exceeds the shareholder's tax liability on the dividend in the country of residence. Any distortion in this regard is a general feature of the ordinary foreign tax credit system and is equally an issue where non-residents derive other types of income.

### 3.1.2.2   Dividend relief at the corporate level

Conceptually, dividend relief at the corporate level works well with scenario 3 in that it produces dividend relief across borders and so is consistent between the taxation of dividends received by resident and non-resident shareholders. However, it raises some serious practical issues. In particular, it substantially erodes source countries' accepted taxing rights. Again, this impact is best demonstrated by an example, and a dividend deduction system is used for this purpose.

A corporation derives 100 domestic source profits and the corporate tax rate is 30%. If a dividend deduction is available and those profits are distributed, the corporation will have no taxable income and pay no corporation tax. This would be the natural result irrespective of whether the

---

[26] Generally regarding these limitations, see Harris & Oliver (2010, pp. 182–90).

shareholder is resident or non-resident. Indeed, it would be clear discrimination to deny a deduction for dividends distributed to non-residents when one is available for dividends distributed to residents. It is also likely that such a denial would breach typical tax treaties.[27]

This means the domestic / source country's taxing rights would be limited to any shareholder tax. This limitation is not of itself a concern, but it becomes one if tax treaties limit that amount to 15%, or especially 5% in the context of dividends distributed to non-resident parents. Historically, 15% is too low and would create a substantial incentive to distribute profits to non-resident shareholders in order to avoid higher corporation tax if the profits are retained. However, because corporate tax rates have decreased in recent years, perhaps a 15% rate is not looking as low as it once might have. The 5% rate, however, is substantially below average corporate tax rates. This issue could be fixed by negotiating higher rates of dividend withholding tax under tax treaties, but doing so has two problems. First, most countries require reciprocity of withholding taxes and so would not be willing to let the other contracting state have a higher rate of dividend withholding tax than they do.[28] Second, if a higher tax rate is negotiated, it would be a high tax on a gross basis, which would increase the discrimination against low-tax-rate non-resident investors and those investors with substantial expenses. The result could be a lot of excess foreign tax credits.

However, if there were sufficient tax liability in the country of the shareholder's residence, the dividend deduction system would produce substantial neutrality. There would be no corporate-level tax, and so economic double taxation of corporate income would be avoided. The source country would retain some tax, which would be a direct tax on dividends distributed. As a result, the country of the shareholder's residence would be obliged to grant direct foreign tax credits for all source country tax levied. The result is a shared but single level of shareholder tax, creating substantial neutrality between domestic and foreign ownership. As noted later, the major problem with shareholder-level dividend relief in scenario 3 is that it does not remove the source country's corporate-level tax and

---

[27] In particular, it is likely to breach OECD Model Arts. 24(4) & (5). Such breach depends on dividends constituting 'other disbursements' (Art. 24(4)) or a resident corporation with resident shareholders being a 'similar enterprise' to one with non-resident shareholders.

[28] Regarding reciprocity of withholding tax rates, see Harris & Oliver (2010, pp. 104–5). Famously, Germany had difficulty negotiating higher rates of dividend withholding tax despite granting dividend relief at the corporate level in the form of a split-rate system; see Harris (1996, pp. 315 & 364) and the references cited therein.

the country of residence of the shareholder may not provide underlying foreign tax relief.

The same observations apply to a split-rate system and a corporation tax credit system. Corporate-level dividend relief systems did (when they existed) tend to apply in a non-discriminatory fashion as between dividends distributed to resident or non-resident shareholders. So, under the former German split-rate system, the lower rate for distributed profits was available irrespective of whether the shareholder was resident or non-resident. Similarly, under the former UK advanced corporation tax system, the corporation tax credit was available irrespective of the identity of the shareholder.[29] To the extent that the US accumulated earnings tax can be viewed as a type of split-rate system, it also does not impose that tax on distributions to non-resident shareholders.

### 3.1.2.3  Dividend exclusion and shareholder differentiation systems

Corporate-level dividend relief systems can produce dividend relief across borders in scenario 3, but only as a result of the sacrifice of taxing rights by source countries. By contrast, a shareholder-level dividend relief system cannot guarantee dividend relief across borders in scenario 3. Whether that occurs depends on the country of the shareholder's residence providing dividend relief. These problems arise no matter which type of shareholder-level dividend relief system is used.

It might seem obvious that a country that adopts a dividend exclusion system will not tax non-residents in receipt of dividends from resident corporations. However, from the perspective of the country of residence of the shareholder, this just means that the dividends do not suffer any tax. The only tax that is suffered is corporation tax, and unless the country of the shareholder's residence grants underlying relief, no foreign tax relief will be available for that tax. The result is commonly a classical treatment: the domestic / source country imposes corporation tax, and the country of the shareholder's residence imposes a full shareholder tax. In this case, non-residents investing in resident corporations are taxed more than residents investing in resident corporations.

Further, as compared with a true classical system, the country of the shareholder's residence might be viewed as having received a windfall tax benefit. That country gets more tax than it would have if the domestic / source country had adopted a classical system. The response of some countries with a dividend exclusion system is to simply tax the

---

[29]  See Harris (1996, pp. 615 & 778–80).

non-resident at the usual dividend withholding tax rates (i.e. not extend the benefits of the dividend exclusion system to non-residents). This is presently the approach of Germany and the US.

Under domestic law, Germany subjects non-resident shareholders in German corporations to a dividend withholding tax of 25% (increased by the surcharge).[30] This withholding tax is reduced under tax treaties. The dividend exclusion available to resident corporate shareholders is not available to non-resident shareholders,[31] although this is required in an EU context by EU law. The same is true with respect to the US dividends-received deduction. The US imposes a 30% dividend withholding tax on dividends distributed to non-residents.[32] Again, this rate is reduced by tax treaties. The tax is on the gross amount and deductions are not permitted. As a result, non-resident corporate shareholders are not entitled to the dividends-received deduction. This treatment is obviously discriminatory. Corporate income distributed to non-resident shareholders is taxed more by the domestic / source country than if the income were distributed to resident corporate shareholders.

It might be thought that such obvious discrimination would breach tax treaties based on the OECD Model, but it does not. As noted earlier at 3.1.2.2, the tax treaty rules based on the OECD Model prohibit discrimination of a resident corporation making payments to non-residents or on the basis that it has non-resident shareholders. As a result, those rules require corporate-level dividend relief systems to grant dividend relief for dividends distributed to non-resident shareholders. However, those rules do not prevent discrimination targeted directly at the non-resident shareholder.[33] The result is form over substance. Despite producing the same substantive result, corporate-level dividend relief systems cannot deny dividend relief for dividends distributed to non-residents, but shareholder-level dividend relief systems can. It was for this reason that a number of countries moved from corporate-level dividend relief systems in the 1980/1990s to shareholder-level systems (i.e. so that they could discriminate against non-residents).

---

[30] EStG (Germany) ss. 43 & 43a. Dividends distributed by resident corporations are treated as having a domestic source; Art. 49(1)5a.

[31] However, Germany will generally reduce this taxation to 15% for non-resident corporate shareholders; EStG (Germany) s. 44a(9).

[32] IRC (US) ss. 881(a) & 1442. Under s. 861(a)(2) dividends have a source in the US if distributed by US (domestic) corporations.

[33] For example, with respect to OECD Model Art. 24(5), see OECD Commentary on Art. 24 para. 78 and Harris and Oliver (2010, pp. 183–4).

The exception to this discrimination in both Germany and the US is where the dividends received by the non-resident are received through a PE (Germany) or US business. Here Germany grants the dividend exclusions available to residents, including a credit for the dividend withholding tax.[34] The US does not impose dividend withholding tax on dividends effectively connected with a US business,[35] and the dividends-received deduction is available because the non-resident is taxed on a net basis. The removal of discrimination in this context is not surprising, because PEs are protected by a different non-discrimination rule in tax treaties that is likely to require the extension of dividend relief.[36]

By contrast, the UK imposes no withholding tax on dividends paid to non-residents. Unlike Germany and the US, it applies the usual exemption from corporation tax for inter-corporate dividends to dividends distributed to non-resident corporate shareholders irrespective of whether those dividends are received through a UK PE. The CCCTB Proposal would not impose tax and would only apply to corporations subject to one of the member state's corporation taxes. The inter-corporate dividend exclusion would apply generally to prevent the imposition of such a corporation tax on distributions to non-resident corporations. However, often the member state tax on distributions to non-resident corporations is not corporation tax per se, but a separate withholding tax. For example, this is the case in Germany. It is usual for EU corporation taxes to apply to PEs of non-residents situated in a member state.

There is little further to add with respect to shareholder differentiation systems. If this takes the form of a final withholding tax, the international system (and its distortions) has essentially been brought onshore. Commonly, the dividend withholding tax rate is selected somewhere near a typical tax treaty rate, such as between 15% and 5%, and that becomes a final tax on dividends distributed to all types of shareholders. A benefit of this system is that resident corporations do not need to identify their shareholders as resident or non-resident. This efficiency benefit is not available if treaty rates are lower than the domestic rate. This is the situation in Germany, where the 25% withholding tax is substantially higher than the rate agreed in many of Germany's tax treaties.

---

[34] The withholding tax constitutes a final tax for non-residents unless imposed with respect to income of a German PE; EStG (Germany) s. 50(3) and KStG (Germany) s. 32(1).

[35] IRC (US) ss. 872(a), 882(a) and 1441(c)(1).

[36] OECD Model Art. 24(3). This requirement for dividend relief is subject to divergent views, which are reflected in a non-committal approach in OECD Commentary on Art. 24 paras. 48–54. Generally, see Harris & Oliver (2010, pp. 186–8).

Shareholder differentiation systems that use multiple dividend tax rates for dividends do not have such an obvious rate for non-resident shareholders, as in the case of a final dividend withholding tax system. In shareholder differentiation systems, it seems that the non-resident rate should, in principle, be no more than the highest rate applicable to a resident. A sensible rate would also be the rate usually used in tax treaties. The US and UK shareholder differentiation systems are on opposite ends of a spectrum in this regard and show little logic. Despite reducing dividend tax rates to no more than 15% for resident individuals, the US maintains the 30% final withholding tax for non-residents.[37] This is likely to be reduced to at least 15% in the context of a tax treaty, but outside that context the taxation of non-residents is at least twice what it is of residents.

In stark contrast, the UK does not tax non-resident individuals in receipt of dividends from UK corporations.[38] So although individuals may be taxed at rates up to 42.5% on dividends, non-residents are typically not taxed at all. As discussed in the context of the dividend exclusion system, this benefit is often taxed away by the shareholder's country of residence. That shareholder may be fully taxable with no foreign tax relief (because no UK tax is paid on the dividend). Despite the UK providing dividend relief, the result may be a classical system. This result is very different from the UK's treaty practice under its former advanced corporation tax system discussed in the next subheading.

### 3.1.2.4 Dividend tax credit and imputation systems

Added difficulties caused by a dividend tax credit system in scenario 3 are again related to that system's propensity to produce surplus relief and mimic corporate-level dividend relief systems. If non-resident shareholders were treated in the same fashion as resident shareholders, they would be granted dividend tax credits and taxed on the grossed-up amount of the distribution at usual non-resident shareholder rates. The problem is that dividend tax credits often exceed non-resident shareholder rates, particularly as reduced by tax treaties. Commonly, dividend tax credits might be granted at 30% of the grossed-up amount of the dividend and non-residents are taxable at half that rate (i.e. 15%). The question is then what to do with the excess.

---

[37] IRC (US) ss. 871(a) & 1441.

[38] The exception is the unlikely scenario in which a non-resident individual receives a dividend through a UK branch; ITA 2007 (UK) ss. 811 and 825.

If the excess is refundable, or at least available for use against other tax liability, the result is effectively the same as a corporate-level dividend relief system. Consider a dividend tax credit system incorporating full dividend relief where the corporate tax rate is 30%. With corporate profits of 100, corporation tax of 30 and a dividend of 70, the shareholder receives 30 in dividend tax credits. A portfolio non-resident shareholder under a tax treaty might be taxed at 15% on the grossed-up amount of 100 (70 dividend + 30 dividend tax credit), making a tax liability of 15. If the dividend tax credits are available to non-resident shareholders, the shareholder has no tax liability and 15 excess dividend tax credits. If that excess is refunded to the non-resident shareholder, the shareholder has a net return of 85 (70 dividend plus 15 refunded credits) – the same as the shareholder's tax rate.

This means that granting refundable dividend tax credits to non-resident shareholders would result in the domestic / source country levying less tax than it would under other forms of shareholder-level dividend relief systems. The amount levied would be the same as under corporate-level dividend relief systems. But although the amount might be the same, the tax consequences might not be. There are two features of refunding dividend tax credits to non-resident shareholders under a dividend tax credit system that might produce results different from those under a corporate-level dividend relief system.

First, as noted earlier at 3.1.2.3, tax treaties do not require shareholder-level dividend relief systems to extend dividend relief to non-resident shareholders, even though they do require that extension by corporate-level dividend relief systems. Especially in the context of a dividend tax credit system, the result is form over substance. Despite producing the same substantive result, corporate-level dividend relief systems cannot deny dividend relief for dividends distributed to non-residents, but dividend tax credit systems can.

This flexibility of the dividend credit system is offset by the second feature that makes such a system different from the corporate-level dividend relief systems it mimics. Dividend tax credit systems are likely to suffer from the same problem as other shareholder-level dividend relief systems when it comes to the tax treatment in the shareholder's country of residence. The 15 residual tax imposed by the domestic / source country in the previous example is imposed at the corporate level. Although a notional shareholder tax is imposed, that tax is fully offset by dividend tax credits. Indeed, the shareholder receives a refund of some corporation tax. As a result, the country of the shareholder's residence may give no direct foreign tax credit (although underlying relief may be available in an appropriate case). As with other shareholder-level dividend relief systems, the result is likely to be a classical treatment. The domestic / source country collects tax equal to the shareholder tax as limited by treaty, and the country of the shareholder's residence collects a full shareholder tax.

The result is that dividend tax credit countries are encouraged to discriminate against non-resident shareholders. Even if they behave in a non-discriminatory fashion (like corporate-level dividend relief systems), they will not secure cross-border dividend relief (unlike corporate-level dividend relief systems). What can be done about this? Countries have followed three approaches. First, as noted either with respect to other shareholder-level dividend relief systems, a dividend tax credit country might just switch to a classical treatment with respect to corporate income distributed to non-resident shareholders. This was the standard approach under former European imputation systems.[39] As noted earlier at 3.1.2.3, this discriminatory feature continues under the current German dividend relief system.

Second, because it is not limited by non-discrimination, a country may switch from the dividend tax credit system to another form of dividend relief for non-resident shareholders. So, for example, Australia switches from its refundable dividend tax credit system for resident shareholders to a dividend exemption system for non-resident shareholders. The exemption is triggered by the Australian imputation system. A dividend withholding tax of 30% is imposed on non-residents,[40] which is typically reduced to 15% under tax treaties. Non-residents are not entitled to dividend tax credits.[41] However, to the extent that a dividend carries dividend tax credits at the maximum rate (corporate tax rate on the grossed-up dividend), the dividend is exempt from withholding tax.[42]

Yet the Australian approach causes difficulties and does not result in cross-border dividend relief. This system ensures that Australia collects its corporation tax on domestic source corporate income distributed to non-residents. However, as Australia understands, the benefit of the shareholder tax exemption is likely to be taxed away by the residence country in situations in which that country does not grant underlying foreign

---

[39] See Harris (1996, pp. 352–3).

[40] Income Tax Assessment Act 1936 (Australia) s. 128B(1) and Income Tax (Dividends, Interest and Royalties Withholding Tax) Act 1974 (Australia) s. 7.

[41] Income Tax Assessment Act 1997 (Australia) s. 207–70. The exception is Australian PEs of non-residents, which are entitled to dividend tax credits and are not subject to withholding tax. Again, this is consistent with the non-discrimination rule for PEs in tax treaties.

[42] Income Tax Assessment Act 1936 (Australia) s. 128B(3)(ga).

tax relief. In these cases, despite the granting of dividend relief, the result is likely to be a classical treatment. Further, the Australian switch in form of dividend relief means that dividend tax credits are less valuable for most non-resident shareholders than they are for resident shareholders. Resident shareholders can receive a reduction in tax liability equal to the corporate tax rate of 30% applied to the grossed-up dividend. Non-residents typically receive a maximum benefit of 15% of the amount of the dividend. As a result, this treatment of non-residents has been a major source of dividend streaming in Australia.

This differential can also have an effect on the receipt of dividends that do not carry dividend tax credits at the maximum rate (unfranked dividends) through an Australian holding corporation. Receipt of an unfranked dividend through an Australian holding corporation would result in a direct imposition of Australian corporation tax on the unfranked part of the dividend at 30%. If the dividend were received directly by the non-resident shareholder, only dividend withholding tax would be applied (typically 15%, but sometimes nil). Australia has a special rule to relieve this distortion, which involves granting an Australian holding corporation wholly owned by a non-resident a deduction when it on-pays certain dividends received to its foreign parent. For this purpose, the Australian subsidiary must maintain a particular account of dividends received.[43] Again, this is a limited example of switching from one form of dividend relief to another (i.e. switching from an imputation system to a dividend deduction system).

Like Australia, the UK usually does not extend dividend tax credits to non-resident shareholders.[44] Further like Australia, it in substance switches to a dividend exemption system for non-resident shareholders, with all the drawbacks that switch involves (see the earlier discussion at 3.1.2.3).

New Zealand has an imputation system similar to the Australian imputation system, and like Australia it does not grant the full value of dividend tax credits to non-resident shareholders.[45] However, rather than adopting an exemption system with respect to non-resident shareholders, New Zealand converts to a limited form of a corporate-level dividend relief system. Corporations may be entitled to a corporation tax credit

[43] Income Tax Assessment Act 1936 (Australia) ss. 46FA and 46FB.
[44] ITTOIA 2005 (UK) s. 397.
[45] New Zealand imposes dividend withholding tax at a 30% rate; Income Tax Act 2007 (New Zealand) s. RF8. This rate is reduced to the general rate of 15% where the dividend carries dividend tax credits at the maximum rate.

with respect to dividends distributed to non-resident shareholders.[46] This is referred to as the 'foreign investor tax credit' regime. Such dividends are still subject to dividend withholding tax (at a rate of 15%), which means that non-resident shareholders would not directly benefit from the corporation tax credit. That benefit is secured by denying the corporation tax credit unless the corporation distributes a special 'supplementary dividend' in the same amount as the credit, but only to non-resident shareholders.[47]

The New Zealand system is designed to achieve cross-border dividend relief in the same manner as do corporate-level systems (see the earlier discussion at 3.1.2.2). The hope is that the non-resident shareholder will receive a direct foreign tax credit for the dividend withholding tax, despite the fact that it is offset by a supplementary dividend. The system smacks more than a little of form over substance, but perhaps no more than the distorting non-discrimination rules of tax treaties based on the OECD Model. The system has remained relatively unchanged since its introduction twenty years ago.

What New Zealand seeks to achieve unilaterally, a country may achieve in a more straightforward manner under its tax treaties. This is the third approach taken to resolve the problems of dividend tax credit systems. This was a standard practice by France, Italy and the UK in their tax treaties from the 1970s through the 1990s.[48] The treaty provisions were complicated, but did not involve complex amendments to domestic law as did the New Zealand foreign investor tax credit regime. The treaties typically involved two features. First, some (but not all) dividend tax credits would be refunded to non-resident shareholders. This meant that the domestic / source country collected somewhat less than its corporation tax on outbound corporate income. Second, the residence country agreed to give the shareholder a direct foreign tax credit for part of this remaining corporation tax. The result was that the foreign shareholder was granted the same level of dividend relief as a resident shareholder. This treaty practice was sufficiently superior to current practice to warrant an example using the former UK practice.

The UK had (and has) the power to grant tax credits to non-residents under tax treaties.[49] It granted its old dividend tax credit under its advanced corporation tax system to numerous non-resident portfolio

---

[46] Income Tax Act 2007 (New Zealand) s. LP2.
[47] Income Tax Act 2007 (New Zealand) s. YA1 definition of 'supplementary dividend'.
[48] This treaty practice is described in Harris (1996, pp. 368–76).
[49] TIOPA 2010 (UK) s. 6(2)(g).

investors (under about forty treaties) and in some cases to non-portfolio investors (on a slightly different basis). The dividend tax credit was typically refunded to treaty partner portfolio shareholders minus the dividend withholding tax of 15% (i.e. paying lip service to the OECD Model).[50] The system looked like this:

| UK Treatment | |
| --- | --- |
| Corporate profits | 100 |
| UK corporation tax | 30 |
| Dividend | 70 |
| Dividend tax credit[51] | 17.5 |
| Grossed-up dividend [70 + 17.5] | 87.5 |
| Withholding tax [15% × 87.5] | 13.125 |
| Refund [17.5−13.125] | 4.375 |
| Return to non-resident | 74.375 |
| Foreign Country Treatment | |
| Shareholder tax [say 40% on 87.5] | 35 |
| Less direct foreign tax credit | 13.125 |
| Net residence tax | 21.875 |
| Net return [74.375−21.875] | 52.5 |

This net return was precisely the same as that received by a 40% shareholder resident in the UK. The system presumed that a non-resident shareholder should be taxed under the dividend relief system applicable where the corporation is resident, not under the system where the shareholder is resident. This is an important point and is returned to in 3.2.2 in the context of the domestic country being the country of the shareholder's residence.

To secure this treatment, the UK had to, in effect, refund 4.375% of its 30% corporation tax, leaving it imposing an effective tax of 25.625. However, it secured the agreement of the other country to grant a direct foreign tax credit of 13.125 for what can only be described as corporation tax (i.e. it secured agreement for the other country to grant underlying foreign tax relief to portfolio shareholders). The effectiveness of this treaty practice in providing cross-border dividend relief should not be underestimated.

---

[50] In tax treaties applying to non-portfolio investors, half the dividend tax credit was granted less a dividend withholding tax of 5%. This style of treaty provision was in issue in Case C-58/01 *Oce Van der Grinten NV* v. *IRC* [2003] ECR I-9809 (ECJ).

[51] The dividend tax credit was equal to the advanced corporation tax payable on the dividend, which was 25% of the dividend.

Consider a country that simply exempts outbound dividends, such as Australia or the UK currently. Such a country would have to have a corporate tax rate of less than 13% to produce a result as good as under this UK tax treaty practice using its former corporate tax rate of 30%.[52] That is a tax rate lower than that which applied in Hong Kong at the time.

This treaty practice was disrupted by the jurisprudence of the ECJ. In essence, the ECJ decided that the domestic / source country did not have to extend dividend tax credits to non-resident shareholders. That country is entitled to impose at least its corporation tax, provided it does not seek to tax the non-resident shareholder (i.e. provided it applies an exemption system).[53] Further, the ECJ decided that the country of the shareholder's residence must grant that shareholder the same dividend relief that the shareholder would receive with a dividend from a corporation resident in that country.[54] The type of dividend relief received in the country where the actual distributing corporation is resident is, therefore, irrelevant.

This outcome is unfortunate, because the ECJ jurisprudence was the driver for the domestic introduction of more arbitrary forms of dividend relief.[55] These forms of dividend relief (largely dividend exclusion and shareholder differentiation systems) have increased tax distortions between the corporate and unincorporated sectors and between debt and equity domestically. As previously noted, these distortions are particularly acute for low-tax rate shareholders, especially tax-exempt institutions. The situation is less neutral, not only domestically but also internationally, at least by comparison with this former tax treaty practice.[56] In turn this situation is spawning suggestions that the full amount of corporate profits cannot be taxed under a corporation tax, and that only economic rents can (i.e. corporate profits beyond a standard rate of return on equity capital).[57] This is viewed as the best way to ensure that tax-exempt institutions are not taxed on their share of equity capital. The downside is that, in doing so,

---

[52] Corporate profits of 100, corporation tax of 13 and a dividend of 87 paid to the non-resident; 40% tax in the country of residence with no foreign tax relief gives a tax liability of 34.8 (87 × 40%) and a net return of 52.2.

[53] See Harris & Oliver (2010, pp. 190–7).

[54] Ibid., pp. 291–6.

[55] See Harris (2010).

[56] Exempt institutions were entitled to the refund of dividend tax credits under these tax treaties and would suffer no further tax in their residence country. Even if they are not subject to dividend withholding tax in the domestic / source country, they are worse off under current dividend exclusion and shareholder differentiation systems.

[57] Mirrlees, Adam, Besley et al. (2011, chapters 17 & 18).

the suggestion becomes that the standard rate of return on capital should be exempt for everyone and not just for tax-exempt institutions. If this suggestion is implemented, it will fundamentally change the nature of income taxation.

### 3.1.3    Foreign income / non-resident shareholders: scenario 4

Scenario 4 involves pasting together the international aspects of scenarios 2 and 3. It deals with both foreign source income and foreign shareholders. The only recognised jurisdiction to tax in this scenario is on the basis of residence of the corporation. If, in a globalising world, this is viewed as a questionable or fragile jurisdiction to tax, then it might be suggested that the resultant tax treatment by the domestic country in scenario 4 should be the same as if the corporation were not resident (i.e. the same as in scenario 8). If corporate residence were seen as a questionable jurisdiction to tax, then the country should not impose any tax at all in scenario 4. A similar conclusion may be reached on various philosophies of corporation tax that might be used to justify dividend relief (see the earlier discussion at 1.3.1 and 2.3.2). If corporation tax is a temporary surrogate for personal income tax or a tax on economic rents, then no tax should be levied in scenario 4. There is no personal income tax for the country of corporate residence in scenario 4, and there are unlikely to be any economic rents in that country.[58]

Scenario 4 is often referred to as the 'flow through' or 'conduit' scenario because income flows from outside the country through a corporation resident in that country to a shareholder outside that country.[59] The question is whether the flow-through country imposes any tax toll on the income on the way through its resident corporation. Seeking any such tax toll is likely to act as a substantial deterrent for locating residence of corporations in that jurisdiction. This is particularly the case for corporations that have a lot of flow-through income, such as holding, treasury or headquarters corporations. Countries that have a reputation for the location of such corporations typically find some way of making sure they do not tax flow-through income.

Flow-through without a tax toll may be achieved simply by putting together scenarios 2 and 3. This is the case with the UK, which has a

---

[58]  Any economic rents arising as a result of locating the corporation's residence in a particular country should give rise to income sourced in that country.

[59]  Generally, see Harris (1996, pp. 381–97).

history of seeking to attract headquarters and other financial corporations. The UK no longer taxes resident corporations on the profits of a foreign PE, nor does it tax dividends from a foreign subsidiary (see the later discussion at 3.2.2). These exemptions are subject to substantial anti-abuse rules. The UK also does not tax outbound dividends. So it is quite easy to flow income through a UK resident corporation without any charge to UK corporation tax. Further, the anti-abuse rules are in the process of being amended to further facilitate this situation.

Depending on other policies, a corporate tax system may only achieve flow-through without a tax toll through implementation of a special scheme. This is the case with the Australian imputation system. Australia's conscious decision to discriminate against Australian corporations deriving foreign source income was discussed earlier at 3.1.1.4. That system backfires when it comes to flow-through income. Australia only grants dividend tax credits for domestic corporation tax, not foreign tax. So an Australian corporation that has only foreign source income will often have no credit in its imputation account and its dividends will have no dividend tax credits attached. The result is that dividend withholding tax will be payable on distribution to a non-resident shareholder (or equalisation tax will be payable). If Australia imposed such a tax toll in the flow-through situation, that would be a powerful disincentive to locate headquarters or holding corporations in Australia.

Therefore, Australia expressly overrides its imputation system in a flow-through scenario. In addition to their franking account (recording Australian corporation tax paid), Australian corporations may maintain a separate account recording 'conduit foreign income'. This account is credited with certain foreign income, including exempt profits of a foreign PE and exempt dividends received from a foreign subsidiary.[60] To the extent that a dividend does not carry dividend tax credits at the maximum rate (unfranked dividends), a corporation can declare that the dividend is paid out of conduit foreign income. The result is that this part of the dividend is also exempt from non-resident dividend withholding tax.[61] Such a declaration has no impact on resident shareholders, who are still fully taxable on the unfranked part of a dividend.

Germany, the US and the CCCTB Proposal do not have a special flow-through regime, and as in the UK, it is a matter of piecing together the treatments in scenarios 2 and 3. The German corporate tax system

---

[60] Income Tax Assessment Act 1997 (Australia) s. 802–30.
[61] Income Tax Assessment Act 1997 (Australia) s. 802–15(1).

may impose a tax toll on flow-through income. In particular, there may be a residual German corporation tax liability with respect to profits of a foreign PE under the German direct foreign tax credit. However, an exemption is often available under a tax treaty. There may also be a residual 5% charge when dividends are received from a foreign subsidiary, which is discussed later at 3.2.2. More importantly, Germany imposes dividend withholding tax on the dividend paid to a non-resident, irrespective of whether it is distributed from foreign source income. The Parent-Subsidiary Directive provides an exception.[62] This means that Germany is not usually a good location for headquarters or holding corporations.

The situation is similar in the US. There may be a residual US corporation tax liability under the US's foreign tax credit regime when a resident corporation derives foreign source income. Further, non-resident dividend withholding tax is imposed on outbound dividends irrespective of whether they are distributed from foreign source income. However, there are some exceptions under recent US tax treaties where distributions from US subsidiaries to treaty partner parent corporations are exempt from dividend withholding tax.

The CCCTB Proposal would typically exempt only 95% of the profits of a foreign PE or dividends received from a foreign subsidiary. This could result in a residual charge to corporation tax on foreign source income. The EU Presidency amendments would increase these to a full exemption, but deny the deduction of expenses. Further, as noted earlier at 3.1.2.3, the CCCTB Proposal would not impose any tax, and so it does not provide for any dividend withholding tax. However, such a tax may be imposed by member states where the distributing corporation is resident, depending on their domestic tax law.

## 3.2   Non-resident corporations

### 3.2.1   Domestic income / non-resident shareholders: scenario 5

Broadly, scenario 5 is analogous to scenario 3 except that the former involves a non-resident corporation and the latter a resident corporation. Both scenarios involve a non-resident investing in the domestic country. From the domestic / source country's perspective, scenario 5 simply involves a non-resident corporation deriving domestic source income.

---

[62]  *Parent-Subsidiary Directive*, Council Directive 90/435/EEC of 23 July 1990.

However, scenario 5 is the first time this book has directly considered the taxation of non-resident corporations. It raises a host of issues that have only been considered thus far on the presumption that the corporation is resident in the subject country. In particular, it raises questions as to taxation when the income is derived in the nature of those discussed in Chapter 1. These are the first matters considered in the following discussion.

Like the other scenarios, scenario 5 also presumes a distribution of corporate income. A major issue with scenario 5 is that this distribution involves a non-resident corporation and a non-resident shareholder and so does not usually involve a domestic country jurisdiction to tax. So although scenario 5 is analogous to scenario 3, it is the one scenario (other than scenario 8) where the dividends are not within the jurisdiction of the country in question. This raises questions as to whether the country can claim to tax those dividends if they are distributed from domestic source profits or simply can tax the profits because they leave the country whether or not they are distributed. Issues arising on the distribution or repatriation of the profits are the second matters considered in this subheading.

### 3.2.1.1 Corporate income when derived

A non-resident corporation will have been identified as a corporation and subcategorised as not resident according to the matters discussed earlier at 1.1. Accordingly, the following discussion focuses on the corporate tax base of a non-resident corporation and its tax treatment when corporate income is derived.

**Corporate tax base**    The earlier discussion at 1.2.1 noted the difference between a global and a schedular approach to calculating the corporate tax base. Inevitably, a schedular approach is adopted with respect to non-resident corporations. This is because, as noted earlier at 3.1.2.1, almost every country distinguishes between taxation of non-residents on a net basis and taxation of non-residents on a gross basis.

So, for example, Germany imposes corporation tax on non-resident corporations with respect to their German source income.[63] German source income is defined in the Personal Income Tax Law and includes numerous heads.[64] Recall that Germany adopts a global approach to the

---

[63] KStG (Germany) s. 2.
[64] EStG (Germany) s. 49.

tax base of resident corporations in that it treats all income of such corporations as business income.[65] This is also true for non-resident corporations, with an important schedularising qualification: the tax on any income of a non-resident corporation that is not attributable to a German PE is satisfied by any withholding tax imposed on that income (i.e. the withholding tax is final).[66] This is the same treatment as for non-resident individuals.

Though different in form, the US approach is similar, although it does not use the PE concept in its domestic law. Non-resident corporations are taxed in the same manner as resident corporations on income effectively connected with the conduct of a trade or business in the US (i.e. on a net basis).[67] Other US source income of non-resident corporations is typically taxed at 30% on the gross amount (reduced by tax treaties).[68] This tax is usually collected by withholding.[69] The US has comprehensive rules for determining whether income has a US source.[70] Again, the treatment with respect to non-effectively connected US source income of non-resident corporations is similar to that imposed on individuals with respect to such income.[71]

The UK approach is again different in form. Non-resident corporations are only subject to corporation tax with respect to profits that are 'attributable' to a UK PE.[72] However, they may be subject to income tax (i.e. the tax applicable to individuals) with respect to other UK source income. This is because non-resident corporations are within the charge to income tax, but are exempt from income tax to the extent that they are subject to corporation tax.[73] Income of non-resident corporations that is not within the charge to corporation tax is typically taxable at the basic rate of 20%.[74] Unlike Germany and the US, the UK source rules and the rules limiting non-residents to income tax only on the basis of source are scattered.[75] So again, except for income derived through a UK PE,

[65]  KStG (Germany) s. 8(2).
[66]  KStG (Germany) s. 32(2).
[67]  IRC (US) s. 882.
[68]  IRC (US) s. 881.
[69]  IRC (US) s. 1442.
[70]  IRC (US) s. 861.
[71]  Contrast IRC (US) ss. 871 and 1441.
[72]  CTA 2009 (UK) s. 5.
[73]  CTA 2009 (UK) s. 3(1)(b).
[74]  ITA 2007 (UK) ss. 10 and 11 (i.e. only individuals are subject to the lower, higher and additional income tax rates).
[75]  These rules appear in each of the heads of charge (schedules) to income tax and include ITTOIA 2005 (UK) ss. 6 (trade carried on in the UK), 264 (income from land in the UK),

non-resident corporations are taxed in the same manner as non-resident individuals.

By contrast, the CCCTB Proposal is limited because it would not impose tax. Profits of an EU PE of a non-resident corporation would (by election) fall within the tax base of the CCCTB Proposal.[76] Other EU source profits of non-resident corporations would fall outside of the Proposal and so be taxed under the usual domestic rules of the member states' tax laws.

As this discussion demonstrates, gross basis taxation for non-resident corporations is typically the same as it is for individuals (i.e. both the tax base and the tax rates). Because gross basis taxation does not involve matters that are peculiar to corporations, it is not considered further. However, taxation of non-resident corporations on a net basis, and particularly profits derived by a non-resident corporation through a domestic PE, is unique to corporations. Accordingly, the following discussion is limited to taxation of PEs of non-resident corporations.

Therefore, an essential issue in scenario 5 is whether the domestic country treats income derived by non-resident corporations through a PE situated there consistently with income derived through a subsidiary resident there (scenario 3). The choice between a PE and a subsidiary is a fundamental in structuring the form of a cross-border investment. Tax treaties based on the OECD Model protect the taxation of PEs and subsidiaries with specific non-discrimination rules. In particular, that taxation cannot be 'less favourable' or 'more burdensome' than that of corporations that are resident and controlled in the domestic country.[77] Broadly, this means that income derived through a PE must be calculated in the same fashion as it would be for resident corporations.

These non-discrimination rules can be problematic when the other major issue of corporate tax base discussed earlier at 1.2 is considered (i.e. calculation of the corporate tax base of corporate groups). The question for present discussion is whether PEs of non-resident corporations can participate in special rules, such as consolidation or group relief, that erode the separate identity of group members. Controversially, the OECD changed the commentary on its non-discrimination rules in 2008 to suggest that this was not required under an OECD Model style treaty.[78]

---

368 (savings and investment income just mentions 'source' of income) and 577 (other income also just mentions 'source').

[76] CCCTB Proposal Art. 6(2).

[77] OECD Model Art. 24(3) & (5), respectively.

[78] Regarding this and generally with respect to OECD Model Art. 24(3) & (5), see Harris & Oliver (2010, pp. 168–76).

Countries adopt widely different practices in their domestic laws in this regard. For example, the US adopts a restrictive approach. Only resident corporations may file a consolidated tax return. As an exception, a non-resident corporation may join a group if it is wholly owned by a resident corporation and that corporation elects for its subsidiary to be treated as a resident corporation (for all corporation tax purposes).[79]

The German *Organschaft* regime is slightly more flexible. As noted earlier at 1.2.3.2, any domestic business can be the head of an *Organschaft*, and this includes a PE of a non-resident corporation. However, only corporations that are organised under German law and are resident in Germany can be a subsidiary under an *Organschaft*.[80] In 2011, after a dispute with the European Commission, the requirement that a corporation be formed under German law was lifted by administrative letter. It is now sufficient that the subsidiary corporation be formed under the law of any EU member state (or state within the European Economic Area). However, the corporation must still have its place of management in Germany. There is also an argument that a nationality non-discrimination clause in a tax treaty may produce the same result.[81]

By comparison, the UK group relief system is substantially more flexible. Non-resident corporations can be members of a group of corporations, but there are restrictions on how group relief works in this case, as discussed earlier at 1.2.3.2. Broadly, the relief is limited to profits, gains and losses of a UK PE of a non-resident corporation. So, for example, only losses from a UK PE can be surrendered by a non-resident corporation for purposes of the loss transfer system.[82] Similarly, such a PE may be the recipient of a loss transfer.[83] Deferral of chargeable gains on the transfer of capital assets between group members is similarly available for a transfer to or from a UK PE of a non-resident corporation.[84]

The CCCTB Proposal would produce a result similar to that in the UK in that EU PEs of non-resident corporations can qualify for consolidation. A PE of a non-resident corporation (whether formed under the law of an EU member state or otherwise) may form the head of a consolidated group or a subsidiary part of a consolidated group.[85]

---

[79]  IRC (US) s. 1504(d).
[80]  KStG (Germany) ss. 14 and 17.
[81]  Dorfmueller (2011).
[82]  CTA 2010 (UK) s. 107.
[83]  CTA 2010 (UK) s. 134.
[84]  TCGA 1992 (UK) s. 171(1A).
[85]  CCCTB Proposal Art. 55.

**Tax treatment**    As with resident corporations, even if a non-resident corporation derives profits through a domestic PE, there is the question as to whether the domestic country will tax the corporation with respect to those profits or tax the corporation's shareholders. Again, as with resident corporations, the usual approach is to impose corporation tax. However, there is a question of the rate at which non-resident corporations are taxed. As a general rule, the PE non-discrimination rule in tax treaties will require application of the rate applicable to resident corporations.[86] So, for example, the simple rule in Germany is that PEs of non-resident corporations are taxed at the same rate as resident corporations. Some countries impose a higher rate as a substitute for dividend withholding tax. That is discussed further at 3.2.1.2.

Further issues arise where a country adopts multiple corporate tax rates or imposes multiple corporate taxes. In the US, for example, a US trade or business of a non-resident corporation is subject to the same taxes as resident corporations.[87] As a result, the US subjects PEs of non-resident corporations to the same progressive rates as resident corporations. In applying these rates, there is no attempt to take into account income of the non-resident corporation other than that effectively connected with the US trade or business.[88] However, if the non-resident corporation is a member of a corporate group, the rate thresholds may be apportioned as discussed earlier at 1.3.2.2. This means that the flat 35% corporate tax rate for qualified personal service corporations (see the earlier discussion at 1.3.2.2) can apply to a US trade or business of a non-resident corporation. Further, the income of such a trade or business may be subject to alternative minimum tax and even accumulated earnings tax if the non-resident corporation has US shareholders.[89]

By contrast, the UK does not grant its small companies rate to non-resident corporations.[90] However, as an administrative matter, it does extend this rate to UK PEs of corporations resident in EU countries or countries with a tax treaty with a non-discrimination provision for PEs. Unlike the US, in determining the amount of relief available, the UK takes into account the entire profits of the non-resident corporation. Further, like the US, it apportions the threshold between corporations associated with the non-resident corporation.[91]

---

[86]  OECD Model Art. 24(3).
[87]  IRC (US) s. 882.
[88]  Title 26 Code of Federal Regulations (US) § 1.882–1(2).
[89]  Title 26 Code of Federal Regulations (US) § 1.532–1(c).
[90]  CTA 2010 (UK) s. 18(a).
[91]  See Harris & Oliver (2010, pp. 170–1).

Situations where a corporate tax system allocates and taxes corporate profits to shareholders might also be applied to non-resident corporations. For example, the US check-the-box regime (see the earlier discussion at 1.1.1.1 and 1.1.4.2) applies to non-resident corporations (corporations formed under foreign laws). This provision is particularly important because if the non-resident corporation disappears for tax purposes and there is an individual behind it, individual tax rates apply and the branch profits tax (discussed later at 3.2.1.2) does not. By contrast, non-resident corporations cannot be an S corporation,[92] and so the pass-through election under the S corporation regime does not apply (see the earlier discussion at 1.3.3.2).

The UK rules for attributing to an individual income derived by a corporation from personal services of that individual (see the earlier discussion at 1.3.3.3) can also apply where a non-resident corporation is used as the intermediary.

### 3.2.1.2    Corporate income when repatriated or distributed

As the earlier discussion at 3.2.1.1 has noted, when corporate income is derived, the majority of countries tax PEs and resident corporations similarly. This is consistent with a comparison of scenario 5 with scenario 3. However, scenario 3 involves an undisputed jurisdiction to tax dividends when distributed to the non-resident shareholder, although dividend relief complicates this jurisdiction. By comparison, scenario 5 involves a distribution by a non-resident corporation to a non-resident shareholder and so does not involve an accepted domestic country jurisdiction to tax. The primary issue in scenario 5 is whether the domestic country treats a non-resident investor consistently whether the income is derived through a resident or non-resident corporation.

A non-resident investor typically has a choice as to whether to invest in the domestic country through a resident or non-resident corporation. If the income to be derived would be subject to a final withholding tax if derived directly by the investor, then it is likely that deriving the income through a non-resident corporation without a PE in the domestic country will produce the same result. In this case, for the reasons discussed earlier at 3.2.1.1, there is no point of comparison between the taxation of income derived through a resident and non-resident corporation, and so there is no point in discussing the potential domestic country taxation of dividends distributed by a non-resident corporation.

---

[92]  IRC (US) s. 1361(b)(1).

It is only where the income is derived by a non-resident corporation through a PE situated in the domestic country that a comparison of distributions of resident and non-resident corporations is worthy of consideration. This is because the taxation in the domestic country when the income is derived is likely to be the same whether the income is derived through a resident or non-resident corporation. As noted, this position is backed up by the non-discrimination rule for PEs in tax treaties.

However, even if PEs and subsidiaries are required by tax treaties to be treated similarly when corporate income is derived, differences appear when corporate income is distributed. This is primarily because of the additional jurisdiction to tax on the basis of the source of dividends in the context of a subsidiary that is not present when simply a PE is involved. This additional jurisdiction is reflected in OECD Model style tax treaties. As noted earlier at 3.1.2, the country of corporate residence has the right to tax dividends at the rates of 5% (direct investors) and 15% (portfolio investors) on the gross amount.[93]

Tax treaties do not usually grant a similar right to tax with respect to PEs. Indeed, it is usual for tax treaties to positively prohibit the taxation of distributions or repatriations of PEs of non-resident corporations or the taxation of such PEs at higher rates than resident corporations.[94] The result is that tax treaties permit and presume that domestic / source countries tax income derived and distributed through a subsidiary more heavily than income derived through a PE.

Some countries simply accept this distorting treatment of PEs and subsidiaries. Germany is such a country. As noted earlier, it imposes a withholding tax on outbound dividends. It does not seek to tax dividends of non-resident corporations or repatriations of profits from German PEs of non-resident corporations. It used to address this issue under its pre-2000 split-rate system by taxing such PEs at a flat rate higher than the distributed profits rate of resident corporations. That system was held to be contrary to the freedom of establishment under EU law.[95] The current system encourages non-resident corporations to derive dividends from German corporations through a German PE. In this way, they can avoid German dividend withholding tax.[96] This avoidance is less important

---

[93] OECD Model Art. 10(2).

[94] OECD Model Arts. 10(5) and 24(3). Regarding the former, see Harris & Oliver (2010, pp. 188–90).

[95] Case C-253/03 *CLT-UFA SA* v. *Finanzamt Köln-West* [2006] ECR I-1831 (ECJ).

[96] For an example of such a structure, see Case C-307/97 *Compagnie de Saint-Gobain, Zweigniederlassung Deutschland* v. *Finanzamt Aachen-Innenstadt* [1999] ECR I-6161 (ECJ).

since the introduction of the Parent-Subsidiary Directive, which exempts outbound non-portfolio dividends within the EU.

If a country wishes to neutralise the treatment of PEs and subsidiaries, there are a number of ways to do so. One approach is to extraterritorially tax dividends of non-resident corporations distributed from profits derived through a domestic country PE. Such an approach conflicts with tax treaties and can be complex. Further, the domestic country may have difficulty enforcing its tax law on a dividend distributed by a corporation outside its jurisdiction to a shareholder outside its jurisdiction. Nevertheless, there are examples of countries claiming jurisdiction to tax over such dividends. The US provides such an example.

The US treats certain dividends of non-resident corporations as having a source in the US; for example, where more than 25% of the corporation's income is 'effective[ly] connected ... with the conduct of a trade or business' in the US. In such a case, the source of the dividends is apportioned between the US and non-US sources based on the ratio of profits from the US and foreign sources during the past three years.[97] The consequence would be that the foreign corporation is required to withhold US tax from its dividends. This withholding can be enforced because of the presence of a trade or business of the non-resident corporation in the US. Such extraterritorial taxation of dividends would be suppressed by an OECD Model style tax treaty.[98]

A simpler manner to neutralise the treatment of PEs and subsidiaries is to impose corporation tax on PEs when income is derived at a higher rate than applicable to resident corporations. This approach is adopted by India (40% vs. 30%) and South Africa (33% vs. 28%),[99] and the former German system mentioned earlier is another example. This approach does not perfectly neutralise the tax treatment of PEs and subsidiaries because the PE suffers the higher tax irrespective of whether it retains or repatriates the profits. As noted, unless specifically catered for, this additional tax should be suppressed in a tax treaty context.[100]

---

[97]  IRC (US) s. 861(a)(2).

[98]  OECD Model Art. 10(5).

[99]  Finance Act, 2012 (India) First Schedule, Part I, para. E (the rates mentioned in the text do not account for surcharge or education cess) and Taxation Laws Amendment Act, 2011 (South Africa) Appendix I para. 4. India intends to replace its higher corporate tax rate for non-resident corporations with a branch profits tax; see BMR Advisors (2011).

[100]  OECD Model Art. 24(3). Regarding Indian and South African tax treaty practice in this regard, see Harris (2010, p. 583).

A different manner to better neutralise the treatment of PEs and subsidiaries is to impose a tax on repatriation of profits by PEs. This tax would be at the same rate as the tax on repatriations of dividends by subsidiaries. It is referred to as a 'branch profits tax', and the US provides an example.[101] It imposes a tax of 30% on the 'dividend equivalent amount' of US branches.[102] This amount comprises the after-tax earnings of the foreign corporation's US trade or business that are not reinvested in the business by the close of the tax year or that are disinvested in a later tax year. Whether earnings are reinvested or disinvested is measured by changes in the equity in the business.[103] Such a tax would usually be suppressed by tax treaties.[104] However, the US typically provides for its branch profits tax in its treaties, and this is confirmed by legislation.[105] US tax treaties usually reduce branch profits tax to the same rate as for dividends distributed by US subsidiaries to treaty partner parent corporations.

A third approach to neutralise the treatment of PEs and subsidiaries is to tax subsidiaries in the same manner as PEs. In this approach the domestic / source country exempts repatriations (dividends) of subsidiaries, just as repatriations of PEs are not taxed (or dividends of non-resident corporations). This is the approach taken by the UK. As noted earlier at 3.1.2, the UK does not seek to tax non-residents with respect to dividends received from UK corporations. This is also broadly true in Australia. Both countries tax resident and non-resident corporations at the same rate, and neither country imposes a branch profits tax.

None of this discussion of neutral treatment of PEs and subsidiaries addresses the question of whether a dividend relief system should be extended to non-resident corporations. At a fundamental level, such an extension is problematic. Dividend relief presumes relief from economic double taxation, but only at the point dividends are distributed. If a country has no jurisdiction to tax with respect to dividends of non-resident corporations, then it is difficult to comprehend how dividend relief would work. It might be possible to treat repatriations of PEs as dividends and apply dividend relief at this point. However, this approach also has difficulties, which are different for corporate-level and shareholder-level dividend relief systems.

---

[101] Other countries imposing branch profits taxes include Canada, France, Indonesia, Spain and Turkey; see ibid.
[102] IRC (US) s. 884(a).
[103] IRC (US) s. 884(b) & (c).
[104] OECD Model Art. 10(5).
[105] IRC (US) s. 884(e).

A corporate-level dividend relief system might suggest that corporation tax imposed on a non-resident corporation should be relieved when the corporation distributes dividends. However, from a practical perspective, it might be difficult to determine when a non-resident corporation distributes dividends and, even if this is possible to determine, when the profits of the domestic country PE (as opposed to other profits) have been distributed. In any case, current tax treaties would exclude taxation of the dividend by the domestic country. In a full dividend relief scenario, the result would be that the domestic country gives up the only tax it levies. Such a refund at the point PE profits are distributed might also play havoc with foreign tax relief provided in the country where the distributing corporation is resident. A corporate-level dividend relief system is unlikely to fare better if it applied to repatriations of PEs. Again, without the right to impose a branch profits type tax, the result would be that the country of the PE would not collect any tax on income derived within its jurisdiction.

Shareholder-level dividend relief in the form of dividend exclusion causes no problems in scenario 5. This is because exclusion is consistent with the lack of jurisdiction to tax dividends of non-resident corporations. However, a shareholder differentiation system does cause problems in scenario 5. Such a system suffers the same difficulties as a corporate-level dividend relief system (i.e. it suggests extra-territorial taxation of dividends distributed by non-resident corporations or a branch profits style tax). However, without such a tax, the domestic country would still retain its corporation tax. This is not true of a dividend tax credit system. If dividend tax credits are refundable and granted at the point of distribution or repatriation, the result would be the same as under a corporate-level dividend relief system.

The difference in tax treatment of income derived by a non-resident through a resident corporation or a domestic country PE may involve more than just the taxation of repatriations. As discussed earlier at 2.5, a country may seek to reconcile corporation and shareholder taxes by imposing an equalisation tax or restricting dividend relief when preference income is distributed. Such a reconciliation is likely to apply in scenario 3 (domestic subsidiary), but a question is whether any such equivalent treatment can be imposed in the context of scenario 5. If a country refunded corporation tax on repatriation by a PE, it would be possible to restrict such relief. But if the reconciliation involves an attempt to impose further tax on the non-resident corporation, it is likely to involve a breach of tax treaties based on the OECD Model.[106]

---

[106]  OECD Model Art. 10(5),

As noted earlier at 3.1.2.4, Australia may deny a non-resident shareholder an exemption from dividend withholding tax where the dividend does not carry dividend tax credits. So Australia does not usually tax dividends of Australian corporations distributed to non-resident shareholders. However, it might impose such a tax if insufficient Australian corporation tax has been paid. This is not true of Australian PEs of non-resident corporations. Here there is no attempt to impose an equivalent of an equalisation tax or branch profits tax where insufficient Australian corporation tax has been imposed. This difference creates non-neutrality between the Australian tax treatment of PEs and subsidiaries. By comparison, the Mexican equalisation tax applies to repatriations by a Mexican PE of a non-resident corporation in the same manner as it applies to dividends distributed by a Mexican subsidiary.[107]

### 3.2.2 Foreign income / resident shareholders: scenario 6

Scenario 6 involves a non-resident corporation deriving foreign source income and distributing that income to resident shareholders. It is comparable with scenario 2, but for the difference in the residence of the corporation. In principle, this scenario involves no recognised jurisdiction to tax when corporate income is derived because both source and residence are outside the domestic jurisdiction. However, some countries exercise some extra-territorial jurisdiction to tax in this case under their controlled foreign corporation rules. This is the first matter considered in the following discussion.

By contrast, the domestic country does have a recognised jurisdiction to tax when the corporate income is distributed (i.e. on the basis of residence of the shareholder). The identification and taxation of distributions were considered earlier at 2.1, 2.2 and 2.3. That consideration presumed a resident corporation making a distribution. Scenario 6 is the first scenario that specifically considers distributions made by non-resident corporations. Non-resident corporations are regulated by foreign corporate law, and this raises the question of whether the same tax rules in this regard should be applied to both resident and non-resident corporations. This is the second matter considered in the following discussion.

Dividends distributed by a non-resident corporation are usually considered to have a foreign source. An exception regarding the US was considered earlier at 3.2.1.2. As foreign source income, tax treaties based on the OECD Model require the domestic country to grant foreign tax relief

---

[107] Income Tax Law (*Ley del Impuesto sobre la Renta*) (Mexico) Art. 193.

for any tax imposed on the dividends by the source country (e.g. by with-holding tax). This tax relief is usually in the form of a direct foreign tax credit.[108] Germany, the UK and the US each unilaterally provide a direct foreign tax credit in this scenario. More problematic is whether any dividend relief is provided, recognising that the foreign profits of the non-resident corporation were subject to foreign corporation tax. In an international setting, such relief is referred to as underlying foreign tax relief. Underlying foreign tax relief is the third matter considered in the following discussion.

### 3.2.2.1 Corporate income when derived: CFC and PFIF rules

Most countries do not tax when a foreign corporation derives foreign income. The exception is where the foreign corporation has shareholders resident in the domestic country and the corporation is used as an abusive tax shelter. Some countries may tax in this case, especially if the foreign corporation is subject to no or a very low corporation tax or if the foreign corporation predominantly derives passive income. The tax shelter problem and the methods by which it can be overcome were considered earlier at 1.3.3. These methods in substance involve attributing corporate income to shareholders irrespective of whether the corporation distributes its income. The tax shelter issue is more acute in an international setting, particularly where foreign corporation tax is substantially below that applicable in the country of the shareholder's residence.

Attribution regimes are typically of two types when projected into an international setting. The most common approach is the use of controlled foreign corporation rules. These rules apply when a foreign corporation is controlled by residents. They typically require calculation of the foreign corporation's income according to domestic rules, and then the resident shareholders are attributed and taxed on their domestic share of the income. This is not the place for a detailed consideration of controlled foreign corporation rules or whether they are consistent with tax treaties or EU law.[109] However, it is important to note two aspects that are related to matters previously discussed. First, there is a need to determine whether the foreign corporation is controlled by residents (i.e. controlled

---

[108] OECD Model Art. 23.

[109] Regarding the practical operation of controlled foreign corporation rules, see Ault & Arnold (2010, pp. 474–785). Regarding tax treaty and EU law issues, see Harris & Oliver (2010, pp. 296–312).

by a particular group of persons). This issue was generally considered earlier at 1.1.5.2 in the context of closely held corporations. Second, controlled foreign corporation rules typically involve the partnership method of allocating corporate profits to shareholders, considered earlier at 1.3.3.2.

Germany, the UK, the US and the CCCTB Proposal have controlled foreign corporation rules. These rules are subject to ongoing review in the EU because of their possible incompatibility with EU law. The oldest of these are the rules in the US, which include in the gross income of resident shareholders certain income ('Subpart F income') derived by a 'controlled foreign corporation'.[110] 'Subpart F income' is a complex concept, but broadly includes passive income and income that has little economic connection with the country of the foreign corporation's residence ('base company' income).[111] A foreign corporation is a controlled foreign corporation if it is more than 50% held (voting power and value) by residents who have at least a 10% interest in the corporation.[112] The holdings of associates are attributed for this purpose.[113]

Similarly, in Germany income of a foreign corporation controlled by resident taxpayers 'is taxable in the hands of each taxpayer in the proportion of the nominal capital of the company allocated to each taxpayer'. Only income for which the corporation is an 'intermediate company' is attributed to the shareholders.[114] Control is determined by reference to more than 50% of the number of shares or voting power.[115] Intermediate company income is defined in a complex fashion, but broadly excludes active income and income taxed at 25% or more.[116] Attribution and taxation to resident shareholders occur irrespective of the level of holding in the controlled foreign corporation. There is an exception for EU establishments.[117]

The UK controlled foreign corporation rules have been in a continuous state of flux since 2007. They were fundamentally reformed in 2012 to focus only on the artificial diversion of profits from the UK. The reform has made the rules horrendously complex and nearly impenetrable. They

---

[110] IRC (US) s. 951.
[111] IRC (US) s. 952.
[112] IRC (US) ss. 951(b) & 957(a).
[113] IRC (US) s. 958.
[114] Foreign Transaction Tax Law (*Aussensteuergesetz*) (Germany) s. 7(1).
[115] Foreign Transaction Tax Law (*Aussensteuergesetz*) (Germany) s. 7(2).
[116] Foreign Transaction Tax Law (*Aussensteuergesetz*) (Germany) s. 8(1).
[117] Foreign Transaction Tax Law (*Aussensteuergesetz*) (Germany) s. 8(2).

impose a corporate tax charge on UK resident corporations that have certain interests in a non-resident corporation controlled by resident persons (a 'CFC').[118] 'Control' is defined broadly and includes 40% ownership if no other person has a 55% interest in the corporation.[119] The charge is only with respect to 'chargeable profits', which are profits that pass any one of five gateway tests.[120]

The first gateway covers profits attributable to functions performed by significant people located in the UK. It has four critical exceptions. Profits do not pass this gateway unless the CFC has assets or bears risks that are managed or controlled from the UK on non-arm's length terms. Profits do not pass if the CFC's business would be 'commercially effective' were the assets or risks to stop being managed or controlled from the UK. Profits do not pass unless there is an avoidance purpose or the CFC only has property business profits or non-trading finance profits.[121] The second gateway deals with non-trading finance profits, being profits from credits on non-trading loan relationships and company distributions. Profits do not pass this gateway if they are only incidental to the CFC's business, measured at a threshold of 5%, or they arise from the investment of funds held for the purposes of the CFC's trade.[122] The third gateway deals with trading finance profits (treasury functions),[123] the fourth with captive insurance[124] and the fifth is specific to banks and relates to capital adequacy requirements.[125]

The gateway rules are followed by a list of outright exemptions from the CFC rules. These include an exemption for CFCs resident in certain listed countries and a de minimis exemption where the CFC's profits are less than £50,000.[126] Another exemption applies where the CFC's accounting profits are no more than 10% of relevant operating expenditure.[127] The CFC charge also does not apply unless the foreign tax is less than 75% of the tax that would have been paid if the corporation were resident in the

---

[118]  TIOPA 2010 (UK) ss. 371AA(3) & 371BA.
[119]  TIOPA 2010 (UK) Part 9A, Chapter 18.
[120]  TIOPA 2010 (UK) s. 371BB.
[121]  TIOPA 2010 (UK) s. 371CA and Part 9A, Chapter 4.
[122]  TIOPA 2010 (UK) ss. 371CB & 371CC and Part 9A, Chapter 5. Under Chapter 9 there may be a complete exemption for profits from loans made between group corporations.
[123]  TIOPA 2010 (UK) s. 371CE and Part 9A, Chapter 6.
[124]  TIOPA 2010 (UK) s. 371CF and Part 9A, Chapter 7.
[125]  TIOPA 2010 (UK) s. 371CG and Part 9A, Chapter 8.
[126]  TIOPA 2010 (UK) Part 9A, Chapters 11 and 12, respectively.
[127]  TIOPA 2010 (UK) Part 9A, Chapter 13.

UK.[128] As a general rule, the gateway tests do not cover capital gains, but there is a separate rule that applies to them.[129]

Where profits do pass a gateway and an exemption does not apply, the chargeable profits are allocated to persons with a 'relevant interest' in the CFC together with any foreign tax paid by the CFC.[130] However, only corporations with a 25% interest in the CFC are charged on their proportionate interest in the chargeable profits, and they get a credit for the foreign tax attributed to them (i.e. an underlying foreign tax credit).[131] There is no direct equivalent of the CFC charge for individual shareholders in non-resident corporations. The CFC rules are adapted to remove the exemption for PE profits in similar circumstances.[132]

The CCCTB Proposal also contains controlled foreign corporation rules. These rules can only apply to 'entities' resident outside the EU that are owned as to 50% by a resident corporation and its 'associated enterprises'. The concept 'asssociated enterprises' was considered earlier at 1.1.5.3. The tax rate applicable to the third country entity must be less than 40% of the average corporate tax rate within the EU, and more than 30% of the entity's income must be passive income from associated enterprises.[133] Where these rules apply, the income of the foreign entity (calculated under the rules of the CCCTB Proposal) is included in the resident corporation's income 'in proportion to the entitlement...to share in the profits of the foreign entity'.[134] The EU Presidency amendments would extend these rules to tax PE profits subject to lower taxation.

A second type of attribution rules are those that apply in a non-controlled setting. The US enacted passive foreign investment company rules in 1986 to counter deferral of taxation through retention in lowly taxed foreign corporations. The primary mechanism to counter the deferral is through allocation of distributions to a shareholder's holding period and imposition of an interest charge for deferral of tax.[135] This style of approach was discussed earlier at 1.3.3.1. The rule only applies to foreign corporations if 75% of their income is passive income or 50% of their

[128] TIOPA 2010 (UK) Part 9A, Chapter 14.
[129] TCGA 1992 (UK) s. 13.
[130] TIOPA 2010 (UK) Part 9A, Chapters 15, 16 and 17.
[131] TIOPA 2010 (UK) s. 371BC. Section 371BD defines a 'chargeable company' in terms of a 25% holding.
[132] CTA 2009 (UK) ss. 18G to 18ID.
[133] CCCTB Proposal Art. 82.
[134] CCCTB Proposal Art. 83.
[135] IRC (US) s. 1291.

assets produce passive income.[136] US shareholders may be taxed irrespective of their level of shareholding or the collective level of US shareholding in the foreign corporation.

This interest charge approach only taxes corporate income when distributed, although in a manner meant to replicate taxation of the shareholder when the income was derived by the foreign corporation. It is possible for US shareholders to avoid the interest charge by electing to be taxed currently on their 'pro rata share of the ordinary earnings' of the foreign corporation.[137] This may be practically impossible unless the shareholder is able to obtain the relevant information. Where the election is made, attribution to and taxation of the shareholder are another example of the partnership method of taxing corporate income to shareholders.

The German controlled foreign corporation rules can also apply in a non-controlled setting. This may happen where the foreign corporation is essentially engaged only in passive investment. In such a case, shareholders with as little as 1% of the shares in the corporation may be attributed and taxed with respect to the corporation's profits. In some cases, even less than a 1% holding may cause attribution.[138] Germany has a separate law regulating investment funds (domestic or foreign), which largely applies to open-ended funds (funds that provide for redemption of shares). Funds regulated by this law have a special tax law that allocates their income to their investors irrespective of distribution.[139] This law applies in priority to the controlled foreign corporation rules.[140] Again, these are examples of the partnership method of taxing corporate income when derived.

### 3.2.2.2   Identification and taxation of distributions

The earlier discussion at 3.2.1 was the first time this book had specifically considered the taxation of non-resident corporations when corporate income is derived. That discussion skated over the issues discussed in Chapter 1, noting any differences from the treatment of a resident corporation. Similarly, this subheading is the first time that this book specifically considers dividends distributed by non-resident corporations. Accordingly, it is appropriate to skate over the issues discussed earlier at 2.1, 2.2 and 2.3 to note any differences that might arise by reason of the corporation being non-resident.

---

[136]  IRC (US) s. 1297.
[137]  IRC (US) ss. 1293 to 1295.
[138]  Foreign Transaction Tax Law (*Aussensteuergesetz*) (Germany) s. 7(6) & (6a).
[139]  Investment Tax Law (*Investmentsteuergesetz*) (Germany).
[140]  Foreign Transaction Tax Law (*Aussensteuergesetz*) (Germany) s. 7(7).

As noted, non-resident corporations are regulated by foreign corporate law. It is inevitable that those foreign laws are both different from domestic corporate law and different from each other. The issue is whether the same tax rules regarding identification and taxation of distributions of resident corporations can or should be applied to distributions of non-resident corporations. As the following discussion demonstrates, the general answer seems to be that countries usually apply the same rules. However, those rules may have to be applied in a different fashion or with a different emphasis because of the differences in underlying corporate law. For example, the corporate laws of different countries are likely to demonstrate wide variations in the treatment of share premiums (many countries no longer have this concept) and returns of capital. The same may be true of the issue of bonus shares and hidden profit distributions and the consequences thereof.

As noted earlier at 2.1, US case law takes a substance approach to identifying who is a shareholder. In principle, the same approach is taken irrespective of whether an interest in a resident or non-resident corporation is being considered. The same is true of the identification of distributions and their taxation. In particular, the concept of earnings and profits applies to both resident and non-resident corporations. Unlike the IRC, the Treasury Regulations make specific reference to 'dividends' being defined in terms of a 'distribution of property as defined in section 317 in the ordinary course of business, even though extraordinary in amount, made by a domestic or foreign corporation to its shareholders out of earnings and profits.[141] Further, attributable profits under the controlled foreign corporation rules are identified in terms of 'earnings and profits of the foreign corporation.'[142] Similarly, the inclusion of dividends in gross income applies equally to dividends of resident and non-resident corporations.[143]

The situation is similar in Germany. The reference to 'income from shares' or 'hidden profit distributions' is not limited by reference to whether the corporation is resident or not resident.[144] Nevertheless, the concepts used are focused on German-style organisations. There must be circumstances in which it may be difficult to apply these concepts to

---

[141] Title 26 Code of Federal Regulations (US) § 1.316–1(a)(1).

[142] IRC (US) s. 952(a)(3). In particular, 'earnings and profits of any foreign corporation ... shall be determined according to rules substantially similar to those applicable to domestic corporations'; s. 964(a).

[143] IRC (US) s. 61(a)(7).

[144] EStG (Germany) s. 20(1)1 and KStG (Germany) s. 8(3).

foreign corporations. For example, it might especially be a problem with a 'repayment of nominal capital', discussed later at 6.1.1.[145]

The position is similar under the CCCTB Proposal. The reference to 'dividends and other profit distributions' makes no distinction between those made by resident or non-resident corporations.[146] The same is true of the reference to 'benefits granted to a shareholder'.[147] These concepts could take on a very different focus depending on the corporate law in question.

In a familiar pattern, the UK is the odd one out. Historically, its definition of 'distribution' only applied to tax liability on distributions of resident corporations. This changed with the tax law rewrite, and now that concept also applies to distributions of non-resident corporations with one important exception. For corporation tax purposes, the charge is on 'any dividend or other distributions' irrespective of whether the distribution is from a resident or non-resident corporation.[148] The same is true with respect to the income tax charge on distributions of resident corporations.[149] This income tax charge expressly applies whether the distribution is 'capital' or not; there is no such prescription in the corporation tax charge.[150]

However, when it comes to non-resident corporations, the income tax charge only applies to 'dividends', and this 'does not include dividends of a capital nature.'[151] This means that all the rules dealing with the distinction between debt and equity instruments and hidden profit distributions do not apply in this context. The results can be confusing.[152] Further, recall that the definition of 'close company' requires the corporation to be resident.[153] So the extension of the concept of distribution in the context of close companies cannot apply to a non-resident corporation; neither can the charge to corporation tax on making a loan to a shareholder of such a company.[154] This differential policy seems to be a result of historic fragmentation and makes little sense from a policy perspective.

---

[145] EStG (Germany) s. 20(1)2.
[146] CCCTB Proposal Art. 4(8).
[147] CCCTB Proposal Art. 15.
[148] CTA 2009 (UK) s. 931A(1).
[149] ITTOIA 2005 (UK) s. 383(1).
[150] Compare CTA 2009 (UK) s. 931A with ITTOIA 2005 (UK) s. 383(3).
[151] ITTOIA 2005 (UK) s. 402.
[152] For an example of the difficulty involving a distribution out of the share premium account of a Cayman Islands company, see *First Nationwide* v. *RCC* [2012] EWCA Civ 278 (CA).
[153] CTA 2010 (UK) s. 442(a).
[154] For example, CTA 2010 (UK) ss. 1064 and 455, respectively.

### 3.2.2.3 Dividend relief: underlying foreign tax relief

Presuming a distribution by a non-resident corporation to a resident shareholder is a dividend and is taxable as such, it remains to consider whether any dividend relief is available with respect to the dividend. This is a question of relief from economic double taxation, which in an international setting is referred to as underlying or indirect foreign tax relief. It is not a question of relief from juridical double taxation, which in an international setting is referred to as direct foreign tax relief and in the context of a dividend will take the form of a direct foreign tax credit.

**Corporate-level dividend relief systems**   Scenario 6 is comparable to scenario 2, except for the residence of the corporation. The difficulties for corporate-level dividend relief systems in scenario 2 were discussed earlier at 3.1.1.3. These difficulties become a complete impossibility in the context of scenario 6. The domestic country has no jurisdiction to tax the corporation, and so relief from corporation tax is not possible because there is no corporation tax imposed by that country. A corporate-level dividend relief system, like a classical system, presumes that dividends are fully taxable in the hands of the shareholder. If the country of the corporation's residence has not provided corporate-level dividend relief, the result will be economic double taxation. The country where the corporation is resident imposes corporation tax, and the domestic country imposes shareholder tax.

There is an important qualification to this treatment. The country of corporate residence may have switched some of its corporation tax for shareholder-level tax. Examples involving Australia, especially New Zealand and, formerly under tax treaty, the UK were given earlier at 3.1.2.4. If the domestic country where the shareholder is resident gives a direct foreign tax credit for the corporate tax 'switched' to a shareholder tax, then cross-border relief from economic double taxation may be provided. This is not really a function of the corporate-level dividend relief system of the domestic country, but an acceptance of the foreign switch under the domestic country's direct foreign tax credit system.

**Shareholder-level dividend relief systems**   Matters are very different if the domestic country provides dividend relief at the shareholder level. Here it does grant relief against shareholder tax, and the question is whether that relief is granted with respect to distributions of non-resident corporations. Historically, underlying foreign tax relief was limited to non-portfolio shareholders (i.e. corporate shareholders with a significant holding in the distributing foreign corporation). However, in the past dozen years or so countries have dramatically changed their position, and it is now common for dividend relief to be extended to dividends of non-resident corporations distributed to resident portfolio shareholders.[155]

For example, Germany extends the same dividend exclusion available with respect to distributions of resident corporations to distributions of non-resident corporations, whether the recipient shareholder is a corporation or an individual. Any German tax liability that arises under these rules may be reduced by a direct foreign tax credit for any foreign tax imposed directly on the distribution.[156] This can leave a country exposed to tax competition, particularly if the distribution comes from a corporation resident in a low-tax country. Germany relies on its attribution rules discussed earlier at 3.2.2.1 to address this issue. In addition, in 2006 Germany introduced anti-hybrid rules that deny dividend relief if the distribution is deductible for the foreign corporation.[157]

The position would be the same under the CCCTB Proposal. The inter-corporate dividend exemption would apply irrespective of whether the distributing corporation is resident or non-resident.[158] Under the Proposal as drafted, 5% of such dividends would be re-included in the tax base on account of expenses.[159] The Proposal contains no provision for a direct foreign tax credit, which may not be surprising considering the Proposal would not impose any tax. It is unclear whether a foreign tax credit would nevertheless be available under the domestic law of the member state that would impose the tax (tax treaties would seem to require this). Again, there would be an issue of harmful tax competition, but like Germany it may be addressed by the attribution rules discussed earlier at 3.2.2.1.

In principle, since 2010 the UK position has been similar. The exemption for inter-corporate dividends is available irrespective of whether the

---

[155] Regarding the difference between portfolio and non-portfolio shareholders (or the lack thereof), see Harris & Oliver (2010, pp. 182–6).

[156] EStG (Germany) s. 34c(1) and KStG (Germany) s. 26(6).

[157] EStG (Germany) s. 3 No. 40 and KStG (Germany) s. 8b(1).

[158] CCCTB Proposal Art. 11(c).

[159] CCCTB Proposal Art. 14(1)(g). Although the EU Presidency amendments would fully exempt inter-corporate dividends, it would add a 10% holding requirement. So there would still be some dividends that remained taxable under the Proposal. Further, the amendments would deny the participation exemption if the distribution were deductible to the distributing corporation; Art. 83a(2).

distribution is from a resident or non-resident corporation.[160] Historically, some protection from harmful tax competition may have been provided by the UK controlled foreign corporation rules, but this is no longer the case since the 2012 amendments (discussed earlier at 3.2.2.1). Since 2005 the UK also has had anti-hybrid rules that deny dividend relief if the distribution is deductible for the foreign corporation.[161] A corporation may elect that the inter-corporate dividend exemption does not apply,[162] in which case an underlying foreign tax credit may be available (discussed later).

Similarly, countries that adopt a shareholder differentiation system may extend the lower tax rates for dividends to dividends received from non-resident corporations. This is the situation in Germany with respect to the 25% final withholding tax: it applies to dividends received from both resident and non-resident corporations. There is a direct foreign tax credit for any foreign tax levied directly on the dividend.[163] The position is more restricted under the US shareholder differentiation system. Lower dividend tax rates are available in scenario 6, but only with respect to dividends distributed by a 'qualified foreign corporation'.[164] This is defined by reference to a corporation eligible for tax treaty benefits under a treaty 'which includes an exchange of information program.'[165] The US Treasury has issued a list of tax treaties that qualify for this purpose.[166] The US also grants a direct foreign tax credit, irrespective of whether the US lower rates are available.[167]

The UK generally extends its lower tax rates for dividends received by individuals to dividends of non-resident corporations. Similarly, it broadly extends its dividend tax credit to such dividends, although not in precisely the same manner as for dividends from resident corporations.[168] A direct

---

[160] CTA 2009 (UK) ss. 931B to 931Q.

[161] CTA 2009 (UK) ss. 931B(c) & 931D(c).

[162] CTA 2009 (UK) ss. 931R.

[163] EStG (Germany) s. 32d(5).

[164] IRC (US) s. 1(h)(11)(B).

[165] IRC (US) s. 1(h)(11)(C)(i). Under (ii), corporations with stock readily tradable on a US securities market are also included. However, under (iii) foreign personal holding companies and passive foreign investment companies are excluded.

[166] IRS Notice 2006–101.

[167] IRC (US) s. 901.

[168] ITTOIA 2005 (UK) s. 397A. Under s. 397AA the tax credit is only available if one of three conditions is met:

- the shareholder holds less than 10% of the shares of the non-resident corporation and the corporation has a share capital

foreign tax credit is available for any foreign tax imposed directly on the foreign dividend.[169]

**Switching forms of dividend relief**   It is also possible that a country switches its domestic form of dividend relief to another form of dividend relief when dividends are received from a non-resident corporation. Classically, this would occur when a country adopting an inter-corporate dividend exemption domestically moved to use an imputation system (i.e. an underlying foreign tax credit system) for receipt of non-portfolio dividends from non-resident corporations. Underlying foreign tax credit systems display all of the usual features of an imputation system, including wash-out of corporate preferences and recording and ordering requirements (see the earlier discusssion at 2.4.3.3 and 2.5). They are typically limited to inter-corporate shareholders of at least 10% on the basis that it would otherwise be difficult for the resident shareholder to identify the foreign tax imposed on the distributing corporation's underlying profits.[170]

The US still switches from a domestic dividend exemption (dividends-received deduction) to an imputation system with respect to non-portfolio dividends from non-resident corporations. US corporations are entitled to an indirect foreign tax credit with respect to dividends received from 10% foreign subsidiaries.[171] The 10% is tested by reference to 'voting stock' of the foreign corporation. The credit is calculated as the proportion that the amount of the dividends bears to the foreign corporation's 'undistributed earnings', a concept that is determined by reference to earnings and profits. This is an example of the simple two pools (profits and tax) approach to recording corporate profits with tax treatment, discussed earlier at 2.5.1.2. It also means that the US implicitly uses a proportionate ordering rule (see

---

- the distributing corporation is an offshore fund (but if 60% of its assets are in interest-bearing assets, individuals receiving distributions will be treated for tax purposes as having received interest and not a dividend or other type of distribution. This means that no tax credit will be available and the tax rates applicable will be those applicable to interest)
- the distributing corporation is resident in a country that has a tax treaty with the UK including a non-discrimination provision and the distribution is not part of a tax avoidance scheme

[169] TIOPA 2010 (UK) ss. 9 & 13.
[170] Regarding the underlying foreign tax credit system, see Harris & Oliver (2010, pp. 286–91).
[171] IRC (US) s. 902.

the earlier discussion at 2.5.2.2). The foreign tax credit is also available for taxes paid by lower tier subsidiaries.[172]

Where a UK corporation elects that the inter-corporate dividend exemption does not apply, an underlying foreign tax credit may be available with respect to a dividend from a non-resident corporation. This is the case if the UK corporation holds at least 10% of the voting power in the distributing corporation.[173] The credit is equal to 'the foreign tax borne on the relevant profits by the company paying the dividend'.[174] 'Relevant profits' are the distributable profits of that period, if the dividend is paid for a specific period. Otherwise, a last in / first out rule is used to identify the foreign profits distributed. Distributable profits are largely determined by reference to profits shown in the foreign distributing corporation's accounts.[175] So the UK requires distributing foreign corporations to record foreign profits for each year with their foreign tax treatment. Again, the earlier discussion at 2.5.1.2 is relevant. Unlike the US proportionate ordering rule, the UK ordering rule is largely discretionary. As with the US, the UK allows an indirect foreign tax credit for foreign tax paid by lower tier subsidiaries.

Although traditionally a switch-over would be from a domestic inter-corporate dividend exemption to an underlying foreign tax credit system for dividends from non-resident corporations, Australia peculiarly does the opposite. Its domestic imputation system applies to inter-corporate dividends (except in a consolidation). However, it adopts an exemption system with respect to dividends received from foreign subsidiaries.[176] As with the UK and the US, the threshold for such relief is a 10% holding in the distributing corporation.

**No-dividend relief: classical treatment**   These examples leave a number of situations in which there is dividend relief for domestic dividends, but no dividend relief for dividends from non-resident corporations (although a direct foreign tax credit will be available). Such discrimination usually does not occur within the EU because it is prohibited by EU law.[177] In other countries, economic double taxation of dividends from

---

[172] For an overview of the US indirect foreign tax credit regime, see Kochman & Rosenbloom (2012).
[173] TIOPA 2010 (UK) s. 14(2).
[174] TIOPA 2010 (UK) s. 58.
[175] TIOPA 2010 (UK) s. 59.
[176] Income Tax Assessment Act 1936 (Australia) s. 23AJ.
[177] See Harris & Oliver (2010, pp. 291–6).

non-resident corporations is more common. So, for example, in the US it may occur for an individual where the dividend is from a non-qualifying foreign corporation. For US corporate shareholders, it may occur where the holding in the non-resident corporation is less than 10%. The same is also true for portfolio dividends received by Australian corporations (i.e. there is no inter-corporate dividend exemption if the shareholding is less than 10%).

The same is true of Australian individuals in receipt of foreign dividends; they are fully taxable on the dividends without dividend relief. There is consistency in this discriminatory treatment with the discriminatory treatment noted in scenario 2 (i.e. the distribution of foreign source income by a resident corporation). It was noted earlier at 3.1.1.4 that the Australian imputation system washes out corporate-level foreign tax relief and the shareholder effectively receives a classical treatment in scenario 2. So a classical treatment in scenario 6 is consistent. By comparison, if a US corporation derives foreign source income and distributes it to resident shareholders, dividend relief is available. As noted, this is not always the case in scenario 6, and so there is less consistency in this regard when compared to Australia.

The CCCTB Proposal would deny the inter-corporate dividend exemption if the distributing foreign corporation is resident in a non-EU country and is subject there to corporate tax at less than 40% of the EU average corporate tax rate, or is subject to a special low tax regime.[178] This would result in a classical treatment (i.e. economic double taxation). In addition, the CCCTB Proposal would make no provision for a direct foreign tax credit for any foreign tax imposed directly on the dividend, such as a dividend withholding tax.

### 3.2.3  Domestic income / resident shareholders: scenario 7

Scenario 7 involves a non-resident corporation deriving domestic source income and distributing it to a resident shareholder. It is similar to a purely domestic scenario (scenario 1) except for the residence of the corporation. It may seem that this is an unlikely scenario, but it is increasingly common as a result of cross-border mergers. Such a merger can involve as a target a resident corporation with resident shareholders (i.e. scenario 1). This type of merger involves the resident shareholders exchanging their shares in the resident corporation for shares in the non-resident corporation. The

---

[178]  CCCTB Proposal Art. 73.

resident corporation then distributes its profits to its new non-resident parent corporation, which in turn distributes at least some of those profits back to the resident shareholders.

Without a specialist regime, scenario 7 involves amalgamating the treatment in scenarios 5 and 6. As a result, it potentially involves five levels of tax. The domestic country is likely to subject the domestic profits to corporation tax. Some countries, like the US, may additionally seek to impose a branch profits tax. The foreign country may impose some residual corporation tax (e.g. under a foreign tax credit system). In addition, the foreign country may impose a dividend withholding tax on the dividend. Finally, the domestic country may impose residual tax on the dividend in the hands of the resident shareholder.

Historically, scenario 7 would result in at least a classical treatment, even if dividend relief would have been available in a purely domestic scenario (scenario 1). This, however, can no longer be presumed. There is a likelihood that the domestic country will now impose no more than its corporation tax (scenario 5) and that it might provide dividend relief for the dividend (scenario 6). Further, as far as the foreign country is concerned, this situation is scenario 4, in which case it may not impose tax on this flow-through income (see the earlier discussion at 3.1.3). So with the right mix of countries, it is possible that dividend relief could be provided in scenario 7. This is particularly likely within the EU.

So, for example, the UK would impose no more than its corporation tax on the foreign corporation and the same may be true in Germany. This is particularly likely as a result of the Parent-subsidiary Directive.[179] Further, both of these countries will apply their shareholder-level dividend relief systems to the dividend received from the foreign corporation. If the foreign country does not tax the flow-through income, the result in both the case of the UK and Germany is no more taxation than would have been levied in a purely domestic scenario.

This is less likely in the case of the US, largely because of the imposition of branch profits tax. As noted, there may also be cases in which the resident shareholder is denied dividend relief. However, the US has a special rule where the dividend from the foreign corporation comes back to a resident corporate shareholder. Dividends paid by a 10% foreign subsidiary (voting power and value) may qualify for the dividends-received deduction in the hands of its US parent.[180] The 70% or 80%

---

[179] *Parent-Subsidiary Directive*, Council Directive 90/435/EEC of 23 July 1990.
[180] IRC (US) s. 245.

dividends-received deduction (see the earlier discussion at 2.4.3.1) is available for a portion of the dividends, determined by reference to the ratio of the subsidiary's undistributed earnings from US sources to its total undistributed earnings.[181]

Just as the Australian imputation system is discriminatory in scenarios 2 and 6, it is also discriminatory in scenario 7. This is largely due to its failure to provide dividend relief with respect to foreign dividends (i.e. scenario 6). This discrimination seems particularly harsh and distorting when the classical treatment is caused by both domestic corporation tax and domestic shareholder tax and the only reason for not providing dividend relief is the residence of the corporation. Generally, the Australian imputation system accepts this discrimination. An isolated and complex exception to this discrimination involves an agreement with New Zealand.

It is possible for a New Zealand resident corporation to maintain a franking account to which is credited Australian corporation tax paid by the New Zealand corporation. The New Zealand corporation may then attach Australian imputation credits to its dividends. These credits are only usable by Australian shareholders in the New Zealand corporation.[182] They are valueless to New Zealand shareholders, and so the benefits of this system are limited to scenario 7. It is possible for Australian resident corporations to do the same thing under the New Zealand imputation system.

### 3.3   Extent of relief: whose corporate tax system?

If all countries adopted a classical system, a classical treatment with respect to the derivation and distribution of cross-border corporate income would be expected. There might be different overall levels of tax depending on comparative corporate tax rates, shareholder tax rates and the method of foreign tax relief provided (whether exemption or foreign tax credit). But there would be agreement on the refusal to provide dividend relief. This presumes that an international perspective is taken and it is agreed that there should be no discrimination against cross-border activity.

The same may be expected if two countries each adopt full dividend relief. There would be the same issues of corporate tax rate and forms of

---

[181] The 100% dividends-received deduction is not available because the foreign subsidiary cannot be a member of a US affiliated group. An exception is where the foreign subsidiary is wholly owned and treated as a US resident corporation.

[182] Generally, see Income Tax Assessment Act 1997 (Australia) Division 220.

foreign tax relief. In addition, as the earlier discussion has demonstrated, there might be difficulties caused by the countries adopting different methods of dividend relief. Corporate-level dividend relief systems suggest relief with respect to income derived by corporations but no relief for shareholder tax. Shareholder-level dividend relief systems suggest no relief with respect to income derived by corporations but relief with respect to shareholder tax. Be this as it may, it still seems clear that dividend relief should be provided in the cross-border scenario if both countries adopt full dividend relief. The same might be suggested if both countries adopt only partial dividend relief, but to the same extent.

But if two countries do not adopt the same level of dividend relief, should a shareholder in a cross-border scenario be granted dividend relief and if so to what extent? The earlier discussion has paid scant attention to jurisdiction to tax based on the residence of the corporation, and examples have been given of cases in which it is becoming increasingly irrelevant. This leaves substantive jurisdictions to tax with the country from where the corporation derives its income and the shareholder's country of residence. Focusing on these, which country's corporate tax system should dominate in determining whether a shareholder should receive dividend relief? An example demonstrates the issues.

A corporation (residence irrelevant) derives income from Country A and distributes it to a shareholder resident in Country B. Country A has a classical system and Country B provides dividend relief. Should the shareholder receive dividend relief? One approach is to suggest that, because other shareholders investing through a corporation into Country A do not receive dividend relief, neither should the shareholder in question. This is a particularly strong argument if the classical corporation tax is shifted onto other economic factors in Country A (e.g. employees or land). Alternately, it might be suggested that, because other Country B resident shareholders receive dividend relief, the shareholder in question should also receive dividend relief irrespective of from where the corporation derives its income. A third argument is that, because the shareholder owes economic allegiance to both countries, the shareholder should receive a treatment that mixes or averages the result in Countries A and B.[183] The same issues arise if the situation is reversed, and Country A provides dividend relief but Country B does not.

These are real issues and for some countries the situation has changed dramatically in the past forty years. Consider the situation in 1980

[183] For example, see Harris (1996, pp. 501–10).

between the UK and the US. At that time, the UK had its advanced corporation tax system and the US a full classical system. The UK extended dividend tax credits to US portfolio shareholders in UK corporations under the treaty practice discussed earlier at 3.1.2.4. This resulted in the US granting a direct foreign tax credit to the shareholders for some of the underlying UK corporation tax. The result was that the US shareholder received dividend relief when investing in a UK corporation, but not when investing in a US corporation. All shareholders in UK corporations received the same level of dividend relief. The reverse was also true. UK investors in US corporations would receive a classical treatment, even though they would receive dividend relief if they invested in a UK corporation. France produced similar results under many of its tax treaties.

The result of this treaty practice was that the level of dividend relief was determined by reference to the corporate tax system of the country in which the investment was made. Things started to change towards the end of the 1990s; the ECJ was particularly influential in this regard. It decided that a dividend relief country was not required to extend dividend relief to shareholders resident in other member states, provided that the dividend relief country did not attempt to tax outbound dividends.[184] In addition, it decided that a dividend relief country was required to extend the same dividend relief with respect to dividends from corporations in other member states as it does with respect to resident corporations.[185] The result was the opposite of the tax treaty practice of the UK, France and some other dividend relief countries.[186] This approach has now spread outside the EU, as the US form of dividend relief demonstrates.

Is this change in focus from the dividend relief system of the country of investment to the dividend relief system of the country of shareholder's residence an improvement? That seems debateable. Consider again the example given earlier. We now have a situation in which a person from a dividend relief country can invest into a classical country and yet still receive dividend relief. This seems bizarre when shareholders resident in the classical country do not receive such relief and so a foreign shareholder could be at an advantage. By contrast, there seems little wrong with granting shareholders resident in the same country different levels

---

[184] For example, see Case C-374/04 *Test Claimants in Class IV of the ACT Group Litigation* v. *IRC* [2006] ECR I-11673 (ECJ).

[185] For example, see Case C-35/98 *Secretaris van Financien* v. *Verkooijen* [2000] ECR I-4071 (ECJ) and Case C-319/02 *Manninen* [2004] ECR I-7477 (ECJ).

[186] Generally regarding these developments, see Harris (2010).

of relief if they are investing into countries that provide different levels of relief.

If countries are slowly harmonising around partial dividend relief systems then perhaps this is just academic. If the levels of dividend relief are broadly similar from country to country then it does not matter which country provides dividend relief. It seems too early yet to say that it does not matter. There is still a wide difference between the Australian full imputation system and the US dividend relief system. There is similarly, a wide difference between the Irish full classical system with a low corporate tax rate and the Brazilian dividend exclusion system with a high corporate tax rate. These differences are overlaid with the disturbing difference in treatment between debt and equity and what it means for exempt institutions investing in corporations. The treatment of debt is often the effective equivalent of a dividend deduction system with little or no investor-level tax in the country in which the funds are used. All these factors suggest that the international order is fragmented, inconsistent, distorting and positively harmful to the allocation and form of investments across borders through corporations.

# 4

# Creating share interests

Thus far, this book has considered the manner in which the artificiality of the corporation has an impact on the taxation of corporate income when derived by a corporation and when distributed by a corporation. In doing so, it has presumed that the ownership structure of the corporation is stable. The book now changes track to consider tax aspects where there is a change in the ownership structure of a corporation. Changes in the ownership structure of a corporation are predominantly affairs of capital, and so tax aspects associated with such changes are not relevant to the extent that a country does not tax capital gains.[1] Nevertheless, all countries face the issues considered in the rest of this book where assets or shares are held as part of a business or on revenue account or where the tax consequences of a change have an impact at the corporate level.

As noted in the introduction, changes of ownership of a corporation also highlight the artificiality of the corporation and, in particular, raise similar duplicity issues as those considered in the earlier chapters. The value of assets held by a corporation and generally the value of a corporation are reflected in the value of share interests held in the corporation. In this sense, shares are true derivatives in that they derive their value from value held at the corporate level. The problems this causes for a tax system can be highlighted with a simple example.

Assume an individual has £100. That is an asset that the tax system must recognise and track the consequences of. Now presume that the individual uses that £100 to subscribe for shares in a corporation. After the shares are issued, there are two assets. The corporation has the actual £100, but now the individual has shares that in a simple case may be

---

[1] Many common law jurisdictions still do not tax capital gains per se (e.g. New Zealand, Singapore and Malaysia), whereas many other jurisdictions do not tax capital gains fully or exempt some types of capital gains, particularly of individuals. This is the case in Germany, for example.

presumed to be worth the same amount (i.e. £100). Instead of seeing one asset, now the tax system must track two sets of assets: the original £100 now held by the corporation and the shares worth £100. Of course, in reality there is only one asset, the original £100, but that asset is reflected in the second asset being the shares. Like so many reflections, the reflective asset (the shares) may be distorted and shaped to the wants of persons controlling the artificial entity that is the corporation. This sort of duplicity, which is a function of the fact that corporations are fictions, is at the heart of the complexity of many corporate tax systems.

The situation becomes worse where corporations hold shares in other corporations. Assume that the corporation that has the £100 (A Co) now subscribes for £100 shares in B Co, and B Co subscribes for £100 of shares in C Co, and C Co in D Co. Now the tax system must recognise and track £500 (the actual £100 plus the A Co, B Co, C Co and D Co shares each worth £100), when in fact there is only £100. Further, presume that D Co makes a profit from use of the actual £100. This profit will be reflected as an unrealised gain in the shares held in D Co, and the shares held in C Co, B Co and A Co. Worse still, if D Co makes a loss, that loss will be duplicated in the value of the shares up the chain. These gains and losses are not real – they are reflective – but nevertheless the tax system must find some way of dealing with them.

Corporate law also has to deal with this sort of issue when facing compensation for wrongs done to a corporation. A wrong suffered by a corporation may also be reflected in the value of its shares and constitute a wrong done to shareholders. Courts have struggled with when to deny a shareholder a right to compensation because the shareholder's loss is merely a reflection of a loss suffered by the corporation.[2] However, it is fair to suggest, at least in the UK, that the corporate law prohibition on recovery of reflective loss is less developed than tax law rules designed to prevent duplicative gains and losses. Again, it must be emphasised that this is a problem that stems directly from the fact that corporations are not real.

As mentioned, the rest of this book is concerned in one way or another with changes in a corporation's ownership structure. The ownership structure of a corporation is altered by dealing in share interests in the corporation. The difficult issue of how a corporate tax system should

---

[2] For example, in the UK see *Johnson* v. *Gore Wood & Co* [2002] 2 AC 1 (HL) and in the US see *Tooley* v. *Donaldson, Lufkin & Jenrette, Inc* (2004) 845 A 2d 1031 (SC Delaware). In Germany, the reflective loss problem appears in AktG (Germany) s. 117(1). Also, see Cahn & Donald (2010, p. 602).

identify shares was discussed earlier at 2.1. This chapter and Chapters 5–8 presume that the investment in question is shares, and so the issues discussed at 2.1 are not repeated.

Share interests may be created, transferred, terminated and varied. This chapter begins by considering tax aspects of the creation of share interests, especially the tax consequences of the issue of shares by a corporation. Shares may be issued for cash or in return for assets. Shares issued for cash raise few income tax issues, but a brief consideration of those issues assists in highlighting the artificial and derivative nature of shares.

Shares issued for assets involve the additional issue of the prospective shareholder disposing of those assets (in return for the shares). Commonly, this is a related party transaction because the corporation is controlled by the person to whom the shares are issued, or by persons related to that person. Such a disposal from one person to another would typically involve a realisation of any gains or losses associated with the assets and so have tax consequences. However, given the artificial nature of the corporation, even after the contribution of the assets in return for shares, there is an argument that the contributor is still in substance (or at least indirectly) the owner of the assets. If this position is accepted, the consequence would be that the contribution of assets to a corporation in return for shares should not be treated as a realisation event, but rather some form of tax relief should be provided.

This chapter first considers the simple issue of shares, whether for cash or in return for assets. In particular, in the case of a contribution of assets it does not presume that the assets are part of a business that is being transferred to the corporation (i.e. it does not presume the incorporation of a business). Many countries have special rules where a person contributes a business in return for shares in a corporation. So it is appropriate to consider the tax consequences of the transfer of a business to a corporation separately. That consideration is discussed under the second heading of this chapter.

## 4.1   Issue of shares

### 4.1.1   In return for cash

The issue of shares for cash is perhaps the simplest scenario in which shares are issued. Inevitably, there are no immediate income tax consequences of such an issue, although there may be transaction tax consequences to be considered (e.g. stamp duty). Nevertheless, the issue of shares, even in this simple scenario, raises a number of structural matters that it is useful to briefly explore. A consideration of these issues aids an understanding of some of the more complex issues considered in the remainder of this book.

The distinction between par value and non-par value shares was mentioned earlier at 2.5.2.1 and involves the question as to whether shares are allocated a set capital amount. In many ways, the par value of a share is a notional or fictitious amount. An acquirer of shares pays the corporation the same amount for an issue whether or not the shares are assigned a par value. In the case of non-par value shares, the price paid is the issue price and most likely will be considered share capital in the hands of the corporation.

In the case of par value shares, only the par value is considered share (or statutory) capital. The par value of shares represents the extent of liability of the shareholder in the context of a limited liability corporation. If the par value is only partly paid on issue (or the shares are limited by guarantee), the shareholder is liable for the remainder in specified circumstances, typically when the directors make a call on the unpaid capital. The issue price in excess of the par value (whether paid up or not paid up) is the premium, which is typically credited to a share premium account or capital reserve.

Most countries adopting the par value approach treat credit in the share premium account in a similar fashion to credit in the share capital account. This similar treatment is particularly important when it comes to returns of capital and the application of any maintenance of capital doctrine. Nevertheless, there can be important differences in the treatment of credit in the share premium account and credit in the share capital account. For example, in most par value jurisdictions it is possible to pay up the par value of bonus shares by using credit in the share premium account (i.e. by transferring credit between the two accounts).[3]

In the EU, par value shares are still the norm. The Second Company Law Directive was amended in 2006 to permit corporations to have shares with an 'accountable par' instead of a notional par value.[4] Although the UK still adheres to par value, Germany now (at least in form) permits no par value

[3] AktG (Germany) s. 207 (subject to the limits in s. 150(4)) and Companies Act 2006 (UK) s. 610.
[4] *Second Company Law Directive*, Council Directive 77/91/EEC of 13 December 1976 Art. 8(1).

shares.[5] As noted at a number of points in this book, in the US corporations are typically regulated by state law. In most US states the adoption of par value for shares is optional. For example, this is the case under the MBCA and under the DGCL.[6] Other examples of countries where par value is not required are Australia and Canada.

Another structural issue concerns the tax classification of the issue of shares. Shares are property, and to a non-lawyer it may seem like shares are disposed of by the issuing corporation to the acquirer. If this were the case, the issue of shares may result in capital gains tax consequences for the issuing corporation. In a worst case scenario, the corporation's cost base in the shares would be nil, and so the whole amount received on issue would constitute a taxable gain of the issuing corporation. Such a tax liability would create a major disincentive for issuing shares and so a major distortion between raising capital by way of debt or equity (share capital).

The issue of debt does not create tax consequences. This is because the funds received when issuing debt are not a profit or gain. The cash received on issue is most often offset by the liability to pay interest and repay the loan funds when the term of the loan expires. Perhaps it is best to think of the receipt of share capital by a corporation in the same fashion. Share capital is received in return for the corporation agreeing to pay dividends and repay the share capital in the case of a liquidation (presuming the corporation to be solvent). Adopting this view is particularly consistent with the corporation being a separate entity from its shareholders. If a transparent view of the corporation is adopted for tax purposes, then it might be suggested that the contribution of share capital to a corporation is no different from the contribution of capital to a business conducted by a partnership or sole trader. On this view, the issue of share capital is not a transaction of sufficient substance so as to require recognition for tax purposes.

Some countries' tax laws recognise the receipt of share capital as an issue and expressly deal with it, whereas other tax laws ignore the issue. US income tax law is particularly explicit in ignoring the receipt of share capital. Capital contributions to a corporation are expressly excluded from the gross income of the corporation.[7] Similarly, US income tax law

---

[5] Companies Act 2006 (UK) s. 10 and AktG (Germany) s. 8(3). No par value shares may be more formal than real in Germany because they are allocated contributed capital on a pro-rata basis.

[6] MBCA (US) s. 2.02 and DGCL (US) s. 102(a)(4).

[7] IRC (US) s. 118(a).

recognizes no gain or loss when a corporation receives money or other amounts in return for the issue of its shares.[8] The CCCTB Proposal is similarly explicit. 'Revenues shall not include equity raised by the taxpayer,'[9] and there is no definition of 'equity'.

In Germany the tax law is less direct. All income of a corporation is treated as business income and calculated according to the business income rules in the Income Tax Law.[10] Under the Income Tax Law, business income is calculated based on profit, which is defined as the difference between the fiscal balance sheet at the start of the year and that at the end of the year. Profits are expressly reduced for capital contributions received, which include share capital received by a corporation.[11]

UK tax law does not directly deal with the treatment of share capital received by an issuing corporation. The issue of shares would be considered an affair of capital, and so only capital gains treatment is relevant. Generally, all gains accruing on the disposal of assets are chargeable gains.[12] Shares are clearly an asset, but there is no definition of 'disposal'. The better view is that a disposal (other than a deemed disposal under the tax law) involves a change in ownership or a divestiture of rights in an asset.[13] On this view, the issue of shares is not a disposal because the corporation does not own the shares prior to their issue. The result is that a corporation does not realise a chargeable gain on the issue of shares.

### 4.1.2   In return for non-business assets

All countries accept that the disposal of local currency is a non-tax event. So if a person pays for the issue of shares with cash, the fact that the person has disposed of an asset (local currency) has no tax consequences. This is not the case where the person pays for the shares in a form other than local cash (e.g. by transferring an asset to the issuing corporation). Here, the person disposes of the asset used to pay for the shares, and in principle, a tax liability may attach to that disposal.

Consider the situation in which the person pays for shares by transferring land to the corporation. The person has disposed of the land, the consideration received for the disposal being the shares. Through one

---

[8]  IRC (US) s. 1032(a).
[9]  CCCTB Proposal Art. 4(8).
[10]  KStG (Germany) s. 8(1).
[11]  EStG (Germany) s. 4(1).
[12]  TCGA 1992 (UK) s. 15.
[13]  For example, see Tiley (2008, p. 709).

means or another, it is likely that the residual position under the tax law is that the person will be treated as having received the market value of the land in respect of the disposal. This will be because the transaction is treated as not having been made at arm's length or because the shares will be valued as increased by the value of the land (taken at market value).

Some countries recognise that this treatment can create a disincentive for contributing assets to a corporation in return for shares, and those countries provide relief from the tax liability that would otherwise arise. At this stage it is presumed that the asset contributed to the corporation is isolated and is not transferred to the corporation as part of a business (i.e. it is presumed that what is transferred is a non-depreciable capital asset). Although some of the rules considered in the present discussion are relevant to the tax treatment on incorporation of a business, that specific tax treatment is considered later at 4.2. The present discussion first considers the situation where an individual contributes the asset to a corporation in return for shares and then the situation in which another corporation contributes the asset to a corporation in return for shares.

### 4.1.2.1   From an individual

Germany provides no express relief where an individual contributes assets to a corporation in return for shares unless the contribution is part of the contribution of a business to the corporation (discussed later at 4.2). However, the German income tax system incorporates a limited scope for the taxation of gains of individuals on the disposal of assets outside a business. This is a function of the schedular system and the fact that the residual income category generally requires an element of recurrence.[14] The shares received by the individual would have a cost equal to the fair market value of the asset transferred.[15] This would also be the cost of the asset in the hands of the corporation.

By contrast, the UK tax system incorporates a comparatively comprehensive taxation of capital gains, including those realised by an individual, although with a substantial annual exemption (in excess of £10,000). Like Germany, the UK has no generally applicable tax relief for individuals contributing passive assets to a corporation. This means that the contribution of a passive asset to a corporation in return for shares might give rise to the taxation of unrealised gains. If the exchange is between connected persons, not at arm's length or the shares received in return cannot

---

[14]  EStG (Germany) s. 22.
[15]  EStG (Germany) s. 6(6).

be valued, the taxation will be of the excess of market value over the cost of the asset.[16]

The US has a special rule on 'corporate organisations' that may provide relief in the present context. Section 351 of the IRC provides,

> No gain or loss shall be recognized if property is transferred to a corporation by one or more persons solely in exchange for stock in such corporation and immediately after the exchange such person or persons are in control... of the corporation.[17]

This provision applies automatically and so at a general level would prevent a person from transferring an asset to a controlled corporation in order to crystallise a loss. The provision is limited to transfers of 'property' and so does not usually apply to shares issued in return for services rendered.[18] However, there is no requirement that the contributed property be used in the context of a business at the time of transfer nor that any other property be transferred at the same time. Special apportionment rules apply where consideration in addition to shares ('boot') is received for the transfer.

A major limitation on this US relief is that after the exchange the transferor must 'control' the corporation. The test for control is similar, but not the same as those discussed in other contexts in this book (e.g. see the earlier discussion at 1.1.5.1). It requires a holding of at least 80% in terms of voting power and also 80% of all classes of shares not entitled to vote.[19] Much tax planning is devoted to manipulating this restriction – especially because section 351 expressly permits more than one person to transfer assets to a corporation and it is their joint holding that counts for purposes of determining whether the control requirement is met. This sort of issue involving difficulty in grouping persons was discussed earlier at 1.1.5.1. Two unrelated persons may transfer assets to a corporation under the protection of section 351 even though the indirect consequence is that they indirectly gain an interest in each other's asset.

As noted in the introduction to this chapter, whenever shares are created there is a duplication of the money or asset that is used to pay for the shares. If a country like the US defers recognition of gain or loss on the transfer of an asset to a corporation in exchange for shares, a difficult

---

[16] TCGA 1992 (UK) ss. 17 & 18.
[17] IRC (US) s. 351(a).
[18] In particular, see IRC (US) s. 351(d).
[19] IRC (US) s. 368(c).

policy issue arises regarding the treatment of disposals after the exchange. Again, this is best illustrated by an example.

Assume an individual owns land that cost $100 but has a market value of $150. The individual contributes the land to a corporation in return for shares, and the tax system in question does not recognise the gain at the point of exchange. The value of the land has now been duplicated for tax purposes: the real land is owned by the corporation, but its value is reflected in the shares issued in exchange for it. This raises two issues for the tax system. The first is what should be the cost of the shares for tax purposes in the hands of the individual who formerly owned the land. The second is what should be the cost of the land for tax purposes in the hands of the corporation. The fundamental question is whether the gain on the land that was deferred should be duplicated (as the value of the land is) or whether after the transfer there should still be only a single gain.

Duplicating the gain may result in economic double taxation in given circumstances; for example, the sale of the land by the corporation and, either before or after that sale, the sale of the shares by the individual (but before the proceeds from the sale of land are distributed). If the land incorporates an unrealised loss, then the problem is rather one of loss duplication. These scenarios primarily involve the sale of shares and so are discussed further at 5.1. If the gain is not duplicated, other problems arise. Here either the land in the hands of the corporation or the shares in the hands of the individual will be given a market value cost for tax purposes. This valuation provides an easy route for avoiding tax as an extension of the example demonstrates.

Presume the real intention of the individual is to sell the land, but if the individual does so directly he or she will be subject to tax on the gain (i.e. taxed on $50). To avoid this tax liability, the individual could transfer the land to a corporation on a no gain basis. It would then be possible to sell either the land or the shares in the corporation (and thereby the land) to the third party. The individual would choose to sell the asset that had been given a market value for tax purposes (i.e. the one that would not give rise to a tax liability). This practice is commonly referred to as 'enveloping' an asset (i.e. wrapping it up in a corporation). The issues discussed in the past few paragraphs are issues inherent in creating shares and are a general theme of the rest of this book.

Perhaps the majority of countries that provide tax relief where assets are contributed to a corporation accept the potential for double taxation. One reason for this is to prevent the type of avoidance mentioned in the last paragraph. Another might be that taxpayers can avoid the double taxation by distributing profits out of a corporation and thereby lowering the share value, discussed further at 5.1.2. The US is such a country. Where section 351 of IRC applies, the shares acquired by the individual take their cost for tax purposes from the property transferred to the corporation.[20] So in the example of the land with a built-in gain of $50, the cost base of the shares in the hands of the shareholder would be $100. Presuming the value of the shares after the transaction equals the value of the land (i.e. $150), the shares also have a built-in gain of $50. This gain would be duplicated at the corporate level. This is because the corporation also takes the land with a cost base equal to the cost base in the hands of the transferring individual (i.e. $100).[21]

### 4.1.2.2 From another corporation

Although there are many situations in which a corporation may contribute an asset to another corporation in return for shares, it is a common occurrence within the context of corporate groups. As a result, there is often an overlap between this scenario and the deferral of transactions in the context of corporate groups, considered earlier at 1.2.3.1. For example, although the UK does not generally provide relief from gains on the contribution of passive assets for shares, the rules for transfer of an asset on a no gain / no loss basis discussed earlier at 1.2.3.1 may apply to transfers between members of a 75% controlled group. The position would be similar under the rules of the CCCTB Proposal, also discussed at that point.

Germany has no express provision for deferral of recognition of transactions between group members, and it has no express deferral for contributions of passive assets in return for shares. However, recall that when it comes to corporations, Germany generally considers their activities to be business activities.[22] Therefore, the rules discussed later at 4.2 in the context of contributions of business assets in return for shares generally apply.

The US position is somewhat complicated. The rules for deferral of transactions in the context of a group of corporations filing a consolidated return (discussed earlier at 1.2.3.1) may apply. It is also possible that section 351 of IRC (discussed earlier at 4.1.2.1 in the context of individuals) applies to contributions of assets by corporations in return for shares

---

[20] IRC (US) s. 358(a).
[21] IRC (US) s. 362(a).
[22] KStG (Germany) s. 8(3).

(i.e. that provision is not limited to individuals making contributions). A further possibility is section 361, which deals with corporate reorganisations. The reorganisation rules are primarily discussed in Chapter 7. The contribution of an asset by a parent corporation to an 80% subsidiary in return for shares might constitute a type 'D' reorganisation.[23] If so, section 361 provides that the parent will recognise no gain or loss on the transfer. It is accepted that there may be overlap between sections 351 and 361 in particular cases.[24]

The distinction between the section 351 relief and the reorganisation rules in the US can be important. If an exchange qualifies under the reorganisation rules, the transferee (issuing corporation) may be able to take over some of the transferor's tax attributes, including loss carry-forwards, earnings and profits position and the cost of trading stock (inventory) and depreciable assets.[25] This will only be the case if the subsidiary receives 'substantially all' of the parent's assets.[26] This relief is primarily focused at the transfer of businesses, but can have application outside this context. There is no similar transfer of tax attributes if section 351 is used.

## 4.2  Transfer of a business: incorporation

This heading considers the transfer of assets to a corporation in return for the issue of shares. However, it focuses on the situation where the assets transferred are the whole or part of a business as a going concern. For some countries, such as the US, and under the CCCTB Proposal, whether or not the assets are the whole or part of a business makes little difference, and the general rules discussed earlier at 4.1.2 apply. For other countries, such as Germany and the UK, there are special concessionary rules for incorporations of a business, particularly by an individual. Sometimes these rules treat all assets of a business in the same manner, such as in Germany. In other cases, each of the different types of assets held by a business must be considered to determine the tax consequences on incorporation. This is the position in the UK.

---

[23] See IRC (US) s. 368(a)(1), defining 'reorganisation'. In form, the incorporation of a subsidiary might also constitute a type 'C' reorganisation, but in such a case s. 368(a)(2)(A) gives primacy to the type 'D' reorganisation provisions. Nevertheless, it is possible for a s. 351 transaction to also constitute a type C reorganisation' see Bittker and Eustice (2003–, para. 12.24[5]).

[24] See Bittker and Eustice (2003–, para. 3.19).

[25] IRC (US) s. 381

[26] IRC (US) s. 354(b)(1).

As a preliminary matter, presuming an individual has an existing business, there is the basic issue of why incorporate the business. There may be many non-tax reasons for incorporation, such as a desire to secure limited liability, raise funds from external sources and provide a mechanism for succession. These are beyond the scope of this book, which is only concerned with tax matters. From a tax perspective, this book has already considered several reasons why an individual might consider incorporation. In particular, the corporate tax rate, especially with respect to retained profits, might be lower than the rate the individual faces if deriving income directly (see the earlier discussion at 1.3). In addition, a corporation has the potential to employ the controller as well as other family members and provides other mechanisms to split income through streaming the payment of dividends, if doing so reduces tax (see the earlier discussion at 2.3.2 and 2.4.1.5).

Germany has a dedicated law dealing with the tax effects of qualifying corporate reorganisations; the Reorganisation Tax Law (*Umwandlungssteuergesetz*). In particular, section 20 applies where 'a business, business division or a partnership holding is contributed to a company...in exchange for newly issued shares in the company'.[27] This provision can apply to both individuals and corporations incorporating a business or part thereof. There is no express requirement (as in the US) that the contributor hold any particular percentage of the recipient (issuing) corporation after the exchange. However, what is transferred must be an entire business or at least a 'business division' (*Teilbetrieb*). Again, this is different from the US rule that applies on an asset-by-asset basis.

The Reorganisation Tax Law has no definition of what constitutes a business division. The expression is interpreted according to judicial decisions, which require that what is transferred is a viable part of a business that is independent from an organizational perspective from the rest of the business. There is no requirement that the business unit be totally independent or that it maintain its own accounts. However, the tax administration requires that a qualifying independent business division must comprise all operational assets necessary for the continuation of the business. In practice, this is decided on a case-by-case basis. Whether what is being transferred is a business division is a common subject of a request for a binding ruling from the tax administration.

As a residual rule, the Reorganisation Tax Law says (since it was tightened in 2006) that the transfer for shares is taken to be for market value,

---

[27] UmwStG (Germany) s. 20(1).

which would realise any gain for the contributor of the asset. This is also
the value that the recipient corporation must recognise in its accounts.
However, a request can be made of the tax administration that the recipient corporation enter the transferred assets at the value entered in the
transferor's tax accounts or any amount between that value and market
value. The value entered in the recipient corporation's accounts cannot
exceed market value.[28]

This valuation of assets by the recipient corporation does not of itself
provide any relief for the transferor (contributor), but it does set the acquisition cost of the assets for the recipient corporation. Section 20 goes on to
deal with the transferor. The value at which the recipient corporation takes
up the assets in its accounts is treated as both the sales proceeds received
by the contributor for the transfer of the assets and the acquisition cost of
the shares received in exchange.[29]

The effect of these rules is similar to that in the US discussed earlier
at 4.1.2.1. Unrealised gains imbedded in assets of a business at the point
of incorporation can be deferred, but those gains are duplicated (i.e. the
assets continue to incorporate the unrealised gain in the hands of the
corporation, and the shares in the corporation also incorporate any such
gain). However, there are several differences from the US provision. The
fact that the contributor (incorporator) need not control the corporation
after the contribution has been mentioned. The German relief is a matter
of taxpayer choice and does not apply automatically, which can be important where losses are imbedded in assets. Further, because the recipient
corporation can value the assets received anywhere between cost and market value, the parties can choose the extent to which any gain is realised.
Unlike the US reorganisation rules, it is not possible in Germany to transfer carried-forward tax losses of the business to the recipient corporation
along with the business.

The flexibility of the German rules also provides some scope for abuse.
Gains on business assets are fully taxable, but gains on shares are often subject to partial taxation for both individuals and corporations (discussed
later at 5.1.3). So it would be possible for a person intending to sell a business to first envelope the business in a corporation and then sell the shares
in the corporation (rather than the business itself) with a tax advantage.
This incentive is overcome by a special rule. If a person defers taxation of
a gain on incorporation and then sells the shares received within seven
years, any gain on the disposal of the shares (up to the amount of the

---

[28] UmwStG (Germany) s. 20(2).
[29] UmwStG (Germany) s. 20(3).

deferred gain) is treated and taxed as business income.[30] This means tax at marginal rates for individuals or full taxation for corporations (in the year of sale of the shares), not the preferential taxation otherwise applicable to gains on the disposal of shares. The amount that may be deemed to be business income in this way is reduced by one-seventh for every year after the incorporation.

The German rules do not distinguish between different types of assets. In particular, depreciation claimed in respect of assets reduces the value assigned to them in the tax balance sheet. The position is fundamentally different in countries that do not use the tax balance sheet approach, such as the UK. In the UK, the effects of incorporation must be considered for each of the different types of assets that may be used in a business. In particular, separate consideration must be given to the transfer of trading stock, capital assets for which capital allowances (depreciation) are available and other capital assets. In addition, the rules for individuals incorporating a business are slightly different from those for a corporation incorporating a business in the form of a subsidiary. These features make the UK approach particularly complex (and confusing).

The contribution of trading stock of an individual to a corporation in return for shares is a disposal of the stock. The individual will have received the shares as consideration for the disposal, and this may give rise to chargeable income of the individual. In addition, if the individual is connected with the corporation, the individual may be required to treat the disposal as having been made for market value.[31] An individual is connected with a corporation if he or she has 'control' of the corporation. 'Connected persons' and 'control' were discussed earlier at 1.1.5.1.

Nevertheless, if the individual is connected with the corporation and the exchange would result in a charge to tax for the individual, relief is available that permits the sale to be treated as taking place at cost (if that is less than market value).[32] The provision providing relief is not without difficulties, but it is widely accepted that it has this effect. This is the value for trading stock (income tax) purposes and does not specify the cost of the shares received from the corporation in return. It is regulated by TCGA 1992. There are no special rules for this purpose, and it appears that it usually is the market value of the trading stock contributed (see the later discussion).

---

[30] UmwStG (Germany) s. 22(1).
[31] ITTOIA 2005 (UK) s. 177(1).
[32] ITTOIA 2005 (UK) s. 178(1).

Next it is easier to consider the contribution of a capital asset for which no capital allowances are available (e.g. land, buildings or goodwill). Here there are two routes available to relief, the difference being in the cost base in the hands of the recipient corporation. The apparently more favourable relief is that in section 162 of TCGA 1992, which applies where an individual 'transfers to a company a business as a going concern, together with the whole assets of the business'. This provision is particularly restrictive as to qualification, and the withholding of any business assets from the transfer will compromise application of the relief. This restriction is particularly problematic with the contribution of assets that might be subject to stamp duty, such as land. As with the German rule, the transferor need not hold any particular percentage of the issuing corporation after the transfer.

Section 162 is on its face compulsory, but section 162A of TCGA 1992 grants the transferor an election to dis-apply section 162. This might happen if the individual wishes to realise a gain in order to use the annual personal exemption.[33] Where it applies, section 162 prescribes that any gain on the transfer of the asset be computed and allocated to the shares received in return (and any other consideration). Any gain allocated to other consideration is chargeable immediately, but that allocated to the shares is not. Rather, the gain allocated to the shares is deducted from their cost when the shares are disposed of. So any gain deferred at the point of exchange will be recaptured when the shares are sold.[34]

What section 162 does not do is prescribe the cost of the contributed assets in the hands of the recipient corporation. Presuming that the exchange is between connected persons or otherwise not at arm's length, it seems the corporation receives a market value cost base.[35] Unlike the US and German examples, this means that the UK approach avoids the doubling of any deferred gain. This also means that the UK has historically had difficulties with the 'enveloping' problem.[36] A number of

---

[33]  The personal exemption from taxation of chargeable gains for individuals is now in excess of £10,000; TCGA 1992 (UK) s. 3. It may also be advantageous to leave the sale price of assets contributed to a corporation outstanding as a loan, which can be drawn down tax free over a number of years instead of paying dividends. This is often the case if there is goodwill transferred to the corporation that has a substantial market value.

[34]  TCGA 1992 (UK) s. 162 sets the cost base of all shares received on incorporation of a business. This includes shares received in return for trading stock and assets for which capital allowances are available. The relief from immediate taxation only applies proportionately to chargeable gains arising on other assets.

[35]  TCGA 1992 (UK) ss. 17 & 18.

[36]  This problem is limited to capital assets for which capital allowances (depreciation) are not available. The tax position (cost) of trading stock and capital assets for which capital

high-profile anti-avoidance cases have involved individuals transferring businesses to a corporation and then shortly afterwards selling the business out of the hands of the corporation.[37] Because the corporation receives a market value cost base, there is no unrealised gain for the corporation with respect to the assets. The gain is still trapped in the shares in the corporation, but they are not likely to be disposed of.

As mentioned, the downside to use of section 162 is that all of the assets of a business must be transferred, and this transfer may have transaction costs. The alternate tax deferral route is to use section 165 of TCGA 1992, which applies to gifts of assets used for the purposes of a trade. This rule provides relief on an asset-by-asset basis, but only applies to the extent that consideration is not received by the contributor in return. So a standard route to use of this relief is to incorporate a company that issues shares to the controlling individual and then for the individual to subsequently contribute assets to the corporation for little or no consideration. Section 165 effectively requires the corporation to take the transferor's cost in the asset transferred and can be contrasted with the potential step-up in cost to market value under the section 162 route. This can result in the usual duplication of any gain imbedded in the asset (and if no shares are issued in return, sometimes worse). This route is most commonly used when the individual does not intend to sell the shares in the recipient corporation in the near future.

In the UK, capital allowances are granted instead of recognising depreciation of assets. The assets for which capital allowances are available are much narrower than accounting depreciation. The capital allowances regime is in many ways independent of, but integrated into income tax and capital gains tax for individuals. There is the usual recapture of excess allowances, meaning that if the loss on a disposal of an asset for which allowances have been granted is less than the allowances granted, the excess must be included in income of the year of disposal (balancing charge).[38] However, a pooling system is used for most types of plant and machinery (few allowances are granted outside these categories); this means that balancing charges are delayed, and not imposed until the

---

allowances are available is not 'stepped up' to market value in the hands of the corporation where a deferral of tax liability is granted to the contributor on incorporation. So in these cases there may be a duplication of unrealised gain at the corporate level and with respect to the shares received in exchange (presuming TCGA 1992 (UK) s. 162 applies).

[37] See *Furniss* v. *Dawson* [1984] AC 474 (HL) and the other cases discussed in Tiley (2008, pp. 117–20).

[38] CAA 2001 (UK) ss. 55 & 247.

balance of expenditure in the pool has been exhausted. The capital allowances regime is not explored in any detail in this book.[39]

Capital gains treatment (as discussed earlier) also applies to assets for which capital allowances are granted and is in many ways independent. It applies on an asset-by-asset basis (in contrast to the capital allowances pooled basis), and the cost of assets is not written down for capital allowances granted.[40] Capital gains treatment tends to be relevant only where a gain is made on the disposal of an asset for which capital allowances have been granted. The overall position in the UK is unnecessarily complex.

If an individual asset for which capital allowances are granted is contributed to a corporation from the business of an individual (in exchange for shares), the disposal receipts are the value of the shares (up to the original cost of the asset contributed).[41] However, any balancing charge is likely to be deferred through the pooling system. This is likely to be different if an individual incorporates the whole of a business, and so all assets in a capital allowances pool are disposed of. The incorporation of a business may give rise to a balancing charge (where the disposal value of plant and machinery is more than its written-down value) and so be a tax liability in the hands of the individual. However, relief independent of that for trading stock or capital gains is provided.

Section 266 of CAA 2001 applies if a person (the corporation) succeeds to a trade that was carried on by another person (the individual) who is connected with the first person. An individual is connected with a corporation if the individual has 'control' of the corporation. 'Connected persons' and 'control' were discussed earlier at 1.1.5.1 and are similar (but not identical) to those used in the context of the trading stock provisions discussed earlier. Where section 266 applies, the individual and the corporation may jointly elect that the plant and machinery are disposed of for a price that would give 'rise to neither a balancing allowance nor a balancing charge'.[42] The corporation then takes over the individual's capital allowances position with respect to the plant and machinery.[43]

As with the trading stock provisions and section 165 of the TCGA 1992, the effect of this relief under the capital allowances provision may be to

---

[39] Generally regarding the capital allowances regime, see Tiley (2008, chapter 24).

[40] TCGA 1992 (UK) s. 41(1). However, any capital loss arising on disposal of an asset is excluded to the extent of capital allowances granted with respect to the asset.

[41] CAA 2001 (UK) ss. 61 & 62.

[42] CAA 2001 (UK) s. 267(2).

[43] CAA 2001 (UK) s. 267(4).

duplicate any gain (by reference to the written-down value of the assets). This will be the case if section 162 applies to also capture the gain in the cost of the shares in the hands of the individual (but an individual may elect for that provision not to apply). As discussed earlier, the only exceptions are capital assets that fall into none of these regimes, where there is the potential for a step-up in cost in the hands of the corporation.

There is one other UK provision worthy of mention where an individual transfers a trade to a corporation (i.e. incorporates a business). Recall from the earlier discussion at 1.2.3.2 that the UK quarantines the use of trading losses carried forward (i.e. they can only be used against future profits of that particular trade).[44] This could be a disincentive to incorporate a trade where the individual is carrying forward losses, because after the transfer of the trade the trading losses in the hands of the individual would be isolated and worthless. A special provision permits the individual to continue to use the trading losses carried forward against any income received by the individual from the corporation to which the trade was transferred.[45] The income from the corporation against which the losses can be used can be any type of income – dividends, rent, interest, employment income or otherwise.

This long and convoluted series of provisions for UK individuals incorporating a business are repeated in a varied form where a corporation seeks to incorporate a business or transfer business assets to another corporation in return for shares. Broadly, there is similar relief for the contribution of trading stock where the transferor and transferee are connected persons.[46] For the transfer of capital assets, a chargeable gain may arise unless the deferral for transfers between group corporations is available; this deferral was discussed earlier at 1.2.3.1. Otherwise, there is no equivalent for corporations to sections 162 and 165 of TCGA 1992, which only apply to individuals.

The capital allowances position is also different where a trade is transferred by one corporation to another corporation. The rules in chapter 1 of Part 22 of CTA 2010 are particularly important in tax planning in the UK. These rules only apply where a trade is transferred between corporations that are under common ownership.[47] Broadly, this requires a 75% level of common ownership, but the test is very different from that applied in the

---

[44] The quarantining rule for individuals is in ITA 2007 (UK) s. 83.
[45] ITA 2007 (UK) s. 86.
[46] CTA 2009 (UK) s. 167.
[47] CTA 2010 (UK) s. 938.

context of group corporations (discussed earlier at 1.2.3).[48] In particular, the testing period of the share ownership is different, as is the manner in which intermediate shareholdings may be looked through.[49]

Where these rules apply, then as with the provision discussed earlier in the context of individuals, the transferee takes over the transferor's capital allowances position with respect to assets transferred. As a result, there is again deferral of any balancing charge.[50] These rules also cover losses carried forward with respect to the trade transferred, which is again different from the situation where an individual transfers a trade to a corporation. Rather than the transferor being able to continue to use the losses against other income, where the transfer of the trade is between corporations the losses are transferred to the transferee.[51] This treatment is only available for trading losses, and other types of losses (including capital losses) stay with the transferor. The importance of this loss transfer rule in tax planning should not be underestimated; it is often used when selling a trade. The trade is transferred to a new subsidiary (hive down) together with any losses. The shares in the new subsidiary are then sold to the buyer, which takes the subsidiary and the losses. This is further considered at 5.2.1.2.

Finally, it is worth briefly mentioning the transfer of a business from a partnership to a corporation. Each of the manners of incorporation relief provided by Germany, the UK and the US can be used when incorporating the business of a partnership; for example, section 351 of the US's IRC and section 20 of Germany's Reorganisation Tax Law. By and large the plethora of rules that apply in the UK can also be used to provide relief. In particular, it is generally accepted that the incorporation relief in section 162 of TCGA 1992 can apply in the context of the incorporation of a partnership interest of an individual.[52]

---

[48] CTA 2010 (UK) s. 941.
[49] CTA 2010 (UK) s. 942. These rules effectively mean that the corporate veil need not be pierced beyond the trading company, but this is possible if it results in qualification. In principle, these rules are more favourable for the taxpayer than the group relief rules.
[50] CTA 2010 (UK) s. 948.
[51] CTA 2010 (UK) s. 944.
[52] For example, see *Gordan* v. IRC [1991] STC 174 (Crt of Session).

# 5

## Transferring share interests

The duplicative nature of corporate assets and their reflection in the value of shares were noted at the start of Chapter 4. That chapter dealt with the creation of shares, and a primary issue was determining the tax value of the reflective asset when shares are issued. It was noted how unrealised gains or losses may be duplicated on the contribution of assets to a corporation. Issues caused by that duplication come to a head when shares are sold or otherwise realised: that is the subject of this chapter. However, issues arising on the transfer of shares are both broader and deeper than the issue of duplication of unrealised gains and losses.

Fundamentally, gains on the disposal of shares may arise from at least three sources. The first has been mentioned (i.e. where the market value of assets held by a corporation has increased but the unrealised corporate gains have not been taxed). Second, gains on the disposal of shares may arise from profits or gains realised at the corporate level that have been taxed. Here it is important to appreciate that cash is an asset and that profits made that have been taxed and are reflected in a corporation's bank account increase the value of shares, just as do unrealised gains on corporate assets. The third source of gains on the disposal of shares is simply the perceived prospects of the corporation. If the outlook of the corporation is positive (corporate opportunities), this may increase the value of shares in the corporation even if those prospects have not been converted into gains or profits or the value of particular assets (other than goodwill).

These different sources of gains on the disposal of shares give rise to different policy considerations when considering how to tax those gains. Balancing each of these three sources of gains are three sources of potential loss on the disposal of shares. A corporate asset may have a market value that is less than the price paid by the corporation for the asset (i.e. an unrealised loss). A corporation may have actually realised a loss (and perhaps obtained tax relief for it); for example, through trading activities. Finally, a corporation may have poor prospects despite its current asset value holding up. Issues raised by gains and losses on the disposal or transfer of shares are discussed under the first heading of this chapter. These are issues raised at the shareholder level from such a transfer.

The transfer of shares is, in law, the transfer of an intangible asset. However, despite the separate legal personality of the corporation and that it is the corporation, not the shareholders, that is the legal owner of corporate assets, in substance it is otherwise. Especially in the context of closely held corporations, shareholders do have an interest in corporate assets, and the value of their shares depends on those assets. It is common to speak of 'indirect ownership' of assets, which is ownership determined on the basis that the corporation is transparent.

Tax systems ascribe many attributes to corporations that are carried forward from year to year.[1] Particularly, these attributes include the tax value of assets (and so unrealised gains and losses), the carry-forward of losses and the carry-forward of excess tax credits. The current shareholders of a corporation have an interest in the tax attributes, and they are the indirect owners of them. Most commonly, individuals are not permitted to sell or transfer tax attributes that are directly ascribed to them. For example, individuals may not sell losses that they are carrying forward to another person or sell credits granted to them. The loss or credit belongs to the individual, and only the individual may use it.

However, if corporate tax attributes are carried forward by a corporation irrespective of who owns the corporation, then the transfer of shares in the corporation will effect an indirect transfer of the tax attributes to the acquirer of the shares. Using the loss example, if a corporation carries forward a loss, the sale of shares in the corporation may effect an indirect transfer of the loss to a new owner. If this is permitted then it creates an inconsistency with the direct position of individuals. Why should an individual be permitted to do something indirectly (sell losses with a corporation) that he or she cannot do directly? For this reason, many countries have rules that restrict the carry-forward of tax attributes by a corporation if there has been a major change in who owns the corporation. Restrictions on carrying forward tax attributes following a change of ownership of a corporation are discussed under the second heading of this chapter. These are issues raised at the corporate level from the transfer of shares.

It has been pointed out that assets held by a corporation are duplicated in shares held in the corporation. This duplication is no clearer than when the controller of a corporation decides to sell a business or assets held by a corporation. Here the controller has the choice of whether to sell the

---

[1]  Regarding tax attributes, see the earlier discussion at 1.1.4.2.

business or assets directly, isolating any tax consequences at the corporate level. Alternately, the controller may sell the shares in the corporation and thereby sell the corporation together with the business or assets. The choice pits the corporate tax consequences of a direct sale against the combined tax consequences at the shareholder and corporate levels of a sale of shares (as considered under the first and second headings of this chapter). In addition, one must consider the tax consequences of either choice for the purchaser. Overall, the situation is a complex mixture of tax considerations. Those considerations – whether to sell shares or a business of a corporation – are briefly considered under the third heading of this chapter.

In passing, it is worth noting that this chapter deals with the direct transfer of shares. However, shares, or at least the interest in the corporation that they represent, may also be transferred indirectly. A brief example illustrates this indirect transfer. Presume the sale of shares in A Co and that A Co holds shares in B Co. The sale of shares in A Co effects an indirect transfer of the shares in B Co. An indirect transfer of shares may also be effected in other ways. For example, the issue of shares in a corporation may effect an indirect transfer of the ownership of the corporation. Similarly, an indirect transfer can be effected by terminating shares in a corporation, such as upon redemption or buy-back. Further, altering the rights attaching to shares may effect a value shift and thereby an indirect transfer of who owns the corporation.

Other parts of this book deal with these matters: the issue of shares in Chapter 4, the termination of shares in Chapter 6 and shifting value from shares in Chapter 8. These indirect methods of transferring share interests also raise issues regarding the carry-forward of corporate tax attributes. Therefore, the issues discussed under the second heading of this chapter may also arise where there is a change of ownership of a corporation arising from an indirect transfer of shares. Because the issues are not fundamentally different whether the transfer of shares is direct or indirect, limitations on the carry-forward of corporate tax attributes on a change of ownership are dealt with as a dedicated topic in this chapter, rather than anywhere else in this book.

## 5.1 Shareholder-level consequences

This heading considers the tax consequences of a transfer of shares at the shareholder level. As a preliminary matter, where a shareholder holds a number of shares in the same corporation and sells only some of them, there is an issue as to how to identify which of the shares has been sold. This is the first matter briefly considered in the following discussion. The discussion then moves to consider the main factors that might be taken into account in determining a tax treatment for gains and losses on the disposal of shares. Most of these factors stem from the artificial and reflective nature of shares. The heading then moves to consider the various options for taxing gains on the disposal of shares. A particularly critical factor in this regard is the interaction between the taxation of gains on the disposal of shares and the taxation of dividends. The heading then proceeds to consider additional international issues that arise where either the corporation or the shareholder is a non-resident.

### 5.1.1   Fungibles: identifying shares

By their nature, shares of a corporation in a particular class are identical. As a result, when a person has acquired more than one share in a particular class, the person holds identical assets. This raises questions when the person comes to sell only part of the shares, especially if the person has paid different amounts for the shares or acquired them at different times. Usually, the person would prefer to sell the shares with the highest cost, so as to minimise the amount of the gain subject to tax. However, if shares held for longer periods of time are subject to a lower rate of tax, it may be the shares held for the longest that the person wishes to sell. There may be differences in the treatment of losses on the disposal of shares that create the opposite effect (i.e. where the person would prefer to sell the shares held for the shortest period).

In this situation, a corporate tax system needs an explicit or implicit rule that identifies which of a set of identical shares a person is treated as selling. This issue is not uniquely related to shares and arises whenever a person holds *fungible* (substitutable) assets with different tax attributes (cost bases). For example, countries often have tax law rules for dealing with the identification of trading stock sold. The issue is the same with shares, but corporate tax systems are less likely to provide a comprehensive answer.

In the absence of any explicit rule, shareholders should be able to select which shares they sell in a particular transaction, and often it will pay to seek tax advice in this regard. For example, shareholders may select the shares they sell in both Germany and Australia (excluding shares held as trading stock (inventory)). However, tax administrations may place a burden on the shareholder to prove and record precisely which shares have been sold. This is the case in the US. If the shareholder fails to 'adequately identify' which shares are disposed of, then the shareholder is treated as selling the shares held for the longest period before more recently acquired shares.[2] Germany has a similar rule for certain jointly held securities.[3]

The UK adopts a different approach. It pools shares in a particular class as a single asset and treats disposals of shares from the pool as a part disposal of the pooled asset:

> Any number of securities of the same class acquired by the same person in the same capacity shall for the purposes of this Act ... be regarded as indistinguishable parts of a single asset growing or diminishing on the occasions on which additional securities of the same class are acquired or ... disposed of.[4]

The effect is to spread the cost base of the shares evenly over the shares. This sort of approach is only possible where the tax consequences on disposal do not depend on for how long the shares were held. For example, it would not work in the US where the tax rate applicable to gains on the disposal of shares is higher for shares that have been held for less than twelve months.

The fungible nature of shares also gives rise to what is referred to as 'wash sales' or 'bed and breakfast' behaviour. A person with an unrealised loss on shares might be tempted to sell those shares just before the end of the tax year in order to realise a loss that might be used against other gains. The person might also like to realise a capital gain if he or she has not used up some personal exempt allowance for the year. When the new tax year comes, the person might reacquire the shares and then is in a position very little different from what he or she was in prior to the sale.

Both the UK and the US have express rules to deal with wash sales. The US rules apply where a person acquires shares within a thirty-day period before or after the disposal of 'substantially identical' shares.[5] The purpose of the rules is to prevent the person from crystallising a loss on the disposal. The UK has similar rules that use a similar period but apply to newly acquired shares that are in the 'same class' as the shares sold.[6] The UK rules target the crystallising not only of losses but also of gains to use up the annual individual exempt amount for capital gains. Neither the

---

[2] Title 26 Code of Federal Regulations (US) § 1.1012–1(c)(1).
[3] EStG (Germany) s. 20(4).
[4] TCGA 1992 (UK) s. 104(1).
[5] IRC (US) s. 1091.
[6] TCGA 1992 (UK) ss. 105 & 106A.

UK nor the US rules are entirely satisfactory, and both cause taxpayers to engage in a fair bit of tax planning to avoid them.

### 5.1.2  Factors in determining tax treatment

Countries adopt a wide variety of approaches to the taxation of gains on the disposal of shares. In the usual way, the reason for the diversity is imbedded in differences as to what taxation of gains on the disposal of shares should be trying to achieve. What a country may seek to achieve in this regard is likely to be fundamentally linked to the manner in which its tax system views corporations and so is linked to matters that have been considered in the earlier chapters of this book.

If a corporation is viewed as completely transparent for tax purposes, there should be no reason to recognise gains or losses on disposal of shares. Everything that happens at the corporate level is attributed to the shareholder. Therefore, this scenario is not considered in the following discussion. It is different if a tax law recognises a corporation as deriving income and requires the corporation to calculate its income for tax purposes. Here gains on the disposal of shares in the corporation are likely to be relevant irrespective of whether the tax law decides to tax the corporation or the shareholders with respect to the corporation's income (see the earlier discussions at 1.3.2 and 1.3.3, respectively).

In the context of a corporate tax system that recognises that a corporation can derive income, the following discussion considers several factors that are relevant in determining a tax treatment for gains on the disposal of shares. Rather than seek to introduce all of those factors at this point, the discussion begins with the most common factor identified, that of economic double taxation of corporate profits. This is illustrated by a simple example that is developed in a way so as to demonstrate other factors that may be relevant in determining a tax treatment.

### Double taxation of retained profits

As mentioned earlier, there are several potential sources of gains that arise on the disposal of shares. One of these is retention of profits by a corporation. Other things being equal, a corporation with retained profits is worth more than a corporation without retained profits, and the share value of the corporation will be comparatively higher. If those retained profits are subjected to tax (whether in the hands of the corporation or the corporation's shareholders), the further taxation of the increase in value of the shares caused by the retention (e.g. on disposal of the shares) is a form of economic double taxation. This is best illustrated with an example.

Presume Bill sets up a corporation with negligible capital, and so the cost base of the shares in the corporation is also negligible (presumed to be nil). Through whatever means, the corporation derives profits of 100, which is subject to corporation tax at a rate of 30%. So after tax the corporation has 70 retained profits, which it credits to its bank account. A potential purchaser of Bill's shares will be willing to pay at least this much for the corporation (i.e. 70). Because his cost base is nil, if Bill receives 70 for the sale of the shares in the corporation the entire amount will constitute a capital gain (i.e. 70). If Bill's marginal tax rate is 40% and capital gains on the disposal of shares are fully taxed, Bill will pay 28 in tax with respect to the sale.

In substance, there is only one economic gain: the corporation's profits of 100. Through the direct taxation of that gain and the taxation of its reflection in the value of the shares, a total of 58 has been paid in tax (30 in the hands of the corporation and 28 on the disposal of the shares). This is precisely the same treatment as would occur under the classical system (see the earlier discussion at 2.3.1). The tax policy question is whether this form of economic double taxation is different from the double taxation of distributed corporate profits and whether it gives rise to the same types of distortions (see the earlier discussion at 2.3.2). Is it possible or appropriate to provide relief from this form of double taxation in the same manner as for the economic double taxation of dividends (see the earlier discussion at 2.4)? If so, what should be the interaction between relief provided for economic double taxation on the disposal of shares and that provided for the economic double taxation of dividends?

At a quick glance, the figures look the same, the problem seems to be the same and it is easy to jump to the conclusion that it *is* the same problem. More subtly, however, this is not the case. Just as the value of shares in a corporation is a mere reflection of real assets held at the corporate level, gains on the disposal of shares are a mere reflection of events at the corporate level, including deriving and retaining profits. By contrast, dividends *are* the real assets of the corporation being transferred by the corporation to the shareholder and not just a reflection of those assets. In the context of the present example, the gain on the disposal of shares is a mere reflection of a potential dividend, and the actual distribution of a dividend will cause that reflection to disappear. This can be demonstrated by an extension of the example.

## Stripping effect of dividends

The derivation and retention of profits cause the value of shares to rise. By contrast, the distribution of profits (without derivation of further gains) causes the value of shares to fall. Indeed, in the lifecycle of a corporation the derivation of profits (or incurring of losses), distributions and gains and losses on the disposal of shares are inextricably linked. At the start of a corporation's life, before it is promised anything, its intrinsic value is nothing. When a corporation is finally liquidated it is also worth nothing. If one were to add up all the gains on the disposal of shares in a corporation during the corporation's life, they should precisely equal all of the losses on disposal of shares in the same corporation.

This simple fact suggests that governments should not expect to collect much, if any, tax from gains on the disposal of shares. Any net tax collected should only arise from differences in the tax rates of various shareholders, restrictions on the use of losses and any net increase in the overall size of the share market in a country. This limited utility of taxation of gains on the disposal of shares for revenue collection purposes raises the fundamental question of why bother taxing such gains at all. Further or in the alternative, if such gains are linked so inextricably to the taxation of corporations and their dividends, why not just tax such gains in the same manner as dividends? The artificiality of the corporation and the nature of interests in corporations mean that answers to these questions are not straightforward. An extension of the example under the previous subheading demonstrates why this is the case.

Bill has made a gain of 70, and the taxation of that gain and the taxation of the corporation's profits giving rise to it have resulted in economic double taxation. However, as discussed earlier, the gain on the shares that caused the double taxation is merely a reflection of potential dividends. So if the retained profits are distributed, will the economic double taxation be resolved; that is, is the double taxation permanent or just temporary awaiting the distribution of dividends?

Presume the purchaser is Ted. Ted paid 70 for the shares in the corporation and so his cost base is 70. Now presume that the corporation distributes the profits (i.e. distributes a dividend of 70). Without dividend relief, that dividend is fully taxable to Ted. If Ted is taxed at a rate of 20%, he pays tax of 14 with respect to the dividend. This results in a third layer of tax and a total tax collection of 72 (30 corporation tax, 28 tax on the disposal and 14 tax on the dividend), despite there being only 100 profits. However, the distribution will cause the value of the shares to drop.

Presuming that the corporation has no other prospects (i.e. its total value was linked to the retained profits), the shares are now worth nothing.

If Ted sold the shares for nothing (or liquidated the corporation) he would realise a loss of 70. This is precisely the same amount as the dividend he was taxed on. If this loss were fully deductible (and such losses usually are not; see the later discussion at 5.1.3), it would offset the inclusion of the dividend in Ted's income and result in no further taxation for the new shareholder (Ted). The only taxation left would be the corporation tax of 30 and Bill's tax on disposal of the shares of 28. This is consistent with the treatment under a classical system, and the system in question is presumed to be such a system. A similar position is reached under a dividend relief system, and this can be illustrated with a slightly altered example.

Presume that the country in question adopts a full imputation system such as the system found in Australia. When the corporation pays corporation tax, 30 will be credited to its imputation account. Credit in an imputation account is a corporate asset, and provided an acquirer of a corporation can use that account to reduce its own tax liability, the acquirer will be willing to pay something for it. The maximum that anyone would be willing to pay should be 30 (i.e. the amount of the credit in the account). Together with the retained profits of 70, this now gives the corporation a maximum value of 100. Presume this is what Ted pays for the corporation, making Bill's gain on disposal of the shares 100 and his tax liability 40. Now the total temporary double taxation is 70 (i.e. 30 corporation tax and 40 tax on disposal).

Ted now has a cost base of 100 in the shares. When he receives a dividend of 70 it now has imputation credits of 30 attached to it (i.e. equal to the corporation tax paid). Ted has total income of 100 (just like the corporation). With a 20% tax rate, this gives rise to a tax liability of 20 with respect to the dividend. The dividend tax credits of 30 cover this liability and produce excess dividend tax credits of 10. If that amount is refundable, Ted has received 80 in total (i.e. a 70 dividend plus a 10 refund of excess credits). Economic double taxation is still evident, now with respect to Bill's tax of 40 and Ted's tax liability of 20 on the distributed profits (corporation tax of 30 less the refund of 10). But consider what happens if Ted now sells the shares.

Again it is presumed (for purposes of simplicity) that the value of the shares after the distribution is nil. So if Ted sells the shares for nothing he makes a capital loss of 100 (having paid 100 for the shares). If that loss can be fully utilised, it entirely offsets Ted's dividend income of 100 (70 dividend plus 30 dividend tax credit). This means that Ted has no tax liability with respect to the receipt of the dividends, just excess dividend tax credits of 30. Presuming these credits are refunded, Ted has received a total of 100 (i.e. a dividend of 70 plus a refund of corporation tax of 30). This is the same amount as he paid for the shares. The only tax that has been paid is that paid by Bill, which was paid at his marginal rate of 40%. The economic double taxation has been reversed and dividend relief instated.

This example is extreme, but it does demonstrate several important points. First, the distribution of dividends strips value out of shares held in a corporation. Second, economic double taxation resulting from the taxation of retained corporate profits and gains on the disposal of shares caused by that retention is, at least conceptually, temporary. Whether it is temporary or not is heavily dependent on the manner in which losses on the disposal of shares may be used. Until such losses are realised and used, the economic double taxation is real and may give rise to a distortion in terms of the time value of money (presuming the government pays no interest on corporation tax when it is refunded). These issues are the same whether a classical or dividend relief system is adopted. The example also demonstrates why countries should not expect to collect much in the way of tax from gains on the disposal of shares.

What this example does not so clearly demonstrate is why a country would bother to go through all these calculations, with a potential high administrative and compliance cost, if little to no tax is at stake. Why not simply exempt gains on the disposal of shares? There are two reasons why matters are not so simple. The first pertains to timing and the second to gains on the disposal of shares that are not attributable to taxed profits retained at the corporate level.

### Timing: whose tax rate?

From a policy perspective, the taxation of gains on the disposal of shares raises complex timing issues. The example discussed earlier involves gains caused by the retention of taxed corporate profits (i.e. potential dividends). It involves the shareholder at the time the profits are derived (Bill) selling shares and the dividend being distributed to another person (Ted). With the addition of the later sale of the shares by Ted, there was the potential resolution of the economic double taxation arising on the initial disposal of the shares by Bill. So the following discussion ignores that feature – economic double taxation. What is left is the usual treatment provided on distribution by the corporate tax system in question (i.e. a classical system or, in the extended example, an imputation system).

When the taxation of dividends was considered in Chapter 2, there was no change in share ownership, so there was only one shareholder marginal tax rate to be considered for analytical purposes. That is not the case with the present example. Now there are two consecutive shareholders, Bill and Ted, and each has a different tax rate (i.e. in the example, 40% and 20%, respectively). A fundamental question is, What is the appropriate tax rate to levy with respect to distributed profits? Should it be the tax rate of the shareholder who held the shares at the time the profits were derived (i.e. Bill) or the tax rate of the shareholder who holds the shares at the time the profits are distributed (i.e. Ted)? And does it matter which tax rate is levied? Which one is the appropriate rate is perhaps open to dispute, but it certainly matters which rate is used.

In the context of this convoluted example, the tax rate ultimately imposed on the distributed corporate profits is consistent with Bill's tax rate; that is, the tax rate of the shareholder at the time the profits are derived (not when they are distributed). This is clearest in the imputation example. After the refund of corporation tax to Ted, the only tax left is the tax paid by Bill of 40, which is equal to his marginal tax rate applied to the entire profits of the corporation. This is true even of the example involving the classical system. The total tax collected is 30 corporation tax and 28 tax on the disposal of the shares, which is consistent with the tax treatment that would have resulted had the dividend been distributed to Bill rather than Ted (i.e. 28 is also equal to a rate of 40% applied to the dividend of 70).

At a conceptual level, this seems like an appropriate result. If the artificiality of the corporation is accepted, then taxation at the rate of the person who holds shares at the time a corporation derives income seems appropriate. But what would happen if, as mentioned earlier, gains on the disposal of shares were simply exempt. This would mean that Bill would not be taxable with respect to the gain on the disposal of the shares. It would also mean that any capital loss made by Ted on a subsequent disposal of the shares would not be recognised. That would simply leave the taxation of the profits in the hands of the corporation (i.e. 30), and the taxation of Ted with respect to the dividend. In the context of a classical system, this would be the taxation of 14 (20% of the dividend of 70) and, in the context of the imputation system, a refund of 10 (30 dividend tax credit less dividend tax liability of 20).

In either case, the situation has fundamentally changed. Instead of taxing in a fashion consistent with the tax rate of the shareholder who holds shares when corporate profits are derived, there is now taxation consistent with the tax rate of the shareholder who holds shares when corporate profits are distributed. Initially, it might seem that this is a simple matter of preference, but that would overlook a potentially serious problem. A fundamental mismatch between the tax treatment of dividends and gains on the disposal of shares in this manner can give rise to serious issues of tax arbitrage.

Such a mismatch provides high tax rate shareholders with a clear incentive to sell shares before a dividend is distributed. The most obvious candidate as a purchaser then becomes a low-rate taxpayer. Tax could be substantially reduced or eliminated by selling shares to low-rate taxpayers before payment of a dividend and reacquiring the shares after the dividend is paid. This is the problem of 'dividend stripping', which is a function of a mismatch between the tax treatment of dividends and that of gains on the disposal of shares. It is discussed in more depth later at 8.3. So although a tax on gains on the disposal of shares may not raise much in the way of revenue directly, it may save a substantial amount by preventing avoidance of taxation of dividends and on corporate profits generally. Indeed, a tax on gains on the disposal of shares may be viewed as a type of anti-avoidance or anti-income shifting rule.

### Unrealised corporate gains: the problem of enveloping

This discussion has presumed that the cause or source of the gain on the disposal of shares is the retention of taxed profits by the corporation. Of course, that is often not the case. Equally, the gain may be attributable to matters that have not been taxed at the corporate level, whether an increase in value of assets or a positive outlook for the corporation's prospects. If the gain is not attributable to the retention of taxed profits, then the issue of double taxation when gains on the disposal of shares are taxed does not arise. At least, that double taxation does not arise at the time the shares are disposed of. Whether it may arise at a later time requires a brief consideration.

Consider the example involving Bill and Ted outlined earlier, with the alteration that the value of the shares is increased to 100 for a reason other than that the corporation derived taxed profits. On the sale of shares to Ted, Bill is taxed at his marginal rate of 40% on the gain of 100, making taxation of 40. Ted's cost base in the shares is 100. Now the corporation sells the asset that has increased in value (potentially its whole undertaking) and realises the gain of 100 that caused the increase in value of the shares. Here again there is double taxation: it is just that the order is reversed. Instead of the corporation tax being paid first and then the tax on the gain on the shares, the tax with respect to the shares is paid first and then the corporation tax. Otherwise, the consequences are the same with one additional observation.

After the corporate realisation, Ted can still draw a dividend that will reduce the value of the shares, which he may sell at a loss. However, note the consequence if full relief is provided for the subsequent loss by Ted on the disposal of shares. In the example provided earlier, it was suggested that the overall effect is taxation in a manner consistent with the person who holds the shares when the corporation derives the profits. This extension to the example shows that more accurately it is taxation in a manner consistent with the person who holds the shares when the gain accrues to the corporation, not the person who holds the shares when the gain is realised. The relevant person is the person who holds the shares at the point that the potential corporate gain (whether or not realised) has an increasing effect on the value of the shares.

The extension of the example once again reinforces that double taxation caused by taxing gains on the disposal of shares is essentially a question of timing. If it is just a question of timing, does that mean that it would be sufficient to rely on corporation tax and dividend taxation and ignore taxation on the disposal of shares? It was pointed out earlier that the lack of taxation of gains on the disposal of shares might cause serious tax planning problems. This is because taxation would be imposed according to the shareholder who holds the shares when dividends are distributed rather than the shareholder who holds the shares at the time the corporate profits are derived. The issues are more serious where the gains accrue but have not been taxed to the corporation before the shares are disposed of.

Consider a tax system where gains on the disposal of assets are generally taxed but there is a specific exemption for shares. In such a system, there is an incentive to hold appreciating assets through a corporation. A corporation is the legal owner of its assets. When the controller of a corporation holding an appreciating asset wishes to sell the appreciated asset, the controller has one of two options: selling it outside or inside the corporation. The controller can sell the asset out of the hands of the corporation, but any gain would be taxed. Therefore the controller is more likely to sell the shares in the corporation because the gain will not be taxed. This is widely referred to as *enveloping* an asset because the asset is wrapped in the corporate form (owned by the corporation). *Enveloping* was mentioned earlier in the context of the creation of shares at 4.1.2.1.

Enveloping is a serious issue that regularly occurs in practice. It can cause practical difficulties because often each corporation holds more than a single asset. It happens more often where corporations have held assets over an extended period. In such a case, to get the benefit of enveloping, a person desiring to indirectly sell an asset held by a corporation often has to strip assets out of the corporation that the purchaser does not require or that the seller does not want to dispose of. This sort of restructuring of a corporation prior to sale is standard work for tax professionals.

Once a valuable asset is enveloped in a corporation, it may stay there permanently, irrespective of how large the gain over the original cost may be. New owners can continue to sell the shares in the corporation without tax consequences, despite this indirectly involving a realisation of a gain on an asset held by the corporation. The distortion between a direct sale by the corporation and an indirect sale of the asset by selling the shares is obvious and is one of the major distortions in corporate tax systems. It is not simply a function of not having a tax on the disposal of shares. The problem with enveloping is unequal treatment of gains on the disposal of assets and those gains on the disposal of shares.

A controller of a corporation has the choice to sell the asset either directly from the corporation or indirectly by selling the shares in the corporation. If the tax consequences are not the same, then one can expect the controller to prefer the type of sale that involves the least amount of tax. Accordingly, if a corporate tax system provides dividend relief and, as a matter of consistency, taxes gains on the disposal of shares in a similar fashion, it will have to face the enveloping issue. The same is true where an asset depreciates. If losses on the disposal of shares are not recognised (because gains are not taxed) or otherwise restricted (e.g. quarantined), the seller may prefer to sell the asset directly from the corporation and recognise the loss at that level.

Nevertheless, it is often the case that just looking at what the seller prefers is overly simplistic. The purchaser also has preferences. For example, consider the situation where the asset that the purchaser wishes to buy is an enveloped depreciable asset. If the purchaser buys the shares, then no additional depreciation may be available (in most countries shares cannot be depreciated). However, if the purchaser buys the depreciable asset directly from the corporation, then this will reset the cost of the asset and higher amounts of depreciation will be available in the future. Similar issues can arise with trading stock and non-depreciable capital assets.

Particularly when a whole business is purchased directly, there are often complex negotiations between the seller and the purchaser in allocating an overall purchase price between assets. These negotiations pit the tax profile of the seller against the tax profile of the buyer. Where the seller's and the buyer's tax profiles oppose one another, there may be little revenue leakage caused by distortions between the direct and indirect sale of an enveloped asset. However, where there is no such opposition the amount of tax to be saved by structuring a sale in a particular manner may be substantial. In any case, the buyer and seller can be expected to engage in tax arbitrage to the extent possible and to structure a deal in the manner that produces the least amount of overall tax. Some of these issues are further reflected on later at 5.3.

At the end of the day, the conceptual issues underlying the taxation of gains on the disposal of shares in the context of a realisation based income tax are intractable. This is not surprising considering that shares are, like the corporations in which they are held, an artificial legal construct. If the source of the gain on the shares has been taxed at the corporate level, then to tax such gains again on the disposal of shares must produce a distortion. If the source of the gain on the shares has not been taxed at the corporate level, then to not tax such gains when the shares are disposed of may produce an unacceptable and distorting deferral of taxation. To distinguish gains on the disposal of shares between those attributable to a source taxed at the corporate level and those not may seem an appropriate response, but it brings with it complicated tax calculations that involve high administrative and compliance costs. This is further explored at 5.1.3. In any case, most commonly those adjustments are inaccurate and do not fully resolve the distortions.

### 5.1.3 Options for tax treatment of gains on disposal of shares

With this conceptual background, the discussion now turns to assess some of the main and commonly used options for the taxation of gains on the disposal of shares. These options are multifarious, and the discussion only considers the main options adopted in practice. In the usual manner, examples of these main options are drawn from the corporate tax systems of Germany, the UK, the US and the CCCTB Proposal, but a number of other practical examples are also referenced.

The discussion begins with the possibility of applying the same type of relief to gains on the disposal of shares as is applied to dividends. Here the treatments are the same, rather than integrated. It is noted that applying the same type of relief is only possible where corporation tax and dividend tax are not closely integrated (i.e. is only available in the context of a classical system and some forms of dividend relief). The second alternative is to seek to integrate the taxation of dividends and gains on the disposal of shares in some shape or form. This may involve adjustment of the taxation on the disposal of shares depending on retained profits and dividends distributed or the sharing of a uniform relief between the taxation of dividends and gains on the disposal of shares.

The other options provide no specific connection between the taxation of gains on the disposal of shares and the taxation of dividends. There may be a dedicated relief provided with respect to gains on disposal of shares, but it may be different from that provided for dividends (if any). Alternately, capital gains generally may be granted some type of tax relief, and gains on the disposal of shares may be covered by this tax relief. Finally, there may be no relief; that is, there is taxation of gains on the disposal of shares (and likely capital gains generally) according to the marginal rate of the shareholder.

### 5.1.3.1   Consistency between taxation of dividends and capital gains on shares

A major option for the taxation of gains on the disposal of shares is to tax them in a fashion consistent with the taxation of dividends. The rationale for this approach is straightforward. A shareholder has various methods of extracting a return from shares. The two major options are to wait for the payment of a dividend or to sell the shares. In many cases, this is a straightforward choice for a shareholder, and that choice may be affected by tax considerations. Unfortunately, and as should be predictable by this stage of the book, matters are not that simple.

Although it is true that dividends and gains on the disposal of shares are similar, they are not the same. It may even be questioned whether they are sufficiently similar so as to justify the same tax treatment. In particular, dividends are typically paid from realised corporate profits, whereas gains on the disposal of shares may be a reflection of those profits but may equally be a reflection of unrealised gains at the corporate level. Further, the taxation of gains on the disposal of shares is inherently a net concept that takes into account at least the cost of the shares and, most often, many other types of expenses. As pointed out earlier at 2.3.1.2, there are many cases in which dividends are taxed on a gross basis. Further, the distribution of dividends, through the stripping effect discussed earlier at 5.1.2, may have a substantial and direct impact on the value of shares and so on gains and losses on the disposal of shares. By contrast, gains and losses on the disposal of shares do not have any direct impact on dividends distributed with respect to those shares.

This lack of equivalence between the dividends and gains on the disposal of shares is underlined by comparing the options for dividend relief, discussed earlier at 2.4. There are several options for dividend relief that simply cannot be replicated with respect to gains on the disposal of shares, at least not in any sensible form. This is generally true of the options for relief at the corporate level. For example, what would be the equivalent of a dividend deduction system for gains on the disposal of shares? Perhaps it would involve granting the corporation a deduction when gains arise on disposal of shares in the corporation. How would that work if the gain is not attributable to the retention of taxed profits by the corporation? Should the deduction be permitted to be carried forward if it cannot be used presently? What should be the treatment when a dividend is subsequently distributed to a shareholder? Should another deduction be available or should some other adjustment be made? The same questions arise for a split-rate system or a corporation tax credit system.

It seems that equivalency between the taxation of dividends and gains on the disposal of shares only makes sense where dividend relief is provided at the shareholder level or where a classical system is used. In particular, equivalency is possible where notional dividend relief is provided at the shareholder level. However, it is essentially impossible wherever dividend taxation depends on corporate-level taxation (i.e. all of the corporate-level forms of dividend relief and the imputation system). In these cases, by contrast, it is theoretically possible to integrate the relief for corporation tax between the taxation of dividends and the disposal of shares. That is considered under the next subheading. The discussion presently considers the possibility of equivalence in the context of the different types of shareholder-level dividend relief systems.

**Dividend exclusion**    If dividends are excluded from income, a similar exclusion or exemption may apply to gains on the disposal of shares. This approach is commonly adopted in Continental Europe for inter-corporate shareholdings and constitutes part of the 'participation exemption'. For example, just as inter-corporate dividends are 95% exempt in Germany, 'profits' on the disposal of shares by one corporation in another corporation are also 95% exempt.[7] As with inter-corporate dividends, the exemption for gains on the disposal of shares does not depend on the level of shareholding in the corporation whose shares are disposed of.

---

[7]  KStG (Germany) s. 8b(2) & (3).

Although these German exemptions are similar, they are not the same. Recall that expenses incurred in deriving 95% exempt dividends are fully deductible, the 5% taxation of dividends being an arbitrary offset for this deduction (see the earlier discussion at 2.4.3.1). By contrast, because it is *profits* or *gains* on the disposal of shares that are 95% exempt, costs incurred with respect to the acquisition or disposal of shares are, in substance, only 5% deductible. Further, should those costs result in a loss on the disposal of shares, the loss is not deductible at all. By contrast, other expenses relating to the holding of shares (such as financing and stewardship costs) are fully deductible.

The CCCTB Proposal is similar, but not the same. Just as dividends received by a corporation are excluded from income, so are 'proceeds from a disposal of shares'.[8] Note that the reference here is to 'proceeds', leaving open the question of costs incurred in acquiring shares. Costs 'relating to the acquisition, construction or improvement of fixed assets' are expressly non-deductible.[9] Shares are a 'financial asset' and so are a 'fixed asset'.[10] This seems to mean that losses on the disposal of shares are not deductible. The outcome seems to be different from the German approach in that there is 5% disparity in the treatment of dividends (95% exempt) and gains on the disposal of shares (fully exempt). The EU Presidency amendments would go some way to equalising the treatment by fully exempting inter-corporate dividends and proceedings from the disposal of shares, but denying a deduction for all costs associated therewith. However, a 10% holding would be required to secure the exemption.

The same is true of the UK participation exemption. As noted earlier at 2.4.3.1, generally the UK fully exempts inter-corporate dividends, and yet financing costs are fully deductible. A similar but more limited exemption is also available for gains on the disposal of shares held by one corporation in another corporation. This exemption applies to shares held on capital account where the disposing corporation holds at least 10% of the shares in the corporation whose shares are disposed of.[11] Part disposals out of a substantial shareholding can continue to qualify for up to twelve months after the 10% threshold has ceased.[12] The 10% threshold is measured by reference to 'ordinary share capital' and an entitlement to 10% of 'profits

---

[8]  CCCTB Proposal Art. 11(d).
[9]  CCCTB Proposal Art. 14(1)(i).
[10]  CCCTB Proposal Art. 4(14) & (15).
[11]  TCGA 1992 (UK) s. 192A giving effect to Sch. 7AC.
[12]  TCGA 1992 (UK) Sch. 7AC para. 7.

available for distribution.[13] Holdings of a 51% group of corporations may be aggregated for purposes of determining this threshold.[14]

The UK relief is only available if the selling corporation is a 'trading company' or a member of a trading group and the corporation whose shares are disposed of is also a trading company.[15] 'Trading company' is obscurely defined as a corporation whose activities do not to any substantial extent include activities other than trading activities.[16]

From a policy perspective, it is not clear why the UK exemption is limited by reference to a 10% holding and to trading activities. This limitation creates a strange dislocation with the broad exemption for inter-corporate dividends. Further, where a gain on disposal of shares would be exempt, a loss on disposal is not recognised.[17] The outcome is that losses on disposal of portfolio holdings of shares or the holding of shares in passive corporations may be recognised (though quarantined).[18] At least the latter of these is the type of loss that is most open to manipulation through the cascading of losses up a corporate chain. The UK now relies on a broad capital loss anti-abuse rule for protection in this regard.[19]

A participation exemption can be an effective tool against the cascading of losses up a corporate chain. As noted at the start of Chapter 4, a loss at the bottom of a corporate chain will be reflected in a reduced value of shares at each link in that chain. Gains may also be duplicated, but given the stripping effect of dividends discussed earlier at 5.1.2, corporate groups generally have a mechanism to resolve issues of double taxation resulting from taxation of gains on the disposal of shares. When it comes to losses on the disposal of shares, however, if they are recognised then corporate groups are likely to plan for duplication. This can place extreme pressure on a corporate tax system.

Corporate groups will seek to use the multiple reflective losses up a corporate chain that are caused by a loss in a corporation at the bottom of that chain. Exactly how or if that can be achieved depends on the corporate tax system in question. Where losses can be transferred within a

---

[13] TCGA 1992 (UK) Sch. 7AC para. 8.
[14] TCGA 1992 (UK) Sch. 7AC para. 9.
[15] TCGA 1992 (UK) Sch. 7AC para. 18.
[16] TCGA 1992 (UK) Sch. 7AC para. 20.
[17] TCGA 1992 (UK) s. 16(2).
[18] Added to this confusion are CTA 2010 (UK) ss. 68–90. These sections provide that, if an investment company incurs an allowable loss for the purposes of corporation tax on the disposal of ordinary shares in a qualifying trading company that it subscribed for, the loss may be set against the corporation's income (i.e. is not quarantined).
[19] TCGA 1992 (UK) s. 16A.

group, using the multiple reflective losses can be a relatively simple matter. Consider a corporate chain where A Co holds shares in B Co and C Co, and B Co holds shares in D Co. D Co incurs a loss, which is reflected in a loss on the shares that B Co holds in D Co and that A Co holds in B Co. Presume that C Co is profitable and that the corporate tax system in question permits the transfer of losses, whether of a revenue or capital nature.

The loss incurred by D Co can be transferred to C Co. Presume that B Co then sells the shares in D Co, realising a loss that is a reflection of the loss incurred by D Co. This loss realised by B Co can then be transferred to C Co. Finally, A Co can sell its shares in B Co, involving a second reflection of the real loss incurred by D Co. This loss incurred by A Co can also be transferred to D Co. The result is three tax losses being transferred to C Co when in reality there was only one loss. Australia faced this type of problem in the late 1990s, and it was one of the reasons why Australia moved in 2002 to a consolidation regime that collapses the identity of subsidiaries.

Even if there is no potential for loss transfer, corporate groups often find ways of using reflective losses to good effect. One approach involves transferring gains to the various loss companies (e.g. through a book value transfer of an asset or pushing the boundaries of domestic transfer pricing rules). More complex techniques involve the use of reorganisation provisions to marry real gains with reflective losses. The bottom line is that if the reflective losses are recognised the tax system is at risk. One of the major benefits of the participation exemption is that it intercepts the problem and stops the reflective losses arising in the first place.

Unfortunately, the downside of the participation exemption is that it also does not tax gains on the disposal of shares. For reasons discussed earlier at 5.1.2, this is not an issue with respect to gains caused by the retention of taxed profits, but can be a big issue with respect to gains on the disposal of shares caused by unrealised corporate profits. So, a country implementing a participation exemption may not have a loss cascading problem, but will have a serious problem with enveloping (discussed earlier at 5.1.2). Both Germany and the UK have problems with appreciating assets being *enveloped* in a corporation and then those assets being subject to continual indirect sale (through the sale of the shares in the enveloping corporation) without substantial taxation. The same would be true under the CCCTB Proposal. Ad hoc rules that countries might use to address this serious tax deferral issue are beyond the scope of this book.

The enveloping problem has an analogy with an issue discussed earlier at 2.4.3: providing dividend relief, especially by way of dividend exclusion or reduced rates, for dividends distributed from profits that have not been subject to full tax at the corporate level. There is an incentive for corporations to derive such income, because overall it is subject to less taxation than income derived by a corporation that is subject to full taxation. This is particularly an issue with hidden profit distributions in a country that does not deem a corporation to realise income as a result of such a distribution (see the earlier discussion at 2.2.2). However, it seems a much more straightforward matter for a controller to cause a corporation not to sell an asset and then sell shares to a third party than it is to engineer a constructive dividend from a source that is not effectively taxed at the corporate level.

The cascading of losses problem is less severe where individuals hold shares directly in the corporation incurring the real loss. Here the maximum is one reflective gain or loss, so often countries are less concerned about it. The German 40% exemption for individuals receiving dividends on shares held as business assets was noted earlier at 2.4.3.1. Broadly, this 40% exemption also applies to sales proceeds on the disposal of those shares.[20] However, the German system also incorporates a substantial amount of inconsistency in this regard following the introduction of the shareholder differentiation system in 2009.

If the individual shareholder holds at least 1% of the shares in a corporation, then the proceeds on the disposal of such shares are treated as business income.[21] Such proceeds are also subject to the 40% exemption system, despite the fact that dividends distributed on such shares are subject to a flat tax rate of 25%.[22] Where sales proceeds are 40% exempt, then only 40% of the cost base of the shares may be deducted.[23] As a result, losses on the disposal of shares that are or are treated as business assets are deductible as to 60% only. However, to this extent the losses are fully deductible against the taxpayer's income and not subject to quarantining.

**Shareholder differentiation**    It is also possible to achieve some consistency between the taxation of dividends and gains on the disposal of shares under a shareholder differentiation system. Again, however, in practice

---

[20]  EStG (Germany) s. 3 No. 40(a).
[21]  EStG (Germany) ss. 16 & 17.
[22]  EStG (Germany) s. 3 No. 40(b) & (c).
[23]  EStG (Germany) s. 3c(2).

this does not achieve complete consistency. In the US, consistency is achieved by including qualifying dividends in a taxpayer's net capital gains (see the earlier discussion at 2.4.3.2). Here, rather than treating gains on the disposal of shares in the same fashion as dividends, dividends are treated in the same fashion as capital gains, including gains on the disposal of shares. So dividends are subject to lower rates ranging to a maximum of 15%.[24]

The consistency in the US is not complete because the amount of dividends included in net capital gains is the gross amount, whereas the amount of gains on the disposal of shares included is the net amount (i.e. after deduction of the cost base of shares). As noted earlier at 2.4.3.2, if an individual wishes to claim a deduction for expenses associated with dividends, he or she must be taxed on the dividend at full marginal rates, and not the reduced rates for capital gains. Further, the reduced rate for capital gains is only available where the asset disposed of has been held for more than twelve months. Losses on the disposal of shares are typically quarantined and may only be set against capital gains, whereas excess expenses in deriving dividends are not so quarantined. The exception for individuals is that capital losses up to $3000 per year are generally deductible.[25]

The German shareholder differentiation system introduced in 2009 is different. Here there is a special tax rate for dividends (and certain other types of capital income) derived outside of a business, typically 25%. The tax rate for gains on the disposal of shares held outside a business is then aligned to this dividend tax rate.[26] (Recall from the earlier discussion that shareholdings of 1% or more are treated as business holdings.) Because gains on the disposal of shares are subject to a special rate, losses on the disposal of shares have to be quarantined and cannot be set against income subject to normal rates, including other types of capital gains. Losses on the disposal of passively held shares may only be set against gains on the disposal of such shares.[27]

Shareholder differentiation is usually applied only in the context of individuals. As a result, applying it to gains on the disposal of shares does not usually involve the extreme of the loss cascading problem. There may

---

[24] IRC (US) s. 1(h).
[25] IRC (US) s. 1211.
[26] This is achieved by including 'profit from the sale of shares' in the definition of 'investment income'; EStG (Germany) s. 20(2). 'Investment income' is generally subject to the flat rate of 25%; EStG (Germany) s. 32d(1).
[27] EStG (Germany) Art. 20(6).

be duplication of a loss (at the corporate level and at the individual share-holder level), but as noted, often the loss at the shareholder level is quarantined. The problem of enveloping unrealised gains in a corporation, however, still exists to a large extent. Corporation tax can be avoided by simply not selling appreciating corporate assets. Taxation of gains on the disposal of shares is then limited to the equivalent of dividends subject to dividend relief. So, for example, in the US individual taxation would be a maximum of 15%. In Germany it would in theory be limited to 25%, but because any holding of 1% or more is a business asset and subject to a different treatment, the shareholder would have no control over whether the corporation holds or sells an asset. In either case, the taxation would be substantially below the highest personal marginal tax rate.

**Dividend tax credit**   Conceptually, it is possible to provide a shareholder a notional tax credit with respect to gains on the disposal of shares that is equivalent to a tax credit received with dividends. However, countries that offer dividend tax credits do not tend to do this. So, an equivalent of the notional dividend tax credit offered by the UK and of the dividend tax credit granted under the Australian imputation system is not granted to shareholders with respect to gains on the disposal of shares.

If the notional dividend tax credit system is changed to an imputation system, then (as noted earlier) even the conceptual possibility of providing tax credits with respect to gains on the disposal of shares is difficult. An imputation system only grants dividend tax credits for corporation tax actually paid at the corporate level. Because gains on the disposal of shares are a reflection of potential dividends, it is not clear whether credit for the corporation tax should be granted with respect to the gain or the potential subsequent dividend. Without complex adjustments (e.g. the cost base of shares), it seems clear that it should not be granted with respect to both. In any case, these issues simply reflect issues in providing consistency between dividends and gains on the disposal of shares under systems that provide corporate-level dividend relief. That is not surprising because, as noted earlier at 2.4.3.3, imputation systems tend to behave in a manner similar to corporate-level dividend relief systems.

### 5.1.3.2   Integration of taxation of dividends and capital gains on shares

Rather than the same relief being applied to dividends and to gains on the disposal of shares, there may be some integration or sharing of relief between these taxing events. This is best demonstrated by reference to corporate-level dividend relief systems and the imputation system. Here the goal is to provide relief by reference to corporation tax and no more. In the context of heading 2.4, the presumption was that the relief for corporation tax would be provided by reference to the distribution of dividends only. However, it is possible that gains on the disposal of shares could be treated as an equal event.

Consider the example developed earlier at 5.1.2. The corporation retains 70 profits that have been subjected to 30 corporation tax. Presume that the country in question adopts a full imputation system, like Australia. When Bill sells the shares and makes a capital gain of 70, it would be possible to impute the 30 corporation tax to the taxation of that gain. Bill would gross up his gain for the imputed corporation tax and have income of 100 and a personal tax liability of 40, which is reduced to 10 by the tax credit of 30. Bill would pay 10 in tax, and the overall tax collected would be consistent with Bill's marginal tax rate; that is, the issue of (temporary) double taxation would not arise at this point.

However, the double taxation issue would arise again when the corporation distributes the dividend of 70 to Ted. It seems inappropriate at this stage to impute the corporation tax for a second time. If the dividend were subject to full taxation without credit, there would again be economic double taxation. This might reverse itself when Ted subsequently sells the shares at a loss. It would be possible to prevent the double taxation from arising at all by permitting Ted to reduce the taxation of dividends by his share of taxed profits retained by the corporation at the time he acquired the shares. The cost base of the shares in the hands of Ted would have to be reduced by the same amount. This would come close to being an accurate system that did not result in double taxation. A corporate-level dividend relief system could be structured in a similar manner. However, the calculations would be excessively complex and potentially open to abuse, and outside of targeted examples, no country has come close to implementing such a system. Rather, countries are more likely to accept (temporary) double taxation or over-compensate with relief that extends to gains on the disposal of shares that are attributable to corporate gains that have not been realised or subject to tax.[28]

It is possible to integrate the taxation of dividends and gains on the disposal of shares in a less precise fashion. As mentioned, it is the taxation of gains on the disposal of shares that reflect taxed profits retained by the

---

[28] For a more detailed discussion of these types of issue in the context of an imputation system, see Harris (1996, pp. 261–4).

corporation that causes the (temporary) double taxation. It is possible to adjust the cost base of shares upwards for such profits and so relieve the double taxation. It would then also be necessary to adjust the cost base of shares downwards when dividends are distributed to ensure that excess relief is not provided.

Unlike the earlier, more complex example, this cost base adjustment approach alters the overall tax rate ultimately imposed on the profits derived through a corporation. In the context of the example, this approach relieves the taxation of Bill with respect to the capital gains, and so ultimately his marginal rate of 40% will not be used. Ted will still be taxable on the receipt of the dividend, potentially with dividend relief. The dividend will reduce Ted's cost base, and so he will not have a subsequent capital loss should he dispose of the shares after the distribution. Overall, the result is likely to be taxation at Ted's margin rate rather than at Bill's marginal rate. The appropriateness of taxation at the rate of the shareholder who holds the shares when dividends are distributed, rather than at the rate of the shareholder who holds the shares at the time the profits accrue to the corporation, was questioned earlier at 5.1.2.

Perhaps because of this questionable effect, in practice the adjustment of the cost base approach tends to be used only in one of two situations. The first scenario is where shareholders are taxed at a flat rate. This was the situation under the former Norwegian RISK system, which operated prior to 2006.[29] Mexico still makes adjustments of this nature. Corporations maintain a taxed profits account from which exempt dividends may be distributed (see the earlier discussion at 2.4.3.1). When profits are retained and the corporation credits its taxed profits account, the shareholders make a proportionate upward adjustment to the cost base of their shares in the corporation.[30]

The second scenario in which an adjustment of the cost base of shares for retained profits tends to be used is where the shareholder has already been taxed by attribution when the profits are derived. This scenario involving the partnership method was discussed earlier at 1.3.3. Here corporate profits are attributed to and taxed at the rate of the shareholders who hold shares at the point the profits are derived (i.e. there is no corporation tax). The cost base of shares is adjusted for this attribution to

---

[29] Regarding the operation of this system, see Harris (1996, pp. 731–2).

[30] Income Tax Law (*Ley del Impuesto sobre la Renta*) (Mexico) Arts. 24 (corporate shareholders) & 151 (individual shareholders).

ensure that the same shareholder is not indirectly taxed with respect to those same profits (by an increase in value of the shares) when the shares are disposed of.

Taxation of gains on the disposal of shares is still appropriate in this scenario in which the cost base of shares is increased for attribution of corporate income. The type of gain on the disposal of shares that is most likely to be taxed is that attributable to gains accruing at the corporate level that have not yet been realised (and so not attributed to the shareholders). Cost base adjustments of this nature are often used with respect to the taxation of partnership income, where the partnership is an income calculation entity although is transparent for purposes of tax liability. Not surprisingly, it is also the method used under the US S corporation regime, which adopts the partnership method for certain closely held corporations. Increases in the cost base of shares in an S corporation for attributed profits and decreases for dividends were discussed earlier at 1.3.3.2.

These types of cost base adjustments may also be made under other types of attribution regimes. So, for example, the US adopts similar adjustments with respect to intergroup shareholdings under its consolidation regime (discussed earlier at 1.2.3). Where a group corporation derives earnings and profits, the cost bases of shareholdings of other group members in that corporation are adjusted upwards.[31] Where the corporation distributes dividends those cost bases are adjusted downwards. The US makes these adjustments because it taxes gains on the disposal of shares by one group corporation in another group corporation. Broadly, that is not the case in Germany or the UK because of their participation exemptions, and the same would be true under the CCCTB Proposal. So these other corporate tax systems do not make equivalent adjustments. Similar adjustments are often made under controlled foreign corporation regimes (see the earlier discussion at 3.2.2.1), but are beyond the scope of this book.

Moving further from precise relief from economic double taxation, excess dividend relief may be available to offset the taxation of gains on the disposal of shares. This is only likely to occur where the excess relief is at the shareholder level. An example may involve a dividend tax credit system where excess credits are not refundable. The excess credits may be permitted to reduce tax payable with respect to gains on the disposal of the shares with respect to which the credits are granted.

Another example may be where a tax-free allowance is granted to a shareholder that is not calculated by reference to dividends distributed.

---

[31] Title 26 Code of Federal Regulations (US) § 1.1502–33.

The current Norwegian 'shielding allowance' (discussed earlier at 2.4.3.1) is an example of this approach. Norway excludes from taxation a standard allowance for dividends calculated by reference to the price paid for shares (not dividends distributed). A shareholder may have excess allowance (e.g. because no dividends are distributed in a particular year). Excess allowance may be carried forward and used to reduce tax liability with respect to shares in future years. If shares are sold, excess Norwegian shielding allowance may be used to reduce the amount of a gain on the shares that is subject to tax.[32]

### 5.1.3.3 Specific relief of capital gains on shares

Rather than seek an equivalence or integration of treatment, a corporate tax system may provide some relief from taxation on the disposal of shares that is independent of the tax treatment of dividends. There are several reasons why a country may wish to take this approach. One reason is to avoid economic double taxation of corporate gains discussed earlier. Another reason is that the taxation of gains on the disposal of shares is a transaction cost and may retard the liquidity of the share market. So a number of countries provide an exemption for gains on the disposal of shares in listed corporations. Mexico provides such an exemption for individuals.[33] None of the corporate tax systems focused on in this study adopts this approach, although there are many cases in which the UK and the US exempt gains on the disposal of shares (e.g. shares held by pension funds and non-residents).

The issues are different for closely held corporations. Here the main issues are building up a business as a retirement fund for the effectively self-employed and intergenerational transfers of such businesses. If retirement savings of employees are tax preferred, there is an argument that the direct or indirect sale of a business by an individual that has been built up over a lifetime should be treated in a similar fashion. Further, if a business is passed from one generation of a family to another, the imposition of a substantial amount of tax on the transfer may severely hamper the capital and operation of the business. The UK addresses this type of issue through the provision of entrepreneur's relief, which provides a tax rate of 10% on qualifying gains.[34] Germany has a similar relief involving an exemption and reduced rate for the disposal of a business (including shares in a

---

[32] Income and Capital Tax Law (*Lov om skatt av formue og inntekt*) (Norway) Art. 10–31.
[33] Income Tax Law (*Ley del Impuesto sobre la Renta*) (Mexico) Art. 109 Item XXVI.
[34] TCGA 1992 (UK) ss. 169H to 169S.

wholly owned corporation) by certain persons over 55 years of age.[35] Further consideration of this style of retirement relief is beyond the scope of this book.

Providing a different form of tax relief for dividends and gains on the disposal of shares may increase the scope for tax arbitrage. Whenever relief is provided for gains on the disposal of shares and is not limited to gains attributable to retained profits taxed at the corporate level, then enveloping unrealised gains in a controlled corporation is a problem. Further, it is likely that a differing tax treatment of dividends and gains on the disposal of shares will affect the choice of a shareholder to wait for dividends or to sell shares and realise capital gains.

Dividends and gains on the disposal of shares are not pure alternatives. However, the countries that adopt a consistent tax treatment between these alternate forms of return from shares (see the earlier discussion at 5.1.3.1) clearly believe they are addressing a tax distortion between them. Whether they can be successful is questionable. At one extreme it is likely that there is a substantial distortion (e.g. where dividends are subject to a classical treatment but gains on the disposal of shares are exempt). The reverse could also be true (e.g. where dividends are treated more favourably than gains on the disposal of shares). In a controlled corporation scenario, it seems difficult to anticipate and neutralise the distortion without some form of adjustment for the extent to which gains on the disposal of shares are attributable to the retention of taxed profits.

### 5.1.3.4 Concessional capital gains taxation

Most countries tax at least some forms of capital gains at a rate that is lower than full marginal rates. This lower tax rate is especially the case for individuals subject to progressive taxation. One of the main rationales for this lower taxation is that capital gains may accrue over a number of years, but are realised in just one year. The result may be to push taxpayers into a higher tax bracket than they ever would have been in, had they realised the gain over the years during which it accrued. A related issue with the taxation of capital gains is that it emphasises the 'lock-in' effect of a realisation-based income tax. Taxpayers may be unwilling to sell an asset that has accrued gains over a number of years for fear of losing a substantial part of their investment in taxation.

---

[35] EStG (Germany) ss. 16(4) & 34.

Some countries have loosened gains on the disposal of shares from their general taxation of capital gains. Germany provides an example of this approach with respect to individuals, discussed earlier at 5.1.3.1. The participation exemption for corporate shareholders (also mentioned at that point) is of a similar nature. However, other countries simply leave gains on the disposal of shares subject to the usual taxation of capital gains treatment, including where capital gains are subject to some form of concessionary tax treatment. This is the position taken with respect to individuals in the UK, the US and Australia.

Prior to 1998, UK individuals were taxed at marginal income tax rates on capital gains, but were permitted to index the cost base of assets for inflation. Between 1998 and 2008 a taper relief system for capital gains was introduced under which the amount of capital gains subject to tax (at marginal rates, but without indexation) decreased depending on how long the asset disposed of had been held. Currently, the UK taxes capital gains of individuals according to a special tax rate structure that is generally more favourable than income tax rates. The general capital gains tax rate for individuals is 18%, with a 28% rate applying to individuals who are in the 40% or 50% rate bands for income tax.[36]

Each of these sets of UK rules, including the current rules, applies equally to capital gains on the disposal of shares. In contrast to most other countries, the UK has a separate substantial exempt amount of capital gains, which is in addition to the personal allowance for income tax purposes. The exempt amount is usually indexed and is currently in excess of £10,000.[37] This general concessionary treatment of capital gains can be similar in quantum, but is far from the same as the provision of dividend relief for individuals. This leaves substantial scope for wealthy individuals planning whether to realise a return from shares in the form of capital gains on disposal or dividends.

Australia is another country that applies the usual concessionary capital gains tax treatment to gains on the disposal of shares. If shares have been held by an individual for more than twelve months, only 50% of the gain is taxable (at marginal rates).[38] Again, although this provides some relief analogous to dividend relief, it is far from the same as Australia's full imputation system. The result is potential tax planning, particularly for higher tax rate individuals.

---

[36] TCGA 1992 (UK) s. 4.
[37] TCGA 1992 (UK) s. 3.
[38] Income Tax Assessment Act 1997 (Australia) ss. 102–3 & 115–100.

The position in the US is different. As discussed earlier at 5.1.3.1, it has taken the peculiar step of treating dividends in the same fashion as capital gains. Capital gains on the disposal of shares are treated in the same concessionary manner as other types of capital gains. Because dividends are treated in the same fashion as any type of capital gain, the quantum of dividend relief provided is necessarily arbitrary (i.e. bears no relationship to corporation tax). The US had a full classical system prior to the intro-duction of this form of dividend relief, which perhaps made the move to capital gains treatment for dividends more straightforward.

By contrast, both the UK and Australia have a long history of divi-dend relief in the form of dividend tax credits. As mentioned earlier at 5.1.3.1, there is real difficulty in creating consistency between the taxa-tion of gains on the disposal of shares and on dividends where dividend relief is provided by way of dividend tax credit, particularly in an impu-tation system. In this context, it is not surprising that both the UK and Australia suffer a real difference in tax treatment between gains on the dis-posal of shares and on dividends. This difference has the potential to cause additional distortions of the variety discussed earlier at 5.1.3.3, including issues pertaining to enveloping and quarantining of losses. Perhaps the only realistic manner in which the UK and Australia could provide accept-able consistency between the taxation of gains on the disposal of shares and dividends is to move away from their current dividend tax credit systems.

In passing, it may be noted that those countries that do not impose taxa-tion on capital gains adopt the approach discussed in this paragraph; that is, a concessional taxation of capital gains on the disposal of shares. In New Zealand, Malaysia and Singapore the general capital gains exemp-tion includes exemption of capital gains on the disposal of shares. His-torically, this could be a substantially different tax treatment from that imposed with respect to dividends, particularly when the classical sys-tem was prevalent during the 1950s to 1980s. This difference gave rise to substantial problems with enveloping and dividend stripping (the latter is discussed later at 8.3). Currently, most countries, including New Zealand, Malaysia and Singapore, do not retain such a substantial distinction. New Zealand ameliorates the distinction by adopting a full imputation system. Historically, Malaysia and Singapore did the same, but since 2008 they have effectively adopted the US approach of treating dividends in the same manner as capital gains. They did so by adopting a dividend exclusion system.

### 5.1.3.5 Full taxation

Gains on the disposal of shares may be subject to full taxation at marginal rates. It is possible that this is a specific treatment for gains on the disposal of shares, but more likely it is a treatment applied to all types of capital gains. This is an uncommon approach with respect to individuals. For reasons discussed earlier at 5.1.3.3 and 5.1.3.4, individuals are usually granted some form of concessionary treatment with respect to the taxation of capital gains or at least gains on the disposal of shares. By contrast, capital gains derived by corporations are often subject to full taxation; the rationale for this approach requires a brief explanation.

Dividends of corporations may be distributed from profits generally, and it does not matter whether those profits are of a capital or revenue nature. If corporations are subject to concessionary taxation of capital gains, some of the profits available for distribution will have suffered a lower amount of tax than other types. Because all profits may become dividends, it is not clear that this treatment is appropriate, and this is one reason for the full taxation of all corporate profits, including capital gains. Full taxation of corporate profits is also consistent with the global approach in corporate financial accounts (see the earlier discussion at 1.2.1). Taxation of corporate capital gains at concessionary rates can also cause issues with some forms of dividend relief, in particular corporate-level dividend relief systems and the imputation system. Australia's full imputation system can be used as an example.

If Australian corporations were subject to lower taxation with respect to capital gains, they would have less tax to credit to their franking (imputation) account. This would mean that when dividends are distributed there would be less corporation tax available to attach as dividend tax credits. The result would be increased shareholder taxation, and ultimately the concession granted with respect to corporate capital gains would be *washed out*. As discussed earlier at 2.4.3.3, this can cause distortions as to distribution policy or at least increased complexity in terms of recording corporate tax and allocating profits as retained or distributed.

Whether these are compelling reasons or not, many if not most countries tax corporate capital gains at full corporate tax rates. This is true of Germany, the UK and the US and would be the case under the CCCTB Proposal. However, when it comes to the taxation of corporations with respect to gains on the disposal of shares, the treatment often diverges. As mentioned earlier at 5.1.3.1, many countries adopt a participation exemption. So, although Germany and the UK impose full corporate taxation of capital gains, many corporate gains on the disposal of shares are exempt. The same would be true under the CCCTB Proposal.

By contrast, the US and, residually in many situations, the UK impose full taxation of gains on the disposal of shares by one corporation in another corporation. This can create a substantial dislocation between the taxation of gains on disposal of shares and of dividends. For example, the US grants dividend relief for inter-corporate dividends by way of an exemption ranging from 70% to 100% (see the earlier discussion at 2.4.3.1), but gains on the disposal of shares are fully taxable. This differing treatment can create an incentive to strip dividends out of a corporation prior to sale of its shares to reduce tax liability with respect to the sale. The same can be true in the UK where the shares are held in non-trading corporations or the shareholding is below the 10% requirement for the substantial shareholder exemption.[39]

It may seem that Australia adopts a more consistent approach in that both dividends and capital gains on the disposal of shares are fully taxable to a corporation. However, tax liability with respect to dividends is commonly covered by dividend tax credits attached to dividends. Where dividend tax credits are attached at the maximum rate, the effect can be similar to an exemption for inter-corporate dividends. Although this may seem to be an uneven treatment likely to create distortions, the Australian imputation system demonstrates that it may not be so. As mentioned earlier, if tax is paid with respect to corporate capital gains, the corporation will have a credit in its franking account that it can pass on as dividend tax credits to its shareholders. The bottom line is that Australia has chosen to allocate corporation tax (and so tax credits for corporation tax) only to dividends and not to gains on the disposal of shares. It is not clear that this choice causes any substantial distortions.

The full taxation of gains on the disposal of shares addresses the enveloping problem. However, it does exacerbate the (temporary) economic double taxation of corporate profits described earlier at 5.1.2. Further, full taxation of gains on the disposal of shares by one corporation in another corporation is likely to mean that capital losses on such disposals are also recognised. As noted earlier at 5.1.2, this can cause problems with

---

[39] Unlike the other corporate tax systems focused on in this study, the UK continues to index the cost base of assets for purposes of calculating capital gains of corporations; TCGA 1992 (UK) s. 53.

loss cascading and is likely to lead to a need for anti-abuse rules. Australia, the UK and the US have each experienced problems in this regard. Details of their specific anti-abuse rules are beyond the scope of this book. These specific rules are backed up with a general quarantining rule under which capital losses may only be set against capital gains.[40]

### 5.1.4 International issues

Finally, it is useful to briefly extend issues pertaining to the taxation of gains on the disposal of shares into an international setting. This extension involves two scenarios. The first is where non-residents dispose of shares in a resident corporation. The second is where residents dispose of shares in a non-resident corporation.

#### Shares held by non-residents

The issue of consistency between the tax treatment of gains on the disposal of shares and dividends extends to the shareholdings of non-residents in resident corporations. As noted earlier at 3.1.2, traditionally many countries impose withholding tax on outbound dividends. Because capital gains are a net concept and sales proceeds are not received from a single person (e.g. in the case of dividends, the corporation), it is not a simple matter to replicate this treatment. Rather, the usual approach is either to tax gains of non-residents on the disposal of shares in resident corporations in full or simply to exempt them. Unless, dividends are treated in the same fashion, there will be inconsistency. In passing, the OECD Model tax treaty permits this form of inconsistency: permitting withholding of tax on dividends paid by resident corporations, but exempting most gains on the disposal of shares in such corporations.[41]

Despite its inconsistent treatment of resident shareholders, the UK corporate tax system incorporates a substantial amount of consistency for non-resident shareholders. Broadly, the UK does not tax capital gains of non-residents unless derived through a branch or PE.[42] This is consistent with the tax treatment of dividends distributed by resident corporations to non-residents, which are effectively exempt in almost all cases. By contrast, the US corporate tax system demonstrates inconsistency. It

---

[40] TCGA 1992 (UK) ss. 2 & 8, IRC (US) s. 1211 and Income Tax Assessment Act 1997 (Australia) s. 102–10.

[41] OECD Model Arts. 10 & 13. Regarding these provisions, see Harris & Oliver (2010, pp. 181–90 & 207–11).

[42] TCGA 1992 (UK) ss. 10 and 10B.

has a general dividend withholding tax of 30% on outbound dividends. However, like the UK, it generally exempts non-residents from taxation of capital gains unless they are connected with a US business.[43]

The German taxation of non-residents with respect to gains on the disposal of shares is complex. A non-resident is a taxpayer with limited tax liability and so is only taxable with respect to income having a German source. Gains on the disposal of shares have a German source if derived through a German PE or if the non-resident shareholder holds at least a 1% interest in the German corporation whose shares are disposed of.[44] This taxation of gains on the disposal of shares is often suppressed by German tax treaties, which by comparison may limit the taxation of dividends, but usually do not eliminate it.

If a non-resident individual shareholder is not taxable on gains on the disposal of shares in a German corporation, there is inconsistency with the 25% withholding tax imposed on dividends of German corporations distributed to such shareholders. If the non-resident individual is taxable, the 40% exemption system applies (see the earlier discussion at 5.1.3.1); this is also inconsistent. If the shares are held by a non-resident corporation through a German PE, the participation exemption should be available (again see the earlier discussion at 5.1.3.1). This would be consistent with the treatment of dividends received by such a corporation. If the shares are not attributed to a German PE and the non-resident corporation holds more than 1% of the shares in the German corporation, it seems the non-resident corporation is taxable. Here there is again inconsistency. If the gains are not taxable, that is inconsistent with the 25% tax on outbound dividends. If the gains are taxable, they are subject to corporation tax rather than the 25% withholding tax.

The CCCTB Proposal would only apply to eligible corporations that opt into the Proposal. At present, eligible corporations include all corporations resident in a member state. They also include third country resident corporations that have a PE in a member state, but the Proposal would apply only with respect to the PE.[45] To the extent the Proposal would apply to a non-resident corporation, there would be a simple consistent system for dividends and capital gains on the disposal of shares. The exemption for inter-corporate dividends and gains on the disposal of shares (see the earlier discussion at 5.1.3.1) would apply. If the Proposal

[43]   IRC (US) ss. 871 & 882.
[44]   EStG (Germany) s. 49(1) No. 2.
[45]   CCCTB Proposal Art. 6.

does not apply to the non-resident shareholder, the treatment would be a matter for the domestic tax law of the country from which the dividend or gain is sourced.

### Shares held in non-resident corporations

As noted earlier at 3.2.2.3, as regards resident shareholders, dividends received from a non-resident corporation are often treated in a manner different from dividends received from a resident corporation. In particular, dividend relief is often available with respect to the latter but not the former. However, there are some important exceptions to this treatment, particularly in the EU and the US.

In the context of gains on the disposal of shares, there is less likely to be a variation in tax treatment depending on whether the shares are held in a resident or non-resident corporation. This is true of all the corporate tax systems focused on in this study. For example, German individuals are entitled to the 40% exemption or the 25% tax rate irrespective of whether the corporation whose shares are disposed of is resident or non-resident. The same is true of the participation exemption for corporations and would be true under the participation exemption in the CCCTB Proposal. In the UK and the US, the reduced rates of capital gains tax for individuals are available for gains on the disposal of shares in non-resident corporations. The UK participation exemption for corporate shareholders is also available for gains on the disposal of shares in non-resident corporations.

Even countries that adopt an inconsistent treatment of dividends received from resident or non-resident corporations tend to adopt a consistent treatment with respect to gains on the disposal of shares. So, for example, the Australian 50% exemption of capital gains on assets held for twelve months or longer applies to gains on the disposal of shares in non-resident corporations. New Zealand's general exemption for capital gains also applies to such gains. The most likely scenario in which there might be inconsistency between gains on the disposal of shares in resident and non-resident corporations is where there is a targeted tax treatment of gains on the disposal of shares. So, for example, the Mexican exemption for gains on the disposal of listed shares mentioned earlier at 5.1.3.3 only applies to corporations regulated by the Mexican stock exchange law.

## 5.2 Corporate-level consequences

As noted in the introduction to this chapter, the transfer of shares in a corporation may be viewed as an indirect transfer of tax attributes of the corporation. To permit the free indirect transfer of corporate tax attributes through the sale of shares may be viewed as inappropriate, particularly if direct transfers of tax attributes are not permitted (e.g. the direct sale of carried-forward losses). It will also give rise to taxpayers seeking to make arrangements with each other to minimise overall tax (i.e. tax arbitrage). As a result, the corporate tax systems of many countries incorporate restrictions on the carry-forward of corporate tax attributes following a change of ownership of the corporation. It is those rules with which this heading is primarily concerned. The corporate tax systems of Germany, the UK and the US incorporate such rules, but notably the CCCTB Proposal does not.[46] So to provide a broader analysis, the basics of the Australian rules are mentioned.

As explained earlier at 1.1.4.2, tax attributes are those features of a tax system that attach to tax subjects and that are carried forward from one tax period to another. Two prime examples are carried-forward losses and the tax value of particular assets. These examples are linked because losses are often calculated by reference to or realised by reason of the tax value of assets disposed of. Inevitably, restrictions on the carry-forward of tax attributes are only triggered if there is a sufficient change in the ownership of the corporation in question. Defining what constitutes a sufficient change is the first matter discussed under this heading. The discussion then moves to consider the types of restrictions that countries impose on the indirect transfer of gains and losses. This discussion also delves deeper into the reasons why countries adopt such restrictions. Third, the heading turns to consider limitations on the carry-forward of other types of corporate tax attributes.

The final matter with which this heading is briefly concerned is how a transfer of shares might affect group corporations. A transfer of shares in a group corporation might cause the corporation to leave the corporate group. The sorts of issues that arise when a member leaves a corporate group are in many ways similar to those that arise on a change of ownership.

### 5.2.1   Defining a sufficient change

The issue for present discussion is what constitutes a sufficient change of a corporation's ownership structure such that restrictions should be placed

---

[46] Although the EU Presidency comments on CCCTB Proposal Art. 43 (losses) note that they should have rules on a change of ownership and merger.

on its ability to carry forward tax attributes. As mentioned, a point of comparison is with the general prohibition on the direct transfer of tax attributes. A problem is that a direct transfer of tax attributes involves a complete change of ownership of the attribute in question, even if only part of the attribute is split off and transferred. However, where an artificial entity like a corporation is involved, that is not the case.

Ownership of a corporation involves an undivided indirect interest in corporate assets and liabilities, including corporate tax attributes. Because of that undivided nature, it is impossible to identify the part of, say, a carried-forward corporate loss that belongs to any particular shareholder. Where there is a transfer of all of the shares in a corporation, it is appropriate to say that there has been an indirect transfer of all of the corporation's tax attributes, and it may be appropriate to deny, say, a loss carry-forward. However, where only a portion of the shares in the corporation are transferred, it is impossible to impose a restriction on the carry-forward of corporate tax attributes without penalising continuing shareholders. This is best illustrated with a simple example based on the carry-forward of losses.

Presume a corporation with a loss carry-forward of 100. It has two shareholders, one holding 60% of the shares in the corporation and the other 40%. It is inaccurate to say that one shareholder indirectly owns 60 of the loss and the other 40 of the loss. Further, if, say, the 60% shareholder sells, it is inaccurate to say that there has been an indirect transfer of 60 of the loss. Rather, both the 60% shareholder and the 40% shareholder hold a proportionate undivided interest in each unit of the loss. So, if the 60% shareholder sells, there is an indirect transfer of a 60% interest in each unit of the loss and not a complete transfer of 60 of the loss.

Presume the 60% shareholder does sell. What should be the response of the corporate tax system? The first issue is whether it should deny any of the corporation's carried-forward loss. As mentioned, if it does not, there is an ability to indirectly transfer this tax attribute, which is inconsistent with an inability to directly transfer (sell) losses. Presume that the response is to limit the amount of loss carried forward. How much should be limited? Should it be the full 100 or the proportionate 60? Neither answer is correct. This can be demonstrated by focusing on a denial of 60, which at first may seem a balanced approach.

Presume the corporation is denied a loss carry-forward of 60 by reason of the change of ownership. Then 40 of the loss remains available in the future, representing the 40% of the shares in the corporation that did not change ownership. However, that 40 does not belong to the continuing

40% shareholder. Rather, the 40% shareholder has an undivided 40% interest in the remaining 40 loss carry-forward. The 40% shareholder has been denied his or her interest in the 60 prohibited loss carry-forward, despite the fact that the 40% shareholder may have had nothing to do with the 60% shareholder selling. Further, the new 60% shareholder has acquired a 60% interest in the remaining 40 loss carry-forward, and so there has been an indirect transfer of the loss to the new shareholder despite an attempt to prevent this.

There is no way to remedy this problem without engaging in complex adjustments that would alter the general nature of a shareholding as an undivided interest in a corporation.[47] The result is that there is an inherent conflict between the holistic nature of corporate tax attributes and the undivided nature of shareholder interests in those attributes. This conflict in turn means that there is no easy or correct answer to what constitutes a sufficient change of ownership in order to trigger carry-forward restrictions. Perhaps for this reason, most countries view restrictions on the carry-forward of corporate tax attributes as an anti-abuse rather than a structural measure and focus their restrictions on an ability to control the corporation. However, this is not always the case, and the German example discussed later provides a good example of an alternate approach. The first part of the following discussion considers what constitutes a sufficient change of ownership to trigger restrictions on the carry-forward of corporate tax attributes.

The potential harshness of a rule based on a change in control for continuing shareholders and the focus on anti-abuse have caused a number of countries to provide exceptions to their restrictions on the carry-forward of corporate tax attributes. In particular, these countries try to identify circumstances in which a corporation is acquired predominantly for its tax attributes and so is abusive. For this purpose, the focus is on the activities of the corporation. If the activities of the corporation do not change sufficiently after the change of ownership, then the view is taken that the corporation was not acquired for its tax attributes. In such a case, the

---

[47] For example, at the time of a change of ownership, corporate losses may be attributed to continuing shareholders in proportion to their shareholdings and then denied at the corporate level. Alternately, losses could continue to be carried forward at the corporate level following a change of ownership, but adjustments made when they are used; for example, an additional tax imposed on the new shareholders' next dividend (perhaps by way of withholding) equal to their share of the corporate tax saved with the corporate losses. In any case, to get at the problem requires moving it from the corporate to the shareholder level.

corporation may be saved from the restrictions. Additional rules that require a sufficient change of corporate activity before restrictions on the carry-forward of tax attributes are imposed are the second matter discussed under this subheading.

### 5.2.1.1 Of ownership

Identifying what is a sufficient change of ownership and the manner in which that is determined for purposes of restricting the carry-forward of corporate tax attributes raises many issues. The present discussion provides an overview of the main issues only. The dominant issue is the threshold that constitutes an ownership change and what is being measured for this purpose. Other issues include the period during which the change is measured and the treatment of changes in small shareholdings. Particularly difficult issues occur where corporations hold shares in other corporations. One question is the extent to which changes up a chain of corporate shareholdings are treated as a change down the corporate chain. There is the related issue of whether a change down a corporate chain should be recognised if there is no change up the corporate chain.

**Threshold issues** Difficulties with selecting any particular threshold for denying the carry-forward of corporate tax attributes were discussed earlier. Because a proportionate approach does not function accurately, the selection of any threshold must be arbitrary. The most commonly selected threshold is the point at which control of the corporation passes, typically defined as in excess of a 50% change in shareholdings. The concept of 'control' of a corporation was discussed earlier at 1.1.5.1, and one issue is whether the tests discussed at that point are used for present purposes. Another relevant threshold might be the threshold at which the corporation is part of a group of corporations for loss relief purposes. This issue was discussed earlier at 1.2.3.

The US threshold is comparatively straightforward and is triggered by an 'ownership change'. It is defined by reference to the 'percentage of the stock' of the corporation increasing 'by more than 50 percentage points, over ... the lowest percentage of stock ... owned by such shareholders at any time during the testing period'.[48] 'Stock' for this purpose does not include non-voting, non-convertible preference shares.[49] To prevent manipulation, regulations provide further qualifications and additions to

---

[48] IRC (US) s. 382(g)(1).
[49] IRC (US) s. 382(k)(6).

the definition of 'stock'.[50] As a general rule, percentage changes in stock are determined by reference to value rather than the number of shares.[51]

By contrast, the UK uses two main thresholds. The UK revenue loss rules are triggered where there is a 'change in ownership', which is broadly defined as one or more persons acquiring 'a holding of the ordinary share capital of the company' that amounts 'to more than half the ordinary share capital of the company'.[52] The ordinary share capital test would be easy to manipulate and is backed up with an anti-abuse rule that applies to persons with extraordinary powers or rights. In this case, other tests may be used, including all share capital and voting power.[53]

In the usual bizarre manner, the UK has a separate and unrelated test for capital loss purposes. TCGA 1992 also has a definition of 'qualifying change of ownership',[54] which includes joining or leaving a 75% group or becoming subject to a different 'control'.[55] This definition is fundamentally different from the test used for revenue loss purposes. The threshold is triggered by going through a group or control barrier and not by reference to the volume of shares changing hands. As a result, a change of ownership can be triggered by making an acquisition that takes the acquirer through a 50% ownership threshold.[56] Unlike the other tests considered here, this change may occur by reason of a single small increase in a shareholding.

Australia is another country that uses a basic 50% change threshold. However, it is couched in terms of the same persons continuing to hold 'more than 50%' of the corporation. So unlike in the UK and the US, this threshold is breached by a 50% change. The Australian rules also incorporate alternate tests to prevent manipulation of the basic threshold: the change is tested by reference to voting power, the right to dividends and the right to receive distributions of capital.[57] There are further rules dealing with arrangements affecting the beneficial ownership of shares.[58] There are also a general change of control test and an income injection test,

---

[50] See Title 26 Code of Federal Regulations (US) § 1.382–2(a)(3) and the references referred to therein.

[51] IRC (US) s. 382(k)(6)(C).

[52] CTA 2010 (UK) s. 719(1).

[53] CTA 2010 (UK) s. 721.

[54] TCGA 1992 (UK) s. 184C.

[55] 'Group of companies' was discussed earlier at 1.2.3.1 and 'control' at 1.1.5.1.

[56] The UK capital loss rules suffer similar aggregation problems to those discussed at 1.1.5.1. In TCGA 1992 (UK) s. 184C(6) the test is control by a person 'whether alone or together with one or more others'.

[57] Income Tax Assessment Act 1997 (Australia) s. 165–12.

[58] Income Tax Assessment Act 1997 (Australia) s. 165–180.

which are of an anti-abuse nature.[59] Less onerous rules apply for testing changes of listed corporations.[60]

So although the US, the UK and the Australian thresholds appear basically similar (being triggered on a change of shareholding of more than 50%), there are substantial differences in the details of determining when the threshold is breached. The German approach is different again, even with respect to the basic threshold. Since the start of 2008, the German rules have two thresholds: one to fully deny the carry-forward of losses and the other to deny a proportion of carried-forward losses.

The test for the full denial of the carry-forward of losses is broadly similar to that used in the US and the UK. It applies where

> more than 50 percent of the subscribed capital, membership rights, ownership rights, or voting rights of a corporation are transferred to a purchaser or related persons, or a comparable situation exists. As a purchaser within the meaning of the sentences 1 and 2 is also a group of purchasers with parallel interests. A capital increase is equal to the transfer of the registered capital if they result in a change in the participation rates in the capital of the corporation.[61]

So like the US and UK approach, there must be more than a 50% change. Similarly, the range of interests in a corporation is broad in an attempt to prevent manipulation of the basic threshold. The German tax administration has released guidance with respect to this rule that gives examples of what might constitute a 'comparable situation'. It might include the acquisition of participation rights, voting agreements, corporate reorganisations, share redemptions or capital reductions.[62]

The test for the proportionate denial of carried-forward losses is more peculiar. It applies where

> more than 25 percent of the subscribed capital, membership rights, ownership rights, or voting rights of a corporation are transferred to a purchaser or related persons, or if a similar situation exists.[63]

Note that, like the 50% change of ownership rule, prima facie the 25% transfer must be to one purchaser (or one purchaser and related persons). Further, this proportionate rule raises several additional issues. One is the

---

[59] Income Tax Assessment Act 1997 (Australia) s. 165–15 and Subdiv. 175-A, respectively.
[60] Income Tax Assessment Act 1997 (Australia) Div. 166.
[61] KStG (Germany) s. 8c(1).
[62] Regarding this guidance, see Weyde (2008).
[63] KStG (Germany) s. 8c(1).

manner in which this rule interacts with the full denial rule. This interaction is relatively straightforward. The full denial of corporate losses rule is an independent rule. So a breach of the 25% rule does not trigger a restart of the calculation of whether there has been more than a 50% transfer under the full denial rule. So, a breach of the 25% rule may trigger a proportionate denial of loss carry-forward, and subsequent transfers taking the breach through the more than 50% threshold will result in the denial of carry-forward of the rest of the losses.

A second issue is the potential multiple applications of the proportionate 25% rule. The proportion of losses denied to the corporation under the proportionate rule increases depending on the percentage of shares sold between 25% and 50%. When the rule is triggered by an acquisition of 25% or more, what is the effect of further subsequent acquisitions? There are two possibilities here: further acquisitions continue to decrease the amount of losses that can be used, or the 25% threshold starts back at zero and there is no further denial until the 25% threshold is reached again. The tax administration guidance mentioned earlier adopts the latter approach. After the 25% threshold has been breached, the acquisition of additional shares by the same acquirer (or related persons) does not increase the pro rata share of disallowed losses. However, a series of acquisitions by one acquirer (or related persons) is treated as one acquisition if they are part of a predetermined plan. There is a rebuttable presumption that such a plan exists for acquisitions occurring within a year.[64]

**Test period**  A change of ownership of a corporation must be tested by reference to a time period. Its duration varies, but may be implicitly limited by reference to the period for which the tax attribute (e.g. loss) can be carried forward. Australia provides an example of an unlimited time period. The period during which changes of share ownership are tested to see if the 50% threshold is breached is the period from the year the loss was incurred to the year that the loss is sought to be used.[65] In theory, because losses can be carried forward indefinitely, it does not matter whether this period is one year or fifty years. In practice, however, there may be a limit on the administrative ability of a corporation to trace ownership changes (especially indirect ownership changes) over such a long period. This is one reason why Australia has less onerous rules for listed corporations.

---

[64] Regarding this guidance, see Weyde (2008).
[65] Income Tax Assessment Act 1997 (Australia) s. 165–12.

The UK and the US have a more realistic period for testing whether the 50% threshold has been breached. Both countries use a three-year test period. In the US, for example, a corporation must test every time there is a change in the level of shares held by a 5% shareholder. The test is whether the percentage of shares in the corporation held by one or more 5% shareholders has increased by more than 50 percentage points when compared to any time within the previous three years.[66]

For revenue loss purposes, the UK rule is similar. Whether there is a change of ownership must be measured at two points, which cannot be more than three years apart.[67] There is no equivalent limitation in the rules restricting the use of capital losses. This is because, as mentioned earlier, this test is fundamentally different from the revenue loss test or the tests in Germany, the US or Australia. The threshold is triggered by going through a control or grouping barrier and not by reference to the volume of shares changing hands.

Germany has a slightly longer testing period of five years. The share transfer (or similar situation) must occur 'within 5 years'.[68] This testing period is used for the purposes of both the proportionate loss denial rule and the full loss denial rule. The five- year test period is straightforward with respect to the latter rule, but its application to the proportionate loss denial rule requires some further explanation. Multiple acquisitions by a single acquirer (or related persons) over a five-year period can be aggregated for the purposes of determining whether the 25% threshold is met. However, once that 25% threshold is breached with respect to a single acquisition (and other acquisitions in a pre-determined plan), the counting of the threshold and the five-year period start again.[69] As mentioned before, however, breaching the 25% threshold does not start a new counting of the threshold or five-year period for the purposes of the full loss denial rule.

**Small shareholdings** The tracking of changes in substantial shareholders can be difficult administratively, but tracking changes of small shareholders can verge on the impossible – especially if the corporation must prove that it has not suffered a change of ownership. Many countries have a mechanism for excluding small shareholdings from counting when

---

[66] IRC (US) s. 382(g)(1) & (i)(1).
[67] CTA 2010 (UK) s. 720(2).
[68] KStG (Germany) s. 8c(1).
[69] See the administrative guidance described in Weyde (2008).

determining whether a corporation has suffered a change of ownership. This seems appropriate when the threshold for change of ownership generally focuses on control: small shareholdings rarely carry a significant control element (unless they are added to a larger shareholding).

The UK and the US provide a good example of ignoring changes in small shareholdings. In the UK, when determining whether there is more than a 50% acquisition of shares,

> there is disregarded a holding of less than 5% unless
>
> (i) it is an addition to an existing holding, and
> (ii) the two holdings together amount to at least 5% of the ordinary share capital of the company.[70]

Similarly in the US, the test is measured by changes in the holdings of 5% shareholders.[71] A '5-percent shareholder' is defined as a 'person holding 5 percent or more of the stock of the corporation'.[72]

Australia also has a rule ignoring small shareholdings, but it is more targeted. It only applies to the test for determining whether listed corporations have suffered a change of ownership. In this context, all shareholdings under 10% are attributed to a single notional shareholder so that changes among small shareholders do not affect the change of ownership test.[73] Although Germany has no legislative rule for small shareholdings, its proportionate loss denial rule is targeted at acquisitions of shares by a single person (and related persons) of at least 25%. Changes in small shareholdings are irrelevant to the application of this rule (unless they are part of a 'group of purchasers').

**Indirect change without direct change**  If restrictions on the carry-forward of corporate tax attributes were limited to direct changes in ownership of the corporation, the restrictions would be easy to avoid. It would be a simple matter of ensuring that corporations with substantial activities were always held by a holding corporation and the *real* shareholders held shares in the holding corporation. If the substantial corporation incurred a loss, the sale of shares in the holding corporation could effect an indirect transfer of the loss without triggering the loss denial restrictions. For these reasons, countries that incorporate restrictions on the carry-forward

---

[70]  CTA 2010 (UK) s. 719(1)[C](b).
[71]  IRC (US) s. 382(g)(1)(A).
[72]  IRC (US) s. 382(k)(7).
[73]  Income Tax Assessment Act 1997 (Australia) s. 166–225.

of corporate tax attributes inevitably cover indirect changes in ownership of the corporation. However, the precise manner in which countries do this varies substantially.

The indirect attribution of rights to particular persons was discussed earlier at 1.1.5.1, and that discussion is relevant for present purposes. The most complex manner in which to calculate indirect changes in ownership is to use the proportionate approach. Germany provides an example of this approach. Both its proportionate and full loss denial rules apply to direct and 'indirect' acquisitions of shares. There is no further legislative direction on what constitutes an 'indirect' acquisition, but it is presumed to involve the proportionate approach.

The US rules on indirect changes in ownership are slightly different in form, but produce a similar proportionate approach. The US has share attribution rules that are similar but not the same as those in section 267(c) of IRC, discussed earlier at 1.1.5.1. For the purposes of determining whether there has been a change of more than 50% of share ownership, shares may be treated as owned by certain related persons. In particular, the holdings of family members are treated as a single holding (and so transfers between them do not count). By contrast, an individual is allocated a proportionate share of stock held 'indirectly' through artificial entities (i.e. other corporations, partnerships, estates or trusts). This involves a proportionate approach. By contrast, no shares are attributed to artificial entities.[74]

Australia also adopts the proportionate approach to tracing changes in ownership, and its more detailed legislative rules are instructive of some of the issues faced with this approach. The Australian continuity of ownership rules incorporate a primary test and an alternate test for attributing voting power, the right to receive dividends or the right to receive capital of a corporation in determining if there is a 50% change. The alternate test is particularly concerned with indirect holdings. Using dividend attribution as an example, if

> there are persons (none of them companies) who (between them) at a particular time have the right to receive for their own benefit (whether directly or indirectly) more than 50% of any dividends that the company may pay, those persons have rights to 'more than 50% of the company's dividends' at that time.[75]

---

[74] IRC (US) s. 382(l)(3)(A) applying and modifying the attribution rules in s. 318(a).
[75] Income Tax Assessment Act 1997 (Australia) s. 165–155(2).

This is expanded upon with a definition of 'indirectly':

> [E]ntities have the right to receive dividends...of a company 'indirectly' for their own benefit if they would receive the dividends...for their own benefit if:
>
> (a) the company were to pay or distribute the dividends...and
> (b) the dividends...were then successively paid or distributed by each entity interposed between the company and those entities.[76]

Testing indirect ownership changes in this fashion can be particularly onerous, and again Australia relaxes the precision of these rules in the context of listed corporations. In particular, it is not necessary to trace ownership through shareholdings of up to 50% that are held by widely held corporations or pension funds and by some other collective ownership entities.[77]

The UK rules on indirect changes in ownership appear less onerous. Unlike the other corporate tax systems discussed, the UK does not refer to 'indirect' changes. Rather, it has a rule that attributes shares held by a corporation if that corporation suffers a change of ownership. If a single person acquires more than half the ordinary share capital of a corporation, that person is treated as acquiring any shares owned by the corporation.[78] For example, presume that A Co holds 55% of the shares in B Co, and individual Z acquires 55% of the shares in A Co. A Co suffers a change of ownership, and as a result the shares held by A Co in B Co are treated as also acquired by Z. The result is that B Co also suffers a change of control, and restrictions on the carry-forward of losses also apply to B Co. This attribution of the shares held by A Co to Z is an example of an absolute approach.

In other cases of a change of ownership (e.g. where a number of shareholders acquire more than 50% of the ordinary share capital of a corporation), the proportionate approach is used. Extending the example in the last paragraph, presume that individual Y acquires 30% of A Co, and individual Z acquires 25% of A Co. A Co has still suffered a change of ownership, and so the shares that it holds in B Co are attributed to Y and Z, but this time proportionately. Y is treated as acquiring 16.5% of the shares in B Co (30% of 55%) and Z as acquiring 13.75% of the shares in B Co (25% of 55%). In the result, only 30.25% (16.5% plus 13.75%) of the

---

[76] Income Tax Assessment Act 1997 (Australia) s. 995–1.
[77] Income Tax Assessment Act 1997 (Australia) ss. 166–240 and 166–245.
[78] CTA 2010 (UK) s. 723(3).

shares in B Co have been acquired, and B Co does not suffer a change of ownership.

Another feature of the UK rules is that they can result in no change of ownership, despite the indirect acquisition of more than 50% of the shares in a corporation. Presume that individual Z owns all of the shares in A Co, which holds all of the shares in B Co. Z sells 40% of the shares in A Co to individual Y. A Co sells 40% of its shares in B Co to Y. Indirectly, Y has acquired 64% of B Co (40% directly and indirectly 40% of A Co's remaining 60%). However, because A Co has not suffered a change of ownership, none of the shares that A Co holds in B Co are attributed to Y. In turn, this means that for UK tax purposes, B Co does not suffer a change of ownership.

Again, these are the rules for revenue losses. The rules for capital losses are fundamentally different. As noted earlier, these are determined by reference to joining or leaving a group of corporations or suffering a change of control. Indirect ownership counts for purposes of determining whether a corporation is a member of a group, which is determined according to the proportionate approach (see the earlier discussion at 1.1.5.1 and 1.2.3.1). Indirect ownership can also count when it comes to determining control, but here the absolute approach is used (see the earlier discussion at 1.1.5.1).

**Direct change without indirect change**  Just as there can be an indirect change without a direct change of ownership of a corporation, there can be a direct change without an indirect change. Here the problem is that, if form rules, the corporation will be denied the carry-forward of its tax attributes despite retaining the same ultimate owners. If this were the rule, it could cause severe problems with corporate reorganisations. For example, presume that A Co holds all of the shares in B Co, which holds all of the shares in C Co, and that C Co has carried forward losses. A transfer of the shares in C Co by B Co to A Co constitutes a direct change of ownership and without more might result in C Co being denied the use of its losses.

The UK seeks to avoid this result with a direct rule:

> A change in the ownership of a company ... is disregarded ... if
>
> (a) immediately before the change in ownership, the subsidiary company is a qualifying 75% subsidiary of another company ... and

(b) although there is a change in the direct ownership of the subsidiary company, the subsidiary company continues after the change to be a qualifying 75% subsidiary of the parent company.[79]

This rule provides a broad scope for reorganising members of a 75% corporate group without losing the carry-forward of revenue losses. A similar result is achieved under the capital loss rules, which are triggered when a corporation joins or leaves a group or suffers a change of control.

Originally, the German change of ownership rule introduced in 2008 incorporated no exception for direct changes in ownership without an indirect change. This caused difficulty, and an exception was introduced in 2010 that partly addresses the issue. The exception applies where the transfer triggering the change of ownership is from one subsidiary to another subsidiary and both are wholly owned (directly or indirectly) by the parent corporation.[80] It does not cover a transfer to or from the parent corporation. This makes the German exception substantially narrower than the UK exception.

By contrast, the US exception is not explicit, but seems to be broader. The attribution of indirect interests through interposed entities for purposes of the change of ownership rule was described earlier as involving the proportionate approach. Often when attribution occurs (e.g. to determine whether a person controls an entity) the entity itself continues to qualify as a shareholder, and this duplicates share interests in the subject corporation. That is, interests in the corporation are treated as owned both by the interposed entity and the person to whom the interests held by the interposed entity are attributed. The US rule on changes of corporate ownership expressly prevents this duplication from happening. When a share held by an entity (such as a corporation) is attributed to a person that holds an interest in that entity, the share is considered as 'no longer being held by the entity from which attributed'.[81] In the result, a restructure within a 50% corporate group should not result in a change of ownership.

Australia achieves a similar result through the distinction between the primary test for change of ownership and the alternate test. As discussed earlier, the alternate test attributes ownership through interposed entities according to the proportionate approach. The primary section imposing the restriction on the carry-forward of corporate losses specifically

---

[79] CTA 2010 (UK) s. 724(1).
[80] KStG (Germany) s. 8c(1).
[81] IRC (US) s. 382(l)(3)(A)(ii).

prescribes whether the primary or the alternate test is to be used. The alternate test is to be used (instead of the primary test) 'if one or more other companies beneficially owned shares or interests in shares' in the corporation being tested.[82] Therefore, in the case of a direct change of ownership of a corporation (partly held by other corporations) without an indirect change, only the alternate test is used and this alternate test will not be met. So similarly to the US, a restructure within a 51% corporate group should not result in a change of ownership.[83]

### 5.2.1.2   Of business / activity

The denial of the carry-forward of corporate tax attributes on a 50% or more change of ownership can have harsh effects. As mentioned, corporations are typically fully denied carry-forward despite suffering substantially less than a full change of ownership. Further, substantial pressure is put on marginal share transfers due to the all-or-nothing nature of the denial. Shares can be freely sold up to the threshold with no consequences. Then the sale of the shares that trigger the threshold results in full denial. Then again, the sale of shares after the trigger has no consequences. This type of all-or-nothing approach is often referred to as a *knife-edge* approach. It may seem that a proportionate denial would be superior to the knife-edge approach. However, conceptual difficulties with a proportionate denial were discussed earlier. Germany's experiment with a proportionate denial is not a clear success, has raised its own problems and can produce arbitrary results.

As mentioned at the start of this subheading, the potential harshness of a *knife-edge* rule based on a change of ownership has caused several countries to ameliorate this rule with an exception based on continuity of corporate activities. Inevitably, it is continuity of business activities that is the focus of the exception. The intent of such an exception is that it helps limit the denial of carry-forward of tax attributes to abusive cases. The presumption here is that, if after a change of ownership a corporation continues its business as usual, then the corporation was not purchased for its tax attributes. However, this presumption is open to serious doubt, and it is clear that a corporation with, say, carry-forward losses can be purchased for its losses despite continuing the same business after the change of ownership.

---

[82]   Income Tax Assessment Act 1997 (Australia) s. 165–12(6).

[83]   The 1% difference between the Australian and the US approach is because the Australian test is 'more than' 50% continuity of ownership.

Further, the basic policy underlying such an exception can be questioned. First, especially in the context of carried-forward losses, the exception encourages corporations to continue inefficient businesses that have been loss making. Restructuring the business so as to make it viable carries with it an increasing risk that one of the corporation's substantial assets (carried-forward losses) may, if taken even a little bit too far, be lost entirely. Further, it replaces a bright-line test with a grey or *mud* test. In a simple situation, it can be clear whether a corporation has suffered a change of ownership or not, even if the change is marginal. However, corporate activities are a question of degree and not absolutes. It can never be clear at the margin when a corporation's activities have changed sufficiently so as to justify the change falling outside the exception to the denial of carried-forward losses rule.

These issues with saving rules based on continuation of corporate activity seem to have had an impact in Germany's change of position in 2008. Until that year, it was possible for a corporation suffering a change of ownership to save its use of carried-forward losses by continuing to use a majority of business assets that were used before the change. However, there were difficulties in determining whether this test was met. This potential saving was swept away from the start of 2008 as part of a reform involving a reduction in the corporate tax rate, limitations on the use of interest and the introduction of the proportionate rule for denial of corporate loss carry-forward following a change of ownership. Just as Germany had difficulties with its former rule, other countries continue to experience difficulties with their saving rules based on continuity of corporate activity.

In the UK, a change of ownership of a corporation is not fatal to the corporation's ability to carry forward revenue losses. In addition, within a 'period of 3 years in which the change of ownership occurs there [must be] a major change in the nature or conduct of a trade carried on by the company'.[84] When added to the time for testing a change of ownership, this means that there may be six years between the time the first shares are sold that eventually trigger the change of ownership and the change in trade that triggers the denial of carried-forward losses. 'Major change in the nature or conduct of trade' is defined in terms of 'a major change in the type of property dealt in, or services or facilities provided

---

[84] CTA 2010 (UK) s. 673(1)(a). As an alternative, the change of ownership must occur 'after the scale of activities in a trade carried on by the company has become small or negligible and before any significant revival of the trade'.

in, the trade, or … a major change in customers, outlets or markets of the trade'. The change can occur as the 'result of a gradual process' that began before the three-year period.[85]

The UK tax administration does not treat a change as major if the corporation simply rationalises its product range (e.g. by withdrawing unprofitable items and replacing them with new items of a kind already being produced). Similarly, no major change may occur if the company makes changes to increase its efficiency or to keep pace with changing technology or management techniques – so-called *organic growth*.[86] Whether there is a major change is a question of fact to be determined by weighing all of the circumstances. Being a question of degree with an all-or-nothing result, the test has proved to be less than satisfactory in its practical application.[87]

It is this rule on saving losses where there is no major change in a trade that is used in conjunction with the rule permitting the transfer of a carried-forward trading loss with the transfer of the trade. As noted earlier at 4.2, this results in the practice known as a *hive down*. A corporation may wish to sell a trade to a third party and sell carried-forward trading losses with it. To do so, the corporation first incorporates a subsidiary (at least 75%) and then transfers the trade and the losses to it under section 944 of CTA 2010. The (now) parent corporation then sells the shares in the subsidiary to the third party, which sale may or may not be taxable depending on how long a time elapsed between the transfer and the sale (see the earlier discussion at 5.1.3.1). Provided the third party does not cause a major change in the trade, the losses can continue to be carried forward and used despite a clear change of ownership of the corporation.[88]

The UK rule works in the context of the UK's schedular system: carried-forward losses continue to attach to the trade that generated them (and are quarantined to use against profits from that trade; see the earlier discussion at 1.2.1 and 1.2.3.2). So when there is a clear change in that trade, application of the rule is quite straightforward. When it comes to the use

---

[85] CTA 2010 (UK) s. 673(4).

[86] Statement of Practice SP 10/91.

[87] For example, see *Willis* v. *Peeters Picture Frames Ltd* [1983] STC 453 (CA). This was an extreme case where a corporation had sold picture frames in the market, but within three years of a takeover 92% of its sales were to members of the acquirer's group on a cost-plus basis. Nevertheless, the finding of fact that there had been no major change was not overturned on appeal.

[88] For an example of a disputed hive down, see *Barkers of Malton Ltd* v. *HMRC* [2008] STC 884 (SCD).

of capital losses, the UK uses a different saving mechanism, which asks whether the change of ownership occurs in connection with an arrangement to secure a tax advantage.[89]

Australia has a rule similar to the UK trading loss rule, but the Australian rule does not sit well in its corporate tax system framework because Australia adopts a global approach. Even if a corporation fails the Australian continuity of ownership test, it can still use its carried-forward losses if it meets the same business test.[90] The same business test requires that at the time a corporation wishes to use a carried-forward loss it 'carries on the same business as it carried on' before the change of ownership.[91] In an infamous ruling, the Australian tax administration suggests that the word 'business' here means the 'business of the company as an entirety, or its "overall business"'.[92] This is a necessary fudge in trying to overlay a schedular feature onto a global system. Otherwise, this exception would be particularly problematic in its application to other types of corporate tax attributes, such as capital losses.[93] The point is that the losses are not attributable to any particular 'business', but reflect an overall global position of a corporation, typically for a tax year.[94]

Australian case law requires that, for the same business test to be met, the 'identical' business must be carried on by a corporation suffering a change of ownership.[95] Any change in *identity* may be sufficient to deny the carry-forward of losses. Minor changes in activity may not cause the test to be failed, and the case is one of weighing up the changes to see if the identity of the corporation is intact. In a high-profile case, the Full Federal Court of Australia held that what was important was to identify

---

[89] TCGA 1992 (UK) s. 184A(1). There are rules for other types of carried-forward losses in CTA 2010 (UK) Part 14, such as losses of corporations with investment business or property business. These rules incorporate variations of the 'major change in trade' test.

[90] Income Tax Assessment Act 1997 (Australia) s. 165–13.

[91] Income Tax Assessment Act 1997 (Australia) s. 165–210(1).

[92] Tax Ruling TR 1999/9 (Australia), e.g. at para. 8.

[93] Income Tax Assessment Act 1997 (Australia) s. 165–96 applies the restrictions on carry-forward of revenue losses (including the saving of the same business test) to capital losses.

[94] This confused position is reinforced in the very next provision in Income Tax Assessment Act 1997 (Australia) s. 165–210(2)(a). It provides that the same business test is not met if the corporation proceeds to derive income from 'a business of a kind that it did not carry on before' the change of ownership. Here the Australian tax administration suggests that 'business' necessarily means 'a particular undertaking or enterprise' (i.e. something less than the corporation's whole undertaking); TR 1999/9, for example, at para. 8. The same business test is also not met if the corporation derives income from a 'transaction of a kind that it had not entered into in the course of its business operations before' the change.

[95] *Avondale Motors (Parts) Pty Ltd* v. *FCT* (1971) 2 ATR 312 (HC).

the nature of the business (which requires a focus on revenue-producing activities).[96] The manner in which a corporation manages the business was not relevant to the same business test. The case involved a change from out-sourced to in-house management of a hotel. The court noted that from the perspective of the hotel's clients there was no discernable change after the new management was in place.

By comparison to the UK and Australian approaches, the nature of the US saving based on continuity of corporate activities is different. In the US, continuity of activity does not fully save a corporation from restrictions on the carry-forward of corporate tax attributes following a change of ownership. Rather, it means that the corporate tax attributes can continue to be used, but at a reduced rate. The slowing down of the rate at which corporate tax attributes can be used under the US rule is discussed later at 5.2.2.1. However, like the UK and Australia, the US fully restricts the carry-forward of corporate tax attributes if a corporation suffers both a change of ownership and fails the continuity of activity test.

The continuity of activity test in the US requires that a corporation 'continue the business enterprise [of the corporation] at all times during the 2-year period beginning on the change date'.[97] Bittker and Eustice suggest that this requirement is intended to have the same application as the business continuity test for corporate reorganisations, discussed later at 7.2.1.1. Therefore, it requires 'the loss corporation to continue its historic business or continue to use a significant portion of its historic business assets for the requisite two-year period'.[98] Some significant business activity must continue, but this need only be for two years. Provided a significant part of the historic business activity is continued, it should not matter whether there are changes in business location, employees or substantial parts of the business.

This US test seems more lenient than that used in the UK or especially Australia. In the UK the corporation must suffer no 'major change in the nature or conduct' of the trade, and in Australia the corporation must continue to conduct the 'same' (identical) business. In the US, there is a three-year testing period for a change of ownership and then a two-year period for continuing a significant part of the business. In the UK, these periods are effectively three years and three years. By contrast, in Australia change of ownership is tested over a potentially limitless period, and similarly, the

---

[96] *Lilyvale Hotel Pty Ltd* v. *FCT* [2009] FCAFC 21 (FFC).
[97] IRC (US) s. 382(c)(1).
[98] Bittker & Eustice (2003–, para. 14.44[5]).

corporation must continue to carry on the same business until such period as the carried-forward losses are used.

### 5.2.2   Limitations on indirect transfer of gains and losses

The activities of a corporation give rise to items that are included or deducted in calculating the corporation's income. Broadly, these activities include the receipt or provision of services and transactions in assets and liabilities. Typically, the receipt or provision of services gives rise to immediate tax consequences and therefore to no carried-forward tax attributes. Services may also give rise to tax consequences over a number of years, but usually when they involve the creation of an intangible asset or liability. Assets and liabilities have a cost that under a realisation-based income tax may be carried forward from one year to the next. That is, the price paid for an asset or amount received for a liability may be used in determining the tax consequences of a future year. The cost of an asset or liability, therefore, is a tax attribute.

The activities of a corporation during a year give rise to income or loss for the year. This outcome incorporates the consequences of realising assets and liabilities during the year, and those consequences are typically determined by reference to the historic cost of assets and liabilities. If the outcome is income, that has an immediate impact by way of taxation of the corporation. However, if the outcome is a loss, that loss may be carried forward in the manner described earlier at 1.2.3.2. The carry-forward of a loss is another type of tax attribute of a corporation, and it is inherently related to the cost of assets and liabilities. Of course, income and loss incorporate many other features such as amounts received for assets and services provided and payments made for liabilities and services received.

Despite the link between the carry-forward of the tax value of assets and liabilities and realised losses, restrictions on the carry-forward of corporate tax attributes following a change of ownership have historically focused on realised losses. The earliest forms of such restrictions only dealt with realised losses, and the current basic rules for such restrictions are still those dealing with realised losses. Accordingly, the following discussion begins with a consideration of restrictions on the carry-forward of realised losses by a corporation following a change of ownership. These restrictions also provide an opportunity to come to terms with the basic rules and issues as regards the change of ownership rules.

These basic rules on realised losses do not explain very well why the indirect transfer of realised losses can be abusive or the scope for abuse with respect to the indirect transfer of gains and losses generally. Many countries have learned by experience that they can have just as many problems with the indirect transfer of unrealised gains and losses as they do with respect to realised losses. Before launching into a consideration of specific rules to deal with this problem, the discussion considers the core of the problem with indirect transfers of gains and losses and lays out the potential for abuse.

The discussion then proceeds to consider more specifically restrictive rules pertaining to unrealised gains and losses following a change in corporate ownership and their relationship with the rules for realised losses. This is done in two parts. The first part deals with the scenario where a loss corporation is acquired by a person with a potential profit. The second part deals with the scenario where a corporation with a potential profit is acquired by a person with a loss.

### 5.2.2.1 Rules for realised losses

Realised losses are typically the primary target of change of ownership rules. In considering these rules, there are three broad areas for discussion. The first involves whether a country applies a single rule or multiple rules. This choice is related to whether the country adopts a global or schedular approach to calculating corporate income (see the earlier discussion at 1.2.1). Second is the question of whether a country adopts an all-or-nothing approach to denying the use of realised losses following a change of ownership or whether there is some graduated mechanism for that denial. The third area of discussion involves temporal issues. The rules focus on carried-forward losses, but there may also be realised (but not yet calculated) losses of the year in which the change of ownership occurs, and there is the issue of what happens where a country permits loss carry-back (as opposed to loss carry-forward).

**One rule or multiple rules**    Germany is a prime example of a country that adopts a single rule for the denial of corporate loss carry-forward following a change of ownership.[99] This is consistent with its global approach to the calculation of corporate income. In form, both the US and Australia also adopt a global approach, but they proceed to then quarantine capital losses and in doing so incorporate a schedular aspect in the calculation of corporate income. Both countries, however, effectively adopt the same

---

[99] KStG (Germany) s. 8c.

rule or use a similar rule for denying the use of capital losses as they do for revenue losses.[100]

By contrast, the schedular approach of the UK means that it has multiple rules. The rules for revenue losses are broadly similar (though not the same), but those for capital losses are very different.[101] In particular, the UK capital loss rules apply to individual losses incurred on the disposal of particular assets, whereas the revenue loss rules apply (as usual) to a net loss position of a particular activity for a particular period.

**Knife-edge or graduated approach**   The usual approach is that the full amount of realised losses is denied if there is a change of ownership. Because the change may be triggered by the transfer of a small shareholding, this rule was described earlier as a *knife-edge* approach. Countries that accept this approach include the UK and Australia. Both countries seek to ameliorate the severity of the knife-edge approach by providing a full exception from the denial of losses where there is continuity of business. These exceptions were discussed earlier at 5.2.1.2, where it was pointed out that the tests of both countries in this respect incorporate inherent difficulties.

By contrast, the US and Germany have rules that provide the potential for a more gradual approach to the limitation on the use of losses following a change of ownership. However, the scope of these rules and the manner in which they graduate the limitation of losses are fundamentally different.

In Germany, where there is more than a 50% change of corporate ownership, carried-forward losses are denied in full. Further, unlike in the UK and Australia, there is no exception for continuity of corporate activities. In addition, there is the German proportionate denial of corporate losses where a single person (and related persons) acquires between 25% and 50% of a corporation, which was discussed earlier at 5.2.1.1.[102] This rule also flatly denies the use of corporate losses without a saving for continuity of corporate activity, but the rule is a proportional denial. So, if a single

---

[100]   In the US, these are IRC (US) ss. 382(a) (revenue losses) and 383(b) (capital losses). The rules for capital losses are prescribed by regulation and 'based on the principles applicable under section 382'; see Title 26 Code of Federal Regulations (US) § 1.383–1. Indeed, these capital loss rules are integrated into the section 382 limitation. In Australia, the rules are Income Tax Assessment Act 1997 (Australia) ss. 165–10 (revenue losses) and 165–96 (capital losses, adopting the revenue loss rules).

[101]   CTA 2010 (UK) Part 14 (ss. 672–730) (revenue losses) and TCGA 1992 (UK) s. 184A (capital losses).

[102]   KStG (Germany) s. 8c(1).

person acquires 30% of a corporation with losses, the corporation loses the right to use 30% of its carried-forward losses. The proportion that is not denied can be used in the usual manner. However, it must be remembered that Germany places a general limit on the rate at which corporations may use losses. In particular, as discussed earlier at 1.2.3.2, carried-forward losses may unrestrictedly reduce profits up to €1 million each year, but beyond this limit the use of losses is restricted to 60% of income.[103]

This can be contrasted with the US approach. Like in the UK and in Australia, under US tax law a corporation is fully entitled to use its losses unless it suffers a 50% change of ownership. In addition, as in those countries, if a corporation does not satisfy the continuity of activity test, the US denies the use of carried-forward losses in full. The difference between the US and the other countries arises where a corporation suffers a change of ownership, but meets the continuity of activity test. Here there is no saving in Germany and the losses are denied in full (because there is no saving for continuity of activity), but in the UK and Australia the losses are saved in full. In this scenario the US adopts a middle ground. Where a corporation suffers a change of ownership but continues with its business operations, the US slows down the rate at which the corporation can use carried-forward losses.

Section 382 of IRC limits the amount of taxable income of a corporation that can be offset by a loss incurred before a change of ownership:

> [T]he section 382 limitation for any post change year is an amount equal to
>
> (A) the value of the old loss corporation, multiplied by
> (B) the long-term tax-exempt rate.[104]

The US rule distinguishes between the 'old loss corporation' and the 'new loss corporation', which are defined in terms of the corporation before and after the change of ownership, respectively.[105] Further, the 'long-term tax-exempt rate' is defined by reference to the average market yield of long-term marketable debt obligations of the US government.[106] In other words, it is meant to represent a standard risk-free return.

The idea behind this rule is to take the value of the loss corporation at the time it is acquired and apply a conservative rate of return to that value.

---

[103]  EStG (Germany) s. 10d(2).
[104]  IRC (US) s. 382(b)(1).
[105]  IRC (US) s. 382(k).
[106]  IRC (US) s. 382(f).

This is the rate at which the corporation is permitted to use its losses after the change of ownership. If the use of losses is restricted to this rate, it is suggested that the corporation could not have been acquired so that its losses could be set against other income that the acquirer diverts to the loss corporation. This seems to be a robust rule that strikes an acceptable balance in an area of competing difficulties. It is sufficiently robust to have been used for post-change consolidation purposes, and Australia also adopts a version of this rule in the context of post-change consolidation (see the later discussion at 5.2.2.3).

If the new loss corporation cannot use its section 382 limitation for a year (e.g. because it is more than the corporation's income), the excess can be carried forward and added to the section 382 limitation for the next year.[107] By contrast, if the corporation post-change does not continue its 'business enterprise' for a two-year period after the change, the section 382 limitation is set to zero for the future.[108] In other words, if the business enterprise is not continued, then the pre-change losses are denied in full.

**Year of change**   Countries that have restrictions on the use of corporate losses following a change of ownership tend to have an apportionment rule for dealing with the year in which the change occurs. The standard approach is to split that year into two tax years: one part before the change and the other after. Taxable income or loss then needs to be calculated for each half. If a loss is realised in the first half, then the usual restriction on the carry-forward of losses applies for purposes of using that loss after the change of ownership. This is the position in the UK and the US.[109] Germany formerly had an express provision to this effect, but it was repealed along with the former rule on carry-forward of losses from the start of 2008.[110] By contrast, Australia has a separate division for this apportionment, but the result is similar to that in the UK and the US.[111]

---

[107]   IRC (US) s. 382(b)(2).

[108]   IRC (US) s. 382(c)(1).

[109]   CTA 2010 (UK) s. 674(3) and IRC (US) s. 382(b)(3). This type of apportionment is not necessary in the context of the UK rule on use of capital losses because, as noted earlier, it denies the use of losses on the individual disposal of capital assets and not a net loss belonging to a particular period; see TCGA 1992 (UK) s. 184A.

[110]   Former KStG (Germany) s. 8(4).

[111]   Income Tax Assessment Act 1997 (Australia) Subdivs. 165-B (revenue losses) & 165-CB (capital losses).

**Carry-back of losses**    Finally, there is the issue of applying the loss restriction rule on a change of ownership to the carry-back of losses. Here the issue is whether a loss that is incurred *after* a change of ownership can be carried back to set off the profits of a year before the change. Again, Germany has no rule expressly prohibiting this practice, but as noted earlier at 1.2.3.2, the carry-back is limited to €511,500.[112] Australia needs no such rule because it does not permit corporations to carry back losses (although a small carry-back is scheduled to be introduced soon). The UK allows a one-year carry-back and it has a rule to prevent a carry-back to before a change of ownership.[113]

Despite its two-year carry-back for revenue losses and three-year carry-back for capital losses, the US has no express rule denying the carry-back of losses to before an ownership change.[114] However, if a person acquires

> control of a corporation ... and the principal purpose for which such acquisition was made is evasion or avoidance of Federal income tax by securing the benefit of a deduction ... then the Secretary may disallow such deduction.[115]

This is the predecessor of section 382 of IRC, but it continues to apply. It seems broad enough to cover an abusive carry-back of losses following a change of ownership.

### 5.2.2.2    Extending to unrealised gains and losses: the core issues

The purpose of this subheading is twofold. It seeks to investigate the mechanics of the problem of indirect transfer of realised losses and, in the course of doing so, explain why that problem is inextricably linked to unrealised gains and losses. The core of the problem is tax arbitrage involving two steps: an indirect transfer of a tax attribute followed by an offset. Especially with respect to the second step, defects in arm's length transfer pricing rules can be a serious problem. With a deeper understanding of the core problem, the discussion proceeds to identify the scope for abuse through the indirect transfer of gains and losses.

**Two-step tax arbitrage**    It was suggested earlier that the indirect transfer of losses may be viewed as inappropriate because tax systems do not permit the direct transfer of losses. So there may be an inconsistency, but that

---

[112]    EStG (Germany) s. 10d(1).
[113]    CTA 2010 (UK) s. 674(1).
[114]    IRC (US) s. 382 apparently only applies to losses carried forward.
[115]    IRC (US) s. 269.

does not really explain *why* an indirect transfer of losses is problematic. An indirect transfer of losses can only be problematic if those losses manage to offset profits of a person who did not indirectly own those losses when they were incurred. That is where the inconsistency lies when compared with the denial of a direct loss transfer. Often, a carried-forward realised loss of a corporation is trapped in the corporation. If the loss cannot be used, there does not seem to be a problem, even if there has been an indirect transfer of the loss. So, if a loss survives a change in corporate ownership, the question becomes how the loss can be used following the change.

One line of investigation is to see if the loss can be transferred or grouped with the profits of other persons after the change of ownership. This involves the specific rules for corporate grouping of losses, which were explored earlier at 1.2.3.2 and are further explored later in the context of a change of ownership. If the loss cannot be moved, another line of investigation is to see if profit can be moved to the loss corporation following a change of ownership. There are many ways in which profit may be moved, all involving a payment from the acquirer (or persons related to the acquirer) to the loss corporation without an equal return consideration.

As noted in the introduction, a payment is any manner in which one person may bestow value on another person. The various manners in which a person can bestow value on another person were explored earlier at 2.2.2 in the context of a corporation seeking to make a hidden profit distribution to a shareholder. That was described as involving a shareholder intercepting corporate income. The same principles apply here. After a loss corporation changes ownership, the new controller might seek to arrange affairs such that the loss corporation *intercepts* income that might otherwise have accrued to the controller (or related persons) directly. This is often referred to as *income injection* of a loss corporation, although it can be similar to a hidden capital contribution.

Income injection may occur by the new controller transferring assets to the loss corporation at an undervalue or acquiring assets from the loss corporation at an overvalue. Assumption or forgiveness of a liability of the loss corporation is another possibility, as is a loan or use of the acquirer's assets for less than market value interest or rent and the provision of services at an undervalue. Again, there is a payment if the provision is in the opposite direction for an overvalue. As noted earlier at 2.2.2.1, the value bestowed may not have crystallised into an actual asset of the payer and may still constitute no more than an opportunity to profit that the controller makes available to the loss corporation.

In the earlier discussion at 2.2.2, the ways in which countries address the hidden profit distribution issue were commonly benchmarked by reference to arm's length pricing under a standard transfer pricing rule. The same is true in the context of a loss corporation following a change of ownership. Indeed, it may be suggested that the application of full transfer pricing rules might prevent much income injection into a loss corporation following a change of ownership. There may still be problems with the transfer of corporate opportunities, at least in terms of identification and pricing. It is perhaps for this reason that a number of countries have a targeted anti-abuse rule for income injection into loss corporations following a change of ownership.[116] This rule may be relevant only where the losses have been preserved due to a continuity of activity test, or the income injection rule might apply in circumstances where there is less than a change of ownership as defined.

This analysis of realised corporate losses following a change of ownership assists in identifying the fundamental nature of the issue underlying the rules that restrict the use of such losses. These rules are concerned with a particular type of tax arbitrage using corporations. There are two essential steps in this arbitrage:

1. Indirect transfer of tax attributes by transferring ownership of a corporation
2. Offset of the corporate tax attribute by one of two routes:
   (i) transfer of the tax attribute by the corporation to the acquirer (or related parties)
   (ii) transfer of an offsetting attribute by the acquirer (or related parties) to the corporation

For the purposes of step 2, the transfer may be directly permitted by the tax law. Equally, however, the corporation and the acquirer may seek to effect the transfer by manipulating prices and opportunities. This may be especially possible in the absence of comprehensive arm's length transfer pricing rules.

---

[116] For example, see Income Tax Assessment Act 1997 (Australia) Subdiv. 175-A. Notably, Australia does not have comprehensive transfer pricing rules that apply domestically.

**Scoping the potential for tax arbitrage and counteracting measures**    Indirect transfer of realised corporate losses on a change of ownership is only one variety of the two-step tax arbitrage identified earlier. This type of tax arbitrage can involve any corporate tax attribute that may be carried forward from one tax period to another. Of particular relevance for present purposes are other types of corporate tax attributes relating to corporate losses. Realised losses are, at their broadest, the outcome of a year's corporate activity. Similarly, such corporate activity may result in profits. More narrowly, the individual activities that make up those profits or losses may involve realised gains or losses.

Further, corporate activities may involve potential gains and losses that are yet to be realised (i.e. unrealised gains and losses), particularly those that would arise on a future disposal of assets and liabilities. Gains and losses on assets and liabilities are typically measured by reference to the historic cost of the assets or liabilities. Until the tax consequences of the cost of an asset or liability have been triggered by realisation, the cost is carried forward. As noted at the start of this heading, that carry-forward represents a tax attribute. By comparing the cost of an asset or liability with its potential market value realisation, an unrealised gain or loss can be determined. An unrealised loss is a potential tax relief, whereas an unrealised gain is a potential tax liability.

Just as realised losses may be arbitraged on a change of corporate ownership, it is possible to arbitrage unrealised gains and losses and even realised gains and profits. All of these types of arbitrage are related and should be considered holistically by a corporate tax system. The basic tax planning involved in the arbitrage is not rocket science and involves assessing the corporate tax attribute to be moved (by sale of the subject corporation) and matching it with a corporate tax attribute of the acquirer (or related persons). In the present context, this means matching gains with losses or losses with gains, and these are the two basic themes. So, the first step in the tax arbitrage involves either a change of ownership of a corporation with a loss (realised or unrealised) or a change of ownership of a corporation with a gain or profit (realised or unrealised). Each of these themes is considered separately in the following discussion.

Countries that wish to address this type of tax arbitrage have a number of possibilities, which revolve around the two steps in the tax arbitrage. At step 1 they can seek to eliminate the corporate tax attribute when a change of ownership occurs. At step 2, although countries may permit a corporation to retain its tax attribute following such a change, they can seek to prevent it from offsetting or being offset by a tax attribute of the acquirer (or related persons). The methods by which such counteracting measures can be implemented vary depending on the step involved and the tax attribute in question.

**Removing the corporate tax attribute**   With respect to counteracting measures at step 1, the treatment of realised losses has already been considered earlier at 5.2.2.1. For carried-forward losses, this is a simple matter of denying carry-forward after a change of ownership. Current-year losses are slightly more complex because they involve dividing the period in which the change of ownership occurs. Carry-back of losses across a change of ownership is even more complex. Here the tax attribute that is carried forward by the corporation across a change of ownership is not a realised loss. Rather, it is a realised profit that retains the potential of being offset (and so resulting in corporation tax refunded) by a loss occurring after the change. It is the potential refund that is the tax attribute that is carried forward, and so any counteracting measure involves denying that potential for refund following a change of ownership.

Unrealised gains and losses have not been specifically considered thus far. Here the tax attribute that is carried forward is the historic cost of, say, the asset or liability in question. That is the feature from the past that may affect the taxation in the future. The only manner in which to remove this tax attribute is to remove the relevance of the historic cost by revaluing the asset to market value at the time a change of ownership occurs. The only comprehensive manner in which to do this is to treat a corporation as realising all of its assets and liabilities for market value at the time its ownership changes. The deemed realised gains and losses would be offset and any carried-forward realised losses used. If the net result is a profit, it would be taxed to the corporation. If the net result is a loss, it would not be available for carry-forward beyond the change. This is the only way of achieving a high degree of consistency with a direct transfer of those assets and liabilities and requires a brief explanation.

When a corporation is sold, the value on sale is derived not from the artificial entity, but rather from the undertaking (e.g. business) conducted by the corporation. If that undertaking were sold directly to an independent third party, the sale would be at market value and involve the transfer of all the assets and liabilities of the undertaking. The sale of the shares in the corporation involves an indirect transfer of the corporation's undertaking, and so the only manner in which to achieve consistency with a direct sale is by treating the corporation as realising all its assets and liabilities at market value when its shares are sold. Note that such an approach also addresses the enveloping problem discussed earlier at 5.1.2.

Countries are generally reluctant to adopt this comprehensive solution.[117] One reason for this reluctance may be the potential that unrealised gains will be taxed in full when perhaps somewhat less than 100% of the corporation may have changed hands. This is no different from the problem with fully denying a corporate loss carry-forward on a change of ownership (i.e. the undivided interest issue discussed earlier at 5.2.2.1). However, this reluctance perhaps demonstrates the willingness of countries to act more arbitrarily when denying a tax relief (the carried-forward loss) than when imposing a tax liability. There are limited examples of taxing deferred gains on intergroup transactions when a corporation leaves a corporate group. These are discussed later at 5.2.4.

Outside of these limited exceptions, the problem, however, is that countries end up adopting inconsistent approaches. The tax attribute that is a carried-forward realised loss is often denied following a change of corporate ownership (unless saved by a continuity of corporate activity test). An ability to claim (after such a change) a refund of corporation tax paid before the change (e.g. by carry-back of losses across a change) is also often denied. However, when it comes to unrealised gains and losses, the tax attributes that are the costs of assets and liabilities of the corporation are usually permitted to be carried forward across a change of ownership. This means that any counteracting measures must take place at step 2 of the tax arbitrage. The interaction between the counteracting measures at step 1 and those at step 2 can result in substantial complexity.

**Removing the ability to offset the tax attribute**     Counteracting measures at step 2 effectively involve quarantining the corporate tax attribute that has been permitted to pass through a change of ownership so that it cannot be offset by a complementary tax attribute of the acquirer (or related persons). These counteracting measures can be complex for two reasons. First, they need to target every method by which two tax attributes may offset each other. As noted earlier, these methods include express permissions under the tax law to transfer tax attributes, particularly between

---

[117] Although there are some examples: Income Tax Act 2001 (Nepal) s. 57(1) and Income Tax Act 2004 (Tanzania) s. 56(1). This may also happen in the US by election under IRC (US) s. 338, mentioned further at footnote 142.

related persons. More obscurely, they also need to cover all indirect methods by which persons may shift gains and losses, including any breaches in comprehensive arm's length transfer pricing rules.

The second reason why these types of counteracting rules tend to be complex is because the quarantining involved is typically limited in some shape or form as to time. For example, unrealised gains and losses on assets to be quarantined are typically identified by reference to the market value of the assets or liabilities at the time of change of ownership. The offsetting tax attribute of the acquirer may also be identified by reference to this time. Further, the quarantining may apply only by reference to a particular time period (e.g. whether the asset is sold or the acquirer ceases to own the corporation within a certain period of time).

### 5.2.2.3 Change of ownership of loss corporation

The scenario for discussion is an analysis of the potential for two-step tax arbitrage where the corporation to be taken over has losses. The position regarding realised losses was considered earlier at 5.2.2.1, and a primary purpose of the present discussion is to extend the consideration to unrealised losses. The counteracting measures adopted by countries for realised losses (discussed at 5.2.2.1) operate at step 1 of the potential tax arbitrage and so cancel the loss if there is a change of ownership. For reasons mentioned earlier at 5.2.2.2, countries tend not to deal with unrealised losses precisely in this fashion. However, there is often at least some relationship between the treatment of realised losses and the treatment of unrealised losses. This relationship is the first matter noted in the following discussion.

The focus of the following discussion is counteracting measures at step 2 of the tax arbitrage. This presumes that at step 1 it has been accepted that the corporate tax attribute is carried forward across a change of ownership. This can be the case with both realised and unrealised losses, especially if losses are preserved by a continuity of corporate activity test (see the earlier discussion at 5.2.1.2). With the loss in the acquired corporation, there is one of two methods of achieving the offset at step 2 of the tax arbitrage. First, the loss corporation may be brought into a consolidation after the change of ownership. If the loss continues to be recognised, it will automatically be brought into the same consolidated entity as profits of the acquirer. The potential to take a pre-change loss into a consolidation post-change is the second matter noted in the following discussion.

If consolidation is not available, then there are two potential methods of securing the offset of profits of the acquirer with the pre-change loss of the acquired corporation. First, the loss may be transferred from the loss corporation to the acquirer. Second, the acquirer may transfer a gain or profit to the loss corporation. These are the third and fourth matters noted in the following discussion.

In passing, the limits of the following discussion should be noted. The issues being discussed are at the sharp end of tax planning and require complex tax rules to prevent tax arbitrage. They involve an intricate simultaneous consideration of multiple rules outlined at various points of this book overlaid with anti-abuse rules. These rules can only be sketched in their broadest outline, and in some cases only the issues are identified rather than the rules that might apply. They are the types of issues that occupy the time of many tax practitioners.

**Limitations on carry-forward of unrealised losses**    Some countries extend their limitations on the use of realised corporate losses following a change of ownership to unrealised losses. This extension typically involves valuing all assets held by a corporation at the time of change and netting off the notional gains and losses. If the net result is a loss, then losses on the assets owned before the change incurred by a disposal after the change may be denied unless a continuity of activity test is met. Although this may be similar to the treatment of realised losses, nevertheless, there are likely to be differences between the two. In particular, if unrealised losses are not realised within a certain period after a change of ownership, restrictions on their use may be lifted.

For example, the US restrictions on the use of losses following a change of ownership also apply to any 'net unrealized built-in loss'. A 'net unrealized built-in loss' exists if the 'fair market value of the assets of [the loss] corporation immediately before an ownership change is ... less ... than ... the aggregate adjusted basis of such assets at such time'.[118] In such a case, the section 382 of IRC limitation applies to the deduction of any loss on a pre-change asset disposed of during the five years after the change. The limit is applied to the amount of the loss not exceeding the amount by which the cost base of the asset exceeded the market value of the asset at the time of change.[119] As with the general rules on realised losses, the limitation will be nil unless the loss corporation maintains its business enterprise for two years after the change.

---

[118]   IRC (US) s. 382(h)(3)(A).
[119]   IRC (US) s. 382(h)(1)(B) & (2)(B).

If the loss corporation has a 'net unrealized built-in gain' rather than a net unrealised built-in loss, this gain may increase the loss corporation's section 382 of IRC limitation and so increase the rate at which carried-forward realised losses may be used after the change.[120] Again, to qualify the gains must be realised within the five years following the change. These rules for net unrealised built-in gains and losses are also applied where the loss corporation enters into a consolidation with the acquirer after the takeover, discussed later.

Australia also adopts this approach with respect to net unrealised losses at the time a corporation suffers a change of ownership. It has a special rule for netting unrealised capital gains and losses at the time of change by reference to the market value of assets held at this time. Capital losses (or deductions) arising in respect of the later disposal of assets held at the time of change may be denied unless the corporation meets the same business test.[121] Australia also has a separate rule for unrealised revenue losses, but it is limited in application to bad debts where the debt is incurred before a change of ownership but is written off after such a change.[122]

The position in Germany regarding unrealised losses is less clear. The German loss carry-forward limitation applies to 'not deducted or not compensated negative revenues (unused losses)'. On the face of it, this appears to be limited to realised losses. Further, from 2010 a specific amendment was made to reduce the amount of losses denied on a change of ownership by the amount of 'hidden reserves of the operating assets of the corporation'. Broadly, the hidden reserves are defined in terms of the total of reported equity (net assets) of the corporation and the market value of shares in the corporation and so is similar to net unrealised gains (after accounting for built-in losses on particular assets).[123] This specific treatment of net unrealised gains seems to suggest that the main prohibition does not apply to unrealised losses. However, the German tax administration did argue that at least some types of unrealised losses were denied under the prior change of ownership limitation.[124]

The UK approach is again disjointed. The rule restricting the use of capital losses following a change of ownership can apply to unrealised losses as well as realised losses. It applies where 'a loss…accrues to the

---

[120] IRC (US) s. 382(h)(1)(A).
[121] Income Tax Assessment Act 1997 (Australia) Subdiv. 165-CC.
[122] Income Tax Assessment Act 1997 (Australia) Subdiv. 165-C.
[123] KStG (Germany) s. 8c(1).
[124] See Sieker (2004).

relevant company ... on disposal of a pre-change asset'.[125] There is no similar rule for revenue losses, which gives rise to a problem with capital allowances (depreciation). Corporations could refuse to claim their entitlement to capital allowances with respect to an asset, thus building up an unrealised loss that could be realised by selling the asset or subsequently claiming allowances. This was an unrealised revenue loss (because capital allowances are deductible against revenue profits) and could be passed on after a change of ownership of a corporation. Further, once realised after such a change, it was possible to transfer the ensuing loss to the acquirer by way of group relief.

This type of unrealised loss arbitrage was addressed in 2010 with yet another targeted anti-abuse rule that is not integrated with the other change of ownership rules. Broadly, the grant of capital allowances may be restricted where there is a change of ownership of a corporation and the written-down value of its assets for capital allowances purposes is more than the balance sheet value of those assets. One of the main purposes of the change must be to obtain a tax advantage.[126] Here a qualifying change is essentially defined by reference to becoming part of a 75% group of corporations and so is very different from either the test for revenue losses or the test for capital losses discussed earlier at 5.2.1.1.[127] The consequence of the rule applying is to quarantine the excess of the written-down value over the balance sheet value of the assets. Capital allowances granted in the future with respect to this excess can only be used against the profits of the trade in which the assets are held.[128] A critical feature of this rule is that the quarantined capital allowances cannot be used in the future for purposes of group relief.

**Consolidation**    If a loss corporation is taken over by another corporation with profits and the losses survive, an important issue is whether those losses may be taken into any consolidation regime available. If so, those losses would automatically be brought to the profits, and there would be a potential for tax arbitrage. Consolidation was considered earlier at 1.2.3.2, where it was noted that the US and Australia have forms of consolidation and that one would be implemented under the CCCTB Proposal.

---

[125]  TCGA 1992 (UK) s. 184A(1)(b).
[126]  CAA 2001 (UK) s. 212B.
[127]  CAA 2001 (UK) ss. 212C to 212I.
[128]  CAA 2001 (UK) ss. 212P & 212Q.

In the US, losses survive a corporate change of ownership if the continuity of activity test is met. However, as noted earlier at 5.2.2.1, the rate at which those losses can be used in the future is restricted each year to the value of the loss corporation at the time of change multiplied by the federally set rate. This rule has also been adapted for consolidation purposes.[129] As a result, the loss corporation with its losses may be taken into a consolidated group with its acquirer and the losses carried forward for use against consolidated income. The losses are still restricted to the value of the loss corporation multiplied by the federal rate, which is the primary protection against tax arbitrage.

Australia adopted a version of these US rules when it implemented its consolidation regime in 2002. If a loss corporation passes the same business test following a change of ownership, the corporation can take carried-forward losses (revenue and capital) into a consolidation with the acquirer (presuming the 100% acquisition threshold is met). However, the rate at which those losses can be used in the consolidation is slowed. This rate is calculated in a different manner from the US rule. Broadly, a loss factor is set by comparing the value of the loss corporation at the time of consolidation to the value of the group as a whole. The brought-in losses may only reduce the consolidated corporate income for any year by a percentage equal to this loss factor.[130]

At present, the CCCTB Proposal does not restrict the ability of a corporation to carry forward losses following a change of ownership, unless the general anti-avoidance rule is triggered. However, the CCCTB Proposal does incorporate a restriction on a corporation taking losses into a consolidation irrespective of whether that corporation suffers a change of ownership. Brought-in losses may not be set against the consolidated tax base generally. Rather, that consolidated tax base is apportioned to various members of the consolidated group under the formula provided by the CCCTB Proposal.[131] Losses that a corporation has when it joins a consolidation may only be 'set off against the apportioned share' of that corporation in any particular year.[132]

---

[129] Title 26 Code of Federal Regulations (US) §§ 1.1502–90 to 1.1502–99.

[130] Income Tax Assessment Act 1997 (Australia) Subdiv. 707-C. These Australian rules only apply to losses brought into a consolidation. Outside of consolidation and unlike the US rules, if the loss corporation meets the same business test the losses can be used after a change of ownership in an unrestricted fashion.

[131] CCCTB Proposal Art. 86.

[132] CCCTB Proposal Art. 64.

It seems that a related rule would apply a similar restriction to unrealised losses. That is, losses on assets held by a corporation before joining a group that are realised by a disposal after joining a group are deducted from that corporation's share of the group's profits and not those group profits per se.[133] This rule is different from the US and Australian rules on unrealised losses. It applies to any loss accruing on such an asset, whether before or after a change of ownership or entry into consolidation. So here there is no marking by reference to market value at any particular time.

Nevertheless, this type of quarantining under the CCCTB Proposal has similarities to those in the US and Australia. The rationale in all three approaches is to limit the use of the losses to income generated (or that might be considered generated) by the loss corporation in the future. The difference between these three corporate tax systems is that each uses a different method for calculating the portion of consolidated income attributable to the loss corporation in consolidation.

**Transfer the loss to a profit**   The scenario for analysis is whether a pre-change loss of a corporation that survives a change of ownership can be transferred to the acquirer. With respect to realised losses, this is not possible in either Germany or the UK. The other corporate tax systems considered in this book do not permit the transfer of losses in any case.

In Germany, only losses incurred by a subsidiary while a profit-pooling agreement (*Organschaft*) is in place can be transferred to the parent corporation (see the earlier discussion at 1.2.3.2). The profit-pooling agreement cannot be in place until the loss corporation is acquired. Accordingly, when a corporation with carried-forward losses is taken into a profit-pooling agreement, those losses continue to be carried forward (presuming no change of ownership), but are frozen outside of the agreement. Each year during the agreement the subsidiary transfers its profits to the parent corporation *before* the use of any carried-forward losses. The only way to use these isolated losses is to wait until the profit-pooling agreement is broken and the loss corporation independently derives profits.

Similarly in the UK, only revenue losses incurred while a corporation is a member of a group may be transferred under group relief. So, although a loss corporation may continue to carry forward its losses after a change of ownership if it suffers no major change in the conduct of its trade, those losses are quarantined within the loss corporation. As noted earlier at 1.2.3.2, those losses may only be used against profits of the trade

---

[133] CCCTB Proposal Art. 61.

that incurred them. Similarly, the UK only permits the transfer of realised capital losses that are incurred when the corporation is part of a group.

The transfer of unrealised losses is less clear-cut. The most obvious scenario involves the loss corporation transferring an asset to the acquirer when the cost of the asset is more than its market value at the time of change of ownership (i.e. the asset incorporates an unrealised loss). Such a transfer would be between related parties, and the question is how that transaction would be valued for tax purposes. There are two options in this regard: value the transaction at market value or value the transaction at historic cost. Neither option is without difficulty.

If the transfer of the asset is valued at market value (e.g. under an arm's length transfer pricing rule), the unrealised loss is prevented from being transferred from the loss corporation to the acquirer. However, this also causes the loss to be crystallised in the hands of the loss corporation, turning the loss from an unusable unrealised loss into a usable realised loss. Once the loss is realised there is the potential that it could be used for group loss relief purposes. If the transfer of the asset is at historic cost, then the unrealised loss is effectively transferred to the acquirer. The acquirer can then sell the asset to a third party, thereby realising the loss as a loss of the acquirer (not the loss corporation). The acquirer could then use the loss against its own profits. Countries vary in how they approach this type of issue.

The rules that need consideration are those for transactions between related parties that were discussed earlier at 1.2.3.1. So, in Germany, arm's length rules for transfer prices between related parties generally mean the crystallisation of loss when the loss corporation transfers the asset to the acquirer. The potential here after a change of ownership seems to be that that loss would then be available for transfer to the acquirer if the acquirer has entered into a profit-pooling agreement (*Organschaft*) with the loss corporation. This is subject to the German change of ownership rules applying to the carry-forward of an unrealised loss.

By contrast and as usual, the position in the UK is relatively confused and depends on the type of asset in question. If the asset is trading stock, there is some scope for triggering a loss in either the loss corporation or the acquirer. Whether a loss can be triggered depends on the value at which the stock is transferred and whether the transfer pricing rules apply or not (see the earlier discussion at 1.2.3.1). Such a loss is transferable if the loss corporation and the acquirer are grouped (75% ownership). Residually, the same is true if the unrealised loss is on a depreciable asset (written-down value for capital allowance purposes is greater than the market value). However, the quarantining rule (discussed earlier) where, by reason of the change of ownership the loss corporation becomes part of a new 75% group, may apply.

If the asset with the unrealised loss is a capital asset, then the residual position is that the asset is treated as sold at market value. This would effect a realisation of the loss for the loss corporation and trigger certain quarantining rules because the transaction is between related persons.[134] More likely, the loss corporation might simply realise the loss after the change of ownership by a sale to a third party and then seek to transfer the loss to the acquirer if they are part of a 75% group.[135] Use of the loss in this manner might be subject to the rule for capital losses following a change of ownership or the general anti-abuse rule for capital losses.[136]

Even the countries that provide consolidation require brief consideration because their shareholding thresholds for consolidation are typically higher than for their restrictions on use of carried-forward losses. The US seems reasonably protected in this regard. The general application of the US arm's length transfer pricing rule should make it difficult to transfer the unrealised loss to the acquirer. Further, a transfer to the acquirer might trigger the quarantining rules for loss crystallisation on transfers to related persons (see the earlier discussion at 1.2.3.1). In any case, the section 382 of IRC limitation applies to a net unrealised built-in loss (see the earlier discussion).

As in the US, it should be relatively difficult to transfer unrealised losses to the acquirer under the CCCTB Proposal due to its arm's length transfer pricing rule. This rule and its limitations were discussed earlier at 1.2.2. If the rule applies, the loss corporation would be treated as transferring the asset at its market value and so would effectively crystallise its loss. However, if the rule does not apply, the parties could use the cost of the asset as the price for the sale and effectively transfer the unrealised loss.

The Australian situation, like that of the UK, is messy and depends on the type of asset in question. If the asset is trading stock or a depreciable asset, there seems some scope for a transfer above market value to effectively transfer the unrealised loss to the acquirer.[137] However, this should not be possible in the case of a capital asset because a general arm's length

---

[134] TCGA 1992 (UK) s. 18.
[135] TCGA 1992 (UK) s. 171A.
[136] TCGA 1992 (UK) ss. 184A and 16A, respectively.
[137] Income Tax Assessment Act 1997(Australia) ss. 70–90 (trading stock) & 40–300 (depreciable assets).

rule for related party transactions should apply.[138] The recognition of capital losses may be deferred if incurred in a transaction between related corporations.[139]

**Transfer a profit to the loss**  Presuming the loss survives the change of ownership and consolidation is not available, it is still possible that the acquirer can transfer a profit into the loss corporation to set against the loss. However, doing so is difficult if a market value rule applies to related party transactions. This would be the case in Germany, at least for realised losses, although there may be some scope for transferring corporate opportunities into a loss corporation. In the case of unrealised losses, as mentioned earlier, the loss corporation might be able to realise the loss after entering into a profit-pooling agreement (*Organschaft*) and transfer it to the acquirer.

Under the messy UK tax law there seems some scope for moving profits into a corporation that has carried forward revenue losses. This scope is limited by the 'major change in the nature or conduct of a trade' test (discussed earlier at 5.2.1.2), which can be triggered by attempts to inject profits into a corporation. Where the corporation has capital losses, the general market value rule for related party transactions prevents the acquirer from moving a capital gain into the corporation. However, if the corporation forms a 75% group with the acquirer, moving a capital gain becomes easy by the transfer at book value rule discussed earlier at 1.2.3.1. As noted at that point, an actual transfer of the asset to the loss corporation is no longer necessary. The acquirer could sell its asset at a profit and simply transfer the capital gain to the loss corporation. Again, this is subject to the general anti-abuse rules for capital losses discussed earlier.

Where the loss corporation has realised capital losses, it is subject to another anti-abuse rule (of an earlier date). Schedule 7A of TCGA 1992 applies where a corporation becomes a member of a group at a time when it is carrying forward capital losses. The pre-group loss can only be used against a gain accruing on the disposal of an asset that the loss corporation held before the grouping or that was acquired from outside the group and is used in any business of the loss corporation.[140] This rule previously

---

[138] Income Tax Assessment Act 1997 (Australia) ss. 112–20 (seller) & 116–30 (acquirer).
[139] Income Tax Assessment Act 1997 (Australia) Subdiv. 170-D, although these rules only apply to related corporations.
[140] TCGA 1992 (UK) Sch. 7A para. 7.

extended to unrealised losses, but that extension was repealed in 2011, and reliance was then placed on the anti-abuse rules referred to earlier.

The general market value rule for related party transactions in the US makes it difficult to transfer a profit into a loss corporation. Transferring profit may be possible through the transfer of corporate opportunities, but in any case the loss corporation would be subject to the section 382 of IRC limitation. The CCCTB Proposal also has a broad market value rule for related party transactions. Where it applies, transferring profits into a loss corporation may be difficult. By contrast, Australia has a more limited and fragmented approach in applying market value to related party transactions in a domestic context. Such a rule is only comprehensive in a capital gains context. However, seeking to 'stuff' profits into a loss corporation may trigger denial of the loss under Australia's income injection test mentioned earlier at 5.2.2.2.[141]

### 5.2.2.4   Change of ownership of profit corporation

As the earlier discussion demonstrates, many countries put multifarious obstacles in the way of using losses after the takeover of a loss corporation. But as any competent tax planner knows; if you cannot bring the loss to the profit, then try to take the profit to the loss. A similar tax arbitrage may be achieved by an acquirer with carried-forward losses acquiring a corporation with profits (the 'target' corporation). If the acquirer can use its losses to shelter the target corporation from tax, then the target corporation is worth more to the acquirer than to a third party that cannot shelter the profits.

As discussed earlier at 5.2.2.2, one method of addressing this variation of the two-step tax arbitrage is to fix the tax liability of the corporation at the time of the change of ownership. This involves treating the target corporation as realising all its assets and liabilities at the point of change and setting off any existing losses. That liability could not be adjusted after the change. Countries are generally reluctant to adopt such a holistic approach to the problem, but the rules discussed at 5.2.2.2 may be relevant in the current context. The reluctance to tax unrealised gains was already mentioned, even though in substance the assets may be viewed as having been indirectly realised. More deeply, these issues are related to taxation of gains on the disposal of shares (discussed earlier at 5.1.2), and this requires some explanation.

---

[141]   Income Tax Assessment Act 1997 (Australia) Subdiv. 175-A.

If a corporation with, say, an unrealised gain is sold, that profit may be reflected in the value of the shares that are sold. Therefore, to tax the corporation on its unrealised gains by reason of the change of ownership may produce an immediate (though potentially temporary) double taxation. The corporation is taxed on its gain, and the shareholder who sells the shares is also taxed on the gain (depending on the cost base of the shares). This type of double taxation would be immediate and more obvious than the type of double taxation that is caused by separating these two events (i.e. realisation by the corporation and separate realisation by the shareholder).[142]

However, the risk of this type of double taxation can be overstated. As discussed earlier at 5.1.3, there are many circumstances in which gains on the disposal of shares are not comprehensively taxed. These circumstances are directly related to the problem of enveloping. Cases where gains on the disposal of shares are not effectively taxed are the cases most open to abuse by tax arbitrage through the takeover of a profit corporation by an acquirer with losses. So, for example, if the existing shareholder of the target corporation is another corporation for which a participation exemption is available, this type of tax arbitrage might be easy to achieve. The same applies to any other type of exempt shareholder and, in particular, non-resident shareholders, who are often protected from taxation on gains on the disposal of shares by tax treaties (if not domestic law).

The following discussion is limited to tax arbitrage involving takeover of a target corporation with unrealised gains, which is the most common scenario. However, depending on the tax law in question, it might be possible to achieve a similar sort of tax arbitrage with realised profits of a corporation subject to a change of ownership. This might happen where, after the takeover, the acquirer can transfer a loss to the target corporation that can be carried backwards across the change of ownership. The discussion first considers the possibility of tax arbitrage where consolidation is available and then where it is not.

**Consolidation**  The present scenario involves a corporation with carried-forward losses acquiring another corporation with an unrealised gain. After the takeover, the corporations consolidate, the profit corporation

---

[142] This type of realisation and double taxation on the takeover of a corporation can occur in the US by election under IRC (US) s. 338. This provision is beyond the scope of this book, but one reason for making such an election is to receive a high cost base in the acquired corporation's assets after the acquisition. This would result, for example, in high amounts of depreciation for the corporation in the future.

realises its gain and the question is whether the pre-acquisition losses of the acquirer can be used to relieve taxation of the pre-acquisition gain of the target corporation. There are two issues here: whether the acquirer's loss can be taken into the consolidation and, if it can, whether there are any restrictions on using the loss against the target corporation's gain.

Broadly, in the US the answers are yes and yes. As a general rule, the US permits corporations to take existing losses into a consolidation.[143] Where it is the loss corporation that is taken over, this permission is subject to the section 382 of IRC limitation, considered earlier at 5.2.2.1 and 5.2.2.3. If the loss corporation has not suffered a change of ownership, the 'separate return limitation year' (SRLY) rules may apply, which effect a quarantining that can be similar to the section 382 limitation.[144] However, there is an exception to the SRLY rules for the parent of the consolidated group and a subsidiary that was effectively an 80% subsidiary at the time the loss was incurred.[145]

The result is that in principle, a loss corporation could acquire a target profit corporation, consolidate and set its pre-existing losses against the profits of its newly acquired subsidiary. This, however, is subject to a special limitation:

If

(1) a corporation acquires ... control of another corporation ... and
(2) either of such corporations is a gain corporation, income for any recognition period taxable year (to the extent attributable to recognized built-in gains) shall not be offset by any preacquisition loss (other than a preacquisition loss of the gain corporation).[146]

This is a quarantining rule that prevents the acquirer's pre-existing losses being set against the target corporation's pre-existing gains, including in a consolidation. It only applies to gains realised within five years of the change of ownership (the 'recognition period').

In Australia the answers would also be broadly yes and yes. Under the Australian consolidation regime the newly acquired profit corporation would become, for tax purposes, a division of the acquirer. The acquirer retains its carried-forward loss, which would be available to set against

---

[143]  Title 26 Code of Federal Regulations (US) § 1.1502–21(b).
[144]  Title 26 Code of Federal Regulations (US) § 1.1502–21(c) (revenue losses) and 1.1502–22(c) (capital losses).
[145]  Title 26 Code of Federal Regulations (US)§ 1.1502–1(f)(2).
[146]  IRC (US) s. 384(a).

future profits of the newly acquired target corporation. However, the unrealised gain of the acquired corporation may well be wiped out on consolidation by rules that reset the tax cost of assets. In broad outline, the price paid for the shares in the target corporation is allocated to the assets and liabilities held by the corporation at the time it enters the consolidation. On consolidation, the separate identity of the target corporation disappears, and the acquiring corporation is treated as holding the assets of the target corporation directly. The value allocated under the cost-setting process is treated as the cost of the assets in the hands of the acquiring corporation.[147]

In the case of a target corporation with an unrealised gain, it is likely that this gain is reflected in the price paid for the shares in the corporation. Accordingly, in principle, the asset would, in the consolidation, be allocated a cost equal to its market value (i.e. a step-up in cost). The result may be that in the consolidation there is no unrealised gain to set the acquirer's loss against. Rather, the presumption is that the gain was realised and taxed at the shareholder level when the existing shareholder sold the shares in the target corporation to the acquirer. Australia does not have a participation exemption for gains on the disposal of shares in resident corporations. These tax cost-setting rules are extremely complex and subject to anti-abuse rules that are beyond the scope of this book.

Under the CCCTB Proposal the answers would be a qualified no and no. The rules for bringing realised losses into a consolidated group were considered earlier at 5.2.2.3, and unlike in the US and Australia, they would also apply to the parent of a group, in the present case the acquirer. So, the acquirer's pre-acquisition loss could only be carried forward to set against the acquirer's post-consolidation share of the consolidated profits.[148] Further, if the target corporation realises its gain at any point in the five years after consolidation, the gain would be attributed directly to that corporation and would not go into the consolidated profits.[149] These rules seem comparatively robust against the type of tax arbitrage being considered. However, it must be remembered that a participation exemption would apply under the CCCTB Proposal, whereas both the US and Australia tax gains on the disposal of shares by one corporation in another corporation.

---

[147] The asset tax-cost setting rules are in Income Tax Assessment Act 1997 (Australia) Div. 705.
[148] CCCTB Proposal Art. 64.
[149] CCCTB Proposal Art. 61.

**Transfer the profit to a loss or vice versa**    In the absence of a consolidation regime, it may be presumed that the acquisition of the target corporation by the acquirer has no effect on the ability of the acquirer to use its losses; the acquirer has suffered no change of ownership. However, the second issue discussed in the context of consolidation remains: are there any restrictions on using the loss against the target corporation's gain? More particularly, is the target corporation's unrealised gain identified and quarantined in any way so as to prevent set-off against the acquirer's loss? If not, how might the gain or loss be moved to be set against the other? The last question is essentially a repeat of the discussion on how a gain or loss may be moved where a loss corporation is acquired (see the earlier discussion at 5.2.2.3), and that discussion is not repeated here.

For example, the US quarantining rule in section 384 of IRC (discussed earlier) is not limited in application to consolidation scenarios, but in principle it does require an 80% acquisition to apply.[150] Where this rule does not apply, the primary defence for the US against the type of tax arbitrage under consideration is its transfer pricing rules. Realised gains and losses cannot be transferred, so the primary risk is an attempt to transfer unrealised gains and losses, and here the transfer pricing rules would need to be negotiated. The position is essentially the same in Australia and under the CCCTB Proposal, although Australia's domestic transfer pricing rules are not as comprehensive as in the US or under the CCCTB Proposal.

In Germany, this type of tax arbitrage seems particularly easy, despite the more formidable restrictions where a loss corporation is acquired. The acquirer's loss is its own and may be carried forward in the usual manner. The shares in the target corporation can be acquired without effecting a realisation of its built-in gain. This means that, if the seller of the shares is entitled to the participation exemption, there will be little to no tax by reason of the sale of the profit corporation. After the acquisition, the profit corporation can enter into a profit-pooling agreement (*Organschaft*) with the acquirer. The profit corporation can then realise its gain, which will be transferred to the acquirer under the agreement. The acquirer can then use its loss against the gain. The only legislative protection that Germany has against this type of planning is the general limitation on use of carried-forward losses (60% above €1 million; see the earlier discussion at 1.2.3.2).

In the UK, the position of the acquirer is similar. It is the acquirer's loss, and because the acquirer does not suffer a change of ownership, the loss is

---

[150] See the definition of 'control' in IRC (US) s. 384(c)(5).

not affected. If the loss is already realised, it cannot be transferred. If the loss is realised by the acquirer after the acquisition, it may be possible to transfer the loss to the profit corporation whether the loss is of a revenue or capital nature (see the earlier discussion at 1.2.3.2). However, there are two rules that might need to be negotiated, depending on the type of gain in question. In the usual way, the UK makes no attempt to coordinate the operation of these rules.

With respect to built-in revenue gains, there is a special rule for the acquisition of corporations engaged in a leasing business. The UK widely recognises a lessor under a finance lease as the owner of the leased asset. This means that it is the lessor (usually a subsidiary of a bank) and not the operating lessee that claims capital allowances (depreciation). The deduction for capital allowances early in a lease usually exceeds rental income. The result is that there is a point during the lease where, from a tax perspective, the lease turns from loss making to being profit making. At this point, the subsidiary, with the potential for profit, could be sold to a corporation with losses. As the newly acquired subsidiary realises its profits, losses could be transferred to it from its loss-making parent.

The UK sought to shut down this type of planning in 2006, but in the usual manner did not get at the core of the conceptual issue. As a result, these rules have been amended on numerous occasions since their introduction. The broad effect of these rules is that the acquired corporation might be required to realise some of its built-in gains to ensure that they are not available for offset by losses of the acquirer.[151] A detailed consideration of these rules is beyond the scope of this book.

In the case of unrealised capital gains, the anti-abuse capital loss rule that is triggered by a change of ownership is reflected in an anti-abuse capital gain rule triggered by such a change. This rule applies where after a change of ownership a gain accrues to a corporation on an asset that it held before the change. If the change is part of an arrangement to secure a tax advantage, the gain may not be offset by a loss accruing to the corporation (e.g. a capital loss transferred in by the acquirer).[152]

### 5.2.3 Limitations on carry-forward of other corporate tax attributes

The discussion at 5.2.2 was solely concerned with the indirect transfer of corporate tax attributes in the form of gains and particularly losses, and

---

[151] CTA 2010 (UK) ss. 382–408.
[152] TCGA 1992 (UK) s. 184B.

even so it was concerned with basic rules only. A corporate tax system may incorporate restrictions on the carry-forward of other tax attributes such as special types of deductions or loss equivalents, tax credits or even a particular status of a corporation for tax purposes. A few of these tax attributes are mentioned here, but the discussion is far from comprehensive.

The US tax law seems most organised in this regard. It has a broad rule for carried-forward tax credits and effectively applies the section 382 of IRC limitation in this regard.[153] This rule applies to the carry-forward of certain business tax credits, the minimum tax credit (for alternative minimum tax purposes) and foreign tax credits. It also applies to carried-forward capital losses.

Other countries' approaches are more hit and miss, but seem more likely to only apply carry-forward limitations to loss equivalents. So, for example, Germany applies its loss limitation rule to the carry-forward of denied interest deductions under the interest barrier and carried-forward losses for trade tax purposes.[154] Outside the context of a trade, the UK restricts the carry-forward of a number of corporate tax attributes on a change of ownership, including debits and deficits under the loan relationship rules, relief for intangible fixed assets and certain expenses.[155]

Foreign tax credits seem less likely to be targeted. Sometimes, this is because they cannot be carried forward, as in Germany and generally in the UK. However, even where they can be carried forward in the UK (foreign tax credits of a foreign PE where exemption is not elected) there is no restriction on a change of ownership. Australia once considered such a rule for foreign tax credits but decided to deny the carry-forward of foreign tax credits.[156]

An interesting issue for countries with imputation systems is whether the credit in the imputation account should be restricted following a change of ownership of a corporation. To do so would introduce a substantial classical element into an imputation system and play havoc with the earlier analysis at 5.1.2 involving the connection between distributions and capital losses. Australia has always permitted the carry-forward of

---

[153] IRC (US) s. 383.
[154] The extension of the loss limitation rule under KStG (Germany) s. 8c to interest carried forward under the interest barrier is in KStG (Germany) s. 8a(1) and to losses for trade tax purposes is in the Trade Tax Law (*Gewerbesteuergesetz*) (Germany) s. 10a. The interest barrier in EStG (Germany) s. 4h was discussed earlier at 2.1.3.
[155] CTA 2010 (UK) ss. 692 to 703.
[156] Income Tax Assessment Act 1997 (Australia) s. 770-75.

credit in a corporation's franking (imputation) account despite a change of ownership. Consistently, subsidiaries that enter into a consolidation transfer their franking account credits to the parent corporation.[157] By contrast, New Zealand does extinguish credit in many accounts of a corporation suffering a 66% change of ownership, including its imputation credit account.[158]

### 5.2.4 Leaving a corporate group

It may be that the corporation whose shares are transferred is a member of a corporate group before the transfer, but not a member of the group after the transfer (i.e. the transfer may cause the member to leave the corporate group). As noted at the start of this heading, the sorts of issues that arise when a corporation leaves a group in many ways resemble those that arise on a change of ownership. There is a threshold of change that will cause a corporation to leave a corporate group, and the leaving may have an impact on the tax attributes of both the leaving corporation and the remaining group members.

The thresholds for forming a corporate group were discussed earlier at 1.2.3. These are typically much higher than the thresholds for restrictions on the carry-forward of corporate tax attributes on a change of ownership discussed earlier at 5.2.1. Indeed, it is possible for a corporation to have to leave a corporate group when it suffers no change of underlying ownership at all. For example, this may happen when the corporation is no longer held by a parent corporation, such as in a corporate division or de-merger (see the later discussion at 7.2.2), even though the corporation is still held proportionately by the parent corporation's shareholders. Accordingly, a transfer of shares may result in a corporate member leaving a corporate group without triggering change of ownership restrictions.

As noted earlier at 1.2.3, tax laws often incorporate rules that erode the identity of members of a corporate group. When a member leaves a corporate group, that member requires a full tax identity, and an issue is whether that member should take with it any tax attributes that have been assigned to the group as a whole. Further, when a corporation leaves a group there is the question of whether tax attributes that have been individually assigned to group members should be denied or adjusted in any

[157] Income Tax Assessment Act 1997 (Australia) Subdiv. 709-A.
[158] Income Tax Act 2007 (New Zealand) ss. OA8 (shareholder continuity requirements) & OB41 (debit to imputation credit account).

way. These are particularly difficult and complex issues and can result in a tax liability. The following discussion provides only a brief outline of these issues and focuses on the issues emphasised in the earlier discussion at 1.2.3 of eroding the identity of group corporations.

The issues discussed earlier at 1.2.3 are in many ways similar to the issues discussed under this heading at 5.2.2 (i.e. the treatment of realised losses and unrealised gains and losses). Group relief potentially dislocates a carried-forward loss from the corporation that incurred it. So, when a corporation leaves a group, there is a question of whether the corporation should take losses carried forward by the group with it and, if so, how much. The situation with respect to unrealised gains and losses is similar. Deferral of recognition of group transactions, discussed earlier at 1.2.3.1, has the potential to dislocate gains and losses and the assets associated with them from the group member that accrued or incurred them. This is particularly clear when an asset is transferred at book value between group members. If a transaction between group members was not recognised when it occurred, the question is whether it should be recognised when one of the parties to the transaction leaves the group.

### 5.2.4.1 Deferred transactions

If a transaction between group members was deferred when it occurred (see the earlier discussion at 1.2.3.1), then the fact that one of the parties to the transaction leaves the group may trigger recognition. This issue does not arise if, as in Germany, the recognition of transactions between group members is not deferred. By contrast, the UK and the US provide examples of recognition of deferred transactions when a corporate member leaves a group. The CCCTB Proposal and Australia adopt a different approach and provide examples of potentially taxing a deferred gain as a gain on the disposal of shares in the leaving member.

The UK permits group corporations to transfer capital assets between themselves on a no gain / no loss basis. The transferee takes over the cost base of the transferor. The result is that an unrealised capital gain or loss may be indirectly transferred from one group corporation to another group corporation. Without a recapture rule, this would provide a simple method for avoiding tax on a sale of an asset while realising a built-in gain to a third party by enveloping the asset in a leaving group member (regarding enveloping, see the earlier discussion at 4.1.2.1). To counter this problem, the UK has a rule that retrospectively recognises and taxes intergroup transactions if the transferee corporation leaves the group within six years of the transfer.[159] There are complex exceptions to this rule when more than one group member leaves at the same time (subgroup break-up).

The US provides a broader example of recognition of deferred transactions. When a US corporation leaves a corporate group it moves from a consolidated return year to a separate return year. The leaving corporation takes with it corporate tax attributes that it has been individually assigned. However, the leaving corporation may have transacted with other members of the corporate group, and gains and losses on these transactions may have been deferred. Leaving the group triggers these gains and losses, whether for the leaving member or the group member that transacted with the leaving member.[160]

The UK and the US target tax consequences at the corporations that were parties to a transaction that received deferred tax treatment. By contrast, Australia and the CCCTB Proposal target the holders of the shares in the corporation that leaves the group. The CCCTB Proposal at present has no rules that restrict the carry-forward of tax attributes on a change of ownership. However, it has a rule similar to that in the UK, which seeks to remove the benefit of a prior transfer of an asset between group corporations at book value when the transferee corporation leaves the group. Unlike in the UK, however, the CCCTB Proposal rule would remove the participation exemption available to the parent corporation selling the shares in the transferee to the extent of any unrealised gain deferred when the asset was transferred.[161] The CCCTB Proposal rule would be excluded if 'it is demonstrated that the inter-group transactions were carried out for valid commercial reasons'.

The Australian rules on leaving a corporate group may produce a similar result, though in a very different manner. Under Australia's pure consolidation approach, when a subsidiary joins a group its shares disappear for tax purposes. When a subsidiary leaves a corporate group then the cost base of its shares have to be reconstructed for tax purposes. The cost base of the subsidiary's shares is, as a general rule, reconstructed from the cost base of the assets held by the subsidiary at the time of its departure from the group.[162] Transactions between group members are not recognised. So, if a subsidiary receives an asset from another group member with a built-in gain, that built-in gain is reflected in the reconstructed cost base

---

[159] TCGA 1992 (UK) s. 179.
[160] Title 26 Code of Federal Regulations (US) § 1.1502–13(d)(1).
[161] CCCTB Proposal Art. 75.
[162] Income Tax Assessment Act 1997 (Australia) Div. 711.

of the subsidiary when it leaves the group. Because Australia does not have a domestic participation exemption, that gain will be taxed when the parent corporation disposes of the shares in the subsidiary.

### 5.2.4.2  Carried-forward losses and other tax attributes

When a corporation leaves a group, an issue is the extent to which the corporation takes any carried-forward losses (or other tax attributes) incurred while the corporation was a member of the group. Typically, this is not an issue for countries that do not consolidate losses at the corporate-group level. So, for example, even while within a group, the UK continues to allocate losses to the group member that incurs the loss. Further, as losses may only be transferred between group members for use in the year in which the loss is incurred, the only corporation that can carry forward a loss is the group member that incurred it. Accordingly, when a corporation leaves a group, it takes its losses with it.

The German position is fundamentally different, even though it also continues to recognise the separate existence of group members for tax purposes. When an *Organschaft* agreement is concluded, all future losses incurred by the subsidiary are attributed to the parent corporation. In this way, it is the parent corporation that carries forward group losses and not the subsidiary. Because these are the parent's personal losses (a point reinforced by the legal nature of the *Organschaft* agreement), a subsidiary takes no share of these losses should it leave the group, irrespective of whether it was the leaving subsidiary that incurred the loss. If the subsidiary has losses carried forward from before the *Organschaft* agreement (which cannot be transferred to the parent), the subsidiary will once again be able to use these losses after exit from the group (presuming no change of ownership).

By contrast, losses of US group corporations are incurred by individual group members, but are consolidated at the group level. When a corporation leaves a corporate group, the leaving corporation may take its share of a carried-forward consolidated corporate loss. Determination of its share is subject to complex regulations, but as a general rule the apportionment is done on the basis of the relative amounts of separate net operating losses that the group member actually incurred.[163]

Some countries that consolidate losses at the group level deny a leaving member a share of group losses. For example, the CCCTB Proposal

---

[163]  Title 26 Code of Federal Regulations (US) § 1.1502–21(b). § 1.1502–22(b) applies similarly to carried-forward capital losses and § 1.1502–79(d) to foreign tax credits.

incorporates a simple rule that '[n]o losses shall be attributed to a group member leaving a group'.[164] However, if the whole group terminates, then carried-forward losses are 'allocated to each group member in accordance with…the apportionment factors applicable to the tax year of termination'.[165] This somewhat arbitrary prescription uses the tax base formulary apportionment rules, but only as applicable in the year of termination and not the year in which the loss was incurred.

Australia adopts a similar approach. Australia's pure form of consolidation means that subsidiaries are considered divisions of the parent corporation. Therefore, losses incurred during a consolidation are losses of the parent corporation. When a subsidiary leaves a consolidated group, all group losses stay with the parent corporation, irrespective of whether the loss carried forward was incurred by the leaving subsidiary.[166] Australia adopts the same approach with respect to credit in the franking (imputation) account. The whole of this credit stays with the parent corporation, and a departing subsidiary leaves with nothing.

## 5.3   Sale of shares versus sale of corporate activity

Shares are derivatives and reflect the value of assets and opportunities of the corporation in which they are held. Shares have no or at least very little intrinsic value in themselves. As noted in the introduction to this chapter, the duplicity that shares create gives the controllers of a corporation a stark choice when they decide to sell the corporation's business as a going concern: whether to sell the business or assets of the corporation directly or to sell the shares in the corporation and thereby sell the corporation together with the business or assets.

It is one thing for the controllers to determine which of these options they prefer, but their preference may be pitted against the preference of the purchaser. This book is not directly concerned with the tax treatment of a sale of a business or undertaking, which is a generic tax issue. Further, this chapter has considered the legal rules that might apply on the transfer of shares. So this subheading does not discuss legal rules or options in either context per se. Rather, it notes that the choice between a direct sale of assets and a sale of shares is a fundamental issue for a corporate tax system that is particularly important in practice. It seeks to briefly outline the main

---

[164]   CCCTB Proposal Art. 69.
[165]   CCCTB Proposal Art. 65.
[166]   For example, see Income Tax Assessment Act 1997 (Australia) s. 707–410.

issues that arise for each option. Tax issues for the seller are considered first, and these issues are then compared to those that may arise for the purchaser.

## Issues for the seller

Because the seller is realising assets, typically the seller's tax consequences of a sale are more immediate than those of the purchaser. It is presumed that the price for a full purchase is little different whether the corporation is purchased or the undertaking of the corporation is purchased. This then leaves two variable factors: the net tax cost of the assets being sold and the tax treatment of any gain or loss resulting from the sale.

It is nearly inevitable that the tax cost of assets held in the target corporation is not the same as the tax cost of the shares held in it. This means that the quantum of gain or loss on sale is different depending on whether the corporation's business is sold directly or the shares in the corporation are sold. If the shares have been held for a long time (e.g. since incorporation), the tax cost of the corporation's assets may be higher than the tax cost of the shares. Alternately, if the shares in the corporation were purchased recently at a time when the corporation had unrealised gains, the tax cost of the shares may be the higher of the two. In any case, it is a standard role for a tax advisor to compare these alternate sales and determine the alternate gains and losses.

It is not, however, sufficient to just determine whether there is a gain or loss on these alternatives. The tax treatment of the gains or losses must also be compared. With respect to a sale of shares, the sale should be homogeneous. There will be a gain or a loss, and the tax treatment will be as discussed previously in this chapter. This may not be the case with a sale of the corporation's business or undertaking. Legally, this is an individual sale of each asset of the business, and the tax consequences of a sale may vary depending on the type of asset in question. Further, a sale of shares results in tax consequences for the shareholder, whereas a sale of the corporation's business results in tax consequences for the corporation (e.g. at the corporation's tax rate).

The sale of trading stock or inventory by a corporation gives rise to full tax consequences. If there is a gain, it will be taxed at the full corporate tax rate; if there is a loss it should be fully deductible. The same is generally true of depreciable assets. If they are sold above their (written-down) tax cost, the excess depreciation to be recaptured (balancing charge) is fully taxable. If they are sold below this value, an extra deduction is granted. Non-depreciable capital assets may be treated differently, usually depending on the type of jurisdiction in question. In a civil law country like Germany, gains and losses on the disposal of capital assets have full tax consequences for the corporation. This would also be the case under the CCCTB Proposal.

However, in common law jurisdictions there may be special rules applying to gains and losses on the disposal of capital assets, even those held in a business. So, in the UK, the US and Australia, capital losses are quarantined, even for corporations, and may only be set against capital gains. Further, in some cases capital gains are treated in a particular fashion. So, for example, the UK still permits corporations to index the cost base of their capital assets for inflation when calculating a capital gain. Some common law jurisdictions extend this treatment to capital gains on the disposal of depreciable assets. The recapture or granting of additional depreciation on disposal is treated as described in the last paragraph, but if the asset is sold above its original cost, the excess is treated as a capital gain (not a revenue gain). This is the situation in both the UK and the US.

Even if the gain on the disposal of the corporation's assets or its shares were the same, the differing tax treatment of these events would mean there would be a difference in tax outcome. In principle, the taxation of corporate gains is usually full, but at the corporate tax rate, which in many cases is lower than the highest personal marginal rate. By contrast, at the shareholder level there may well be exemptions and reduced rates for gains on the disposal of shares (as discussed earlier at 5.1.3). For example, if gains are involved and the shareholder is another corporation, the existence of a participation exemption (as in Germany, the UK or under the CCCTB Proposal) may be particularly attractive. The same is true of the UK's personal exemption if the shareholder is an individual. However, the situation may be reversed if losses are involved. If losses on the disposal of shares are quarantined or denied, the seller may prefer to sell the corporation's assets rather than its shares.

As discussed earlier at 5.1.2, the existence of an exemption or reduced taxation at the shareholder level may have an impact on whether a corporation chooses to realise gains or not. Where such concessions mean that *enveloping* is attractive, the controllers of a corporation have an incentive to trap unrealised gains in corporations and only dispose of the assets indirectly by selling shares in the corporation. This may mean that, over a period of time, the tax cost of a corporation's assets is intentionally caused to be substantially below that of the tax cost of shares in it. That is, the availability of enveloping may be a cause of imbalance between these competing costs.

It is one thing to take into account the potential for losses on the disposal of the corporation's assets or its shares. However, it may also be the case that the corporation has carried-forward losses, and the effect of a sale on this type of valuable tax attribute must be considered. A sale of the corporation's assets leaves the carried-forward loss trapped in the corporation (still owned by the seller) and separated from the business that incurred it. If the corporation has no other income-earning activity then, looking to the future, the seller has an incentive to inject income into the corporation in order to use the losses. This may be difficult if the country quarantines the carry-forward of losses (e.g. as the UK does with trading losses).

By contrast, if the shares in the corporation are sold, the loss stays with the corporation and so leaves the seller. However, because there is likely to have been a change of ownership of the corporation, the restrictions on the carry-forward of losses following such a change must be considered (as discussed earlier at 5.2). This may have particular implications for the purchaser, especially if the purchaser is required to cause the corporation to continue its pre-change activities.

### Competing interests of the purchaser

From a commercial perspective, it is often the case that acquiring assets of a corporation's business is more favourable to a prospective purchaser than acquiring the shares in the corporation. This is because the purchaser can select only those assets it requires and need not purchase the entire business of the corporation. Contrast a sale of shares where the purchaser effectively buys all of the corporation's assets, including its carried-forward tax attributes. This relates to the point made earlier that the sale of a business is essentially a series of individual disposals of the assets comprising the business. As a result, although the parties may agree on an overall price for the business, as a general rule the sale price must be apportioned between each of the assets being transferred.

The sale price needs to be apportioned because each of the assets transferred needs a tax value in the hands of the purchaser and the seller needs to determine the tax consequences of disposal of particular assets. For the purchaser, it is this apportioned value that is used for the purposes of depreciation and for calculating any gain or loss on a future disposal of the assets. In the absence of a specific tax law rule, the apportionment process will be a matter to be determined by the parties to the sale. There may be some general limits as to the manner in which the parties make the apportionment (e.g. there may be some test of reasonableness).[167] However, parties usually have substantial flexibility in this regard, and negotiating the apportionment by the parties is often an important task performed by tax advisors. An apportionment commonly forms a schedule to a business sale agreement.

In apportioning an overall price to particular assets the buyer and seller may have conflicting interests. The purchaser usually wishes to allocate as much of the sale price as possible to those assets on which the purchaser can claim immediate or full tax relief. For example, the purchaser might wish to allocate a maximum amount to trading stock, if that is to be sold imminently. Next in line would be depreciable assets, especially those assets on higher rates of depreciation. A purchaser is likely to give lowest priority to capital assets for which a deduction is not available unless realised.

This order of allocation may not, however, be favourable to the seller. Large allocations to trading stock and depreciable assets may give rise to large immediate tax liabilities. Allocations to capital assets may be more favourable, particularly if they are taxable at concessionary rates or the seller has quarantined capital losses that can be used against them. Because the seller is selling individual assets, there is also the possibility that the seller might be entitled to some concessionary treatment on the acquisition of assets that replace the assets sold (e.g. a deferral of any gain). Therefore, the seller may prefer that greater amounts are allocated to this type of asset.

Despite these issues of attribution, the effect of an asset sale is usually to step up the value of the assets to market value for tax purposes. This step-up of value maximises the amount available as a deduction for trading stock, the amount of depreciation available, and it minimises any gain on the subsequent disposal of assets. This can be contrasted with a share sale. Such a sale typically does not increase the cost base of the assets in the hands of the corporation that is sold. So the purchaser may be acquiring an indirect tax liability if the assets of the corporation have unrealised gains. The same may be true of carried-forward losses (realised or unrealised). All these matters may have an impact on the overall price paid for the shares.

---

[167] For example, in the UK see CAA 2001 (UK) s. 562 and TCGA 1992 (UK) s 53(4).

# 6

# Terminating share interests

Chapter 4 discussed how the issue of shares duplicates, for tax purposes, the assets of a corporation because corporate assets are reflected in the value of shares. Chapter 5 discussed the difficult policy issues that arise for a corporate tax system when those reflective assets (shares) are transferred. A substantial part of the discussion in Chapter 5 involved comparing the tax treatment of gains on disposal of these reflective assets with the tax treatment of corporate distributions discussed in Chapter 2. Indeed, one of the issues discussed in Chapter 5 was whether there should be some form of integrated tax treatment of gains on the disposal of shares and dividends (see the earlier discussion at 5.1.3.2). If there were ever any doubts about the need to consider the integration of these events, they are put to rest when shares are terminated.

Gains on disposal of shares and on the distribution of corporate profits have thus far been considered as separate taxing events. The termination of shares often collapses these gains into a single event. For example, this happens where a solvent corporation with retained profits is liquidated. Liquidation distributions are both consideration for the disposal of shares in the corporation and a distribution of profits (or return of capital). The collapsing of gains into a single event also can happen where the corporation buys its own shares, often called a partial liquidation. The result is that there is a direct link between this chapter and Chapters 2 and 5. In addition, terminations of shares end the reflection of real assets caused when shares are created. So this chapter is also linked to Chapter 4 in that it involves the reversal of the duplication of corporate assets discussed there.

This chapter is concerned with terminations of shares. However, as mentioned earlier at 2.1, one view is that a share is simply an amalgam of individual rights. As a result, it seems possible to terminate a part of a share (e.g. by terminating or restricting certain rights attached to the share). This is the first matter discussed in this chapter. This scenario involves neither the termination of the whole share nor the termination of the corporation in which the shares are held.

The chapter then moves to consider terminations of shares in their entirety. The first scenario considered is the termination of shares where termination of the corporation itself is not anticipated. A corporation cannot exist without members, and so this scenario involves the termination of some of the corporation's shares, but not all of them. The discussion considers the tax treatment of redemptions of shares (e.g. where the corporation has issued shares on terms as to their redemption and cancellation). It also considers a corporation buying its own shares (share buy-back), because the corporate law of many countries anticipates that a corporation must cancel shares that it buys in itself.

The termination of shares may also be part of a process involving the termination of the corporation itself. Shares cannot exist without a corporation, and so the termination of a corporation necessarily involves the termination of its shares. The formal process leading up to the termination of a corporation and its shares is referred to as liquidation or winding up. The actual termination or dissolution of a corporation and its shares occurs when the corporation is struck off the register of corporations (presuming the corporation is a registered corporation). This is one matter, but there are a host of other issues that arise in the process of liquidation and dissolution. These are discussed under the third heading of this chapter.

## 6.1 Partial share termination

The particular rights that typically attach to shares are the right to share in a division of profits, the right to a subordinated return of capital and the right to vote in a general meeting of members of the corporation (see the earlier discussion at 2.1). In principle, any of these rights may be terminated, but with varying consequences. Under corporate law, it is unlikely that a corporation can unilaterally terminate a shareholder's right to dividends or to vote at a general meeting.[1] This means that these types of terminations are unlikely to occur without shareholder compensation.

If the shareholder receives further rights in the corporation as consideration for the termination of dividend or voting rights, this is a corporate reorganisation and is considered later at 7.1. If the shareholder receives cash, then this may still be a reorganisation, and the rules discussed at 7.1 apply. Unless the amount is debited to the corporation's share capital

[1] In some cases, corporate law may not even permit such a termination. Rights may be suspended by reason of dire economic circumstances of a corporation; for example, when a corporation is put into receivership or liquidation (see the later discussion at 6.3.1).

account, the cash payment is likely to be a distribution of profits and so be classified as a dividend for tax purposes. Whether in this case there is also a partial disposal of the shares is more difficult and depends on the tax law in question. If the shareholder consents to the termination with no consideration, there is likely to be a shift of value from the shares in question to other shares in the corporation. Value shifts are considered later at 8.2.

The most common type of partial termination of share rights is a termination of a right to receive a return of share capital. The form and consequences of such a termination may be different depending on whether the corporate law in question still recognises shares as having a par value or not. Par value allocates a particular amount of share capital to each share, and (subject to rights to share premiums) this allocation defines the capital rights attaching to such shares. By contrast, capital rights attaching to non-par value shares are generally a right to share (on a defined basis; e.g. proportionally) in the corporate pool of share capital.

In contrast to other share rights, most commonly a corporation does not need the permission of a particular shareholder to cancel rights to a return of capital. Nevertheless, there is a special procedure that a corporation follows to cancel share capital. Sometimes it is simply by means of a special resolution (e.g. resolution of 75% of members entitled to vote). Sometimes directors may need to certify the solvency of the corporation. In other cases, the approval of a court may be required.

So, for example, for private companies in the UK a special resolution is needed together with a solvency statement by the directors. For public companies the requirement is a special resolution and court approval.[2] In Germany, capital reduction may be effected by special resolution, but creditors must be given six months to demand security, and payments to shareholders cannot be made until this time expires.[3] In the US, the general position is that the directors of a corporation can make a distribution to shareholders (whether of profits or capital) provided they are satisfied as to the corporation's solvency.[4]

Whether the shareholder receives any compensation on a cancellation of share capital depends on the financial circumstances of the corporation. If the net value of the corporation's assets is more than its outstanding share capital, it is likely that the shareholder will receive a payment for

[2] Companies Act (UK) s. 641.
[3] AktG (Germany) ss. 222 & 225.
[4] DGCL (US) ss. 154 & 170 and MBCA (US) s. 6.40.

the cancellation (i.e. the shareholder will receive a return of capital). If the shares have a par value, this return of capital will directly reduce that par value, and so the amount that the shareholder may receive as a return of capital in the future. If the shares have no par value, then the return of capital will reduce the capital pool from which the shareholder may claim a return of capital in the future. The tax treatment of returns of capital is the first matter discussed under this heading.

If, however, the net value of the corporation's assets is less than the amount standing in the corporation's share capital account, there may be no payment to the shareholder as compensation for the cancellation of capital. Rather, amounts standing to the credit of the share capital account may simply be cancelled. This is a method by which corporations that have permanently lost part of their share capital may formally recognise that fact. If a corporation may only make distributions out of profits, cancelling lost capital may be the only mechanism by which it can put itself into a position to pay any dividends in the future. Cancellation of share capital is the second matter discussed under this heading.

### 6.1.1 Returns of capital

At its simplest, share capital is an investment made in a corporation in order to secure a return in the form of dividends. A simple return of the funds invested (presuming it to be no more than the amount invested) is not typically a taxing event under an income tax because it does not involve a gain. Rather, if the return involves a termination of the investment, the investor must go through a reconciliation process. If the amount received is more than the cost base of the investment, the investor realises a gain; if it is less the investor realises a loss. Returns where only part of an investment is realised can cause income tax headaches.

Returns of share capital are typically cash payments made by a corporation to a shareholder.[5] As a cash payment made with respect to shares, returns of capital can be a substitute for dividends, particularly if the return does not involve the termination of the whole investment (i.e. cancellation of the shares). If substitution is a straightforward matter, then corporations may manipulate the payment of dividends and returns of share capital so as to minimize shareholder taxation (i.e. dividend streaming may be a problem; see the earlier discussion at 2.4.1.5). The fundamental question is whether the form of a return of capital, as a partial

---

[5] In-kind returns of capital are possible, but not considered.

termination of an investment in shares, is recognised for tax purposes or whether the tax law re-characterises that payment as a dividend.

The manner in which a corporate tax system allocates payments made by a corporation between dividends and returns of capital was discussed earlier at 2.5.2.1. As noted at that point, countries are more likely to accept a corporate law classification of a payment as a return of share capital if such returns are not easily substitutable with dividends. Corporate law may make it difficult for corporations to return capital to their shareholders; this is classically the case in countries where corporate law still follows the maintenance of capital approach, such as in Germany and the UK. As noted earlier, in these countries it is not easy to return capital to shareholders because formalities must be followed (special resolutions, court orders, rights of creditors, and so on). In these cases, dividends and returns of capital are not easily substituted.

In Germany, 'repayment of nominal capital' is specifically excluded from income from investment (dividends).[6] Further, the tax law specifies no realisation event in the case of a return of capital. Inevitably, however, the return of capital reduces the shareholder's cost base in the shares. It is presumed that the same approach would apply under the CCCTB Proposal. Returns of capital are not mentioned in the definition of 'revenues'.[7]

Similarly in the UK, returns of capital are specifically excluded from the definition of distribution.[8] However, there may be capital gains consequences. Under section 122(1) of TCGA 1992,

> Where a person receives ... in respect of shares in a company any capital distribution from the company ... he shall be treated as if he had in consideration of that capital distribution disposed of an interest in the shares.

The cost base of the shares is apportioned based on the market value of what is received and on the market value of what remains of the shares.[9] The result may be a chargeable capital gain. A chargeable gain may be avoided if the capital payment is small when compared to the value of the shares, normally accepted to be about 5%. In this case only the cost base of the shares is written down.[10] However, if the capital payment exceeds the cost base of the shares there is an immediate chargeable gain.[11]

---

6   EStG (Germany) s. 20(1)No. 2.
7   CCCTB Proposal Art. 4(8).
8   CTA 2010 (UK) s. 1000(1)B.
9   TCGA 1992 (UK) s. 42.
10   TCGA 1992 (UK) s. 122(2).
11   TCGA 1992 (UK) s. 122(4).

If a country has liberalised its corporate law so that shares do not have a par value and there is no strict capital maintenance requirement, it may need protection from dividend streaming. As noted earlier at 2.5.2.1, this protection may take one of two forms. First, corporate law may be broadly accepted, but overridden with dividend treatment in cases of perceived abuse. The Australian capital streaming rules discussed at 2.5.2.1 are an example. If these rules do not apply, then the Australian definition of 'dividend' specifically excludes a payment debited to the corporation's 'share capital account'.[12] If not a dividend, the return of capital reduces the shareholder's cost base in the shares in question. If that cost base is exceeded, the excess is a capital gain.[13]

Alternately, general law classification as to what constitutes a return of capital may be irrelevant for tax law purposes. This includes a situation such as generally in the US where there is often no formal corporate law distinction between a profit distribution and a capital distribution. The US profits-first rule is an example of a tax law rule that stands independent of general law classification. It was discussed earlier at 2.5.2.1. All corporate distributions are taxable as dividends to the extent of earnings and profits even if the distribution may be viewed as a return of capital.[14] Where all earnings and profits are considered distributed, further distributions reduce the cost base of shares. Distributions in excess of the cost base are treated as an immediate taxable gain.[15] An additional German example involving returns of hidden capital contributions was also discussed earlier at 2.5.2.1.

There is another scenario in which corporate law classification of a payment as a return of capital may be overridden by a tax law, irrespective of whether the corporate law classification involves a strict maintenance of capital approach or not. This involves the capitalisation of profits. Returns of capital that are identified with capitalised profits are commonly treated as dividends. How this treatment is achieved under a tax law differs from country to country and depends on how the capitalisation was treated in the first place. Capitalisation of profits commonly occurs in the context of the issue of bonus shares, which are discussed later at 7.1.2.

Germany adopts a comprehensive approach to returns of capital from capitalised profits that breaks with a corporate law classification. For tax

---

[12] Income Tax Assessment Act 1936 (Australia) s. 6(1) definition of 'dividend' para. (d).
[13] Income Tax Assessment Act 1997 (Australia) s. 104–135.
[14] IRC (US) ss. 301 and 316(a).
[15] IRC (US) s. 301(c)(3)(A).

purposes, Germany requires corporations to record capitalised profits as a separate entry in their share capital account.[16] A return of capital from the separate entry is then treated as a dividend.[17] The reverse situation is not expressly covered (unless it occurs within the same tax year); that is, where the corporation returns capital and then capitalises profits.

The UK adopts a more fragmented approach that in general respects the corporate law classification of returns of capital, even in the case of capitalised profits. There is, however, a special rule where a corporation returns capital that was not fully paid up with new consideration. The major example of capital not paid up with new consideration is the capitalisation of profits that occurs when bonus shares are issued. Where this happens, the tax law provides that '[d]istributions made afterwards by the company in respect of shares representing the bonus share capital are not treated as repayments of share capital'.[18] This rule is excluded where the repayment occurs more than ten years after the capitalisation (unless the corporation is a close company).[19] There is a similar rule providing dividend treatment of a capitalisation where the return of capital occurs before the capitalisation.[20]

The US and the CCCTB Proposal have no equivalent to these German and UK rules. In the US, capitalisations of profits do not decrease a corporation's earnings and profits and so do not decrease the profits pool from which dividends are distributed on a profits-first basis. So a return of capitalised profits in the US should in principle result in dividend treatment. Under the CCCTB Proposal, because dividends are essentially exempt, that capitalised profits might be distributed as a return of capital would seem to be of little consequence.

### 6.1.2   Cancellation of capital

A corporation may cancel amounts standing in its share capital account without any capital payment if the credit in that account is more than the net value of the corporation's assets. This is only likely to be important in countries where corporate law still requires maintenance of capital, such as in Germany and the UK. In this case, the loss of capital may have to

---

[16] KStG (Germany) s. 28(1).
[17] KStG (Germany) s. 28(2) and EStG (Germany) s. 20(1)No. 2.
[18] CTA 2010 (UK) s. 1026(2). The difficult issue of determining when a repayment of capital is considered to be in respect of particular shares is dealt with in s. 1026(4).
[19] CTA 2010 (UK) s. 1026(3).
[20] CTA 2010 (UK) s. 1022.

be made up before any dividend is distributed. This could mean that a corporation that has suffered substantial losses would not be in a position to distribute dividends for years, which might have a serious effect on the corporation's share price. Cancelling share capital reduces this pressure and may put the corporation into an immediate position to distribute dividends (e.g. where the cancelled share capital creates a profits reserve).

The primary tax issue arising on a cancellation of capital is the tax treatment of distributions made from any profits reserve created on the cancellation. In the UK, this is dealt with by a specific provision that applies only for corporation tax purposes:

> A distribution made out of a reserve arising from a reduction of share capital is to be treated as if it were made out of profits available for distribution otherwise than by virtue of the reduction.[21]

This means that such a distribution qualifies for the inter-corporate dividend exemption, which is the intent of the provision. The provision does not cover the treatment of individual shareholders, which is left in a confused split state.[22]

The German approach appears to be different. As noted earlier at 6.1.1, it specifically requires a corporation to maintain for tax purposes a record of capitalised profits as a 'separate entry' from contributed share capital.[23] Returns of capital from this separate entry are treated as dividends (having originated from profits).[24] If there is only a cancellation of share capital (without a payment to the shareholder), the separate entry is also debited. Nothing further is required; the original capitalisation of profits has simply been reversed.

If, however, the capital reduction exceeds the corporation's special entry (capitalised profits), then contributed share capital must be reduced. When contributed share capital is reduced without an actual payment to the shareholder, there is a credit in the capital contributions account discussed earlier at 2.5.1.1.[25] Distributions out of this account are not treated

---

[21] CTA 2010 (UK) s. 1027A.

[22] The issue is whether dividends are of a capital nature if distributed from a profit reserve created with the cancellation of share capital. Dividends of resident corporations are chargeable to income tax whether or not they are of a capital nature; ITTOIA 2005 (UK) s. 383(3). Dividends of non-resident corporations are not chargeable to income tax if they are of a capital nature; s. 402(4).

[23] KStG (Germany) s. 28(1).

[24] EStG (Germany) s. 20(1) No. 2.

[25] KStG (Germany) s. 28(2).

as dividends.[26] Although the Germany rules are convoluted, their effect is the opposite to that of the UK corporation tax treatment. Any profit reserves created by a cancellation of contributed share capital is credited to the capital contributions account. This ensures that any distribution of these profit reserves created with share capital retains its non-dividend treatment.

These issues do not arise under US tax law because corporate law is generally irrelevant in determining distribution treatment. If there is a cancellation of share capital, it does not result in an increase in earnings and profits, and so there is no increase in the pool that might be treated as a dividend on distribution (the source of the issue in Germany and the UK). There is, however, an exception that applies where a corporation with a deficit in its earnings and profits is subject to reorganisation under federal bankruptcy law or similar proceedings. In this case, if shareholders have their interest in the corporation extinguished, the earnings and profits deficit is 'reduced by an amount equal to the paid-in capital which is allocable to the interest of the shareholder which is so terminated or extinguished'.[27]

These issues also would not arise under the CCCTB Proposal. The Proposal contains no rules dealing with reductions of share capital. It seems that a distribution from a profits reserve created by the cancellation of share capital would be an 'other profits distribution'.[28] This is unlikely to be of any concern because of the general exemption for dividends under the Proposal.

## 6.2    Share termination only: redemptions and share buy-backs

Rather than terminating just part of a share, the whole of a share may be terminated. This heading considers the termination of shares in full, but in a scenario in which the ongoing existence of the corporation is anticipated. This can occur where the shares are issued on terms of their redemption (i.e. redeemable shares). Even where shares are not issued on such terms, most countries' corporate laws now provide a mechanism whereby corporations can agree with shareholders to buy back their own shares.[29]

---

[26]  EStG (Germany) s. 20(1)No. 1.

[27]  IRC (US) s. 312(l)(2).

[28]  CCCTB Proposal Art. 4(8).

[29]  For example, see AktG (Germany) s. 71, Companies Act 2006 (UK) s. 690, DGCL (US) s. 160 and MBCA (US) s. 6.31.

There are three primary factors that a tax law might take into account when dealing with a share termination. Two pertain to the source of the funds used by the corporation for the acquisition. The corporation may use retained profits, share capital or a mixture of both for this purpose. If it uses retained profits, the corporate tax system must make a decision as to whether to treat any part of the price paid by the corporation for the shares as a dividend or not. In any case, there is a disposal of shares by the shareholder, and the corporate tax system must decide how to treat the cost base of the shares disposed of. This sets up the potential fusing of two tax events discussed in the introduction to this chapter (dividends and disposal of shares).

The corporate tax systems of most countries provide a mixture of dividend and disposal or just disposal treatment for redemptions and buy-backs. The following discussion first considers share redemptions and then the rules for share buy-backs.

### 6.2.1 Share redemptions

As mentioned, redeemable shares are those that are issued on terms that they will be redeemed in certain events. The primary example of such an event is effluxion of time (e.g. five-year redeemable shares). The usual procedure is that the capital that is contributed when the redeemable shares are issued is repaid when the shares are redeemed. So unless the shares are issued at a discount or redeemed at a premium, the redemption of shares should not give rise to the issue of whether the corporation has distributed a dividend. The corporate tax systems focused on in this study all reach this position, but for different reasons.

In Germany, the disposal of shares by a shareholder, whether to a third party or the corporation itself, is generally respected, and that is the tax treatment the shareholder receives. So the shareholder is treated as disposing of redeemable shares when they are redeemed, with a potential gain or loss. This treatment is subject to the rules on hidden profits distributions (see the earlier discussion at 2.2.2). So if the redeemable shares are issued or redeemed not at arm's length and value passes to the shareholder, the excess amount may be treated as a dividend for tax purposes. Any amount treated as a dividend would not constitute consideration for disposal of the shares. To the extent that Germany treats dividends and gains on the disposal of shares in a similar fashion (see the earlier discussion at 5.1.3.1), the identification of a dividend may be of little consequence.

The CCCTB Proposal has no dedicated rules for redemptions of shares. As with the German hidden profits distribution approach, it is possible that redemption proceeds might constitute a 'dividend' or other 'profits distribution'.[30] However, to the extent that distributions and proceeds on the disposal of shares are treated similarly under the Proposal (i.e. exempt), whether there is a dividend or not may make little difference.

The US has dedicated rules dealing with share redemptions that are fundamentally different and yet may produce similar results as those in Germany. The residual position is that redemption proceeds are a corporate distribution.[31] This means that if the corporation has earnings and profits the proceeds constitute a taxable dividend (see the earlier discussion at 2.5.2.1). However, there are several circumstances in which dividend treatment is excluded and the redemption proceeds are treated as consideration on the disposal of the shares only.[32]

These circumstances include where the distribution constituting the redemption is not 'essentially equivalent to a dividend'. The meaning of this phrase has been the subject of substantial administrative and judicial interpretation.[33] Another important exception to dividend treatment is where the distribution constituting the redemption proceeds is 'substantially disproportionate' with respect to the shareholder. This is defined in terms of shareholders reducing their interest in the corporation by more than 20%. This exception does not apply if they still hold 50% of the corporation after the redemption.[34] In the usual manner, holdings of related parties are attributed to the shareholders for the purposes of determining these thresholds.[35]

The UK approach is again unnecessarily messy. It is possible that a dividend can arise on the redemption of shares because the corporation makes a 'distribution out of assets . . . in respect of shares'.[36] However, if all that the shareholder receives on redemption is a return of share capital, there is no dividend. This is because the amount of the distribution is reduced by any amount that 'represents repayment of capital on the shares'. If, however, the shareholder receives more on redemption than was received by the corporation when the redeemable shares were issued, the excess may

---

[30] CCCTB Proposal Art. 4(8)
[31] IRC (US) s. 302(d).
[32] IRC (US) s. 302(a).
[33] In this regard, see Bittker & Eustice (2003–, para. 9.05) and the references cited therein.
[34] IRC (US) s. 302(b).
[35] IRC (US) ss. 302(c) & 318.
[36] CTA 2010 (UK) s. 1000(1)B.

be a distribution and taxed as such. This is not a concern for corporate shareholders because they are generally exempt from tax on intercorporate dividends (see the earlier discussion at 2.4.3.1).

There may also be capital gains consequences from the redemption of shares. Here, the (somewhat confusing) conventional wisdom seems to be that there is in general no 'disposal' of the shares because the corporation does not own the shares after redemption (rather they expire or are cancelled). Instead, reliance must be placed on one of two specific rules. The first deems a disposal where an asset is surrendered or expires.[37] The second is the provision discussed earlier at 6.1.1 that deals with capital payments made by corporations to shareholders.[38] Either could give rise to a tax charge if the redemption proceeds exceed the shareholder's cost base in the shares.

In the case of individuals, the consideration received for a disposal is reduced by any amounts subject to income tax.[39] So, if an individual has a dividend as a result of the redemption of shares, the consideration received for the disposal of shares is reduced by the dividend and there is no double taxation. By contrast, corporate shareholders in receipt of redemption proceeds are effectively excluded from a chargeable gain arising to the extent that the proceeds constitute an exempt dividend.[40] This is different from the treatment of share buy-backs for corporate shareholders, which is discussed later.

If the redemption of shares would result in a dividend for tax purposes, the UK provides the potential to avoid dividend treatment if certain conditions are met. The exception applies where the company whose shares are redeemed is an 'unquoted trading company'. The redemption must be for the 'benefit' of the company's trade and not for the purpose of distributing profits or avoiding tax.[41] There are many conditions attached to the application of this exception, including corporate residency requirements, that the shareholder has held the shares for at least five years and that the shareholder's holding in the corporation must be substantially eliminated by the redemption. The result of the exception is that the redemption is treated purely as a disposal of the shares (i.e. none of the redemption proceeds constitutes a dividend).

---

[37] TCGA 1992 (UK) s. 22.
[38] TCGA 1992 (UK) s. 122.
[39] TCGA 1992 (UK) s. 37.
[40] TCGA 1992 (UK) ss. 22(4) and 122(6).
[41] CTA 2010 (UK) s. 1033.

## 6.2.2   Share buy-backs

As mentioned in the introduction to this heading, most corporate laws now permit, within limits, corporations to buy their own shares. This involves shares that were not issued on terms of redemption and so is different from the situation considered earlier at 6.2.1. Nevertheless, the issues and often the tax law rules are the same in the case of a share buy-back as they are in the case of the redemption of shares.

One difference may relate to a corporation buying back its own shares that are listed on a stock exchange. Here, the anonymity of dealings on the stock exchange may mean that dividend treatment is impossible or at least inappropriate. Dividend treatment should not be imposed on a shareholder if the only reason for that treatment is that the corporation purchased the shares and this was a matter that the shareholder could not know about. Countries generally provide disposal-only treatment of on-market share buy-backs. A country may have special tax rules for on-market purchases, such as in the case of Australia,[42] or the disposal-only treatment may be simply a function of the manner in which the country's general rules apply.

Another difference between a share redemption and a share buy-back involves the treatment of the shares after the event. Shares are typically extinguished or cancelled by the process of share redemption, whereas in the case of a share buy-back this need not be the case. Although many corporate laws require the cancellation of shares bought back by corporations, many others permit (within limits) corporations to hold their own shares and reissue them. Shares held by a corporation in itself that can be reissued are referred to as 'treasury shares'. Treasury shares raise the issue of whether the corporation can make a gain or loss for tax purposes when it deals in its own shares (e.g. where there is a difference between the price at which shares are bought back and the price at which they are reissued).

In Germany, the tax treatment of share buy-backs is the same as that for share redemptions. The shareholder receives disposal-only treatment provided there is no hidden profits distribution. A hidden profits distribution is particularly unlikely in the case of on-market buy-backs. The treatment of the shares in the hands of the corporation depends on whether the shares are purchased to reduce capital or not. If they are, there are no direct tax consequences for the corporation, although if the purchase proceeds exceed the par value of the shares the excess must be deducted

---

[42]   Income Tax Assessment Act 1997 (Australia) Div. 190.

from the capital contribution account (as to which see earlier at 2.5.1.1). If a corporation buys its own shares, but not for purposes of capital reduction, then the corporation will hold the shares as current assets. When the shares are sold by the corporation, the corporation may make a gain or a loss that has tax consequences.[43]

Similarly, the US provisions dealing with share buy-backs are the same as those dealing with share redemptions. Again, the sales proceeds may constitute a dividend unless one of the exceptions applies. In particular, an on-market buy-back is unlikely to be 'essentially equivalent to a dividend' and is likely to be 'substantially disproportionate' with respect to the shareholder. The result should be disposal-only treatment. In contrast to the German approach, US tax law expressly provides that a corporation cannot make a gain or loss on the disposal of treasury shares.[44]

As is the case with share redemptions, the CCCTB Proposal incorporates no special rules for share buy-backs.

The UK position is again a mess. In principle, the same provisions apply (or are at least relevant) as in the case of a share redemption. There is no express provision dealing with on-market share buy-backs, and on the face of it, it seems that the dividend treatment rules could apply. However, commonly the sale by the shareholder on-market is to a market-maker and not directly to the share purchaser. It seems that such a sale is recognised for tax purposes (and not treated as a bare agency), and so the dividend treatment rule cannot apply because it is the market-maker and not the corporation that purchases the shares. Market-makers hold shares as trading stock, and so the rules that may produce dividend treatment do not apply to them.

UK corporate law also recognises the potential for corporations to hold their own shares as treasury shares. However, this position is not recognised by tax law, which provides that the acquisition of its own shares by a corporation 'is not to be treated as the acquisition of an asset'.[45] As a result, a corporation cannot make a gain or loss on the reissue of treasury shares. When the shares are bought back, for tax purposes the corporation's share capital account is reduced by the par value of the shares. When the shares are reissued, then, for tax purposes, the corporation's share capital account

---

[43] This treatment of treasury shares is not without doubt due to the 2010 German tax administration's withdrawal of a decree dating from 1998.

[44] 'No gain or loss shall be recognized to a corporation on the receipt of money or other property in exchange for stock (including treasury stock) of such corporation'; IRC (US) s. 1032(a).

[45] Finance Act 2003 (UK) s. 195(2).

(and share premium account) is increased by the consideration received.[46] The result of this process may be a dislocation between the share capital account for corporate law purposes and that account for tax law purposes.

In the UK the treatment of individual shareholders is broadly the same whether their shares are redeemed or bought back by the corporation. However, if the shareholder is a corporate shareholder that treatment is slightly different. This occurs where the shares held by a corporation are bought back for more than their nominal value and where the rules on repurchase of shares by non-quoted trading companies do not apply. As discussed earlier at 6.2.1, such a situation may give rise to a dividend. As an inter-corporate dividend, that dividend is generally exempt. As discussed at 6.2.1, in the case of share redemptions there are effectively no capital gains consequences from the disposal of the shares. That is not the case with a share buy-back.

In the case of a share buy-back in the UK, section 931RA of CTA 2009 specifically provides that the 'fact that a dividend or other distribution is exempt does not prevent it from being taken into account in the calculation of chargeable gains'. Further, the specific rules in TCGA 1992 that exclude capital gains treatment for corporate shareholders in the case of share redemptions do not apply in the case of share buy-backs.[47] This is because, unlike with share redemptions, in the case of a share buy-back there is a 'disposal' because the corporation does acquire the shares. This means that the general rules for 'disposal' of assets apply. The consideration for the disposal is not reduced by the amount of the purchase price that is a dividend because that dividend does not fall 'into account as a receipt in computing income'.[48] This is because of the inter-corporate dividend exemption. The result is that the gain of a corporate shareholder on the redemption of shares is not taxable, whereas the gain of a corporate shareholder on a share buy-back is. The inconsistency is well known, but currently accepted.

## 6.3  Corporate termination: liquidations and related proceedings

A termination of shares may also result from the termination of the corporation itself. Most commonly this occurs when the corporation is liquidated, but a corporation can cease to exist in other circumstances. One

---

[46] Finance Act 2003 (UK) s. 195(4) & (8).
[47] That is, TCGA 1992 (UK) ss. 22 and 122 do not apply.
[48] TCGA 1992 (UK) s. 37(1).

such situation is where a corporation is fused (merged) into another corporation. These cases do not really involve a termination of the shareholder's investment in the corporation, but rather a variation of that investment into another form. Variations of share interests are considered in Chapter 7, so the present discussion is limited to liquidations.

The termination of a corporation by liquidation is typically preceded with a formal procedure. These procedures are usually of two types, one for solvent corporations and another for insolvent corporations. The appointment of a liquidator for insolvent corporations may be preceded by other types of proceedings for corporations in financial distress. These may involve the appointment of receivers and administrators. The types of proceedings available differ from country to country. All of these different types of procedures may have tax consequences for the corporation prior to its ceasing to exist. Particularly important issues can arise where a corporation in financial distress is part of a corporate group. A brief overview of these corporate-level consequences is found in the first matter discussed under this heading.

The termination of shares in an insolvent corporation gives rise to few tax issues for the shareholder. Generally, it involves a loss on disposal of the shares by the shareholder and gives rise to the same tax consequences as in other cases of disposal of shares. The liquidation of solvent corporations raises additional issues. In this case, the shareholder is likely to receive liquidation distributions representing a return of share capital and, potentially, the distribution of retained profits. Here there is again the possibility of two tax events occurring at the same time: the distribution of profits and the disposal of shares. The tax treatment of distributions and disposals of shares in liquidation is the second matter discussed under this heading.

### 6.3.1 Corporate consequences

The appointment of a liquidator or other administrator in a corporate liquidation or related procedure may raise a host of issues under specific tax laws. The following discussion provides a brief consideration of the types of issues that arise in three categories. The first is whether such a procedure affects the general manner in which corporate income is calculated. The second is whether the change of control that comes with the appointment of a liquidator or administrator has any effect on corporate tax attributes and especially on the corporation's status as a member of a corporate group. The third issue discussed is whether the appointment has any impact on, from the corporation's perspective, the tax treatment of corporate distributions and especially in-kind corporate distributions.

## Calculation of corporate income

The appointment of a liquidator or other administrator does not of itself affect the corporation's separate personality. In principle, therefore, the tax liability of a corporation continues to be calculated in the standard fashion, and the corporation's tax attributes such as losses continue to be carried forward in the usual manner. This is especially the case for countries that adopt the global approach to corporate income calculation, such as in the US, Germany and under the CCCTB Proposal. Germany has a specific provision to this effect.[49] Unlike the other countries, Germany provides that the tax period for liquidation is the total liquidation period and not particular tax years.[50] The CCCTB Proposal specifies that 'proceeds of liquidation' are included in the tax base.[51]

Some issues may arise where a country adopts a schedular approach to the calculation of corporate income; the UK provides an example. In principle, the profits of a corporation arising in the course of an insolvency proceeding are chargeable to corporation tax under the usual rules. However, the UK tax administration takes the view that when a corporation goes into liquidation (solvent or insolvent) it ceases to trade. This means that the commencement of liquidation affects the application of tax rules that depend on the continuation of a corporation's trade.

One such UK rule is the entitlement to the lower corporate tax rate, which largely depends on whether the corporation trades or not (see the earlier discussion at 1.3.2.2). A corporation in liquidation is not entitled to this lower rate unless it falls within a limited exception. The exception applies to the accounting period after a liquidator is appointed.[52] Another such rule involves the carry-forward of trading losses, which may only be set against the profits of the trade in which the loss was incurred. The ceasing of trade on the appointment of a liquidator means that the corporation loses the right to carry forward trading losses. However, the cessation of trade also triggers an increase in the carry-back of trading losses from one year to three years.[53]

---

[49]  KStG (Germany) s. 11(6).
[50]  KStG (Germany) s. 11(1).
[51]  CCCTB Proposal Art. 4(8).
[52]  CTA 2010 (UK) s. 34(5).
[53]  CTA 2010 (UK) ss. 37 & 39.

These UK rules are only applied where a corporation is placed in liquidation. They do not apply where the corporation is the subject of other pre-liquidation insolvency proceedings, such as receivership or administration. Here the corporation's trade does not cease, and so the lower corporate tax rate would continue to be available and trading losses could continue to be carried forward.

### Change of control

A liquidator or, in pre-liquidation proceedings, an administrator is appointed with some if not complete power over corporate activities. So the appointment of a liquidator or administrator constitutes, at least in substance, a change of control of a corporation. A question is whether a change of control of this type has any impact on the carry-forward of tax attributes by the corporation in question. The answer is generally no, but this is an issue that requires investigation under the specifics of tax laws.

The carry-forward of corporate tax attributes following a change of ownership of a corporation was considered earlier at 5.2. In form, the appointment of a liquidator or administrator does not involve a direct or indirect transfer of shares. So, if the restrictions on the carry-forward of tax attributes are simply triggered by a transfer of shares, they will not be triggered by the appointment of a liquidator or administrator. This is the position in Germany where the appointment of a liquidator does not trigger the change of ownership rules because there is no 'transfer' of membership rights and such an appointment is unlikely to constitute a 'comparable situation'. In Germany carried-forward losses may reduce any corporate income in liquidation.

The position in the US is broadly the same with one qualification. The US permits shareholders in a corporation to treat their shares as disposed of where the shares have become worthless (discussed later at 6.3.2.1).[54] If the shareholder owns 50% of the shares in the corporation and then treats the shares as worthless, the shareholder is also treated as a different shareholder for purposes of determining whether the corporation has suffered an ownership change.[55] Of course, this is not directly connected with the appointment of a liquidator, but such an appointment might cause the shareholder to crystallise a loss on the shares by declaring them

---

[54] IRC (US) s. 165(g). This rule does not apply if the shareholder holds 80% of the shares in the corporation.
[55] IRC (US) s. 382(g)(3)(D).

worthless. The result could be a change of ownership of the corporation and the imposition of restrictions on loss carry-forward.

By contrast, in the UK a corporation may lose its right to use carried-forward losses after the commencement of liquidation. First, as mentioned earlier, the appointment of a liquidator causes the cessation of trade of the corporation and so the carry-forward of trading losses. In any case, the appointment of a liquidator or other administrator raises questions as to whether that person acquires 'extraordinary rights or powers under any document regulating the company'.[56] If so, the corporation might be treated as suffering a change of ownership and would only be permitted to continue to use its losses if it has continuity of activity (see the earlier discussion at 5.2.1.2).

Further under the UK rules, if a corporation placed in liquidation is a holding corporation, this can affect corporations further down the corporate chain. The appointment of a liquidator is accepted as constituting a change in the beneficial ownership of the corporation's assets.[57] It is the 'beneficial ownership' of shares that matters for the purposes of determining whether there is a change of ownership of a corporation.[58] So the appointment of a liquidator to a holding corporation triggers a change of ownership of the corporation's subsidiaries. The subsidiaries are only permitted to continue to use any carried-forward losses if they meet the continuity of activity test (see the earlier discussion at 5.2.1.2).

In the usual fragmented way, different considerations arise under the UK capital loss rules. The UK limitations on the carry-forward of capital losses depend on a corporation joining or leaving a 75% group or becoming subject to a different control. With respect to the first of these conditions, the appointment of a liquidator might constitute a change of ownership and so change the group status of the corporation. However, there is a specific rule that a group continues to exist for capital gains purposes, notwithstanding the commencement of liquidation.[59] As for becoming subject to a different control, this requirement may well be met by the appointment of a liquidator or administrator.[60] However, the additional requirement to trigger restrictions on use of capital losses (i.e. that the appointment be for a tax avoidance purpose) is unlikely to be met.

---

[56] CTA 2010 (UK) s. 721(2).
[57] *CIR v. Olive Mill Spinners Ltd* (1963) 41 TC 77 (ChD).
[58] CTA 2010 (UK) s. 726.
[59] TCGA 1992 (UK) s. 170(11).
[60] TCGA 1992 (UK) s. 288(1) defining 'control' in terms of CTA 2010 (UK) ss. 450 & 451.

The change of control consequent upon the appointment of a liquidator or administrator may also affect whether a corporation falls within some subcategory of corporation. For example, it may affect whether a corporation is a closely held corporation or a member of a corporate group.

In the UK for example, it seems that a liquidator or administrator might be viewed as 'controlling' a corporation. Nevertheless, the appointment of a liquidator or administrator does not cause a corporation to become a close company (see the earlier discussion at 1.1.5.2). This is because the liquidator or administrator is neither a participator (effectively a shareholder) nor a director. Similarly, in the US such appointments do not affect whether a corporation is a personal holding company or an S corporation, both of which are determined on the basis of who owns the shares in a corporation.

Status as a member of a corporate group is a bit more complex. In the US, the appointment of a liquidator or administrator does not break a corporate group. The 80% threshold is measured by reference to value of shares or voting power, and neither is formally affected by the type of control exercised by a liquidator or administrator. The German position is similar with respect to its group relief (*Organschaft*) system. The test for grouping is based on voting power attaching to shares.[61] However, it seems that the profit-pooling agreement may be terminated under corporate law if one of the parties is not in a position to meet its obligations under it.[62]

The position under the CCCTB Proposal is the opposite. It provides that

> [a] company in insolvency or liquidation may not become a member of a group. A taxpayer in respect of which a declaration of insolvency is made or which is liquidated shall leave the group immediately.[63]

Leaving the group would give rise to certain tax consequences with respect to assets disposed of after leaving or costs incurred before.[64] A corporation leaving a group is not entitled to take any part of a group-consolidated loss with it.[65] Further, there is a special rule for leaving group members that have benefited from intergroup transfers of assets incorporating

---

[61] The question arises whether there may be a change in voting power for subsidiaries of corporations in liquidation or administration. Often it is the liquidator or administrator of a parent corporation who exercises voting power over shares held in subsidiaries.

[62] AktG (Germany) s. 297.

[63] CCCTB Proposal Art. 56.

[64] CCCTB Proposal Arts. 67 and 68.

[65] CCCTB Proposal Art. 69.

unrealised gains in the previous six years. To the extent of these gains, the participation exemption for the disposal of shares by the parent corporation would be withdrawn.[66]

The UK position is partway between these extremes. As mentioned, the appointment of a liquidator results in a change in the beneficial ownership of corporate assets. This change, in turn, breaks the grouping with any subsidiaries of the corporation (though not so obviously with the corporation's parent). This is because the requirement (also in the grouping rules) that the parent corporation own shares in the subsidiary beneficially will not be met.[67] In the result, transfer of losses with in a group (see the earlier discussion at 1.2.3.2) may no longer be available after the appointment of a liquidator. Appointment of a liquidator also means that the corporation cannot transfer losses with the transfer of a trade in a *hive down* to a subsidiary, as described earlier at 5.2.1.2. The same is not necessarily true of pre-liquidation insolvency proceedings, but there is some doubt as to whether grouping is broken in any case by reason of a change in control.[68]

The rules for capital gains groups were mentioned earlier (i.e. there is an express provision that a group continues notwithstanding the commencement of liquidation). This means that the transfer of capital assets between members of the group after liquidation can still be made on a no gain / no loss basis (see the earlier discussion at 1.2.3.1). Such transfers may give rise to tax consequences where a corporation in liquidation is struck off (ceases to exist). This will cause the corporation to leave a corporate group, and there is a retrospective charge on gains deferred by group transfers within the previous six years.[69] This is analogous to the rule in the CCCTB Proposal, discussed earlier. Similarly, the commencement of liquidation does not affect the holding requirements for the purposes of the substantial shareholder exemption (see the earlier discussion at 5.1.3.1).[70]

### In-kind distributions to shareholders

A liquidation of a solvent corporation will involve distributions to shareholders. If such distributions are in cash, the only tax issues that arise involve the tax treatment of the shareholders, discussed later at 6.3.2. However, further issues arise where such distributions are made in-kind (i.e.

---

[66]  CCCTB Proposal Art. 75.
[67]  CTA 2010 (UK) s. 1154(6).
[68]  CTA 2010 (UK) s. 154.
[69]  TCGA 1992 (UK) s 179.
[70]  TCGA 1992 (UK) Sch. 7AC para. 16.

the corporation distributes assets to its shareholders). Because the corporation is disposing of an asset, there may be tax consequences for the corporation. Because the corporation does not receive any direct consideration in respect of the disposal, such a distribution raises questions of whether the disposal is treated as made at market value (i.e. whether an arm's length transfer pricing rule may apply).

In the absence of a specific rule, the general rules for transactions with shareholders apply. Potential corporate-level consequences of distributions to shareholders were considered earlier at 2.2.2. In Germany, the distributing corporation is required to account for the market value of the assets distributed by the corporation. This may involve the realisation of any previously unrealised gains (or losses).

In the UK, the distribution of an asset by a corporation in liquidation is an affair of capital. In the case of trading stock or the recapture of excess depreciation (balancing charge), it is not clear that a corporation would have to recognise any unrealised gain.[71] However, unrealised capital gains may have to be recognised due to the market value rule for bargains not made at arm's length.[72] Yet, as mentioned earlier, if the distribution is of a capital asset to a parent corporation, then deferral of any gain may be possible. The result may be similar under the CCCTB Proposal, where it is not clear that the arm's length transfer pricing rule would apply to all in-kind distributions in liquidation.

By contrast, the US has dedicated rules dealing with in-kind distributions in a corporate liquidation. Such distributions are treated as made at 'fair market value' and so may result in the corporation realising gains (or, subject to limitations, losses).[73] An exception applies for liquidation distributions made by a subsidiary to its 80% parent corporation.[74] In such a case, the parent corporation takes over the subsidiary's cost base in the assets.[75]

### 6.3.2 Shareholder consequences

It remains to consider shareholder-level tax consequences of a termination of a corporation by liquidation. As mentioned, they potentially involve

---

[71] The line of enquiry is similar to that used in the context of the transfer of business assets on incorporation and involves the question of whether the corporation and the shareholder are connected persons (see the earlier discussion at 4.2).

[72] TCGA 1992 ss. 17 & 18.

[73] IRC (US) s. 336.

[74] IRC (US) s. 337.

[75] IRC (US) s. 334(b).

two features: a disposal of shares and distributions made by the corporation in the lead-up to its termination. The tax treatment may differ depending on whether the corporation is solvent or not. Each is considered in turn.

### 6.3.2.1   Insolvent corporations

The dissolution of an insolvent corporation is unlikely to involve any distribution to shareholders, and so only the disposal of shares is briefly considered. From a technical perspective, shares in such a corporation only cease to exist when the corporation is dissolved or struck off the register. However, liquidation of an insolvent corporation often involves formal steps of an imprecise nature, and there can be a substantial period of time between the onset of insolvency and the final termination of a corporation, which potentially may last years. Therefore, a number of countries specifically permit a shareholder in an insolvent corporation to declare a disposal of their shares when the shares become worthless.

For example, this is the case in the US under the rule mentioned earlier at 6.3.1. If a share

> which is a capital asset becomes worthless during the taxable year, the loss resulting therefrom shall, for purposes of this subtitle, be treated as a loss from the sale or exchange, on the last day of the taxable year, of a capital asset.[76]

There are certain restrictions on using this rule where the shareholder holds 80% of the corporation in question. So this rule may facilitate the realisation of a loss on shares and applies irrespective of whether the corporation ultimately ceases to exist.

The UK has a similar rule of wider application. A person may claim that an asset has become of 'negligible value'. The claim results in a deemed disposal and reacquisition of the asset at the value stated in the claim.[77] This rule is commonly used to crystallise losses on shares that have become worthless due to the insolvency of the corporation. Again, it applies irrespective of whether the corporation ultimately ceases to exist. By contrast, the Australian rule is more restrictive. A shareholder can only realise a loss when a liquidator or an administrator of the corporation declares in writing that there is no likelihood that shareholders will receive any (further) distribution.[78]

---

[76]  IRC (US) s. 165(g)(1).
[77]  TCGA 1992 (UK) s. 24(1A) to (2).
[78]  Income Tax Assessment Act 1997 (Australia) s. 104–145(1).

There is no equivalent to these provisions under German tax law or under the CCCTB Proposal. However, in Germany it is still possible to claim a deduction with respect to a loss in value of shares by claiming extraordinary depreciation, so long as the shares are held as part of a business.[79] This is only relevant where and to the extent that gains and losses on the disposal of shares are recognised. So, for example, it may be a mechanism by which an individual shareholder recognises loss of value of shares in an insolvent corporation. It is of no relevance where a participation exemption is available, such as in both Germany and under the CCCTB Proposal. Gains are not taxable, and so losses (including depreciation) are not deductible.[80]

### 6.3.2.2 Solvent corporations

These provisions on the crystallisation of losses on shares are generally inapplicable in the case of a solvent corporation. The general rules considered in this book in Chapters 2 and 5 for distributions and disposals of shares apply to shareholders of a solvent corporation until it is placed in liquidation. Ultimately, however, the liquidation means a disposal of shares, and from a tax perspective, the primary question for consideration is the extent to which any such disposal is integrated with distributions received by a shareholder in the course of the liquidation.

Some countries provide full integration. Corporate distributions in the course of liquidation are treated only as consideration on the disposal of shares irrespective of whether they are distributed from share capital or retained profits. Alternately, distributions of profits may be singled out and treated in the same manner as any other distribution of dividends. This alternative leaves open the question of the tax treatment of the ultimate disposal of shares. Each of these options is considered in turn.

**Disposal-only treatment** The UK and the US are examples of countries that treat liquidation distributions as received solely in consideration for the disposal of shares. No part of a liquidation distribution is treated as a dividend even if it is made out of profits. This means that preliquidation distributions of profits and distributions of profits in liquidation are treated differently, which may give rise to tax planning opportunities. In particular, if liquidation distributions are treated more favourably, there may be an incentive to liquidate small corporations regularly as a

---

[79] EStG (Germany) s. 6(1)No. 1.
[80] KStG (Germany) s. 8(3) and CCCTB Proposal Arts. 40 & 41. The EU Presidency amendments would remove Art. 41 (exceptional depreciation).

tax-efficient method of distributing profits. The controllers can then start up a new corporation conducting similar activities – the so-called *phoenix corporation* problem.

The effect is the opposite if liquidation distributions are taxed more heavily than dividend distributions. Here, either the corporation will not be liquidated, or the controllers will ensure that any available profits are distributed prior to putting the corporation into liquidation (pre-liquidation stripping). In particular, this disposal-only treatment can interfere with more accurate forms of dividend relief.

Consider, for example, if Australia adopted this approach (it does not) with its full imputation system. Corporation tax paid with respect to retained profits before a corporation goes into liquidation may be reflected in credit in the corporation's franking (imputation) account. If no part of a liquidation distribution is treated as a dividend, then that credit is never imputed to any shareholder. If gains on the disposal of shares were taxable in full, the result would be permanent economic double taxation of profits distributed in the liquidation. This example demonstrates that there can be much work for tax advisors in planning the liquidation of solvent corporations.

The UK does not have a full imputation system, and it does not tax capital gains on the disposal of shares in full. Nevertheless, the tax treatment of dividends and that of liquidation distributions are different, and this gives rise to some level of tax planning. Distributions of profits received in the course of liquidation are a receipt of capital and so do not give rise to income.[81] This is reflected in an exclusion from the definition of 'distribution'. 'A distribution made in respect of share capital in a winding up is not a distribution of a company'.[82]

This provision is not without its difficulties. In particular, it only applies to 'winding up' a corporation, and the UK tax administration is of the opinion that it only applies to a formal liquidation under the insolvency law. It does not include an informal distribution of all of a corporation's assets followed by an application to the Companies Registrar to strike the corporation off the register as a defunct company.[83] However, in 2012 a concession of the UK tax administration was enacted to exclude distributions made in anticipation of dissolving a corporation from the definition of 'distribution'.[84]

---

[81] *IRC* v. *Burrell* [1924] 2 KB 52 (CA).
[82] CTA 2010 (UK) s. 1030.
[83] This striking-off procedure is in Companies Act 2006 (UK) ss. 1000–1011.
[84] CTA 2010 (UK) s. 1030A. Such distributions cannot exceed £25,000.

This leaves liquidation distributions in the UK subject to capital-gains-only treatment and so governed by the rule on capital distributions discussed earlier at 6.1.1. Section 122 of TCGA 1992 applies to each liquidation distribution. Technically, this produces a series of disposals of a part interest in a share each time a liquidation distribution is received. Each time such a distribution is received, the cost base of the share is apportioned according to the market value of what is received and the market value of what is left of the share.[85] Little importance will attach to this process unless the liquidation distributions are made in different tax years.

The US has a similar provision that prescribes that '[a]mounts received by a shareholder in a distribution in complete liquidation of a corporation shall be treated as in full payment in exchange for the stock'. Dividend treatment is specifically excluded.[86] The phrase 'complete liquidation' is not defined. Bittker and Eustice suggest that a formal proceeding or dissolution of the corporation is not required.[87] So this is very different from the approach to the UK rule.

Also different from the UK treatment is where the shareholder receives a number of liquidation distributions. Here the US tax administration permits distributions to first reduce the cost base of the shares. It is only when this cost base is exceeded that any excess constitutes a capital gain.[88] Again unlike in the UK, that capital gain is taxed by the US in a similar fashion and at similar rates as a dividend. Note, however, how the liquidation has reversed the usual US ordering rule. Usually, distributions of profits are considered distributed before returns of capital because of the profits-first rule (see the earlier discussion at 2.5.2.1). On liquidation, returns of capital are effectively treated as received first, followed by amounts that are taxed in a similar fashion to dividends.

**Dividend and disposal treatment**   Rather than treating liquidation distributions as solely received for the disposal of shares, a corporate tax system may treat any distributions of profits in liquidation as dividends. This is the approach adopted by Germany. The definition of investment income includes 'payments derived from the dissolution of a company…as far they do not involve a repayment of nominal capital'.[89] So the usual dividend treatment discussed earlier at 2.4 applies to distributions of profits by a corporation in liquidation.

---

[85]   TCGA 1992 (UK) s. 42.
[86]   IRC (US) s. 331.
[87]   Bittker & Eustice (2003–, para. 10.02).
[88]   Ibid. (para. 10.03[1]) and the references cited therein.
[89]   EStG (Germany) s. 20(1) No. 2.

This leaves open the question of the treatment of the disposal of shares, which occurs when the corporation is struck off. The question that arises in this case is what is the consideration received on the disposal of the shares. Clearly, it includes the return of share capital, but does it include any of the liquidation distribution treated as a dividend? In Germany, only the return of capital is treated as consideration received on disposal of shares in a corporate liquidation.[90] Generally, this is less than the cost base of the shares and so gives rise to a loss on disposal. However, there may be cases when the return of capital is more than the cost base, particularly if the shareholder has previously claimed depreciation with respect to the shares. In this case, a gain may be realised and would be taxed in the usual manner (see the earlier discussion at 5.1.3).

These rules in Germany apply to both individual and corporate shareholders. In the case of corporate shareholders, the treatment is largely irrelevant due to the participation exemption, although the residual taxation of 5% of dividends and gains on disposal may have some effect. By contrast, the CCCTB Proposal only mentions 'liquidation' twice, and neither instance is relevant in the current context.[91] On the face of the Proposal, it seems that a 'profit distribution' could include a distribution of profits in liquidation.[92] However, again the existence of the participation exemption is likely to mean that no tax consequences attach to the receipt of liquidation distributions under the Proposal. Both dividends and gains on the disposal of shares are generally exempt (although the EU Presidency amendments would narrow the exemption to 10% holdings).

Australia is another country that treats distributions of profits in liquidation as a dividend for tax purposes.[93] Further, liquidation distributions are 'frankable dividends' and so may have dividend tax credits attached to them.[94] This relieves (but does not eliminate) the possibility that imputation credits are stranded at the corporate level and lost when a corporation is dissolved. If all the credit in the franking (imputation) account is used in liquidation distributions, this may mean that all corporation tax paid during the life of the corporation has been credited to shareholders. In other

---

[90] For example, see EStG ss. 16(1) & 17(4).

[91] One is in CCCTB Proposal Art. 56 with respect to the expulsion of group members (discussed earlier at 6.3.1). The other is Art. 4(8), which specifies that 'proceeds of liquidation' are included in revenue.

[92] CCCTB Proposal Art. 11(c).

[93] Income Tax Assessment Act 1936 (Australia) s. 47.

[94] A liquidation distribution is a frankable dividend under Income Tax Assessment Act 1997 (Australia) s. 202–40 because it is not excluded under s. 202–45.

words, unless a shareholder has been denied the benefits of a dividend tax credit at some point, no corporate income derived during the life of the corporation has been subjected to economic double taxation (unless franking credits have been wasted).

Australia demonstrates a different peculiarity when it comes to the treatment of the disposal of shares following liquidation. As noted earlier, Germany reduces the consideration received in respect of that disposal by the amount treated as a dividend (i.e. only the return of capital is treated as consideration on disposal). Australia does not do this and continues to count the full amount of the liquidation distribution as consideration on disposal of the shares. It is only if the disposal results in a capital gain that Australia seeks to rectify the double counting of the distribution of profits. A gain on the disposal of the shares is reduced by any amount included in income; in this case the liquidation dividend (and not the dividend as grossed up by imputation credits).[95] The point is that this reconciliation rule only reduces a gain and does not increase a capital loss on the disposal of shares. In the result, the German approach is much more likely to give rise to a (justifiable) loss on the disposal of shares in liquidation than the Australian approach.

[95] Income Tax Assessment Act 1997 (Australia) s. 118–20(1B)(b).

7

Varying share interests

Chapters 1–3 considered the constant holding of a share interest that is not altered, whereas Chapters 4–6 considered the creation, transfer and termination of share interests. These holdings and dealings of share interests were presumed to be real, both in form and in substance. For example, on a creation of shares, it was presumed that a new investment in a corporation was created. By contrast, if the shares were terminated, it was presumed that those shares did not continue in some other form. The last two chapters of this book seek to break this alignment of form and substance between these two states of share interest (i.e. holding and dealing in share interests).

This chapter looks at the scenario in which there is in form a dealing in a share interest, whether a creation, transfer or termination of the interest. Before this dealing, the investor has a share interest of a particular quantum, and after the dealing the investor still has a share interest of a particular quantum, but in a different form. That is, in form there is a change of share interest, but in substance there is not, or at least the share interest before the change can be identified with a share interest after the change. For present purposes, this is referred to as a 'variation' of share interest, although 'corporate reconstruction' and 'corporate reorganisation' are also phrases used to cover the types of matters discussed in this chapter.

This chapter considers the issue of whether a share interest that has changed has changed enough to justify the realisation of any gain or loss built into the interest. The type of event that occurs involves exchanging an existing share interest for a new or varied share interest. For the purposes of this chapter, these forms of share interest are referred to as the 'existing share interest' and the 'replacement share interest', respectively. The question is whether the realisation event (the exchange) should be recognised or whether the replacement share interest should just be identified with the existing share interest. In other words, this chapter is primarily concerned with whether deferral or roll-over relief is available. The justifications for this relief can be made in various ways, often on the basis of not retarding sensible corporate reorganisations. From a conceptual perspective, the question is largely one of whether substance should prevail over form, and so there is a link with the types of issues that arise on incorporation (see Chapter 4).

There are only so many manners in which a share interest can be varied, the variation being triggered by the potential realisation event mentioned in the preceding paragraph. These different options for variation centre on the share interest(s) before the event and the share interest(s) after the event. First, the investor may have a particular type of share interest before the event that is substituted for a different type of share interest by the event. Second, the investor may have one share interest before the event that is split into two or more interests by the event. Third, the investor may have two or more share interests before the event that are consolidated into a single share interest by the event. The following discussion considers each of these different options.

The discussion initially assumes that these variations take place with respect to share interests in a single corporation. That is, the share interest(s) in a particular corporation before the event is varied into share interest(s) in the same corporation after the event. However, this book has continually noted how corporate tax systems question the separate legal identity imbued on corporations by corporate law. If corporations are recognised as artificial legal constructs then it is a small step to say that the arguments for deferral or roll-over of variation of shares interests in the *same* corporation can be extended to a situation involving more than one corporation. So, a share interest in a corporation that is substituted into a share interest or interests in one or more other corporations may be sufficiently similar so as to justify non-recognition of realisation. The same may be true where share interests in two corporations are varied into share interests in a single corporation. This line of approach raises the difficult issues of the tax treatment of corporate mergers and divisions (de-mergers).

This chapter is structured under two primary headings. The first deals with variation of share interests involving a single corporation. This provides a simple scenario in which to discuss the three main methods for varying share interests and to identify the core issues that arise for each. After that consideration, the second heading ventures into a brief discussion of variations of share interests involving two or more corporations. Here the particular focus is on various methods for merging or de-merging corporations.

In passing, the CCCTB Proposal has no particular rules that apply in the scenarios discussed in this chapter (although the EU Presidency amendments suggest that it should have some). So the discussion ignores that Proposal unless there is some particular provision worthy of mention. The Mergers Directive may be of relevance in the context of EU law,[1] but that Directive is only concerned with cross-border mergers and so is not the focus of this chapter.[2]

## 7.1   Within a corporation

### 7.1.1   Substitution

The present discussion presumes that a person has a particular share interest in a corporation and that, through a particular event, that interest is substituted for a different interest in the same corporation. The primary issue for discussion is whether the substitution constitutes a realisation event such that a gain or loss may be realised by reason of the substitution. Many countries provide some form of relief in this regard, and there are two primary factors that arise with respect to the relief. The first pertains to the scope of the permitted substitution (i.e. what is being substituted for what). The second pertains to triggering the substitution and whether it is done by agreement or option.

#### Scope of substitution

A country that provides relief on the substitution of share interests must determine the type of share interests that qualify. The chapter has been careful thus far to use the phrase 'share interests' rather than 'shares'. The blurred distinction between shares and other types of corporate investment, particularly debt, was discussed earlier at 2.1 in the context of identifying corporate distributions. In practice, the rules discussed at that point may or may not have relevance in the context of relief for share substitutions. It is a different question to ask whether they should have relevance.

There is perhaps a stronger case for providing relief if the return on the existing share interest is the same as that which will be derived on the replacement share interest. If dividends are derived on each and the tax treatment is the same, perhaps there is reason to accept that nothing

---

[1] *Mergers Directive*, Council Directive 90/434/EEC of 23 July 1990 (consolidated as 2009/133/EC).

[2] Generally regarding the Mergers Directive, see Harris & Oliver (2010, pp. 416–51).

much has changed in substance and that deferral relief should be provided for the substitution realisation event. The situation is not so clear if the tax treatment of the return on the investment changes by reason of the substitution event; this is particularly the case where debt is substituted for equity (shares) or vice versa. There is a fundamental difference between deductibility of interest and full taxation in the hands of the investor on the one hand and non-deductibility of dividends and potential dividend relief in the hands of the investor on the other. Such a change in treatment may be viewed as so substantial as to trigger tax consequences when one type of interest is substituted for the other.

Different countries adopt different approaches to these issues. Historically, Germany had a rule permitting deferral of recognition on the replacement of an asset. This was a broad rule that could cover the replacement of one type of security for another type of security.[3] This relief was repealed in 1999, and since then the exchange of securities has been, in principle, a taxing event. As a result, the general rules for disposal of share interests apply, including the limited taxation of individuals and, for corporate investors, the participation exemption where the existing interest is shares.

By contrast, the US has broad reorganisation rules that may provide relief in the substitution scenario. These were briefly introduced in the context of creating share interests (see the earlier discussion at 4.1.2.2):

> No gain or loss shall be recognized if stock or securities in a corporation a party to a reorganization are, in pursuance of the plan of reorganization, exchanged solely for stock or securities in such corporation or in another corporation a party to the reorganization.[4]

Critical for present purposes, the definition of 'reorganization' includes a 'recapitalisation' or Type E reorganisation.[5] 'Recapitalization' is not defined, but has been broadly interpreted as the 'reshuffling of a capital structure within the framework of an existing corporation'.[6]

The reference to 'stock or securities' means that the US rule is broad enough to cover exchanges of shares, debentures for shares and shares for debentures.[7] If other property is received in the exchange, then there may

---

[3] Former EStG (Germany) s. 6b.
[4] IRC (US) s. 354(a)(1).
[5] IRC (US) s. 368(a)(1).
[6] *Helvering v. Southwest Consolidated Corp* (1942) 315 US 194 (SC) at 202.
[7] Generally, see Bittker & Eustice (2003–, para. 12.27).

be partial recognition of a gain.[8] Outside of that, the investor simply transfers the cost base of the existing share interest to the replacement share interest.[9]

The UK rules are similar (originally based on the US rules), but at least in form they are more limited:

> [A] reorganisation shall not be treated as involving any disposal of the original shares or any acquisition of the new holding or any part of it, but the original shares (taken as a single asset) and the new holding (taken as a single asset) shall be treated as the same asset acquired as the original shares were acquired.[10]

'Reorganisation' is defined in terms of a 'reorganisation or reduction of a company's share capital'. Note that the existing share interest must be 'shares'. There is no useful definition of 'shares', which therefore takes its general law meaning and so is far more limited than the type of interests in a corporation discussed earlier at 2.1 in the context of distribution treatment. However, the replacement share interest can be 'shares in and debentures of the company'.[11] As in the US, where the investor receives some consideration other than the new holding, a capital gain may be realised.[12]

Although a UK reorganisation can involve the substitution of shares for debt, the provisions do not expressly apply to the substitution of debt for shares. This is remedied by a specific provision that extends the reorganisation rules to the 'conversion of securities', which includes a conversion 'effected by a transaction or occurring in consequence of the operation of the terms of any security'.[13]

The conversion or substitution of debt into equity may raise other issues for a corporate tax system. In times of economic crisis, controllers of corporations are often required to 'retire' debt they are owed and replace it with shares, often of a lower face value to the debt that is replaced. Doing so involves forgiving an element of corporate debt, and an issue is whether the corporation may have to recognise income as a result of the forgiveness. In the US the forgiveness constitutes income if the amount of debt forgiven is more than the market value of the replacement

---

[8]  IRC (US) s. 356(a)(1).
[9]  IRC (US) s. 358(a).
[10] TCGA 1992 (UK) s. 127.
[11] TCGA 1992 (UK) s. 126(1).
[12] TCGA 1992 (UK) s. 128(3).
[13] TCGA 1992 (UK) s. 132.

shares.[14] By contrast, in the UK such a forgiveness may not be treated as income if the release is in consideration for shares forming part of the ordinary share capital of the debtor corporation.[15]

### Triggering the substitution: options and convertible notes

A share interest may be issued on terms that specify the circumstances in which it converts into another share interest. The conversion may be at the choice of one of the parties. The share interest may constitute nothing more than an option that may convert into a share interest. Alternately, the option may be imbedded in another security, such as in the case of convertible notes or debentures. If a share interest does not incorporate terms as to its conversion, then (outside of insolvency arrangements) it is likely that the interest can only be substituted for another share interest by agreement between the parties. That is what has been presumed thus far, and so the present discussion briefly considers whether there are any special rules for convertible securities and options.

Germany has no express rules that cover the conversion of convertible securities and the exercise of share options. Again the risk is that such a conversion may trigger a realisation, but it seems much will depend on how the exercise is accounted for. In the case of share options, the acquirer may capitalise the value of the shares as the price paid plus any option premium (at its depreciated value, if relevant).[16] For the issuing corporation, the option premium would be recognised as income when the option is exercised or expires.[17] In the case of convertible notes, the instrument would commonly be bifurcated into its option and debt components.[18] The option would be treated as discussed. The conversion of the note may give rise to tax consequences, depending on whether the market value of the shares is more or less than the face value of the debt.

The situation is different in the US. The IRC expressly provides that amounts received by a corporation in exchange for options to acquire its stock are not taxable, even if the option remains unexercised.[19] For the acquirer, the cost of the option is added to the cost of the shares if the option is exercised, but there is no attempt to tax any increase in the

---

[14] IRC (US) s. 108(e)(8).
[15] CTA 2009 (UK) s. 322(4).
[16] Amann (2001, p. 388).
[17] Ibid., p. 390.
[18] Ibid., p. 400.
[19] IRC (US) s. 1032(a).

value of the option at the time of exercise.[20] If the option is imbedded in a debt security, then as in Germany there would be bifurcation between the option and the debt, but this time as prescribed by statute.[21] Again, the rules regarding options mean that the corporation recognises no income in respect of the option part of the convertible security. The security holder also does not have to recognise any gain on conversion, but the statutory basis for this provision is not clear. The cost base of the security is included in the cost base of the shares on conversion.[22]

In the UK, the general rules for options apply to options to acquire shares.[23] In particular, if the option is exercised, then the granting and exercise of the option are treated as a single disposal when the option is exercised. This means that the acquirer's cost base of the shares includes any price paid for the option. For the corporation, this means that any price paid for the option is treated as paid in consideration for the shares and so need not be recognised. If the option is not exercised, the corporation is taxable on any price paid for the option as a capital gain. The holder of an expired option is only permitted a capital loss on certain types of options, typically those listed on a stock exchange. As for convertible notes, the treatment of the note holder is the same as for debt converted into shares by agreement.[24] As in Germany and the US, a corporation issuing convertible notes typically bifurcates them into a debt instrument and an option for corporation tax purposes under the loan relationship rules.[25]

### 7.1.2  Splitting: focus on bonus shares

A variation of share interest may involve the splitting of an existing share interest. This type of variation may involve the surrender of the existing share interest followed by the issue of two or more new share interests. For countries with par value shares, this variation could involve the splitting of a share with a par value of, say, $10 into two shares with a par value of $5. The analysis of this type of share split is essentially the same as that

[20]  Bittker & Eustice (2003–, para. 4.62[3]).
[21]  IRC (US) s. 1273(c)(2).
[22]  Bittker & Eustice (2003–, para. 4.61) noting non-recognition of conversion of convertible notes as a long-term administrative practice and referring to Rev. Rul. 72–265, 1972–1 CB 222.
[23]  TCGA 1992 (UK) s. 144.
[24]  TCGA 1992 (UK) s. 132 applying to a conversion 'occurring in consequence of the operation of the terms of any security'.
[25]  CTA 2009 (UK) s. 415.

considered in the substitution case, discussed earlier at 7.1.1. So, for example, the reorganisation rules of the UK and the US would apply in such a scenario.

The more common form of share split involves the issue of bonus shares or stock dividends.[26] That a bonus share issue can be functionally equivalent to a share split can be illustrated with a simple example. Presume that a corporation with a market value of 100 has issued 10 shares. Notionally, each share is worth 10. If the corporation makes a one-for-one bonus issue, each shareholder will receive an additional share for each share. The total number of shares is now 20, but the value of the corporation has not increased. So each of the 20 shares is now worth 5, and the value of the existing shares has decreased: the value of the existing shares has been *split* or *shifted* between the original shares and the bonus shares.

This example once again emphasises the artificial nature of the corporation and the derivative nature of share interests in it. These types of value shifts can cause headaches for a corporate tax system, a matter further explored in Chapter 8. The example in the preceding paragraph is rather extreme. There can be sound commercial reasons why a corporation issues bonus shares. Management may feel that the corporation is undervalued, and the issue of bonus shares often sends a message to the market about the confidence of management in the corporation's outlook. As a result, particularly for listed corporations, a bonus share issue does not necessarily result in the devaluation of existing shares, at least not in proportion to the bonus share issue.

It is true that the issue of bonus shares can be functionally equivalent to a share split. However, this is only fully true if the bonus share issue is, as presumed in the earlier example, proportionate to the holding of existing shares. By contrast, if the bonus share issue is disproportionate, then the value that is shifted by the issue of the bonus shares is shifted unequally as between the existing shareholders. The percentage interest in the corporation of a shareholder that receives bonus shares will increase, and that of a shareholder that does not receive bonus shares will decrease. To this extent, a disproportionate issue of bonus shares can be functionally equivalent to a transfer of a share interest. It is this difference between bonus shares acting as a share split or as a share transfer that causes many countries to treat proportionate and disproportionate issues of bonus shares differently for tax purposes.

---

[26] 'Bonus shares' and 'stock dividends' are often used interchangeably. The former term is used for the purposes of this book.

Another important feature of the issue of bonus shares is that it may or may not trigger a capitalisation of profits. This can have important tax implications for subsequent corporate distributions and is the first matter considered by the following discussion. The discussion then considers proportionate distributions of bonus shares and disproportionate distributions of bonus shares.

### Bonus shares and the capitalisation of profits

When a corporation issues bonus shares, it distributes additional shares to existing shareholders for no additional consideration. What else is involved in the issue of bonus shares depends on whether the shares have a par value. If shares do not have a par value, the corporation usually has a choice as to whether to distribute bonus shares with or without a capitalisation of profits. It is also possible to capitalise profits without issuing bonus shares or directly affecting the rights attached to particular shares.

However, in par value jurisdictions, whenever bonus shares are issued, an amount equal to the par value of the bonus shares must be transferred to the corporation's share capital account. This amount is typically transferred from retained profits, and so the process is referred to as a capitalisation of profits. However, as noted earlier at 4.1.1, in some jurisdictions (such as Germany and the UK) it is also possible to pay up an issue of bonus shares from the corporation's share premium account. In par value jurisdictions, it is not possible to increase the share capital account without issuing new shares or increasing the par value of existing shares.

The difference between these approaches is important for determining the tax consequences of an issue of bonus shares and subsequent corporate distributions. Distributions from profits are typically taxable as dividends, whereas distributions of capital are not (see the earlier discussion at 6.1.1). If no part of a bonus share that capitalises profits is treated as a dividend, then the corporation may be able to distribute those profits in the future as a return of capital subject to non-dividend treatment. If there is a substantial inconsistency between the taxation of dividends and the taxation of returns of capital, then the capitalisation of profits, including by way of bonus share issue, can give rise to tax arbitrage.

Because of this risk of tax arbitrage, some countries, such as Germany and the UK, do not respect a corporate law capitalisation of profits for corporate tax law purposes. As discussed earlier at 6.1.1, both countries treat certain returns of capital proximate to a capitalisation of profits as a dividend for tax purposes. By contrast, these issues do not arise in the US because corporate distributions are taxable to the extent of the tax law concept of earnings and profits. Capitalisations of profits do not decrease earnings and profits.

Neither approach is particularly satisfactory. One involves recording capitalisations of profits for tax law purposes, and the other involves a special record of all corporate profits for tax law purposes (whether capitalised or not). Both involve a break with the recording of share capital for corporate law purposes. Further, both require ordering rules (see the earlier discussion at 2.5). A different approach might treat all capitalisations of profits as a dividend distribution. If the capitalisation of profits is taxed like a dividend then a subsequent return of the capitalised profits can be treated as a return of capital without the risk of tax arbitrage. Of course, that risk may still arise from other factors, such as the streaming of returns of capital where corporate law does not have a strict maintenance of capital requirement.

Treating capitalisations of profits as dividends for tax purposes may facilitate consistency between records of share capital for corporate law and tax law purposes. However, it may cause other problems, particularly for countries that adopt no par value shares. If a corporation capitalises profits without a bonus share issue or without allocating those profits to particular shares, who should be taxed on the deemed dividend? Even if bonus shares are issued on a capitalisation, should shareholders be personally liable for tax on the capitalisation, even though they do not receive any additional value in their shares (e.g. as in a proportionate bonus share issue)?

These issues may be insurmountable, especially for particular types of dividend relief systems and the classical system. However, they are not so problematic with respect to some arbitrary types of shareholder-level dividend relief systems (i.e. those that isolate tax consequences at the corporate level). So, for example, capitalisations of profits are not particularly an issue for dividend exclusion systems. The profits would not have been taxed had they been distributed, so there is no problem with letting them be capitalised and then treated as a return of capital on distribution.

The same can also be true of a dividend relief system incorporating a final shareholder withholding tax. Here there may be a notional allocation of dividends to shareholders, but the tax consequences of dividend distributions are isolated at the corporate level through the withholding of the dividend tax. So even if a country has no par value shares, a corporation could be made liable for dividend withholding tax whenever it capitalises profits. As noted earlier at 2.4.3.2, the final dividend withholding tax system is particularly popular amongst developing countries.

Treating capitalisations of profits as dividends subject to that withhold-ing can also be simple and has the advantage of maintaining consistency between corporate law and tax law when it comes to recording share capital.[27]

### Proportionate bonus share issues

Bonus shares are commonly distributed to the shareholders in proportion to existing holdings (i.e. a proportionate issue of bonus shares). The major tax issue here is whether such a distribution constitutes a taxable dividend and, if not, why not. The policy reasons as to why proportionate issues of bonus shares might not be treated as a distribution were discussed ear-lier. Such a distribution is effectively a share split, and so the fundamental nature of the shareholder's investment in the corporation has not changed. This is again a case where the form (i.e. that the shareholder is getting shares for no consideration) is inconsistent with the substance. It remains to consider what tax laws provide for in this regard.

Neither Germany, the UK nor the US taxes proportionate issues of bonus shares. However, the legal reason for not taxing these shares is dif-ferent in each case. In the UK, proportionate bonus share issues are not taxable as a dividend because nothing says they should be. Old case law suggests that a distribution of bonus shares is an affair of capital and so does not constitute income in the hands of the shareholder.[28] Bonus shares might nevertheless be taxable as a dividend if they fall within the statutory definition of 'distribution' (see the earlier discussion at 2.1 and 2.2). How-ever, this is not the case. Bonus shares are not viewed as a 'dividend' or even as a 'capital dividend'.

Another possibility is a 'distribution out of assets' of the corporation.[29] This does not apply because bonus shares do not deplete the assets of a corporation; the asset value of the corporation remains the same. So, as a general rule, the issue of bonus shares is not treated as a dividend in the UK. Yet there are a number of exceptions, even with respect to propor-tionate bonus share issues. Bonus shares that are redeemable are treated as a dividend. The same is true where what is distributed is not shares, but paid-up debentures.[30]

---

[27] For example, capitalisations of profits are treated as dividends under Internal Revenue Act 2000 (Ghana) s. 2(3), Income Tax Act 2058 (2001) (Nepal) s. 53 and Income Tax Act 2004 (Tanzania) s. 2 (definition of 'distribution').

[28] *IRC* v. *Blott* [1921] 2 AC 171 (HL).

[29] CTA 2010 (UK) s. 1000(1)B.

[30] CTA 2010 (UK) s. 1000(1)C & D.

By contrast, in Germany a distribution of bonus shares would be treated in the same manner as cash distributions, giving rise to distribution and a reinvestment in the capital of the company.[31] However, there is a specific tax law that permits corporations to make a tax-free distribution of bonus shares. Where a corporation increases share capital through the capitalisation of reserves, the shares received by the shareholder are not income for income tax purposes.[32] The structuring of share capital under German corporate law is more restrictive than in the UK or the US; in particular, there is no express provision for the issue of redeemable shares.[33]

By contrast, the express residual rule in the US is that bonus shares are not taxable:

> Except as otherwise provided in this section, gross income does not include the amount of any distribution of the stock of a corporation made by such corporation to its shareholders with respect to its stock.[34]

However, the exceptions are important, and where they apply they generally produce dividend treatment (presuming the corporation has earnings and profits). In particular, the exclusion from gross income does not apply to disproportionate distributions of bonus shares. These distributions involve the distribution of property to some shareholders and an 'increase in the proportionate interests of other shareholders in the assets or earnings and profits of the corporation'.[35] There are, therefore, two parts to this provision: the distribution of property to some and the distribution of shares to others. One without the other does not result in dividend treatment. The US exclusion from gross income does not extend to bonus issues of debentures, although it may extend to bonus issues of redeemable shares, unless they are convertible into ordinary shares.[36]

Irrespective of whether bonus shares constitute a dividend, bonus shares constitute a new asset acquired by shareholders that must be tracked for tax purposes. Therefore, bonus shares need a cost base. If the tax law provides nothing in this regard, there could be problems. In form,

---

[31] EStG (Germany) s. 20(1)No. 1.
[32] Law on Fiscal Measures to Increase Nominal Capital from Corporate Funds (*Gesetz über steuerrechtliche Maßnahmen bei Erhöhung des Nennkapitals aus Gesellschaftsmitteln*) (Germany) s. 1.
[33] AktG (Germany) s. 57(1) specifically prohibits refunding capital contributions to shareholders unless the procedure for corporation purchase of its own shares is followed. See also Cahn & Donald (2010, pp. 267–70).
[34] IRC (US) s. 305(a).
[35] IRC (US) s. 305(b)(2).
[36] IRC (US) s. 305(b)(5).

the shareholder has paid nothing for the bonus shares, and so the cost base would be nil (unless the deemed market value rule is applied). The existing shares would have gone down in value and so might be sold at a loss. This would create an easy method by which to manufacture artificial capital losses. Value would be shifted from the existing shares to the bonus shares, perhaps crystallising profit in the bonus shares, but at the expense of the existing shares. If the bonus issue were large compared to the existing shares, the existing shares might be disposed of for a large loss, despite the fact that the shareholder's percentage interest in the corporation may have changed little, if any.

Corporate tax systems adopt different approaches to dealing with this issue, which are related to the general manner in which the system identifies which shares have been disposed of. As noted earlier at 5.1.1, the UK generally adopts a pooling system. As a result, if the bonus shares are of the same class as the existing shares, the bonus shares are simply added to the same pool and so, on disposal, are attributed a proportionate amount of the cost base of the pool. If the bonus shares are of a different class from the existing shares (and are still not a dividend), then the reorganisation rules specifically apply.[37] In this case, the cost base of the existing shares is apportioned between those shares and the bonus shares.[38] The reorganisation rules also seem to apply if the bonus issue is a dividend (e.g. when they are redeemable securities), but it is not clear that the amount taxed as income is added to the cost base apportioned.[39]

In Germany, where bonus shares are tax free, the law specifically provides that the cost base of the existing shares is apportioned between the existing shares and the bonus shares according to their par value.[40] If the bonus shares are a dividend, the shares are treated as a distribution to the shareholder and then as a contribution to the corporation, meaning the shares will have a cost equal to the amount of the dividend. The approach is the same in the US. Where bonus shares are exempt, the cost base of the existing shares is apportioned between those shares and the

---

[37] TCGA 1992 (UK) s. 126(2)(a). In form, the reorganisation rules apply to all proportionate bonus share issues, but they are superseded by the pooling rules for shares in the same class.

[38] TCGA 1992 (UK) s. 130.

[39] TCGA 1992 (UK) s. 17(1)(a) would treat the redeemable securities as acquired at market value, but this seems to be excluded by s. 128(2).

[40] Law on Fiscal Measures to Increase Nominal Capital from Corporate Funds (*Gesetz über steuerrechtliche Maßnahmen bei Erhöhung des Nennkapitals aus Gesellschaftsmitteln*) (Germany) s. 3.

bonus shares.[41] If the bonus shares are a dividend, then the cost base of the shares is the amount of the dividend.[42]

Briefly, the same issues that arise on the issue of bonus shares arise when the corporation allocates rights to acquire shares, especially where the right is granted on favourable terms (i.e. a rights issue). Presuming that in accordance with any pre-emption rights the rights issue is proportionate, it may also split value from existing shares. Rights issues are commonly tradable, and so shareholders can sell their rights at a profit. Some countries specifically extend their tax treatment of bonus shares to the receipt of a rights issue. So, for example, in the US rules on bonus shares, 'stock' is defined to include a right to acquire stock.[43]

The UK adopts a slightly different approach. The distribution of a rights issue is still not 'out of the assets' of the corporation and so is not a dividend for tax purposes. The subsequent sale of rights to acquire shares is effectively treated as a part disposal of the existing shares.[44] This treatment ensures a spreading of the cost base of the shares and that not all of the consideration received for the sale is taxable as a capital gain.

Germany appears to adopt a different approach. It treats as income from capital any profits from the disposal of 'claims by the holder of the right giving rise to the underlying right if the corresponding ... shares are not disposed of.[45] This treatment seems to apply to the sale of a right to acquire shares. The provision goes on to prescribe that this treatment replaces the taxation of any dividend that would otherwise arise. The result seems to mean that the grant of the right to acquire shares is not a dividend, but any profit on the sale of such a right is taxable as income from capital. The rules for determining this profit appear to permit allocation of the cost base of the shares between the shares and the right to acquire further shares.[46]

### Disproportionate bonus share issues

It remains to consider the tax treatment where bonus shares are distributed to shareholders in a disproportionate manner. As an initial point, this should not arise in Germany because its corporate law incorporates a requirement of shareholder equality, and it requires that bonus shares are

---

[41] IRC (US) s. 307.
[42] IRC (US) s. 301(d).
[43] IRC (US) s. 305(d)(1).
[44] TCGA 1992 (UK) s. 123.
[45] EStG (Germany) s. 20(2) No. 2(a).
[46] EStG (Germany) s. 20(4).

distributed in proportion to existing holdings.[47] In both the UK and the US, disproportionate issue of bonus shares results in dividend treatment.

As noted earlier, the US rules generally prescribe dividend treatment for a disproportionate issue of bonus shares. One particular scenario in which this can arise is where shareholders are granted the choice of whether to receive a cash dividend or bonus shares. The US specifically provides that such 'stock in lieu of cash' elections are treated as dividends.[48] It does not matter whether the election is 'exercised before or after the declaration' of the dividend. This provision ensures dividend treatment of shares issued under bonus share plans, where the shareholder makes an election to receive bonus shares in lieu of future cash dividend distributions.[49] Bonus shares taxed as dividends receive the usual dividend tax treatment, including the lower rates for individual shareholders and the dividends-received deduction for corporate shareholders.

The situation in the UK is essentially the same. It has a specific rule for shares issued 'in lieu of a cash dividend', and these rules also apply to 'bonus share capital issued ... in respect of shares in the company of a qualifying class'.[50] A 'qualifying class' is a class of share that carries 'the right to receive bonus share capital', whether according to the terms of issue or 'otherwise'.[51] This rule is targeted at schemes in the nature of bonus share plans. These 'stock dividends' are subject to an express charge to income tax rather than being charged as dividends.[52] The lower rates of dividend tax nevertheless apply. Further, although there is no dividend tax credit as such, shareholders are treated as having paid tax at the dividend ordinary rate (10%) and gross-up is required.[53] The cost base of the shares is the amount subject to charge.[54] The overall result is very similar to dividend treatment. There is no equivalent charge for corporate shareholders, reflecting the inter-corporate dividend exemption.

---

[47]  AktG (Germany) ss. 53a & 216(1), respectively.
[48]  IRC (US) s. 305(b)(1).
[49]  A distinction is sometimes made between bonus share plans and dividend reinvestment plans. The former involves the issue of new shares that dilute the capital of all shareholders, whereas the latter involves existing shares bought back by the corporation in the market with cash paid out by the corporation.
[50]  CTA 2010 (UK) s. 1049(1).
[51]  CTA 2010 (UK) s. 1049(2).
[52]  ITTOIA 2005 (UK) s. 411.
[53]  ITTOIA 2005 (UK) s. 414.
[54]  TCGA 1992 (UK) s. 142.

### 7.1.3 Consolidation

It is also possible that shares are consolidated. Inevitably, this involves the disposal or surrender of two or more shares in return for the issue of a single new share. Commonly this can happen when shares of a small par value are consolidated into a single share of a greater value. Here there typically is no issue of dividend treatment, but only the exchange of an existing holding in return for a new holding of shares. Accordingly, the issues and rules discussed earlier at 7.1.1 are relevant. In particular, the reorganisation rules in both the UK and the US would apply in such a scenario.

## 7.2 More than one corporation

This heading extends variation of share interests to scenarios involving two or more corporations. As mentioned in the introduction to this chapter, if the separate identity of a corporation is questioned, as it has been throughout this book, then the rationale for providing roll-over or deferral relief for variations of share interest in a single corporation may be extended to situations involving two or more corporations. These scenarios typically involve the corporations concerned being related (e.g. a parent and a subsidiary corporation). This is hardly surprising because group corporations are one of the major scenarios in which the separate identity of the corporation is questioned (see the earlier discussion at 1.1.4).

As with the first heading, there are three primary manners in which a variation may involve two or more corporations. In a substitution scenario, the existing share interest may be in one corporation, but the replacement share interest may be in another corporation. Most commonly, this scenario occurs when two corporations are merged, which is the first matter discussed under this heading. In a splitting scenario, a person may hold an existing share interest in one corporation and receive an additional share interest in another corporation. Most commonly, this occurs when two corporations are divided (de-merged), which is the second matter discussed under this heading. It is also possible for shares in two corporations to be consolidated into a share in a single corporation, but this scenario is discounted for purposes of the following discussion.[55]

---

[55] A consolidation of the shares of two corporations might occur, for example, when a stapled stock structure is dismantled. A stapled stock structure commonly involves the ability

In passing, as noted at the start of this chapter, the CCCTB Proposal as drafted has no particular rules for mergers and divisions. Accordingly, to provide a broader platform for comparison, the Australian rules on mergers and divisions are briefly considered.

### 7.2.1 Merger

A corporate merger involves the amalgamation of shareholders of two separate corporations under one single corporation. A merger can occur in a number of ways, but the following discussion only focuses on the two most common manners: the merger by share exchange and merger by fusion. A share exchange merger occurs where one corporation (the merged corporation) acquires the shares of a second corporation (the merging corporation), and as consideration for the acquisition, the one corporation issues its shares to the shareholders of the second corporation.

A merger by fusion (also referred to as a 'formal' or 'statutory merger') is different in that the shares in the merging corporation are not transferred to the merged corporation. Rather, (i) the assets of the merging corporation are transferred to the merged corporation, (ii) as consideration the merged corporation issues shares to the shareholders of the merging corporation and (iii) the merging corporation is then dissolved without liquidation. Many jurisdictions, especially civil law jurisdictions, expressly provide a special corporate law procedure whereby one corporation is fused into another corporation and dissolved without using the standard corporate liquidation or winding-up procedure. For example, a flexible fusion procedure is possible in Germany and the US.[56] By contrast, fusions are not possible in many common law jurisdictions, including the UK and Australia, unless a court order is obtained (in which case they are referred to as a 'scheme of arrangement').[57]

A major difference between a merger by share exchange and a merger by fusion is that a merger by share exchange may involve only some of the shareholders of the merging corporation. If not all shareholders engage in the exchange, then after the merger the merged corporation will not

---

to trade in shares in one corporation depending on trading in the shares of another corporation and, particularly, where shares in a subsidiary are stapled to shares in a parent corporation.

[56] *Umwandlungsgesetz* (Reorganisation Law) (Germany) s. 20, DGCL (US) s. 251(a) and MBCA (US) ss. 11.02 & 11.07.

[57] The scheme of arrangement procedure appears in Companies Act 2006 (UK) Parts 26 and 27 (ss. 895–941) and Corporations Act 2001 (Australia) s. 411.

be the sole shareholder in the merging corporation, because there will be shareholders in the merging corporation that continue their shareholding across the merger. This cannot happen in a merger by fusion. Here the merger must involve all of the shareholders of the merging corporation because that corporation ceases to exist after the merger.

A merger involves tax issues for each of the three players involved: the shareholders, the merged corporation and the merging corporation. These issues arise whether the merger is by way of share exchange or fusion. In particular, the issues involved are as follows:

(i) A disposal of the shares of the merging corporation
(ii) An acquisition of those shares or, in a merger by fusion, of the assets of the merging corporation by the merged corporation
(iii) An acquisition of the merged corporation's shares by the shareholders, and
(iv) Questions as to the continuation of the tax attributes of the merging corporation

If relief from the usual consequences of these events (e.g. as previously discussed in this book) is to be provided, there is the additional issue of threshold requirements for that relief. These threshold requirements are discussed first and then the tax consequences for each of the three players.

In passing, it is noted that mergers often involve the use of additional corporations (e.g. a holding corporation). This use can be important for several tax reasons, including the form of financing the acquisition and future strategies for exit from the acquisition. However, the use of holding corporations in the context of a merger is beyond the scope of this book.

### 7.2.1.1 Threshold for relief

A merger involves a change of form of investment where the substance of the investment may not change sufficiently for the tax law to recognise the change as a taxing event. Accordingly, the tax issues are similar to those raised on incorporation, discussed earlier in Chapter 4. As noted in that chapter, the threshold for incorporation relief typically focusses on the level of share ownership after incorporation, the incorporation of a business (or identifiable part thereof) or a combination of both. Some countries draw a formal connection between incorporation relief and merger relief and the thresholds used for each. For example, Germany incorporates both forms of relief in the dedicated tax law (*Umwandlungssteuergesetz*) on reorganisation, discussed earlier at 4.2. However, most countries (including Germany) focus on the level of share ownership post-merger when determining the threshold for merger relief.

In the context of a share exchange, country practices vary widely as to the level of shareholding that must be achieved by the merged corporation in the merging corporation after the merger. The US and Australia have quite high thresholds, broadly at 80%, whereas the UK at the other extreme has a very low threshold, which simply requires that a general offer be made for the shares of the merging corporation. The form of the threshold is critical in determining the tax consequences of the merger for the merging corporation's shareholders. If the merged corporation must acquire a certain percentage of the merging corporation, then the merging corporation's shareholders may not know at the time of acceptance of the share exchange whether merger relief will be available. This is because whether the relief is available for a particular shareholder will depend on the number of shareholders accepting the exchange. Accordingly, the type of threshold used may affect whether a shareholder has to unconditionally accept an exchange before becoming aware of whether other shareholders have accepted the exchange.

As mentioned, in the US relief for a merger by share exchange broadly requires that the merged corporation acquires 80% of the merging corporation. This is prescribed by paragraph (B) of the definition of 'reorganization' (a type B reorganisation).[58] In particular, the merged corporation must acquire 'control' of the merging corporation, which is defined in terms of '80 percent of the total combined voting power of all classes of stock entitled to vote and at least 80 percent of the total number of shares of all other classes of stock of the corporation'.[59] This provision appears to require direct ownership of the 80% by the merged corporation. As an additional requirement, the consideration given by the merged corporation for the exchange must be 'solely … all or a part of its voting stock'.[60] So the merged corporation cannot mix cash consideration with the issue of its shares or the transfer becomes taxable.

The 80% requirement is not prescribed under a type C reorganisation. A type C reorganisation can also be used to facilitate a merger, especially where the merger by fusion route is not available. It involves the merging corporation transferring 'substantially all of [its] properties' to the merged corporation 'solely' in return for shares in the merged corporation. This

[58]  IRC (US) s. 368(a)(1)(B).
[59]  IRC (US) s. 368(c).
[60]  IRC (US) s. 368(a)(1)(B).

would leave the merged corporation partly owned by its original share-holders and partly by the merging corporation and, so indirectly, by its shareholders.[61] However, the merging corporation is then required to dis-tribute its shares in the merged corporation to its shareholders and be liquidated (unless waived by the tax administration).[62] What constitutes 'substantially all' of the merging corporation's property has been the sub-ject of substantial judicial discourse. The US tax administration accepts that 90% of the market value of net assets and 70% of gross assets is substantial.[63]

Under either a type B or C reorganisation the consideration given by the merged corporation must be 'solely' its own voting stock. This is not the case where a type A reorganisation is used. A type A reorganisation involves 'a statutory merger or consolidation'.[64] Here the merged corpo-ration can use non-voting shares and securities as consideration, and it can use even money or other property without causing disqualification as a reorganisation. This substantial flexibility caused the legislature and the courts to impose some general restrictions on the use of the reorganisa-tion procedure in order to safeguard its intent. As a result, qualification as a statutory merger under the corporate law of a US state is not by itself sufficient to qualify as a reorganisation under the federal income tax law.

In particular, the merged and merging corporations must be 'a party to a reorganization', and the reorganisation must be in pursuance of a 'plan of reorganization'.[65] Regarding the latter, although the 'plan' need not be written, typically it is formalised. Further, the reorganisation must have a business or commercial purpose. The courts also require the shareholders to have a significant continuing ownership interest in the acquiring cor-poration, and they look to the period of ownership by shareholders both pre- and post-merger.[66]

Australia also has a quite high threshold of acquisition of the merging corporation by the merged corporation, but it is not ameliorated, as in

---

[61] IRC (US) s. 368(a)(1)(C).
[62] IRC (US) s. 368(a)(2)(G).
[63] Bittker & Eustice (2003–, para. 12.24[2]).
[64] IRC (US) s. 368(a)(1)(A). A merger or consolidation requires compliance with US state corporate laws. In particular, a merger involves the merged corporation absorbing the merging corporation (e.g. by the merging corporation transferring its assets to the merged corporation and then being dissolved). A consolidation involves multiple merging cor-porations transferring their assets to a new (merged) corporation and then the merging corporations being dissolved.
[65] IRC (US) s. 354(a)(1). 'Party to a reorganization' is defined in s. 368(b).
[66] Bittker & Eustice (2003–, para. 12.21).

the case of the US, by other rules. Merger relief is available where under a 'single arrangement' the merged corporation becomes 'the owner of 80% or more of the voting shares' in the merging corporation. Generally, the merged corporation must directly hold the 80%, but (unlike in the US) holdings of other members within a wholly owned corporate group count for this purpose. There is no requirement, as in the US, that the shareholders only receive shares in the merged corporation as consideration for the exchange. However, to qualify, all of the owners of voting shares in the merging corporation must be eligible to participate in the exchange on 'substantially the same terms'.[67] Australia has no special rule for mergers by fusion because that is only possible under corporate law with court approval.

The threshold for merger relief by share exchange in Germany is lower. Relief is available where the merged corporation acquires 'directly the majority of voting rights' in the merging corporation.[68] Any existing shares held prior to the merger count for purposes of determining whether the majority is obtained. As in the US, the threshold must be met by a direct holding. Unlike in the US, but like in Australia, it is possible for the shareholders to receive other forms of consideration for the exchange than just shares in the merged corporation. Germany has separate rules for mergers by fusion, which require compliance with the German law on reorganisations (*Umwandlungsgesetz*). In addition (and unlike for share exchanges), tax relief is only available where any consideration received constitutes exclusively shares in the merged corporation.[69]

UK corporate law does not generally facilitate a merger by fusion without court authorisation (scheme of arrangement). However, in the context of a merger by share exchange, the UK has the lowest level of shareholding requirement of the countries presently under consideration. Merger relief is available in one of three scenarios:

(i) After the merger the merged corporation holds 'more than 25% of the ordinary share capital' of the merging corporation.

(ii) The merged corporation issues its shares in the exchange 'as the result of a general offer' made to shareholders of the merging corporation

---

[67] Income Tax Assessment Act 1997 (Australia) s. 124–780. Certain exceptions to these requirements apply to takeovers and schemes of arrangement under the Corporations Act 2001 (Australia). It is also possible to secure merger relief within a wholly owned group of corporations by using Income Tax Assessment Act 1997 (Australia) Subdiv. 124-G (share exchanges) or 126-B (asset transfers).

[68] UmwStG (Germany) s. 21(1).

[69] UmwStG (Germany) s. 11.

and 'in the first instance on a condition such that if it were satisfied [the merged corporation] would have control of [the merging corporation]'.

(iii) After the merger the merged corporation holds 'the greater part of the voting power' of the merging corporation.[70]

The ordinary share capital and voting power thresholds are determined by aggregating shares held pre-merger with those acquired as a result of the merger. The respective holdings, however, must be held directly (indirect holdings do not count). The relief extends to exchanges of 'shares or debentures', but any other type of consideration results in disqualification. Merger relief is only available if the reorganisation is for bona fide commercial reasons and does not form part of a scheme in which one of the main purposes is to avoid tax.[71]

UK tax law also contains a flexible provision for relief that can apply where one corporation transfers a business to another corporation and the recipient corporation issues shares to the transferor corporation's shareholders.[72] As with US type C reorganisations, this UK provision can be used in a merger-type scenario. However, unlike a US type C reorganisation, the UK rule does not require the merging corporation to be liquidated. This UK rule also requires that the reorganisation is for bona fide commercial reasons and does not form part of a scheme in which one of the main purposes is to avoid tax.

### 7.2.1.2   Consequences for the shareholder

In the absence of relief, a shareholder in a merger by share exchange or fusion disposes of shares in the merging corporation and acquires shares in the merged corporation. The consideration received for the disposal is the shares in the merged corporation, and the consideration given for the acquisition is the shares in the merging corporation. Presuming these shares are taken at their market value (the usual rule), the result may be a gain or loss on the disposal of the shares in the merging corporation and a market value cost base for the shares acquired in the merged corporation.

Invariably, merger relief provides that no gain or loss is recognised by the shareholder on the disposal and that the cost base of the shares in the merging corporation is transferred and used as the cost base of the

---

[70]   TCGA 1992 (UK) s. 135(2). Section 138 provides a dedicated clearance procedure with the UK tax administration for assessing whether these tests are met.
[71]   TCGA 1992 (UK) s. 137.
[72]   TCGA 1992 (UK) s. 139.

shares in the merged corporation. This is commonly referred to as 'roll-over relief'. The relief generally means that any gain or loss built into the shares in the merging corporation is rolled over into the shares held by the shareholder in the merged corporation. There are, however, two primary issues regarding the form of merger relief for shareholders. The first is the extent to which the shareholder has an option to elect for the relief or not. The second is the extent of the relief and whether the relief is all or nothing or there is the possibility of realising a partial gain or loss.

In the US, the rules on merger by share exchange are in principle compulsory, and the shareholder has no option to elect whether they apply or not. Of course, it is possible to manufacture a share exchange so that the conditions for the rules to apply are not met, in which case the usual rules for disposals and acquisitions apply. However, where the conditions discussed earlier at 7.2.1.1 are met then,

> [n]o gain or loss shall be recognized if stock or securities in a corporation a party to a reorganization are, in pursuance of the plan of reorganization, exchanged solely for stock or securities in such corporation or in another corporation a party to the reorganization.[73]

The cost base rules for the shareholder are the same as those used in the context of a reorganisation involving a single corporation discussed earlier at 7.1.1 (i.e. in the usual case the cost base of the shares in the merging corporation is used as the cost base of the shares in the merged corporation).[74]

The approach in the UK is similarly compulsory in form. Where the conditions discussed earlier at 7.2.1.1 are met, then the reorganisation rules discussed earlier at 7.1.1 are applied 'with necessary adaptations as if [the merging company and the merged company] were the same company and the exchange were a reorganisation of its share capital'.[75] This means that the shares acquired by the shareholders in the merged corporation are treated for tax purposes as a continuation of the shares previously held in the merging corporation.

As noted earlier at 7.2.1.1, it is also possible in the UK to engage in a reconstruction that involves the merging corporation transferring its business to the merged corporation and the merged corporation (as consideration) issuing shares to the merging corporation's shareholders. In such a case, then provided the shareholders either retain their shares in the

---

[73]  IRC (US) s. 354(a)(1).
[74]  IRC (US) s. 358(a).
[75]  TCGA 1992 (UK) s. 135(3).

merging corporation or those shares are cancelled, the reorganisation provisions are triggered.[76] This means that the shares acquired by the shareholders in the merged corporation, together with any continuing shares
in the merging corporation, are treated for tax purposes as a continuation
of the shares held in the merging corporation prior to the merger.

The Australian rules are both more flexible and, in other respects, more
rigid. In principle, the shareholder has a choice as to whether to receive no
gain / no loss treatment, but the shareholder may not elect to roll over a
loss.[77] Where an election is available and is made, no gain is recognised,
and the cost base of the shares in the merging corporation is transferred
to and treated as the cost base of the shares in the merged corporation.[78]
Partial relief is granted where the consideration for the exchange includes
something other than shares in the merged corporation.[79]

The German rules for the treatment of shareholders in a merger by
share exchange take a different approach. That treatment depends on the
book value allocated by the merged corporation to the shares received
in the merging corporation after the merger. This rule takes the same
approach as is used on incorporation, discussed earlier at 4.2. As a general
rule, the merged corporation must take up these shares at market value.
However, the tax administration may permit the merged corporation to
take up these shares at anywhere between the transferring shareholder's
cost base in the shares and market value.[80]

The value at which the merged corporation takes up the shares in the
merging corporation in its accounts is then treated as 'the proceeds of sale
of the acquired shares and as the acquisition cost of the shares received
in exchange'.[81] The German approach is interesting because it means that
there is a direct ability to manipulate the amount of gain or loss recognised
by the shareholder. The degree of recognition is dependent on the value
at which the merged corporation takes up the shares in the merging corporation in its accounts. In any case, gain is recognised to the extent that
the shareholder receives consideration for the exchange other than shares
in the merged corporation (an exchange involving so-called boot).

There is the potential that, for an individual shareholder, the shares held
in the merging corporation do not have the same character as the shares

---

[76] TCGA 1992 (UK) s. 136.
[77] Income Tax Assessment Act 1997 (Australia) s. 124–780(3).
[78] Income Tax Assessment Act 1997 (Australia) s. 124–785.
[79] Income Tax Assessment Act 1997 (Australia) s. 124–786.
[80] UmwStG (Germany) s. 21(1).
[81] UmwStG (Germany) s. 21(2).

received in the merged corporation (e.g. where one set of shares are held as business assets and the other as investment assets). If the shares held in the merging corporation were held as business assets, Germany treats any disposal of shares in the merged corporation within seven years of the exchange as having a business character. However, the amount of any gain treated as a business gain is reduced proportionately over the seven years if the shares in the merged corporation are actually held as investment assets.[82] This is similar to the rule that Germany uses for incorporation relief, which was discussed earlier at 4.2.

In the US, the rules for shareholders are the same whether a merger by share exchange or a merger by fusion is involved. By contrast, Germany repeats its provisions separately for each of these types of merger. In particular, in the case of a merger by fusion, the shareholder can seek permission of the tax administration to defer any recognition of gain and use the cost base of the shares in the merging corporation as the cost base of the shares in the merged corporation after the fusion.[83] It seems there is no option (as there is in a merger by share exchange) to use a value between that cost base and market value and the seven-year proportioning rule is not applied. Rather, the shares in the merged corporation seem to take their character from the shares in the merging corporation.

### 7.2.1.3  Consequences for the merged corporation

Whether the merger is by way of share exchange or fusion, the merged corporation acquires assets. In the former case it acquires shares in the merging corporation and, in the latter, the assets of the merging corporation. The question for present discussion is what the cost base of those assets is in the hands of the merged corporation. The answer to this question is relatively straightforward in the case of a merger by fusion. However, a merger by share exchange raises similar issues as to duplication of gains and losses that arise on incorporation, discussed earlier in Chapter 4.

In the context of a merger by fusion, the merging corporation disposes of its assets to the merged corporation and is then dissolved. It is inevitable that the merging corporation and the merged corporation are treated symmetrically with respect to this transfer. If the transfer does not trigger tax consequences for the merging corporation – and, as discussed later at 7.2.1.4, it typically does not – then the merged corporation takes up the

---

[82]  UmwStG (Germany) s. 22(1).
[83]  UmwStG (Germany) s. 13.

merging corporation's assets at the same cost base (tax value) as was the case in the hands of the merging corporation.

So, in the context of a merger by fusion in the US, this provision applies:

> If property was acquired by a corporation in connection with a reorganization to which this part applies, then the basis shall be the same as it would be in the hands of the transferor, increased in the amount of gain recognized to the transferor on such transfer.[84]

The position is broadly the same in Germany. The merged corporation takes over the tax values of the merging corporation's assets as recorded in the merging corporation's final balance sheet. In this way, as in the US, the merged corporation assumes the merging corporation's acquisition cost, depreciation and other tax characteristics of the transferred assets.[85]

The position is partially the same in the UK when a business is transferred from a merging corporation to a merged corporation as part of a reconstruction. For the purposes of capital gains, the transfer is treated as taking place at a consideration that secures neither gain nor loss for the transferring merging corporation.[86] This treatment does not extend to trading stock and relief from balancing charges for depreciable assets unless the merging and the merged corporations are already connected or within a 75% group, respectively (see the rules discussed earlier at 1.2.3.1). This is just another example of the UK's fragmented approach to asset valuations for tax purposes.

The position is not so straightforward in the context of a merger by share exchange. The duplication of assets for tax purposes when they are enveloped in a corporation (e.g. by incorporation) was discussed earlier at the start of Chapter 4. Mergers by share exchange are an example of this duplication because they insert another link in the corporate chain between real assets and ultimate shareholders. As noted earlier at 7.2.1.2, where merger relief for a share exchange is available, any gain built into the shares held in the merging corporation is rolled over into the shares held in the merged corporation after the merger. However, unlike in the case of a fusion, the merging corporation and the shares in it continue to exist. Post-merger, those shares in the merging corporation are held by the merged corporation, and the issue is what tax value should be assigned to them.

---

[84] IRC (US) s. 362(b).
[85] UmwStG (Germany) s. 12.
[86] TCGA 1992 (UK) s. 139.

As in the incorporation scenario, there is one of two choices for this valuation, and neither is entirely satisfactory. The shares held by the merged corporation in the merging corporation may take their cost base from the cost base of the transferring shareholder in the merging corporation. This approach duplicates any pre-merger gain or loss built into the shares. Alternately, the merged corporation may be given an uplift in the cost base to market value. This approach opens up tax avoidance opportunities whereby the merged corporation can, post-merger, sell the merging corporation for cash without any tax liability. Doing so may be viewed as objectionable because, when viewed as a whole, the former shareholder in the merging corporation has changed both the form and substance of the investment without incurring any tax liability (i.e. the rationale for granting merger relief is not met in such a case). These sorts of tax avoidance issues also arise where the inter-corporate participation exemption (see the earlier discussion at 5.1.3.1) is broad enough to cover the post-merger disposal of shares in the merging corporation by the merged corporation.

The US is a major example of a country that requires the merged corporation to use the transferring shareholders' cost base for the shares that it acquires in the merging corporation and where this requirement has significant tax consequences. This is by reason of section 362(b) of IRC, which was reproduced earlier. For example, any gain built into shares in a merging corporation pre-merger is duplicated post-merger (i.e. in the shares held by the shareholders in the merged corporation and in the shares held by the merged corporation in the merging corporation). Where the latter shares are subsequently sold by the merged corporation, the gain is taxable without relief by way of, for example, a participation exemption.

Germany adopts the same approach, but in its case the subsequent sale is 95% protected from taxation by the participation exemption. As noted earlier at 7.2.1.2, the merged corporation may, with tax administration permission, take up the shares in the merging corporation at anywhere between the transferor shareholder's cost base and the market value of the shares. The value at which it takes up the shares is treated as the price paid by the merged corporation for the shares in the merging corporation. So, to the extent that the shareholder has a built-in gain and the cost base of the shareholder is taken up, that gain will in principle be duplicated. However, this will be of little consequence because any gain of the merged corporation on the subsequent sale of the shares in the merging corporation is typically protected from taxation as to 95% by the participation exemption (see the earlier discussion at 5.1.3.1).

The position in the UK is different and broadly the same as the position it adopts with respect to relief on incorporation of a business (see the earlier discussion at 4.2). Although there is an express rule for rolling over any gain (or loss) of the shareholder on the exchange into the shares held in the merged corporation post-merger, there is no rule for how to deal with the shares in the merging corporation held by the merged corporation. This means the general rules apply, and because this is a non-arm's length transaction, the merged corporation should take up the shares in the merging corporation at market value.[87] The importance of this step-up has been somewhat reduced since the introduction of the substantial shareholder exemption for disposals of shares by one corporation in another corporation (see the earlier discussion at 5.1.3.1). Nevertheless, the step-up continues to be of significance where this exemption is not available.

Australia takes the peculiar approach of sitting somewhere between the duplication of any built-in gain and, as in the UK, a step-up to market value for the shares held by the merged corporation in the merging corporation. As with the US, this position is particularly important in Australia because it does not have a general participation exemption for the disposal of shares in one corporation by another corporation. The residual position in Australia is the same as in the UK (i.e. a step-up, in which the merged corporation takes up the shares in the merging corporation at market value). This is on the presumption that the merged corporation 'gives' its shares in respect of acquiring the shares in the merging corporation.[88] However, there are exceptions to this residual rule where the merged corporation must take up the shares in the merging corporation at the same cost base as the transferring shareholder.

The provisions enacting the exceptions are complex, but broadly involve two scenarios.[89] This first is where a particular shareholder (together with associates) holds a 30% stake in the merging corporation before the merger and also holds a 30% stake in the merged corporation after the merger. This is known as the 'significant stakeholder' exception. The second scenario involves the situation where the merging corporation is much bigger than the merged corporation before the merger. Broadly, this exception applies if the shareholders in the merging corporation end up holding 80% of the merged corporation post-merger. It does not apply

---

[87] TCGA 1992 (UK) s. 17. Alternately, the merged corporation may be viewed as having 'given' its own shares as consideration for the acquisition; s. 38.
[88] Income Tax Assessment Act 1997 (Australia) s. 110–25(2).
[89] Income Tax Assessment Act 1997 (Australia) s. 124–782.

if either corporation is widely held, although there have been difficulties with this qualification. This is known as the 'common stakeholder' exception.[90]

Recall that merger relief in Australia is not compulsory and typically depends on the election of the transferring shareholder. However, where the shareholder falls within the significant or common stakeholder exceptions, then the election of the shareholder could affect the future tax liability of the merged corporation. This is because that corporation will inherit the (duplicated) built-in gain of the transferring shareholder. Accordingly, where either of these exceptions to a step-up in cost base applies, the election for shareholder roll-over is a joint one. That is, if the shareholder is a significant or common stakeholder, the shareholder is only entitled to merger relief if the shareholder and the merged corporation jointly elect.[91]

### 7.2.1.4   Consequences for the merging corporation and survival of tax attributes

When the merging corporation is considered, the difference between a merger by fusion and a merger by share exchange becomes dramatic. In a merger by fusion, the merging corporation ceases to exist. Such a merger effects a consolidation of the identity of the merging and merged corporations – not just for tax purposes (see the earlier discussion at 1.1.4.2) but also for corporate and general law purposes. There are two primary issues for a merging corporation with respect to a merger by fusion. The first is whether the corporation realises any gain by reason of transfer of its assets to the merged corporation under the arrangement. The second is what happens to any continuing tax attributes of the merging corporation post-merger, such as the carry-forward of losses or credits.

The US tax law presumes that a merger by fusion involves four steps. The first is the transfer of the assets of the merging corporation to the merged corporation. The second is that in return the merged corporation issues shares to the merging corporation. The third is that the merging corporation distributes these shares in the merged corporation to its own shareholders. The fourth is that the merging corporation is then dissolved. All of these issues are dealt with in section 361 of IRC on a non-recognition basis. In particular,

---

[90]  'Significant stakeholder' and 'common stakeholder' are defined in Income Tax Assessment Act 1997 (Australia) s. 124–783.
[91]  Income Tax Assessment Act 1997 (Australia) s. 124–780(3)(d).

[n]o gain or loss shall be recognized to a corporation if such corporation is a party to a reorganization and exchanges property, in pursuance of the plan of reorganization, solely for stock or securities in another corporation a party to the reorganization.[92]

The provision goes on to state the following:

[N]o gain or loss shall be recognized to a corporation a party to a reorganization on the distribution to its shareholders of property in pursuance of the plan of reorganization.[93]

As for the remaining tax attributes of the merging corporation, many of them may be carried forward by the merged corporation after a merger by fusion (i.e. the transferee of the merging corporation's assets). These attributes include net operating and capital losses as well as the balance of earnings and profits (but not apparently excess foreign tax credits).[94] However, presuming there has been a 50% change of ownership of these attributes as a result of the merger, the limitations in section 382 of IRC apply. These limitations were discussed earlier at 5.2 in the context of a corporate takeover by share acquisition. The US adopts a particularly admirable consistency in applying its section 382 limitations to changes of ownership caused by simple cash acquisition or merger by fusion or share exchange and any subsequent tax consolidation of entities.

Germany used to adopt a similar approach with respect to the treatment of mergers by fusion, but it was changed in 2006 due to perceived abuses and the reduction in corporate tax rate. As with other forms of reorganisation, the transfer of assets by the merging corporation to the merged corporation is generally considered made at market value. This transfer may crystallise a gain to the merging corporation. However, with the permission of the tax administration, the transfer may be considered made at anywhere between the market value and the merging corporation's book value of the assets.[95]

Historically, it was also possible to transfer any carried-forward loss of the merging corporation to the merged corporation, but this is now expressly prohibited, as is the transfer of certain other tax attributes.[96] However, in many cases it may still be possible to use such losses by a

---

[92] IRC (US) s. 361(a). Gain may be realised to the extent consideration received for the assets is not solely shares in the merged corporation; s. 361(b).
[93] IRC (US) s. 361(c).
[94] IRC (US) s. 381.
[95] UmwStG (Germany) s. 11.
[96] UmwStG (Germany) s. 12(3) applying s. 4(2).

merging corporation that realises gains on the transfer of its assets to the merged corporation. This occurs where the book value of the assets is below their market value and the merging corporation takes up the assets at their market value in its final balance sheet. Any losses (and other tax attributes) not used in this manner are lost with the dissolution of the merging corporation.

By contrast, in a merger by share exchange, the merging corporation continues to exist and hold its assets and other tax attributes unless an express rule provides otherwise. The rules of major concern in this regard are those dealing with limitations on the use of corporate tax attributes following a change of ownership, considered earlier at 5.2. In Germany, the UK, the US and Australia these rules may be triggered by reason of a merger by share exchange where the shareholder qualifies for roll-over relief.[97]

### 7.2.2   Division

A variation of share interests may also result in a shareholder that holds shares in a single corporation before the variation holding shares in two or more corporations after the variation. This is most commonly referred to as a division or de-merger. Divisions are broadly of one of two types. The first involves the simple situation in which a parent corporation holds shares in a subsidiary, and the parent distributes those shares by way of dividend to its shareholders. The parent corporation ceases to hold the subsidiary, and after the distribution the shareholders hold both shares in the parent corporation and in the former subsidiary corporation. The primary issues that arise in this case are whether the distribution is treated as a taxable dividend, whether the disposal of the shares in the subsidiary by the parent corporation is a taxable event and how to determine the cost base of the shares in the subsidiary acquired by the shareholder.

The second major form of division involves the transfer of a business from an existing corporation to a new corporation in return for that new corporation issuing shares to the existing corporation's shareholders. After the division, the shareholders hold both shares in the existing corporation and shares in the new corporation. The business

---

[97] Although the UK has a special rule in TCGA 1992 s. 181 that relieves a merging corporation from a charge under s. 179 where certain conditions are met. Section 179 was discussed earlier at 5.2.2.2.

transferred to the new corporation may be a business carried on directly by the existing corporation, or it may be a business carried on by a subsidiary of the existing corporation. For the purposes of simplicity, the former is presumed in the following discussion. This division by assets transfer also raises issues of recognition of a dividend and the cost base of the shares in the new corporation after the division. In addition, such a division raises questions as to the taxability of the transfer of the business to the new corporation.

Consistent with the earlier discussion of mergers, the following discussion first considers thresholds that countries use in providing relief from the residual tax consequences of a division. The discussion then turns to consider the consequences for the shareholder receiving the new shares. It next considers the tax consequences for the corporation in which the shareholders holds shares prior to the division, referred to as the 'distributing corporation'. It then turns to consider the tax consequences for the corporation whose shares are acquired by the shareholders as a result of the division, referred to as the 'distributed corporation'.

### 7.2.2.1 Threshold for relief

The threshold for de-merger relief typically focuses on the same issues as merger relief and incorporation relief (i.e. level of share ownership, transfer of a business (or identifiable part thereof) or a combination of both). However, in the case of de-merger relief, the focus is on the holding or business before the de-merger rather than after the de-merger. Which aspect is focused on depends on whether the de-merger is by way of distribution or asset transfer.

In the case of a de-merger by way of distribution, de-merger relief typically depends on the distributing corporation having a particular level of holding of shares in the distributed corporation. The level of holding can vary dramatically from country to country. The US seems to have a particularly high threshold. De-merger relief applies where

(A) a corporation...distributes to a shareholder, with respect to its stock,...solely stock or securities of a corporation...which it controls immediately before the distribution,

(B) the transaction was not used principally as a device for the distribution of the earnings and profits...

(C) the requirements...relating to active businesses...are satisfied, and

(D) as part of the distribution, the distributing corporation dis- tributes … all of the stock and securities in the controlled corporation held by it.[98]

The immediate requirement that the distributing corporation control the distributed corporation is again a reference to an 80% holding.[99] The rule is subject to many anti-avoidance requirements, and the focus is on pro- viding relief in circumstances where the de-merger serves a corporate business purpose.[100] As for requirement (C), this broadly requires the distributing corporation and the distributed corporation to have actively conducted business for at least five years.[101]

The strictness of this US rule is ameliorated in other ways. US de- merger relief expressly applies 'whether or not the distribution is pro rata with respect to all of the shareholders of the distributing corporation'.[102] This means that de-merger relief can be used as a means of dividing a cor- poration (and its subsidiaries) between two groups of shareholders in a non-proportionate manner. This rule can be particularly useful in settling disputes between different groups of shareholders.

These US rules for relief in the context of a de-merger by distribution do not use the reorganisation rules, which are so important in dealing with other types of variations of share interest. However, the reorganisa- tion rules may be used in the context of a de-merger by way of asset trans- fer. In particular, such a de-merger may amount to a Type D reorganisation involving the

transfer by a corporation of all or a part of its assets to another corporation if immediately after the transfer the transferor, or one or more of its share- holders (including persons who were shareholders immediately before the transfer), or any combination thereof, is in control of the corporation to which the assets are transferred; but only if, in pursuance of the plan, stock

---

[98] IRC (US) s. 355(a)(1). Requirement (D) may also be met if the distributing corporation disposes of 80% of the shares in the distributed corporation and the de-merger is not part of a tax avoidance plan.

[99] IRC (US) s. 368(c).

[100] See, for example, Title 26 Code of Federal Regulations (US) § 1.355–2. Further, IRC (US) s. 355(e) denies relief if the division was part of a plan for someone to acquire 50% or more of the distributing or distributed corporation. This may be assumed if such an acquisition occurs two years before or two years after the de-merger.

[101] IRC (US) s. 355(b). There is a special rule for holding corporations with active subsidiaries.

[102] IRC (US) s. 355(a)(2)(A).

or securities of the corporation to which the assets are transferred are distributed in a transaction which qualifies under section 354, 355, or 356.[103]

Typically, the distributing corporation will transfer its assets to the distributed corporation in return for shares in the distributed corporation. Then the distributing corporation engages in a de-merger by distribution by distributing the shares in the distributed corporation to its own shareholders. As discussed earlier, this can be done on a non-pro-rata basis.

The UK also has comparatively high thresholds for de-merger relief. In the case of a de-merger by distribution, relief is only available where the distributing corporation distributes to its shareholders shares in a 75% subsidiary.[104] Further, the shares distributed cannot be redeemable and must 'constitute the whole or substantially the whole' of the distributing corporation's holding of ordinary shares and voting rights in the distributed corporation.[105]

The UK's approach is similar in providing relief for a de-merger by asset distribution. That relief is available for

a distribution which consists of both of the following-

(a) the transfer by a company to one or more other companies ... of ... a trade or trades, or ... shares in one or more companies which are 75% subsidiaries of the company making the transfer, and
(b) the issue of shares by the transferee company or companies to all or any of the members of the company making the transfer.[106]

In addition, the distributing corporation must retain no more than a 'minor interest' in the trade transferred to the distributed corporation, or where a subsidiary is transferred, substantially all of the shares in subsidiary must be transferred to the distributed corporation.[107]

Relief under the UK rules is also subject to some general requirements, whether the de-merger is by way of distribution or asset transfer. Similar to the approach in the US, a commercial purpose is necessary, and each corporation must be engaged in a trade or a holding corporation of a corporation engaged in a trade. Disproportionate distributions to the distributing corporation's shareholders are not expressly prohibited, but there are general anti-abuse rules that need to be negotiated, including as

---

[103]  IRC (US) s. 368(a)(1)(D).
[104]  CTA 2010 (UK) s. 1076.
[105]  CTA 2010 (UK) s. 1082(1).
[106]  CTA 2010 (UK) s. 1077(1).
[107]  CTA 2010 (UK) s. 1083.

to cessation or sale of trade after the de-merger.[108] A dedicated clearance procedure with the tax administration is available.[109]

The Australian rules are both more flexible and more restrictive than the UK and US approaches. The Australian de-merger relief rules are focused on de-mergers by way of distribution rather than by way of asset transfer. However, it may be possible to effectively receive relief for a de-merger by way of asset transfer if that transfer occurs in the context of a wholly owned group. In the context of a de-merger by distribution, relief is available if a head entity and its 20% subsidiaries (by income, capital or voting)[110] distribute at least 80% of their shares in one of those sub-sidiaries to the shareholders of the parent corporation.[111] The disposal can also be achieved by way of share issue and cancellation in the distributed subsidiary.

The Australian relief is only available if 50% (by market value) of the dis-tributing corporation's capital assets are used in business.[112] Further, the relief is only available where the shares in the distributed corporation are distributed to shareholders in proportion to their interests in the distribut-ing corporation before the de-merger.[113] So unlike the UK and the US, Australia requires a proportionate distribution. In addition, the Australian rules expressly provide that no cash or other benefits can be distributed in the de-merger other than the shares in the distributed corporation.[114]

The German rules are quite different from those of the other countries, and there is a close connection with their approach taken with respect to incorporation, discussed earlier at 4.2. In particular, just as the Australian rules do not expressly cover de-mergers by asset transfer, the German de-merger rules do not expressly cover de-mergers by distribution of shares in a subsidiary. However, the German rules do cover de-mergers by trans-fer of assets. Further, and unlike the other countries, there is no express requirement as to level of holding of shares in the distributed corporation either before or after the transfer of assets to it, whether by the distributing corporation or the shareholders in the distributing corporation. Rather, as in the case of incorporation, Germany relies on the concept of the transfer of a business or 'business division' (*Teilbetrieb*). The concept of a 'business

---

[108]  CTA 2010 (UK) s. 1081 and see the definition of 'trade' in s. 1099.
[109]  CTA 2010 (UK) s. 1091.
[110]  Income Tax Assessment Act 1997 (Australia) s. 125–65.
[111]  Income Tax Assessment Act 1997 (Australia) s. 125–70(1).
[112]  Income Tax Assessment Act 1936 (Australia) s. 44(5).
[113]  Income Tax Assessment Act 1997 (Australia) s. 125–70(2).
[114]  Income Tax Assessment Act 1997 (Australia) s. 125–70(1)(c).

division' and the need for it to be separately viable were discussed earlier at 4.2.

The German de-merger relief rules are defined by reference to the transfer of assets in a 'splitting, spin-off or partial transfer'.[115] These terms are defined by reference to the Reorganisation Law.[116] In particular, a spin-off involves the distributing corporation transferring assets to the distributed corporation in return for the distributed corporation issuing shares to the shareholders of the distributing corporation. However, relief is only available where what is transferred to the distributed corporation is a business or business division and the distributing corporation retains a business or business division. Interests in partnerships and shares in wholly owned subsidiaries are treated as a business division for this purpose.[117] The Reorganisation Law requires that the members of the distributing corporation approve the de-merger. If the distribution is not proportionate to their holdings in the distributing corporation, the approval must be unanimous.[118]

As with de-merger relief in other countries, the German relief is subject to substantial anti-abuse rules. One such rule denies the relief if the business division was created during the three years before the merger by a transfer of assets that did not itself constitute a business division. Broadly, this is targeted at 'enveloping' a group of assets that are not a business division in a wholly owned partnership or subsidiary that is deemed to be a business division.[119] Further, the merger must not be used as a preparation for the sale of shares. Merger relief is retrospectively denied if, within five years of a de-merger, more than 20% of the shares in the distributed corporation are sold. Further, merger relief is not available unless the shares in the distributing corporation have existed for at least five years prior to the merger.[120]

### 7.2.2.2 Consequences for the shareholder

A shareholder in a de-merger by distribution or asset transfer receives shares in the distributed corporation. In the absence of relief, many countries treat this as a dividend and tax it as such. In addition, there is the issue of the cost base of the new shares in the hands of the shareholder.

---

[115] UmwStG (Germany) s. 15(1) first sentence.
[116] UmwStG (Germany) s. 1 referring to the concepts in the Reorganisation Law (*Umwandlungsgesetz*) (Germany) ss. 123 and 174.
[117] UmwStG (Germany) s. 15(1) second and third sentences.
[118] Reorganisation Law (*Umwandlungsgesetz*) (Germany) s. 128.
[119] As to 'enveloping', see the earlier discussion at 4.1.2.1.
[120] UmwStG (Germany) s. 15(2).

Although the shareholder will typically pay nothing for these shares, most countries would accept that whatever amount is treated and taxed like a dividend is the cost base of the shares. From the shareholder's perspective, de-merger relief typically ignores the dividend treatment. Further, it takes the cost base of the shares held by the shareholder in the distributing corporation before the de-merger and spreads it across the shares held in the distributing and distributed corporations post de-merger, typically in proportion to market value.

However, the two primary issues that arise for shareholders in the context of merger relief also arise for shareholders in the context of de-merger relief. One issue is the extent to which the shareholder has an option to elect for the relief or not. The second is the extent of the relief and whether the relief is all or nothing or whether there is the possibility of recognising and being taxed on a partial dividend.

In the US, the approach is similar to that for merger relief. De-merger relief is in principle compulsory and the shareholder has no option to elect whether it applies. In a de-merger by distribution, the US rule provides that 'no gain or loss shall be recognized to (and no amount shall be includible in the income of)' the shareholder on the receipt of the shares in the distributed corporation.[121] The effect of this rule is to avoid dividend treatment. This rule also applies to a de-merger by asset transfer, which, as mentioned earlier at 7.2.2.1, presumes that the shares in the distributed corporation are first issued to the distributing corporation, which in turn distributes them to its own shareholders. The US permits a shareholder to receive other consideration in a de-merger by distribution that does not qualify for relief. This other consideration ('boot') is expressly given distribution treatment and so may result in a dividend under the usual rules.[122]

Presuming de-merger relief is provided to a shareholder, the cost base of the shares held in the distributing corporation before the de-merger is apportioned over the shares held in the distributing and distributed corporations after the de-merger. The apportionment of basis is prescribed in regulations.[123] As a general rule, the allocation is proportionate to the fair market value of the shares.[124] These rules apply whether the de-merger is by way of distribution or by way of asset transfer.

---

[121] IRC (US) s. 355(a)(1).
[122] IRC (US) s. 356(b).
[123] IRC (US) s. 358.
[124] Title 26 Code of Federal Regulations (US) § 1.358–2(a).

The UK rules are similar, although perhaps slightly more prescriptive. A distribution of shares in the distributed corporation under a qualifying de-merger (whether by way of distribution or assets transfer) is an 'exempt distribution'.[125] 'An exempt distribution is not a distribution of a company'.[126] Because such a distribution is also not a 'dividend' or 'income' within the ordinary meaning of those terms, a qualifying de-merger distribution is not directly taxable.

In the case of a de-merger by distribution and presuming the shares in the distributed corporation are received on capital account, these shares are not treated as a 'capital distribution' received with respect to the shares held in the distributing corporation.[127] This excludes the rule that capital distributions are treated as a partial realisation of the shares with respect to which they are received.[128] Rather, the reorganisation rules apply

> with necessary modifications ... as if [the distributing] company and the subsidiary whose shares are transferred were the same company and the distribution were a reorganisation of its share capital.[129]

The result is that the cost base of the shares held in the distributing corporation before the de-merger is spread across the shares held in both the distributing and distributed corporations after the de-merger.[130]

The rules for de-merger by asset transfer are similar, though not the same. Here the UK rules anticipate that the distributed corporation issues its shares directly to the shareholders of the distributing corporation, rather than, as in the US, issuing them to the distributing corporation that then distributes the shares to its own shareholders. This process may constitute a 'scheme of reconstruction', although only if the shareholders are issued with shares in the distributed corporation 'in proportion to ... their relevant holdings in' the distributing corporation.[131] If it is a scheme of reconstruction, then again the reorganisation rules are applied as though the distributing and the distributed corporations were the same corporation.[132]

---

[125] CTA 2010 (UK) ss. 1076 and 1077, respectively.
[126] CTA 2010 (UK) s. 1075.
[127] TCGA 1992 (UK) s. 192(2)(a).
[128] That is, TCGA 1992 (UK) s. 122, discussed earlier at 6.1.1.
[129] TCGA 1992 (UK) s. 192(2)(b).
[130] TCGA 1992 (UK) s. 130.
[131] TCGA 1992 (UK) s. 136(1).
[132] TCGA 1992 (UK) s. 136(2).

In the context of a merger, Australia gives the shareholders the choice as to whether to receive tax relief. In the context of a de-merger, this choice is in the hands of the distributing corporation. The distributing corporation may, in effect, elect that all shareholders receive dividend treatment.[133] If no such election is made, then the shares received in a qualifying de-merger (a 'de-merger dividend') are 'not assessable income'.[134] In the usual manner, the cost base of the shares in the distributing corporation is apportioned between the shares held in the distributing and distributed corporations after the de-merger. The apportionment is according to the market value of the shares.[135] It is not clear that any additional cost base is received should the distributing corporation elect for dividend treatment of its shareholders.

Again, the German treatment is somewhat different from that in the other countries. Where a de-merger qualifies under the Reorganisation Tax Law, that law applies the relief provisions that are applicable to mergers by fusion.[136] These were discussed earlier at 7.2.1.2. There seems to be no express provision that excludes dividend treatment. However, if tax relief is available (with the permission of the tax administration), the shares in the distributed corporation 'take the place of' shares in the distributing corporation. Taken literally, this rule seems to exclude dividend treatment and produce a cost base spreading.[137] In particular, the tax administration requires the spreading of the cost base of the shares in the distributing corporation across the shares held in the distributing and distributed corporations after de-merger. The apportionment may be according to the exchange ratio in the de-merger plan, but is otherwise performed according to the fair market value of the shares.[138]

### 7.2.2.3 Consequences for the distributing corporation

In a de-merger by way of distribution, the distributing corporation disposes of its shares in the distributed corporation. Without relief, this could give rise to a tax liability if the cost base of the shares is less than their

---

[133] Income Tax Assessment Act 1936 (Australia) s. 44(2).

[134] Income Tax Assessment Act 1936 (Australia) s. 44(4).

[135] Income Tax Assessment Act 1997 (Australia) ss. 125–80 and 125–90.

[136] UmwStG (Germany) s. 15(1).

[137] UmwStG (Germany) s. 13(2).

[138] Federal Ministry of Finance (Bundesfinanzministerium) Decree of 11 November 2011 concerning the application of the Reorganisation Tax Law (IV C 2 – S 1978-b/08/10001) paras. 15.42 and 15.43. The decree is available at http://www.bundesfinanzministerium.de (accessed 16 July 2012).

market value. The same could be true of a de-merger by way of asset transfer. In this case, the distributing corporation may receive shares in the distributed corporation in consideration for the transfer of assets to the distributed corporation and then distribute those shares to its own shareholders. In addition, a de-merger by asset transfer also involves a transfer of assets by the distributing corporation to the distributed corporation. De-merger relief typically extends to disregard any gain or loss made by the distributing corporation with respect to these disposals.

For example, US tax law prescribes that 'no gain or loss shall be recognized to a corporation on any distribution to which' de-merger relief applies.[139] This rule covers any distribution of shares in the distributed corporation, whether in a de-merger by way of distribution or by way of assets transfer.[140] Further, relief is provided for the transfer of assets to the distributed corporation by the distributing corporation in a de-merger by way of assets transfer. As mentioned earlier at 7.2.2.1, such a de-merger may qualify as a type D reorganisation. As such, the usual rules on reorganisations apply, and so if the assets are transferred 'solely for stock or securities' in the distributed corporation, then '[n]o gain or loss shall be recognized' by the distributing corporation.[141]

By contrast, the UK provides no express relief for a corporation distributing shares in a subsidiary in the course of a de-merger by distribution. However, the participation exemption (discussed earlier at 5.1.3.1) is often available. By contrast, relief may be secured in the context of a de-merger by way of asset transfer. As noted earlier at 7.2.2.2, the UK rules anticipate that the distributed corporation will issue its shares directly to the shareholders of the distributing corporation, and this may constitute a 'scheme of reconstruction'. As a result, the same provision as discussed earlier at 7.2.1.3 may apply to treat the transfer of assets from the distributing corporation to the distributed corporation as taking place at a consideration that secures neither gain nor loss for the transferring distributing corporation.[142] As noted at that point, this treatment does not extend to trading stock or depreciable assets unless the distributing and distributed corporations are related.

---

[139] IRC (US) s. 355(c)(1).
[140] Although shares distributed in a de-merger by assets transfer would also be covered by IRC (US) s. 361(c)(1).
[141] IRC (US) s. 361(a)(1). Regarding this provision, see the earlier discussion at 7.2.1.4.
[142] TCGA 1992 (UK) s. 139.

The Australian rules provide a focus that is the reverse of the UK focus. The Australian rules provide clear relief for the distributing corporation with respect to the disposal of shares in the distributed corporation in the context of a de-merger by way of distribution. Any 'capital gain or capital loss' that a distributing corporation makes from the disposal of shares in the distributed corporation 'is disregarded'.[143] By contrast, there is no express relief for the transfer of assets by a distributing corporation to a distributed corporation in the context of a de-merger by way of assets transfer. However, such relief may be available if the distributing and distributed corporations are part of a wholly owned group.

As for Germany, as noted earlier at 7.2.2.2, the rules on mergers by way of fusion are applied to de-mergers by way of assets transfer. This means that the transfer of assets by the distributing corporation to the distributed corporation is generally considered as made at market value. This transfer may crystallise a gain to the distributing corporation. However, with the permission of the tax administration, the transfer may be considered made at anywhere between the market value and the distributing corporation's book value of the assets.[144] If book value is used, the distributing corporation will realise no gain from the transfer.

### 7.2.2.4 Consequences for the distributed corporation and survival of tax attributes

In a simple de-merger by way of distribution, very little happens to the distributed corporation. It retains its separate existence and all of its assets. It does, however, suffer a change of ownership, although if the distribution is proportionate, it will not be a change in underlying (indirect) ownership. This change of ownership may trigger restrictions on the carry-forward of tax attributes (discussed earlier at 5.2.2 and 5.2.3), but in many cases these restrictions are not triggered. Perhaps more importantly, such a de-merger may cause the distributed corporation to leave a corporate group (typically a grouping with the distributing corporation), and so the considerations discussed earlier at 5.2.4 may be relevant.

These issues also arise in the context of a de-merger by way of asset transfer, with the same considerations applying. In addition, the distributed corporation acquires the assets transferred to it by the distributing corporation. In the usual manner, if this transfer has received non-recognition treatment in the hands of the distributing corporation, the

---

[143] Income Tax Assessment Act 1997 (Australia) s. 125–155.
[144] UmwStG (Germany) s. 11.

distributed corporation will take over the distributing corporation's cost base with respect to the assets. So, because such a de-merger is a reorganisation under US tax law, the cost base of the assets received by the distributed corporation will be the 'same as it would be in the hands of the' distributing corporation.[145]

Similarly, in the UK the distributed corporation takes over the cost base of the assets in the hands of the distributing corporation, at least in respect of capital assets.[146] This is also the case in Germany if the distributed corporation takes up the assets received at the book value of the transferring distributing corporation.[147] As noted earlier, Australia has no special rules for transfers in the course of a de-merger by way of assets transfer.

German de-merger relief only applies in the context of a de-merger by way of assets transfer and only if the assets transferred and those that remain with the distributing corporation constitute an independently viable business (see the earlier discussion at 7.2.2.1). Further, the de-merger must comply with the formal corporate law requirements of the Reorganisation Law (*Umwandlungsgesetz*). When these requirements are met, then any loss carried forward by the distributing corporation may be split between it and the distributed corporation. The allocation is based on the fair market value of the assets transferred when compared to the fair market value of all of the assets of the distributing corporation prior to the de-merger.[148]

It is possible to achieve a similar result in the UK within a 75% group through the use of the hive-down procedure (discussed earlier at 4.2). Where a trade is transferred to the distributed corporation by the distributing corporation and they are both within a 75% group, any carried-forward losses of the trade may also be transferred to the distributed corporation. The distributed corporation may then be de-merged. By contrast, in the US, despite a de-merger by way of assets transfer constituting a reorganisation, the rules discussed earlier at 7.2.1.4 regarding transfer of tax attributes in a merger by way of fusion do not apply.[149]

---

[145] IRC (US) s. 362(b).
[146] TCGA 1992 (UK) s. 139(1).
[147] UmwStG (Germany) s. 12.
[148] UmwStG (Germany) s. 15(3).
[149] See IRC (US) s. 381(a) and Bittker & Eustice (2003–, para. 11.12[5]).

# Dividend and capital stripping and value shifting

This book has focused on three primary artificialities faced by a tax system that derive from the nature of a corporation. The first is the artificiality of the corporation as a separate income-deriving entity. This was the focus of Chapter 1. The second is the artificiality of the corporation as a separate source of income in the form of dividends. This was the focus of Chapter 2. The third is the artificiality of interests in corporations as a separate form of asset from the assets held by corporations. This was the focus of Chapters 4–7, which discussed dealings in share interests.

These artificialities interact in various ways. The primary outcome from the interaction of the first two artificialities (corporation deriving income and source of dividend income) is the problem of economic double taxation of distributed corporate income. This was discussed earlier at 2.3 and 2.4. The primary outcome from the interaction of the first and third artificialities (corporation deriving income and derivative nature of shares) is the problem of economic double taxation of gains on the disposal of shares. This was discussed earlier at 5.1.2 and 5.1.3. What is yet to be discussed directly is the interaction of the second and third artificialities (source of dividend income and derivative nature of shares). That interaction is the focus of this chapter.

Chapter 6 noted how payments by a corporation on a termination of shares can conflate the distribution of corporate profits and the disposal of shares into a single event. Outside of terminations of share interests, dividends and gains on the disposal of shares are separate events, but are inherently linked in at least two ways. First, a shareholder, especially a controlling shareholder, often has a choice between receiving dividends and deriving a gain on the disposal of shares. Second, as noted earlier at 5.1.2, the distribution of dividends has a stripping effect on the value of shares and so may erode potential gains on their disposal. This means that if these two artificialities interact (i.e. a particular arrangement involves both dividends and a disposal of shares), which event occurs first may be critical in determining the tax treatment of particular persons.

Assuming that a corporation has profits available that can be used to distribute dividends, there are three primary orders that might affect the tax liability of shareholders. First, shares may be sold at a value inflated by the corporate profits, and then dividends are distributed to the purchaser. This scenario involves the sale of a potential income stream in the form of dividends and might particularly be used by a shareholder who favours capital gains over dividends. Second, dividends may be distributed to the shareholder who then sells the shares at a value deflated by the dividends. This is often referred to as 'capital stripping' and might particularly be used by a shareholder who favours dividends over capital gains. Third, there may be a combination of the first two scenarios. This scenario involves the sale of shares with an inflated value, the stripping of that value by the purchaser receiving dividends and the resale of those shares at a deflated value back to the original owner. This is often referred to as a 'full dividend strip' and might be used by a shareholder who favours capital gains but who does not really want to part with ownership of the corporation.

This chapter considers each of these three scenarios in turn. In passing, it may be noted that this chapter is fundamentally concerned with issues of substance over form and with the fungibility of dividends and gains on the disposal of shares.[1] As noted earlier at 5.1.3.1, it may be argued that if dividends and capital gains on the disposal of shares were taxed in the same manner, the tax problems raised by fungibility would be resolved. A primary issue for consideration in this chapter is whether that claim is necessarily the case.

The issues discussed in this chapter are complex and often interact with broader concepts underlying the income tax law, generally including those developed by case law. Those broader concepts are beyond the scope of this book, and the following is only a brief consideration of the issues in question. Because at this stage the CCCTB Proposal does not have express rules dealing with the situations covered by this chapter and because there

---

[1] Earlier, this book considered the fungibility of dividends with some other returns. It considered the fungibility of returns, including dividends, on hybrid instruments (at 2.1). It considered the fungibility of dividends with other payments to shareholders and, in particular, constructive dividends (at 2.2). It considered the problem of dividend streaming where dividends are taxed differently from other types of payments from corporations (at 2.4.1.5). It considered the fungibility of dividends with returns of capital (at 2.5.2.1). Those scenarios differ from the ones considered in this chapter in that in each of them there was a presumption that there was no alteration to the shareholder's interest in the corporation (i.e. no share dealing was involved).

has been no opportunity to develop case law in this respect, it is not considered.

## 8.1    Dividends into capital: just the disposal

The scenario for consideration involves a corporation with profits available for distribution. Here the shareholder wishing a return on shares has a choice: wait for a distribution of the profits or sell the shares and realise the value of the profits in the form of a capital gain. Of course, these are not equal choices (see the earlier discussion at 5.1.3.1). One involves a continuing interest in the corporation and questions of deduction of costs incurred in deriving the dividends (e.g. interest on money borrowed to acquire the shares). The other involves a departure from the corporation, consideration received not just for the retained profits of the corporation but also for its potential earnings (including unrealised gains) and the deduction of the cost of the shares in calculating the gain. Especially in closely held corporations, the amount subject to tax can be wildly different, even before account is taken of any difference in treatment between the taxation of dividends and the taxation of gains on the disposal of shares.

Considering these fundamental differences, it is not surprising that as a general rule corporate tax systems accept the form of a disposal of shares, even if the taxpayer's primary intention is to realise his or her share of retained profits of a corporation. There are, however, two primary scenarios that require further investigation – where a corporate tax system may hesitate to recognise this form as a simple capital gain when an interest in the shares of a corporation inflated with profits is disposed of. The first scenario is where what is disposed of is not a full interest in the shares, but only the right to receive dividends. This is especially the case when the disposal of the right to receive dividends is only temporary. The second scenario is where the corporation whose shares are disposed of has already declared a dividend but the dividend has not yet been paid by the time of the disposal.

A potential third scenario is where the corporation does not have realised profits, but has unrealised gains that have not been taxed at the corporate level. Here, to distribute a dividend might require the corporation to realise the profits and incur a corporation tax liability, as well as a shareholder tax liability on the distributed dividends. By contrast, a simple sale of the shares may give the shareholder access to the unrealised gain in the corporation without a corporation tax liability. This is the enveloping problem, which was considered earlier at 5.1.2. The related question of whether a corporation that suffers a change of control should be considered to realise its assets was discussed earlier at 5.2.2.2. These issues are not pursued again as a separate matter here.

### 8.1.1 *Disposal of dividends*

Disposal of the right to receive dividends (or any income stream) raises difficult questions for a tax system. The first question is the tax treatment of the disposal: is the transaction taxable and what character does it have? The second is one of attribution; that is, when the corporation pays a dividend on the shares, who is treated as receiving it: the assignor or the assignee? Another question relates to the treatment for the assignee of any consideration paid for the right: can it be amortised or deducted in any other fashion?

The US has no specific statutory rules dealing with the disposal of the right to receive dividends. Rather, the dominant feature for consideration is the complex and sometimes obscure assignment of income doctrine as it applies to assignments of property.[2] Because the disposal of the right to receive dividends is not a transfer of the income-producing property (i.e. the shares), the transfer of the right to receive dividends is unlikely to be respected for tax purposes. This means the transferor of the right is likely to remain liable to tax with respect to the receipt of the dividends. This is clearly the case where there is a gratuitous transfer of the right to receive dividends, but the situation is more complex where consideration is received for the transfer. In the latter case US courts have often held that the payment for the right is an advance or loan from the transferee to the transferor, in which case the transferor would only recognise dividend income when the dividends were actually paid (to the transferee). However, if the transaction is concluded at arm's length, there is some scope for recognising that the transferor must account for the sale proceeds as income.[3]

By contrast, common law jurisdictions based on the UK tradition have historically hesitated to recognise a gain from the sale of an income stream as income. It was quite possible to sell the right to receive dividends and expect the sale to be treated as an exempt capital gain.[4] However, some

---

[2] Generally regarding the application of the assignment of income doctrine, see Bittker & Lokken (1999–, chapter 75).

[3] See Bittker & Eustice (2003–, para. 8.07[1][d]) and the references cited therein.

[4] *Paget* v. *IRC* [1938] 2 KB 25 (CA). This approach was reinforced as late as *IRC* v. *John Lewis Properties plc* [2002] EWCA Civ 1869 (CA) (assignment of rent income for six years held to be capital).

common law jurisdictions moved on from this approach some time ago to find such payments as income in nature.[5] Since 2009 the UK has had a comprehensive statutory rule that applies to treat the value of a transferred income stream as income. In the usual fragmented UK fashion, these rules are rewritten separately for income tax and corporation tax purposes. The consequence is that consideration received for the transfer or, if more, its market value is treated as income of the seller.[6] Nevertheless, the treatment of consideration on the sale of a dividend stream as income does not necessarily mean that the income is characterised as dividends or taxed as dividends. In both the UK and Australia, the consideration is generically characterised and taxed as income and so would not have the character of dividends.[7]

Further, treatment of consideration on the sale of a dividend stream as income does not mean that the dividends received by the acquirer of the stream are treated as dividends for tax purposes. In particular, receipt of the dividends by the acquirer may not be taxed as dividends if the tax law requires receipt of the dividend by a person who is a shareholder. Technically, this is the case in the US where 'dividend' is defined in terms of a distribution to a 'shareholder'.[8] The same is true in Australia, where the receipt of the dividend by the assignor would not be taxed as a dividend because it is not received by a 'shareholder'.[9] However, it may be effectively treated in the same fashion because of the rules for 'non-share equity interests'.[10] Even if the tax law treats the assignee as receiving dividends, this does not mean that the recipient is entitled to any dividend relief available for dividends. For example, the fact that the shares are not transferred may make it difficult for the recipient of dividends to satisfy the 'at risk' rules that pre-empt dividend relief in both the US and Australia (see the earlier discussion at 2.4.3).

By contrast, the position is different in the UK, where the tax law simply charges 'dividends' without expressly requiring that they be received by a shareholder. For example, in the case of an individual, the UK will charge

---

[5] For example, see the Australian case of *FCT* v. *Myer Emporium Ltd* (1987) 163 CLR 199 (HC). Income Tax Assessment Act 1936 (Australia) s. 102CA now covers these types of income assignments.

[6] ITA 2007 (UK) Part 13 Chapter 5A (ss. 809AZA to 809AZG) and CTA 2010 (UK) Part 16 Chapter 1 (ss. 752 to 757).

[7] ITA 2007 (UK) s. 809AZB, CTA 2010 (UK) s. 753 and Income Tax Assessment Act 1936 (Australia) s. 102CA(1).

[8] IRC (US) s. 316(a).

[9] Income Tax Assessment Act 1936 (Australia) ss. 6(1) (definition of 'dividend') and 44(1).

[10] See Income Tax Assessment Act 1936 (Australia) s. 43B and the earlier discussion at 2.1.2.

the person 'to whom the distribution is made … or … the person receiving or entitled to the distribution'.[11] Dividend relief in the UK typically follows from the receipt of a payment that is properly characterised as a dividend.

Germany has no express assignment of income provision in its income tax law, and the rules on attribution of income are determined by the words used with respect to each source of income subject to tax. In particular, investment income 'is attributed to the person who is the (beneficial) owner of the underlying capital'. This means that if 'only the bare right to income (e.g., a dividend on stock or interest on a bond), is transferred, the income remains taxable to the holder of the underlying asset'.[12] However, where a right to receive dividends has been transferred under a usufruct, it is the transferee / usufructuary (not the transferor) that is treated as receiving the dividends.[13] Dividend treatment including dividend relief follows the correct attribution of dividend income. Receipt of a payment for the income stream, although not a dividend, may still constitute other income.

A special German rule applies to the sale of dividend coupons. Investment income includes profit from the sale

> of dividend coupons and other claims by the holder of the ordinary rights,
> if the accompanying shares or other shares are not sold at the same time.
> Taxation shall replace taxation in accordance with paragraph 1.[14]

This means that the consideration received by the seller of the right to receive dividends is treated as a dividend in the hands of the seller and the seller may be entitled to dividend relief with respect to this payment. Further, this treatment excludes dividend treatment of the actual dividends, whether in the hands of the seller or the purchaser. This does not mean, however, that the actual dividends received by the purchaser are not income. They may nevertheless be treated as other income (not dividends), and a question would be whether the price paid for the right could be deducted or amortised.

### 8.1.2 Sales cum-dividend

The distinction between dividends and gains on the disposal of shares also blurs where shares are sold at a time when a dividend has been declared but

---

[11] ITTOIA 2005 s. 385.
[12] Ault & Arnold (2010, p. 329).
[13] EStG (Germany) s. 20(5).
[14] EStG (Germany) s. 20(2) No.2(a).

not paid. In this context, share markets often make a distinction between the sale of shares cum-dividend (where the purchaser has the right to the next dividend) or ex-dividend (where the seller retains the right to the next dividend). Generally, sales of shares ex-dividend do not raise issues of turning dividends into gains on the disposal of shares because the dividend is received by the seller, who was the shareholder at the time the dividend accrued. This is not necessarily true in the context of sales of shares cum-dividend and here we need to distinguish between two situations depending on who is the shareholder on the record date (i.e. the date the corporation uses for determining who gets the dividend).

In the first scenario, the purchaser is the shareholder on the record date and will receive the dividend. Here, unless the tax law re-characterises, the seller manages to 'sell' the expectant dividend for disposal proceeds. This seems to be the case in the UK. The purchaser both receives and is entitled to the dividend.[15] This is also the position in the US:

> When stock is sold between the time of declaration and the time of payment of the dividend, and the sale takes place at such time that the purchaser becomes entitled to the dividend, the dividend ordinarily is income to him. The fact that the purchaser may have included the amount of the dividend in his purchase price in contemplation of receiving the dividend does not exempt him from tax. Nor can the purchaser deduct the added amount he advanced to the seller in anticipation of the dividend. That added amount is merely part of the purchase price of the stock.[16]

The position seems to be the same in Australia. However, in both the US and Australia the purchaser's entitlement to dividend relief will depend on holding the shares at risk for the requisite holding period (usually 45 days; see the earlier discussion at 2.4.3).

The position in Germany requires further consideration. As noted earlier at 8.1.1, the person taxable with respect to dividends is the shareholder and

> [t]he shareholder is the individual to whom the shares...are attributable pursuant to section 39 of the Tax Code at the time of the resolution ordering the distribution of profits.[17]

Under section 39 of the Tax Code, attribution generally follows legal ownership. Without more, the seller is the owner at the time the dividend is

---

[15]  ITTOIA 2005 s. 385.
[16]  Title 26 Code of Federal Regulations (US) § 1.61–9(c).
[17]  EStG (Germany) s. 20(5).

declared and so would be considered to receive the dividend. However, section 39 goes on:

> If another than the owner exercises control over economic goods in a way that he can exclude the owner for the useful life of the goods from the economic enjoyment of the goods, then the economic goods are to be added to him.[18]

In many cases, this may well be true of a purchaser of shares cum-dividend, in which case the purchaser will be treated as the shareholder and as receiving the dividend. Dividend relief follows dividends and so is available to a person to whom dividends are attributed.

In the second scenario, the seller is still the shareholder on the record date and receives the dividend even if by the payment date the purchaser is now the formal owner of the shares. However, due to the cum-dividend terms of the sale, if the seller receives the dividend the seller must pass the dividend on to the purchaser (i.e. the purchaser is entitled to the dividend). The US has a general rule dealing with this scenario: 'When stock is sold after the declaration of a dividend and after the date as of which the seller becomes entitled to the dividend, the dividend ordinarily is income to the seller'.[19]

The UK rules are similar, though more prescriptive. Under the UK manufactured dividend rules, the actual dividend is included in the income of the recipient seller. However, the payment of the dividend to the purchaser may be deductible to the seller and treated as a dividend in the hands of the purchaser for which dividend relief is available. In the usual way, these rules are repeated for both income tax and corporation tax.[20] These rules have been continuously restricted in recent years due to perceived abuses.

The German rules applicable to this second scenario are the same as those applicable to the first. The difference in this second scenario is that the seller is not only the shareholder at the time of the dividend resolution but is also the recipient of the dividend. Nevertheless, because the seller must pass on the dividend it is possible that the purchaser qualifies as the economic owner of the shares and so the dividends. Australia reaches this

---

[18] AO (Germany) s. 39(2).

[19] Title 26 Code of Federal Regulations (US) § 1.61–9(c). The exception is where 'the seller receives the dividends only because the seller retains legal title to the stock to secure payment'. In such a case the purchaser is taxable on the dividend received and adjustments are made to the consideration for the sale. See Bittker & Eustice (2003–, para. 8.07[2][a]).

[20] ITA 2007 (UK) ss. 573 to 577 and CTA 2010 (UK) ss. 782 to 789.

conclusion expressly, if only in the context of listed shares. The Australian rules deem the purchaser of the shares to receive the dividend (paid to the seller) as shareholder. This means that the purchaser may qualify for dividend tax credits as long as the purchaser subsequently holds the shares at risk for 45 days. This deemed receipt only applies to shares sold cum-dividend on an approved Australian stock exchange.[21]

## 8.2   Capital re-characterised: value shift then disposal

The earlier discussion at 8.1 presumed a shareholder wishing to turn dividends into capital gains. This may particularly happen where gains on the disposal of shares are taxed less than dividends, which often occurs in the context of the taxation of individuals. However, the opposite can occur. A shareholder may be taxed less on dividends than on the disposal of shares, in which case there is an incentive to distribute dividends prior to an intended sale of shares in a corporation. The distribution of dividends prior to sale reduces the value of the shares and so reduces any gain (or may increase a loss) that may be realised on the disposal of the shares. This is commonly referred to as 'capital stripping', although as is discussed, reducing the value of shares may be achieved through other mechanisms.

A tax preference for dividends over gains on the disposal of shares can particularly be in issue in the context of the sale of shares by a corporate shareholder. Some countries try to treat dividends and sales of shares by corporate shareholders similarly. This is the case with the German participation exemption. Other countries adopt a diametrically opposed treatment such as the US and Australia, which tax the sale of shares by corporate shareholders (and recognise losses) but to a large extent do not tax dividends received by such shareholders. This can also happen in the UK because the breadth of the exemption for inter-corporate dividends is wider than it is for gains on the disposal of shares by corporate shareholders.

The current discussion presumes a shareholder that wishes to sell shares or otherwise divest him- or herself of an interest in shares. It is also presumed that such a disposal will give rise to a taxable gain that the shareholder wishes to avoid. To achieve this reduction in the gain, the shareholder needs to reduce the value of the shares prior to sale. Value can be removed directly from the shares by altering or diluting the rights attached to the shares. This is referred to a 'direct value shifting'. Value can be

---

[21]   Income Tax Assessment Act 1997 (Australia) s. 216–5.

indirectly removed from shares by altering the value of the corporation in which the shares are held. This is referred to as 'indirect value shifting'.

Value shifting is a problem where a shareholder seeks to reduce the taxation of a gain on an intended disposal of shares. It can also be a problem where a shareholder seeks to manufacture a loss and then crystallise the loss through a sale of shares even if the shareholder (and associates) does not end up parting with the interest in the corporation. The point is that value shifting can be used to reduce a gain or manufacture a loss. In either case there is a concern that the tax system is being manipulated.

Value shifting emphasises the artificial nature of the corporation and how easy it is to manipulate that form and the interests in it. Therefore, it is more of a problem in jurisdictions that are prone to accepting form over substance. So it is not surprising that the UK and Australia have comprehensive rules dealing with value shifting, the US has a limited number of rules while German does not have any express rules. The following discussion briefly considers direct value shifting and then indirect value shifting.

In passing, it may be noted that the primary tax policy issue considered in both Chapters 4 and 7 was whether a formal change in investment that occurs without a substantial change in the economic substance of the investment is sufficient so as to justify tax consequences arising from the change. In many ways, this heading focuses on the reverse of that. Value shifting often involves a scenario in which there has been, in substance, a transfer of an interest in shares, but there is no legal disposal event to which to attach tax consequences. Value shifting often involves the issue of shares or the alteration or termination of rights attached to shares. It may be thought of as an informal method of transferring share interests. As such, value shifting rules often involve a tax law deeming a disposal of shares where one does not exist from a formal legal perspective.

### 8.2.1 Direct value shift

A direct value shift involves adjusting the rights attached to a share interest in a corporation in a way that gives rise to an increase in value of other shares in the corporation. For example, in the famous Australian case of *Peabody*, value was removed from ordinary shares in a corporation by converting them to 1% preference shares. The value was deposited in certain exempt shares in the corporation held by an associate.[22] Both sets of shares

---

[22] *FCT v. Peabody* (1994) 181 CLR 359 (HC).

were disposed of in a public floatation of the corporation. Such a blatant manipulation of shareholder rights may not be possible under the corporate law of many countries where shareholders are guaranteed certain minimum rights. However, as the Australian case demonstrates, it is possible under the corporate law of many other countries.

A direct value shift may also be achieved without a direct alteration of rights attached to shares. In particular, it may be achieved by a corporation issuing shares at undervalue (including bonus shares). If shares are issued at a value less than the proportionate value of the corporation that the shares represent, there will be a shift of value from existing shares to the new shares (see the earlier discussion at 7.1.2). For countries that have statutory pre-emption rights in their corporate law, these rights will have to be waived by the existing shareholders for the issue of shares to proceed. Unless the form of such a transaction is looked through, an arm's length pricing rule will not be sufficient to address this type of manipulation. That rule would only deem the new shareholder to have paid market value for the shares. Something further would be needed to address the tax arbitrage (e.g. a deemed dividend or a deemed sale of part of the existing shares).

The tax arbitrage arises because two interests in a corporation are not taxed in the same manner. In *Peabody*, it was the difference between shares that were taxable and shares that were exempt (because they were acquired before the taxation of capital gains was introduced). This sort of difference happens often. For example, shares held by other corporations or non-resident persons are often exempt, whereas shares held by individuals are often taxable. One shareholder may have a loss that can be used against a gain on the disposal of shares, whereas another may not.

In addressing direct value shifting, whether by express rules or through anti-avoidance doctrines, an issue is how it should be characterised. In substance it appears to involve the disposal of an interest by a shareholder in the corporation to another or new shareholder in the corporation. The problem is that the artificial personality of the corporation sits in the way, with the consequence that there may in form be no disposal of an interest in the shares from which the value is shifted. The corporation may simply have granted addition rights to another, with the result that there is less attributable to the residual rights of those shares.

Direct value shifting most commonly occurs between shares held by related persons (or the same person). This means that if there is a tax law response in this case, it is most likely to be a disposal of the shares from which the value is shifted for a market value consideration. This is what happens under the UK direct value shifting rule. It applies where

> a person having control of a company exercises his control so that value passes out of shares in the company owned by him or a person with whom he is connected ... and passes into other shares in or rights over the company.

In such a case, the value shift is treated as 'a disposal of the shares ... out of which the value passes'.[23] The Australian rules are broadly similar to those in the UK, although to suffer consequences under the Australian rules the person must be an 'active participant' in the scheme that produces the value shift.[24]

By contrast, Germany appears to have no express rules to deal with direct value shifting. Rather, it would rely on addressing any abuse through general rules such as the hidden profits distribution rules (see the earlier discussion at 2.2.2) and the general anti-avoidance rule.[25] The US also has no direct express provisions targeting direct value shifts. However, regulations have been issued under section 305(c) of IRC that treat 'a wide variety of transactions as 'constructive' or 'deemed' distributions of stock with respect to the stock of any shareholder whose proportionate interest in the corporation's earnings or assets is increased by the transaction.'[26] This might create dividend income in an appropriate case. More generally, where a shareholder permits an erosion of share rights so as to benefit another shareholder, that action or inaction may be construed as a taxable gift to the beneficiary, though not a taxable dividend.[27] Such a result would not be available in many jurisdictions because they do not, in principle, tax gifts. In both Germany and the US consideration must also be given to transfer pricing rules, which may treat shareholders eroding their rights in favour of a related party as receiving a market value consideration.

Direct value shifting can also be used as a method of tax arbitrage between unrelated parties. However, in such a case it can be presumed that the person suffering a devaluation of his or her shares will require some form of market value compensation for that devaluation. In this case, identifying and characterising that compensation are the primary issues. In some instances this may involve allocation of the compensation

---

[23] TCGA 1992 (UK) s. 29(2).
[24] Income Tax Assessment Act 1997 (Australia) Division 725.
[25] AO (Germany) s. 42(1).
[26] Bittker & Eustice (2003–, para. 8.41[3]).
[27] Ibid., para. 8.41[7]).

to the shareholder by constructive receipt (e.g. where the compensation is actually received by a related party). Most countries would find a way of taxing the compensation if it is identified as the price paid for the alteration of the rights attaching to the devalued shares and allocated to the shareholder.

In the UK, the direct value shifting rule discussed earlier can apply to value shifts between unrelated parties. All that is required is a person exercising control over a corporation so as to cause the value shift. The beneficiary need not be a related party. Where the rule is triggered the deemed disposal of the devalued shares is treated as having been made for market value. Similarly, the Australian direct value shifting rules can apply as between unrelated parties. However, in this case, although there must be a controller, any of the active participants can cause the value shift.[28]

### 8.2.2  Indirect value shift

In contrast to direct value shifting, indirect value shifting involves taking value out of a corporation and thereby reducing the value of its shares. There are two simple and related mechanisms by which it might be done. The broader category is any transfer of value (payment) by the corporation for inadequate consideration (i.e. a gift). This transfer might even involve the gifting of tax attributes, such as the transfer of losses (where that is available) for no consideration. The second category is the distribution of dividends, which like the first, involves the transfer of value when there is no direct return to the corporation of an equal amount. The following discussion first considers the distribution of dividends to indirectly devalue shares and then considers devaluation by corporate gift.

In passing, it is noted that it is also possible to indirectly take value out of a corporation and thereby indirectly reduce the value of the shares in the corporation. This might happen where there is no formal payment to or by the corporation to constitute a gift, but value has been moved into or out of an asset of the corporation with no formal transfer. The most likely example that could fall within this category of indirect value shift is where value is shifted out of or into a share held by the corporation (i.e. a second or downstream phase of direct or indirect value shifting). This indirect form of devaluing a corporation is not considered separately.

---

[28] Income Tax Assessment Act 1997 (Australia) s. 725–65.

### 8.2.2.1 By distribution

The scenario for consideration involves a shareholder wishing to sell shares in a corporation and causing the corporation to distribute dividends prior to sale in order to reduce the gain on disposal (or increase a loss on disposal). This is only likely to be beneficial from a tax perspective if dividends are subject to less tax than gains on the disposal of shares. If the profits that are distributed were derived by the corporation while the shareholder held the shares, it may be thought that there is no abuse. However, the enveloping nature of a corporation (see the earlier discussion at 5.1.2) can cause particular difficulties in this regard. An example demonstrates these difficulties.

Presume A Co holds shares in B Co. B Co has a valuable asset that is worth substantially more than it cost (built-in gain). Due to the derivative nature of shares that gain is also built into the shares. A Co wishes to sell the shares in B Co (indirect transfer of the asset). If A Co is entitled to a participation exemption with respect to the sale, enveloping is a problem. This is the case in Germany and can be the case in the UK where the substantial shareholder exemption is available. By contrast, the US and Australia, and in some cases the UK, will tax the gain made on the sale of shares, and so enveloping is not such a problem. The gain on the asset (which is indirectly sold) is not taxed, but its reflective gain in the shares may be. However, if incorporate dividends are exempt, this can cause a different problem.

Here the incentive is to strip as much value as possible out of the corporation in the form of exempt dividends prior to the sale of the corporation. In some cases this might be facilitated by revaluing the asset. From an accounting and corporate law perspective, this revaluation might produce profits that can be distributed. Some countries' tax laws might recognise and tax such a profit to the corporation, but others do not tax because the asset has not been realised (only revalued). The actual funds for the dividend might be found through borrowing, either independently or even through loans from the purchaser of the shares. Depending on the corporate law and the position of the corporation in question, the availability of profits might not even be necessary to distribute an exempt dividend for tax purposes.

The point is that if gains on the disposal of shares are taxed more heavily than dividends there is an incentive to find ways of distributing dividends in order to reduce such gains. If left to their own devices, taxpayers may manipulate the situation so that the tax treatment of dividends is available, at least to some extent, for gains on the disposal of shares. A country that generally permits enveloping and taxes dividends and gains on the disposal of shares similarly may feel that there is nothing to be done in this case. This seems to be the position of Germany. However, enveloping can be a serious problem.

By contrast, despite creating an incentive for corporate shareholders to favour dividends over capital gains, the US has no express rules dealing with capital stripping by distribution of dividends. However, case law principles may treat the stripping dividend as additional sales proceeds, particularly if the funds used to pay the dividend come indirectly from the purchaser.[29]

Other countries may feel a need to do something. For example, the UK has a provision that applies where one corporation has a 10% shareholding in another corporation and a distribution is made that has the effect 'that the value of the holding is…materially reduced.'[30] However, this provision is targeted at the manufacture of capital losses and only applies to reduce a capital loss on the devalued shares 'to such extent as is just and reasonable'.[31] The provision does not apply to increase a gain on the disposal of the shares and does not apply to individuals who hold shares. The provision is entitled and particularly targeted at the practice of dividend stripping (see the later discussion at 8.3.2).

The UK also has a broader rule (reformulated in 2011) that applies to arrangements with a tax avoidance purpose, whereby shares held by one corporation in another corporation are 'materially reduced' and then disposed of.[32] The arrangements must involve more than an exempt inter-corporate dividend to a large corporation. Where the rule applies, consideration received on disposal of the shares is increased by 'such amount as is just and reasonable'. So this might increase a gain as well as reduce a loss on disposal. It does not apply to disposals of shares by individuals, although another rule may apply if an individual has managed to derive a tax-free benefit under an arrangement that materially reduces the value of shares prior to disposal.[33]

Australia also has express rules dealing with indirect value shifting.[34] These rules apply where a non-arm's length dealing occurs between a

---

[29]  See Bittker & Eustice (2003–, para. 8.07[2][a]) referring to *Waterman Steamship Corp* v. *United States* (1970) 430 F.2d 1185 (5th Cir).

[30]  TCGA 1992 (UK) s. 177(1).

[31]  TCGA 1992 (UK) s. 176(4).

[32]  TCGA 1992(UK) s. 31.

[33]  TCGA 1992(UK) s. 30.

[34]  Income Tax Assessment Act 1997 (Australia) Div. 727.

corporation and another person that results in a reduction in value of shares or loans in the corporation. The corporation and the beneficiary of the value shift must be connected, generally defined by reference to holding 50% of the corporation or being subject to 50% common control. As with the situation in the UK, these rules do not apply if the value shifted 'consists entirely' of a dividend.[35] The Australian rules also do not apply where they overlap with certain other rules and to certain small corporations. Where the rules apply, they adjust downwards the cost base of the shares that are devalued and increase upwards any shares that are increased in value.

### 8.2.2.2 By corporate gift

The scenario in question involves taking value out of a corporation by causing the corporation to part with assets in circumstances that do not involve, at least in form, a dividend. The purpose of the corporate gift is to reduce the value of the shares in the corporation. A simple example of such a scenario is where a person holds shares in both A Co and B Co. The person then causes A Co to make a gift to B Co (e.g. by the transfer of an asset at undervalue). This causes the value of the shares in A Co to decrease and the value of the shares in B Co to increase. The person may then sell the shares in A Co at a reduced gain or loss. Provided the person does not sell the shares in B Co (which now incorporate an unrealised gain), the person has managed to artificially reduce his or her tax liability on the disposal of A Co.

Because value has left A Co at the instruction of its controller, some countries such as the US may characterise the gift as a constructive dividend from A Co to the person and then as a contribution of capital by the person to B Co. Bittker and Eustice note case law for this treatment involving 'purported loans, purported businesses expenses, purported purchases of assets, and outright diversions. However, where transactions between affiliates are effected at arm's length, there should be no constructive distribution'.[36] Similarly, Germany may address this situation through its concept of hidden profits distribution:

> Because constructive dividends may be assumed also based on contractual relationships between sister companies the consequence of entering into contractual relationships not at arm's length are that (i) a hidden profit distribution takes place by the company whose equity is affected to the joint

---

[35] Income Tax Assessment Act 1997 (Australia) s. 727–250.
[36] Bittker & Eustice (2003–, para. 8.05[10]).

shareholder and (ii) a constructive contribution by the joint shareholder to the sister company which is tax neutral.[37]

A potential problem with this approach is that the shareholder may be entitled to dividend relief with respect to the deemed dividend, especially if the person is a corporation and an inter-corporate dividend exemption is available.

If gains on the disposal of shares are to be taxed appropriately, what is needed is a rule that adjusts the cost base of the shares held by the person (i.e. a decrease in the cost base of the shares in A Co in the amount of the gift and an increase in the cost base of the shares in B Co). This could happen in the US; for example, where the corporation from which value is shifted has no earnings and profits, the deemed distribution would effectively reduce the cost base of the shares held in that corporation. Germany seems to address this issue by treating a 'concealed capital contribution of shares in one incorporated company into another incorporated company' as a sale of shares.[38] The existence of minority shareholders can cause particular difficulties in this regard.

Other countries feel a need to more specifically address this sort of situation in their tax law. For example, the UK has a special rule dealing with 'depreciatory' transactions whereby the value of shares is 'materially reduced'. The provision expressly covers reductions caused by a 'disposal of assets at other than market value by one member of a group of companies to another' and certain other transactions.[39] The limit to transactions between 'group' corporations (defined in the usual way by reference to 75% ownership) makes the provision quite narrow. As with the rule on stripping value by way of distribution (discussed earlier at 8.2.2.1), this provision only applies to reduce a capital loss on the devalued shares 'to such extent as is just and reasonable'.[40]

The broader value shifting rules discussed earlier at 8.2.2.1 may also have application in the context of value shifting by way of corporate gift. Both the UK and Australian indirect value shifting rules are generally targeted at stripping share value by way of corporate gift rather than by way of distribution of a dividend: both are excluded where an arrangement involves no more than the distribution of a dividend. As noted, the

---

[37]   Whittmann (1983–, para. 32.05[2][d][i]).
[38]   EStG (Germany) s. 17(1). The effect seems to be the same under the Corporate Income Tax Law, although with different wording; KStG (Germany) s. 8b(2).
[39]   TCGA 1992 (UK) s. 176(1).
[40]   TCGA 1992 (UK) s. 176(4).

UK rules require an avoidance purpose, although the Australian rules do not.[41]

## 8.3 Disposal, value shift, disposal: stock lending, repos and the full strip

Finally, the interplay between gains on the disposal of shares and dividends may involve a combination of the scenarios considered earlier at 8.1 and 8.2. As noted at the start of this chapter, this scenario involves the sale of shares with an inflated value, the stripping of that value by the purchaser receiving dividends and the resale of those shares at a deflated value back to the original owner. The circularity of this third scenario emphasises the artificiality of the corporation and the substitutability of gains on the disposal of shares and dividends. Indeed, this scenario raises the fundamental question of whether the temporary holder of the shares should be considered a shareholder at all for tax purposes. This issue is clearly demonstrated in the tax treatment of stock lending and share repurchase agreements, the first matter briefly discussed. The discussion then considers the potentially abusive practice of dividend stripping.

### 8.3.1 Stock lending and share repurchase agreements

Under a stock lending agreement, a lender temporarily transfers shares to a borrower of the shares. In a simple case, the loan of the shares might be in return for the borrower paying a fee. However, the shares might also be transferred as security for funds loaned to the transferor by the transferee (i.e. a legal mortgage of shares). Share repurchase agreements are similar, being in economic substance (though not form) a secured loan. When the agreement is completed the transferee re-transfers the shares (or at least similar securities) back to the transferor.

The issue for present consideration is the treatment of any dividends received by the transferee while the transferee is the legal owner of the shares. Any such dividends are usually credited under the agreement in favour of the transferor, either as an increase in the fee payable by the transferee for the facility or, in the case of security for a loan of funds, against amounts payable by the transferor to the transferee such as interest. It is this crediting or set-off that raises the question of whether the

---

[41] TCGA 1992(UK) ss. 30 & 31.

transferee should receive dividend tax treatment with respect to such dividends or whether this treatment should be reserved for the transferor.

The US respects the secured financing nature of legal mortgages of shares. Further, for US tax purposes share repurchase agreements

> are treated as secured loans notwithstanding their legal form. That is, the repo 'seller' is treated as borrowing money from the repo 'buyer,' and the transfer of securities from the repo seller to the repo buyer is treated as the equivalent for tax purposes of the pledge of collateral by the repo seller to the repo buyer.[42]

This means that the transferee under these types of agreements is not treated as receiving the dividends, but only their financing charge as income. Rather, the transferor is treated as the person deriving the dividends received by the transferee during the term of the transfer.[43]

Germany has a simple rule in this regard. If dividends 'are attributable to a ... creditor, then that individual shall be deemed to be the shareholder.'[44] So, if a stock lending or share repurchase agreement creates a debtor / creditor relationship and under that agreement dividends are attributable to the transferor of the shares, that person will be treated as the shareholder.

The UK has dedicated rules for stock lending and share repurchase agreements, although they vary somewhat in their technical application. In a simple case involving a corporate share repurchase agreement, the sale and repurchase are effectively ignored. The borrower of the funds (transferor of the shares) is treated as receiving the dividends on the shares and may be entitled to dividend relief with respect thereto.[45] The lender of the funds (transferee of the shares) is treated as not owning the shares or receiving dividends, but as receiving interest equal to the financing charge shown in its accounts.[46] The sale and repurchase are ignored for purposes of recognition of capital gains and losses on disposal of shares.[47]

---

[42] Nijenhuis (2011, pp. 5–6).
[43] See Bittker & Eustice (2003–, para. 8.07[1][b]) and the references cited therein. The treatment is different where the shares are 'sold short' and the transferee on sells the shares to a third party. These are treated as 'securities loans'. Nijenhuis (2011, p. 6) notes that 'repos and securities loans traditionally have been analyzed under separate bodies of law. ... The precise dividing line between repos and securities loans under current law is unclear, and in many cases as a practical matter is driven by the form of the transaction'.
[44] EStG (Germany) s. 20(5).
[45] CTA 2009 (UK) s. 550.
[46] CTA 2009 (UK) ss. 545 and 551, respectively.
[47] Finance Act 2007 (UK) Sch. 13 paras. 6 and 11.

In the usual fragmented way, the UK has different rules for individuals participating in such arrangements. These rules are slightly different as they apply to stock lending and share repurchase agreements, but unlike the corporate rules the transfer of the shares is not ignored for purposes of determining who receives payments. Rather, the rules override the dividend treatment of the transferee and treat the transferee as paying a manufactured dividend to the transferor.[48] The rules ignore the capital gains effects of the transfer and retransfer.[49] The treatment of corporations engaged in stock lending will commonly fall under the corporate share repurchase agreement provisions. If it does not, stock lending will fall under a treatment that is broadly the same as that applying to individuals.[50]

Australia has similar, though less prescriptive rules. In particular, if the transfer of the shares is for less than twelve months it is ignored, although any fee payable for the facilitation of the arrangement is assessable.[51] For the purposes of the imputation system, any dividend received by the transferee under a securities lending agreement is 'taken to have been made' to the transferor as a shareholder and not to the transferee.[52] It is important that these provisions are complied with because, if they are not, the transferee will receive the dividends but will not be entitled to dividend tax credits because it is unlikely that the shares will be held at risk for forty-five days (see the earlier discussion at 2.4.3.3).

### 8.3.2  Full strip

Securities lending and share repurchase agreements serve a bona fide commercial function in the securities industry. By contrast, although similar in terms of events, dividend stripping is a practice that may be viewed as an intentional manipulation of the tax system for tax avoidance purposes. In its most serious form it has historically involved tax arbitrage between taxpayers in a tax system in which there is low or no taxation of gains on the disposal of shares, especially those held on capital account.

In its most abusive form (and prior to the introduction of a barrage of anti-abuse rules), dividend stripping involved a high-rate individual selling shares in a controlled corporation inflated with profits and not being

---

[48] ITA 2007 (UK) Part 11 Chapters 3 and 4 (ss. 592–605).
[49] TCGA 1992 (UK) s. 263A.
[50] CTA 2010 (UK) Part 17 Chapter 5 (ss. 805–812).
[51] Income Tax Assessment Act 1936 (Australia) s. 26BC.
[52] Income Tax Assessment Act 1997 (Australia) s. 216–10.

taxed on the resultant capital gain. The acquirer was a share trader who was entitled to dividend relief when the corporation distributed dividends (the profits were stripped by way of extraordinary dividend), such as an inter-corporate dividend exemption. This meant that the profits had been removed from the corporation and indirectly received by the high-rate individual in circumstances in which there was no tax payable. The 'kick in the teeth' for the tax administration was the next step.

The share trader had stripped the value out of the corporation through the distribution of dividends. In substance this was simply a return of the price paid for the shares, but the receipt of the dividend would not reduce the cost of the shares. So when the share trader subsequently disposed of the shares (often back to the original owner or an associate) the share trader made a large loss. If the shares were held as trading stock this would be a revenue loss. So the risk was that the tax system would get no tax on any of these transactions, but might have to provide relief to the share trader for what was in effect an artificial loss.[53]

There are many variations on this theme, some involving other transactions such as liquidations and share buy-backs and some involving stripping value by other means such as non-arm's length pricing and others involving timing differentials. Many countries responded with a barrage of increasingly complex rules before turning to addressing the structural features of their tax systems that facilitated the worst features of dividend stripping. This is not the place to engage in a comprehensive analysis of complex dividend stripping rules. It is sufficient to outline the broad ways in which countries might respond to this sort of behaviour.

The US had problems with dividends stripping, particularly through the use of the dividends-received deduction for inter-corporate dividends. This was primarily addressed in 1958 with the holding period requirement to qualify for that deduction, a requirement that was strengthened in 1984.[54] In the same year a rule was enacted that provides that if a 'corporation receives any extraordinary dividend with respect to any share of stock and such corporation has not held such stock for more than 2 years' the cost base of the shares is reduced by the non-taxed part of the dividend.[55] The non-taxed part is the part for which the dividends-received deduction is available (see the earlier discussion at 2.4.3.1). An 'extraordinary

---

[53]   This practice is well illustrated by the UK case of *Griffiths* v. *J P Harrison (Watford) Ltd* [1963] AC 1 (HL) and the Australian case of *Rodwell* v. *FCT* (1963) 111 CLR 106 (HC).
[54]   See Bittker & Eustice (2003–, para. 5.05[7][c]).
[55]   IRC (US) s. 1059.

dividend' is generally one that exceeds 10% of the cost of the shares. There is no equivalent provision for individuals in receipt of extraordinary dividends. In an appropriate case the anti-abuse rule in section 269 of IRC might also apply. It 'provides for the disallowance of deductions and other tax benefits when tax avoidance is the principal purpose for the acquisition of control of a corporation or for certain transfers of property from one corporation to another'.[56]

In the UK, dividend stripping is addressed through the transactions in securities provisions. These have a long and chequered history, and like so many other provisions in UK income tax law they now appear in quite different forms for income tax and corporation tax purposes.[57] The provisions are cast in anti-abuse terminology and so require a main purpose of obtaining a tax advantage or are excluded where the transaction is for 'genuine commercial reasons'. The legislation outlines obscure circumstances in which the provisions apply. However, generally they apply where there is a transaction in securities under which a person realises shares in a corporation in return for consideration that represents distributable amounts of the corporation. The consequence of the rules applying is that the tax administration has the power to issue a 'counteraction notice' removing a tax advantage that the transaction might otherwise give rise to.

Australia had a similar problem with dividend stripping, especially in the years before capital gains tax.[58] It addressed it by making sure that 'dividend stripping' (an undefined term) and a scheme 'in the nature of dividend stripping' are treated as producing a tax benefit to which Australia's general anti-avoidance rule applies.[59] This could have implications for the original seller, who might be treated as receiving income taxable at full marginal rates rather than deriving a capital gain from the disposal of shares taxed at concessional rates. Further, the actual dividend paid to the stripper will be denied the benefits of the imputation system. In particular, the recipient stripper is not entitled to an imputation credit with respect to a dividend received as part of the scheme.[60]

Germany had substantial problems with dividend stripping under its former imputation system and had a dedicated (if somewhat ineffective)

---

[56] See Bittker & Eustice (2003–, para. 14.41[1]).
[57] ITA 2007 (UK) Part 13 Chapter 1 (ss. 682 to 713) and CTA 2010 (UK) Part 15 (ss. 731–751). Generally, see Tiley (2008, pp. 1075–84).
[58] See Parsons (1985, paras. 6.81–6.141).
[59] Income Tax Assessment Act 1936 (Australia) s. 177E.
[60] Income Tax Assessment Act 1997 (Australia) s. 207–145.

rule to deal with it.[61] The dividend stripping rule was removed with the imputation system from 2001. The general anti-avoidance rule may have some continued application in this area.[62]

[61] Former EStG (Germany) Art. 50c.
[62] AO (Germany) s. 42(1).

# REFERENCES

Almand, K. & D. Sayers (2009), 'Hot topics in thin capitalisation' *Tax Journal*, No. 968, 5–6

Alworth, J. (2010), 'International capital taxation: Commentary', in Mirrlees et al. (eds), 998–1008

Amann, R. (ed.) (2001), *German tax guide* (The Netherlands: Kluwer Law International)

American Bar Association (2010), *Model Business Corporation Act: Official text with official comments and statutory cross-references revised through December 2010*, Corporate Laws Committee (US: ABA)

Andres, C., A. Betzer & M. Goergen (2012), 'Dividend policy, corporate control and the tax status of the controlling shareholder', 18 November 2011, available at http://ssrn.com/abstract=1978771

Ardizzoni, M. (2005), *German tax and business law* (London: Sweet & Maxwell)

Auerbach, A. (2006), 'Who bears the corporate tax? A review of what we know', in J. Poterba (ed.), *Tax policy and the economy*, NBER Book Series, Vol. 20 (Cambridge: MIT Press), 1–40

Auerbach, A., M. Devereux & H. Simpson (2010), 'Taxing corporate income', in Mirrlees et al. (eds.), chapter 9

Ault, H. & B. Arnold (eds.) (2010), *Comparative income taxation: a structural analysis*, 3rd edition (The Netherlands: Kluwer Law International)

Avery Jones, J. (1991), 'Bodies of persons', *British Tax Review*, 1991, 453–65

Avery Jones, J. (2011), 'Defining and taxing companies 1799 to 1965', in J. Tiley (ed.), *Studies in the history of tax law*, Vol. 5 (Oxford: Hart Publishing), 1–42

Avery Jones, J., P. Harris & D. Oliver (eds.) (2008), *Comparative perspectives on revenue law: essays in honour of John Tiley* (Cambridge: Cambridge University Press)

Bierce, A. (2010), *The devil's dictionary of Ambrose Bierce*, complete and unabridged special edition (Texas: El Paso Norte Press)

Bishop, C. (2011), 'The series LLC: tax classification appears in rear view', *Tax Notes*, Vol. 130, No. 3, Suffolk University Law School Research Paper No. 10–62, available at http://ssrn.com/abstract=1709445

Bittker, B. and Eustice, J (2003–), *Federal income taxation of corporations and shareholders* (US: RIA)

Bittker, B. and Lokken, L. (1999–), *Federal taxation of income, estates and gifts* (US: RIA)

BMR Advisors (2011), 'DTC countdown – the ALL NEW branch profit tax and the minimum alternate tax', *Worldwide Tax Daily*, 1 July 1, 2011 WTD 128–28

Bramwell, R. et al. (2009, loose-leaf), *Taxation of companies and company reconstructions*, 9th edition (London: Sweet and Maxwell)

Cahn, A. & D. Donald (2010), *Comparative company law* (Cambridge: Cambridge University Press)

Canada (2010), 'The taxation of corporate groups', Department of Finance Consultation Paper, November 2010, available at http://www.fin.gc.ca/activty/consult/tcc-igs-eng.pdf

Carmichael, D., R. Whittington & L. Graham (2012), *Accountants' handbook: financial accounting and general topics* (Hoboken, New Jersey: John Wiley & Sons)

Cooper, G. (2011), *A few observations on managing the taxation of corporate groups – the Australian experience*, Sydney Law School Research Paper No. 11/36, available at http://papers.ssrn.com/sol3/papers.cfm?abstract_id=1868650###

Crawford, C. and J. Freedman (2010), 'Small business taxation', in Mirrlees et al. (eds), chapter 11

Curtis, R. (2011), 'A simple life', *Taxation*, Vol. 168, No. 4331, 16–19

Daiber, C. (2003), 'Germany's new law eliminating tax preferences has far-reaching consequences', *Worldwide Tax Daily*, 7 August, 2003 WTD 152–7

Dine, J. & P. Hughes (2007–) (eds.), *Gore-Browne on EU company law* (Bristol: Jordans)

Dodge, J. (2012), *Deconstructing Haig-Simons income and reconstructing it as objective ability-to-pay income*, FSU College of Law, Public Law Research Paper No. 595, available at http://ssrn.com/abstract=2053275

Dorfmueller, P. (2011), 'Germany waives dual domestic link requirement for EU/EEA-incorporated Organschaft subsidiaries', *Worldwide Tax Daily*, 5 April, 2011 WTD 65–3

Eckhardt, T. & U. Woywode (2004), 'German tax authorities issue guidance on classification of U.S. LLCs', *Worldwide Tax Daily*, 1 April, 2004 WTD 63–1

Endres, D, & A. Miles (2004), 'German Supreme Tax Court rejects application of transfer pricing rules to domestic transaction', *Worldwide Tax Daily*, 8 September, 2004 WTD 174–4

European Communities (1970), *Corporation tax and individual income tax in the European communities* (van den Tempel, A.), Competition - Approximation of Legislation Series No. 15 (Brussels: Studies)

Fischer, H. & A. Lohbeck (2012), 'Branch report: Germany', in *International Fiscal Association* (2012), 307–27

Fuller, J. (2010), 'U.S. tax review', *Worldwide Tax Daily*, 4 October, 2010 WTD 191–11

Gordon, R. & J. Hausman (2010), 'International capital taxation: commentary', in Mirrlees et al. (eds), pp. 1009–27

Griffith, R., J. Hines & P. Sørensen (2010), 'International capital taxation', in Mirrlees et al. (eds), chapter 10

Hanlon, M. & J. Hoopes (2012), 'What do firms do when dividend tax rates change? An examination of alternative payout responses to dividend tax rate changes', 23 May 2012, available at http://ssrn.com/abstract=2065628

Harris, P. (1996), *Corporate/shareholder income taxation and allocating taxing rights between countries: a comparison of imputation systems* (Amsterdam: IBFD)

Harris, P. (1998), 'Dividend streaming', *Australian Tax Review*, Vol. 27, 132–47

Harris, P. (1999), 'An historic view of the principle and options for double tax relief', *British Tax Review*, 469–89

Harris, P. (2006), *Income tax in common law jurisdictions: from the origins to 1820* (Cambridge: Cambridge University Press)

Harris, P. (2010), 'Cross-border dividend taxation in the 21st century: the [ir]relevance of tax treaties', *British Tax Review*, 573–88

Harris, P. (2011), 'Company, person, body of persons, entity: what's the difference and why?', *British Tax Review*, 188–209

Harris, P. (2012), 'The CCCTB GAAR: a toothless tiger or Russian roulette?', in Weber, D. (ed.), chapter 15

Harris, P. (forthcoming), *Income tax in common law jurisdictions: 1820 to present*

Harris, P. & J. D. Oliver (2008), 'Family connections and the corporate entity: income splitting through the family company', in Avery Jones, Harris & Oliver (eds.), 244–87

Harris, P. & J. D. Oliver (2010), *International commercial tax* (Cambridge: Cambridge University Press)

HMRC (2012a), 'U.K. describes simpler income tax for small businesses', *Worldwide Tax Daily*, 17 May, 2012 WTD 97–27

HMRC (2012b), 'U.K. issues IR35 Intermediaries Legislation compliance guidance', *Worldwide Tax Daily*, 10 May, 2012 WTD 91–25

Holmes, K. (2001), *The concept of income – a multi-disciplinary analysis* (Amsterdam: IBFD)

Huizinga, H. (2010), 'Taxing corporate income: commentary', in Mirrlees et al. (eds), 894–904

Institute for Fiscal Studies (1991), *Equity for companies: a corporation tax for the 1990s* (Capital Taxes Group) (London: Institute for Fiscal Studies)

International Fiscal Association (ed.) (2012), *The debt-equity conundrum*, IFA Cahiers de droit fiscal international, Vol. 97b (The Hague: Sdu Uitgevers)

Juneja. R. & I. Crosbie (2011), 'Canada to amend income tax act to clamp down on stapled securities', *Worldwide Tax Daily*, 22 July, 2011 WTD 141–1

Kaserer, C., M. Rapp & O. Trinchera (2011), 'Payout policy, taxes, and corporate insiders: evidence from the German Tax Reform 2001', 2 March 2011, available at http://ssrn.com/abstract=1801286

Kochman, N. & D. Rosenbloom (2012), ' The new US foreign tax credit rules', *Bulletin for International Taxation*, Vol. 66, No. 4/5, 221–8

Laux, C. & C. Leuz (2009), 'The crisis of fair-value accounting: making sense of the recent debate', *Accounting, Organizations and Society*, Vol. 34, 826–34

Mazansky, E. (2012), 'New rules for tax on dividends (domestic and foreign) and other company distributions', *Bulletin for International Taxation*, Vol. 66, No. 3, 170–6

McClure, C. E. (1979), *Must corporate income be taxed twice?* (Washington, DC: The Brookings Institution)

Mill, J. (1871), *Principles of political economy* (London: Longmans)

Mintz, M. (2010), 'Taxing corporate income: commentary', in Mirrlees et al. (eds), 905–13

Mirrlees, J., S. Adam, T. Besley, et al. (eds) (2010), *Dimensions of tax design: The Mirrlees Review*, Institute for Fiscal Studies (Oxford: Oxford University Press), available at http://www.ifs.org.uk/mirrleesReview/dimensions

Mirrlees, J., S. Adam, T. Besley, et al. (2011), *Tax by design: The Mirrlees Review* (Oxford: Oxford University Press), available at http://www.ifs.org.uk/mirrleesReview/design

Montagu, G. (2001), 'Is a foreign state a body corporate?', *British Tax Review*, 421–48

Mullis, K. (2011), 'Check-the-box and hybrids: a second look at elective U.S. tax classification of foreign entities', *Worldwide Tax Daily*, 31 October, 2011 WTD 210–14

Nakazato, M., M. Ramseyer & Y. Nishikori (2010), 'Japan', in Ault & Arnold, 93–110

Nicodème, G. (2009), *Corporate income tax and economic distortions*, EC Taxation Paper, D (2009) 33065 – EN, available at http://ec.europa.eu/taxation_customs/resources/doc…tion_paper_15_en.pdf

Nijenhuis, E. (2011), 'Repos, the technical taxpayer rules, and foreign tax credit splitter rules (Section 909)', available at http://ssrn.com/abstract=1799479

Norr, M. (1982), *The taxation of corporations and shareholders* (Deventer: Kluwer)

OECD (1992–), *Model tax convention on income and on capital*, Committee on Fiscal Affairs (Paris: OECD)

OECD (1995–2000), *Transfer pricing guidelines for multinational enterprises and tax administrations* (Paris: OECD)

OECD (2010–), 'Revenue statistics: comparative tables', *OECD Tax Statistics* (database) doi:10.1787/data-00262-en; accessed 16 July 2012

Office for National Statistics (2010), 'Share ownership survey 2008', *Statistical Bulletin*, 27 January, available at http://www.statistics.gov.uk

Office for National Statistics (2012), 'Ownership of UK quoted shares 2010', *Statistical Bulletin*, 28 February, available at http://www.statistics.gov.uk

Parsons, R. W. (1985), *Income taxation in Australia: principles of income, deductibility and tax accounting* (Sydney: The Law Book Company)

Passant, J. (2011), 'Economic rent and taxation – a lawyer's guide', 23 January 2011, available at http://ssrn.com/abstract=1987571

Ring, D. (2012), 'Branch report: United States', *International Fiscal Association*, 771–91

Schanz, D. & H. Theßeling (2011), 'The influence of tax regimes on distribution policy of corporations – evidence from German tax reforms', 3 March 2011, available at http://ssrn.com/abstract=1775942

Schön, W. (2008) (ed.), *Taxation and corporate governance*, MPI Studies on Intellectual Property, Competition and Tax Law, Vol. 3 (Heidelberg: Springer)

Schön, W. (2010), 'Germany', in Ault & Arnold, 65–91

Schön, W., T. Beuchert, A. Erker, et al. (2009), *Debt and equity: what's the difference? A comparative view*, Max Planck Institute for Intellectual Property, Competition & Tax Law Research Paper No. 09–09, available at http://ssrn.com/abstract=1457649

Seligman, E.R.A. (1914), *The income tax: a study of the history, theory, and practice of income taxation at home and abroad* (New York: MacMillan Company)

Seligman, E. (1927), *The shifting and incidence of taxation*, 5th ed (New York: Columbia University Press)

Sieker, K. (2004), 'German tax review: recent changes affect use of losses', *Worldwide Tax Daily*, 22 January, 2004 WTD 14–5

Simpson, J. (chief ed.) (2000–), *Oxford English dictionary* (Oxford: Oxford University Press), available at www.oed.com

Southern, D. (2012), 'Branch report: United Kingdom', *International Fiscal Association*, 749–69

Sparagna, G. (2004), 'Branch report: United States', in International Fiscal Association (ed), *Group Taxation*, IFA Cahiers de droit fiscal international, Vol. 89b (Amersfoort: Sdu Fiscale & Financiële Uitgevers), 711–29

Suarez, S. (2012), 'Using tax losses within a Canadian group of companies', *Worldwide Tax Daily*, 2 April, 2012 WTD 63–15

Sullivan, M.A. (2011), 'International tax reform should precede domestic efforts in U.S', *Worldwide Tax Daily*, 20 January, 2011 WTD 14–33

Surrey, S. & P. McDaniel (1985), *Tax expenditures* (Cambridge, MA: Harvard University Press)

Symons, S. & N. Howlett (2010), 'Analysis – total tax contribution & the hundred group', *Tax Journal*, No. 1022, 29 March, 21–3

Tiley, J. (2008), *Revenue law*, 6th edition (London: Hart Publishing)

Tiley, J. (2010a), 'Law and tax law, judges and statutes', *British Tax Review*, 55–82

Tiley, J. (2010b), 'United Kingdom', in Ault & Arnold (eds.), 145–72

Ting, A. (2012), *The taxation of corporate groups under consolidation: an international comparison* (Cambridge: Cambridge University Press)

Truman, M. (2006), 'What's in a name?', *Taxation*, Vol. 158, No. 4085, 181

UK (2011), 'A simpler income tax for the smallest businesses', Office of Tax Simplification discussion paper, July 2011, available at http://www.hm-treasury.gov.uk/d/ots_tax_for_small_business_discussion_paper.pdf

US Treasury (2003), 'General explanations of the administration's fiscal year 2004 revenue proposals', (Blue Book) February 2003

Vanistendael, F. (1996), 'Legal framework for taxation', in V. Thuronyi (ed.), *Tax law design and drafting*, Vol. 1, 15–70

Waltman, J. (1980), 'Origins of the Federal Income Tax', *Mid-America: An Historical Review*, Vol. 62, No. 3, 147–60

Weber, D. (ed.) (2012), *CCCTB: Selected issues*, EUCOTAX Series on European Taxation (The Netherlands: Kluwer Law International)

Weyde, D. (2008), 'Germany issues final guidance for rule disallowing use of losses', *Worldwide Tax Daily*, 21 August, 2008 WTD 163–1

Whittmann, H. (1983–), 'Taxation', chapter 32 in D. Campbell, C. Campbell and F. Rüster (eds.), *Business transactions in Germany* (New York: Matthew Bender)